The Four Major Cults

The Four Major Cults

Christian Science

Jehovah's Witnesses

Mormonism

Seventh-day Adventism

by

ANTHONY A. HOEKEMA

Professor of Systematic Theology
Calvin Theological Seminary, Grand Rapids, Michigan

William B. Eerdmans Publishing Company   *Grand Rapids, Michigan*

Second printing, October 1965

PHOTOLITHOPRINTED BY CUSHING - MALLOY, INC.
ANN ARBOR, MICHIGAN, UNITED STATES OF AMERICA

To Ruth

Contents

Preface

THIS BOOK GREW OUT OF A TEACHING NEED. WHILE TEACHING A course in the cults to seminarians, I came to the conviction that to meet the challenge of the cults today, we need to understand the teachings of the cults in their totality, so that the various doctrines can be seen to fit into a certain theological pattern. The type of treatment here used, therefore, is analogous to that employed in textbooks on Christian doctrine. I also felt that to do full justice to the cults discussed and to be completely fair in reproducing their teachings, such a systematic treatment should be based exclusively on primary source materials.

The question arises, Why *four* major cults? The answer is twofold. First, the method used requires a rather thorough treatment of a few cults, rather than a summary discussion of a large number. Secondly, among the major cults I have selected the four largest and most influential, so that one may readily see what various cults have in common, and so that the phenomenon of cultism may be better understood.

The main purpose of this book, then, is to set forth in a systematic way the doctrinal teachings of Christian Science, Jehovah's Witnesses, Mormonism, and Seventh-day Adventism. Though Seventh-day Adventism does teach a number of doctrines in common with evangelical Protestant churches, and is therefore considered by most writers on the subject to be nearer to the evangelical position than are the other three groups, it is my conviction that Seventh-day Adventism is a cult and not a branch of evangelical Christianity. The reasons for this evaluation are given in Chapter 6.

The order in which these four cults are taken up is chronological. Since the Mormon Church was organized and incorporated in 1830, Mormonism is discussed first. Next in order is Seventh-day Adventism, since this denomination held its first General Conference in 1863. Because the Christian Science Church was incorporated in 1879, Christian Science is treated next. Last in order comes the discussion of Jehovah's Witnesses, whose first corporate organization, Zion's Watch Tower Tract Society, was incorporated in 1884.

The discussion of each cult follows this pattern: first, a brief history of the cult is given; next, the question of the source of authority appealed to by the cult is taken up; and, finally, the doctrines taught by the cult are expounded in the order of the customary divisions of Christian theology: God, man, Christ, salvation, the church, the last things. The same general doctrinal headings have been used with each cult treated, so as to facilitate comparison. Though this book was written to serve a teaching need, an attempt has been made to write it in such a way that persons without specialized theological training may use it with profit.

In setting forth the doctrinal views of the cults discussed, I have used primary source material exclusively (writings by the original founders of the cult and doctrinal works by past and present cult leaders). Whenever there was uncertainty about what was being taught on a particular doctrinal point, information was obtained directly from the cult involved. In many cases material has been quoted directly from cult publications; in other instances these sources have been paraphrased. In all cases, references to the source materials used are given in the footnotes. Readers desiring to do further research in cult teachings are urged to work directly with these sources, since this is the most satisfactory way of finding out exactly what the cults teach.

In five appendices certain cult teachings are singled out for critical evaluation. These teachings are: the alleged genuineness of the *Book of Mormon* as an additional sacred scripture, the investigative judgment and scapegoat doctrines in Seventh-day Adventism, Seventh-day Adventist teachings on the Sabbath, the Jehovah-Witness denial of the deity of Christ, and the teachings of both Seventh-day Adventists and Jehovah's Witnesses on soul-extinction in the intermediate state and on the final annihilation of the wicked.

In addition to the above, I have set forth in Chapter 1 what lessons we can learn from the cults, in Chapter 6 what are the distinctive traits of the cult, and in Chapter 7 how we should approach the cultist. The bibliography has been made sufficiently complete so that it can serve as an aid to further research on the cults discussed.

Though I have sought always to be fair and accurate, in a study of this sort there are bound to be many shortcomings and inadequacies. I shall be grateful if inaccuracies or misstatements are called to my attention.

I should like to express my sincere appreciation to those officials in the four groups involved who have willingly answered correspondence, supplied information, and provided literature. I should like, further, to express my indebtedness to various authors who have written on the cults.

I acknowledge with gratitude the helpfulness of the library staff at Calvin College and Seminary. A special word of appreciation is extended to the Rev. Nicholas Vogelzang, Christian Reformed Home Missionary at Salt Lake City, for his help in obtaining important recent literature on Mormonism.

I wish to thank those of my colleagues at Calvin Seminary who have read parts of the manuscript, and my students, whose comments in class discussions have helped to remove ambiguities and weaknesses. A particular word of thanks is extended to Mr. Calvin Bulthuis of the Wm. B. Eerdmans Publishing Company for his exceptional helpfulness.

Through this study the amazing love of Jesus Christ, my Savior, has become more real and more precious to me than ever before. May the Lord use this book for the advancement of His kingdom and for the glory of His grace. May He particularly use it to lead many from the errors of the cult into the truth as it is in Christ.

—ANTHONY A. HOEKEMA

Grand Rapids, Michigan
August, 1963

ABBREVIATIONS

ASV	American Standard Version
Glaubenswelt	*Die Glaubenswelt des Sektierers*
The Great Controversy	*The Great Controversy Between Christ and Satan*
KJ	King James Version
NWT	*New World Translation,* 1961 ed.
Paradise Lost	*From Paradise Lost to Paradise Regained*
Questions on Doctrine	*Seventh-day Adventists Answer Questions on Doctrine*
Religion for Mankind	*What Has Religion Done for Mankind?*
RSV	Revised Standard Version
Survival After Death	*What Do the Scriptures Say about "Survival After Death?"*
You May Survive Armageddon	*You May Survive Armageddon into God's New World*
Your Will Be Done	*"Your Will Be Done on Earth"*

(Note: All Scripture quotations not otherwise identified are from the American Standard Version.)

CHAPTER ONE

The Challenge of the Cults

YOU MAY HAVE HEARD THE EXPRESSION, "THE CULTS ARE THE unpaid bills of the church." Though this statement does not tell the whole story, there is a great deal of truth in it. Cults have sometimes arisen because the established churches have failed to emphasize certain important aspects of religious life, or have neglected certain techniques. Though one may assign many reasons for the rapid growth of the cults, one reason we may be sure of: people often find in the cults emphases and practices which they miss in the established churches.

This is not to suggest that where the cults differ from the churches, the cults are invariably right and the churches are always wrong. One of the main purposes of this book will be to expose the many pernicious anti-Christian teachings which the cults are disseminating throughout the world today. As James Orr has somewhere remarked, however, every heresy which has obtained wide acceptance has been so accepted because of the grain of truth which was found in it.

Whereas this study will be chiefly concerned to point out the doctrinal aberrations of the cults, we may profitably begin by asking ourselves what we can learn from these movements. For there are certainly things we can learn from them. If we can somehow abstract the points which follow from the motivations and

1

teachings of the cults involved, we may see in these emphases a certain challenge to the established churches. Some of these emphases may even serve as rebukes to the church, accusing fingers pointing at its failures and shortcomings, its coldness and its lack of zeal.[1]

(1) One of the first things we may learn from the cults is *the importance of having definite convictions about matters of faith.* This is a strong characteristic of the cults. If you ask a cultist what he believes, he will be glad to tell you. In fact, he is usually eager to tell you whether you ask him or not. Though there are exceptions to this rule, a cultist usually not only knows what he believes, but is convinced that these beliefs matter supremely.

This combination of knowledge and conviction is perhaps one of the leading reasons why the cults grow so rapidly. People who "stand for nothing and fall for everything" are an easy prey for the cults. Nominal church members who have been exposed to very little systematic Bible teaching may easily get the impression that the cultist can provide them with real insight into the meaning of the Scriptures. If all the cultist encounters when he talks to people is a spiritual and intellectual vacuum, he will meet little resistance and win many converts.

It is precisely at this point that the church faces one of its greatest challenges. The cults challenge the churches to a more thorough and more effective program of indoctrination. The churches must train their members so that they know what they believe and have deep convictions about these matters. Though, strictly speaking, only the Holy Spirit can implant and sustain these deep convictions, the church nevertheless has a responsibility in this area. Doctrinal instruction must be pursued with vigor. The children and young people of the congregation must be trained in the faith of the fathers in classes for doctrinal instruction. Though this training must be solid and thorough, it must not be merely an intellectual process, but the kind of instruction which will make these doctrines meaningful and vital. We must deepen conviction as well as impart information.

(2) A second lesson we may learn from the cults is *the importance of knowing the Scriptures.* Jehovah's Witnesses readily quote Scripture passages when occasion requires. Other cultists,

---

[1] To those interested in delving further into this aspect of the cults, I suggest the following: Charles S. Braden, "What Can We Learn from the Cults?" *Religion in Life,* XIV, No. 1 (Winter, 1944-45), 52-64; John E. Kuizenga, "The Cults: Phenomenon and Challenge," *Theology Today,* I, No. 1 (April, 1944), 34-46; J. K. Van Baalen, "The Unpaid Bills of the Church," in *Chaos of Cults* (4th ed.; Grand Rapids: Eerdmans, 1962), pp. 390-398.

too, can very quickly supply Bible verses, complete with references, to buttress their teachings. This Scripture quoting is usually done quite glibly and often out of context so that it is actually a perversion of Scripture. Yet, by contrast, the inability of many church members to quote Bible passages in support of their beliefs stands out in bold relief. How many Christians are able, at a moment's notice, to adduce Biblical passages which refute cult teachings? Granting at once that a mere quotation of a Bible passage is not sufficient, is there not, however, real value in having at our fingertips Scripture texts which support the doctrines we embrace? The rapid growth of movements like the Jehovah's Witnesses make more thorough Scripture memorization on the part of both pastors and people a highly desirable thing. Young people, too, should be trained not only in the understanding of Christian doctrines, but also in the ability to find and quote Scripture passages on which these doctrines are based.

The superficial and misleading treatment of Scripture found in the cults ought also to make all church members insist that theological seminaries provide thorough training, not only in the doctrines to which Christians are committed, but also in the defense of these doctrines from the Scriptures. Doctrines, in fact, ought to be taught "exegetically" — that is, in such close relationship to Scripture that the student realizes that they are drawn from the Bible, not imposed upon the Bible. Only in this way will future pastors be adequately trained to meet cultists, who often claim to be more true to Scripture than the established churches are. Needless to say, we canot insist too strongly on a ministry trained in the original languages of the Bible. Only in this way can a pastor meet, and train his people to meet, cultists who glibly affirm, "The original Greek says so and so!" Though theological students may sometimes become impatient at the many hours they are compelled to spend in learning the niceties of Greek and Hebrew grammar and exegesis, they will be profoundly thankful for their solid training in these languages when they come face to face with cultists.

(3) A third feature of the cults which we should be eager to emulate is their *zeal for witnessing*. Much though we may deplore the witnessing methods of many cultists, it is undeniably true that these groups are gaining adherents in droves because they go out after them! This is particularly true of Jehovah's Witnesses, for whom door-to-door witnessing is an integral part of their religion. Cultists not only hold definite convictions, but they witness enthusiastically about them, in season and out of season. We may find much fault with the way in which these people witness: I am certainly not recommending the methods used, the tactics em-

ployed, or the goals envisaged (many cults, for example, work with converted natives on mission fields in the attempt to lure them away from the Christian church which has evangelized them). What must never be forgotten, however, is that cultists are getting out into the highways and byways, talking to others about their beliefs, leaving their literature, inviting people to their meetings, offering to start instruction classes. It would appear that the cults are generally pursuing a much more diligent and systematic program of witnessing, both at home and abroad, than are the churches.

What a pity it is that often the members of the established churches keep so quiet about their faith, whereas the cultists peddle their perversions far and wide. What a pity that church members are often silent Christians, while cultists are usually enthusiastic propagandists for their faith! John E. Kuizenga has put the matter very vividly: "The man who sells popcorn may have a steam-whistle that can be heard for blocks, and the 'good humor' ice cream carts may tinkle through every town and hamlet . . . but Christianity is something Christians can be silent about in all languages."[2]

Here, too, the cults point an accusing finger at the churches. Why is it, they say to us, that you have lost that passion for witnessing which was so characteristic of early Christianity? It has often been said that one reason for the rapid spread of Christianity in its early days was that every believer was a witness. How different the situation is today! Charles S. Braden surmises that "probably more people have been won to the Christian faith by the witness of some who hold it than by any one other means."[3] If this is so — and there is no reason for thinking that it is not so — we are confronted anew today with the urgent necessity of training people to witness for Christ, and of praying that the Holy Spirit may fill us with greater zeal for such witnessing.

(4) The cults make a much more effective *use of the printed page* than do the established churches. Christian Scientists have their reading rooms in every good-sized city; you will find copies of Christian Science literature in every public library and in many public places. Seventh-day Adventists have 44 publishing houses producing literature in 220 languages. A constant stream of books, booklets, and periodicals pours forth from Mormon presses. Jehovah's Witnesses publish their books in 50 languages and their chief periodical, *The Watchtower*, in 62; in January of 1962 they claimed to have distributed during the previous year 14,650,615

[2] *Loc. cit.,* p. 44.
[3] *Loc. cit.,* p. 56.

pieces of literature and 105,281,876 individual magazines![4] One stands amazed at the amount of printed material the cults send into the world.

How much more the churches could do with the printed page than they are doing today! What Protestant church can claim that more than 17 million copies of one of its doctrinal books have been printed? What Protestant magazine dares to claim a circulation of more than 3,850,000? Yet these claims are made by Jehovah's Witnesses for their book, *Let God Be True*, and for their best-known periodical, *The Watchtower*. Here, therefore, we see another area in which the cults challenge the churches, and another reason for their phenomenal growth.

(5) Another element in the challenge of the cults is *the strong sense of urgency* which is characteristic of many of them. Especially in the millennial and adventist cults there is a strong conviction that the end of the world is very near and that, therefore, what has to be done in the way of witnessing must be done now. The Battle of Armageddon, so say Jehovah's Witnesses, is just around the corner; since they believe that all those who die in this great battle will never be raised, it is imperative that they witness to people while they still have the opportunity.

Needless to say, those who do not share the theology of the cults will not share their particular type of urgency either. Yet, though we may not agree that "Armageddon is just around the corner," do not we Christians believe that the day of grace in which we now live will not last forever? Is it not true that for each individual the moment of death is the moment when for him the day of grace is over — and may not that moment come any time? How strong is our expectation of the Second Coming of Christ? Braden puts it very strikingly when he says: "One could well believe from much of the preaching he hears that it would be nice if men were to become Christian, but that really there is nothing urgent about it."[5] If we felt more of a sense of urgency, our message, too, would be more compelling.

(6) The cults challenge us also by *the large role they assign to laymen*. Laymen are given much important work to do by the cults. Mormons claim to have no professional clergy; it is distinctive of their position to maintain that every male Mormon above the age of 20 may hold either the Aaronic or the Melchizedek priesthood. It is also well-known that many Mormon young people devote two years of their lives to mission work at their own expense (or at the expense of their relatives). "Probably

4 *The Watchtower*, LXXXIII, No. 1 (Jan. 1, 1962), p. 25.
5 *Loc. cit.*, pp. 59f.

the greater part of the propagation of the Mormon gospel has been done by what the churches would call laymen but who are ordained Mormon priests."[6]   In the Jehovah's Witness movement lay members, both men and women, are expected to become "publishers," and to devote a certain number of hours each week to ringing doorbells and distributing literature.   Though not ordained in the usual sense, all members who engage in this type of door-to-door witnessing, including teen-agers, are called *ministers*.

Are the established churches using their laymen to the best advantage? Or are we missing some real opportunities here? Most of the members of our churches have, of course, no opportunity to obtain seminary training.   Are we providing enough opportunities for lay witnessing?   Or are many of our laymen members of the "hearing church" only — to say nothing about the "sleeping church"?   The cults challenge us to re-examine the role of laymen in our evangelistic and missionary activities.

(7) Another way in which the cults challenge us is by *the sense of dedication* found in their members.   When one encounters a cult, one meets people who are completely committed to a cause — committed in a way which puts many a church member to shame.   Many Mormon young people, as we have seen, give two years of their lives to the cause.   Jehovah's Witnesses not only spend many hours a week witnessing for the movement (132,695, 540 hours throughout the world in 1961, according to the January 1, 1962, *Watchtower*), but many of them work virtually for room and board only in the printing plants, in the offices, and on the farms.   Seventh-day Adventists claimed in 1961 that they were carrying on mission work in 195 countries out of a total of 220[7] — eloquent testimony to the fact that this movement, too, claims many dedicated people willing to forego the comforts of life in America in order to bring the Seventh-day Adventist witness to the world.

Do we in the established churches have this kind of dedication to the Kingdom of Christ?   One may certainly point to many dedicated people within the churches, but the question cannot be dodged: are all of our people, by and large, possessed by this kind of dedication?   One can, of course, always find excuses, but is there any real reason why a Mormon or a Jehovah's Witness should be more wholeheartedly committed to his cult than a Christian should be devoted to the glorious Kingdom of our Lord and Saviour Jesus Christ?

[6] Charles S. Braden, *These Also Believe* (New York: Macmillan, 1960), p. 434.
[7] *Yearbook of the Seventh-Day Adventist Denomination* (Washington: Review and Herald, 1961), p. 340.

(8) The cults teach their people *definite techniques for witnessing.* Jehovah's Witnesses, for example, have weekly "service meetings" at which they give their members specific training in methods of witnessing; in addition to this they have published a volume (*Qualified to be Ministers,* 1955) dealing particularly with such matters as methods of study, methods of speaking, meeting objections, distributing literature, conducting home Bible studies, conducting meetings, organizing new congregations, and so on. Hardly a detail is left to chance in this book; everything is spelled out. A person who has studied this volume carefully will have taken a substantial course in witnessing methods.

We may find much fault with the techniques advocated in books of this sort. Yet by means of such books and by means of meetings of the kind described above, the cults are training their people for witnessing in a far more effective way than most churches train their members for this task. We are inclined to preach and talk in glittering generalities. We tell people to do more religious reading, but often fail to give them guidance in what to read or how to read. We tell people to witness, but do not teach them how to witness. We urge people to be more expressive about their faith, but give them little or no guidance as to what they should say.

Here, again, the cults challenge us. They are usually quite definite about what they want people to do and quite specific in their instructions. We might well consider whether in the churches we should not be much more practical than we usually are, and whether we should not take greater pains to tell people how they should pray, study the Bible, and witness to others about Christ.

(9) Cultists are *willing to endure ridicule.* Jehovah's Witnesses are not afraid of being thought queer, eccentric, or peculiar. Seventh-day Adventists are not afraid to defy convention by observing the seventh day as their Sabbath instead of the first. Both Mormons and Adventists are willing to be thought different from others, in that they refuse to drink certain beverages or eat certain foods.

Here, too, the cults present a challenge. Without defending for a moment the teachings on which their unconventionalities are based, we may yet find something to emulate in their willingness to endure ridicule. I am not saying that we should try to be different just for the sake of being different, like beatniks. But are we not often at the other extreme? Most church members are terribly afraid to be different. We desperately crave social approval. We want to go along with the crowd; we want to be in step. We so easily forget that the great creative figures in the history of the church have always been ready to defy convention. Our Lord Jesus Christ Himself thundered against many of the traditions of His day. Paul was willing to be a fool for Christ's sake.

Martin Luther dared to defy the political and religious leaders of his day, saying, "Here I stand; I cannot do otherwise — so help me God!". We shall not make much of an impression upon the world if we are as similar to unbelievers as peas in a pod. We can stand something of the spirit of the cultist who dares to be different, despite the pressures of social convention.

(10) We may also learn from the cults that *the Christian faith has a contribution to make to good health.* Without for a moment endorsing the principles which motivate Christian Science and other faith-healing cults, I venture to suggest that one reason why movements of this sort have gotten such hold on people is that churches have often failed to emphasize the relation between religion and health. Needless to say, I do not wish in any way to minimize the important role played in healing by the physician, the ministry of medicine, or the amazing resources of the modern hospital. But, as Braden puts it, "When science has done all it can, there is still a powerful ministry which religious faith brings to sick folk."[8] In fact, we can go back to the Bible itself to learn that there is a close relationship between a healthy mind and a healthy body: "A merry heart doeth good like medicine" (Prov. 17:22).

Recent years have witnessed the rise of the science of psychosomatic medicine. From this science we have learned that mental and emotional tensions may result in definite physical ailments, stomach ulcers being a notorious example. We have learned that there are such things as "adjustive ailments" — physical maladies which originate in the desire to escape reality. On the other hand, psychiatrists and psychotherapists are emphasizing more than ever before the tremendous resources for both mental and physical health which are to be found in a vital religious faith.

Here, then, is a final challenge from the cults. From movements like Christian Science we can learn anew that religious faith does have much to do with physical health and with the process of healing. Pastors should be fully convinced that their prayers and their ministry to the sick are as vitally important in the healing process as is the care of doctors and nurses. Every pastor can testify that he has witnessed amazing answers to prayer in critical illnesses — answers which have baffled medical science. What one Christian doctor used to say is as true today as it ever was: "We only set the bones; God must do the healing." While being grateful for the ministry of medicine, let the church not neglect the ministry of prayer.

---

[8] "What Can We Learn from the Cults?" p. 63.

CHAPTER TWO

Mormonism

HISTORY

THERE IS PROBABLY NO AMERICAN RELIGIOUS GROUP WHICH HAS had a more colorful or fascinating history than the Mormons. The Mormon trek to Salt Lake City in 1846-47, for example, has become an integral part of the American saga of the settlement of the West. I shall reproduce here only as much of this history as will enable us to place Mormonism into its proper setting, and will serve to acquaint us with its outstanding leaders.[1]

JOSEPH SMITH

Joseph Smith, Jr., was born on December 23, 1805, in Sharon, Vermont, the third son of Joseph and Lucy Smith. In 1817, when Joseph was 11, the family settled near Palmyra, New York, not far from present-day Rochester. A few years later most of the members of the family had joined the Presbyterian church, but Joseph was undecided as to which church he should join. There was so much strife among the denominations, he felt, that he could not decide who was right and who was wrong.

In describing the following events, I am drawing upon Smith's own autobiography as reproduced in one of the sacred books of

[1] Readers desiring more complete treatments of Mormon history are referred to the biographical and historical titles listed in the bibliography.

9

Mormonism, *Pearl of Great Price,* under the heading, "Extracts from the History of Joseph Smith, the Prophet" (pp. 46-57). While puzzling about which church to join, so Smith tells us, he read James 1:5, "If any of you lack wisdom, let him ask of God, that giveth to all men liberally, and upbraideth not; and it shall be given him."[2] Accordingly, he continues, I retired to the woods, knelt down, and began to pray. Suddenly two "Personages" appeared. One of them pointed to the other and said, "This is my Beloved Son. Hear Him!" In answer to the question as to which of the "sects" was right, the one Personage who had addressed me, so Smith goes on, said that I was to join none of them, since "they were all wrong," and since "all their creeds were an abomination in his sight" — that, in fact, those professing their faith in these various "sects" were all corrupt and hypocritical.[3] This vision, Smith alleges, occurred in the early spring of 1820. It will be observed that Smith would then have been only 14 years old.

On September 21, 1823, Smith continues, I had a second vision. A personage appeared at my bedside who was glorious beyond description. He said that he was a messenger sent from the presence of God, and that his name was Moroni; that God had a work for me to do, and that "my name should be had for good and evil among all nations, kindreds and tongues." He told me that a book had been deposited, written on golden plates, giving an account of the former inhabitants of this continent and containing "the fulness of the everlasting Gospel" as delivered by the Saviour to the ancient inhabitants of this land. He also said that there were "two stones in silver bows — and these stones, fastened to a breastplate, constituted what is called the Urim and Thummim — deposited with the plates," adding that God had prepared these stones for the purpose of translating this book.[4]

---

[2] Joseph Smith, *The Pearl of Great Price* (Salt Lake City: Church of Jesus Christ of Latter-Day Saints, 1952), p. 47.

[3] *Ibid.,* p. 48.

[4] *Ibid.,* pp. 50, 51. It will be observed that in the Bible the Urim and Thummim are mentioned as means whereby the will of the Lord was ascertained in certain judicial matters (Num. 27:21, I Sam. 28:6, I Sam. 14:41 in RSV). No reference is ever made in the Old Testament to their use as an aid in translating documents. In Smith's vision, however, the Urim and Thummim were stones affixed to silver bows so as to look like a pair of spectacles. From p. 55 of *The Pearl of Great Price* we learn that the Urim and Thummim were used by Smith as means whereby he translated the characters on the golden plates (cf. Mormon 9:34 in the *Book of Mormon*; also *Doctrine and Covenants* [Salt Lake City, 1952], sections 8 and 9). It is thus obvious that Joseph Smith's understanding of the use of the Urim and Thummim was quite different from that of the Old Testament writers. It is also important to note that, according to Smith's own admission, the characters on the golden plates could not be translated without the aid of the Urim and Thummim.

In the vision, Smith says, I was shown exactly where the plates had been deposited. That same night the heavenly messenger appeared again twice, each time repeating the same message.[5]

The next day, Smith continues, I went to a hill outside the village where we lived (called the hill Cumorah) and found the golden plates deposited in a stone box with the Urim and Thummim and the breastplate. I was not permitted to take them out at this time, however, but was told by the angel, who had reappeared, that I should come back to this place every year at this time for the next four years.[6] Finally, however, on September 22, 1827, I was given the plates by the heavenly messenger, with instructions to keep them carefully until he, the angel, should call for them again.[7]

It should be mentioned here that some months previous to this date, on January 18, 1827, Smith had been married to Emma Hale, of Harmony, Pennsylvania, having eloped with her after Emma's father had refused to give his consent to their marriage. The "official" reason for this refusal, according to Smith's autobiography, was the persecution which attended Smith because of the vision he claimed to have seen.[8] Fawn M. Brodie, however, in her biography of Joseph Smith, gives documentary evidence to prove that the real reason for Mr. Hale's refusal was that at this time Smith's only occupation was that of digging for money with the help of a "peepstone" into which he would gaze to determine the location of the treasure.[9]

Smith goes on to tell us that because of the persecution which followed his reception of the plates he decided to move to the house of his wife's father in Harmony, Pennsylvania. There he began to copy the characters off the plates and, by means of the Urim and Thummim, to translate some of them.

At about this time Mr. Martin Harris, a New York farmer who was befriending Smith and was planning to finance the publication of the book which would result from the translation of the plates, wanted to have some assurance that the plates were genuine and that they were being translated correctly. Though Harris was first under the impression that the characters on the golden plates were Hebrew, Smith explained to him that they were actually an altered or "Reformed" Egyptian.[10] To satisfy Harris, Smith gave him the characters that had been copied from the plates; Har-

[5] *Pearl of Great Price*, p. 52.
[6] *Ibid.*, p. 53.
[7] *Ibid.*, p. 54.
[8] *Ibid.*, p. 54.
[9] *No Man Knows My History* (New York: Knopf, 1957), pp. 29-33; see also her Appendix A, pp. 405-18.
[10] Cf. Mormon 9:32, 33.

ris then took these characters, together with a translation of them, to a certain Professor Charles Anthon in New York City. According to Smith's autobiography, Professor Anthon identified the characters supposedly copied from the plates as "Egyptian, Chaldaic, Assyriac, and Arabic," and affirmed that the translation of them was correct, "more so than any he had before seen translated from the Egyptian."[11]

In April of 1829, Smith continues, a former schoolteacher, Oliver Cowdery, joined me. I now commenced to translate the Book of Mormon, and he began to copy down what I told him to write. In May of 1829 we went into the woods to pray. While we were praying, a heavenly messenger, who identified himself as John the Baptist, descended and conferred upon both Oliver and myself the priesthood of Aaron. Both of us now began to prophesy and to understand the true meaning of the Scriptures.[12]

Shortly after this, so it is claimed, the Melchizedek, or higher, priesthood was also conferred upon Joseph Smith and Oliver Cowdery at a place along the banks of the Susquehanna River, by Peter, James, and John.[13]

On one of the opening pages of every copy of the *Book of Mormon,* the reader will find the so-called *Testimony of Three Witnesses.* Smith had been told that he was not to show the plates to anyone except to certain witnesses who were to be designated by divine revelation.[14] Joseph Fielding Smith tells the story of these three witnesses. After the translation of the *Book of Mormon* had been completed, the following three men desired to be the witnesses of the golden plates: Oliver Cowdery, David Whitmer, and Martin Harris. These three men went out into the woods with Smith and knelt in prayer. Suddenly an angel stood before them, holding the plates in his hands and turning them leaf by leaf.[15]

---

11 *Pearl of Great Price,* p. 55. It should be observed that to combine Arabic script and Egyptian characters (whether hieroglyphic, hieratic, or demotic) would be a linguistic monstrosity. Further, note the letter from Charles Anthon to E. D. Howe, reproduced by Walter Martin, in which Anthon asserts, "The whole story about my having pronounced the Mormonite inscription to be 'reformed Egyptian hieroglyphics' is perfectly false." *The Maze of Mormonism* (Grand Rapids: Zondervan, 1962), p. 42.

12 *Pearl of Great Price,* pp. 56-57.

13 Joseph Fielding Smith, *Essentials in Church History* (Salt Lake City: Deseret News Press, 1953), p. 69. Mr. Smith is the President of the Council of the Twelve Apostles and the official church historian of the Mormon Church.

14 See Ether 5:2-4, II Nephi 27:12-13, and cf. *Doctrine and Covenants* 5:11ff.

15 J. F. Smith, *op. cit.,* pp. 72-77 (cf. *Doctrine and Covenants,* Section 17). Robert F. Boyd, in "Mormonism," *Interpretation,* X, No. 4 (Oct., 1956), informs us that two of these men, Whitmer and Cowdery,

Apparently not satisfied with the witness of these three men, Smith later called eight other witnesses to view the plates and to give their testimony — a testimony which one will also find in every authentic copy of the *Book of Mormon*.[16]

On March 26, 1830, the *Book of Mormon,* now complete, was first placed on sale in the Palmyra bookstore. The first printing was financed by Martin Harris, who had had to mortgage his farm to pay for it.

On April 6, 1830, at Fayette, New York, the "Church of Jesus Christ of Latter-day Saints" was officially organized; that same year the church was incorporated. There were but six members at first, the oldest being only thirty-one years of age. Smith and Cowdery ordained each other as elders. Within a month the number of members had jumped to forty.

Since the *Book of Mormon* contained the story of the ancestry of the American Indians, it was but natural that the early Mormons should feel a sense of mission to the Indians.[17] Accordingly, a number of Mormons now went to Kirtland, Ohio (not far from present-day Cleveland, on the Lake Erie shore); here the Mormon gospel was preached and a number of converts were baptized. Later a temple was built at Kirtland. New revelations were now coming to "the prophet" on many subjects. While the group was at Kirtland, Smith compiled and published the first edition of a second Mormon sacred book, *Doctrine and Covenants.*

---

were later charged by their fellow Mormons as thieves and counterfeiters, and that the other witness, Martin Harris, later changed his solemn testimony to the following statement: "Why, I did not see them as I do that pencil case, yet I saw them with the eye of faith. I saw them just as distinctly as I saw anything about me — though at the time they were covered over with a cloth" (p. 431; see Brodie, *op. cit.,* p. 78; and cf. James H. Snowden, *The Truth About Mormonism* [New York, 1926], pp. 71ff.). All three of these witnesses later became apostates from the Mormon Church, though two of them, Cowdery and Harris, were eventually rebaptized (Brodie, p. 78; see *Essentials in Church History*, pp. 208-209, and note b). The question cannot be suppressed: how much weight is to be attached to a testimony coming from men of this sort?

[16] J. F. Smith, *op. cit.,* pp. 77-78. It is significant to note that four of these eight witnesses were Whitmers, relatives of the David Whitmer who had signed the first testimony; that Hiram Page, a fifth, had married a Whitmer daughter; and that the other three were members of "the prophet's" own family: his father and his brothers Hyrum and Samuel. One is not impressed with the impartiality of this group. Three of these eight witnesses later left the Mormon Church (*ibid.,* p. 209, note b). Further, it is to be remembered that the "divine revelations" alluded to in n. 14, above, had only specified that there were to be three witnesses who were to see the plates. One wonders by what authority Smith now obtained the testimony of these eight additional witnesses. Did he, perhaps, have some doubts as to the reliability of the first three?

[17] Charles S. Braden, *These Also Believe* (New York: Macmillan, 1960), p. 427.

Not satisfied with the Bible, Smith also at this time worked on a revision of the King James Version of the Scriptures.

Mormons had already begun moving farther west, to Jackson County, Missouri, where the city of Independence was located. Smith now received a revelation telling him that Jackson County, Missouri, was "the land of promise, and the place for the city of Zion."[18]   Hence many of Smith's followers now began to settle in Independence, Missouri.   The non-Mormon residents of Independence, however, did not take kindly to the claim that God had chosen this land for the Mormons.   Mobs began to attack the Mormons; consequently they went north and founded the town of Far West, Missouri.

Here, too, however, troubles continued.   After a number of battles had been fought between the settlers and the Mormons, the state militia intervened.   Smith and other Mormon leaders were imprisoned.   Eventually, however, the Mormons all escaped and joined the other "saints," who had by this time moved east to Illinois.   Here, in 1839, Joseph Smith chose a site on the Mississippi River, about fifty miles above Quincy, as their new home.   He called it Nauvoo (which, he asserted, was Hebrew for "beautiful place").   At this time Smith organized the so-called Nauvoo Legion, a small standing army, permitting himself to be called its lieutenant- general. Here, in Nauvoo, the construction of another Mormon temple was begun, and intense missionary activity continued.

Trouble began for Smith, however, when the *Nauvoo Expositor,* an anti-Mormon paper, began to publish material which was unfavorable to the Mormons.   Smith therefore ordered his men to destroy the *Expositor's* press and to burn every copy of the paper that could be found. When the owners of the press complained to the governor of the state about this wanton destruction of their property, Smith was arrested.   He was released, but later rearrested, together with his brother Hyrum, and was taken to the city jail in Carthage, Illinois, a few miles from Nauvoo.   On June 27, 1844, a mob attacked the jail and killed both Joseph and Hyrum Smith. The opponents of Mormonism thus hurt their cause, since Smith now became in Mormon eyes a martyred hero.

BRIGHAM YOUNG

After Smith's death, the burning question of the day was: who would become the new Mormon leader?   Very little thought had been given to the subject of succession in the presidency since it had been assumed that Smith still had many years to live. Sidney

18 *Doctrine and Covenants,* 57:1-2.

Rigdon, who had become a member of the church in Kirtland, Ohio, and had worked in close association with Joseph Smith since that time, first presented his claim to be the new "guardian" of the church, basing his claim on the fact that he had been named the first counselor to President Smith. At a later meeting, however, Brigham Young claimed that the authority of the presidency now rested with the twelve apostles, of which group he was the president. The Mormons accepted his leadership, and thus Young (1801-1877) became the second president of the Mormon church.[19]

Having been notified by the State of Illinois that they had to leave Nauvoo, the Mormons, under the leadership of Brigham Young, made plans to move to the west. One of the Mormons described their journey from Nauvoo to the west as "four hundred wagons moving to — we know not where." In early February of 1846 the epic journey to the west began. There were many hardships along the way: cold, exposure, storms, Indians, quarrels, apostasy, inadequate food and clothing. On July 24, 1847, the caravan arrived at the Salt Lake Valley in Utah; when President Young first saw the valley, he expressed his satisfaction in the memorable words, "This is the place!" He then proceeded to locate the site of the proposed new city (since known as Salt Lake City) about ten miles east of the lake.

Salt Lake City has been the headquarters of the Mormon Church ever since. Between 1856 and 1860 some 3,000 converts pushed handcarts from Iowa City, then the end of the railroad, to the Salt Lake Valley — a distance of about 1300 miles. Through Young's leadership a revolving fund was set up to finance immigration from foreign countries, particularly Great Britain and the Scandinavian countries. In 1877, when Brigham Young died, there were 140,000 Mormons.[20]

THE MORMON CHURCH

The Church of Jesus Christ of Latter-day Saints is today divided into approximately 370 stakes, 2800 wards, and 500 independent branches. A stake is a larger grouping of churches comparable to a diocese, presbytery, or classis; the average number of members in a stake is about 4,000, though this number may vary widely. A ward is comparable to a local organized church; the average number of members in a ward is approximately 600, though it may run as high as 1200. An independent branch is a

---

[19] Joseph Fielding Smith, *op. cit.,* pp. 385-89.
[20] Hartzell Spence, "The Mormon Church," *Reader's Digest,* April, 1958, p. 190.

"ward in embryo," comparable to a new church not yet organized; the membership of an independent branch usually runs from 50 to about 200 persons. In addition to the groupings just named, there are also mission branches and full-time missions.[21]

In a letter from Spencer W. Kimball, dated May 7, 1963, it was stated that the world membership of the Mormon Church as of December 31, 1962 was 1,965,786.[22] Of this number, Mr. Kimball continued, approximately 1,713,322 were found in the United States, and approximately 252,464 were to be found outside the United States. As of December, 1962, therefore, the foreign membership of the Mormon Church is approximately one-eighth of the total membership; thus about seven out of every eight Mormons in the world today are to be found in the United States. This is in sharp contrast to the situation which obtains in Seventh-day Adventism, where approximately three out of every four members are to be found outside the United States, and to that which obtains among Jehovah's Witnesses, where approximately two out of every three members are outside the United States.[23]

In the United States, the greatest number of Mormons are to be found in Utah, but there are members of the group in virtually every state of the Union. Outside of the United States, Mormons are most numerous in Canada, Mexico, the British Isles, Germany, and Scandinavia, although there is a considerable membership in South America and in the Pacific Islands. Mormons have twelve temples now in operation: four in Utah (at Salt Lake City, Logan, Manti, and St. George); one in Mesa, Arizona; one in Idaho Falls, Idaho; one in Los Angeles, California; one in Cardston in the Canadian province of Alberta; and one each in the Hawaiian Islands, England, New Zealand, and Switzerland. There is a temple now under construction in Oakland, California. In these temples, which may be entered only by Mormons in good standing, two types of ceremonies, very important in present-day Mormonism, are performed: celestial marriage and baptism for the dead. The

[21] The above information was obtained from a letter from Spencer W. Kimball of the Council of Twelve Apostles, dated April 16, 1963, and from a Church Statistical Report contained in the April 13, 1963, issue of the *Church News,* an official organ of the Mormon Church.

[22] This figure is also found in the Statistical Report referred to above. According to this report, 115,834 converts were baptized in stakes and missions during 1962, and there was a net increase during the year of 142,125 members.

[23] Exact figures will be given when these other groups are taken up. One is puzzled by the Mormon figures, which seem to imply either that Mormons have not been as active in foreign mission work as have these other two groups, or that they have not been as successful in winning converts. One can, of course, understand the desire of many foreign converts to Mormonism to move to the Mormon "Zion" on the North American continent. Perhaps this is the explanation for the disparity just mentioned.

best-known Mormon temple is the one at Salt Lake City, built between the years 1853 and 1893 and located on Temple Square. The other prominent building on Temple Square is the Tabernacle, open to the public, from which the world-famous Tabernacle Choir broadcasts every Sunday morning.

Mormons recognize two orders of priesthood: the lesser, called the Aaronic priesthood, and the greater, known as the Melchizedek priesthood. Every male Mormon may belong to one or the other of these two priesthoods, provided that his understanding of the teachings of the church and his daily life are in conformity with church requirements. One must, however, be at least twelve years old to be eligible for the Aaronic priesthood and at least nineteen to be eligible for the Melchizedek priesthood. The office-bearers with the highest authority must be members of the Melchizedek priesthood. The highest governing body of the church is the so-called First Presidency, consisting of the President of the Church and two Counselors to the President. The current President of the Mormon Church is David O. McKay. Next in the line of authority is the Council of Twelve Apostles, of which Joseph Fielding Smith is currently the president.

> They [the Council of Twelve] constitute a quorum whose unanimous decisions are equally binding in power and authority with those of the First Presidency of the Church. When the First Presidency is disorganized through the death or disability of the President, the directing authority in government reverts at once to the Quorum of the Twelve Apostles, by whom the nomination to the Presidency is made.[24]

It is a well-known fact that many Mormons dedicate two years of their lives to missionary service. According to an authoritative Mormon source, there are currently about 12,000 Mormon missionaries in the field. These include a few older couples and a sprinkling of young women. Most of these, however, are young men. About one-third of Mormon young men between the ages of 19 and 25 go on these missions. Less than 5 per cent of the girls go out; they are not encouraged to go, since missionary work is deemed to be primarily the work of men holding the priesthood.

> All of these missionaries, or their parents, or their close friends, pay their expenses. The Church does not support any missionaries. The work is entirely a free-will offering on the part of all who go out. Their living expenses will range anywhere between $75 and $125 a month per person, depending

---

[24] James E. Talmage, *Articles of Faith* (Salt Lake City: Church of Latter-day Saints, 1960), p. 210.

on the locality in which they are living and the cost of living in such localities.[25]

It is of interest to note that tithing is mandatory for Mormons (see *Doctrine and Covenants,* 119 and 120). In accordance with the so-called "Word of Wisdom" found in *Doctrine and Covenants,* 89, Mormons are not permitted to use tobacco, to drink liquor in any form, or to drink tea or coffee.

Elmer T. Clark, in his *Small Sects in America,* lists five groups which have split off from the Mormons. Of these the largest is the Reorganized Church of Jesus Christ of Latter-day Saints, which has its headquarters at Independence, Missouri. This body, which broke away from the other Mormons when the followers of Brigham Young moved to Salt Lake City, claims to be the real and legal successor of the church founded by Joseph Smith. Frank S. Mead, in the 1961 edition of his *Handbook of Denominations in the United States,* lists their membership as totalling 174,000.

SOURCE OF AUTHORITY

The Pearl of Great Price, one of the Mormon sacred books, contains a series of statements written by Joseph Smith, entitled "The Articles of Faith" (p. 59). These articles are still authoritative for the Mormon Church today. In fact, they form the basis for one of the best-known Mormon doctrinal works: *A Study of the Articles of Faith,* by James E. Talmage. Article 8 of these Articles of Faith reads as follows: "We believe the Bible to be the word of God as far as it is translated correctly; we also believe the Book of Mormon to be the word of God."

Mormons, therefore, have many reservations as to the correctness of past and present Bible translations. It is to be observed, however, that they do not make a similar reservation with regard to the *Book of Mormon,* since they contend that Joseph Smith was the inspired translator of the latter. The following quotation from James E. Talmage, one of the most authoritative writers on Mormon doctrines, will bear out this point:

> It is noticeable that we make no reservation respecting the Book of Mormon on the ground of incorrect translation. To do so would be to ignore attested facts as to the bringing forth of that book. Joseph Smith the prophet, seer, and revelator, through whom the ancient record has been translated into our modern tongue, expressly avers that the trans-

[25] Letter to the author from Mark E. Peterson of the Council of Twelve, dated July 6, 1962. The figures given in the previous paragraph have also been taken from this letter.

lation was effected through the gift and power of God, and is in no sense the product of linguistic scholarship.[26]

We may note that here already we have a point at which Mormons consider the *Book of Mormon* to be superior to the Bible: there are said to be errors of translation in the Bible, whereas no such errors are said to exist in the *Book of Mormon*.[27]

BIBLE VERSION

We consider next the question of the version of the Bible used by the Mormon Church. Before we can discuss this question, however, we must remind ourselves of the previously mentioned fact that, while the Mormons were in Kirtland, Ohio, Joseph Smith worked on a revision of the King James version of the Bible. What was the nature of this revision? On the basis of Article 8 of the Articles of Faith, one would assume that this revision of the Bible would involve nothing more than possible improvements in the English translation. As a matter of fact, this is the impression given by Mormon author John A. Widtsoe: "The prophet Joseph Smith, from the beginning of his ministry, gave some time to revising passages in the Bible which had been translated incorrectly or so rendered as to make the meaning obscure."[28]

This impression, however, is quite contrary to fact. What Smith did when he revised the Bible was not at all merely a matter of improving the translation, as we shall see. Neither did Smith's work bear the slightest resemblance to textual criticism, in which Widtsoe also affirms that he was engaged.[29] Textual critics carefully compare one Bible manuscript with another in the attempt to establish which of various readings of a given passage was the original one. What Smith did, however, had nothing whatever to do with manuscript study of this sort; it was rather a complete rewriting of certain Bible passages in the light of supposed new revelations.

The Reorganized Church of Jesus Christ of Latter-day Saints, a group which severed relations with the main Mormon body in 1844 and was organized as a separate body in 1853, has pub-

---

[26] *The Vitality of Mormonism* (Boston: Gorham Press, 1919), p. 127.

[27] This is a strange claim, indeed, in view of the fact that some 3,000 changes have been made in the text of the *Book of Mormon* since the publication of the first edition! For a more extended discussion of this point, see Appendix A.

[28] *Evidences and Reconciliations,* arranged by G. Homer Durham (Salt Lake City: Bookcraft, 1960), p. 117.

[29] *Ibid.,* p. 118.

lished Joseph Smith's revision of the King James Bible.[30]   Even
a casual perusal of this volume will reveal that Smith made a
great many changes in the Bible text which went far beyond
mere "translation" corrections.   One notices these changes already in the opening chapters of Genesis.   These chapters are
recast as a direct revelation to Moses in which God speaks in the
first person: "And I, God, said, Let there be light, and there was
light" (Gen. 1:6, Inspired Version).   Completely new material
is inserted into Genesis 3:   the story of Satan's coming before
God and offering to be sent into the world to redeem mankind,
if only he can receive God's honor. When this offer is refused
by God, Satan rebels against God (Gen. 3:1-5, Inspired Version).
An entirely new section is added which describes Adam's baptism
by immersion (Gen. 6:67, Inspired Version).   A long new section is added, giving the prophecy of Enoch (Gen. 6:26-7:78, Inspired Version), and telling that not only Enoch but an entire
group of saints, the people of Zion, were taken up into heaven.
Furthermore, in these early chapters of Genesis such distinctive
Mormon doctrines are revealed as the pre-existence of the souls
of all men (Gen. 2:6, 9, Inspired Version); the teaching that
if man had not sinned he would not have been able to propagate
himself (Gen. 6:56, Inspired Version); the teaching that the
children of Canaan were made black as a curse for their sins
(Gen. 7:10, Inspired Version); and the teaching that the earth
shall have rest for a thousand years after the Lord returns (Gen.
7:72, Inspired Version).[31]

Smith revised many more sections of the Bible, both in the
Old Testament and in the New.[32]   One of the most significant
additions was the insertion into Genesis 50 of a passage in which
his own future appearance was predicted: "And that seer will

[30] INSPIRED VERSION: *The Holy Scriptures, Containing the Old and New
Testaments*: An Inspired Revision of the Authorized Version, by Joseph
Smith, Junior.   A New Corrected Edition. Independence, Mo.: Herald
Pub. House, 1955 (originally published in 1867).   The reason why this
version was published by the Reorganized Church is as follows: the original manuscript of this revision was in the possession of Emma Smith,
widow of Joseph Smith, Jr.   She refused to follow Brigham Young's leadership, and also refused to turn over this manuscript to the main Mormon
body.   Mormons claim, however, that a copy of this revision, made by
John M. Bernhisel, is in the possession of the Utah Church (Joseph Fielding Smith, *Answers to Gospel Questions* [Salt Lake City; Deseret Book Co.,
1958], II, 206).

[31] It is revealing to note that in this supposedly superior bit of divine rev-
elation such grammatical errors occur as "for as I, the Lord God, liveth"
(Gen. 3:30), and "surely the flocks of my brother falleth into my hands"
(Gen. 5:18).

[32]   For further details, see George B. Arbaugh, *Revelation in Mormonism*
(Chicago: University of Chicago Press, 1932), Chap. 8.

I bless . . . and his name shall be called Joseph, and it shall be after the name of his father . . . for the thing which the Lord shall bring forth by his hand shall bring my people unto salvation."[33]

It is quite evident, therefore, that what Smith did when he revised the Bible was something far more drastic than merely correcting its translation. The question must therefore now be asked: which version of the Bible do Mormons accept? As we have seen, the Reorganized Church, the largest of the Mormon splinter groups, uses Smith's Inspired Version as its official text. The Mormon Church,[34] however, does not use the Inspired Version; its official Bible version is the King James. Authorities in the Mormon Church, however, make it very clear that they do accept the changes made in the King James Version by Joseph Smith. Note what Joseph Fielding Smith, currently President of the Council of Twelve Apostles, has to say about this:

> The reason why the Church of Jesus Christ of Latter-Day Saints has not published the entire manuscript [of the Inspired Version of the Bible] is not due to any lack of confidence in the integrity of Joseph Smith, or doubt as to the correctness of the numerous additions and changes which are not in the Authorized Version of the Bible. The members of the Church do accept fully all of these and additions as having come by divine revelations to the Prophet Joseph Smith.[35]

Compare also the following statement by the same author:

> The revision of the Bible which was done by Joseph Smith at the command of the Lord was not a complete revision of the Bible. There are many parts of the Bible in which the Prophet did not change the meaning where it is incorrect. . . . However, all that he did is very helpful for the major errors have been corrected.[36]

Why, then, has not the Mormon Church, like the Reorganized Church, adopted Smith's Inspired Version as its official Bible? Mormons give at least two reasons for this:

(1) The Inspired Version has not been published by the Mormon Church because it was never completed. Smith, it is alleged, wished to complete the revision, but was prevented from doing so by persecution and mob violence.[37] This is,

---

[33] Gen. 50:33, Inspired Version. Cf. II Nephi 3:15.
[34] The expression, "the Mormon Church," shall always be used to designate the Salt Lake City Mormons; whenever the word "Mormon" is used without further qualification, it refers to this group. The expression "Reorganized Church" will be used for the group which has its headquarters in Independence, Missouri.
[35] *Answers to Gospel Questions,* II, 207.
[36] *Doctrines of Salvation* (Salt Lake City: Bookcraft, 1956), III, 191.
[37] Joseph Fielding Smith, *Answers to Gospel Questions,* II, 207.

however, rather strange reasoning. If certain errors in the Bible
have been corrected by Smith, as is alleged, why continue to use
an erroneous version? Why not use as many of the "corrections"
as there are?

(2) The Inspired Version is not used by the Mormon Church
because there are such differences between this version and the
versions in common use that the employment of the former
would be a hindrance in mission work. The King James Version
is therefore said to "give us a common ground for proselyting
purposes."[38] This answer is also hard to understand. Do the
missionaries then intend to deceive people as to which Bible
they accept? Furthermore, why not eliminate the *Book of Mormon,* then, since this would, on the ground mentioned above,
constitute an even greater hindrance? Besides, even if missionaries should go out with a King James Version, why should
not the church publish the Inspired Version for use by Mormons
only?

(3) A third reason may be added: an important section of the
Inspired Version, the so-called Book of Moses (which is an
exact copy of the opening chapters of Genesis in the Inspired
Version, containing the additional material referred to above),
has been incorporated into the Mormon sacred book, *Pearl of
Great Price.* This part of Smith's revised Bible, therefore, the
Mormons do retain — though alongside of the King James version
of these chapters, which is quite different, as we have seen.

We conclude from this discussion that the statement made
in Article 8 of the Articles of Faith is not honest and not true:
"We believe the Bible to be the word of God as far as it is
translated correctly. . . ." Mormons believe no such thing.
They hold that the Bible as we have it is not correct on a number
of significant points and that some serious omissions are found
in it. They do not therefore consider the Bible as such to be
either complete or authoritative in its unemended form. More
honest than Article 8 is the following statement by Mormon
author Bruce R. McConkie:

> The Book of Moses, a work containing eight chapters and
> covering the same general period and events as are found in the
> first six chapters of Genesis, contains much of this restored
> truth. The 1st and 7th chapters of Moses are entirely new
> revelations having no counterpart in Genesis. The other
> chapters in Moses cover the same events recorded in the first
> six chapters of Genesis, but the account revealed in latter-days
> has been so enlarged, contains so much new material, and so
> radically changes the whole perspective of the Lord's dealings

[38] *Ibid.*

with Adam and the early patriarchs that for all practical purposes it may be considered as entirely new matter. The whole view of the creation of all things; of pre-existence and the purpose of life; of Adam and his fall; of the primeval revelation of the gospel to man; of the terms and conditions in accordance with which salvation is offered to the living and the dead; of Enoch, his ministry and his establishment of Zion; and of Noah, his priesthood and ministry — the whole view and perspective relative to all these things is radically changed by the new revelations in the Book of Moses. This book, which is also contained in the Prophet's Inspired Version of the Bible, is one of the most important documents the Lord has ever revealed.[39]

Honest and forthright is also the following quotation from Joseph Fielding Smith: "Guided by the *Book of Mormon, Doctrine and Covenants,* and the Spirit of the Lord, it is not difficult for one to discern the errors in the Bible."[40]

We may thus note a second respect in which Mormons consider their sacred books to be superior to the Bible: the Bible as it stands is not only full of errors but is in dire need of supplementary material and revised readings, which have been supplied, at least in part, by Joseph Smith.

At this point the reader is referred to Jesus' Parable of the Rich man and Lazarus, found in Luke 16:19-31. It will be recalled that the rich man, after he lifted up his eyes and found himself in Hades, asked that his brothers be given an additional revelation besides what was in the Bible: namely, that Lazarus be sent to them from the realm of the dead. Abraham, however, replied: "If they hear not Moses and the prophets, neither will they be persuaded, if one rise from the dead" (v. 31). Here Christ clearly disavowed the need for a source of revelation additional to the Bible. The "Moses and the prophets" of which Jesus spoke, furthermore, were not Joseph Smith's emended version, but the Old Testament as we have it. Apparently the Mormons wish to be wiser than Christ Himself.

More needs to be said on this point, however. Mormons arrogate to Joseph Smith an authority which was not claimed even by Jesus Christ: namely, the authority to alter the text of Scripture! When Christ confronted Satan in the wilderness, He answered the tempter by quoting three passages from the Book of Deuteronomy, prefixing these quotations with the words, "It is written" (Mt. 4:4, 7, 10). By these prefixed words our Lord indicated the finality and unchangeability of the words of

---

[39] *Mormon Doctrine* (Salt Lake City: Bookcraft, 1958), pp. 509-10.
[40] *Doctrines of Salvation,* III, 191.

Scripture. Christ further affirmed the inviolability of the law
(which word here probably stands for the entire Old Testament)
in Luke 16:17, "But it is easier for heaven and earth to pass
away, than for one tittle of the law to fall." Christ emphatically
asserted the inviolability of the Scriptures in John 10:35, "The
scripture cannot be broken. . . ." Never did our Lord take it
upon Himself to alter one word of the Old Testament Scriptures,
nor did He ever suggest that a time was coming when certain Old
Testament passages would be altered through further revelation.
Yet Joseph Smith dared to assume authority which Christ never
claimed — dared to tamper with the Word of God. The reader
may judge for himself what this fact tells us about the attitude
of the Mormon Church toward the Bible.

We have already observed in the preceding paragraphs that
the Bible as it stands is not sufficient for the Mormons. In
addition to emending and revising the text of the Scriptures,
however, Mormons have added to them three additional sacred
books: *The Book of Mormon, Doctrine and Covenants,* and *The
Pearl of Great Price.* Let us examine each of these in turn.

THE BOOK OF MORMON

The Book of Mormon, it will be recalled, was referred to in
Article 8 of the Articles of Faith: "We also believe the Book of
Mormon to be the word of God." This book takes pains to assert
its own *raison d'être.* In I Nephi 13:28 an angel is said to have
revealed to Nephi that "after the book [the Bible] hath gone forth
through the hands of the great and abominable church,[41] . . . there
are many plain and precious things taken away from the book. . ."
We have already seen that Smith attempted to supply some of
these "plain and precious things" by revising the Bible. However, Mormons teach that an entirely new book was necessary to
complete God's revelation to man. This point is made clear in
a section of the *Book of Mormon* where God is quoted as saying
through Nephi:

> Thou fool, that shall say: A Bible, we have got a Bible, and
> we need no more Bible. . . . And because that I have spoken
> one word ye need not suppose that I cannot speak another. . . .
> Wherefore, because that ye have a Bible ye need not suppose
> that it contains all my words; neither need ye suppose that I
> have not caused more to be written.[42]

41 Presumably the Roman Catholic Church — see Bruce McConkie,
Mormon Doctrine, p. 130.
42 II Nephi 29:6, 9, and 10.

Bruce McConkie, therefore, is only echoing the *Book of Mormon* when he makes the startling statement: "One of the great heresies of an apostate Christianity is the unfounded assumption that the Bible contains all of the inspired teachings now extant among men."[43]

What is the *Book of Mormon* all about? Briefly, it is an account of two great waves of immigration to the American continents. The first of these, described only in the Book of Ether, was that of the nation of the Jaredites. They left from the region around the Tower of Babel at about 2,250 B.C. Jared's brother, a prophet, was told by the Lord to build eight barges for the ocean trip. These barges were supposed to be as long as a tree, and were to be made "exceeding tight, even that they would hold water like unto a dish" (Ether 2:17). When Jared's brother informed the Lord that there would not be sufficient air in the barges to allow the occupants to breathe, the Lord said to him,

> Behold, thou shalt make a hole in the top, and also in the bottom; and when thou shalt suffer for air thou shalt unstop the hole and receive air. And if it be so that the water come in upon thee, behold, ye shall stop the hole, that ye may not perish in the flood (Ether 2:20).

These eight barges, driven by the wind for three hundred forty-four days, landed at exactly the same time and at exactly the same place: the West Coast of Central America. Here, in America, the Jaredites founded a widespread civilization and built many cities; we are particularly informed that "they also had horses, and asses, and there were elephants and cureloms and cumoms; all of which were useful unto man, and more especially the elephants and cureloms and cumoms" (Ether 9:19). The Jaredites, however, did not get along well with each other; they engaged in savage battles, in one of which two million mighty men, plus their wives and children, were slain! (Ether 15:2). The war continued to rage so furiously that finally there were only two warriors left: Coriantumr and Shiz. In the final battle Shiz was killed; the passage describing Shiz's death contains the following interesting detail: "And it came to pass that after he [Coriantumr] had smitten off the head of Shiz, that Shiz raised upon his hands and fell; and after that he had struggled for breath, he died" (Ether 15:31). Coriantumr, though seriously wounded in this battle, survived and lived with the people of Zarahemla for "nine moons" (Omni 21). The only other survivor of the Jaredites was the prophet Ether, who recorded the history

---

[43] *Op. cit.,* p. 79.

of his people on twenty-four plates.   Thus the Jaredites were
completely obliterated from North America.

The second, and more important, immigration to America
was that of Lehi and his descendants.   Lehi, a Jewish prophet of
the tribe of Manasseh, was forced to leave Jerusalem in 600 B.C.
because of persecution occasioned by his testimony against the
wickedness of the Jews and his prediction of the impending
destruction of Jerusalem.   Lehi, his wife, and his four sons
therefore left Jerusalem and went to live in the region bordering
on the Red Sea.   In obedience to God's command Lehi's sons
were sent back to Jerusalem in order to obtain from a certain
Laban a set of brass plates containing the five books of Moses,
various prophecies, and Lehi's genealogy (the so-called Brass
Plates of Laban).   As Lehi and his sons journeyed on, they came
to the shore of the ocean, where Nephi, one of the sons, proceeded
to build a ship in response to a divine revelation telling him to
do so.   The entire group now entered the ship and began to sail
eastward, with the aid of a ball containing a spindle which pointed
out the way in which they should go, which Lehi had previously
found on the ground (I Nephi 16:10).[44]   In course of time they
landed on the west coast of South America.   (By this time the
Jaredites had exterminated themselves.)

Of the sons of Lehi the most prominent were Nephi and
Laman.   The family of Laman and that of his brother Lemuel
were continually in rebellion against the Lord and against His
commandments; consequently the Lord cursed them and caused
"a skin of blackness" to come upon them (II Nephi 5:21).   Since
the Lamanites, as the descendants of Laman are called, were the
ancestors of the American Indians, it is evident that, according
to Mormon teaching, the American Indians are not of the
Mongolian race — as most anthropologists declare — but are
actually dark-skinned Israelites of the tribe of Manasseh.[45]

The other descendants of Lehi, however, who had begun to
call themselves Nephites (after Nephi, whom they recognized as

[44] One of the more obvious anachronisms of the *Book of Mormon*. The
mariner's compass was not invented until the 12th century A.D.
[45] See Talmage, *Articles of Faith,* pp. 260, 284. One wonders why, if
this is the case, the skin of the Lamanites is said to have turned *black.*
A Mormon missionary once answered this question by saying that in the
days when the plates on which the *Book of Mormon* is based were written
there was no word for brown!   One would expect, however, that the "inspired translation" would correct this detail.   The implications of this
teaching about the origin of dark-pigmented skin are rather unflattering
to these races, to say the least.   It is also interesting to note that, according
to Mormon teaching, "when the Lamanites fully repent and sincerely receive the gospel, the Lord has promised to remove the dark skin" (Joseph
Fielding Smith, *Answers to Gospel Questions,* III, 123).

their king), did not rebel against God's commandments. Gradually the Nephites migrated to Central and North America. Here they founded a great civilization and built large cities. In A.D., 34 in fulfillment of a prophecy made earlier by Nephi (I Nephi 12:6ff.), the Lord Jesus Christ Himself came down from heaven, prescribed baptism by immersion, called and commissioned twelve disciples, instituted the sacrament of bread and wine, and uttered many teachings, including virtually the entire Sermon on the Mount (III Nephi 11:28). Though at the time of Christ's appearance all the inhabitants of the land were converted (IV Nephi 2), and though there was peace and harmony between the Lamanites and the Nephites for two hundred years (IV Nephi 17ff.), after this period hostility again arose between these two groups, and there was constant warfare. In A.D. 385 the two groups assembled for a final battle near the hill Cumorah (located by present-day Mormons in upper New York State). In this battle the Lamanites killed all the Nephites except one — Moroni, whose father's name had been Mormon.

Mormon had been writing down the history of his people, the Nephites, on golden plates. The process of recording this history had begun with Nephi, the son of Lehi, and had been continued by other Nephite historians. Nephi had begun engraving two kinds of plates: larger plates, containing a secular history of the Nephites, and smaller plates, containing their spiritual history. Mormon, who lived in the fourth century A.D., had abridged the larger plates of Nephi and had added to this abridgment the smaller plates of Nephi *in toto.* This entire collection of golden plates Mormon hid in the hill Cumorah before the battle of Cumorah. After the battle, Moroni, the only Nephite survivor, added some additional plates, containing the books of Ether and Moroni, and buried them also in the hill Cumorah. This happened in A.D. 421. Fourteen hundred years later, so Mormons claim, in the years 1823-27, Moroni, now changed into an angel (though he is sometimes called a resurrected being), appeared to Joseph Smith, told him where the plates were hidden, and permitted him to take them.

In Appendix A the question of the genuineness of the *Book of Mormon* will be taken up in greater detail. Suffice it here to note that this book is not only recognized by Mormons as the word of God alongside of the Bible, but is actually thought to be superior to the Bible. For proof of the latter statement, the reader is reminded of what is said by Mormons about the imperfections inherent in all Bible translations and the lack of these imperfections in the *Book of Mormon,* and also about the many "plain and precious things" which have been removed from the Bible. Note also the following statement by Joseph Smith: "I told the brethren that the Book of Mormon was the most correct of any book on earth, and the keystone of our religion, and a man would get nearer to God by abiding by its precepts, than by any other book."[46] "Any other book" obviously includes the Bible. Here, therefore, in the words of their inspired "prophet," Mormons claim that they have a sacred book which can bring one nearer to God than even the Bible itself. It may be presumed, therefore, that if there should be disagreement between the King James Version of the Bible and the *Book of Mormon,* Mormons would follow the latter in preference to the former.

OTHER SACRED BOOKS

In addition to the *Book of Mormon,* however, Mormons recognize two other sacred books. These are actually more important doctrinally than the *Book of Mormon,* since they contain some of the most distinctive doctrines of present-day Mormonism. The first of these is *Doctrine and Covenants.* This volume, which was first published in its present form in 1876, contains 136 sections or chapters, each of which is divided into verses. These sections all contain revelations alleged to have been given through Joseph Smith, except for Section 136, which was a revelation given through President Brigham Young. The current version of *Doctrine and Covenants* also includes the Manifesto prohibiting polygamy issued by President Wilford Woodruff in 1890. These "revelations" deal with such doctrines as the nature of God, the church, the priesthood, the millennium, the resurrection, the state of man after death, the various grades of salvation, and so on. Many of these "revelations" are addressed to specific persons, and deal with very specific matters. So, for example, Section 19 is addressed to Martin Harris and instructs him to "pay the debt thou hast contracted with the printer" (v. 35). In Section 104 a "revelation" is given concerning the disposition of certain lots and houses in Kirtland, Ohio, along with the individuals to whom these properties are assigned (vv. 20-46). In Section 132, the famous section on plural marriage, a specific word is addressed to Joseph Smith's wife, telling her that she must stand ready to receive the additional wives that have been given to her husband, on pain of everlasting destruction (vv. 52-54). The particular significance of *Doctrine and Covenants* for present-day Mormonism is that it contains revelations about baptism for the dead (Sections 124, 127, 128), about

---

[46] Statement made by Smith on November 28, 1841. Reproduced in *Teachings of the Prophet Joseph Smith,* ed. Joseph Fielding Smith (Salt Lake City: Deseret Book Co., 1958), p. 194.

celestial marriage (Section 132, vv. 19 and 20), and about plural marriage or polygamy (132:61, 62; cf. the Woodruff Manifesto, pp. 256-257). The *Book of Mormon,* it should be observed at this point, says nothing about either baptism for the dead or celestial marriage, and denounces polygamy as a practice abominable in the sight of the Lord (Jacob 2:24, 27).

The second of these additional sacred books is the *Pearl of Great Price,* a small volume containing the following writings: (1) The Book of Moses, a work of eight chapters covering the same general period as that covered by the first six chapters of Genesis. This book, as was previously indicated, is a copy of the opening chapters of Smith's "Inspired Version" of the Bible; its contents have been described above (see p. 20). (2) The Book of Abraham, purporting to be a translation from an Egyptian papyrus. This document, representing a later stage in Smith's theological development, clearly teaches polytheism, rewriting the first chapter of Genesis in polytheistic fashion: "And they (the Gods) said: Let there be light" (4:3). This book, supposedly written by Abraham while he was in Egypt, tells about the star Kolob, which is said to be the greatest of all the stars and the one nearest to God (3:3, 9, 16), about the pre-existence of souls (3:22), about the plan to prepare an earth for these souls (3:24), about the plan to subject these souls to a period of probation on earth (3:25), and about the organization of matter whereby the heavens and the earth were formed (4:1).[47] (3) An extract from Joseph Smith's translation of the Bible (Chapter 24 of Matthew). (4) Extracts from the History of Joseph Smith, the Prophet — the section of Smith's autobiography which narrates the discovery of the plates and the translation of them. (5) The Articles of Faith.

FURTHER REVELATIONS

Such, then, are the Mormon sacred books. Even these additional writings, however, do not mark the end of divine revelations for Mormons. In *Doctrine and Covenants* 107 the office of president of the church is described as follows:

> And again, the duty of the President of the office of the High Priesthood is to preside over the whole church, and to be like unto Moses — Behold, here is wisdom; yea, to be a seer, a

---

[47] It will be observed that the Mormons thus have three official accounts of creation: the one found in the King James Version of the Bible; the one found in Chapter 2 of the Book of Moses, which gives the creation story in the first person; and the one found in Chapter 4 of the Book of Abraham, which teaches polytheism. One wonders which account is now to be considered the most authoritative.

revelator, a translator, and a prophet, having all the gifts of God which he bestows upon the head of the church (vv. 91, 92).

It is also stated by a prominent Mormon author, however, that the counselors to the president, the Council of Twelve Apostles, and usually the Patriarch of the Church are likewise sustained as "prophets, seers, and revelators."[48] This same author explains that the revelations received by officers lower than the president of the church (and here he includes bishops and stake presidents as well as those mentioned above) concern the duties of their particular offices; only the president of the church can receive revelations for the guidance of the church as a whole.[49]

Summing up, we have observed that Mormons do not at all accept the Bible as their final authority for doctrine and life; they relegate the Bible to an inferior place of authority. Their own emendations of the Bible and their own sacred scriptures are considered to be superior in value to the Bible. In fact, even their president is believed to possess the power of receiving further revelations which could conceivably alter the doctrines accepted by the Mormon Church.

We must at this point assert, in the strongest possible terms, that Mormonism does not deserve to be called a Christian religion. It is basically anti-Christian and anti-Biblical. The Mormon contention that "after the book [the Bible] hath gone forth through the hands of the great and abominable church . . . there are many plain and precious things taken away from the book. . ." (I Nephi 13:28), is completely contrary to fact. The many copies of Old Testament manuscripts which we now possess do vary in minor matters — the spelling of words, the omission of a phrase here and there — but there is no evidence whatsoever that any major sections of Old Testament books have been lost. The manuscripts found among the Dead Sea Scrolls, generally dated from about 200 to 50 B.C., include portions of every Old Testament book except Esther; studies have revealed that these documents — older by a thousand years than previously discovered Old Testament manuscripts — are substantially identical to the text of the Old Testament which had been previously handed down. As far as New Testament manuscripts are concerned, the oldest of which go back to the second century A.D., the situation is substantially the same. The variations that are found in these manuscripts — all copies of the originals or of copies made from the originals — are of a relatively minor

---

[48] Widtsoe, *Evidences and Reconciliations*, p. 256.
[49] *Ibid.*, pp. 101, 102.

nature. There is no indication whatever that any large sections of material found in the originals have been lost. Most of the manuscript variations concern matters of spelling, word order, tense, and the like; no single doctrine is affected by them in any way.[50] There is, further, not a shred of evidence to show that any translations of the Bible, including the fourth-century Vulgate, which became the official medieval Roman Catholic version, omitted any portions of these manuscripts or failed to reproduce any major sections of the Bible.

The Bible itself, moreover, clearly indicates that it is the final revelation of God to man, and that it does not need to be supplemented by additional revelation. We have already noted Christ's reference to Moses and the prophets as giving sufficient revelation for man's salvation (Lk. 16:19-31; see above, p. 23). When the risen Christ appeared to the disciples from Emmaus, He did not find it necessary to give them additional revelations, but "beginning from Moses and from all the prophets, he interpreted to them in all the Scriptures the things concerning himself" (Lk. 24:27). The finality of the revelation that came through Jesus Christ is strikingly expressed in Hebrews 1:1 and 2:

> God, having of old times spoken unto the fathers in the prophets, by divers portions and in divers manners, hath at the end of these days spoken unto us in his Son. . . .

God's revelation through Christ is here described as climactic and definitive — the claim that further revelations would have to be given to the church 1800 years later by Joseph Smith clearly contradicts the thrust of this passage!

The question might be asked: If Jesus Christ was the culmination of God's revelation to man, why was it necessary for the apostles to write the Bible books which have become incorporated into our present New Testament? The answer is that the apostles had to present to the world their witness to Jesus Christ, so that we might believe on Him on the basis of their testimony. The purpose of the apostolic witness is well expressed by the Apostle John:

> That which was from the beginning, that which we have heard, that which we have seen with our eyes, that which we beheld, and our hands handled, concerning the word of life (and the life was manifested, and we have seen, and bear witness, and declare unto you the life, the eternal life, which was with the Father, and was manifested unto us); that which we have seen and heard declare we unto you also, that ye also

---

[50] For more technical information on these matters, cf. books on textual criticism like Frederick Kenyon's *Our Bible and the Ancient Manuscripts*, rev. by A. W. Adams (New York: Harper, 1958).

may have fellowship with us: yea, and our fellowship is with the Father, and with his Son Jesus Christ (I Jn. 1:1-3).

This testimony having been given by the apostles of the first century after Christ, what need is there for an additional testimony by someone living in the nineteenth century? Our Lord Himself taught that the word of the apostles was to be sufficient to lead men to faith: "Neither for these only [the apostles] do I pray, but for them also [all other believers] that believe on me through their word" (Jn. 17:20). The Bible further indicates that the entire church is "built upon the foundation of the apostles and prophets" (Eph. 2:20). In this passage the word *prophets* stands for the chief Old Testament agents of revelation, and the word *apostles,* for the chief New Testament agents of revelation. Since these two groups constitute the foundation of the church, the need for the work of another prophet arising eighteen centuries later is definitely excluded.

In Revelation 22:18 and 19 the following statement is made:

I [Jesus Christ] testify unto every man that heareth the words of the prophecy of this book, If any man shall add unto them, God shall add unto him the plagues which are written in this book: and if any man shall take away from the words of the book of this prophecy, God shall take away his part from the tree of life, and out of the holy city, which are written in this book.

It must be granted at once that these words apply specifically to the Book of Revelation to which they are appended. If one adds to the words of this book, Jesus here says, God shall add to him the plagues which are written in the book. One may ask at this juncture whether Section 76 of *Doctrine and Covenants,* which purports to give further revelations about the three kinds of heavenly blessedness, is not an adding to the Book of Revelation. Furthermore, note that these words of Jesus set forth in unmistakable terms the finality and inviolability of a book of the Bible. The question may well be asked whether these words do not, by implication, also teach the finality and inviolability of the other books of the Bible. If one may not add anything to the Book of Revelation, on what ground is it permissible to add material to other Biblical books?

In answer to the Mormon contention that a church without further revelation is a church completely without divine guidance, we may say that Christ has promised to be with His church always, even to the end of the world (Mt. 28:20); and that the Holy Spirit has been given to the church forever (Jn. 14:16), by whose guidance the church continues to live and work. This constant leading of the Spirit, however, does not necessitate the production of new sacred books, since the Spirit now guides the church by means of the inscripturated Word.

I conclude by stating once again that by adding to the Holy Scriptures their additional sacred books, the Mormons have undermined and overthrown "the faith which was once for all delivered unto the saints" (Jude 3).

DOCTRINES

We proceed now to examine the doctrines of Mormonism, following the order of the customary divisions of theology: God, man, Christ, salvation, the church, the last things. Since I am concerned to be as fair and objective as possible in setting forth these doctrines, I shall base this exposition exclusively on Mormon sources.

At this juncture it should be made clear that it is not my primary intention to refute the various unscriptural elements in these doctrines. It is my conviction that to do a thorough job of refuting all the errors of even the four cults treated in this book would require not just a volume, but a set of volumes. Furthermore, it is my considered judgment that a thorough refutation of the doctrines of any cult will require a thorough knowledge of the Bible and a thorough grasp of the whole of Christian doctrine. To try to set forth the type of comprehensive doctrinal teaching required to refute the cults in a volume of the size of this one is neither wise nor practicable. It should further be added that what is needed first of all by the person who wishes to oppose and attack the teachings of the cults is a clear understanding and somewhat systematic grasp of exactly what the cults teach.

For the reasons given above, I do not intend to include in the doctrinal treatment of the cults a point-by-point refutation of their errors. Though there will be instances when such refutation will be attempted, and though certain cultist teachings will be given detailed treatment in the appendices, I will generally consider my purpose accomplished if the doctrinal teachings of each cult have been expounded with some degree of thoroughness.[51]

---

[51] If the reader wishes to find more extensive discussions, from a conservative theological point of view, of the doctrinal issues raised by the cults and of the relevant Scriptural passages, he is referred to the following works on Christian doctrine:

Works by writers of Reformed persuasion: Herman Bavinck, *The Doctrine of God* (Grand Rapids: Eerdmans, 1951); *Our Reasonable Faith* Eerdmans, 1956). Louis Berkhof, *Systematic Theology* (Eerdmans, 1953). G. C. Berkouwer, various volumes in the series, *Studies in Dogmatics* (Eerdmans, 1952—). A. A. Hodge, *Outlines of Theology* (originally published in 1860; reprinted by Eerdmans in 1957). Charles Hodge, *Systematic Theology*, 3 vols. (originally published in 1871; reprinted by

DOCTRINE OF GOD

THE BEING OF GOD

Mormonism Denies the Trinity. Mormonism teaches that the Persons of the Trinity are not three Persons in one Being, as historic Christianity has always taught, but three separate Beings. Here, at the very outset of our doctrinal discussion, we encounter one of the baffling aspects of Mormon theology: its inconsistency. One may find, for example, many statements in Mormon sacred writings which affirm the unity of God; statements of this sort, however, are nullified by later "revelations" which affirm that Father, Son, and Holy Spirit are three distinct Beings.

The *Book of Mormon,* for example, clearly teaches the doctrine of the Trinity in agreement with historic Christianity: "And now, behold, this is the doctrine of Christ, and the only and true doctrine of the Father, and of the Son, and of the Holy Ghost, which is one God, without end" (II Nephi 31:21). ". . . Every thing shall be restored to its perfect frame . . . and shall be brought and be arraigned before the bar of Christ the Son, and God the Father, and the Holy Spirit, which is one eternal God . . ." (Alma 11:44). Note also the concluding sentence of the *Testimony of Three Witnesses*: "And the honor be to the Father, and to the Son, and to the Holy Ghost, which is one God." Compare now with the preceding the following statements, made by Joseph Smith in 1844:

> I will preach on the plurality of Gods. I have selected this text [Rev. 1:6, in the King James Version] for that express purpose. I wish to declare I have always and in all congregations when I have preached on the subject of the Deity, it has been the plurality of Gods. . . .

Eerdmans in 1940). Wm. G. T. Shedd, *Dogmatic Theology,* 3 vols. (originally published in 1888; reprinted by Zondervan in 1953).

Works by Baptist writers: Augustus Hopkins Strong, *Systematic Theology* (Philadelphia: Judson Press, 1907). Henry Clarence Thiessen, *Lectures in Systematic Theology* (Eerdmans, 1949).

Works by Methodist writers: John Miley, *Systematic Theology,* 2 vols. (New York: Hunt and Eaton, 1893). Wm. B. Pope, *A Compendium of Christian Theology,* 3 vols. (New York: Phillips and Hunt, 1881). Miner Raymond, *Systematic Theology,* 3 vols. (Cincinnati: Hitchcock and Walden, 1877). Richard Watson, *Theological Institutes,* 2 vols. (New York: Carlton and Porter, 1857).

Works by Nazarene writers: Aaron M. Hills, *Fundamental Christian Theology,* 2 vols. (Pasadena: C. J. Kinne, 1931). Henry Orton Wiley, *Christian Theology,* 3 vols. (Kansas City: Nazarene Publishing House, 1940).

Works by Lutheran writers: John Theodore Mueller, *Christian Dogmatics* (St. Louis: Concordia, 1934). Franz Pieper, *Christian Dogmatics,* 3 vols. (St. Louis: Concordia, 1950).

> I have always declared God to be a distinct personage, Jesus Christ a separate and distinct personage from God the Father, and that the Holy Ghost was a distinct personage and a Spirit: and these three constitute three distinct personages and three Gods. . . .
>
> Many men say there is one God; the Father, the Son and the Holy Ghost are only one God. I say that is a strange God anyhow — three in one, and one in three! It is a curious organization. . . . All are to be crammed into one God, according to sectarianism. It would make the biggest God in all the world. He would be a wonderfully big God — he would be a giant or a monster.[52]

At this juncture we face a real problem. Joseph Smith himself once said that the *Book of Mormon* was the most correct of any book on earth (see above, p. 28). In the light of Smith's later revelation, however, the *Book of Mormon* is here revealed as having been in error, since it contains the "sectarian" teaching that God is one. We must challenge Mormons at this point either to retract Smith's later statement, and thus to admit that their prophet was in error, or to acknowledge that the *Book of Mormon* was in error in affirming the unity of God. Mormons have no right to maintain the errorlessness of both the *Book of Mormon* and Joseph Smith.

Mormonism Denies the Spirituality of God. "The Father has a body of flesh and bones as tangible as man's; the Son also; but the Holy Ghost has not a body of flesh and bones, but is a personage of Spirit" (*Doctrine and Covenants* 130:22). Thus, though an exception is made in the case of the Holy Spirit, it is clearly taught that both Father and Son have material bodies. ". . . It is clear that the Father is a personal being, possessing a definite form, with bodily parts and spiritual passions."[53] In fact, this same author goes on to say, "We affirm that to deny the materiality of God's person is to deny God; for a thing without parts has no whole, and an immaterial body cannot exist."[54] One wonders at this juncture how Mormons can believe that the Holy Spirit exists. If "an immaterial body cannot exist," how can the Holy Spirit exist, who "has not a body of flesh and bones"? To be consistent, Mormons should deny either the existence of the Holy Spirit or the truth of the Talmage statement last quoted

The fact that, according to Mormons, God has a material body

---

[52] Sermon on "The Christian Godhead — Plurality of Gods," delivered on June 16, 1844; quoted in *Teachings of the Prophet Joseph Smith*, pp. 370, 372.
[53] James E. Talmage, *Articles of Faith*, p. 41.
[54] *Ibid.*, p. 48.

(with the exception of the Holy Spirit) implies that sex distinctions must also apply to God. This is what is actually taught in the Mormon sacred scriptures: "In the image of his own body, male and female, created he them . . ." (Book of Moses 6:9). John A. Widtsoe, a prominent Mormon author, puts it this way: "In accordance with Gospel philosophy there are males and females in heaven. Since we have a Father, who is our God, we must also have a mother, who possesses the attributes of Godhood."[55] This thought, that we have a mother in heaven as well as a father, is given poetic expression in the third stanza of a well-known Mormon hymn, "O my Father":

> I had learned to call thee Father,
>   Through Thy Spirit from on high;
> But, until the key of Knowledge
>   Was restored, I knew not why.
> In the heavens are parents single?
>   No; the thought makes reason stare!
> Truth is reason; truth eternal
>   Tells me, I've a mother there.[56]

Mormonism Teaches That There Are a Great Many Gods in Addition to Father, Son, and Holy Spirit. The first thing we should note is that here again we see a certain evolution in Mormon doctrinal teachings. In the Book of Moses, allegedly revealed to Joseph Smith in 1830, the first chapter of Genesis is reproduced with the name of God in the singular: "And I, God, said: Let there be light; and there was light" (2:3; see rest of chapter). In the Book of Abraham, however, supposedly translated in the summer of 1835,[57] the first chapter of Genesis is reproduced again, this time with the name of God in the plural: "And they (the Gods) said: Let there be light; and there was light" 4:3); the plural form, Gods, continues throughout the remainder of this chapter, as well as throughout Chapter 5. If we are to receive the later revelation as the more authoritative, it would appear that the earlier revelation, which spoke of God in the singular, was in error.

Smith tried to justify this translation of the creation account by pointing out that the Hebrew word usually translated God, *Elohim,* is in the plural.[58] Though this is true, the plural as it here occurs is recognized by all Hebrew scholars as a plural of

---

[55] *A Rational Theology,* 6th ed. (Salt Lake City: Deseret Book Co., 1952), p. 69.
[56] Quoted from Ben E. Rich, *Mr. Durant of Salt Lake City* (Salt Lake City: Deseret News Press, 1952), p. 77.
[57] Joseph Fielding Smith, *Essentials in Church History,* p. 184.
[58] *Teachings of the Prophet Joseph Smith,* p. 371.

majesty, referring to the one true God.⁵⁹ The very fact that the Hebrew verb forms which have *Elohim* as their subject are almost invariably in the singular number proves that the author of Genesis intended to speak of a single God and not of a plurality of gods.

In the sermon on "The Christian Godhead — Plurality of Gods" previously referred to, Joseph Smith declared:

> . . . The doctrine of a plurality of gods is as prominent in the Bible as any other doctrine. It is all over the face of the Bible. It stands beyond the power of controversy. A wayfaring man, though a fool, need not err therein.
>
> Paul says there are Gods many and Lords many. I want to set it forth in a plain and simple manner; but to us there is but one God — that is, *pertaining to us.* . . .
>
> The heads of the Gods appointed one God for us; and when you take [that] view of the subject, it sets one free to see all the beauty, holiness and perfection of the Gods.⁶⁰

It is quite clear from these statements that, according to Smith's latest revelations, there are a great many gods, but that one god has been appointed particularly for the people who inhabit this earth.

To the same effect are statements attributed to Brigham Young, the second president of the church, who, according to Mormon teaching, was also a "revelator" and therefore also spoke with infallible authority. The following pronouncement is very clear in its implications:

> How many Gods there are, I do not know. But there never was a time when there were not Gods and worlds, and when men were not passing through the same ordeals that we are now passing through. That course has been from all eternity, and it is and will be to all eternity.⁶¹

According to this passage, the world we live in is not the only world there is, but there have been a great number of worlds and also a great number of gods.

From a more recent Mormon author we learn that there has been an infinite succession of gods which have come into being through a process of generation: "The Prophet taught that our Father had a Father and so on. Is this not a reasonable thought, especially when we remember that the promises are made to us

---

⁵⁹ See, for example, Francis Brown, S. R. Driver, and Charles A. Briggs, *Hebrew and English Lexicon of the Old Testament* (Boston: Houghton Mifflin, 1907), p. 43.

⁶⁰ *Teachings of the Prophet Joseph Smith,* pp. 370, 372.

⁶¹ *Discourses of Brigham Young,* arranged by John A. Widtsoe (Salt Lake City: Deseret Book Co., 1954), pp. 22-23.

that we may become like him?"[62]   An illuminating discussion
of the relation of these various gods to each other will be found
in Chapter 12 of John A. Widtsoe's *A Rational Theology*. From
this chapter we learn that the various gods are in an order of
progression, that there are some in almost every conceivable
stage of development, that God, angel, and similar terms "denote
merely intelligent beings of varying degree of development" (p.
66), and that God the Father is simply the supreme God —
that is, the god who has reached the highest stage of development.
The difference between angels and gods is thus one of degree,
and that between God the Father and the other gods is likewise
one of degree.   He is simply the god who has progressed the
farthest and is therefore superior to the other gods — the other
gods will never be able to catch up with him.   Mormonism thus
embraces a polytheism of the rankest kind.

Mormonism Also Teaches That the Gods Were Once Men. In
his famous King Follett Discourse, delivered in 1844 at the
funeral of Elder King Follett, Joseph Smith made the following
statement:

> God himself was once as we are now, and is an exalted man,
> and sits enthroned in yonder heavens! . . .   If you were to
> see him today, you would see him like a man in form. . . .   He
> was once a man like us; yea . . . God himself, the Father of us
> all, dwelt on an earth, the same as Jesus Christ himself did. . . .[63]

Smith does not tell us when the Father dwelt on an earth;
the expression "an earth," in fact, suggests that he dwelt on a
different earth than the one we inhabit.   To the same effect is
the following statement by a Mormon writer:

> Mormon prophets have continuously taught the sublime
> truth that God the Eternal Father was once a mortal man who
> passed through a school of earth life similar to that through
> which we are now passing.   He became God — an exalted
> being — through obedience to the same eternal Gospel truths
> that we are given opportunity today to obey.[64]

It is quite obvious from these quotations that Mormons flatly
deny such distinctively Christian doctrines as the immutability
of God, the eternity of God, and the transcendence of God —
His absolute distinctness from man.   What their view amounts to
is that all gods first existed as spirits, came to an earth to receive
bodies, and then, after having passed through a period of probation on the aforesaid earth, were advanced to the exalted position

---

[62] Joseph Fielding Smith, *Doctrines of Salvation,* I, 12.
[63] *Teachings of the Prophet Joseph Smith,* pp. 345-46.
[64] Milton R. Hunter, *The Gospel through the Ages* (Salt Lake City:
Deseret Book Co., 1958), p. 104.

they now enjoy in some heavenly realm. When commenting on the thought that God is said to exist from eternity to eternity, Joseph Fielding Smith observes: "From eternity to eternity means from the spirit existence through the probation which we are in, and then back again to the eternal existence which will follow."[65] Thus every god has passed through a cycle similar to that which we observe in the incarnation of Jesus Christ. The uniqueness of Christ's incarnation is thus completely repudiated.

Mormonism Teaches That Men May Become Gods. In the same King Follett Discourse to which reference has just been made, Joseph Smith said,

> Here, then, is eternal life — to know the only wise and true God; and you have got to learn how to be Gods yourselves, and to be kings and priests to God, the same as all Gods have done before you, namely, by going from one small degree to another, and from a small capacity to a great one; from grace to grace, from exaltation to exaltation, until you attain to the resurrection of the dead, and are able to dwell in everlasting burnings, and to sit in glory, as do those who sit enthroned in everlasting power.[66]

This extremely blunt and much criticized statement, however, is only a logical development of what is found in *Doctrine and Covenants,* Chapter 132. In verse 37 of this section we are told that Abraham and the other patriarchs, because they did what they were commanded, now sit upon thrones and are not angels but gods. In verses 19 and 20 of this chapter, furthermore, we are taught that those who shall marry according to the new and everlasting covenant, whereby they are sealed to their spouses for eternity, shall after this life become gods.

That this is still accepted Mormon teaching is shown in the following statement by Joseph Fielding Smith: ". . . We have to pass through mortality and receive the resurrection and then go on to perfection just as our Father did before us."[67] Lorenzo Snow, fifth president of the Mormon Church, expressed this same truth epigrammatically: "As man is, God once was; as God is, man may become."[68] Widtsoe sums the matter up very neatly when he tell us, "In short, man is a god in embryo."[69]

According to Mormonism, therefore, man is a god in the making. He, too, was once a spirit-creature; he then came to this earth to receive a physical tabernacle; after a period of earthly

---

[65] *Doctrines of Salvation,* I, 12.
[66] *Teachings of the Prophet Joseph Smith,* pp. 346-47.
[67] *Doctrines of Salvation,* I, 12.
[68] *Millennial Star,* 54, 404; quoted in Hunter, *op. cit.,* pp. 105-106.
[69] *A Rational Theology,* p. 26.

probation he dies and is raised again; if he has passed the probation, he shall gradually advance to the status of godhood. In Mormon theology, therefore, not only is God dragged down to the level of man, but man is at the same time exalted to potential deity. All ultimate differentiation between God and man has been done away with in this system, which now promises to its adherents what Satan, through the serpent, once promised to Eve: "Ye shall be as God" (Gen. 3:5).

In this connection, something should be said about the so-called "Adam-God theory." The following statement by President Brigham Young has often been quoted:

> When our father Adam came into the Garden of Eden, he came into it with a celestial body, and brought Eve, one of his wives, with him. He helped to make and organize this world. He is Michael, the Archangel, the Ancient of Days, about whom holy men have written and spoken — He is our father and our God, and the only God with whom we have to do.[70]

By many non-Mormons this statement has been understood as implying that Adam was identical with God the Father (*Elohim*). Joseph Fielding Smith, however, goes to great lengths to indicate that President Young's statement should not be thus understood. Referring to passages in *Doctrine and Covenants* in which Adam is called Michael and is said to have been the Ancient of Days (27:11; 78:15-16), Smith insists that Young only meant to say that Adam was the pre-existent spirit known as Michael, who helped Elohim and Jehovah (another name for Christ) form this earth. Adam also became the father of the physical bodies of the members of the human race, and was given the keys of salvation. Hence the human family is immediately subject to Adam. It is in this sense that Adam may be thought of as "the only god with whom we have to do." This does not mean, however, Smith continues, that Adam is to be identified with God the Father.[71]

One may well question whether Joseph Fielding Smith has interpreted Brigham Young correctly. After all, the statement, "He is our father and our God, and the only God with whom we have to do," seems hard to fit into the type of interpretation Smith advances. If, however, we accept Smith's interpretation as representing the current Mormon view, we get this picture: Adam was a spirit who was pre-existent as the Archangel Michael. In this pre-existent state he must have had a number of wives, since Eve

---

[70] *Journal of Discourses*, I, 50; quoted in Smith, *Doctrines of Salvation*, I, 96.
[71] *Doctrines of Salvation*, I, 96-101.

is called "one of his wives." He helped God the Father and Jesus Christ make and organize this earth. He was then placed on this earth, and was given a physical body, so that he and Eve (who was also given a body) could become the progenitors of the physical bodies of the members of the human race (whose spirits had been previously begotten by Elohim). Adam was also given the keys of salvation, and he was assigned dominion over every living creature. On account of these facts, Adam may be recognized as "a god" — as one to whom we are to be subject. Yet Adam is subordinate to Jesus Christ, and Christ is, in turn, subordinate to God the Father (Elohim). It is specifically stated that Mormons do not worship Adam or pray to him, but that they worship Elohim.[72]

To suggest that Adam is a god is, however, in gross contradiction to the Scriptures, which teach us that Adam was the first created man, the father of the human race, through whose fall into sin all men have come under condemnation (Rom. 5:12-21). The suggestion that Adam is to be looked up to as a god robs the fall of all its seriousness, and obliterates completely the distinction between the Creator and the creature.

THE WORKS OF GOD

Decrees. It can hardly be expected that Mormons, with their view of the plurality of gods and of the changeableness of God, could have anything resembling the historic Reformed doctrine of predestination. We find, accordingly, that Mormon writers are extremely critical of this doctrine:

> Predestination is the false doctrine that from all eternity God has ordered whatever comes to pass, having especial and particular reference to the salvation or damnation of souls. Some souls, according to this false concept, are irrevocably chosen for salvation, others for damnation; and there is said to be nothing any individual can do to escape his predestined inheritance in heaven or in hell as the case may be.[73]

McConkie insists, however, that Mormons do believe in fore-ordination: "To carry forward his own purposes among men and

---

72 *Ibid.,* p. 106. Not all Mormons would agree with Smith's interpretation of Brigham Young's words, however. In 1950 W. Gordon Hackney, a faculty member at Brigham Young University, published a pamphlet of twenty-two pages entitled *That Adam-God Doctrine,* in which he vigorously defended the teaching that Adam is our Heavenly Father, and that Adam and Eve were the parents, not only of our physical bodies, but also of our spirits in the pre-existent world.

73 Bruce R. McConkie, *Mormon Doctrine,* p. 530. Similar sentiments are expressed by Joseph Fielding Smith in an article entitled "Apostate Doctrine of Predestination" (*Doctrines of Salvation,* III, 286).

nations, the Lord *foreordained* chosen spirit children in pre-existence and assigned them to come to earth at particular times and places so that they might aid in furthering the divine will."[74] He then goes on to show, from both Mormon and Christian Scriptures, that the following were foreordained to their spiritual callings: Joseph Smith, Abraham, Jeremiah, Christ, Mary, John the Baptist, and all holders of the Melchizedek priesthood. He makes it very clear, however, that there is no compulsion involved in this foreordination, but that persons who are so foreordained retain their free agency. "By their foreordination the Lord merely gives them the opportunity to serve him and his purposes if they will choose to measure up to the standard he knows they are capable of attaining."[75]

From this and other discussions of predestination by Mormon writers, it becomes quite evident that these authors do not understand what this doctrine really teaches. Interpreting predestination as tantamount to fatalism, they reject it. If, however, the foreordination which they teach really means nothing more than an opportunity to serve the Lord, one wonders what is the real difference between this foreordination and the invitation to salvation which, so they affirm, comes to all men.[76] If, on the other hand, there is a real foreordination of these individuals to the tasks for which they have been chosen, this must be more than a mere opportunity for service. The Mormon doctrine of foreordination does justice neither to the sovereignty of God nor to the certainty of planned events, as taught in Scripture. Was the Lamb "slain from the foundation of the world" (Rev. 13:8) merely given an *opportunity* to die on the cross?

Creation. Mormonism rejects the doctrine of creation out of nothing, or *ex nihilo,* affirming that what the Bible calls creation was simply a reorganization of matter which had always existed. Note the following statement from *Doctrine and Covenants*: "For man is spirit. The elements are eternal, and spirit and element, inseparably connected, receive a fulness of joy. . ." (93:33). The word *elements* here means material elements, as the following quotation from Smith's King Follett Discourse will reveal:

> You ask the learned doctors why they say the world was made out of nothing; and they will answer, "Doesn't the Bible say he *created* the world?" And they infer, from the word create, that it must have been made out of nothing. Now, the

[74] McConkie, *op. cit.,* p. 269.
[75] *Ibid.*
[76] LeGrand Richards, *A Marvelous Work and a Wonder* (Salt Lake City; Deseret Book Co., 1950), pp. 358-61.

word create came from the word *baurau,* which does not mean to create out of nothing; it means to organize; the same as a man would organize materials and build a ship. Hence we infer that God had materials to organize the world out of chaos — chaotic matter, which is element, and in which dwells all the glory. Element had an existence from the time he had. The pure principles of element are principles which can never be destroyed; they may be organized and reorganized, but not destroyed. They had no beginning, and can have no end.[77]

Present-day Mormon writers are committed to this view. Bruce McConkie says, "To *create* is to *organize.* It is an utterly false and uninspired notion to believe that the world or any other thing was created out of nothing. . . ."[78] John A. Widtsoe puts it this way: "God, the supreme Power, cannot conceivably originate matter; he can only organize matter. Neither can he destroy matter; he can only disorganize it."[79]

When we reflect on the fact that the gods were once mortal men, we must come to the conclusion that matter is actually more eternal, at least in origin, than the gods. For the gods did not exist as gods from eternity, but matter did. Furthermore, it would appear that all the gods except the head of the gods had a beginning, for Joseph Smith, in his sermon on the plurality of gods, insisted that the proper translation of Genesis 1:1 was, "In the beginning the head of the Gods brought forth the Gods."[80] Matter, however, as we have just seen, had no beginning. In Mormon theology, therefore, matter is more ultimate than the gods.

Before the gods "created" this earth, or any other earths, they "created" a spirit world. "For I, the Lord God, created all things, of which I have spoken, spiritually, before they were naturally upon the face of the earth" (Moses 3:4). This spirit world, as Joseph Fielding Smith indicates, includes the spirits of all men, but also the "spirits" of animals and plants:

> We were all created untold ages before we were placed on this earth. We discover from Abraham 3:22-28, that it was before the earth was formed that the plan of salvation was presented to the spirits, or "intelligences." This being true, then man, animals and plants were not created in the spirit at the time of the creation of the earth, but long before.[81]

[77] *Teachings of the Prophet Joseph Smith,* pp. 350-52.
[78] *Mormon Doctrine,* p. 156.
[79] *A Rational Theology,* p. 12. Cf. his *Evidences and Reconciliations,* p. 150.
[80] *Teachings of the Prophet Joseph Smith,* p. 371.
[81] *Doctrines of Salvation,* I, 76.

McConkie adds to this the thought that these spirit-creatures had a part in the natural "creation":

> There is no revealed account of the spirit creation. . . . That this prior spirit creation occurred long before the temporal or natural creation is evident from the fact that spirit men, men who themselves were before created spiritually, were participating in the natural creation.[82]

Before the earth on which we live was "created," many other worlds were "created," each with its own inhabitants:

> This earth was not the first of the Lord's creation. An infinite number of worlds have come rolling into existence at his command. Each is called *earth;* each is inhabited with his spirit children; each abides the particular law given to it; and each will play its part in the redemption, salvation, and exaltation of that infinite host of the children of an Almighty God.[83]

In order to understand how this earth was "created," we must note the distinction Mormons make between Elohim and Jehovah. For Mormons Elohim is the name given to "God the eternal Father."[84]   Jehovah is, for Mormons, another name for Christ in his pre-incarnate state.[85]

How, now, do Mormons picture the "creation" of this earth? A council of the gods was held on the star Kolob, at which the organization of this earth was planned.[86]   The Book of Abraham tells the story: Abraham was shown a number of souls that were in existence before the earth had been formed (3:22, 23).   The book continues:

---

[82] *Mormon Doctrine*, p. 158.

[83] *Ibid.,* p. 157; cf. Moses 1:29, 35; 7:30.

[84] McConkie, *op. cit.,* p. 207.   One wonders, however, whether this Father also had a Father.   Joseph Smith once said, "Where was there ever a son without a father?   And where was there ever a father without first being a son? . . .   Hence if Jesus had a Father, can we not believe that He had a Father also?" (*Teachings of the Prophet Joseph Smith,* p. 373).   On the basis of this statement, there can be no end to this infinite regression — every father one can think of must have had a father, and this must hold for the gods as well.

[85] McConkie, *op. cit.,* p. 359.   It should be noted here that the distinction Mormons make between Elohim and Jehovah is completely untenable.   Mormons are apparently oblivious of the fact that in many Old Testament passages Elohim and Jehovah (or Yahweh) appear together as designating the same being.   So, for example, in Gen. 2:7, rendered in the King James: "And the Lord God [Hebrew: Yahweh Elohim] formed man of the dust of the ground. . . ."   Cf. Gen. 2:4, 5, 8, 16, 18, 21, 22, and so on.   The expression, "the Lord God," appears even in Joseph Smith's Revised Version, and in Chapter 3 of the Book of Moses!

[86] George Arbaugh, on p. 107 of his *Revelation in Mormonism,* quotes a poem of Joseph Smith's in which he states this fact.

> And there stood one among them that was like unto God [presumably Christ], and he said unto those who were with him: We will go down, for there is space there, and we will take of these materials, and we will make an earth whereon these may dwell. . . .
>
> And then the Lord said: Let us go down. And they went down at the beginning, and they, that is the Gods, organized and formed the heavens and the earth (3:24; 4:1).

The gods labored for six days; each of these days, however, was a thousand years long — since a thousand earth years is equivalent to a day on the star Kolob.[87]

Jesus Christ, or Jehovah, "created" this earth, under the direction of his Father, Elohim. He was helped in this process by Michael, who was Adam in his pre-existent form. Joseph Fielding Smith adds: "I have a strong view or conviction that there were others also who assisted them. Perhaps Noah and Enoch; and *why not Joseph Smith*, and those who were appointed to be rulers before the earth was formed?"[88] McConkie adds to the group of those who assisted in this "creation" also Abraham, Moses, Peter, James, and John.[89] The "creation" of this earth was thus a kind of co-operative venture between the gods and the spirits of certain pre-existent men. One can therefore by no means speak of "creation" in the Mormon sense as exclusively the work of God or the gods — unless one wishes to view these pre-existent human spirits as already gods in the making.

After this earth has passed away, others will be organized, and so on, *ad infinitum*: "And as one earth shall pass away, and the heavens thereof, even so shall another come; and there is no end to my works, neither to my words" (Moses 1:38).

The Providence of God. It is difficult to see how there can be a real doctrine of divine providence in Mormon theology, since there are so many gods, and since these gods are continually progressing and therefore changing. The doctrine of providence does not, in fact, appear to play any prominent part in Mormon thinking about God. Though much is made of God's care for his saints and of his divine direction of their history, we do not find *providence* listed as a major topic in most Mormon doctrinal books. An exception to this rule is the *Doctrine and Covenants Commentary,* which contains a paragraph about the providence of God in a comment on section 3:3, "Remember, remember that it is not the work of God that is frustrated, but the work of men. . . ." In this paragraph God's providence is described as follows: "He

---

87 Smith, *Doctrines of Salvation,* I, 78-79.
88 *Ibid.,* p. 75. See also p. 74.
89 *Op. cit.,* p. 157.

[God] preserves and governs all His creatures, and directs their actions, so that the ultimate results will serve the ends He has in view."[90]

One is constrained, however, to raise certain questions: If matter is more eternal than even the highest of the gods (since even the highest god was a man before he became a god), what gives the highest god the right and the power to preserve and govern the material universe? Since the spirits of pre-existent men had a part in the work of "creation," is it not natural to expect that the spirits of other pre-existent men, or the spirits of these same men in their exalted state, should have a part in the work of providence? Since there are many gods, to which god must the work of providence be ascribed? If the work of providence must be ascribed to the highest of the gods, does not this work of providence then include the preservation and government of the other gods as well? If it does not, who preserves and governs them? And if the highest god was once a man as we are now, who was in providential control of the universe at the time this god was only a man? As a matter of fact, if this highest god, as Mormons teach, once dwelt on an earth in the process of becoming a god, and if the earths were all "organized" by gods, where did the earth come from to which the first god had to go before he could become a god?

DOCTRINE OF MAN

MAN IN HIS ORIGINAL STATE

Man's Pre-existence. As we have seen, Mormons teach that before men inhabited this earth, they existed as spirits. Talmage, in fact, sees in this a parallel between our existence and that of Christ: "Yet Christ was born a child among mortals; and it is consistent to infer that if His earthly birth was the union of a preexistent or antemortal spirit with a mortal body such also is the birth of every member of the human family."[91] It will be recalled that according to Moses 3:5 all things were "created" spiritually before they were naturally upon the face of the earth.

The question now arises: how did these pre-existent spirits of men originate? It is quite common to read in Mormon literature that these spirits were begotten by God the Father. For example, note the following statement from *Doctrine and Covenants*: ". . . By him [the Only Begotten Son], and through him, and

---

[90] Hyrum M. Smith and Janne M. Sjodahl, *Doctrine and Covenants Commentary* (Salt Lake City: Deseret Book Co., 1960), p. 18.
[91] *Articles of Faith*, p. 193.

of him, the worlds are and were created, and the inhabitants thereof are begotten sons and daughters unto God" (76:24). To the
same effect is the following statement by Brigham Young: "Our
Father in Heaven begat all the spirits that ever were, or ever will
be, upon this earth; and they were born spirits in the eternal
world."[92] A statement by the First Presidency of the Church
(Joseph F. Smith, John R. Winder, Anthon H. Lund) adds the
thought that a divine mother was involved in the origin of spirits
as well as a divine father:

> "All men and women are in the similitude of the universal
> Father and Mother, and are literally the sons and daughters of
> Deity"; as spirits they were the "offspring of celestial paren-
> tage."[93]

The foregoing gives one the impression that these pre-existent
spirits were begotten and not "created," and that there is hence a
real difference between the origin of these spirits and that of
the animals or of the earth. Joseph Fielding Smith, in fact, makes
precisely this observation in one of his books.[94] Yet in the Book
of Abraham we find the word *organized* used to indicate the way
in which these spirits came into existence — and it will be recalled
that the word *organized* is the word commonly used to indicate
the way in which the earth came to be: "Now the Lord had shown
unto me, Abraham, the intelligences that were organized before
the world was; and among all these there were many of the
noble and great ones. . ." (3:22). The word *organized* suggests
that previous to the "begetting" or "organizing" of these spirits
their substance must have been in existence. We would expect to
find Mormons teaching this, since, as we have noted, they repudiate
creation out of nothing. This is precisely what we find in Mormon
writings. Note the following statement from *Doctrine and Covenants*: "Man was also in the beginning with God. Intelligence,
or the light of truth, was not created or made, neither indeed can
be" (93:29). Joseph Fielding Smith puts it this way: "The
intelligent part of man was never created but always existed."[95]
Mr. McConkie, quoting *Doctrine and Covenants* 93:29, interprets
"intelligence" as standing for a "self-existent spirit element":

> Unless God the Father was a personal Being, he could not have
> begotten spirits in his image, and if there had been no self-

---

[92] *Discourses of Brigham Young*, p. 24. Cf. Smith, *Doctrines of Salvation*, I, 62-63, 90, 106.
[93] Joseph Fielding Smith, *Man: His Origin and Destiny*, pp. 351, 355;
quoted by McConkie, *Mormon Doctrine*, p. 530.
[94] *Doctrines of Salvation*, I, 63.
[95] *Ibid.*, p. 12.

existent spirit element, there would have been no substance from which those spirit bodies could have been organized.[96]

In the light of the above it would seem that the begetting of these pre-existent human spirits means the organization into "spirit bodies" of self-existent spirit elements which were always there.[97] Thus there would seem to be two eternally existent substances: matter and spirit. But, according to *Doctrine and Covenants*, spirit is only a refined form of matter: "There is no such thing as immaterial matter. All spirit is matter, but it is more fine or pure, and can only be discerned by purer eyes. . ." (131:7). If spirit is only matter which is "more fine or pure," one would presume that intelligence is also a purer form of matter. We conclude that there is only one eternally existent substance: matter; this substance exists, however, in both a coarse and a refined form. Where either the matter or the distinction just alluded to came from, however, Mormons do not divulge.

This pre-existent life was an infinitely long period of "probation, progression, and schooling."[98] All the spirits probably had an equal start, but some outstripped the others in the quality of their pre-existent life,[99] and became noble and great ones (Abraham 3:22). The reason for the discrimination between races is found in the conduct of spirits in the pre-existent state:

> There is a reason why one man is born black and with other disadvantages, while another is born white with great advantages. The reason is that we once had an estate before we came here, and were obedient, more or less, to the laws that were given us there. Those who were faithful in all things there received greater blessings here, and those who were not faithful received less.[100]

The Image of God. Moses 6:9 reads: "In the image of his own body, male and female, created he them. . . ." This passage makes it quite clear that Mormons understand the expression "image of God" as applying primarily to man's physical nature. LeGrand Richards, in his *A Marvelous Work and a Wonder,* takes issue with those who would understand the image of God as applying only to man's spiritual nature. He insists that the appearance of the Father and the Son in human form to Joseph

---

[96] *Mormon Doctrine*, pp. 530-31. By "spirit bodies" Mr. McConkie means bodies which "were made of a more pure and refined substance than the elements from which mortal bodies are made."

[97] At this point the question cannot be suppressed: If these self-existent spirit elements always existed, what is the difference between men and gods, since, as we saw, all the gods except one have also been "brought forth" by the head of the gods?

[98] McConkie, *op. cit.,* p. 531.

[99] Smith, *Doctrines of Salvation,* I, 59

[100] *Ibid.,* p. 61. Cf. McConkie, *op. cit.,* pp. 476-77.

Smith proved beyond a doubt that God the Father has a body exactly like man's body. He also adduces Genesis 5:3 to establish this point: "And Adam lived an hundred and thirty years, and begat a son in his own likeness, after his image; and called his name Seth." Since in this passage image and likeness must have reference to the body, so Richards argues, the expression "image of God" must have a similar reference (pp. 16-17). The non-Mormon cannot help wondering at this point, however, how the deity of the Holy Spirit can be safeguarded in Mormon theology. It would seem from the above that man is more like God the Father and hence more divine than the Holy Spirit, who has no body at all.

Man's Existence on the Earth. Adam, who before his sojourn on this earth was Michael, the Archangel, received from God a tabernacle of flesh, made from the dust of this earth.[101] Eve, who was also a pre-existent spirit before her incarnation, was likewise given a body by God, and was joined to Adam in the new and everlasting covenant of marriage (Moses 3:20-25). Both Adam and Eve were created with immortal bodies — bodies that were not subject to death (II Nephi 2:22). Mormons claim to have solved the vexing problem of the location of the Garden of Eden. It was located, according to them, in Independence, Missouri — the very place where the New Jerusalem will be built in the latter days.[102] The reason why the cradle of civilization later moved to the Mesopotamian area, according to Mormons, is that at the time of the Flood Noah's ark was driven by the wind from the American continent to Asia.

MAN IN THE STATE OF SIN

The Fall of Man. Mormons teach that if Adam and Eve had not partaken of the forbidden fruit they would have had no children:

> And now, behold, if Adam had not transgressed he would not have fallen, but he would have remained in the Garden of Eden. . . .
> And they would have had no children; wherefore they would have remained in a state of innocence, having no joy, for they knew no misery; doing no good, for they knew no sin. . . .
> Adam fell that men might be; and men are, that they might have joy (II Nephi 2:22-25).

---

[101] Smith, *Doctrines of Salvation*, I, 90. On p. 92 the author informs us that though Adam was in the flesh at this time there was no blood in Adam's body before the fall.
[102] *Ibid.*, III, 74.

If this be granted, the fall must have been a good thing, since without it there would have been no human race. It seems hard to understand, however, why marriage was instituted by God before the fall, as Mormons admit.[103]   Apparently, for Mormons, marriage before the fall was not intended as a means for propagating the race.

Eve first disobeyed God by eating of the forbidden fruit.   At this juncture Adam found himself in a dilemma.   Previously God had commanded him and Eve to multiply and replenish the earth. Since Eve had now fallen into the state of mortality and Adam had not, they were in such dissimilar conditions that they could not remain together.   If they should not remain together, however, they would be unable to fulfill God's command to replenish the earth.   On the other hand, to yield to Eve's request to eat the fruit would also be tantamount to disobedience.   Adam, however, "deliberately and wisely decided to stand by the first and greater commandment; and, therefore, with understanding of the nature of his act, he also partook of the fruit. . . ."[104]   Instead of doing wrong, therefore, Adam really did a wise thing when he ate the forbidden fruit.

Accordingly, in the Book of Moses we find Adam saying, "Blessed be the name of God, for because of my transgression my eyes are opened, and in this life I shall have joy . . ." (5:10). Eve likewise rejoices at the fall, saying, "Were it not for our transgression we never should have had seed, and never should have known good and evil, and the joy of our redemption. . ." (5:11).   Joseph Fielding Smith, therefore, is only echoing the Mormon Scriptures when he says, "The fall of man came as a blessing in disguise, and was the means of furthering the purposes of the Lord in the progress of man, rather than a means of hindering them."[105]

At this point the question arises: Was the eating of the forbidden fruit sin?   Brigham Young asserts that it was: "How did Adam and Eve sin?   Did they come out in direct opposition to God and to his government?   No.   But they transgressed a command of the Lord, and through that transgression sin came into the world."[106]   Joseph Fielding Smith, however, prefers not to speak of Adam's transgression as a sin:

> I never speak of the part Eve took in this fall as a sin, nor do I accuse Adam of a sin.   One may say, "Well [,] did they not break a commandment?"   Yes.   But let us examine

103 Smith, *Doctrines of Salvation*, I, 115.
104 Talmage, *Articles of faith*, p. 65.
105 *Doctrines of Salvation*, I, 114.
106 *Discourses of Brigham Young*, p. 103.

the nature of that commandment and the results which came out of it.

In no other commandment the Lord ever gave to man, did he say: "But of the tree of the knowledge of good and evil, thou shalt not eat of it, nevertheless, thou mayest choose for thyself."[107]

It is true, the Lord warned Adam and Eve that to partake of the fruit they would transgress a law, and this happened. But it is not always a sin to transgress a law. I will try to illustrate this. The chemist in his laboratory takes different elements and combines them, and the result is that something very different results. He has changed the law. . . . Well, Adam's transgression was of a similar nature, that is, his transgression was in accordance with law.[108]

In the light of the above, therefore, we observe that for Mormons Adam's sin was not really a sin, and the fall was not really a fall. The fall was rather a step upward: a means for providing billions of pre-existent spirits with mortal tabernacles, and a necessary stage in man's ultimate exaltation to godhood. Mormons therefore view Adam not as the one responsible for the curse which now rests upon the earth, but rather as someone for whom they are to be profoundly grateful:

Father Adam was one of the most noble and intelligent characters who ever lived. . . . He is the head of all gospel dispensations, the presiding high priest (under Christ) over all the earth; presides over all the spirits destined to inhabit this earth; holds the keys of salvation over all the earth; and will reign as Michael, our prince, to all eternity.[109]

We, the children of Adam and Eve, may well be proud of our parentage.[110]

It can be understood that this view of the fall has profoundly affected Mormon theology. By this reinterpretation of the significance of the fall, Mormons have repudiated the deep seriousness of Adam's sin and have minimized the importance of the work of Christ. Instead of contrasting Adam with Christ, as the Scriptures do (see Rom. 5:12-21), Mormons place Adam alongside of Christ as one who played a role almost as important as that of Christ in enabling man to reach his exaltation.

Original Sin. Article 2 of the Mormon Articles of Faith reads as follows: "We believe that men will be punished for their own sins, and not for Adam's transgression." Mormons, therefore, do not accept the doctrine of original sin. Talmage explains

---

[107] Quoted from Moses 3:17. The final clause has been added to the text by Joseph Smith.
[108] *Doctrines of Salvation*, I, 114.
[109] McConkie, *op. cit.*, p. 17
[110] Widtsoe, *Evidences and Reconciliations*, p. 195.

that bodily weakness, disease, and death have come into the world because of the disobedience of Adam and Eve, but that we are not accounted sinners because of the transgression of our first parents.[111]

Mormons further teach the complete sinlessness of infants: "Every spirit of man was innocent in the beginning; and God having redeemed man from the fall, men became again, in their infant state, innocent before God" (*Doctrine and Covenants* 93:38). Joseph Smith had a vision in the year 1836 in which the following truth was made clear to him: "And I also beheld that all children who die before they arrive at the years of accountability, are saved in the celestial kingdom of heaven."[112] Joseph Fielding Smith explains that the age of accountability has been set by the Lord at eight years, referring to *Doctrine and Covenants* 68:27 for proof.[113]

Mormons admit that Christ was the only person who ever lived without sin.[114] Since the pre-existent spirits of men are held to have been sinless in the beginning, and since children are considered to be without sin until they reach the age of eight, one wonders where the universal tendency to sin comes from. It would seem that the only explanation left is the common Pelagian one: imitation of other sinners. It is certainly clear that Mormons deny both original guilt and original pollution; they are thus completely Pelagian with respect to the doctrine of original sin.

Free Agency. One of the most prominent aspects of the Mormon doctrine of man is the insistence that man is a free agent: that is, that man does not act out of compulsion, but that every man is free to act for himself. This teaching is repeatedly stated in the Mormon scriptures: "I . . . have given unto the children of men to be agents unto themselves" (*Doctrine and Covenants* 104:17). Free agency is ascribed by Mormons to God, to pre-existent spirits, and to man:

> Agency is the ability and freedom to choose good or evil. It is an eternal principle which has existed with God from all eternity. The spirit offspring of the Father had agency in pre-existence and were thereby empowered to follow Christ or Lucifer according to their choice. It is by virtue of the exercise of agency in this life that men are enabled to undergo the testing which is an essential part of mortality.[115]

---

[111] *Articles of Faith*, pp. 474-75. This follows logically from Mormon teaching about the fall. Why should Adam's "sin" be imputed to us if it was not really a sin in the first place?
[112] *Teachings of the Prophet Joseph Smith*, p. 107.
[113] *Doctrines of Salvation*, II, 53.
[114] McConkie, *op. cit.*, p. 665.
[115] *Ibid.*, p. 25.

The great sin of Satan was that he tried to take away man's free agency. The Book of Moses pictures Satan as coming before God in the beginning and saying: "Behold, here am I, send me, I will be thy son, and I will redeem all mankind, that one soul shall not be lost . . . wherefore give me thine honor" (4:1). The third verse of this chapter thus describes Satan's pernicious error: "Wherefore, because that Satan rebelled against me, and sought to destroy the agency of man, which I, the Lord God, had given him, . . . I caused that he should be cast down. . . ."

Free agency is therefore "an essential part of the great plan of redemption."[116] "It [free agency] is the only principle upon which exaltation can come. It is the only principle upon which rewards can be given in righteousness."[117]

In the light of what was said about the fall, it is clear that Mormons do not admit that man lost his ability to choose and to do the good through the fall. He is still able at every moment to make the right choices or to repent of whatever wrong choices he may have made. Here again the basically Pelagian nature of Mormon theology becomes evident.

DOCTRINE OF CHRIST

THE PERSON OF CHRIST

The Pre-existence of Christ. Mormons, as we have seen, identify Christ with Jehovah. Jehovah existed prior to his incarnation as the "first-born" of the myriads of pre-existent spirits. The following statements from James Talmage, in his *Articles of Faith,* make this clear: "Among the spirit-children of Elohim the firstborn was and is Jehovah or Jesus Christ to whom all others are juniors" (p. 471). "Jesus Christ is not the Father of the spirits who have taken or yet shall take bodies upon this earth, for He is one of them. He is The Son as they are sons or daughters of Elohim" (pp. 472-73). Note also the following statements from *Doctrine and Covenants*:

> And now, verily I say unto you, I was in the beginning with the Father, and am the First-born;
> And all those who are begotten through me are partakers of the glory of the same, and are the church of the First-born.
> Ye were also in the beginning with the Father. . . (93:21-23).

From these statements it is evident that, for Mormons, the only difference between Christ and us is that Christ was the first-born of Elohim's children, whereas we, in our pre-existence, were

[116] *Ibid.,* p. 25.
[117] Smith, *Doctrines of Salvation,* I, 70.

"born" later. The distinction between Christ and us is therefore
one of degree, not one of kind.

If the devil and the demons were also spirit-children of Elohim,
it must follow that they, too, are Jesus' brothers. This is exactly
what one Mormon writer says: "As for the Devil and his fellow
spirits, they are brothers to man and also to Jesus and sons and
daughters of God in the same sense that we are."[118] One could
therefore even say that, for Mormons, the difference between Christ
and the devil is not one of kind, but of degree!

The Divinity of Christ. From the foregoing it has already become evident that in Mormon theology Jesus Christ is basically
not any more divine than any one of us. We have previously
noted that Mormons deny the Holy Trinity: Father, Son, and
Holy Spirit, so they teach, are not one God but three gods. It
remains further to note that Christ is not considered equal to the
Father: "Jesus is greater than the Holy Spirit, which is subject
unto him, but his Father is greater than he."[119] Though it is said
that Christ "created" this earth under the Father's direction, it is
also said that certain pre-existent spirits, like Adam and Joseph
Smith, helped him. Further confirming Mormonism's denial of
the essential deity of Christ is the following statement by Mormon
elder B. H. Roberts:

> The divinity of Jesus is the truth which now requires to be
> reperceived . . . the divinity of Jesus and [the divinity] of all
> other noble and saintly souls, insofar as they, too, have been
> inflamed by a spark of Deity — insofar as they, too, can be
> recognized as manifestations of the Divine.[120]

When we recall that the goal of Mormon eschatology is for man
to attain godhood,[121] we conclude that the Christ of Mormonism
is a far cry from the Christ of the Scriptures. Neither his divinity
nor his incarnation are unique. His divinity is not unique, for it
is the same as that to which man may attain. His incarnation is
not unique, for it is no different from that of other gods before
him, who were incarnated on other earths; nor is it different from
that of man, who also was a pre-existent spirit before he was incarnated on this earth.

The Virgin Birth of Christ. One finds occasional references in
Mormon writings to the Virgin Mary. One wonders, however,
whether Mormons are entitled to use this term, since they insist

---

[118] John Henry Evans, *An American Prophet* (New York: Macmillan,
1933), p. 241.
[119] Joseph Fielding Smith, *Doctrines of Salvation,* I, 18.
[120] *Teachings of the Prophet Joseph Smith;* p. 347, last paragraph of
n. 3.
[121] McConkie, *op. cit.,* p. 294.

that the body of Jesus Christ was literally begotten, though they grant that he was conceived by Mary. When the question is asked, By whom was this body begotten? Mormons are put "on the spot." There exists a rather embarrassing statement by Brigham Young which seems to give the impression that the body of Jesus Christ was begotten by Adam (who presumably possessed some kind of body at the time):

> When the Virgin Mary conceived the child Jesus, the Father had begotten him in his own likeness. . . . And who is the Father? He is the first of the human family; and when he [Christ] took a tabernacle, it was begotten by his Father in heaven, after the same manner as the tabernacles of Cain, Abel, and the rest of the sons and daughters of Adam and Eve. . . .
>
> Jesus, our elder brother, was begotten in the flesh by the same character that was in the Garden of Eden, and who is our Father in Heaven. . . .[122]

The statements: "the first of the human family," "after the same manner as the tabernacles of Cain, Abel, and the rest of the sons and daughters of Adam and Eve," and "the same character that was in the Garden of Eden," certainly give the casual reader the impression that President Young intended to say that the body of Jesus was begotten by Adam.

Joseph Fielding Smith, however, goes into this question at great length, insisting that Brigham Young did not mean to teach that the body of Christ was begotten by Adam. He bends over backwards in his attempt to prove that Young really meant to say that the body of Christ was begotten by our heavenly Father who is distinct from Adam.[123] On another page Smith expresses himself very plainly:

> Our Father in Heaven is the Father of Jesus Christ, both in the spirit and in the flesh. . . . I believe firmly that Jesus Christ is the Only-Begotten Son of God in the flesh. . . . Christ was begotten of God. He was not born without the aid of Man, and that Man was God.[124]

Talmage, in his *Articles of Faith,* expresses the same opinion: ". . . Elohim is literally the Father of the spirit of Jesus Christ and also of the body in which Jesus Christ performed his mission in the flesh. . ." (p. 466). ". . . He [Christ] is essentially greater than any and all others, by reason . . . of His unique status in the flesh as the offspring of a mortal mother and of an immortal, or resurrected and glorified, Father" (p. 472).

It is difficult for non-Mormons to grasp at first reading what is

---

[122] *Journal of Discourses,* I, 50-51; quoted in Smith, *Doctrines of Salvation,* I, 102.
[123] *Doctrines of Salvation,* I, 101-106.
[124] *Ibid.,* p. 18.

being said here, since we are not accustomed to thinking of God the Father as having a physical body. What these men are saying is that, according to Mormon theology, the body of Jesus Christ was the product of the physical union of God the Father and the Virgin Mary. One shudders to think of the revolting implications of this view, which brings into what is supposed to be "Christian" theology one of the most unsavory features of ancient pagan mythology! The reader may judge for himself whether Mormons are still entitled to say that they believe in "the Virgin birth."[125]

Christ's Polygamous Marriage. According to Mormon doctrine, Jesus Christ was no more essentially divine before his incarnation than any of us. As we shall see when we discuss the Mormon doctrine of salvation, "there can be no exaltation to the fulness of the blessings of the celestial kingdom outside of the marriage relation."[126] Couples whose marriages have not been sealed for eternity become angels and not gods in the life to come; only those sealed to each other for eternity become gods (*Doctrine and Covenants* 132:19, 20). This would imply that if Jesus Christ was not married during his earthly life, he could not rise higher than an angel in the next life.[127]

We are therefore not surprised to find the following statements attributed to one of the members of the first Council of Twelve Apostles, Orson Hyde:

> If at the marriage of Cana of Galilee, Jesus was the bridegroom and took unto him Mary, Martha and the other Mary, it shocks not our nerves. If there was not attachment and familiarity between our Saviour and these women, highly proper only in the relation of husband and wife, then we have no sense of propriety.[128]

> We say it was Jesus Christ who was married whereby He could see His seed before He was crucified. I shall say here that before the Saviour died He looked upon His own natural children as we look upon ours. When Mary came to the sepulchre she saw two angels and she said unto them "they have taken away my Lord or husband."[129]

---

[125] One may well question whether Joseph Fielding Smith's interpretation of Brigham Young's remark really conveys what Young intended to say. Be that as it may, Smith's substitute explanation of the birth of Jesus Christ is no more acceptable to a Bible-believing Christian than is the conception attributed to Young which Smith has attempted to refute.

[126] Smith, *Doctrines of Salvation,* II, 65.

[127] Gordon H. Fraser, *Is Mormonism Christian?* (Chicago: *Moody Press,* 1957), p. 61.

[128] *Journal of Discourses,* II, 81-82; quoted in Fraser, *op. cit.,* p. 62.

[129] *Journal of Discourses,* IV, 210; quoted in Fraser, *op. cit.,* p. 63. It should be added that we do not find this alleged marriage of Christ mentioned in the Mormon sacred books, or alluded to in Mormon doctrinal studies.

THE WORK OF CHRIST

The Atonement. According to Mormon theology, Adam's fall demanded an atonement; such an atonement was necessary to satisfy divine justice. "He had offered Himself, in the primeval council in heaven, as the subject of the atoning sacrifice made necessary by the foreseen transgression of the first man. . . ."[130] Hence Christ came to earth to make this atonement. This atonement was completely voluntary on Christ's part, and consisted particularly in His death by crucifixion. Talmage speaks of "the vicarious nature of his death as a foreordained and voluntary sacrifice, intended for and efficacious as a propitiation for the sins of mankind, thus becoming the means whereby salvation may be secured."[131]

We have observed, however, that for Mormons Adam's transgression was really a wise decision, and the fall was actually a blessing in disguise (above, pp. 49-51). When we are now told that the fall required an atonement, we are inclined to ask, Why? Mormons answer as follows: One of the results of the fall was that it brought physical death into the world; Christ's atonement was therefore necessary to deliver us all from death by providing for us all the right to be raised from the dead. A second result of the fall, however, was the introduction of spiritual death:

> Wherefore, I, the Lord God, caused that he [Adam] should be cast out from the Garden of Eden, from my presence, because of his transgression, wherein he became spiritually dead, which is the first death, even that same death which is the last death, which is spiritual, which shall be pronounced upon the wicked when I shall say: Depart, ye cursed (*Doctrine and Covenants* 29:41).

The atonement was necessary also in order to deliver us from this spiritual death.[132]

Mormons, accordingly, distinguish two main effects of the atonement: *general salvation* and *individual salvation*. *General salvation* is salvation from death through resurrection; this comes to everyone. Joseph Fielding Smith, who also uses the expression

---

[130] Talmage, *Articles of Faith*, p. 79.
[131] *Ibid.*, p. 74. Cf. Chap. 4 in its entirety.
[132] Note at this point a glaring inconsistency in Mormon doctrine. On the one hand it is said that the fall was a blessing in disguise, that Adam acted wisely, that his transgression was in accordance with law, and that the fall was necessary in order to enable man to propagate the race, so that myriads of pre-existent spirits could obtain mortal tabernacles and advance to exaltation. But now we are told that the fall was so calamitous an occurrence that it inflicted spiritual death with its consequent curse upon man. Apparently Mormons wish both to overthrow and to retain traditional theological thinking about the fall, as suits their purpose.

unconditional redemption to designate this, gives the following explanation of it:

> We need a little more explanation as to just what we mean by unconditional redemption. That means to restore us from this mortal state to the immortal state; in other words, to give unto us the resurrection. That comes to every creature, not only to men but also to the fish, the fowls of the air, and the beasts of the field. . . . All of them had spiritual existence before they were placed upon the earth; therefore they are to be redeemed.[133]

No condition needs to be fulfilled for man to receive salvation in this sense — this is a gift forced upon all mankind, which no one can reject.[134]

The second effect of the atonement is *individual salvation* (or, in Joseph Fielding Smith's words, *conditional redemption*). What salvation in this sense means will become evident as we discuss Mormon soteriology and eschatology; let it suffice here to say that it means escape from hell and entrance into one of the three Mormon heavens. *Individual salvation* will be given only to those who believe and obey. Certain classes, however, are excused from these requirements: children who die before the age of eight, and those "who have died not knowing the will of God concerning them, or who have ignorantly sinned" (Mosiah 3:11).

The Extent of the Atonement. The answer to the question about the extent of the atonement depends on which effect of the atonement is being contemplated. If one is thinking of *general salvation,* as defined above, the extent of the atonement is absolutely universal. There will be a resurrection for everyone, including even the animals. If one is thinking of *individual salvation,* however, certain qualifications must be made. Talmage expresses himself on this point as follows:

> But besides this universal application of the atonement, whereby all men are redeemed from the effects of Adam's transgression both with respect to the death of the body and inherited sin, there is application of the same great sacrifice as a means of propitiation for individual sins through the faith and good works of the sinner.
>
> The individual Effect of the Atonement makes it possible for any and every soul to obtain absolution from the effect of personal sins, through the mediation of Christ; but such saving intercession is to be invoked by individual effort as manifested

---

[133] *Doctrines of Salvation,* II, 10-11.
[134] Note that at this point the crucial principle of free agency is surrendered.

through faith, repentance, and continued works of righteousness.[135]

Since, for Mormons, not all will attain individual salvation, the
effect of the atonement in this sense is not universal. In this sense
the atonement, though intended for all, is efficacious only for those
who believe and obey.

Mormons often claim to believe that Christ died to save everybody. When this claim is made, the non-Mormon must first determine in what sense the word *save* is here used. If it is used as
meaning *general salvation,* all it means to say is that Christ died
so that everyone may be raised from the dead. According to
Mormon teachings, however, as we shall see more clearly under
the next doctrinal heading, Christ's atonement does not determine
where man will go after the resurrection, since this is determined
by man's own actions. Mormon theology thus leaves us with a
Christ who does not really save in the full, Biblical sense of this
word, but only gives man an opportunity to save himself from hell.

There is another way in which Mormons limit Christ's power
to save. Joseph Fielding Smith writes:

> Joseph Smith taught that there were certain sins so grievous
> that man may commit, that they will place the transgressors
> beyond the power of the atonement of Christ. If these offenses
> are committed, then the blood of Christ will not cleanse them
> from their sins even though they repent. Therefore their
> only hope is to have their own blood shed to atone, as far as
> possible, in their behalf.
> ... Man may commit certain grievous sins — according to his
> light and knowledge — that will place him beyond the reach of
> the atoning blood of Christ. If then he would be saved he
> must make sacrifice of his own life to atone — so far as in
> his power lies — for that sin, for the blood of Christ alone
> under certain circumstances will not avail.[136]

In the case of grievous sins, therefore, man must add his own blood
to the blood of Christ to atone for his transgression. One wonders
who is to determine when a sin has become so heinous as to require this kind of "blood atonement." What deficiency in the
sacrifice of Christ makes it inadequate to atone for such sins?

Doctrine of Salvation

Individual Salvation. We have already noted the distinctions
Mormons make between general and individual salvation. How,
now, does one receive individual salvation? Mormons vigorously

---

[135] *Articles of Faith,* pp. 86-87, 89.
[136] *Doctrines of Salvation,* I, 135, 134.

reject the doctrine of justification by faith. James Talmage, in fact, calls this a "pernicious doctrine," and states, "The sectarian dogma of justification by faith alone has exercised an influence for evil."[137] Articles 3 and 4 of the Articles of Faith read as follows:

> 3. We believe that through the Atonement of Christ, all mankind may be saved, by obedience to the laws and ordinances of the Gospel.
> 4. We believe that the first principles and ordinances of the Gospel are: first, Faith in the Lord Jesus Christ; second, Repentance; third, Baptism by immersion for the remission of sins; fourth, Laying on of hands for the gift of the Holy Ghost.

Putting these two articles together, it appears that, in Mormonism, one is saved by faith plus works, with emphasis on the works. Mormons insist that one must have faith in the Lord Jesus Christ; it must not be forgotten, however, that faith in Christ and faith in Joseph Smith must go together.[138] Very revealing, in fact, is the following statement from *Doctrine and Covenants*: "Joseph Smith, the Prophet and Seer of the Lord, has done more, save Jesus only, for the salvation of men in this world, than any other man that ever lived in it" (135:3).

The main emphasis in Mormon soteriology, however, is on works. Because of the general effect of Christ's atonement, every man shall receive immortality — that is, shall be raised from the dead. Not every man, however, shall receive salvation in the individual sense — that is, shall go to one of the three Mormon heavens. Salvation in this sense depends on one's merits:

> Salvation is twofold: General — that which comes to all men irrespective of a belief (in this life) in Christ — and, Individual — that which man merits through his own acts through life and by obedience to the laws and ordinances of the gospel.[139]

Mormons distinguish various degrees of salvation. The highest is sometimes called *eternal life* and sometimes *exaltation*. To gain eternal life means to partake of the same life which the Father possesses. Receiving exaltation means to become like God — or, in blunter, but more accurate language, to become a god. To become eligible for this highest degree of salvation, however, one must obey all the commandments of God:

> Very gladly would the Lord give to every one eternal life, but since that blessing can come only on merit — through the faithful performance of duty — only those who are worthy shall receive it.

---

[137] *Articles of Faith*, p. 479.
[138] Smith, *Doctrines of Salvation,* II, 302-3.
[139] *Ibid.,* I, 134.

.... To be exalted one must keep the whole law.

.... To receive the exaltation of the righteous, in other words [,] eternal life, the commandments of the Lord must be kept in all things.[140]

It has apparently never occurred to Mr. Smith that no one can "keep the commandments of the Lord in all things." Does not the Apostle John say, "If we say that we have no sin, we deceive ourselves, and the truth is not in us" (I John 1:8)?

Celestial Marriage. A very important point to remember in this connection, however, is that to receive the fullness of exaltation a man must have a wife and a woman must have a husband. Complete fulfillment of the commandments of God requires that a couple must be sealed to each other for both time and eternity in a temple ceremony.[141] This leads to a consideration of the doctrine of celestial marriage — one of the key doctrines of Mormonism. By way of background we should note what is said in Section 132 of *Doctrine and Covenants*. In verses 15 and 16 of this section we read that, if a man should marry a wife not by the word of the Lord, this marriage will not be in force when the parties have died; hence, when these parties have left the present world, they are not gods but only angels in heaven, destined to minister everlastingly to those who are more worthy than they. Verses 19 and 20 go on to state that if, however, a man shall marry a wife by the word of the Lord, and this marriage is sealed to them by him who is anointed, this marriage shall be of full force when the parties are out of this world; they shall receive glory, "which glory shall be a fulness and a continuation of the seeds forever and ever. Then shall they be gods, because they have no end...."

This implies that, for Mormons, there are two kinds of marriage: marriage for time, and marriage for eternity (or celestial marriage). A marriage for time — one that is not performed in a temple — will be dissolved by death. People so married will be single in the life to come, and will there live as angels, not as gods; their children will be left without parents in the future life, unless they are adopted by parents who have been sealed for eternity. Those, however, who have been married in a temple have been sealed to each other for eternity; their union will last forever. Parents who have been so sealed to each other "will have eternal claim upon their posterity, and will have the gift of eternal increase, if they obtain the exaltation.... All who obtain this exaltation will have the privilege of completing the full measure of

---

[140] *Ibid.,* II, 5, 6.
[141] *Ibid.,* II, 43-44.

their existence and they will have a posterity that will be as innumerable as the stars of heaven."[142]   Children born to such
parents while the latter are in the state of exaltation, Smith says
on another page, will be spirit children, not clothed upon with
tabernacles of flesh and bones.[143]   In the light of all this, it is therefore not surprising to find Bruce McConkie saying:

> The most important single thing that any member of the Church
> of Jesus Christ of Latter-day Saints can ever do in this world
> is to marry the right person by the right authority in the right
> place.[144]

It would appear from the above that no one can receive complete
fullness of salvation, including the attainment of the status of godhood, unless he or she has been married to someone by means of
a temple ceremony.   Exceptions to this rule are, however, allowed
for.   Realizing that the woman does not usually take the initiative
in a marriage proposal, Joseph Fielding Smith states that if a
woman has remained single against her wishes, but would be perfectly willing to obey the ordinance of celestial marriage if an
opportunity should present itself, no blessing shall be withheld
from her — in other words, she can still attain to the state of
exaltation.[145]   The same author mentions another exception: a
faithful Mormon wife whose husband shows no interest in the
Mormon Church will be given to another husband in the life to
come, and will thus receive all the blessings of the celestial kingdom.[146]

It is quite clear, therefore, that Mormons have substituted for
the Biblical doctrine of salvation by grace alone the unscriptural
teaching of salvation by works.

DOCTRINE OF THE CHURCH AND SACRAMENTS

DOCTRINE OF THE CHURCH

Mormons teach that the Church of Jesus Christ was in a state
of apostasy until the Mormon Church was founded in 1830.   This
apostasy began already in the early centuries of the Christian era
and was not rectified even by the Reformation, since the Reformers
had no direct revelations from heaven.   The Lord, however, re-

---

[142] *Ibid.,* II, 44.
[143] *Ibid.,* II, 68.
[144] *Mormon Doctrine,* p. 111.   Note that celestial marriage thus appears
to be more important to Mormons than faith in Jesus Christ.
[145] *Doctrines of Salvation,* II, 76.
[146] *Answers to Gospel Questions,* III, 24.   It is important to note in
this connection that the *Book of Mormon,* which is supposed to contain
"the fulness of the everlasting Gospel" (see above, p. 10), says nothing
whatever about the doctrine of celestial marriage.

established His church in the last days through the Prophet Joseph Smith who, together with Oliver Cowdery, received both the Aaronic and the Melchizedek priesthood. This event Mormons designate as "the Restoration of the Church"; hence they call their own organization, "The Restored Church." James Talmage gives expression to Mormon convictions about the church when he says:

> The Latter-day Saints declare their high claim to be the true church organization, similar in all essentials to the organization effected by Christ among the Jews. This people of the last days profess to have the Priesthood of the Almighty, the power to act in the name of God, which power commands respect both on earth and in heaven.[147]

The Mormon Church claims to be the only true church because it is, so it contends, the only church since the time of Christ which has received divine revelation (through Joseph Smith and others), and which may still continue to receive divine revelation through its presidents. Joseph Smith himself was once asked, "Will everybody be damned, but Mormons?" His answer was, "Yes, and a great portion of them, unless they repent, and work righteousness."[148] In the same vein, Brigham Young once said, ". . . Every spirit that does not confess that God has sent Joseph Smith, and revealed the everlasting gospel to and through him, is of Antichrist. . . ."[149] Orson Pratt, one of the early apostles of the Mormon Church, asserted that it is bold impudence for the non-Mormon churches to call themselves Christian churches, since

> They have nothing to do with Christ, neither has Christ anything to do with them, only to pour out upon them the plagues written. . . . All who will not now repent, as the authority is once more restored to the earth, and come forth out of the corrupt apostate churches and be adopted into the Church of Christ and earnestly seek after the blessings and miraculous gifts of the gospel shall be thrust down to hell, saith the Lord God of Hosts.[150]

These quotations speak for themselves. Mormons claim that they are the only group of God's true people on earth, and that those not in this group must enter it, either while still living or after they have died, in order to be saved.[151] In common with all

---

[147] *Articles of Faith*, p. 204.
[148] *Teachings of the Prophet Joseph Smith*, p. 119.
[149] *Discourses of Brigham Young*, p. 435.
[150] Series of Pamphlets, No. III, p. 8, and No. V, p. 8; quoted in Henry C. Sheldon, *A Fourfold Test of Mormonism* (New York: Abingdon Press, 1914), p. 99.
[151] "If it had not been for Joseph Smith and the restoration, there would be no salvation. There is no salvation outside The Church of Jesus Christ of Latter-day Saints" (McConkie, *Mormon Doctrine*, p. 603).

cults, Latter-day Saints repudiate the Biblical truth of the universality of the church: the doctrine that the true church of Jesus Christ is not to be identified exclusively with any one earthly organization, but that it includes members of various denominations scattered throughout the earth. By relegating all of present-day and most of past Christendom to the status of apostasy, Mormonism reveals its utterly anti-Scriptural sectarianism.

DOCTRINE OF THE SACRAMENTS

Baptism. Mormons teach that baptism is absolutely necessary for salvation; it is therefore one of the "ordinances of the Gospel" which must be obeyed if one would be saved (compare Article 4 of the Articles of Faith). Note the following statements from *Doctrine and Covenants*: ". . . Thou shalt declare repentance and faith on the Savior, and remission of sins by baptism. . ." (19:31). "Verily, verily, I [Christ] say unto you [Joseph Smith], they who believe not on your words, and are not baptized in water in my name, for the remission of their sins, that they may receive the Holy Ghost, shall be damned. . ." (84:74). It is clear that, for Mormons, one can obtain remission of sins only through baptism, which rite must have been preceded by repentance. If sins are committed after one has been baptized, the *law of forgiveness* requires the following: godly sorrow for sin, abandonment of sin, confession of sin, restitution for sin, and obedience to all law.[152]

In distinction from the Bible, the Mormon scriptures precisely define the mode of baptism: it is to be by immersion (3 Nephi 11:26; *Doctrine and Covenants* 21:74). As a matter of fact, one of the additions Joseph Smith made to the Book of Genesis in his revision of the Bible was the episode of Adam's baptism by immersion![153]

Infant baptism is opposed, since little children "are not capable of committing sin" (Moroni 8:8); hence they "need no repentance, neither baptism" (v. 11). In this chapter, supposedly a letter from Mormon to his son Moroni, the further statement is made: ". . . He that supposeth that little children need baptism is in the gall of bitterness and in the bonds of iniquity, for he hath neither faith, hope, nor charity; wherefore, should he be cut off while in the thought, he must go down to hell" (v. 14). It is further specified in *Doctrine and Covenants* 68:27 that children shall be baptized when they are eight years old.

Baptism for the Dead. This is one of the distinctive doctrines of the Mormon Church. Though the Book of Mormon, which is

---

152 McConkie, *op. cit.*, pp. 271-73.
153 Moses 6:51-68; cf. Inspired Version, Gen. 6:52-71.

supposed to contain "the fulness of the everlasting Gospel," says nothing about this practice, Joseph Smith supposedly received revelations about this matter after the *Book of Mormon* had been "translated." The earliest of these revelations is said to have been received by Smith on January 19, 1841 (Section 124 of *Doctrine and Covenants*); a later revelation occurred, it is alleged, in September of 1842 (Section 128). The substance of these "revelations" was as follows: Malachi 4:5 and 6 state that Elijah the Prophet will come before the great and dreadful day of the Lord, to turn the heart of the fathers to the children, and the heart of the children to their fathers. This passage is interpreted to mean that, unless there is a "welding link" of some kind or other between the fathers and the children, the earth will be smitten with a curse (*Doctrine and Covenants* 128:18).[154]

What is this "welding link"? It is baptism for the dead, spoken of by the Apostle Paul in I Corinthians 15:29. Since baptism is essential for salvation, and since many have died before the church was "restored" under Joseph Smith, it seems inevitable that most of the dead will be lost. However, the living may be baptized as substitutes for the dead — that is, for those who died without a knowledge of the restored gospel (128:5). The manner of this baptism is also by immersion, in a font which has been built beneath the surface of the ground to simulate the graves of the deceased (128:12 and 13). These baptisms must be performed in a temple (124:28-37), and must be carefully recorded; ideally there should be three witnesses present at every such baptism (128:3).

Baptism for the dead is an ordinance which was instituted from before the foundation of the world (124:33). This is a matter so important that the salvation of the living depends upon it: "for their [the ancestors'] salvation is necessary and essential to our salvation" (128:15). In fact, Joseph Smith said at one time: "Those saints who neglect it [baptism for the dead] in behalf of their deceased relatives, do it at the peril of their own salvation."[155] Very consistently, therefore, Joseph Fielding Smith denounces the

---

[154] Mormons believe that the promise that Elijah would be sent to the earth before the dreadful day of the Lord would come was literally fulfilled. They insist that on April 3, 1836, in the Kirtland Temple, there appeared to Joseph Smith and Oliver Cowdery, in succession, Christ Himself, Moses, Elias, and Elijah. [Smith apparently did not realize that Elias was the Greek form of the Hebrew name Elijah.] Elijah explained that he was there in fulfillment of the prophecy of Malachi; and that he was committing "the keys of this dispensation" into the hands of Smith and Cowdery (*Doctrine and Covenants* 110). It is the bestowal of these keys, Mormons claim, which gives them the right and the authority to practice baptism for the dead.

[155] *Teachings of the Prophet Joseph Smith,* p. 193.

Reorganized Church as an apostate church because it does not practice baptism for the dead.[156]

Mormons must, therefore, work for the salvation of the dead of their own lineage as far back as they can go.[157]   If the dead accept the baptism performed for them, this baptism is credited to their account, just as if they had acted for themselves.[158]   Not all the dead who are baptized by proxy will attain exaltation, however, but only those among them who are worthy of celestial glory, since salvation will be based on merit.[159]   It should also be mentioned that, according to Mormon teaching, Christ will bring the Gospel to those in the spirit world who did not have an opportunity to hear it while they were on earth; these spirits may then repent of their sins and believe in Christ.   Even though one then repents, however, he still cannot be saved unless someone has been baptized for him.[160]

It will be noted that this doctrine not only enhances the prestige of the Mormon Church as the only agency on earth through which men can be saved, but that it also enables Mormons to become, at least in part, "saviors" of their deceased relatives.

The Lord's Supper.   Christ is said to have instituted the Lord's Supper among the Nephites (III Nephi 18:3).   In administering the Lord's Supper, Mormons follow specific directions given in their sacred books (Moroni, Chapters 4 and 5; *Doctrine and Covenants* 20:76-79).   They make one exception in following these directions, however; whereas the directions call for the use of wine, they use water instead.   To support this practice they adduce *Doctrine and Covenants* 27:2, "For, behold, I say unto you, that it mattereth not what ye shall eat or what ye shall drink when ye partake of the sacrament. . . ."   The words of explanation which introduce this section inform us that in August of 1830 Joseph Smith was on his way to purchase wine from some non-Mormons, since he did not have any at the moment.   He was then met by a heavenly messenger, who gave him the revelation just quoted, adding that he must not purchase wine or strong drink from his enemies.

This sacrament is administered weekly.   All baptized members of the church in good standing, eight years old and older, must partake.[161]   Warnings are sounded against partaking unworthily;

---

156 *Doctrines of Salvation,* I, 265ff. See also the tract by the same author, "The 'Reorganized Church' vs. Salvation for the Dead" (Salt Lake City: Deseret News Press).
157 *Doctrines of Salvation,* II, 167.
158 *Ibid.,* II, 162.
159 *Ibid.,* II, 185-86.
160 *Ibid.,* II, 162, 182, 191.
161 *Ibid.,* II, 348.

such a partaking is said to bring damnation to the soul (3 Nephi 18:29).

Talmage explains that the Lord's Supper is not a means for securing the remission of sins, but is (1) a testimony of our faithfulness and our determination to keep God's commandments, and (2) a means whereby we receive "a continuing endowment of the Holy Spirit."[162]

DOCTRINE OF THE LAST THINGS

THE GATHERINGS

Article 10 of the Articles of Faith briefly sums up Mormon eschatology: "We believe in the literal gathering of Israel and in the restoration of the Ten Tribes; that Zion will be built upon this [the American] continent; that Christ will reign personally upon the earth; and, that the earth will be renewed and receive its paradisaical glory."

We shall consider first the so-called "gathering" doctrine referred to in the opening words of this article. Talmage explains that Mormons believe in the "severely literal fulfilment of prophecies relating to the dispersion of Israel."[163] Various Old Testament prophecies referring to the gathering of Israelites from captivity are literally interpreted by Mormons as pointing to a series of gatherings which shall occur before the Lord's return. In confirmation of this, they refer to the alleged appearance of Moses to Joseph Smith and Oliver Cowdery in the Kirtland Temple in 1836, at which time Moses committed to them "the keys of the gathering of Israel from the four parts of the earth, and the leading of the ten tribes from the land of the north" (*Doctrine and Covenants* 110:11). Though this gathering is to concern remnants of the nation of Israel, Gentiles are to have a part in it, and may thus share in the blessings of it.[164]

This gathering will involve three distinct phases:

(1) *The Gathering of Ephraim.* Ephraim, Joseph's younger son, it is said, received the birthright in Israel after Reuben, the oldest son of Jacob, had lost the birthright by his transgression.[165] The *Book of Mormon,* it is further claimed, came to Ephraim, since Joseph Smith was "a pure Ephraimite."[166] Ephraim, there-

---

162 *Articles of Faith*, p. 175.
163 *Articles of Faith*, p. 336.
164 *Ibid.*, pp. 334-36.
165 Smith, *Doctrines of Salvation*, III, 250-51.
166 *Ibid.*, III, 253. This claim is made despite the fact that Smith was of English descent on his father's side and of Scotch descent on his mother's side! It might be noted here that Mormons understand the expression, "the stick of Ephraim," which occurs in Ezek. 37:16, as a Biblical designation of the *Book of Mormon.*

fore, now holds the priesthood. Ephraim has received "the fulness
of the everlasting gospel."[167] Ephraim must therefore be "gathered first to prepare the way, through the gospel and the priesthood, for the rest of the tribes of Israel when the time comes for
them to be gathered to Zion."[168] Since most of the members of
the Mormon Church today are said to be Ephraimites,[169] it is
obvious that the gathering of Ephraim is going on at the present
time. Ephraim is being gathered in America, to Zion, which was
divinely designated as the gathering-place on the North American
Continent.[170] Strictly speaking, Zion is the city of Independence,
Missouri, within which a site for the temple was divinely revealed
to Joseph Smith (*Doctrine and Covenants* 57:1-5). However, the
divine purpose to make this city the gathering place for Ephraim is
now being held in abeyance; hence Ephraim is being gathered today
in the region of the Rocky Mountains. Zion, however, shall yet
be established on the chosen site.[171]

(2) *The Gathering of the Jews.* Mormons distinguish between
the Jews, who are descendants of the Kingdom of Judah, and the
Israelites, who are descendants of the ancient Kingdom of Israel.
A second phase of the "gathering" is that the Jews, as above defined, will be gathered in Palestine, in fulfillment of the predictions
of the prophets. Mormons contend that the return of many
Jews to Palestine in recent years indicates that this prophecy is
now being fulfilled. The center of this gathering is the city of
Jerusalem, which will be rebuilt before Christ returns. Most of
the Jews who are being gathered to Jerusalem, however, will not
receive Christ as their Redeemer until He manifests Himself to
them in person.[172] After Christ has returned to earth, there will be
two capitals over which He shall reign during the millennium: Zion
(or Independence, Missouri) on the American Continent; and
Jerusalem in Palestine.[173]

(3) *The Gathering of the Lost Ten Tribes.* There will be one
more gathering before Christ returns, namely, that of the lost ten
tribes of Israel. These tribes, it is believed, are still hidden somewhere "in the land of the north." Christ, it is said, went to min-

---

[167] *Ibid.,* III, 252.
[168] *Ibid.*
[169] *Ibid.* One wonders on what grounds Mormons base this assertion
The implication of this is that not only the American Indians, as has been
previously stated, but most members of the Mormon Church are actually
Israelites!
[170] Talmage, *Articles of Faith,* p. 352.
[171] *Ibid.,* p. 353.
[172] Smith, *Doctrines of Salvation,* III, 9.
[173] *Ibid.,* III, 69-70. Just how Christ, in His physical body, will be able
to rule from both capitals simultaneously, we are not told.

ister to them after his visit to the Nephites.[174]   Before Christ returns, these ten tribes will be regathered and will be led to Zion,[175]
where they will receive the crowning blessings from those of Ephraim, the "first-born of Israel," who by this time will all have been
gathered in Zion.[176]

When all these gatherings shall have been completed, Christ will
return to earth to set up His millennial kingdom.   Before the
millennium is discussed, however, something should be said
about the return of the City of Enoch.   In a section which Joseph
Smith added to the Book of Genesis, reproduced in *The Pearl
of Great Price* as the Book of Moses, we read that Enoch, a
preacher of righteousness in the antediluvian world, built a city
which was called the City of Holiness, or Zion (Moses 7:19).
This city, in process of time, was taken up into heaven (v. 21;
cf. v. 69).   Verse 62 of this chapter describes the future
gathering of the elect from the four quarters of the earth into a holy
city, which shall be called "Zion, a New Jerusalem."   In verse
63 we read, "And the Lord said unto Enoch: Then shalt thou
and all thy city meet them there. . . ."   Verse 64 indicates that
after this has happened the earth shall rest for a thousand years.
From this passage we gather that, according to Mormon teachings,
this heavenly city will return to the earth just before the millennium (or, perhaps, shortly after the millennium has begun,
as McConkie thinks).[177]   Talmage is of the opinion that the
New Jerusalem which the Apostle John sees descending out of
heaven, according to Revelation 21:2, is actually the City of Enoch
coming down to earth.   He adds: ". . . The people or Zion of
Enoch and the modern Zion, or the gathered saints on the western
continent, will become one people."[178]

THE MILLENNIUM

According to Article 10 of the Articles of Faith, Mormons
believe that Christ will reign personally upon the earth.   This
reign will occur during the millennium.   Mormons believe that
there will be two resurrections: one at the beginning and one
at the end of the millennium.   At the beginning of the millennium
the believing dead will be raised (*Doctrine and Covenants*
88:97, 98); these shall be caught up to meet the returning Lord
in the air, and shall descend with Him.   At this time the "saints
that are upon the earth, who are alive, shall be quickened and be

---

[174] Talmage, *Articles of Faith,* p. 340.
[175] *Ibid.,* p. 341.
[176] Smith, *Doctrines of Salvation,* III, 252-3.
[177] *Mormon Doctrine,* p. 774.
[178] *Articles of Faith,* p. 352.

caught up to meet Him."[179]   Among those who are raised at this
time will be included the heathen who were groping for the
light, but did not hear the Gospel (45:54).   This resurrection
Mormons call "the first resurrection."

As the millennium begins, all the wicked shall be "burned as
stubble" (29:9); this does not mean annihilation, however,
but sudden death.   During the entire millennium the spirits of the
wicked will remain in the prison-house of the spirit world.   Here
they will be able to repent and to cleanse themselves through the
things they shall suffer.[180]

A great era of peace will now be ushered in.   Satan will be
bound, and his power will be restrained.   There will be no enmity
between man and beast; love will rule supreme.[181]   Men will
be mostly zealous in the service of their reigning Lord.   Yet
sin will not be wholly abolished, nor will death be banished.[182]
All who continue to live during the millennium will reach the
age of one hundred years, and will then suddenly be changed to
immortality, and be "caught up" (*Doctrine and Covenants* 101:30,
31).   Since resurrected saints are also living on the earth at this
time, mortal and immortal people shall be living side by side.

The great work of the millennium will be temple work: baptism
for the dead.   During the millennium mortals will be able to be
baptized for all those who have lived from the beginning of time.
Mortals will be directed in this work by the resurrected saints
and the Saviour.[183]

Though the wicked are no longer on the earth, many non-Mormons who have lived "clean lives" and were therefore not put to
death when Christ returned will also be among those who enjoy
the millennium.   During the millennium the Gospel must be
preached to them "until all men are either converted or pass
away."[184]

At the end of the millennium all the wicked will be raised.[185]

---

[179] *Doctrine and Covenants* 88:96.   Apparently Joseph Smith did not
realize that the word "quicken" means "to make alive"!   Why should
those already alive still have to be "quickened"?
[180] Smith, *Doctrines of Salvation*, III, 59-60.
[181] Talmage, *Articles of Faith*, p. 369.
[182] *Ibid.*, p. 371.
[183] Smith, *Doctrines of Salvation*, III, 58-59.   A Genealogical Society,
with headquarters in Salt Lake City, is gathering genealogical statistics in
order to prepare for this millennial temple work.   According to the
Statistical Report found in the April 13, 1963, issue of the *Church News,*
genealogical records microfilmed in 13 countries during the year 1962
were equivalent to 154,174 printed volumes of approximately 300 pages
per volume!
[184] *Ibid.*, I, 86.
[185] Talmage, *Articles of Faith*, p. 390.

This will be the second resurrection. Also at this time Satan will be loosed and will again assert his power; some of those living on the earth will follow Satan in his last attempt to deceive the nations, and will thus become Sons of Perdition. The hosts whom Satan will gather will include some from the inhabitants of the earth, and some from among the wicked dead who have just been raised. A last great battle will be fought, in which Satan and his hosts will be defeated.[186]

THE FINAL STATE

At the end of the millennium the earth will be dissolved. It shall then be renewed, or "raised with a resurrection," thus becoming "a celestial body, so that they of the celestial order may possess it forever and ever."[187] According to Talmage the earth will then become "a celestialized body fit for the abode of the most exalted intelligences."[188] It will then no longer be opaque, as at present, but, like the sun and the other stars, full of light and glory. In fact, all the great stars that we see, including our sun, are celestial worlds — worlds that have passed on to their exaltation.[189]

What will be the final state of man? We should first note that, after the renewal of the earth, death will be completely banished.[190] There will, however, be quite a difference in the final state of various types of beings. Section 76 of *Doctrine and Covenants* is an important source of Mormon teachings on the final state. The heading prefacing this section states that before this vision came, Joseph Smith and Sidney Rigdon had concluded from various previous revelations that heaven must include more kingdoms than one.

Mormon theology assigns beings in the final state to four different groups. The first of these groups consists of the so-called *Sons of Perdition*. These are again divided into two classes: (a) The devil and his angels. The devil (Lucifer, a brother of Christ) rebelled against God (Elohim) in the pre-existent state, and enticed one-third of the spirits to follow him in his rebellion. In punishment for this rebellion, these spirits remain without bodies eternally,[191] and are denied redemption through Christ, since

---

186 Smith, *Doctrines of Salvation*, I, 87.
187 *Ibid.,* I, 87-88.
188 *Articles of Faith*, p. 375.
189 Smith, *Doctrines of Salvation*, I, 88-89.
190 Talmage, *Articles of Faith*, p. 378.
191 How does this harmonize with the Mormon view of the Holy Spirit, who is also said to be without a body?

they have lost the power of repentance.[192] (b) Human beings whose sins have also placed them beyond "the present possibility of repentance and salvation."[193] These are people who "have known the power of God in this mortal life and then, having full knowledge of the power and purposes of God, rebel against Him, putting Jesus Christ to open shame."[194] Their transgression is also described as the unpardonable sin, or as the blasphemy against the Holy Spirit.[195]

The Sons of Perdition, the human members of whom, according to one Mormon source, are "but a small portion of the human race,"[196] will be permanently consigned to hell. There they are "doomed to suffer the wrath of God, with the devil and his angels, in eternity"; for their sin "there is no forgiveness in this world nor in the world to come" (*Doctrine and Covenants* 76: 33, 34). Their torment will be endless, for "their worm dieth not and the fire is not quenched, which is their torment — and the end thereof, neither the place thereof, nor their torment, no man knows" (76:44, 45).[197]

The Sons of Perdition constitute the only group which shall not be redeemed (76:38). Those who are redeemed, however, will spend eternity in one of three different kingdoms, in each of which are to be found many gradations of glory. Beginning with the highest of these kingdoms, they are as follows:

(1) *The Celestial Kingdom.* This kingdom, which will be located on this earth after its renewal, "is prepared for the righteous, those who have been faithful in keeping the commandments of the Lord, and have been cleansed of all their sins."[198] Most of those who enter this kingdom (though not all) receive full exaltation; those who receive this exaltation constitute the "Church of the First-born" (*Doctrine and Covenants* 76:54); they are gods (76:58). They shall dwell in the presence of God and his Christ forever and ever (76:62). It will be remembered that those who reach this blessed state shall live with the spouses

[192] Smith, *Doctrines of Salvation*, II, 219.
[193] Talmage, *Articles of Faith*, p. 409.
[194] Smith, *Doctrines of Salvation*, II, 219-20.
[195] *Ibid.*, II, 221.
[196] Smith and Sjodahl, *Doctrine and Covenants Commentary*, p. 453.
[197] That the Sons of Perdition shall suffer endlessly is also clearly taught by II Nephi 9:16. What puzzles non-Mormons, however, is the statement quoted above: "the end thereof . . . no man knows." It is possible to construe this sentence as meaning that nobody knows whether there will be an end, implying that there may be an end to their torment after all. Puzzling, too, is *Doctrine and Covenants* 19:10-12, where we are told that *endless punishment* is so called simply because it is the punishment of the Endless One. We are forced to conclude that there is some ambiguity in Mormon teaching on the question of eternal punishment.
[198] Joseph Fielding Smith, *Answers to Gospel Questions*, II, 208.

to whom they have been sealed for eternity, and with the children
to whom they have been so sealed; they shall also continue to
procreate children in the celestial state (though these shall be
spirit children). It might be noted at this point that those who
go into the Terrestrial and Telestial Kingdoms shall be denied the
power of propagation, and shall live in "single blessedness," not
as members of family groups.

(2) *The Terrestrial Kingdom.* This kingdom will be located
on some sphere other than the earth, presumably another planet.[199]
Into this kingdom the following will go:

1. Accountable persons who die without law. . .;
2. Those who reject the gospel in this life and who reverse
their course and accept it in the spirit world;[200]
3. Honorable men of the earth who are blinded by the crafti-
ness of men and who therefore do not accept and live the gospel
law;
4. Members of the Church of Jesus Christ of Latter-day Saints
. . . who are not valiant, but who are instead lukewarm in their
devotion to the Church and to righteousness.[201]

Joseph Fielding Smith adds the comment that "all who enter
this kingdom must be of that class who have been morally clean."[202]
People in this kingdom will be ministered to by those in the
Celestial Kingdom (*Doctrine and Covenants* 76:87). They will
"receive of the presence of the Son, but not of the fulness of the
Father" (76:77).

(3) *The Telestial Kingdom.* This kingdom will be found on
still another earth.[203] "Into this kingdom will go all of those
who have been unclean in their lives. . . . These people who
enter there will be the unclean; the liars, sorcerers, adulterers, and
those who have broken their covenants."[204] These are people who
say they are of Paul, of Apollos, or of Cephas (*Doctrine and Covenants* 76:99.[205] They "receive not the gospel, neither the testimony

---

[199] *Ibid.,* II, 210.
[200] It will be noted that here Mormons adopt the unscriptural position
that people who have rejected the gospel in this life will have another opportunity to accept it after death.
[201] McConkie, *Mormon Doctrine,* p. 708. Reference is made to *Doctrine
and Covenants* 76:71-80.
[202] *Answers to Gospel Questions,* II, 209. One wonders what Smith
means by "morally clean." Is one who rejects the gospel in this life to be
considered "morally clean"?
[203] *Ibid.,* II, 210.
[204] *Ibid.,* II, 209.
[205] It should be noted here that if any group is guilty of the sin rebuked
by Paul in the passage here alluded to (I Cor. 1:12), it is the Mormons!
By placing a merely human leader, Joseph Smith, far higher than Paul or
Apollos or Cephas — almost as high as Jesus Christ, in fact — and by
accusing all those who belong to Christian churches of corruption, hy-

of Jesus, neither the prophets, neither the everlasting covenant"
(76:101). "These are they who are cast down to hell and suffer the
wrath of Almighty God until the fulness of times" (76:106). "Yet
these, after they have been punished for their sins and have been
turned over to the torments of Satan, shall eventually come forth,
after the Millennium, to receive the telestial kingdom."[206]   These
people, in other words, will not be raised until the end of the
millennium.   They will be quite numerous: their number will
be as great as the sand on the seashore (*Doctrine and Covenants*
76:109).   They shall be "judged according to their works, and
every man shall receive . . . his own dominion, in the mansions
which are prepared" (76:111).   These "receive not of his
[God's] fulness in the eternal world, but of the Holy Spirit,
through the ministration of the terrestrial" (76:86). "They shall
be servants of the Most High; but where God and Christ dwell
they cannot come, worlds without end" (76:112).

Opportunity will be given for advancement within each of these
three kingdoms.   As regards the possibility of progression from one
kingdom to another, Talmage declares that the scriptures make
no positive affirmation.[207]   On this point, however, Joseph Fielding Smith is much more dogmatic than Talmage: "It has been
asked if it is possible for one who inherits the telestial glory to
advance in time to the celestial glory.   The answer to this question is, No!"[208]

Summarizing the above, we cannot in the strict sense of the
term call the Mormons Universalists, since they do hold that
some human beings (though their number is very small) will be
consigned to everlasting punishment in hell, along with the devil
and his angels.   One could, however, call Mormons virtual
Universalists since, according to their teaching, the vast majority
of the human race will attain to some kind of salvation.

---

pocrisy, and apostasy (see *Pearl of Great Price*, p. 48, v. 19), Mormons
are doing precisely what the erring factions in Corinth were doing.   Only
they are saying, "We are of Joseph."

[206] *Answers to Gospel Questions*, II, 209.   See *Doctrine and Covenants*
88:100-101.

[207] *Articles of Faith*, p. 409.

[208] *Doctrines of Salvation*, II, 31.

APPENDIX A

THE BOOK OF MORMON

In the preceding chapter the question of the necessity for revelations additional to the Bible was touched upon. In this appendix we shall discuss the question of the genuineness of the *Book of Mormon* as an additional sacred scripture which purports to give additional revelation from God. We shall look at this matter from two points of view: the languages in which the plates basic to the *Book of Mormon* are said to have been written, and the transmission of the *Book of Mormon*.[1]

THE LANGUAGES OF THE BOOK OF MORMON

Mormons claim that the *Book of Mormon* is a book of divine revelation, given us by God in addition to the Bible. Let us see whether the facts concerning the alleged writing and transmission of the *Book of Mormon* bear out this claim. The Bible, as we know, was written in languages which were known and spoken by many: Hebrew, Aramaic, and Greek. The Old Testament was written in the Hebrew language which was spoken in Palestine at the time when these writings were produced, with the excption of a few short sections in Aramaic (six chapters of the Book of Daniel and two passages in the Book of Ezra). The New Testament was written in Greek, which was at that time the common language of the Roman Empire and the literary language of Palestine. Although there was a time when the differences between the Greek of the New Testament and classical Greek led some scholars to presume that the former was a special kind of "Holy Ghost Greek," particularly devised by God for

---

[1] In the bibliography one will find a list of books dealing particularly with the *Book of Mormon*. To these may be added George B. Arbaugh's *Revelation in Mormonism*, E. D. Howe's *Mormonism Unveiled*, and Chapters 3 and 4 of James H. Snowden's *The Truth About Mormonism*. These volumes bring up such matters as contradictions between the *Book of Mormon* and the Bible, between the *Book of Mormon* and the other sacred books of Mormonism, and between the *Book of Mormon* and various statements by Joseph Smith; the so-called Spaulding-Rigdon theory of the origin of the *Book of Mormon;* and the relation between the *Book of Mormon* and archaeological discoveries on the American continent. Since these topics are adequately treated by other writers, this appendix will not touch upon them, but will deal with some aspects of the genuineness of the *Book of Mormon* which have not been fully dealt with elsewhere.

the purpose of communicating His revelation to man, the discovery during the last sixty years of thousands of extra-Biblical
papyri dating from New Testament times, mostly commercial
documents written in Greek, has proved that the Koine Greek
of the New Testament was simply the everyday language which
was in common use throughout the empire at that time.[2]

If, now, God intended to issue another set of sacred books,
it would be expected that He would do so in another well-known
language, the existence and character of which would be testified
to by extra-canonical documents. Mormons claim, however, that
the language in which the plates allegedly original to the *Book
of Mormon* were written was "Reformed Egyptian" (Mormon
9:32); two verses later the following qualification is added: "But
the Lord knoweth the things which we have written, and also that
none other people knoweth our language; therefore he hath prepared means for the interpretation thereof." "Reformed Egyptian," therefore, is not a known language; neither do we possess
documents or inscriptions of any sort which attest the existence
of this language or help us understand its character. Is it
likely that God would give us His newest and allegedly greatest
Book of Scripture in a language completely unknown?

The force of this objection will be more fully realized as we
reflect a bit further. The existence of manuscript copies of the
books of the Bible in Hebrew, Aramaic, and Greek enables
Bible scholars to study the Bible in these original languages. As
anyone who has ever attempted to translate from one language to
another knows, a translation is never a precise reproduction of
the original text. Certain fine shades of meaning are invariably
lost in translation, since one can never fully express in the second
language everything that is expressed in the first language. Because we do have Biblical manuscripts in the original languages,
however, Bible scholars (including ministers trained in Greek
and Hebrew) can study the Bible in the original, and thus recap-
ture the fine shades of meaning which the authors of the Bible
(and, we should add, the Holy Spirit who inspired them) intended
to convey. All this, however, is impossible in the case of the
Book of Mormon, for there are no manuscript copies of the original
documents from which this book was allegedly translated. Does
it seem likely, now, that God would give us His latest sacred
book in a manner so different from that in which He gave us the
Bible? Why did God cause copies of Hebrew and Greek manuscripts of the books of the Bible to be preserved in greater

---

[2] J. H. Moulton and G. Milligan, *The Vocabulary of the Greek Testament Illustrated by the Papyri* (Grand Rapids: Eerdmans, 1957), pp. xi-xii.

number than those of any other ancient book, whereas in the case of the *Book of Mormon* He purportedly left with us only an English translation?

The existence of an extra-Biblical literature in the languages of the Bible constitutes a strong testimony to the genuineness of the Biblical writings. This type of testimony, however, is completely absent in the case of the *Book of Mormon,* since there exists no literature in "Reformed Egyptian." What assurance have we, then, that "Reformed Egyptian" was actually spoken and actually written? We must simply take one man's word for this: namely, that of Joseph Smith. Further, the existence of manuscripts in the original languages of the Bible and the existence of an extra-Biblical literature in these languages enable Biblical scholars to study the grammar of these languages and to engage in lexicographical studies. All of this type of study, however, is impossible in the case of "Reformed Egyptian." Why do we have no lexicons of "Reformed Egyptian," no grammars of "Reformed Egyptian," as we do have Hebrew lexicons and Hebrew grammars, Greek lexicons and Greek grammars? Does it seem likely that God went to all the trouble of having these additional revelations recorded in "Reformed Egyptian," only to allow all further traces of this language to disappear?

More should be said, however, about the "Reformed Egyptian" language. Nephi, who is alleged to have engraved the first "Reformed Egyptian" sacred plates, was a Jew who, it is said, lived originally in Jerusalem at about 600 B.C. At that time both the spoken and written language of the Jews was Hebrew.[3] It would be expected, therefore, that Nephi, his brothers, and his father, Lehi, would also speak and write in Hebrew. However, *mirabile dictu,* we find that Nephi, after having arrived in America, began to write on golden plates in "Reformed Egyptian!" Not only so, but we find that the "Brass Plates of Laban" which Lehi and his sons had taken with them were also written in the Egyptian language! As was mentioned, these brass plates supposedly contained the five books of Moses, the genealogy of Lehi, and "many of the prophecies from the beginning down to and including part of those spoken by Jeremiah."[4] Mosiah 1:4 tells us that the language of these plates was "the language of the Egyptians."

We are to understand, then, that Nephi and his brothers found

---

[3] For example: the Siloam Tunnel Inscription (7th century, B.C.) and the Lachish Letters (early 6th century, B.C.) were written in Hebrew. Further, as is well known, Bible books written around this time, like Jeremiah, Ezekiel, and Habakkuk, were written entirely in Hebrew.

[4] McConkie, *Mormon Doctrine,* p. 97; cf. Alma 37:3.

in Jerusalem in the sixth century B.C. a set of brass plates containing large sections of the Hebrew Scriptures translated into some form of Egyptian. Leaving aside the question of the kind of writing materials used (to which we shall return), we ask at this time: Where did this Egyptian translation come from? What body of Egyptian scholars did this translating? For what purpose was this translation made? If the Egyptian language was so commonly used in Palestine at this time that an Egyptian translation of the Scriptures was required, why have we heard nothing about this? And why do we have no record of this Egyptian translation — which, if it were to be found, would rival, if not surpass, the Septuagint[5] in importance?

We now ask the further question: Where did Lehi and his sons learn to read the Egyptian language so that they could decipher these brass plates? And where did Nephi learn the Egyptian language well enough to write it on the golden plates? In I Nephi 1:2 we hear Nephi saying, "Yea, I make a record in the language of my father, which [the language?] consists of the learning of the Jews and the language of the Egyptians." But where did Lehi learn "the language of the Egyptians"? Were not Lehi and his sons Hebrew-speaking Jews? Mormon missionaries have told the author that the reason Nephi and the Nephites wrote in Egyptian was that they were descendants of Joseph (who was the father of Manasseh), and that Joseph had lived in Egypt. True enough, but the entire nation of Israel had lived in Egypt for over 400 years; yet they did not speak and write Egyptian but Hebrew. Moses himself, who was trained in all the culture of the Egyptians, wrote not in Egyptian but in Hebrew. Why, then, should Nephi, who apparently had never lived in Egypt, write in Egyptian? Why should this small group of Jews from the tribe of Manasseh form a linguistic exception to the prevalence of Hebrew in Palestine?

One could counter, of course, that God could have caused them to learn Egyptian miraculously. But why this unnecessary miracle, when they already possessed a language, namely, Hebrew? And, further, since the plates were later to be miraculously translated into English by Joseph Smith, and were not to be left on earth, why, if there was to be a linguistic miracle, did not the Nephites learn to talk and write English? Then there would have been no need for a "translation."

This brings us to the further question of the character of this "Reformed Egyptian" language in which Nephi and subsequent

---

[5] The translation of the Old Testament into Greek, prepared in Alexandria, Egypt, in the third and second centuries B.C.

Nephite scribes reportedly recorded the history of their nation. The official description of this language and of its characters is found in Mormon 9:32, "And now, behold, we have written this record according to our knowledge, in the characters which are called among us the reformed Egyptian, being handed down and altered by us, according to our manner of speech." So this was allegedly a somewhat altered form of an earlier pure Egyptian language, written in characters which had undergone a process of alteration. Unfortunately, we possess no samples of these characters; we can only surmise what type of script this is supposed to have been. One wishes that Moroni had specified whether the original Egyptian script which the Nephites had somewhat altered was hieroglyphic, hieratic, or demotic.[6] Whichever form it was, however, it seems reasonably sure that it was not an alphabetic script, since none of the three above-mentioned types of Egyptian are either syllabic or alphabetic.[7] This means that any of these types of Egyptian script would be extremely difficult to learn or to use, having a great number of characters picturing various objects and actions. This fact, plus the fact that in Egypt writing was not practiced by the common people but only by the priestly classes,[8] makes it all the more amazing that Lehi and his sons were able to read and write Egyptian.

This raises the question: Why did God choose to use this language and this script for His alleged latest book of revelation? Why, in other words, did God make Nephi and his descendants change from Hebrew to Egyptian? One can very easily understand why the change from Hebrew to Greek was made when the New Testament manuscripts were written: Greek was then the common language of the Greco-Roman world, the language in which the gospel would be able to command the widest hearing. There is a second reason: Greek is more highly inflected than Hebrew, having, for example, seven tenses instead of the two found in Hebrew, and thus providing opportunity for many additional shades of meaning. The language of the New Testament, therefore, is well adapted to convey the more advanced revelation about God and the plan of salvation which is given in the New Testament. But now the question begins to pinch: why the shift from Hebrew to Egyptian? The reason cannot

---

[6] The three main types of Egyptian writing. Hieroglyphic began to be used about 3,000 B.C., and had passed out of use by 600 B.C. Hieratic was used alongside of hieroglyphic, and continued to be employed until the third century A.D. Demotic, a cursive derivative of hieratic, was used from about the 8th century B.C. to the 5th century A.D. See David Diringer, *The Alphabet* (New York: Philosophical Library, 1948), pp. 59, 64-67.

[7] *Ibid.,* p. 67.

[8] *Ibid.,* p. 37.

be found in the suggestion that this was to be the language of the new land where they were going, since the land was at this time presumably uninhabited. As far as the Nephites themselves were concerned, what good reason would there be for their not continuing to talk and write in Hebrew, which they already knew and understood? Furthermore, neither can the reason be found in any possible superiority of the Egyptian language over the Hebrew as a mode of conveying divine revelation. For, as we have seen, all the types of Egyptian script were non-alphabetic, whereas Hebrew is a language written in alphabetic script. Does it seem likely, now, that God would, for His alleged final sacred book, shift from an alphabetically written language like Hebrew to a more primitive, non-alphabetically written language like Egyptian, which would be obviously less precise in conveying fine shades of meaning than either Hebrew or Greek? If, finally, Egyptian were a language in some respects superior to Hebrew, and admirably suited to convey the new and final revelation, why did God permit all traces of this language to be lost and all these original documents to be removed from the earth? If God's intent from the beginning was to leave with us only an English translation of these documents, why could not this translation have been just as effectively made from Hebrew as from "Reformed Egyptian"?

The *Book of Mormon* raises another major linguistic problem, however. Moroni, as we have seen, supposedly completed his father Mormon's records, and added two books of his own, one of which was the Book of Ether. The latter was supposed to be an abridgment by Moroni of the twenty-four plates of Ether (Ether 1:2). Ether was a prophet of the Jaredites, and one of the last survivors of that race. The Jaredites, however, did not speak Egyptian; they "retained a tongue patterned after that of Adam."[9] The Book of Ether itself tells us that, at the time of the confusion of tongues at the tower of Babel, the language of the Jaredites was not confused, though all other languages were (1:33-37). Since Ether was a Jaredite, it seems reasonable to suppose that he wrote in the language of the Jaredites — a language which must have been utterly different from "Reformed Egyptian." Here is another amazing linguistic phenomenon: without supernatural help, such as was allegedly supplied to Joseph Smith when he did his work of translation, Moroni, whose language was "Reformed Egyptian," was able to decipher and abridge plates written in the language of the Jaredites, a language akin to that spoken by Adam and Eve!

[9] McConkie, *Mormon Doctrine,* p. 393.

Moroni, in fact, must have been quite a linguist. Apparently he knew Hebrew too. For note what he says, according to Mormon 9:33,

> And if our plates had been sufficiently large we should have written in Hebrew; but the Hebrew hath been altered by us also; and if we could have written in Hebrew, behold, ye would have had no imperfection in our record.

Talmage concludes from this statement that the Nephites continued to be able to read and write in Hebrew until the time of their extinction.[10] This was also a remarkable achievement! According to Talmage's comment, the Nephites remained bilingual for a period of a thousand years (from 600 B.C. to A.D. 421), able to read and write both in "Reformed Egyptian" and in Hebrew. They thus did far better than the Palestinian Jews, who after the captivity generally no longer used Hebrew as the language of everyday life, but more and more used Aramaic instead.[11] What a pity, further, that these Hebrew-reading Nephites did not have a copy of the Old Testament Scriptures in the Hebrew, but had to depend on an Egyptian translation on brass plates!

We are interested, now, in knowing why Moroni (and his father Mormon) did not write the plates in Hebrew, which would, according to the last part of Mormon 9:33, have resulted in a more perfect type of record. The reason given is that the plates were not large enough. A strange reason indeed. Why did not Moroni and Mormon simply write the Hebrew in smaller letters? Or why did they not make larger plates? If the record would have been more perfect in Hebrew, and if the Nephites could read Hebrew, why did not these men exert every effort to convey the revelation in the best possible medium?

When we attempt to reconstruct the scene, the reason given seems more strange still. If one knew two languages and were trying to decide in which of these two languages he should write certain important material, does it seem likely that the crucial factor in making this decision would be the size of the plates on which he were writing? Would not the deciding factor rather be the writer's greater competence in one language or the other? Or if — as seems highly unlikely — one's competence would be equal

---

10 *Articles of Faith*, p. 292.

11 Frederic Kenyon, *Our Bible and the Ancient Manuscripts*, rev. by A. W. Adams (N.Y.: Harper, 1958), p. 94. This Nephite linguistic phenomenon is all the more remarkable when we reflect on the fact that the Palestinian Jews largely lost their ability to use Hebrew during their 70-year sojourn in Babylonian captivity, whereas the American Nephites allegedly kept up their Hebrew during a 1000-year stay in a foreign land, *while at the same time using "Reformed Egyptian" as their main language!*

in both, would not the language chosen be the one which would most effectively convey the material to be transmitted? According to Moroni's statement, that language would have been Hebrew. And yet Hebrew was not chosen. Does this seem likely?

Does it seem likely, further, that God would allow His revelation to be written in a language which would leave a somewhat imperfect record simply because of a lack of room on the plates? If it was important that the best possible record should be made — and why shouldn't it be? — why did not God see to it that Mormon and Moroni were provided with a sufficient quantity of large plates?

The Transmission of the Book of Mormon

We concern ourselves next with the question of the transmission of the documents allegedly basic to the *Book of Mormon*. Here, too, we shall find a number of improbabilities. In the sixth century B.C. the most common forms of writing material in Palestine were papyrus and leather (or animal skin); the Hebrews also wrote on wood and potsherds. Rare examples of Mesopotamian clay-tablets with cuneiform writing have been found in Palestine, but these were obviously the work of foreigners.[12] The most common form in which books were made in those days was the roll, made of leather or papyrus, in which the various sheets were sewn or pasted together.[13] So common was this method of making books that the expression "roll of the book" (*megillath-seepher*) is often used in the Bible to describe a book. Note particularly that this expression is used several times in the thirty-sixth chapter of the book of Jeremiah — a book written around the sixth century B.C. It is quite obvious, further, that the roll mentioned in Jeremiah 36 was not made of metal, since the king cut it into pieces with a penknife. It should, of course, be mentioned that writing on metal was not completely unknown, since a copper scroll has been discovered at Qumran. This scroll, however, was not a plate but a roll, and is dated much later than 600 B.C., being generally ascribed to the first century B.C.

In view of the above facts, does it seem likely that brass plates containing a large section of the Old Testament in Egyptian would be found in Palestine in 600 B.C.? We have previously discussed the problem of the language reputedly inscribed on these plates; the

[12] G. Ernest Wright, *Biblical Archaeology* (Philadelphia: Westminster Press, 1957), p. 197. Cf. Merrill F. Unger, *Archaeology and the Old Testament* (Grand Rapids: Zondervan, 1956), p. 275. Also Jack Finegan. *Light from the Ancient Past,* 2nd ed. (Princeton University Press, 1959), pp. 389-90.
[13] Wright, *op. cit.,* p. 197. Cf. Frederic Kenyon, *op. cit.,* pp. 37-38.

use of metal plates as writing material for an extensive document such as that described above, however, presents a problem as great as that of the language. The only other instance of writing on metal which is commonly known is the copper scroll of Qumran, as noted above; but even this was a roll, not a plate.[14]

A similar question could be asked about the "golden plates" on which the Nephite records were made. Manuscripts from Central America and Mexico dating from pre-Columbian times were generally on coarse cloth or on paper.[15] Great numbers of these pre-Columbian manuscripts are known to have been burned by fanatical Spanish priests — hence they could not have been made of metal.[16] Does it seem likely, then, that the prehistoric inhabitants of the American continent would have kept their records on golden plates?

We have observed previously that no copies of the original plates from which Joseph Smith "translated" have been preserved; Mormons contend that Smith had to return these plates to the custody of Moroni.[17] This brings us to the question of translation. Joseph Smith, who had not been trained in "Reformed Egyptian," was nevertheless able to translate all these writings into English. Mormons claim, as we know, that Smith did this translating in a supernatural way, with the aid of the "Urim and Thummim."[18] Here, already, as we have seen, there is great disparity between the Bible and the *Book of Mormon*. In giving us the Bible, God gave us manuscripts in Hebrew and Greek which we can translate with the aid of lexicographical helps. Does it seem likely that God would completely change His method and give us, in the instance of His later and reputedly superior revelation, only a translation but not the original language? Does it seem likely that an un-

---

[14] It should be mentioned, however, that a bronze blade from the eleventh century B.C. has been found at Gebal or Byblos on the Mediterranean coast, containing an inscription in Phoenician-Hebrew script. Also, bronze arrowheads of the same period have been found near Bethlehem, each of them containing two words in the Phoenician-Hebrew script (*Views of the Biblical World*, International Publishing Co., 1960, II, 91). It should be noted, however, that these metal objects are a far cry from the type of "brass plates" described in the *Book of Mormon*, that the date of these objects is about five centuries before 600 B.C., and that the writing found on them is not Egyptian but a kind of early Hebrew. Note also that the blade was discovered at Byblos, which is some 160 miles north of Jerusalem, and that neither the blade nor the arrowheads present any kind of analogy for the writing of entire books on metal.

[15] Diringer, *op. cit.*, p. 125.

[16] *Ibid.*

[17] McConkie, *op. cit.*, p. 300.

[18] See above, p. 10 and n. 4 on that page.

trained man can by looking through stones translate foreign characters?

We must next examine the nature of this alleged translation. It will be recalled that, according to Talmage, no reservation may be made respecting the *Book of Mormon* on the ground of incorrect translation, since this translation was effected through the gift and power of God.[19] This means, then, that Joseph Smith's translation differs from all other translations that have ever been made; it was inspired directly by God and is therefore completely errorless. This means, too, that the original manuscript of Smith's translation must be the authoritative one, since it embodies the translation as it is alleged to have come directly from God. No changes therefore may be tolerated in this original translation, since a single change would be sufficient to upset the theory that this was an errorless translation. The fact of the matter is, however, that a great many changes have been made in the *Book of Mormon* since the original edition of 1830 was published.[20] In comparing just the first chapter of this 1830 edition with the first chapter of the 1950 edition, I have noted nine changes, exclusive of punctuation. A number of these changes correct obvious grammatical errors. For example, "my father had read and saw" has been changed to "my father had read and seen"; "thy power, and goodness, and mercy is over all the inhabitants of the earth" has been changed to "thy power, and goodness, and mercy are over all the inhabitants of the earth"; "the tender mercies of the Lord is . . ." has been changed to "the tender mercies of the Lord are. . . ." Does the following sentence sound as though it has been inspired by God? "And when Moroni had said these words, he went forth among the people, waving the rent of his garment in the air, that all might see the writing which he had wrote upon the rent . . ." (Alma 46:19). The sentence has been changed to read: ". . . waving the rent part of his garment in the air, that all might see the writing which he had written upon the rent part. . . ." There have even been doctrinal corrections.

---

[19] See above, pp. 18-19.

[20] Lamoni Call, in a book written in 1898, claimed that 2,038 corrections had been made in the *Book of Mormon* subsequent to the original edition (Arbaugh, *Revelation in Mormonism*, p. 50, n. 23). Arthur Budvarson, however, contends that by 1959 there had been over 3,000 changes (*The Book of Mormon Examined*, published by the Utah Christian Tract Society of La Mesa, Calif., 1959; p. 12).

An authentic copy of this original edition has been printed by the Deseret News Press in Salt Lake City: Wilford C. Wood, ed., *Joseph Smith Begins His Work*, Book of Mormon, 1830 First Edition (Deseret News Press, 1958). This volume contains no verse divisions.

On page 25 of the 1830 edition we read, "And the angel said unto me, behold the Lamb of God, yea, even the Eternal Father!" This has been corrected to read: "Behold the Lamb of God, yea, even the Son of the Eternal Father!" (I Nephi 11:21).

Does it seem likely that God would "inspire" a translation in which both grammatical and doctrinal corrections would have to be made? Mormons have no right to regard the grammatical errors as excusable on the ground of Smith's lack of formal education, for this entire translation is alleged to have been made "through the gift and power of God," and is said to be "in no sense the product of linguistic scholarship."[21] When there are occasional grammatical errors in our Bible translations — such as the notorious King James rendering of Matthew 16:15, "But whom say ye that I am?" — we have no difficulty in admitting that the translators, perhaps misled by the accusative case of the interrogative pronoun in the Greek, were in error. After all, no translator is inspired. But Mormons cannot admit even a single grammatical error in Smith's original translation.

Another difficulty we have with Smith's "translation" is the presence in it of at least 27,000 words from the King James Version of the Bible.[22] Does it seem likely that passages on the golden plates would be translated by divine inspiration in language precisely like that of the King James Bible?

We consider finally the testimony of Professor Charles Anthon, found in *Pearl of Great Price,* regarding the genuineness of the characters taken from the plates and the accuracy of the translation.[23] It will be recalled that when Anthon was shown the characters with their translation, he said, according to Smith's autobiography, that the translation was "correct, more so than any he had before seen translated from the Egyptian" (*Pearl of Great Price,* p. 55). However, in Mormon 9:34 we read, "But the Lord knoweth . . . that none other people knoweth our language; therefore he hath prepared means for the interpretation thereof." If the latter statement be correct, how could Professor Anthon know that the translation was correct? If, on the other hand, he could make a judgment as to the accuracy of the translation, it is not true that "none other people knoweth our language."

Both Budvarson and Walter Martin reproduce the letter sent to Mr. E. D. Howe by Professor Anthon on February 17, 1834, in which the professor completely denies the truth of the statements

---

21 Talmage, *Vitality of Mormonism,* p. 127.
22 Budvarson, *op. cit.,* p. 22.
23 See above, pp. 11-12.

attributed to him in the *Pearl of Great Price.*[24]   Even apart from
the existence of this letter, however, it will be obvious to any
well-informed person that Professor Anthon could not have said
what he is alleged to have said in *Pearl of Great Price.*   For, according to this document, Anthon said, after he saw some characters supposedly copied from the golden plates, that these characters were: "Egyptian, Chaldaic, Assyriac, and Arabic" (p. 55).
One would have expected a learned man, however, to designate
which type of Egyptian script the characters represented: hieroglyphic, hieratic, or demotic.   If we assume, now, that "Assyriac"
stands for Assyrian, and that "Chaldaic" stands for some form of
Aramaic, we may note that the professor is reported as saying
that characters representing four different languages would provide
a readable kind of writing!   The matter is still further complicated when we observe that the cuneiform script used by the
Assyrians, though it did employ syllabic signs and vowels, never
became an alphabetic script,[25] that none of the three types of
Egyptian writing were alphabetic scripts, and that both Aramaic
and Arabic were written in alphabetic scripts.   Does it seem likely
that sense could be made out of characters from four different
languages, two of which were written in alphabetic scripts, whereas the other two were not?   To use an illustration, this would be
like trying to write a sentence by putting letters from our own
English alphabet next to some Hebrew consonants, some Japanese
characters, and some Chinese characters!   Is it not by this time
clear that Professor Anthon, if he were any kind of scholar at
all, could not possibly have said what the *Pearl of Great Price* reports him as having said?   We may thus dismiss this supposedly
learned testimony as completely valueless.

We conclude that there are so many improbabilities and absurd-
ities in the story of the alleged "coming forth" of the *Book of
Mormon* that it cannot possibly have been a genuine vehicle of
divine revelation.   In the words of a Mormon writer,

> This book [The *Book of Mormon*] must be either true or
> false. . . .   If false, it is one of the most cunning, wicked, bold,
> deep-laid impositions ever palmed upon the world, calculated
> to deceive and ruin millions who would sincerely receive it as
> the word of God, and will suppose themselves securely built
> upon the rock of truth until they are plunged with their families
> into hopeless despair.[26]

---

[24] Budvarson, *op. cit.*, pp. 39-40; Walter R. Martin, *The Maze of
Mormonism* (Grand Rapids: Zondervan, 1962), pp. 42-44.
[25] Diringer, *op. cit.*, p. 43.
[26] Orson Pratt, *Divine Authenticity of the Book of Mormon;* quoted in
Budvarson, *op. cit.*, p. 7.

It is my earnest conviction that, in the light of the evidence presented in this appendix, the *Book of Mormon* is precisely what Orson Pratt says it might be in the latter part of the above quotation.   It is, I believe, one of the most cunning and wicked impositions ever palmed upon the world.[27]

[27] An abbreviated version of this appendix has been prepared by the author in the form of a 15-page tract entitled *The Bible and the Book of Mormon*. This tract, which is addressed to Mormons and is intended for use in evangelistic work with Mormons, can be obtained in quantities from the Back to God Tract Committee, 2850 Kalamazoo Ave., Grand Rapids, Mich., 49508.

CHAPTER THREE

Seventh - day Adventism

HISTORY

WILLIAM MILLER

THOUGH WILLIAM MILLER (1782-1849) NEVER JOINED THE SEV-enth-day Adventist movement, the history of Seventh-day Adventism has its roots in Miller's prophecies. Miller was born in Pittsfield, Massachusetts, in 1782. While he was still young, his family moved to Low Hampton, New York, close to the Vermont border. Though he had been reared in a Christian home, Miller became a complete skeptic, rejecting the Bible as divine revelation. After a term in the army he turned to farming, and became a respected member of the Low Hampton community. In 1816 he was converted from his skepticism. During the next two years he studied the Bible intensively with the aid of Cruden's Concordance, but without the help of commentaries. In 1818 he wrote down the conclusions to which he had arrived, which ended with this statement: "I was thus brought, in 1818, at the close of my two-year study of the Scriptures, to the solemn conclusion, that in about twenty-five years from that time [1818] all the affairs of our present state would be wound up."[1] In other words, Miller concluded

---

[1] Leroy Edwin Froom, *The Prophetic Faith of our Fathers* (Washington: Review and Herald, 1954), IV, 463.

from his Bible study that the world would come to an end in 1843.

Hesitant about publicizing so startling a conclusion, he under-took four more years of Bible study, which confirmed his previous judgment. In 1831, at the request of a friend, he publicly stated his views. This led to frequent requests to speak, so that in 1834 he became a full-time Baptist preacher. As can be understood, he preached chiefly on prophecy and the Second Coming of Christ. As can also be understood, he soon had quite a following.

Involved in the "winding up" of the affairs of the world was, of course, the expected return from heaven of the Lord Jesus Christ. Miller did not at first set an exact date for Christ's re-turn, but affirmed that this event would occur "about 1843." Later, however, he specified that this return would take place some time during the Jewish year running from March 21, 1843 to March 21, 1844.[2]

How did Miller arrive at this date? In Daniel 9:24-27 he found the prophecy of the "seventy weeks" which are there predicted as extending from the commandment to rebuild Jerusalem (v. 25) to the time when the anointed one shall be cut off (v. 26). Miller took the starting point for these seventy weeks to be the decree of Artaxerxes spoken of in Ezra 7:11-26 which permitted Ezra to go back to Jerusalem, this decree being dated in his Bible (ac-cording to the Ussher chronology) as having been issued in 457 B.C. He assumed that in prophetic writings of this sort a day stood for a year.[3] On this basis seventy weeks, which would be equivalent to 490 days, would represent 490 years. And 490 years after 457 B.C brings us to A.D. 33, the year when, according to Ussher, Christ was crucified.

In Daniel 8:14 there is a reference to 2300 evenings and morn-ings which must elapse before the sanctuary shall be cleansed. Miller assumed that the cleansing of the sanctuary alluded to in this prophecy meant Christ's return to earth. In agreement with the principle stated in the preceding paragraph, he took the 2300 evenings and mornings as standing for 2300 years. He also as-sumed that the 2300 years started at the same time as the 70 weeks. And 2300 years after 457 B.C. brings us to A.D. 1843, the year when, according to Miller, Christ would return.[4]

---

[2] Francis D. Nichol, *The Midnight Cry* (Washington: Review and Herald, 1945), p. 169.

[3] Froom, *op. cit.,* IV, 473.

[4] *Ibid.* Seventh-day Adventists still follow Miller's method of calcu-lation — see *Seventh-day Adventists Answer Questions on Doctrine* (Washington: Review and Herald, 1957), pp. 268-95. The only difference is, as we shall see, that they have a different interpretation of the cleansing of the sanctuary than Miller did.

It should be noted at this time that this calculation rests on five unproved assumptions: (1) that a day in prophetic writings always represents a year; (2) that the 70 weeks and the 2300 days began at the same time; (3) that this starting date was 457 B.C.;[5] (4) that in figuring the *terminus ad quem* we need make no allowance for the fact that March 21, 0 B.C., would actually be March 21, A.D. 1, thus throwing the calculation off by one year; and (5) that the cleansing of the sanctuary spoken of in Daniel 8:14 stands for Christ's return to earth.[6]

When the designated year arrived, however, the Lord did not return, and there was intense disappointment in the ranks of the so-called "Millerites." Miller, though dumbfounded at the failure of his calculations, was still sure that he had been right. He said,

> Were I to live my life over again, with the same evidence that I then had, to be honest with God and man, I should have to do as I have done. . . . I confess my error, and acknowledge my disappointment; yet I still believe that the day of the Lord is near, even at the door; and I exhort you, my brethren, to be watchful, and not let that day come upon you unawares.[7]

In August of 1844, however, Samuel S. Snow, one of the Millerite leaders, launched the so-called "seventh-month movement." He had become convinced that the 2300 days of Daniel 8:14 were to end not in the spring of 1844, as Miller had supposed, but in the fall of that year. Specifically, he predicted that Christ would return on October 22, 1844, which would be our calendar equivalent of the Jewish Day of Atonement for that year.[8] The "seventh-month movement" — so called because Tishri, the month in which the Day of Atonement fell, was the seventh month of the Jewish

[5] If we were inclined to engage in this type of calculation (which most of us probably are not), it should be noted that the decree of Artaxerxes spoken of in Ezra 7 had nothing to do with the rebuilding of Jerusalem. Yet Daniel spoke of the "commandment" (literally, "word," *dabhar*) to restore and to build Jerusalem. It would seem that Artaxerxes' decision to permit Nehemiah to go back to the city of his fathers' sepulchres, so that he might rebuild it (Neh. 2:5-8), would be much more to the point. But this happened thirteen years after 457 B.C., in 444 B.C. Seventh-day Adventists, however, still defend Miller's choice of 457 B.C.

[6] It is interesting to note that the word translated "cleansed" in the King James Version of Dan. 8:14 is actually the Niphal form of the Hebrew verb *tsadaq*, which means to be right or righteous. Hence the RSV renders the last part of the verse, "then the sanctuary shall be restored to its rightful state"; and the Berkeley version has "then the rights of the sanctuary shall be restored." Many commentators accordingly understand the passage as a prediction of the recovery of the Jerusalem temple from Antiochus Epiphanes by Judas Maccabeus in 165 B.C.

[7] Sylvester Bliss, *Memoirs of William Miller*, p. 256; quoted in Nichol, *The Midnight Cry*, p. 171.

[8] Froom, *op. cit.*, IV, 799-800.

ecclesiastical year — rapidly gained momentum; before long virtually all the followers of Miller had accepted this re-interpretation of the 2300-day prophecy, including, finally, even Miller himself.[9] As October 22 approached, excitement mounted. Groups of Millerites gathered in their homes and in their meeting-places, expecting the Lord to return some time that day. As October 22 ended, however, and Christ did not return, the disappointment of the Millerites was overwhelming. In fact, this day is usually referred to in their history as the day of "The Great Disappointment."[10] Many now gave up the "Advent" faith; but others still clung to it.

Hiram Edson

As we continue our discussion of the history of Seventh-day Adventism, we must further take note of three individuals who played key roles in the development of this movement. The first of these is Hiram Edson of Port Gibson, New York (not far from Rochester). A group of "Millerite" believers met at Edson's house, about a mile south of Port Gibson, on October 22, 1844, to wait for Christ's return. Among those closely associated with Edson at that time were a physician, Dr. Franklin B. Hahn, and a student in his early twenties, O. R. L. Crosier. On the following morning most of the believers, greatly disappointed, returned to their homes. With those who remained, Edson went to his barn to pray. They prayed until they felt assured that light would be given them and that their disappointment would be explained.[11]

After breakfast Edson decided to go out to comfort the other Adventists with the assurance they had received through prayer. Edson and a companion (who is surmised by most Adventist writers to have been Crosier) walked across the corn field adjoining the farm on their way to their first destination. At this point I quote from a manuscript written by Edson himself:

> We started, and while passing through a large field I was stopped about midway of the field. Heaven seemed open to my view, and I saw distinctly and clearly that instead of our High Priest coming out of the Most Holy of the heavenly sanctuary to come to this earth on the tenth day of the seventh month, at the end of the 2300 days, He for the first time entered on that day the second apartment of that sanctuary; and that

[9] *Ibid.*, pp. 818-20.
[10] Walter R. Martin, *The Truth About Seventh-day Adventism* (Grand Rapids: Zondervan, 1960), p. 29.
[11] Arthur W. Spalding, on pp. 91-105 of his *Captains of the Host* (Washington: Review and Herald, 1949), gives a vivid account of this entire episode and of the events connected with it.

He had a work to perform in the most holy before coming to this earth.[12]

Edson told his companion about his vision, which appeared to both of them to be the Lord's answer to their prayer of that morning. In the light of this vision, Edson now realized that there was a heavenly sanctuary corresponding to the Old Testament earthly sanctuary which had been patterned after it, and that there were two phases in Christ's heavenly ministry, just as there had been two phases in the sanctuary ministry of Old Testament priests. In other words, the light now dawned upon him that, instead of Christ's having come out of the holy of holies of the heavenly sanctuary to this earth at the end of the 2300 days, he had simply for the first time passed from the holy place of the heavenly sanctuary into the heavenly holy of holies. So Miller had not been wrong in his calculations, but simply in thinking that the sanctuary which was to be cleansed at the end of the 2300-day period was a sanctuary on earth — or, perhaps, the earth itself.

During the next several months Edson, Hahn, and Crosier set themselves to earnest Bible study, particularly with regard to the sanctuary ministry as described both in the Old Testament and in the book of Hebrews. Crosier wrote up his conclusions on the subject in an article which appeared in the Cincinnati *Day-Star,* an Adventist publication, under date of February 7, 1846. Froom, in his *Prophetic Faith of our Fathers,* gives a digest of this article.[13] Crosier explained that we must see in the work of Christ a fulfillment of the work of the Old Testament priests. In the daily work of these priests, when they presented the daily offerings to God and brought the blood of these offerings into the holy place, sprinkling it before the veil or applying it to the horns of the altar of incense, they were only transferring iniquity from the people to the sanctuary (p. 1232).[14] On the Great Day of Atonement, however, the sanctuary was cleansed. This happened, so Crosier continued, when the high priest entered the holy of holies and sprinkled the blood of the slain goat upon the mercy seat (p. 1232).[15] After the sanctuary had been cleansed, the sins of

---

[12] From a fragment of a manuscript on his life and experiences, by Hiram Edson; quoted by Nichol, *The Midnight Cry,* p. 458.

[13] Vol. IV, pp. 1228-34. He also gives his own understanding of the views of Crosier and Edson, expanding somewhat on the Crosier article, on pp. 896-900.

[14] Froom gives his own interpretation of the meaning of these actions when he says, "Thus in symbol the sins of the people were borne into the sanctuary, to the entrance of the Most Holy, thus 'polluting' the sanctuary" (pp. 896-97).

[15] The reader will note at this point a most peculiar inconsistency. Whereas the application of sacrificial blood to the altar of incense in the

the people were then put on the head of the scapegoat which was sent away into the wilderness (p. 1232). There were thus two phases in the ministry of the Old Testament priests: the first (the daily ministry, which had to do with the holy place) led to the forgiveness of sins; the second, however (the yearly ministry, which had to do with the holy of holies), led to the blotting out of sins (p. 1232).[16]

These two phases of priestly ministry, Crosier continued, are also to be seen in the work of Christ. Throughout the centuries of the Christian era Christ had been doing a work comparable to the daily ministry of the priests, which work resulted in the forgiveness of sin but not in the blotting out of sin (p. 1233). The process of blotting out sin began on October 22, 1844, when Christ entered the holy of holies of the heavenly sanctuary, an action which was comparable to the work of the high priest on the Day of Atonement. However, since the cleansing of the sanctuary was not complete until the sins of the people had been laid on the scapegoat — who, Crosier explained, typified not Christ but Satan — the last act of Christ's priestly ministry will be to take the sins from the heavenly sanctuary and to place them on Satan (pp. 1233-34). Only after this has happened will Christ return (p. 1234).[17]

Later in Adventist history the concept of Christ's having entered the heavenly holy of holies was to be expanded into the so-called "investigative judgment" doctrine, which we shall examine later. Already at this time, however, Adventists had found a solution to the "Great Disappointment," and had laid the groundwork for their later teachings on Christ's present ministry in the heavenly sanctuary.[18]

---

holy place is said to *pollute* the sanctuary (since the sins of believers are thus brought into the sanctuary), the application of sacrificial blood to the mercy seat in the holy of holies is said to *cleanse* the sanctuary. Why should the same ritual procedure pollute in the one case and cleanse in the other?

[16] This distinction between forgiveness and blotting out should be carefully noted; it plays an important part in subsequent Seventh-day Adventist theology.

[17] Froom adds that the Crosier article represented the views, not only of Crosier himself, but also of Edson and Hahn. He further states that the article was endorsed by such prominent Adventist leaders as Joseph Bates and Ellen G. White; it may thus be taken as representative of Adventist thought at this time.

[18] It should be noted at this time that William Miller, who died in 1849, never accepted Crosier's teachings about Christ's sanctuary ministry (Froom, *op. cit.*, IV, 828-9). It is also significant to note that Crosier himself later repudiated his earlier teachings on the sanctuary (*ibid.*, p 892, n. 18).

JOSEPH BATES

A second person prominent in the early history of Seventh-day Adventism was Joseph Bates. This man, during twenty-one years at sea, had advanced from cabin boy to captain and ship owner. He had been converted to Christianity on board ship. After retirement he took up residence in Fair Haven, Massachusetts, where he joined the Christian Connection Church. From 1839 onward Bates was in the forefront of the Advent movement. Through the reading of an article on the Sabbath by Thomas M. Preble in the Portland (Maine) *Hope of Israel* of February 28, 1845, Bates became convinced that the seventh day was the proper Sabbath for Christians to observe.[19]

Previous to this time a group of Adventists in Washington, New Hampshire, had been influenced by some Seventh-day Baptists to embrace the seventh day as the Sabbath. This all began through the influence of a woman — Mrs. Rachel Oakes. She, having become a Seventh-day Baptist, was attending an Adventist communion service in Washington one Sunday in the winter of 1843. After the preacher, Frederick Wheeler, had called upon all his hearers to "obey God and keep His commandments in all things," Mrs. Oakes almost arose to object. Afterwards she told the preacher that she had wanted to ask him to put the cloth back over the communion table until he was willing to keep *all* the commandments of God, *including the fourth.* Knowing that Mrs. Oakes was a Seventh-day Baptist, Wheeler promised her that he would do some serious thinking and earnest studying on the Sabbath question. In March of 1844 he arrived at the conclusion that the seventh day was the proper Sabbath, and began to observe it. Shortly afterwards the leaders of the Adventist group in Washington accepted this view, and began to observe the seventh day. The Washington, New Hampshire, Adventists were thus the first Adventists to observe the seventh day.[20]

After Joseph Bates had arrived at his conclusions about the Sabbath Day, he heard about what had happened at Washington, New Hampshire, and visited the leaders there, including Frederick Wheeler. This visit strengthened Bates's convictions about the Sabbath Day.[21]

Early in 1846 Bates wrote a forty-eight-page tract entitled *The Seventh-day Sabbath, a Perpetual Sign.* In it he argued that the seventh-day Sabbath had been prefigured in creation, ordained in Eden, and confirmed at Mount Sinai. In 1847 he wrote a second

[19] Froom, *op. cit.,* IV, 953-55.
[20] *Ibid.,* pp. 944-47.
[21] *Ibid.,* pp. 947-48.

edition of this tract, in which he discussed the messages of the three angels of Revelation 14:6-12. The third angel mentioned in this passage threatens dire punishments upon those who worship the beast and his image, and who receive his mark on their foreheads (v. 9). Identifying the beast with the Papacy, and arguing that it was the Papacy which had changed the Sabbath from the seventh day to the first, Bates concluded that those who still kept the first day as the Sabbath were worshiping the papal beast and would thus receive his mark. The obedience to God's commandments required by the third angel, Bates continued, was to consist particularly in the observance of the seventh day.[22]

In January, 1849, Bates issued a second tract, entitled *A Seal of the Living God.* Noting that, according to Revelation 7, the servants of God were sealed on their foreheads, Bates concluded that the seventh-day Sabbath was the seal of God here spoken of. From the fact that the number of the sealed spoken of in this chapter is 144,000, Bates drew the conclusion that the "remnant" who keep the commandments of God — in other words, the faithful Adventists — would number only 144,000.[23]

Thus there was added to the Adventist movement an emphasis on the keeping of the seventh day as the Sabbath. Though at first Bates's argument on the Sabbath did not appeal to Ellen Harmon and James White (who were to become prominent Adventist leaders), later they also accepted this position.[24] It was therefore now taught by Adventists that the keeping of the seventh day was the "seal of God," the characteristic mark of all of God's true children. The observance of the first day of the week as the Lord's Day, however, was interpreted as an action which would make one liable to receive the "mark of the beast," and to drink the cup of God's anger.

ELLEN G. WHITE

The third important figure who played a leading role in the history of Seventh-day Adventism was Ellen G. White (1827-1915). Ellen Gould Harmon was born in 1827 in Gorham, Maine, some ten miles north of Portland. While Ellen was still a child, her family moved to Portland. Here they were members of the Chestnut Street Methodist Church. When Ellen was nine years old, while going home from school, she was struck in the

---

[22] *Ibid.,* pp. 956-58.
[23] *Ibid.,* p. 958. Walter Martin indicates, however, that this early restriction of the remnant to 144,000 has been repudiated by the Seventh-day Adventist denomination (*The Truth About Seventh-day Adventism,* p. 34, n. 12).
[24] Froom, *op. cit.,* p. 959.

face by a stone thrown by an older girl. She was unconscious for three weeks; her nose was broken and her face was disfigured. ". . . The shock to her nervous system and the illness which followed, with succeeding complications, continued for years to make her an invalid and to present a constant threat to her life."[25]

In 1840 and in 1842 William Miller lectured in Portland on the Second Advent. After having attended these lectures, the Harmon family accepted Miller's teachings, and were, as a result, disfellowshiped from the Methodist church. It was after the Great Disappointment of 1844 that Ellen had her first vision: in December of that year, while visiting with some other Adventist women at the home of a friend, and while kneeling in prayer, she saw in a vision the Advent believers traveling along a lighted pathway until they reached the shining City of God. Jesus was the guide and leader of this group, which grew to become a great company.[26] Shortly after this, a second vision revealed that, though she was bound to encounter disbelief and calumny, she must now tell others what God had shown her.[27] She now began a life of public witnessing, counseling, teaching, and writing. On August 30, 1846, she married James White, a young Adventist preacher who had been active in the Millerite movement. From this union four sons were born.[28]

Soon there was a sizable group of Advent believers around Portland, Maine, who began to recognize that Mrs. White was being uniquely guided by the Holy Spirit — that, in fact, she was a true prophetess, whose visions and words were to be followed. Others in the Advent movement came to accept Mrs. White's leadership.

Mrs. White's husband stated that during the earlier part of her ministry she had from one hundred to two hundred "open visions" in twenty-three years. These "open visions," however, decreased as the years passed, later guidance coming to her through messages in her waking hours or through dreams. Almost every aspect of the belief and activity of the Seventh-day Adventists was encouraged or inspired by a vision or word from Mrs. White. Thus, in February of 1845, she had a vision of Jesus entering into the holy of holies of the heavenly sanctuary, confirming Hiram Edson's vision received in October of the preceding year.[29] On April 7, 1847, she had a vision in which she was taken first into the holy place, and then into the holy of holies of the heavenly sanctuary.

---

[25] Spalding, *op. cit.,* p. 62.
[26] Froom, *op. cit.,* IV, 979, 981-82.
[27] *Ibid.,* p. 980.
[28] Francis D. Nichol, *Ellen G. White and her Critics* (Washington: Review and Herald, 1951), p. 36.
[29] *Ibid.,* p. 178.

There she saw the ark and the Ten Commandments in the ark, with a halo of glory around the Sabbath commandment.[30] This vision, therefore, confirmed Joseph Bates's teachings about the seventh day. In her voluminous writings Mrs. White commented on such diversified subjects as salvation in all its phases, sacred history, Christian doctrine, the home and society, health, education, temperance, evangelism, finance, world missions, the organization of the church, and the inspiration of the Bible.[31]

The attitude of present-day Seventh-day Adventists toward Mrs. White is well expressed in the following statement, in which Francis Nichol describes the second of two distinguishing marks which set the Advent movement apart: "The belief that God gave to this movement, in harmony with the forecast of prophecy, a manifestation of the prophetic gift in the person and writings of Mrs. E. G. White."[32] Still more official is the following statement, taken from Article 19 of the "Fundamental Beliefs of Seventh-day Adventists":

> That the gift of the Spirit of prophecy is one of the identifying marks of the remnant church. . . . They [Seventh-day Adventists] recognize that this gift was manifested in the life and ministry of Ellen G. White.[33]

In a later section of this chapter we shall examine this claim in order to see what light it sheds on the question of the source of authority for Seventh-day Adventism.

THE SEVENTH-DAY ADVENTIST CHURCH

We have just reviewed the teachings of three Millerite Adventist groups: the group headed by Hiram Edson in western New York State, which emphasized the doctrine of the heavenly sanctuary; the group in Washington, New Hampshire, which, along with Joseph Bates, advocated the observance of the seventh day; and the group around Portland, Maine, which held that Ellen G. White was a true prophetess, whose visions and words were to be followed by the Adventists. These three groups fused to form the Seventh-day Adventist denomination.[34] It might be added that the three teachings developed by these groups (the Sabbath, the sanctuary, and the spirit of prophecy) formed the basis for the emergence of the new theological system known as Seventh-day

---

[30] *Ibid.,* p. 189, n. 2.
[31] Froom, *op. cit.,* IV, 985-86.
[32] *Ellen G. White and her Critics,* p. 22.
[33] *Questions on Doctrine* (this abbreviation will be used from now on for the book, *Seventh-day Adventists Answer Questions on Doctrine*), p. 16.
[34] Froom, *op. cit.,* IV, 845-47.

Adventism,[35] and continue to be among the most distinctive doctrines of that movement.

Through the missionary efforts of Joseph Bates, Adventist groups were started in Jackson, Michigan, and in Battle Creek, Michigan; soon the latter town became the location for the first headquarters of the movement. In 1860 the name *Seventh-day Adventist* was adopted as the official name of the denomination; in May of 1863 the first General Conference, with representatives from all the state conferences except Vermont, was held in Battle Creek. We recognize the year 1863, therefore, as the date of the official organization of the Seventh-day Adventist denomination.[36] In 1903 both General Conference Headquarters and the Review and Herald Publishing Association were moved to Takoma Park, a suburb of Washington, D. C.[37]

After evangelistic work had been begun in the western and southern areas of the United States, a period of tremendous foreign expansion began, which was well under way by 1903. Seventh-day Adventist missionaries were sent to Europe, to Africa, to Australia, the South Sea Islands, South America, the Orient, Southern Asia, Central America, and the Middle East.[38] In their 1961 Yearbook Seventh-day Adventists claim that they are carrying on work in 195 out of the 220 countries in the world recognized by the United Nations, and that therefore only 25 countries have not yet been entered by them.[39]

The following figures about their membership have been culled from the 1961 *Yearbook*. This publication lists a world membership of 1,194,070, and gives the total number of churches as 12,707 (p. 343).[40] If we subtract figures given for the Canadian Union Conference (p. 27) from those given for North America (p. 343), we arrive at the following figures for the United States: 311,535 members, and 3,002 churches. It is of particular interest to note that their world membership is approximately four times

---

[35] *Ibid.,* p. 848.
[36] *The Story of our Church,* Prepared by the Department of Education, General Conference of Seventh-day Adventists (Mountain View, Calif.: Pacific Press, 1956), pp. 215-20.
[37] *Ibid.,* pp. 256-61. The *Review and Herald* (full title: *Advent Review and Sabbath Herald*) is the official church paper of the denomination.
[38] *Ibid.,* pp. 267-374.
[39] *1961 Yearbook of the Seventh-day Adventist Denomination* (Washington: Review and Herald, 1961), p. 340.
[40] The figures published in the 1961 *Yearbook* are for the year ending Dec. 31, 1959. The 1962 *Yearbook,* which gives figures for the year ending Dec. 31, 1961, lists a world membership of 1,307,892, and gives the total number of churches as 13,369. In two years, therefore, the denomination has grown by 113,822 members, an average increase of 56,900 per year.

as large as their United States membership; another way of putting this is to say that three out of every four Seventh-day Adventists are to be found outside the United States. These figures, needless to say, point up the tremendous missionary activities of this group.[41]

There are approximately 6,000 ordained ministers in the denomination, and more than 3,000 licensed ministers.[42] ". . . The Seventh-day Adventists are said to have more missionaries active on foreign fields than any other mission body except Methodists who have a few over 1500; the Adventists [have] in excess of 1400."[43] There are 44 Seventh-day Adventist publishing houses, which publish 309 periodicals in 218 languages[44]; the total number of languages used in oral work only is reported as 573.[45]

Seventh-day Adventists have a radio program, *The Voice of Prophecy,* and a television program, *Faith for Today.* They are very active in educational and medical enterprises; the 1961 Yearbook lists 4,426 elementary schools, 333 colleges and academies, 106 hospitals and sanitariums, 104 clinics and dispensaries, and 26 old people's homes and orphanages (p. 345).

It should be further observed that this movement has experienced a number of splits. The Seventh-day Adventist denomination is the largest and fastest-growing group of Adventists. In an article on "Adventists" in the *Twentieth Century Encyclopedia of Religious Knowledge,* Elmer T. Clark lists six Adventist bodies in addition to the Seventh-day Adventists. Of these the largest is the Advent Christian Church, which in 1951 had a membership of approximately 30,000.

SOURCE OF AUTHORITY

The first question we take up as we begin to study the doctrinal teachings of Seventh-day Adventism is that of their source of authority. The main teachings of Seventh-day Adventists are summarized in a set of twenty-two statements entitled "Fundamental Beliefs of Seventh-day Adventists."[46] Article 1 of these *Fundamental Beliefs* reads as follows:

[41] It will be remembered that about one-eighth of the total membership of the Mormon Church is outside the United States — a situation quite different from that which obtains in Seventh-day Adventism.

[42] Walter Martin, *The Truth About Seventh-day Adventism,* p. 36. Licensed ministers may preach but may not administer the sacraments or perform marriage ceremonies.

[43] *Ibid.*

[44] *1961 Yearbook,* p. 346.

[45] *Ibid.,* p. 342.

[46] These can be found in the *Church Manual,* the *Yearbook,* and also in *Questions on Doctrine.*

> That the Holy Scriptures of the Old and New Testaments were given by inspiration of God, contain an all-sufficient revelation of His will to men, and are the only unerring rule of faith and practice (2 Tim. 3:15-17).

Seventh-Day Adventists Answer Questions on Doctrine is a recent exposition of the teachings of this church, prepared by "a representative group of Seventh-day Adventist leaders, Bible teachers, and editors." The authors explain that the book contains answers to questions which have been raised about Seventh-day Adventist teachings and that these answers are given within the framework of the *Fundamental Beliefs* to which reference has just been made. They add, "In view of this fact, these answers represent the position of our denomination in the area of church doctrine and prophetic interpretation" (p. 8). It is further stated that the officers of the General Conference of Seventh-day Adventists have endorsed this volume, and have recommended it for general use (p. 10). Hence we shall consider this book to be an authentic and reliable source of information about Seventh-day Adventist teachings. Let us now note what the authors have to say about the matter of the source of authority:

> Seventh-day Adventists hold the Protestant position that the Bible and the Bible only is the sole rule of faith and practice for Christians. We believe that all theological beliefs must be measured by the living Word, judged by its truth, and whatsoever is unable to pass this test, or is found to be out of harmony with its message, is to be rejected.[47]

So far, therefore, it would appear that Seventh-day Adventists agree with all conservative Protestants in accepting the Bible as the sole rule of faith and life, and as the ultimate source of authority.

When the question is asked, "Do Seventh-day Adventists regard the writings of Ellen G. White as on an equal plane with the writings of the Bible?", the answer given begins as follows:

> 1. That we do not regard the writings of Ellen G. White as an addition to the sacred canon of Scripture.
> 2. That we do not think of them as of universal application, as is the Bible, but particularly for the Seventh-day Adventist Church.
> 3. That we do not regard them in the same sense as the Holy Scriptures, which stand alone and unique as the standard by which all other writings must be judged.[48]

In further explication of this point, the authors of *Questions on Doctrine* go on to say:

---

[47] *Questions on Doctrine*, p. 28.
[48] *Ibid.*, p. 89.

> Seventh-day Adventists uniformly believe that the canon of
> Scripture closed with the book of Revelation. We hold that all
> other writings and teachings, from whatever source, are to
> be judged by, and are subject to, the Bible, which is the spring
> and norm of the Christian faith. We test the writings of Ellen
> G. White by the Bible, but in no sense do we test the Bible
> by her writings.[49]

In fact, these authors support their contention by quoting statements from Mrs. White herself, such as the following:

> I recommend to you, dear reader, the Word of God as the rule
> of your faith and practice. By that Word we are to be judged.[50]
> Little heed is given to the Bible, and the Lord has given a
> lesser light to lead men and women to the greater light.[51]

As we have previously noted, however, Seventh-day Adventists
do claim that Mrs. White had the gift of prophecy, and that this
gift of prophecy is one of the identifying marks of the remnant
church.[52] From Revelation 12:17 (in the King James Version)
they gather that this remnant church has "the testimony of Jesus
Christ"; and from Revelation 19:10 they learn that "the testimony
of Jesus is the spirit of prophecy." Since, now, the Spirit of prophecy (at this point, contrary to the King James Version, they capitalize the word *spirit*) manifests Himself in the gift of prophecy,
and since, as they believe, Mrs. White had this gift of prophecy,
they conclude that the Seventh-day Adventist denomination must
be the remnant church of which Revelation 12:17 speaks.[53]
Though not placing Mrs. White into the same category as the
writers of the canon of Scripture, the authors of *Questions on Doctrine* compare her to the "prophets or messengers who lived con-
temporaneously with the writers of the two Testaments, but whose
utterances were never a part of Scripture canon."[54] The Seventh-
day Adventist evaluation of Mrs. White is summed up in the
following words:

> While Adventists hold the writings of Ellen G. White in
> highest esteem, yet these are not the source of our expositions.
> We base our teachings on the Scriptures, the only foundation of

---

[49] *Ibid.,* pp. 89-90. To the same effect are statements by Francis D.
Nichol, leading Seventh-day Adventist apologist, in *Ellen G. White and her
Critics,* pp. 87-90.

[50] *Early Writings,* p. 78; quoted in *Questions on Doctrine,* p. 90.

[51] *Review and Herald,* Jan. 20, 1903; quoted in *Questions on Doctrine,*
p. 93. The implication is that Mrs. White herself is the "lesser light."

[52] See above, p. 98.

[53] *Questions on Doctrine,* pp. 95-96.

[54] *Ibid.,* pp. 90-91. Among the examples given of this type of person
is John the Baptist. It will be recalled, however, that some of his
utterances did become a part of the canonical Scriptures: e.g., Mt. 3:2,
7-12.

all true Christian doctrine. However, it is our belief that the Holy Spirit opened to her mind important events and called her to give certain instructions for these last days. And inasmuch as these instructions, in our understanding, are in harmony with the Word of God, which Word alone is able to make us wise unto salvation, we as a denomination accept them as inspired counsels from the Lord.[55]

We are thankful to note that Seventh-day Adventists *claim* that they do not add any writings to the Sacred Scriptures, and that in this way, theoretically at least, they distinguish themselves from a group like the Mormons. It must be said, however, that their use of Mrs. White's writings and their avowed acceptance of her "prophetic gift" are not consistent with this claim. In substantiation of this judgment I offer the following considerations:

(1) Though Seventh-day Adventists claim that they test Mrs. White's writings by the Bible,[56] they assert, on another page of the same volume, that the instructions which she gave the church are in harmony with the Word of God.[57] The latter statement is not qualified in any way; they do not say that *most* of her instructions were in harmony with the Bible, or that her instructions were *generally* in harmony with God's Word — they simply state: "these instructions, in our understanding, are in harmony with the Word of God. . . ." This latter assertion, however, actually nullifies the former. How can one honestly claim to test the writings of a person by the Word of God when one already assumes, as a foregone conclusion, that these writings are in harmony with that Word?

(2) Though Seventh-day Adventists claim to test Mrs. White's writings by the Bible, they call her writings "inspired counsels from the Lord," and say that "the Holy Spirit opened to her mind important events and called her to give certain instructions for these last days."[58] If this is so, however, who may criticize her writings? If they are inspired, they must be true. If her instructions come from the Holy Spirit, they must be true. How, then, could anyone dare to suggest that any of her instructions might be contrary to Scripture? Could messages come from the Holy Spirit which would be contrary to the Word which that same Spirit inspired? Could "inspired counsels from the Lord" be in contradiction to the Lord's Scriptures? Again we must conclude that by describing Mrs. White's instructions as they do, Seventh-day Adventists negate their assertion that they test her writings by the Bible.

[55] *Ibid.,* p. 93.
[56] *Ibid.,* p. 90.
[57] *Ibid.,* p. 93.
[58] *Ibid.*

(3) Though Seventh-day Adventists claim to test Mrs. White's writings by the Bible, they insist that the gift of prophecy which she possessed, and with which she therefore enriched their group, is a mark of the "remnant church."[59] This means that this gift sets the Seventh-day Adventists apart from all other groups. But other Christian groups also have the Bible. What, therefore, sets the Seventh-day Adventists apart is what they have in addition to the Bible, namely, the gift of prophecy as manifested in Mrs. White. But if they test Mrs. White's writings by the Bible, as they say, and if the Bible is really their final authority, what do they really have which sets them apart from other groups? It is quite clear at this point that Seventh-day Adventists do not really test Mrs. White's writings by Scripture, but use them alongside of Scripture, and find in their use a mark of distinction which sets them apart from other groups.

(4) Though Seventh-day Adventists claim to test Mrs. White's writings by the Bible, they maintain that these writings "are not of universal application, as is the Bible, but [are] particularly for the Seventh-day Adventist Church."[60] But, we ask, why are they not of universal application? If her writings are tested by Scripture, there should be nothing in them which is contrary to Scripture; if this is so, why should not all her writings be of universal application? Why should not all Christians be bound to accept them, as all Christians are bound to accept the Bible? If her instructions were from the Holy Spirit, why were they not for everyone? Does the Holy Spirit ordinarily work this way? Does He give instructions and counsels for one body of believers only, which are not binding on others? Putting the question another way, if these instructions are not of universal application, are they really from the Holy Spirit? Are they really in perfect agreement with Scripture?

At this point Seventh-day Adventists really claim to have a special source of divine guidance which is not shared by other groups of believers. Is this really much different from the claims of the Mormons?

(5) Though Seventh-day Adventists claim to test Mrs. White's writings by the Bible, their actual usage of her writings nullifies this claim. Instead of testing her writings by the Bible, they use statements from her writings to substantiate their interpretation of Scripture. Typical of their method, for example, is their treatment of the Investigative Judgment, one of the key doctrines of

---

[59] *Ibid.*, pp. 95-96. The question of what they understand by this "remnant church" will be taken up in greater detail when we examine their doctrine of the church.

[60] *Ibid.*, p. 89.

their faith.   Under the heading, "Investigative Judgment as Part
of the Program of God," the necessity for this investigative judgment (made by Christ before the end of the world) is "proved"
by a reference to two passages of Scripture which are ordinarily
taken to refer to the final judgment at the end of time (Dan. 7:10,
and Rev. 20:12).   No attempt is made to explain these passages;
they are, in fact, not even quoted — a simple reference is considered sufficient.   Soon, however, a passage from Mrs. White is
quoted in full, to prove that there must be an "investigative judgment" prior to the final judgment:

> There must be an examination of the books of record to
> determine who, through repentance of sin and faith in Christ,
> are entitled to the benefits of His atonement.   The cleansing of
> the sanctuary therefore involves a work of investigation — a
> work of judgment.   This work must be performed prior to the
> coming of Christ to redeem His people; for when He comes,
> His reward is with Him to give to every man according to his
> works.[61]

Is this, now, testing Mrs. White's writings by the Bible?   Or is
this interpreting the Bible by the writings of Mrs. White?

As a matter of fact, Seventh-day Adventists quote more from
Mrs. White than from any other author.   *Questions on Doctrine*
is virtually studded with quotations from Mrs. White.   To give
an example, Chapter 6 of *Questions on Doctrine,* dealing with
"The Incarnation and the 'Son of Man,' " contains the following
number of quotations from Mrs. White: one on page 51, one on
page 53, two on page 54, five on page 55, one on page 56, four on
page 57, one on page 58, three on page 59, ten on page 60, eight
on page 61, two on page 62, one on page 63, and two on page 65!
The same practice characterizes other Seventh-day Adventist writings.   Walter Martin quotes a statement from Wilbur M. Smith
which reads in part as follows:

> I do not know any other denomination in all of Christendom
> today that has given such recognition, so slavishly and ex-
> clusively, to its founder or principal theologian as has this com-
> mentary [the new Seventh-day Adventist commentary] to the
> writings of Ellen White.   At the conclusion of every chapter in
> this work is a section headed, "Ellen G. White Comments,"[62]

As a further illustration of the actual usage of Mrs. White's
writings made by Seventh-day Adventists, I instance their recent

---

[61] *The Great Controversy,* p. 422.   The above discussion will be found
on pp. 420-422 of *Questions on Doctrine.*
[62] From a letter to Martin, quoted in the latter's *Truth About Seventh-
Day Adventism,* pp. 95-96.   At this writing, Mr. Smith is Professor of
English Bible at Fuller Theological Seminary.

publication entitled *Principles of Life from the Word of God.*[63]
This is a textbook on Seventh-day Adventist doctrinal teachings,
intended for classroom use.   The method used is that of questions
and answers.   Usually the question is answered by a reference to
a passage from the Bible, followed by a quotation from one of
Mrs. White's writings.   Frequently, however, no Scripture passage
is given in answer to a question; there is only a quotation from
Mrs. White.   One can hardly turn a page of this book without
finding several quotations from Mrs. White; she is virtually the
only authority quoted, alongside of the Bible.   Quite in agreement
with the plan of the book, a paragraph from the introductory statement to the student reads as follows:

> This new book, "Principles of Life From the Word of God,"
> has been written for the express purpose of giving you the facts
> upon which to make your everyday decisions and to solve life's
> complex problems.   It is written for you.   The greater part of
> the evidences cited are from the Bible or the spirit of prophecy
> — our two main sources of divine wisdom.

The expression, "the spirit of prophecy," in the last sentence above
is intended to designate the writings of Mrs. White.   When these
writings are thus described as one of their "two main sources of
divine wisdom," are not Seventh-day Adventists actually recog-
nizing Mrs. White's teachings as a second source of authority
alongside of Scripture?

It is also significant to note that nowhere in Adventist literature do we read the admission that Mrs. White may have been in
error on any point of doctrine.   Francis D. Nichol, in *Ellen G.
White and her Critics,* goes to great lengths to defend Mrs. White
from various types of charges made against her, but nowhere in
his 703 pages admits that Mrs. White could have been in error
on a doctrinal matter.   He does grant in one instance that she
was wrong, but this was not a doctrinal matter; it was, so Nichol
explains, an exercise of private judgment.[64]   Does it seem reasonable to hold that a woman who wrote as many volumes of Scriptural exposition and doctrinal comment as Mrs. White did could
never be wrong?

[63] Prepared by the Department of Education of the General Conference
of Seventh-day Adventists, and published by the Pacific Press Publishing
Association of Mountain View, Calif., in 1952.   It was reprinted as
recently as 1960.
[64] In the matter of advising the construction of the Battle Creek Health
Reform Institute (pp. 495-504).   Martin attacks the assertion that this
was merely a matter of "private judgment," since, so he contends,
the point on which she admitted she was wrong had been introduced with
the formula "I was shown" — the customary way of indicating something which came to her through the "Spirit of prophecy" (*op. cit.,* pp.
105-107).

In further substantiation of the point which is being made, I quote from D. M. Canright, who was a Seventh-day Adventist for twenty-eight years, but left the movement because he became convinced that it was in error. Mr. Canright, who was personally acquainted with both Mr. and Mrs. White, and who therefore had first-hand knowledge of the movement, has set forth his objections to Seventh-day Adventism in a volume entitled *Seventh-day Adventism Renounced.*[65] In this book he quotes a statement by Mrs. White in which she equated her writings with those of the prophets and apostles: "In ancient times God spoke to men by the mouth of prophets and apostles. In these days he speaks to them by the Testimonies of his spirit."[66] Canright further quotes a statement from the Advent *Review* of July 2, 1889, to this effect: "We [Seventh-day Adventists] will not neglect the study of the Bible and the *Testimonies.*" He adds the following comment:

> This illustrates the place they assign her [Mrs. White's] writings, viz., an appendix to the Bible. She occupies the same relation to her people that Mrs. Southcott did to hers, Ann Lee to the Shakers, and Joe Smith to the Mormons.[67]

Mr. Canright goes on to say that anyone in the Advent movement who rejects or opposes the "testimonies" of Mrs. White is branded as a rebel fighting against God.[68] He observes:

> There is not a doctrine nor a practice of the church, from the observance of the Sabbath to the washing of feet, upon which she has not written. That settles it. No further investigation can be made on any of these matters, only to gather evidence and construe everything to sustain it. How, then, can their ministers or people be free to think and investigate for themselves? They can not, dare not, and do not.[69]

On a previous page he says:

> Among themselves they [the Seventh-day Adventists] quote her [Mrs. White] as we do Paul. A text from her writings is an end of all controversy in doctrine and discipline. It is common to hear them say that when they give up her visions they will give up the Bible too, and they often do.[70]

---

[65] Originally published in 1889 by Fleming H. Revell, later published by B. C. Goodpasture, and reprinted in 1961 from the 1914 edition by Baker Book House of Grand Rapids.

[66] Testimony No. 33, p. 189; quoted by Canright on p. 135. "Testimonies" was the name commonly given to Mrs. White's specific instructions for the church.

[67] *Seventh-day Adventism Renounced* (1961 printing), p. 135.

[68] *Ibid.,* p. 135.

[69] *Ibid.,* pp. 136-37.

[70] *Ibid.,* p. 135.

Is it any wonder, then, that Canright feels compelled to assert: "Thus they [the Seventh-day Adventists] have another Bible, just the same as the Mormons have. They have to read our old Bible in the light of this new Bible."[71]

One can understand, of course, that Mr. Canright would be very critical of a movement which he himself had left. Even if we allow for some overstatement in his utterances, however, the statements made by Seventh-day Adventists in their recent doctrinal volume, and the actual use they make of Mrs. White's writings, are sufficient to establish the conclusion that Seventh-day Adventists do actually place Mrs. White's writings above the Bible, even while claiming that they do not. What is really determinative for their theological position is not careful, objective, scholarly searching of the Scriptures, but the teachings and visions of Ellen G. White, which are, for them, the court of final appeal. On the question of their source of authority, therefore, we must reluctantly insist that Seventh-day Adventists do not bow before the Scriptures as their ultimate authority in matters of faith and life.[72]

DOCTRINES

DOCTRINE OF GOD

BEING OF GOD

On the doctrine of the being of God Seventh-day Adventists do not differ from historic Christianity. We are thankful that in this respect they are not at all in the same category as Mormons, Christian Scientists, or Jehovah's Witnesses, all of whom deny the doctrine of the Trinity. Seventh-day Adventists clearly affirm the Trinity, as Article 2 of their *Fundamental Beliefs* reveals:

> That the Godhead, or Trinity, consists of the Eternal Father, a personal, spiritual Being, omnipotent, omnipresent, omniscient, infinite in wisdom and love; the Lord Jesus Christ, the Son of the Eternal Father, through whom all things were created and through whom the salvation of the redeemed hosts will be accomplished; the Holy Spirit, the third person of the Godhead, the great regenerating power in the work of redemption (Mt. 28:19).

[71] *Ibid.*, p. 136.
[72] Needless to say, the relationship of this group to Mrs. White has crucial bearing on the question, much discussed of late, of whether Seventh-day Adventism is to be considered a cult, or whether it is to be classed with the historic Christian churches. The inclusion of Seventh-day Adventism in this volume already indicates the author's judgment on this matter. This question will be taken up in detail, however, in Chapter 6.

It will be noted from this statement that the personality and infinity of God the Father is clearly attested, as well as the personality and full deity of the Holy Spirit. The deity of Jesus Christ, though implied in Article 2, is plainly asserted in Article 3: "That Jesus Christ is very God, being of the same nature and essence as the Eternal Father."

WORKS OF GOD

Decrees. Though Seventh-day Adventists claim that they are neither Calvinist nor totally Arminian in their theology,[73] a careful examination of their writings reveals that they quite definitely reject the Calvinistic view of God's decrees. They explicitly repudiate the position that men "are not all created with a similar destiny; but eternal life is fore-ordained for some, and eternal damnation for others."[74] Their rejection of this statement would seem to imply that they believe that men were all created with a similar destiny, and that the varied destinies of men (the certainty of which they acknowledge) were not in any way foreordained. Their position on this matter, as explicitly stated on another page, is that God foreknew but did not foreordain the salvation of those who are to be saved:

> ... As our eternal Sovereign God, He is omniscient. He knows the end from the beginning. Even before the creation of the world He knew man would sin and that he would need a Savior. Moreover, as Sovereign God, He also knows just who will accept and who will reject His "great salvation."[75]

In agreement with this, they affirm in an earlier section of the book that they believe "that man is free to choose or reject the offer of salvation through Christ; we do not believe that God has predetermined that some men shall be saved and others lost."[76]

The position, however, that God foreknows who will believe but has not foreordained the actions of men is definitely the Arminian one and not the Calvinistic. It is therefore more accurate to say that Seventh-day Adventists are Arminians on this point than to suggest, as they do, that they stand somewhere between Calvinism and Arminianism.

Creation. Seventh-day Adventists believe "that God created the world in six literal days"; they add, "we do not believe that

---

[73] *Questions on Doctrine,* p. 405.
[74] Calvin, *Institutes,* III, 21, 5; quoted in *Questions on Doctrine,* p. 406. Their discussion of Calvin's position here, restricted as it is to two brief quotations, is quite unsatisfactory, and takes no account of the Reformer's teaching on human responsibility.
[75] *Questions on Doctrine,* p. 420.
[76] *Ibid.,* p. 23.

creation was accomplished by long aeons of evolutionary pro-
cesses."[77] They therefore conduct a vigorous polemic against
evolutionary teachings of various sorts, and also against the
suggestion that the creative process could have involved long
aeons of time.[78]

Providence. Belief in Divine Providence is clearly expressed
by Seventh-day Adventists: ". . . God is the Sovereign Creator, up-
holder, and ruler of the universe, and He is eternal, omnipotent,
omniscient, and omnipresent."[79]

DOCTRINE OF MAN

MAN IN HIS ORIGINAL STATE

The Creation of Man. Seventh-day Adventists accept fully the
Genesis account of the creation of man. In agreement with
Genesis 1:26 they teach that man was created in the image of
God. Carlyle B. Haynes, one of their writers, explains what is
involved in the image of God: man had a free will, the power of
intelligent action, the authority to exercise dominion on the
earth, and the faculty of knowing, loving, and obeying his
Creator.[80]

The Constitutional Nature of Man. Seventh-day Adventists
are very critical of the commonly held conception that man consists of two aspects — a physical aspect called *body,* and a non-
physical aspect called *soul* or *spirit.* Since their views on this
matter have reference both to the constitutional nature of man
and to the question of man's existence after death, we shall begin
examining their teachings on this subject at this point, but shall
return to them when we come to their doctrine of the last things.

In *Questions on Doctrine* (p. 23) we read the following:
". . . Man was endowed at creation with conditional immortality;
we do not believe that man has innate immortality or an immortal
soul." To know what Seventh-day Adventists understand by the
term *soul,* we must turn to their answer to Question 40 in the
above-named book. On the basis of studies of both the Hebrew

---

[77] *Ibid.,* p. 24.

[78] See, for example, Chap. 33 of Wm. H. Branson's *Drama of the Ages*
(Washington: Review and Herald, 1950); and pp. 467-89 of Francis
Nichol's *Answers to Objections* (Review and Herald, 1952).

[79] *Questions on Doctrine,* pp. 21-22. Cf. Nichol, *Answers to Objections*
p. 457.

[80] *Life, Death, and Immortality* (Nashville: Southern Publishing Associa
tion, 1952), p. 49.

word *nephesh* and the Greek word *psuchee,* as these occur in the Bible, the authors of this volume conclude that there is nothing in the use of either of these words which implies a conscious entity that can survive the death of the body.[81] They insist that *soul* in the Bible refers to the individual rather than to a constituent part of the individual, and that it is therefore more accurate to say that a certain person *is* a soul than to say that he *has* a soul.[82] "The Scriptures teach," the authors summarize, "that the soul of man represents the whole man, and not a particular part independent of the other component parts of man's nature; and further, that the soul cannot exist apart from the body, for man is a unit."[83]

What these authors are driving at is that, in their judgment, there is no soul which survives after the body dies. This point is made crystal-clear by Carlyle Haynes. Taking his point of departure from Genesis 2:7 ("The Lord God formed man of the dust of the ground, and breathed into his nostrils the breath of life; and man became a living soul," KJ), Haynes says:

> The union of two things, earth and breath, served to create a third thing, soul. The continued existence of the soul depended wholly upon the continued union of breath and body. When that union is broken and the breath separates from the body, as it does at death, the soul ceases to exist.[84]

The authors of *Questions on Doctrine* also discuss the word *spirit* as it occurs in the Bible. After giving a brief word study of the Hebrew word *ruach* and the Greek word *pneuma,* they conclude that neither word ever denotes a separate entity capable of conscious existence apart from the physical body.[85] The conclusion of their study of this matter is: "Seventh-day Adventists do not believe that the whole man or any part of him is inherently immortal."[86]

MAN IN THE STATE OF SIN

The Fall. Seventh-day Adventists teach "that man was created sinless, but by his subsequent fall entered a state of alienation and depravity."[87]

Original Sin. It is held by this group that the results of Adam's sin were transmitted to all succeeding generations.

---

[81] *Questions on Doctrine,* pp. 512-14.
[82] *Ibid.,* p. 513.
[83] *Ibid.,* p. 515.
[84] *Op. cit.,* p. 54.
[85] Pp. 515-17.
[86] *Ibid.,* p. 518.
[87] *Ibid.,* p. 22.

> Sin . . . is an inheritance. Men are born sinners. Through
> disobedience, Adam's nature became changed. He was no
> longer a holy and righteous being, but a sinful being. And this
> sinful nature must, of necessity, be transmitted to his children
> as an inheritance.[88]

Branson further comments that to this inherited sin Adam's
posterity have added the guilt of their own transgressions.
Seventh-day Adventists thus distinguish, in common with most
Christian churches, between original sin and actual sin.

When the question is asked, What effect does this sinful nature
have on man's ability to accept salvation through Christ, it is difficult to find an unambiguous answer. On the one hand, Seventh-
day Adventism teaches that man is dead in sin, and that therefore
even the initial promptings to a better life must come from God.[89]
On the other hand, it affirms "that man is free to choose or reject
the offer of salvation through Christ. . . ."[90] Putting these two
statements together, we conclude that initial promptings to a better
life must come, somehow, to every man, or at least to every man
who hears the gospel, and that then man must make his own choice
as to what he will do in response to these promptings. The decisive
factor in determining who will be saved is thus not God's
sovereign grace but man's free choice. The position of Seventh-
day Adventism on this point would again appear to be basically
the Arminian one.[91]

DOCTRINE OF CHRIST

THE PERSON OF CHRIST

Deity of Christ. As has been stated, Seventh-day Adventists
unequivocally affirm the full deity of Jesus Christ. Their view
of Christ is summarized in Article 3 of their *Fundamental Beliefs*:

> That Jesus Christ is very God, being of the same nature and
> essence as the Eternal Father. While retaining His divine
> nature He took upon Himself the nature of the human family,
> lived on the earth as a man, exemplified in His life as our

[88] Branson, *op. cit.,* p. 43.
[89] *Questions on Doctrine,* p. 107.
[90] *Ibid.,* p. 23.
[91] Arminians teach that there is a universal or common grace which
comes to all men, enabling them, if they wish, to accept Christ. That
this is the teaching of Seventh-day Adventism is shown by the following
explanation: "Christ is the true light, who 'lighteth every man that cometh
into the world' (Jn. 1:9). This light, in some way known only to
Divine Providence, penetrates the darkness of human hearts and kindles
the first spark of desire after God. If the soul begins to seek for God,
then 'the Father which hath sent me [Christ]' will 'draw him [the seeker]'
(Jn. 6:44)" (*Ibid.,* pp. 107-8).

example the principles of righteousness, attested His relationship to God by many mighty miracles, died for our sins on the cross, was raised from the dead, and ascended to the Father, where He ever lives to make intercession for us.

Note that the incarnation of Christ is clearly asserted, that His miracles are recognized, that His substitutionary death, resurrection, ascension, and intercession are all affirmed. So far there would appear to be no difference between their teachings and those of historic Christianity.

Seventh-day Adventists do apply the Biblical name Michael not to a created angel, but to the Son of God in His pre-incarnate state;[92] they thus distinguish themselves from the Mormons, who find in the name Michael a designation for the pre-existent Adam. Though some earlier Adventist writers had contended that the Son was not wholly equal to the Father, and that the former must have had a beginning in the remote past (a form of Arianism), the denomination today officially affirms Christ's complete equality with the Father and the pre-existence of the Son from eternity.[93]

The Human Nature of Christ. According to many writers, Seventh-day Adventists teach that, in becoming incarnate, Christ assumed a polluted human nature. This allegation is made, for example, by John H. Gerstner in his *Theology of the Major Sects* (p. 127), and he adds some quotations to support his charge. Walter Martin, however, contends that Seventh-day Adventists have now repudiated this position, that one must consider *Questions on Doctrine* as giving their latest statement on this point, and that anyone who continues to make this charge is unfair to them, since he is using outdated sources.[94] What shall we say about this matter?

If one reads carefully pages 53-64 of *Questions on Doctrine,* one gathers that the authors of this volume definitely wish to remove the impression that, according to Seventh-day Adventist teaching, Christ assumed a polluted human nature. A great many quotations from Mrs. White are cited, both on these pages and in an Appendix at the back of the book, to prove that Mrs. White really meant to say not that Christ possessed a sinful human nature, but that He assumed a human nature which had been weakened by sin. Statements from Mrs. White are quoted to the effect that, though Christ took upon Himself man's nature in its fallen condition, He did not in the least participate in its sin, and that we should have no misgivings in regard to the perfect sinlessness of the

[92] *Ibid.,* pp. 71-83.
[93] *Ibid.,* pp. 46-49.
[94] *The Truth About Seventh-day Adventism,* pp. 86-88.

human nature of Christ.[95]   Another one of Mrs. White's statements is: "Do not set Him [Christ] before the people as a man
with the propensities of sin. . . .   He could have sinned; He
could have fallen, but not for one moment was there in Him an
evil propensity."[96]   It should be observed here that Christian
theologians have usually insisted that we must not say that
Christ could have sinned.   Yet we here face the question of
the reality of Christ's temptation.   Though I believe that it is
more proper to say that Christ could not sin than to suggest that
He could have sinned, the real difficulty with Adventist teaching
does not lie here.

In spite of the laudable attempt on the part of the authors of
Questions on Doctrine to eliminate all ambiguity on this matter,
there remain some real difficulties on the question of the sinlessness of Christ's human nature.   One of these difficulties is
that Mrs. White's teaching was not consistent on this point.   Both
on page 61 and on page 654 of *Questions on Doctrine* the following
statement of Mrs. White is quoted with approval: "He [Christ]
took upon His sinless nature our sinful nature."[97]   If we analyze
this statement, we conclude that, according to Mrs. White, Christ
assumed in addition to His divine, sinless nature a human nature
which was sinful.   Yet this is precisely what Mrs. White is said
not to have taught.   Would it not be far better for Seventh-day
Adventists to admit that Mrs. White was in error when she made
this statement?

A further difficulty is that there exist a number of statements
by Seventh-day Adventist authors clearly asserting that Christ
inherited tendencies to sin.   One of the best known is the statement by L. A. Wilcox to the effect that Christ conquered over
sin "in spite of bad blood and an inherited meanness."[98]   Though
the discussion of this matter in *Questions on Doctrine* implies that
the denomination would now repudiate this statement, nowhere
in the book are we definitely told that this has been done.   Further,
in 1950 William Henry Branson, who served from 1950 to 1954
as President of the General Conference of Seventh-day Adventists,
published a book entitled *Drama of the Ages*.   In this book, which
can certainly not be called an "outdated source," the following
statement occurs:

[95] *Questions on Doctrine,* p. 659.   The quotation is from *Signs of the
Times,* June 9, 1898.
[96] *Questions on Doctrine,* p. 651.   The quotation is from the *Seventh-
day Adventist Bible Commentary,* V, 1128.
[97] From *Medical Ministry,* p. 181.
[98] From *Signs of the Times,* March, 1927; quoted by Martin, *op. cit.,*
p. 86.

> The Catholic doctrine of the "immaculate conception" is
> that Mary, the mother of our Lord, was preserved from original
> sin. If this be true, then Jesus did not partake of man's
> sinful nature (p. 101).

The author clearly indicates that he does not deem this Catholic
doctrine to be true. It then follows that, in his judgment, Jesus
did partake of man's sinful nature. We find no indication in *Questions on Doctrine* that this recent statement has been repudiated
by the denomination. On the question, therefore, of the sinlessness of Christ's human nature, we conclude that there is still
much ambiguity in Seventh-day Adventist teaching.[99]

THE WORK OF CHRIST

The Atonement of Christ. Seventh-day Adventists teach the
vicarious, substitutionary atonement of Christ. In Article 8 of
the *Fundamental Beliefs* their position is set forth as follows:

> The law cannot save the transgressor from his sin, nor impart
> power to keep him from sinning. In infinite love and mercy,
> God provides a way whereby this may be done. He furnishes
> a substitute, even Christ the Righteous One, to die in man's
> stead, making "him to be sin for us, who knew no sin; that we
> might be made the righteousness of God in him" (2 Cor. 5:21).

To the same effect is the following statement from *Questions on
Doctrine*: ". . . The vicarious, atoning death of Jesus Christ, once
for all, is all-sufficient for the redemption of a lost race" (p. 22).
Crystal-clear is the summary found in the same volume (p. 396):

> We take our stand without qualification on the gospel plat-
> form that the death of Jesus Christ provides the *sole* propitia-
> tion for our sins; that there is salvation through no other means
> or medium, and no other name by which we may be saved;
> and that the shed blood of Jesus Christ *alone* brings remission
> for our sins.

On the question of the extent of the atonement, their position
is clearly the Arminian one: Christ died not just for the elect,
but for everyone. ". . . We believe that the sacrificial atonement
was made on the cross and was *provided* for all men, but that in
the heavenly priestly ministry of Christ our Lord, this sacrificial
atonement is *applied* to the seeking soul."[100]

At this point we must raise a question which is often raised;
it is an important one for a proper understanding of Seventh-day

---

[99] This question is carefully and competently treated in Chap. 4 of
Herbert S. Bird's *Theology of Seventh-day Adventism* (Grand Rapids:
Eerdmans, 1961). This volume is, in fact, one of the ablest evaluations
of Seventh-day Adventist doctrines which has appeared.
[100] *Questions on Doctrine,* p. 348.

Adventist teachings: Was the atonement finished on the cross? When one reads Seventh-day Adventist literature, one frequently comes across statements to the effect that the atonement was not completed on the cross, that the atonement is still going on, or that there will be a final atonement after Christ's work on the cross. Note, for example, the following quotations from Mrs. White:

> Today He [Christ] is making an atonement for us before the Father.[101]

> Now, while our great High Priest is making the atonement for us, we should seek to become perfect in Christ.[102]

> The blood of Christ, while it was to release the repentant sinner from the condemnation of the law, was not to cancel the sin; it would stand on record in the sanctuary until the final atonement. . . .[103]

> Attended by heavenly angels, our great High Priest enters the holy of holies, and there appears in the presence of God, to engage in the last acts of His ministration in behalf of man, — to perform the work of investigative judgment, and to make an atonement for all who are shown to be entitled to its benefits.[104]

The authors of *Questions on Doctrine* attribute this way of speaking about the atonement to the fact that earlier Adventist writers had a wider conception of the word atonement than do most Christian theologians today. These earlier writers, so it is said, wished to understand the word atonement as applying not just to the sacrifice of Christ once made on the cross, but also to the application of that atonement to sinners. It is in the latter sense that we are to understand expressions like those cited above.[105]

> When, therefore, one hears an Adventist say, or reads in Adventist literature — even in the writings of Ellen G. White — that Christ is making atonement now, it should be understood that we mean simply that Christ is now making application of the benefits of the sacrificial atonement He made on the cross; that He is making it efficacious for us individually, according to our needs and requests.[106]

The difficulty with the above explanation, however, is that Mrs. White had a sufficiently adequate command of the English language to be able to say "applying atonement" instead of "making

---

[101] *Manuscript 21,* 1895; quoted in *Questions on Doctrine,* p. 685.
[102] *The Great Controversy Between Christ and Satan* (Mountain View: Pacific Press, 1911), p. 623.
[103] *Patriarchs and Prophets* (Mountain View: Pacific Press, 1913), p. 357.
[104] *The Great Controversy,* p. 480.
[105] *Questions on Doctrine,* pp. 341-48.
[106] *Ibid.,* pp. 354-55.

atonement." Seventh-day Adventists, by an explanation like the one reproduced above, are introducing confusion into our theological terminology. In the statement about the atonement on page 22 of *Questions on Doctrine* it is said that the vicarious, atoning death of Christ is sufficient for the redemption of a lost race. Here the word atoning obviously does not mean what Christ did after His death on the cross, but refers to what He did on the cross. Why confuse the issue by suggesting that this word may have an additional meaning?

The real reason why Seventh-day Adventists speak of Christ's present work as being a work of atonement lies in their seeing in the heavenly ministry of Christ since 1844 a fulfillment of what was done in Old Testament times by the high priest on the great Day of Atonement. Since what the priest did on that day was an atonement, it is assumed by them that they may speak of what Christ is doing now in the heavenly holy of holies as an atonement. This brings up the question of Seventh-day Adventist teachings on the investigative judgment, to which we now turn.

The Investigative Judgment. It will be recalled that reference was made above to O. R. L. Crosier's *Day-Star* article of February 7, 1846, in which the groundwork for the doctrine of the investigative judgment was laid.[107] Later Adventist writers, including particularly Mrs. White, built upon this foundation the doctrine of the investigative judgment. That is, what Crosier called "the process of blotting out sin" — which, he said, Christ began on October 22, 1844, when He entered the holy of holies of the heavenly sanctuary — was called by later Adventists a process of judgment, or of investigative judgment. On the cross, it was said, Christ brought the sacrifice whereby atonement was *provided;* after His ascension, He *applied* this sacrifice. This work of application, again, had two phases. From the time of His ascension to October 22, 1844, Christ did a work comparable to the daily ministry of the Old Testament priests, which resulted in the forgiveness of sin but not in the blotting out of sin. At the latter date, however, Christ entered upon the "judgment phase" of His ministry whereby He blots out sin — a work comparable to that of the high priest on the Day of Atonement.[108]

Seventh-day Adventists devote two of their twenty two *Fundamental Beliefs* to the investigative judgment. After having said that the true sanctuary, of which the tabernacle on earth was a type, is the temple of God in heaven, and that the priestly work of Christ is the antitype (or fulfillment) of the work done by Jewish

107 Above, pp. 93-94.
108 *Questions on Doctrine,* p. 389.

priests in the earthly sanctuary, Article 14 of the *Fundamental Beliefs* goes on to assert:

> . . . this heavenly sanctuary is the one to be cleansed at the end of the 2300 days of Daniel 8:14, its cleansing being, as in the type, a work of judgment, beginning with the entrance of Christ as the high priest upon the judgment phase of His ministry in the heavenly sanctuary, foreshadowed in the earthly service of cleansing the sanctuary on the day of atonement.

Article 16 describes the work of the investigative judgment in greater detail:

> . . . The time of the cleansing of the sanctuary, synchronizing with the period of the proclamation of the message of Revelation 14, is a time of investigative judgment; first, with reference to the dead, and second, with reference to the living. This investigative judgment determines who of the myriads sleeping in the dust of the earth are worthy of a part in the first resurrection, and who of its living multitudes are worthy of translation (I Peter 4:17, 18; Dan. 7:9, 10; Rev. 14:6, 7; Lk. 20:35).[109]

What, now, does this investigative judgment mean? During this time of judgment, which began in 1844 and is still going on, the names of all professing believers who have ever lived are brought up, beginning with those who first lived on this earth. When a name has been singled out, that person's life is carefully scrutinized. The "books" mentioned in Revelation 20:12 ("and books were opened") are assumed to be books of record, in which both the good deeds and the bad deeds of every man have been recorded. These records are carefully examined.[110]

Christ now acts as the Advocate of His people, pleading cases which have been committed to Him. When the name of a true child of God comes up in the judgment, the record will reveal that every sin has been confessed and forgiven, and that the individual concerned has tried to keep all of God's commandments. Such an individual will then be "passed" in the investigative judgment; it will then have been determined that this person is worthy

---

[109] The *Fundamental Beliefs* can be found on pp. 11-18 of *Questions on Doctrine*.

[110] *Questions on Doctrine*, pp. 435-38. It is not made clear, however, who examines these records. From the fact that this is called the judgment phase of Christ's ministry, one would gather that Christ is the examiner. Christ is, however, as we shall see, called the Advocate who pleads the cases of His people. If He is the Advocate in the investigative judgment, why should this aspect of Christ's work be called the "judgment phase" of His ministry? One senses at this point a basic confusion in Adventist thought between the work of Christ as priest and His work as judge.

[111] *Ibid.*, pp. 441-42.

of a part in the first resurrection.[111] It is, of course, to be expected
that not all professing believers will pass this test.

An important point to note here is the distinction Seventh-day
Adventists make between the forgiveness of sins and the blotting
out of sins.[112] When a man repents and believes, so they teach,
his sins are forgiven, but not yet blotted out. His "forgiven" sins
are still on record in the heavenly sanctuary, even after he has
confessed them and after they have been forgiven. This, they
contend, is what was taught us by the Old Testament typology:
when the priests brought the blood of the sin-offerings into the
holy place, they simply transferred the iniquities of the people to
the sanctuary. Taking their cue from the Parable of the Unmerciful Servant in Matthew 18:23-35, Seventh-day Adventists
teach that one's forgiveness can be cancelled after it has been
bestowed, as was the case with the unmerciful servant. Note the
following statement from *Questions on Doctrine*:

> The actual blotting out of sin, therefore, could not take place
> the moment when a sin is forgiven, because subsequent deeds
> and attitudes may affect the final decision. Instead, the sin
> remains on the record until the life is complete — in fact,
> the Scriptures indicate it remains until the judgment.[113]

This leads us to the next question: if the sins of a believer are
only forgiven when he repents but are not then blotted out, when
are his sins blotted out? To this question we get an ambiguous
answer. On the one hand it is clear that the sins of believers will
not be blotted out until their names have come up in the investigative judgment. This will not happen until after they have lived
their lives, so that all their deeds may be taken into consideration.
In fact, so Adventists teach, one cannot even say that a man's
record is closed when he comes to the end of his days:

> He is responsible for his influence during life, and is just as
> surely responsible for his evil influence after he is dead. To
> quote the words of the poet, "The evil that men do lives after
> them," leaving a trail of sin to be charged to the account. In
> order to be just, it would seem that God would need to take
> all these things into account in the judgment.[114]

On the basis of this last statement, it appears that the investigative
judgment will not take place until a considerable time after a person's death.[115] When a believer has been accepted by God in

---

[112] It will be remembered that Crosier had already made this distinction.
See above, p. 94.
[113] P. 441. See pp. 439-41.
[114] *Questions on Doctrine*, p. 420.
[115] From Article 16 of the *Fundamental Beliefs*, quoted above, we learn,
however, that the investigative judgment of those believers who will

the investigative judgment, his sins are no longer held against him.

Some Seventh-day Adventist statements give one the impression that the blotting out of sin occurs when one has been accepted in the investigative judgment. This is the conclusion one draws from the following assertion:

> When He [Christ] confesses before God and the holy angels that the repentant sinner is clothed in the robe of His own spotless character . . . no one in the universe can deny to that saved man an entrance into the eternal kingdom of righteousness. Then, of course, is the time for his sins to be blotted out forever.[116]

Satan as the Scapegoat. It becomes apparent from other Adventist statements, however, that one cannot really say that the sins of the person described above have been totally blotted out when he has been accepted in the investigative judgment. These sins still have some sort of existence. They will not really be blotted out until the time of the "final eradication" or "final blotting out" of sin, which will occur just before Christ's return to earth, and will consist in the placing of the sins of all men, both righteous and wicked, on Satan. Let us listen to Mrs. White on this:

> When Christ, by virtue of His own blood, removes the sins of His people from the heavenly sanctuary at the close of His ministration [the investigative judgment], He will place them upon Satan, who, in the execution of the judgment, must bear the final penalty.[117]
>
> When the investigative judgment closes, Christ will come, and His reward will be with Him to give to every man as his work shall be. . . . As the priest, in removing the sins from the sanctuary, confessed them upon the head of the scapegoat, so Christ will place all these sins upon Satan, the originator and instigator of sin. The scapegoat, bearing the sins of Israel, was sent away . . .; so Satan, bearing the guilt of all the sins which he has caused God's people to commit, will be for a thousand years confined to the earth . . . and he will at last suffer the full penalty of sin in the fires that shall destroy all the wicked. Thus the great plan of redemption will reach its accomplishment in the final eradication of sin. . . .[118]

These statements leave us with no choice but that of concluding that, according to the prophetess of Seventh-day Adventism, sin is

---

still be living when Christ returns to earth will have been completed before the Second Coming, so that they may be translated to glory when the millennium begins.

[116] *Questions on Doctrine*, p. 442.
[117] *The Great Controversy*, p. 422.
[118] *Ibid.*, pp. 485-86.

not really eradicated from this earth until it has been laid on Satan.

Another Seventh-day Adventist writer specifically calls this transaction with Satan the "final blotting out of sin":

> The final service, in the second apartment [of the tabernacle], on the Day of Atonement, symbolized the concluding judgment-hour phase of Christ's ministry, preparatory to the final blotting out of sin. . . . And the scapegoat . . . symbolized Satan, the instigator of sin, who after the atonement was finished through the substitutionary sacrifice, bears his share of responsibility for all sins, and is banished at last into the abyss of oblivion.[119]

The Froom statement suggests that Satan will bear his share of responsibility, not just for the sins of believers, but for all sins. The same thought is found on page 400 of *Questions on Doctrine*. All sins, not just the sins of God's people, will thus be laid on him by Christ. And only in this way will sin finally be blotted out of God's universe.

Seventh-day Adventists derive this teaching from their interpretation of the second goat of Leviticus 16. This chapter describes the ritual of the Day of Atonement. Two goats were to be brought to the high priest; he, in turn, was to cast lots upon the goats: "one lot for Jehovah, and the other lot for Azazel" (Lev. 16:8; the King James Version has "for the scapegoat"). After the high priest had completed the work of bringing the blood of the slain first goat into the holy of holies, he laid both of his hands upon the second goat, and then proceeded to confess over him all the sins of the people of Israel. The second goat was then sent away into the wilderness. Seventh-day Adventists interpret the word Azazel used in this chapter (the Hebrew word translated *scapegoat*) as meaning Satan. They maintain further that this ceremony typified what will happen to Satan at the end of time:

> One [goat] typified our Lord and Savior Jesus Christ, who was slain as our substitute and vicariously bore our sins with all the guilt and punishment entailed. . . . The other goat, we believe, stood for Satan, who is eventually to have rolled back upon his own head, not only his own sins, but the responsibility for all the sins he has caused others to commit.[120]

These authors go on to make a point of the fact that the live goat was not slain, and therefore did not provide any propitiation for the sins of the people. So, they continue,

---

[119] Froom, *Prophetic Faith of our Fathers,* IV, 898-99.
[120] *Questions on Doctrine,* p. 399.

Satan makes no atonement for our sins.   But Satan will
ultimately have to bear the retributive punishment for his responsibility in the sins of all men, both righteous and wicked.[121]

Seventh-day Adventists therefore completely repudiate the suggestion that Satan is in any sense our sin-bearer, or that he makes
atonement for our sins in any way.   Christ, so they say, is the
only one who made atonement for our sins.[122]   Yet they contend
that sin is not completely eradicated from the earth until all sin
has been laid on Satan.

Summarizing, we must say that the Seventh-day Adventist view
of the atonement of Christ contains conflicting emphases.   While
insisting, along with all evangelical Christians, that the vicarious
death of Christ was sufficient for the redemption of a lost race,
they have supplemented this pivotal doctrine of historic Christianity
with their teachings on the investigative judgment and the placing
of sins on Satan.   While wishing to maintain that men are saved by
grace alone, Seventh-day Adventists have cast a shadow over that
claim by their views on the investigative judgment, since they assert
that it is this judgment, with its examination of man's life and
work, which *determines* whether a person shall be saved or not.
The investigative-judgment doctrine impugns the sovereignty of
God, since it implies that neither God the Father nor Christ
knows who are truly God's people until after this examination has
been concluded.   The distinction between the forgiveness of sins
and the blotting out of sins which Seventh-day Adventists make
jeopardizes the security of the child of God, and makes it impossible for anyone to know, even in the hour of his death, whether
he is saved or not.   And the conception that the sins of all men
are to be laid on Satan assigns to Satan an indispensable role in
the blotting out of sin, thus detracting from the all-sufficiency of
Christ.

A more detailed evaluation of Seventh-day Adventist teachings
on the investigative judgment and on Satan as the scapegoat will
be found in Appendix B.[123]

---

[121] *Ibid.*, p. 400.
[122] It must not be forgotten, however, that Adventists use the word
atonement in an ambiguous way.   Mrs. White even said, it will be recalled,
that the blood of Christ did not cancel the sin of the penitent, but that
this sin would stand on record in the sanctuary until the *final atonement*
(see above, p. 116, n. 103).
[123] Able treatments of these teachings will be found in Chap. 5 of
Bird's *Theology of Seventh-day Adventism*, and in Chap. 9 of Norman
F. Douty's *Another Look at Seventh-day Adventism* (Grand Rapids: Baker
1962).

DOCTRINE OF SALVATION

JUSTIFICATION AND SANCTIFICATION

How is man saved, according to Seventh-day Adventism? At first glace, their position looks very sound.

> . . . That which saves is grace alone, through faith in the living Christ. And similarly, that which justifies is His free and blessed grace. We likewise believe in works, and in full obedience to the will and commandments of God. But the works in which we believe, and that we seek to perform, are the result, or fruitage, of salvation, not a means to salvation, in whole or in part. And the obedience that we render is the loving response of a life that is saved by grace. Salvation is never earned; it is a gift from God through Jesus Christ.[124]

What about justification? It is defined as follows: "When we accept Him [Christ] we are justified. That is, His righteousness is imputed to us, and we stand before God just as though we had never sinned."[125] In Article 8 of the *Fundamental Beliefs* we read: ". . . one is justified, not by obedience to the law, but by the grace that is in Christ Jesus." Note also the following statement: "We cannot be justified at all by any kind of works. Justification is wholly an act of God, and we are but the recipients of His unbounded grace."[126] So far it would appear that Seventh-day Adventist soteriology is basically the same as that of Calvin and Luther.

What about sanctification? It is difficult to find a single, clear definition of sanctification in *Questions on Doctrine*. On page 23 we are told "that man is sanctified by the indwelling Christ through the Holy Spirit." From page 410 we learn that, whereas the first work of grace is justification, the continuing work of grace is sanctification. From page 388 we gather that ". . . while justification is *imputed* righteousness, sanctification is *imparted* righteousness." So far the statements quoted have pictured sanctification as a work of God. Man's responsibility in his own sanctification, however, is stressed in the following words from page 387:

> While Christ is "made unto us wisdom, and righteousness, and sanctification, and redemption" (I Cor. 1:30), yet the only ones who are perfected or sanctified are those who fully accept of His grace. . . . When we accept Him we are justified. . . . But only those who follow on and experience Him as an indwelling power, and who continually appropriate His grace for victory over their sinful natures, are sanctified or perfected.

---

[124] *Questions on Doctrine,* p. 102. Cf. p. 108.
[125] *Ibid.,* p. 387.
[126] *Ibid.,* p. 116.

It is thus clear that man must continually appropriate God's grace and experience Christ's indwelling power in order to be sanctified.

The word *perfected* in the above quotation puzzles the non-Adventist reader. The statement could be read so as to teach that sanctification means sinless perfection, and to imply that unless one has attained such a state, he has not really been sanctified. Do Seventh-day Adventists teach this? One does not find a clear answer to this question in *Questions on Doctrine*. On the one hand, their insistence that Christians must confess every sin, and that these confessions of sin will play an important part in the investigative judgment, leads one to think that they do not envision sinless perfection as possible on this earth. On the other hand, by applying to themselves as a group the words of Revelation 12:17, "which keep the commandments of God," they seem to imply that they are actually keeping God's commandments perfectly, in distinction from other groups.

Though they are not clear on this point, it does not appear that Seventh-day Adventists are perfectionists. The writings of Mrs. White teach that the last vestiges of sin will not be removed from man until the resurrection from the dead has occurred. A very striking exception to this rule, however, is found in Seventh-day Adventist teachings about the so-called "time of trouble." M. L. Andreasen, in his book, *The Sanctuary Service,* maintains that the last generation of Christians on the old earth will live completely without sin, and thus give a final demonstration of what God can do with humanity.[127] Making frequent use of Revelation 14:12 ("Here is the patience of the saints; here are they that keep the commandments of God . . .," KJ), Mr. Andreasen claims that this last generation is the group spoken of in the Bible as the 144,000 (p. 315). He contends, in fact, that in this final demonstration men will follow the example of Christ Himself and "prove that what God did in Christ, He can do in every human being who submits to Him" (p. 299). According to this author, therefore, it will be possible for at least one generation of men to live lives as sinless as that of Jesus Christ!

It should further be stated at this point that Seventh-day Adventists decisively reject the doctrine of eternal security, namely, that if one has once been regenerated and justified, he cannot fall away from grace in such a way as to be lost. It will be recalled that, according to *Questions on Doctrine* (p. 441), the actual blotting out of sin cannot take place the moment a sin is forgiven,

[127] P. 302. I quote from the 2nd ed., published by Review and Herald Pub. Ass'n in 1947. This teaching is, however, also found in the writings of Mrs. White. See *The Great Controversy,* pp. 425, 613-14, and 623; cf. Douty's discussion of this point in *op. cit.,* pp. 74-75.

because subsequent deeds and attitudes may affect the final decision. The expression, "subsequent deeds," tells us that by doing wrong deeds a person may lose the forgiveness he has received — which forgiveness would, we take it, be tantamount to justification. To the same effect is the following statement: commenting on Ezekiel 18:20-24, the authors of *Questions on Doctrine* affirm,

> In these verses, two men are brought to view. The one, a wicked man who turns from his sin and becomes obedient to God. He is forgiven; and if he walks in the way of righteousness, none of his former sins will ever be mentioned unto him. The other, a righteous man who turns from the path of righteousness, and goes back into sin. If he continues in iniquity, none of his previous manifestations of goodness will ever be mentioned. He forfeits all the blessings of salvation and goes down into death (p. 415).

The last sentence clearly suggests that this man did have salvation, but has now lost it.

Seventh-day Adventists thus teach that, though one is justified by grace alone, through believing in Christ and having His righteousness imputed to us, it is possible for a person, through subsequent sinful deeds and attitudes, to lose this justification and still be eternally lost. This would imply that the only way one can be sure of retaining his justification is to continue to do the right kind of deeds and maintain the right attitudes throughout the rest of his life. It will be granted, of course, that, according to Adventists, one can only do these deeds and maintain these attitudes through divine grace. But the question now arises: when we look at salvation in its totality, is this salvation for the Seventh-day Adventist due to God's grace alone, or is it due partly to God's grace and partly to man's faithfulness in keeping God's commandments? It is this point which we must now examine more closely.

THE QUESTION OF LEGALISM

Harold Lindsell has contended that the Seventh-day Adventists are guilty of the error of "Galatianism" — that is, that man is saved partly by the work of Christ and partly by the keeping of the law. He bases this conclusion particularly upon their teachings about the keeping of the Sabbath Day. He supports his contention by quoting the following statement from page 449 of Mrs. White's *Great Controversy*:

> . . . In the last days the Sabbath test will be made plain. When this time comes anyone who does not keep the Sabbath will receive the mark of the beast and will be kept from heaven.[128]

[128] "What of Seventh-day Adventism?", *Christianity Today*, April 14. 1958, p. 13.

After making further quotations from Seventh-day Adventist writings, including *Questions on Doctrine,* Lindsell summarizes as follows: ". . . If men now or later must keep the Sabbath to demonstrate their salvation or to prevent their being lost, then grace is no more grace. Rather, we are saved by grace and kept by works."[129]

Mr. Lindsell's charge, therefore, is that the Seventh-day Adventists are guilty of a kind of legalism — not the extreme kind, in which one would claim to be saved wholly by his keeping of the law, but a mixed kind, in which one teaches that he is saved by grace but kept by works. The same type of charge is made by Herbert S. Bird, only he bases it on the doctrine of the investigative judgment. He cites a statement by William Branson: "A Christian who through faith in Jesus Christ has faithfully kept the law's requirements will be acquitted; there is no condemnation, for the law finds no fault in him."[130]   Bird concludes that, for Seventh-day Adventism, it is the keeping of the commandments that constitutes the sinner's title to heaven — "his keeping of them through faith in Jesus Christ, to be sure, but his keeping of them none the less."[131]   And on the last page of his book he expresses the judgment that the "sanctuary position" of this movement "evinces a notion of the way of salvation which is considerably less than all of grace. And we have Paul's word for it that if it be so, it is not of grace at all."[132]

It is my conviction that the charges made by Lindsell and Bird are valid, and that Seventh-day Adventists, though they claim to teach salvation by grace alone, are guilty of the kind of mixed legalism to which these writers point. I base this conviction on the following grounds:

(1) *The doctrine of the investigative judgment.* We appreciate the insistence of Seventh-day Adventists that we are saved by grace alone — an insistence which distinguishes them, at least in theory, from the Mormons. But we must add that their acceptance of the doctrine of the investigative judgment, which is not taught in Scripture, has made it impossible for them really to maintain this insistence. For, in the last analysis, the Adventists teach that it is not the work of Jesus Christ done once for all on the cross, but their faithful keeping of God's commandments and their faithful confession of every single sin that determine whether they are saved or lost. Sinful deeds committed subsequently to their having accepted Christ may cause God to cancel His forgiveness. If

[129] *Ibid.,* p. 15.
[130] *Drama of the Ages,* p. 351; quoted in Bird, *op. cit.,* p. 90.
[131] Bird, *op. cit.,* p. 90.
[132] *Ibid.,* p. 132.

even the posthumous influence of a person must be taken into account in determining whether he can pass the investigative judgment or not, surely he is not saved by grace alone.

(2) *Teachings on the Sabbath.* The question of whether Seventh-day Adventists are right in claiming that the seventh day is the proper Lord's Day for us to observe will be treated in Appendix C. Here we shall examine features of their teachings about the Sabbath Day which support the charge of legalism. Note first that Seventh-day Adventists virtually elevate the Fourth Commandment above all other commandments. It will be recalled that Mrs. White reported a vision in which she saw a halo of glory around the Fourth Commandment (above, pp. 97-98). Mrs. White in her writings pictures the Sabbath as the great test of loyalty, which will divide the inhabitants of the earth into those who obey God and those who submit themselves to earthly powers and consequently receive the mark of the beast.[133] D. M. Canright reflects upon his own experience as an Adventist when he writes:

> I was long impressed with the fact that we Adventists preached very differently from the apostles. For instance, we were always preaching and writing about the Sabbath, while Paul in all his fourteen epistles mentions it but once, Col. 2:16, and then only to condemn it![134]

Note further that, according to Seventh-day Adventism, in the latter days all who refuse to keep the seventh day will receive the mark of the beast and be lost. Though Joseph Bates had taught that all those now keeping the first day as the Sabbath will receive the mark of the beast, the Adventist group has undergone a slight shift in thinking on this point. It is now taught that devout Christians of all faiths who sincerely trust in Christ as Saviour and are following Him according to their best light are saved even though they keep the first day.[135] Just before the return of Christ, however, Sunday observance shall be enforced by law.[136] The world shall then be enlightened concerning the obligation of the true Sabbath.[137] Anyone who shall *then* transgress God's command to

---

[133] *The Great Controversy*, p. 605.
[134] *Seventh-day Adventism Renounced*, p. 86.
[135] *Questions on Doctrine*, p. 184.
[136] *Ibid.* It seems hard to imagine such a situation in a world where Sunday is being treated more and more like any other day of the week, particularly by governmental agencies.
[137] We are not told by Mrs. White, from whose writings these words are quoted, how this enlightenment shall take place. It seems as though some kind of additional revelation will then be received. The clear implication is that Scripture is not really decisive on this point. If so, why this additional enlightenment?

keep the seventh day will thereby be honoring Popery above God, and will receive the mark of the beast.[138]

This means, therefore, that in the last days people will not be saved unless they keep the seventh-day Sabbath. At this juncture, certainly, people will be saved at least in part by works. Mere faith in Christ will then not be sufficient.

DOCTRINE OF THE CHURCH AND SACRAMENTS

DOCTRINE OF THE CHURCH

A distinguishing feature of Seventh-day Adventist ecclesiology is that they call themselves the "remnant church." This fact is referred to in next to the last sentence of Article 19 of the *Fundamental Beliefs*: ". . . the gift of the Spirit of prophecy is one of the identifying marks of the remnant church." This fact is also explicitly affirmed in the Seventh-day Adventist *Church Manual*. Among the questions which a candidate for baptism must answer in the affirmative is the following: "Do you believe that the Seventh-day Adventist Church constitutes the remnant church. . .?"[139]

What is meant by the "remnant church"? Revelation 12:17 reads as follows in the King James Version: "And the dragon was wroth with the woman, and went to make war with the remnant of her seed, which keep the commandments of God, and have the testimony of Jesus Christ." Seventh-day Adventists say: We are that remnant, or last segment, of the woman's seed of which the Bible here speaks. We are the remnant that keeps the commandments of God because we, in distinction from other Christians, keep the seventh day as the Sabbath. We have the testimony of Jesus Christ: in Revelation 19:10 the testimony of Jesus is defined as "the spirit of prophecy," and we have the Spirit of prophecy in the person of Ellen G. White. We have been raised up by God to proclaim the message of the seventh-day Sabbath shortly before the end of the world in such a way as to declare to all that the keeping of this day is now God's will for His people.[140]

---

[138] *Ibid.* The material is quoted from Mrs. White's *Great Controversy*, p. 449. The desperate wickedness of people who receive the mark of the beast, therefore, will be that they worship God on Sunday! One sees here to what lengths one may go when he allows an idea to run away with him.

[139] *Church Manual*, issued by General Conference of Seventh-day Adventists, 1959; pp. 57-58.

[140] *Questions on Doctrine*, pp. 186-96; particularly p. 191. They add, on the last-named page, that this application of the Revelation passage to themselves is the logical conclusion of their system of prophetic interpretation.

This, of course, brings up immediately the question of whether Seventh-day Adventists believe themselves to be the only true people of God, to the exclusion of all others, including all the major denominations of Christendom. To this question we get an ambiguous answer. On the one hand, the authors of *Questions on Doctrine* assert that they have never sought to equate their church with the church invisible — "those in every denomination who remain faithful to the Scriptures" (p. 186). Seventh-day Adventists, these authors further point out, do not believe that they alone constitute the true children of God (p. 187), that they are the only true Christians in the world, or that they are the only ones who will be saved (pp. 191-92). Elsewhere the authors say: "We fully recognize the heartening fact that a host of true followers of Christ are scattered all through the various churches of Christendom, including the Roman Catholic communion" (p. 197).

On the other hand, however, these authors contend that the Protestant Reformation was incomplete, that God wants certain new truths to be emphasized now which were not proclaimed at the time of the Reformation (p. 189), and that God has given these new truths to the Seventh-day Adventist movement. The heart of this new message is the proclamation of the seventh day as the Sabbath (p. 189). This new message must now be brought to all, even to those orthodox Christians who accept the teachings of the Reformation, for only in this way can Christians prepare for the great test of loyalty which will come in the last days (p. 195).

Do Seventh-day Adventists now really believe that the vast majority of Christians who observe the first day of the week instead of the seventh belong to the universal church of God's true people? Theoretically, they do. We appreciate their willingness to make this statement, which Mormons and Jehovah's Witnesses are unwilling to make. But, once again, we find that their doctrines are not consistent with this statement. For if the seed of the woman spoken of in Revelation 12 is the Christian church, and if the remnant of her seed is the *last segment* of that seed, and if the Seventh-day Adventist Church is that last segment, what conclusion can one arrive at except that other Christian groups are not members of the seed of the woman? If they are, why don't they belong to the remnant?

Furthermore, if the message of the seventh-day Sabbath is now so important that God has raised a special people for its proclamation, and if the keeping of this day is now God's will for all His people, how can men and women who refuse to heed this message still be counted as God's true people? How can Seventh-day Adventists say that there are people "in every denomination who remain faithful to the Scriptures" (p. 186), when these people fail to obey the most important commandment of the Decalogue? How can Adventists contend that these alleged members of the true church outside their fold are "living up to all the light God has given them" (p. 192)? They have the Bible, do they not? Doesn't the Bible give sufficient light on the matter of the seventh day? The authors of *Questions on Doctrine* try to get out of this dilemma by saying, "We respect and love those of our fellow Christians who do not interpret God's Word just as we do" (p. 193). This statement gives the impression that the question of the first day or the seventh is a minor matter on which differences of interpretation may be tolerated. But on another page we are told that Seventh-day Adventists have been raised up by God precisely for the purpose of proclaiming to the world the message of the seventh-day Sabbath! This implies that those Christians who interpret the Word as permitting a first-day Sabbath are dead wrong! How, then, can such utterly mistaken and misguided people be recognized as being faithful to the Scriptures and as belonging to the true church of Jesus Christ?

Since this is a point of great importance, let us look at the matter from another angle. In *Questions on Doctrine* we are told that one who refuses to recognize the deity of Jesus Christ can neither understand nor experience salvation in its fullness. Then follows this statement: "Not only is he disqualified for membership [in the Seventh-day Adventist Church] by his very unbelief, but he is already outside the mystic body of Christ, the church" (p. 45). We take it that by "the mystic body of Christ, the church," the authors mean the invisible church as described above (see p. 129). It is clear, then, from this assertion that one who denies the deity of Christ cannot, according to Seventh-day Adventists, be a member of the invisible church. According to other statements made by these same authors, however, Christians who fail to observe the seventh-day Sabbath can be recognized by Adventists as belonging to the invisible church. Putting these two types of statement together, it would seem that, for Seventh-day Adventists, the observance of the seventh-day Sabbath is far less important than the affirmation of the deity of Jesus Christ. Yet they contend at the same time that God has raised up their movement for the specific purpose of proclaiming to the world the message of the seventh-day Sabbath! The statement in *Questions on Doctrine* (p. 193) about respecting and loving fellow Christians who do not interpret the Bible as the Adventists do, implies that the difference of interpretation about the seventh day is something of

such minor importance that it does not hinder one from being included in the invisible church. But if this is so, what reason is
there for Seventh-day Adventists to claim that they alone are the
remnant church? We conclude that Seventh-day Adventists have
no right to claim that they believe that the invisible church is
wider than their own fellowship, while at the same time insisting
that they are the remnant church of God's most faithful people.
They should either repudiate the remnant church concept, or their
alleged belief in the invisible church; they cannot with honesty
hold on to both.

When Adventists claim that Sunday-keeping Christians can be
excused for their transgression of the Fourth Commandment because they are living up to the best light they have, we wonder what
they mean. Would deniers of the deity of Christ be excused, since
they are living up to the best light they have? If this is not so, as
we have seen, why should deniers of the seventh-day Sabbath be
excused? The light they live by is the Bible — must this Bible now
be damned with faint praise by the expression "the best light they
have"? Do Seventh-day Adventists claim to have a *better* light
than the Bible? Is this better light, perhaps, provided by the teaching of Mrs. White? And are they now consistent with their alleged
dependence on the Bible *alone* as their guide for faith and practice?

We conclude, then, that Seventh-day Adventist teachings on the
remnant church are not consistent with their claim that they recognize the existence of an invisible or universal church of Christ
which is larger than their fellowship. It should be added that their
application of the concept "remnant church" to themselves is
neither exegetically nor doctrinally defensible. To begin with
the exegetical matter, the idea that Revelation 12:17 refers to a
"remnant church" is based on a misinterpretation of the Greek
of this passage. The King James Version, to be sure, translates
here: "the dragon . . . went to make war with the remnant of her
seed." The Greek here, however, does not use either the word
leimma (translated *remnant* in Rom. 11:5) or the word *hupoleim-
ma* (translated *remnant* in Rom. 9:27, a rendering of the Hebrew
she'ar in Isa. 10:22), but rather the plural, *hoi loipoi,* literally, "the
rest of them." In the American Standard Version, the expression
hoi loipoi is in every instance translated "the rest." Here, in Revelation 12:17, the expression is rendered in the American Standard: "the rest of her seed"; both the Revised Standard Version and
the New English Bible have "the rest of her offspring." The usual
interpretation of this passage is that, after having failed to wipe
out the church (represented by the woman), Satan (represented by
the dragon) now makes war against certain *individual believers*:

"the rest of her seed."[141]   To read a separate church into this phrase, "the rest of her seed," is completely unwarranted.

Doctrinally the concept of the remnant church is also indefensible. The Scriptures speak about the one body of Christ with its many members (Eph. 4:4-16; I Cor. 12:12-27), and specifically warn against the sin of exalting oneself above other members of the body of Christ (I Cor. 1:12-13; 3:1-7, 21-23). True, the New Testament does speak of a remnant, in Romans 11:5, "Even so then at this present time also there is a remnant (*leimma*) according to the election of grace." But this is not a remnant *within* the invisible church — this remnant is identical with the invisible church, as far as its Jewish members are concerned. The thought that Seventh-day Adventists are a specific "remnant group" within the invisible or universal church, who are to be distinguished from the rest of the body of Christ as the only really pure and true manifestation of that body, is reminiscent of movements like Montanism, Novatianism, and Donatism, which also claimed to be the true church within the church; and of seventeenth-century pietism, which similarly claimed to be a kind of *ecclesiola in ecclesia* ("a little church within the church"). This is not, however, the Scriptural view of the church. If one wishes to use the term *remnant* at all, as applied to the church, Scriptural usage dictates that the term can only be used to designate the entire invisible church, comprising all true believers, wherever these are found.[142]

DOCTRINE OF THE SACRAMENTS

Baptism. Seventh-day Adventists are opposed to infant baptism, holding that faith, repentance, and acceptance of Christ as Saviour are prerequisites to baptism, and that infants cannot meet these requirements.[143] Article 5 of the *Fundamental Beliefs* specifies that baptism should follow repentance and forgiveness of sins,[144] that by

[141] This interpretation is found, for example, in R. C. H. Lenski's *Interpretation of St. John's Revelation* (Columbus: Wartburg Press, 1943); W. Hendriksen's *More Than Conquerors* (Grand Rapids: Baker, 1940); and in Albert Barnes's *Notes on the Book of Revelation* (London: Routledge, 1857).

[142] For additional details on the Seventh-day Adventist view of the remnant church, see below, pp. 396-400.

[143] Branson, *Drama of the Ages,* pp. 167-68.

[144] But how does the church know when a person has truly received the forgiveness of his sins? Can the church read a man's heart? A more accurate expression of this point is found in Article 11 of the Baptismal Vow: ". . . Do you desire to be so baptized as a public expression of your faith in Christ and in the forgiveness of your sins?" (*Church Manual,* p. 57).

its observance faith is shown in the death, burial, and resurrection of Christ, and that the proper form of baptism is immersion. *Questions on Doctrine* further specifies that this must be a single, not a triple, immersion (p. 23).

The *Church Manual* requires that thorough instruction in the fundamental teachings of the church be given to every candidate for baptism (pp. 46, 48), and that before the person is baptized there be a public examination, conducted either in the presence of the church or before the church board (p. 49). The *Manual* further lists the thirteen questions constituting the Baptismal Vow, which the candidate must answer in the affirmative (pp. 56-58).

It is expected of the candidate for baptism that he or she shall, in addition to expressing faith in the Trinity, in Jesus Christ as Saviour, and in the Bible as God's inspired Word, also assent to such distinctive Seventh-day Adventist teachings as the seventh-day Sabbath (Question 6), the Spirit of prophecy (Question 8), and the remnant church (Question 13). It is also expected that he will support the church with his tithes and offerings (Question 10) — tithing is thus mandatory for church membership. Of special interest and significance is Question 7: "Do you believe that your body is the temple of the Holy Spirit and that you are to honor God by caring for your body in abstaining from such things as alcoholic beverages, tobacco in all its forms, and from unclean foods?"

It is to be observed that Seventh-day Adventists thus make total abstinence from liquor and tobacco a requirement for church membership. The *Church Manual,* in fact, lists "among the grievous sins for which members shall be subject to church discipline," the following: "the use, manufacture, or sale of alcoholic beverages," and "the use of tobacco or addiction to narcotic drugs" (pp. 225-26). One wonders by what ethical standards Seventh-day Adventists can equate the use of tobacco with such sins as murder, adultery, and stealing (see p. 225). In view of Paul's words in I Timothy 4:4 ("Every creature of God is good, and nothing is to be rejected, if it be received with thanksgiving"), what right does this church have to make total abstinence from every form of alcoholic beverage a requirement for baptism?

Under the "unclean foods" from which candidates for baptism must promise to abstain are included such beverages as coffee and tea, and such meats as pork, ham, shrimp, lobster, and clams. It will be noted that the meats prohibited are those which the Old Testament called unclean. Seventh-day Adventists say that they are well aware of the fact that the ceremonial law which contained these prohibitions was abolished in New Testament times, but contend that God counseled His people against these articles of diet, both in Mosaic and pre-Mosaic times, because He knew that they were not best for human consumption.[145] Hence, they maintain, Seventh-day Adventists prohibit these foods for health reasons.

No one can object when a church wishes to improve the health of its members. But when one must agree to abstain from certain foods before he may be baptized, these prohibitions have been given a religious sanction which takes them out of the category of mere health measures. To make abstinence from certain foods a condition for church membership is adding requirements to those the Scriptures set before us: true repentance, a living faith in Jesus Christ, and an earnest resolve to do God's will. The position of the Seventh-day Adventist Church on these so-called unclean foods is condemned not only by I Timothy 4:4-5, the first part of which was quoted above,[146] but also by Colossians 2:16-17, "Let no man therefore judge you in meat, or in drink, or in respect of a feast day or a new moon or a sabbath day: which are a shadow of the things to come; but the body is Christ's."[147]

The Lord's Supper. It seems strange that no mention is made of the Lord's Supper in the *Fundamental Beliefs.* According to the *Church Manual,* however, Seventh-day Adventists are to observe the Lord's Supper once every three months (p. 111). This service is announced on the preceding week, at which time the members of the congregation are urged to prepare their hearts and to make sure that matters are right with one another (p. 111). An unusual feature of their Lord's Supper celebration is that it is always preceded by the ordinance of footwashing. Mrs. White taught that, when Jesus washed the disciples' feet prior to His institution of the Lord's Supper, He was not simply teaching the disciples a lesson in humility; He was instituting a religious ceremony (p. 115).[148] Branson, in fact, maintains that this ordinance symbolizes the "lesser cleansing" in distinction from baptism, which is the "greater cleansing" — footwashing thus pictures the forgiveness of sins which have accumulated since baptism.[149] The *Manual* further states that the men and women are separated for this ordinance, each

---

[145] *Questions on Doctrine,* p. 623.

[146] Note particularly the preceding context, where "commanding to abstain from meats" (v. 3) is listed as a "doctrine of demons" (v. 1).

[147] See F. F. Bruce's excellent comment on these verses in his *Commentary on Colossians* (Eerdmans, 1957). For a good treatment of the whole question of "unclean foods" in Seventh-day Adventism, see Chapter 7 of Bird's *Theology of Seventh-day Adventism.*

[148] Quoted from *The Desire of Ages,* p. 650.

[149] *Op. cit.,* pp. 183-84. Note that Branson's explanation here implies that Seventh-day Adventists are not perfectionists.

member washing the feet of the person next to him (pp. 111-12).[150]

The *Manual* calls the Lord's Supper itself a memorial of the crucifixion of Christ (p. 114). Yet it is more than a mere sign; it also strengthens faith: "participation [in the Lord's Supper] by members of the body is essential to Christian growth and fellowship" (p. 55). The *Church Manual* further specifies that every member shall attend the Lord's Supper (p. 114); when people who are visiting the church wish to take part in the service, they shall not be forbidden (p. 113). Seventh-day Adventists use unleavened bread and unfermented wine in the Lord's Supper (p. 114). Any bread or wine which is left over after the service is to be disposed of as follows: the bread is to be burned and the wine is to be poured out (p. 116).

Doctrine of the Last Things

Individual Eschatology

The State of Man after Death. When we examined the Seventh-day Adventist doctrine of man, we learned that Adventists do not believe that man, either as a whole or in part, is inherently immortal, or that man has a soul which can survive the death of the body. We noted also that they interpret the Biblical word *soul* (*nephesh* or *psuchee*) as meaning the entire individual rather than an immaterial aspect of man, and that it is therefore better to say that a person *is* a soul than that he *has* a soul.[151]

What, now, does this position imply as to the state of man after death? We find the answer in Article 10 of the *Fundamental Beliefs*: "That the condition of man in death is one of unconsciousness. That all men, good and evil alike, remain in the grave from death to the resurrection." Here is the way one Seventh-day Adventist author explains their position on this matter:

> The teaching of the Bible regarding the intermediate state of man is plain. Death is really and truly a sleep, a sleep that is deep, that is unconscious, that is unbroken until the awakening at the resurrection.
>
> In death man enters a state of sleep. The language of the Bible makes clear that it is the whole man which sleeps, not merely a part. No intimation is given that man sleeps only as to his body, and that he is wakeful and conscious as to his soul. All that comprises the man sleeps in death.[152]

Note that, according to Mr. Haynes, it is not the soul that

---

[150] Cf. Branson, *op. cit.*, p. 185.
[151] See above, pp. 110-11.
[152] Carlyle B. Haynes, *Life, Death, and Immortality*, p. 202.

sleeps, but man.   The same position is taken by the authors of
Questions on Doctrine (pp. 511-32).   It is therefore not quite
accurate to say, as some do, that the Seventh-day Adventists teach
the doctrine of *soul-sleep,* since this would imply that there is a
soul which continues to exist after death, but in an unconscious
state.   A more precise way of characterizing their teachings on
this point is to say that the Adventists teach *soul-extinction.* For,
according to them, *soul* is simply another name for the entire individual; there is, therefore, no soul that survives after death. After
death nothing survives; when man dies he becomes completely
nonexistent.

Seventh-day Adventists do teach that there will be a resurrection
of all men.   The authors of *Questions on Doctrine* state that the
time interval between death and the resurrection is negligible, since
there is no consciousness in the so-called "intermediate state":

> While asleep in the tomb the child of God knows nothing.
> Time matters not to him.   If he should be there a thousand
> years, the time would be to him as but a moment.   One who
> serves God closes his eyes in death, and whether one day or
> two thousand years elapse, the next instant in his consciousness
> will be when he opens his eyes and beholds his blessed Lord.
> To him it is death — then sudden glory (pp. 523-24).

Conditional Immortality.   Article 9 of the *Fundamental Beliefs*
sets forth the Adventist position on immortality:

> That "God only hath immortality" (I Tim. 6:16).   Mortal
> man possesses a nature inherently sinful and dying.   Eternal life
> is the gift of God through faith in Christ (Rom. 6:23). . . .
> Immortality is bestowed upon the righteous at the Second Com-
> ing of Christ, when the righteous dead are raised from the
> grave and the living righteous translated to meet the Lord.
> Then it is that those accounted faithful "put on immortality"
> (I Cor. 15:51-55).

Seventh-day Adventists thus believe in *conditional immortality*:
immortality is bestowed upon believers at the Second Coming of
Christ.   Man possesses no inherent immortality, and man has no
immortal soul.   Immortality in the absolute sense is possessed only
by God.   Immortality in a relative sense is bestowed only upon
certain people — namely, those who believe.   Unbelievers will
be raised from the dead after the millennium, but they will not receive immortality.   They will be raised only to be annihilated.[153]

---

153 Jehovah's Witnesses, as we shall see, take virtually the same position
on the intermediate state as do Seventh-day Adventists.   Note that acceptance of the doctrine of conditional immortality implies a denial of eternal
punishment.   In Appendix E these doctrines (soul-extinction, conditional
immortality, and the annihilation of the wicked) will be critically evaluated.

GENERAL ESCHATOLOGY

The Return of Christ. As their denominational name indicates, the Second Coming of Christ is one of the cardinal doctrines of the Adventist faith. Seventh-day Adventists believe in the literal, physical, audible, visible, and personal return of Christ.[154] They look upon this Second Coming as "the great hope of the church, the grand climax of the gospel and plan of salvation."[155] Whereas Seventh-day Adventism owes its origin to the attempt by William Miller to set the date for Christ's return, present-day Adventists no longer try to set such a date. In *Questions on Doctrine* they now affirm: ". . . We believe that our Lord's return is imminent, at a time that is near but not disclosed" (p. 463).

It is clearly affirmed that the Return of Christ will be a single coming, not a two-stage advent. Seventh-day Adventists therefore differ from dispensational premillennialists in rejecting a pretribulational secret rapture — that is, in rejecting the doctrine that the church will be secretly and silently snatched from the earth before the Great Tribulation (p. 454). Though they agree with premillennialists that there will be a millennium, they deny that this millennium will be marked by an earthly reign of Christ over the converted Jewish nation; they therefore see no particular prophetic significance in the establishment of the modern state of Israel in Palestine (pp. 234-35). In fact, they indicate ten respects in which they differ from dispensational premillennialism (pp. 239-40).

The Battle of Armageddon. The final conflict among the nations will be the Battle of Armageddon. Taking their cue from Revelation 16:12-16, Seventh-day Adventists contend that the history of this world will be brought to an end in this great battle, called in Scripture "the battle of that great day of God Almighty."[156] The warfare between nations which has always marked man's history will culminate in this great battle, which will be fought in the plain of Megiddo in central Palestine. This will not, however, be simply a war between nations: "At Armageddon international, inter-racial, and inter-religious strife will give place to that phase of man's effort to retain the dominion of this earth described in Rev. 19:19, as a contest between the armies of earth and the armies of heaven."[157] Since the three symbolic characters mentioned in Revelation 16:13 (the dragon, the beast, and the false prophet) represent the false religious systems of the

---

[154] *Questions on Doctrine,* pp. 449-54, 463.
[155] *Fundamental Beliefs,* Article 20.
[156] Branson, *op. cit.,* p. 525. Cf. Carlyle B. Haynes, *The Return of Jesus* (Washington: Review and Herald, 1926), p. 279.
[157] Haynes, *Return of Jesus,* p. 287.

world, both heathen and professed Christian, the Battle of Armageddon will be a "holy war" between God and His people on the one side, and the devil and his people (apostate Christians as well as the devotees of false religions) on the other side.[158]

This war will be interrupted and brought to a sudden end by the personal and visible return of Jesus Christ.[159]   Christ will now break the nations with a rod of iron and "dash them in pieces like a potter's vessel," thus utterly defeating His enemies.[160]   At this time the day of salvation will be past.[161]   The beast and the false prophet are now cast alive into the lake of fire.   All the unrighteous who have not by this time been killed in battle are now put to death, being "destroyed by the brightness of Christ's visible presence."[162]

The Binding of Satan.   The binding of Satan spoken of in Revelation 20:1-3 now occurs.   This is interpreted to mean that Satan is consigned by divine command to the desolate earth, which is understood to be the "abyss" or "bottomless pit" of Revelation 20:3.   As we have seen, the wicked or unrighteous have by this time all been put to death.   This has left only believers on the earth.   They, however, as we shall see in a moment, are about to be translated to heaven.   Thus, during the millennium which is about to begin, the earth will be completely desolate of human habitation.   To this desolate earth Satan, with his fallen-angel companions, will be confined for a thousand years.   This will give him ample time to ponder on the results of his rebellion against God.[163]

This teaching must be seen in connection with Seventh-day Adventist doctrine about Satan as the one upon whom the sins of the world will be laid.   As we have seen, the Adventists see a parallel between what happened to the second goat on the Day of Atonement and what will be done to Satan after Christ returns.   Just as the so-called scapegoat was sent away into an uninhabited wilderness after the sins of the people had been confessed over his head, so Satan, after the sins of the world have been placed upon

[158] Branson, *op. cit.,* pp. 531-33.
[159] Haynes, *Return of Jesus,* p. 287.
[160] *Ibid.,* pp. 287, 295.
[161] Branson, *op. cit.,* p. 536.   Note that Seventh-day Adventists do not teach the possibility of a second chance to be saved after one has died, or after this point in history has been reached.   On this point see *ibid.,* p. 211.
[162] *Questions on Doctrine,* pp. 491-92.   From p. 495 we learn that Christ at this time does not actually come all the way down to the earth, but remains in the air.
[163] *Ibid.,* p. 492.   Cf. also Branson, *op. cit.,* pp. 551-54; and Haynes, *The Return of Jesus,* pp. 295-303.

him, will be banished to the desolate earth, which during the millennium will be a dreary, uninhabited wilderness.[164]

The Special Resurrection. Seventh-day Adventists believe in three resurrections, one special and two general. The two general resurrections are those of believers and unbelievers, respectively, the former occurring at the beginning of the millennium, the latter at the end of the millennium. Before discussing these, however, we must take note of the special resurrection, which will occur before either of the two general resurrections. It will take place just before the Second Coming of Christ, and will involve some unbelievers and some believers. We therefore interrupt the chronological sequence briefly at this point in order to describe this special resurrection.

The first of the two groups to be raised at this time consists of those who were responsible for the trial and crucifixion of Christ. Basing her comment on Revelation 1:7, Mrs. White says,

> "They also which pierced Him" (Rev. 1:7), those that mocked and derided Christ's dying agonies, and the most violent opposers of His truth and His people, are raised to behold Him in His glory, and to see the honor placed upon the loyal and obedient.[165]

The second of these two groups consists of those who "died in the faith of the third angel's message." In a personal letter (June 4, 1963) sent to the author by Mr. Thomas H. Blincoe of Andrews University at Berrien Springs, Michigan (the Seventh-day Adventist Theological Seminary), the following statement was made:

> In Revelation 14:13, just at the close of the third angel's message of Revelation 14:9-12, there appears this beatitude: "Blessed are the dead which die in the Lord from henceforth." We believe that all those who die in the Lord "in the faith of the third angel's message" will be granted a singular blessing in the form of being raised in the special resurrection before the glorious return of Christ and will thus have the privilege of seeing Him come. The third angel's message began to be preached about 1846.

The above statement is based on the following words from Mrs. White:

> Graves are open, and "many of them that sleep in the dust of the earth . . . awake, some to everlasting life, and some to shame

---

[164] *Questions on Doctrine,* pp. 498-501; see also Ellen G. White, *The Great Controversy,* p. 658

[165] *The Great Controversy,* p. 637. Since all the unrighteous who are not killed in the Battle of Armageddon will be destroyed by the brightness of Christ's presence, and since all the wicked will be raised at the end of the millennium, it would appear that the individuals brought to life in this phase of the special resurrection will be raised twice: once now, and once at the end of the millennium.

and everlasting contempt" (Dan. 12:2). All who have died in the faith of the third angel's message come forth from the tomb glorified, to hear God's covenant of peace with those who have kept His law.[166]

As we saw earlier,[167] the third angel's message of Revelation 14 is interpreted by Seventh-day Adventists as requiring the observance of the seventh day. Those who have "died in the faith of the third angel's message," therefore, must be the faithful members of the Seventh-day Adventist denomination who have passed away since 1846 (and any others who have been heeding this message since that time). It appears, then, that loyal and obedient Seventh-day Adventists will be granted a special, pre-Second-Advent resurrection, so that they may have the privilege of seeing Christ's return.

The Resurrection and Transformation of Believers. After Christ has returned and after Satan has been bound, there occurs the general resurrection of believers. Seventh-day Adventists follow the Revised Standard Version in translating Revelation 20:4 as follows: "they [the souls of those who had been beheaded] came to life again, and reigned with Christ a thousand years."[168] At this point, therefore, all true believers who died before 1846, and all who died in the Lord since 1846 but who "never heard and came under the conviction of the truth revealed by the third angel's message,"[169] will be raised. It will be remembered, however, that this is not strictly a resurrection, since there are no souls of these believers which are still in existence. Actually, since no aspect of these believers is still in existence, and since therefore these individuals have been completely annihilated, it would seem to be more accurate to call their restoration to life a *new creation* rather than a resurrection. God, it may be presumed, now creates them anew on the basis of His memory of what they were like before they died.[170]

After this resurrection, all believers who are still alive (and only believers are left alive at this point) will be transformed and glorified. Now both the resurrected believers and the transformed be-

---

[166] *Ibid.,* It is made clear that both groups just described will be raised before Christ's actual return. See on this point also *Principles of Life from the Word of God,* pp. 327-28, 480-81.

[167] See above, pp. 95-96.

[168] *Questions on Doctrine,* p. 493. It should be observed, however, that the Greek word used here, *ezeesan,* can also be rendered simply *they lived,* and is so rendered both by the King James and American Standard Versions.

[169] Letter from Thomas Blincoe referred to above.

[170] *Questions on Doctrine,* pp. 493-94.

lievers will be caught up in the clouds to meet Christ in the air; after this they are taken up by Him to heaven.[171]

The Millennium. At this point the millennium begins, during which the saints will reign with Christ in heaven for a thousand years. On this point Seventh-day Adventists distinguish themselves from premillennialists, who picture the millennium as involving an earthly reign by Christ in Palestine over a kingdom consisting chiefly of converted Jews. For the Adventists, the millennial reign is neither earthly nor Jewish, but heavenly.[172]

During this millennial period the saints engage in a work of judgment. This thought is derived from Revelation 20:4, "And I saw thrones, and they sat upon them, and judgment was given unto them." The question now arises: what is the nature of this judgment? The investigative judgment has been completed as far as believers are concerned. As far as unbelievers are concerned, decisions regarding their punishment have not yet been finally arrived at. Seventh-day Adventists teach that during the millennium the saints engage, together with Christ, in a work of judgment, a work which involves "a careful investigation of the records of evil men and a decision regarding the amount of punishment due each sinner for his part in the rebellion against God."[173]

One wonders how there can be variations in the amount of punishment meted out to the wicked when, according to Seventh-day Adventist teaching, all the wicked will be annihilated. Their answer is that this variation will be evident in the amount of suffering which will precede the annihilation of the wicked.[174]

The Resurrection of the Wicked. In the King James Version Revelation 20:5a reads as follows: "The rest of the dead lived not again until the thousand years were finished." Seventh-day Adventists interpret this verse to mean that the wicked will be raised at the end of the millennium. At this time Christ, accompanied by all the saints, will descend to earth again — only now He will not remain in the air, but will come all the way down to earth. He will now command all the wicked dead to arise. In answer to this summons all the unbelieving dead are brought back to life, and begin to spread over the earth, having the same rebellious spirit which possessed them in life.[175]

---

171 *Ibid.,* pp. 494-96.
172 *Ibid.,* pp. 479-80, 495.
173 *Ibid.,* pp. 496-98.
174 *Ibid.,* p. 498.
175 *Ibid.,* p. 504. The retention of this rebellious spirit is difficult to understand in view of the fact that, according to Adventist teaching, their death meant their complete annihilation, and their so-called resurrection is really a new creation.

Satan Loosed. Through the resurrection of the wicked, Satan is loosed for a "little season" (Rev. 20:3). His enforced idleness now over, he sees the innumerable host of resurrected unbelievers, and determines to make one last attempt to overthrow God's kingdom. Deceiving the risen wicked into thinking that they can take the city of God by force, Satan gathers his hosts into battle array for a final, futile assault upon the "camp of the saints" — the new Jerusalem which has just descended with Christ from heaven. In this great battle the entire human race meets face to face, for the first and the last time.[176]

Satan, the Demons, and the Wicked Annihilated. This great battle — not to be confused with the Battle of Armageddon at the beginning of the millennium — ends in Satan's final defeat. Fire comes down from God out of heaven and annihilates Satan, his evil angels, and all the wicked. This annihilation Seventh-day Adventists call the second death; before the annihilation, however, there will be gradations of suffering, depending upon the guilt of the person or demon involved. Since Satan is the most guilty of all God's creatures, he will suffer the longest and will therefore be the last to perish in the flames.[177] At the end of this period of suffering, however, all those who have rebelled against God will have been wiped out of existence:

> . . . The finally impenitent, including Satan, the author of sin, will, by the fires of the last day, be reduced to a state of non-existence, becoming as though they had not been, thus purging God's universe of sin and sinners.[178]

Seventh-day Adventists thus reject the doctrine of hell as it has always been taught by historic Christianity. They do claim, however, to believe in eternal punishment; annihilation, they say, can be called eternal punishment because it is eternal in its results.[179]

---

[176] *Ibid.*, p. 505.
[177] *Ibid.*, pp. 498, 534; Branson, *op. cit.*, p. 567.
[178] *Fundamental Beliefs*, Article 12. If this is so, one wonders why God went to all the trouble of "raising" the wicked. Would it not have been simpler just to leave them in the state of nonexistence to which their physical death had reduced them?
[179] *Questions on Doctrine*, p. 539. A critical evaluation of these teachings on future punishment will be found in Appendix E. See the competent refutation of these doctrines in Norman Douty, *op. cit.*, pp. 142-159, and in Bird, *op. cit.*, pp. 53-63.
At this point it should be noted that Seventh-day Adventists differ from historic Christianity in denying the doctrine of the public Day of Judgment. The great Protestant creeds affirm that there will be a Day of Judgment after Christ returns to earth, and after the resurrection of both believers and unbelievers has taken place. All persons who have ever lived shall then appear before the judgment-seat of Christ, to be publicly judged on the basis of their personal relationship to Christ during this life, and on the basis of their works (see Augsburg Confession, Part I,

The New Earth. "In the conflagration which destroys Satan and his hosts, the earth itself will be regenerated and cleansed from the effects of the curse."[180] So out of the ruins of the old earth there will spring forth a new earth, which the redeemed will occupy as their everlasting home.

> . . . God will make all things new. The earth, restored to its pristine beauty, will become forever the abode of the saints of the Lord. The promise to Abraham, that through Christ he and his seed should possess the earth throughout the endless ages of eternity, will be fulfilled.[181]

On this new earth Christ will reign supreme, and all the saints shall forever serve, obey, and glorify Him.[182]

Art. 17; Belgic Confession, Art. 37; Westminster Confession, Chap. 33 — or 35, in more recent editions).

Seventh-day Adventists, however, deny that there shall be a public judgment of the sort described above. The judgment referred to in Rev. 20:12 they understand as meaning the investigative judgment which is going on now (*Questions on Doctrine,* p. 421). They distinguish, however, between *investigative judgments* and *executive judgments* (p. 422). There are, according to them, two phases in the process of judgment: the *investigative judgment* of believers, which is going on now, which will be completed before Christ's Second Coming, and which will be followed by the *executive judgment* of believers that will occur at the Second Coming; and the *investigative judgment* of unbelievers, which will be carried on during the millennium, and which will be followed by the *executive judgment* of unbelievers, to take place after the millennium. In each case the executive judgment is simply the execution of the sentence of judgment which has been determined by the investigative judgment.

[180] *Fundamental Beliefs,* Article 21.

[181] *Ibid.,* Article 22.

[182] *Ibid.* Cf. *Questions on Doctrine,* pp. 507-8; and Branson, *op. cit.,* pp. 573-82. For additional details on Seventh-day Adventist eschatology, see below, pp. 400-403.

THE INVESTIGATIVE JUDGMENT AND THE SCAPEGOAT DOCTRINE IN SEVENTH-DAY ADVENTISM

THE INVESTIGATIVE JUDGMENT

Having previously set forth what Seventh-day Adventists teach about the investigative judgment and about Satan as the antitype of the Old Testament scapegoat, I should like in this appendix to subject these doctrines to a Scriptural evaluation. The very first thing we should remember about these teachings is that they arose as the result of a mistake. It was William Miller's erroneous interpretation of Daniel 8:14, it will be recalled, which was the occasion for the formation of these theological constructions. Miller understood the "cleansing of the sanctuary" of Daniel 8:14 to mean Christ's return to earth; he further understood the 2300 evenings and mornings mentioned in this passage as standing for 2300 years; and, using the year 457 B.C. as the starting date for the 2300 years, he predicted that Christ would return from heaven some time between March 21, 1843, and March 21, 1844. Later Miller, following the leadership of Samuel Snow, moved the date ahead to October 22, 1844.[1]

When Christ did not return to earth on this date, Miller himself was convinced that he had been mistaken. On the following morning, however, Hiram Edson had a vision of Christ entering the holy of holies of the heavenly sanctuary. On the basis of this vision he now began to reinterpret Miller's prediction as having had reference not to Christ's return to earth, but to Christ's entrance into the second apartment of the heavenly sanctuary in order to cleanse it. This reinterpretation was adopted by Adventist leaders and became the basis for Seventh-day Adventist teachings on the investigative judgment and on Satan as the antitype of the scapegoat.[2] Mrs. White had a vision confirming this reinterpretation in February of 1845, and Mr. Crosier expanded this reinterpretation into an article in an Adventist periodical in February of 1846 — and thus the doctrine was firmly entrenched as an irrevocable part of Seventh-day Adventist theology.

No Bible expositor, however, had ever found this teaching in

[1] See above, pp. 89-92.
[2] See above, pp. 92-94.

144

the Bible previous to this time. No individual or group outside the Seventh-day Adventists has ever taught it since that time. As we shall see, there is no Biblical basis for this doctrine. The conclusion is inescapable that Seventh-day Adventist teaching on the investigative judgment was simply a way out of an embarrassing predicament. Instead of admitting, as Miller himself did, that a very serious error had been made in Scripture interpretation, these Adventist leaders clung frantically to the date Miller had set, and gave to that date a meaning which he himself never acknowledged. The doctrine of the investigative judgment, therefore, one of the key doctrines of Seventh-day Adventism, was a doctrine built on a mistake!

Closer scrutiny of the eighth chapter of Daniel's prophecy will reveal that verse 14 says nothing about either the return of Christ from heaven or His entrance into the holy of holies of the heavenly sanctuary. The chapter itself indicates that the two-horned ram which Daniel saw in his vision (v. 3) stood for the kings of Media and Persia (v. 20). The he-goat (v. 5) is interpreted by the angel as standing for the king of Greece (v. 21). Obviously, then, the casting down of the ram by the he-goat (v. 7) stands for the defeat of the Medo-Persian empire by Greece. It is presumed by most interpreters that the coming up of four horns on the head of the he-goat instead of the one great horn (v. 8) stands for the division of Alexander the Great's empire into four kingdoms after the latter's death (see v. 22).

What, now, is to be understood by the "little horn, which waxed exceeding great, toward the south, and toward the east, and toward the glorious land" (v. 9)? Verse 23 gives us the answer: this little horn stands for a person, "a king of fierce countenance." In the light of what verses 11 and 12 tell us, we may be reasonably sure that this person was Antiochus Epiphanes, ruler of Syria from 175-164 B.C., who did cast down the Jewish sanctuary (v. 11) by profaning it, and who did take away the continual burnt offering (v. 11) by stopping all Jewish sacrifices in the temple and substituting pagan sacrifices for them. Daniel now hears one holy one asking another, "How long shall be the vision concerning the continual burnt-offering, and the transgression that maketh desolate, to give both the sanctuary and the host to be trodden underfoot?"[3]

---

[3] Verse 13, in the ASV. The expression "to be trodden underfoot" is a translation of a Hebrew noun, *mirmas,* and means literally, "for trampling." The reader's attention is called to this word, since it is obvious that the sanctuary here spoken of is not a heavenly one. A heavenly sanctuary cannot be trampled underfoot.

The answer to this question is given in verse 14: "And he said unto me, Unto two thousand and three hundred evenings and mornings; then shall the sanctuary be cleansed" (ASV). It has been noted previously that the Hebrew word translated *cleansed* is actually the Niphal form of the verb *tsadaq,* which in the Qal means *to be right or righteous*; in the Niphal the verb therefore means *to be put right*.[4] It is unfortunate that the word came to be translated *be cleansed,* since the Hebrew verb usually rendered cleansed is not used here at all.[5] The Brown-Driver-Briggs Hebrew lexicon suggests that this part of the verse be translated: "the holy place shall be put right" (p. 842); the RSV, as previously observed, renders: "then the sanctuary shall be restored to its rightful state." The thought of this verse is not cleansing from sin, but restoration to its right and proper condition or use.

The part of verse 14 which gives the length of time designated reads literally as follows: "Until evening morning two thousand and three hundreds." The words for evening and morning are in the singular, and there is no connective between them. The previous reference to the continual burnt offering — offered every morning and every evening — implies that these words in verse 14 have reference to these two daily sacrifices. The fact that these offerings had been stopped, and that the question was asked, "How long?" implies that the answer will be in terms of the number of these daily burnt offerings. Thus the obvious and natural interpretation of the words "until evening morning two thousand and three hundreds" is: until 2300 morning and evening burnt offerings. Since two of these occurred every day, this means 1150 days.

This number of days, according to Jewish reckoning, would be equivalent to three years and some 50 or 60 days. By comparing I Maccabees 1:54 and 59 with 4:52-53, we learn that a period of exactly three years elapsed between the offering of the first heathen sacrifice upon the altar of burnt offering in the temple court and the resumption of regular sacrifices on this altar after the temple had been won back from Antiochus Epiphanes by Judas Maccabeus (from Dec. 25, 168 B.C. to Dec. 25, 165 B.C.). However, the order to stop offering the

[4] See above, p. 91, n. 6.

[5] *Taheer* in the Pi'el. It is significant that it is this verb which is used in Lev. 16 — the chapter which describes the ceremonies of the Day of Atonement. It is used once (v. 19) of the cleansing of the altar which is before Jehovah (probably the altar of burnt-offering), and once (v. 30) of the cleansing of the people from their sins. Certainly if Daniel meant to refer to the kind of cleansing which was done on the Day of Atonement, he would have used *taheer* instead of *tsadaq.*

regular morning and evening sacrifices on this altar had been given some time prior to Dec. 25, 168 B.C.; thus we can account for the additional 50 or 60 days.[6] In the light of what was said above about the meaning of the verb here used, does it not seem natural and obvious that Daniel 8:14 predicts the restoration of the earthly sanctuary to its rightful and proper use after a period of desecration by a heathen king? The 2300 evenings and mornings, then, picture the period of a little more than three years during which this desecration occurred, and the "putting right" of the sanctuary refers to the end of this period of desecration, on the 25th day of December, 165 B.C.[7]

The doctrine of the investigative judgment, as taught by Seventh-day Adventists, ought therefore to be rejected by all Christians, and by the Adventists themselves, as unscriptural and untrue. For this assertion I advance the following reasons:

(1) The doctrine of the investigative judgment *is based on a mistaken interpretation of Daniel 8:14.* It has been shown above that when Seventh-day Adventists find in Daniel 8:14 a prediction of a cleansing of the heavenly sanctuary by Christ, which cleansing was to begin on October 22, 1844, they are reading something into this passage which simply is not there.

(2) This doctrine *is based on a mistaken understanding of the Old Testament sacrificial system.* This misunderstanding reveals itself, first, in the supposition that the sprinkling of the blood of the daily or occasional sacrifices by the Old Testament priests polluted the sanctuary, whereas the sprinkling of the blood of the goat slain on the Day of Atonement cleansed the sanctuary. We have noted above that Crosier advanced this conception in his *Day-Star* article, and that L. E. Froom, in his own elaboration of Crosier's ideas, likewise accepted it (above, p. 93). We find this same conception in *Questions on Doctrine* (pp. 431-32). Why, however, should the sprinkling of sacrificial blood in one

[6] G. Ch. Aalders, *Het Boek Daniel* (in *Korte Verklaring* series; 2nd printing; Kampen: Kok, 1951), pp. 178-79.

[7] This interpretation of Daniel 8:14 is the one advanced by Aalders, the late Professor of Old Testament at the Free University in Amsterdam, in the volume mentioned above. See also J. K. Van Baalen, *Chaos of Cults* (4th ed.; Grand Rapids: Eerdmans, 1962), p. 233, n. 9. C. F. Keil, in his *Commentary on Daniel* (Edinburgh: Clark, 1891) and Edward J. Young in his *Prophecy of Daniel* (Grand Rapids: Eerdmans, 1953) are both of the opinion that the 2300 evenings and mornings must be interpreted, not as 1150 days, but as 2300 days. Yet both understand the "cleansing" or "putting right" of the sanctuary as referring to its restoration to proper use after its desecration by Antiochus Epiphanes. Both therefore agree basically with the interpretation advanced above (though differing on the time period involved), and disavow the Seventh-day Adventist interpretation of this passage.

instance pollute the sanctuary, and in the other instance cleanse it? Why should such sprinkling of blood mean, in one instance, that the sin involved was now recorded in the sanctuary, and, in the other instance, that the sin was removed from the sanctuary?

We may press this point a bit further. If the blood of sin offerings, for instance, when sprinkled upon the altar of burnt offering, served to transfer the offerer's guilt to the altar and thus to pollute the altar, why should not the blood of the slain goat on the Day of Atonement, when sprinkled upon the mercy seat, serve to transfer the guilt of the people to the mercy seat and thus to pollute the mercy seat? On the other hand, if the blood sprinkled upon the mercy seat served to remove guilt, why should not blood sprinkled upon the altar of burnt offering at the time of every ordinary sin-offering serve to remove guilt?

When Seventh-day Adventists say, "When the blood was sprinkled, the sin was recorded in the sanctuary," adding that it was only on the Day of Atonement that the accumulated record of the sins of the year was removed from the sanctuary,[8] we must reply that they have completely failed to grasp the significance of the sprinkling of the sacrificial blood upon the altar. The Bible itself makes quite clear what the significance of this sprinkling was. After warning the people against eating blood, the Lord through Moses gave the reason for this prohibition: "For the life (*nephesh*) of the flesh is in the blood; and I have given it to you upon the altar to make atonement (*kapper*) for your souls (*naphshootheekhem*); for it is the blood that maketh atonement (*yekappeer*) by reason of the life (*nephesh*)" (Lev. 17:11). The verb *kipper* in the Pi'el means to cover over, or to make propitiation. The verse just quoted states clearly that the blood upon the altar made propitiation for the souls of the offerers; there is no indication whatever that this happened only on the Day of Atonement. If this blood when applied to the altar made propitiation for the offerer and covered his sin, on what ground can Adventists claim that the application of blood to the altar meant that the sin of the offerer was now recorded in the sanctuary?

Note how Patrick Fairbairn, whose two-volume *Typology of Scripture* is one of the classic works on this subject, explains the symbolism of the sprinkling of blood upon the altar:

> Having with his own hands executed the deserved penalty on the victim, the offerer gave the blood to the priest, as God's representative. But that blood had already paid, in death, the penalty of sin, and was no longer laden with guilt and pollution. The justice of God was (symbolically) satisfied concerning it;

[8] *Questions on Doctrine,* p. 432.

and by the hands of His own representative He could with
perfect consistence receive it as a pure and spotless thing,
the very image of His own holiness, upon His table or altar.
In being received there, however, it still represented the blood
or soul of the offerer, who thus saw himself, through the action
with the blood of his victim, re-established in communion with
God, and solemnly recognized as received back to the divine
favor and fellowship.[9]

One might still ask, however: If the daily sacrifices served to
propitiate for sin so that no record of these sins was left in the
sanctuary, why was a Day of Atonement necessary? What
Seventh-day Adventists teach on this point will be evident from
the following quotation:

> On the Day of Atonement, when the blood of the goat was
> sprinkled upon all the furniture of the sanctuary as well as
> upon the altar of burnt offering, the accumulated record of
> the sins of the year were [should be: was] removed. . . . The
> sins of the Israelites, recorded in the sanctuary by the shed
> blood of the sacrificial victims, were removed and totally
> disposed of on the Day of Atonement.[10]

In reply, it may be pointed out that, according to Leviticus 16:33,
the high priest on the Day of Atonement had to make atonement
(*kipper*) for the holy sanctuary, the tent of meeting, the altar
(of burnt offering), the priests, and "all the people of the
assembly." If, now, as Seventh-day Adventists claim, the purpose
of these ceremonies was to remove accumulated sins which had
been recorded, they would have to grant that these accumulated
sins had been recorded upon the people as well as in the sanctuary.
But the whole thrust of their argumentation is that by the daily
sacrifices the guilt of these sins was taken from the people and
transferred to the sanctuary.[11]   It should also be noted that both
in verse 16 and verse 33 of this chapter the Hebrew word used
to describe the atonement that was made for the sanctuary on
the Day of Atonement is *kipper.* In this chapter, according to

---

[9] II, 275. The quotation is from the 10th ed. (New York: Tibbals, n.d.).
Cf. Louis Berkhof, *Biblical Archaeology* (3rd ed., Grand Rapids: Smitter,
1928), p. 146; and G. F. Oehler, *Theology of the Old Testament*, trans.
George E. Day (New York: Funk & Wagnalls, 1883), pp. 276-281.
The last author adds the thought that the sprinkling of the blood represents symbolically the self-surrender of the offerer to God. See also J.
D. Douglas, ed., *The New Bible Dictionary* (Grand Rapids: Eerdmans,
1962), pp. 1120-22.
[10] *Questions on Doctrine*, p. 432.
[11] "The individual sinner was forgiven and thus freed from his sin,
but in the bloodstains of the sanctuary he could perceive in type a
record of the misdeeds that he would fain see blotted out and removed
forever" (*Questions on Doctrine*, p. 432).

the Adventists, *kipper* means the complete removal of sins from the sanctuary. But why, then, does the word not have the same meaning in Leviticus 17:11, quoted above, where it refers to every application of blood upon the altar?

If, however, the daily sacrifices did serve to propitiate for sin (on the basis, of course, of the sacrifice of Christ which was to come), why were the ceremonies of the Day of Atonement necessary? To this question a twofold answer may be given: (i) This general expiation for sin would serve to cover those sins, both of the people and of the priests, for which offerings had not been made during the previous year;[12] and (ii) the entrance of the high priest into the holy of holies was a prediction of the future removal of the evil which separated the people from God, and an anticipation of the work of our great High Priest, Jesus Christ, who was to enter in "once for all into the holy place, having obtained eternal redemption" (Heb. 9:12).[13] We conclude, therefore, that the contention of Seventh-day Adventists, that the daily offerings served to transfer sins to the sanctuary, and that the sacrifices of the Day of Atonement served to remove these sins and thus to cleanse the sanctuary, is not in harmony with the facts. Since this contention is basic to their construction of the investigative judgment, we observe at this point that one of the pillars on which this doctrine rests has been overthrown.

A second misunderstanding of the Old Testament sacrificial system found among Seventh-day Adventists is the view that the morning and evening sacrifices of the continual burnt-offering represented atonement *provided*, whereas the individual sacrifices brought by the worshipers represented atonement *appropriated*.[14] For the continual burnt-offering, the so-called *tamidh*, was not primarily an expiatory sacrifice; rather, in common with all burnt-offerings, it was a sacrifice which typified the consecration of the worshiper to God. Thus this offering was better calculated to symbolize atonement *appropriated* than atonement *provided*. On the other hand, among the individual sacrifices brought by the worshipers in Old Testament times were the sin-offerings, aimed at providing expiation for sins whose effects terminated primarily

---

[12] C. F. Keil and F. Delitzsch, *Commentary on the Pentateuch*, trans. James Martin (Edinburgh: Clark, 1891), II, 395.

[13] *Ibid.*, p. 402. We could add that this communal sin-offering bore the same general relation to the individual offerings of the people that a congregational confession of sin on Sunday morning bears to the individual confessions of the members. Neither the ceremonies of the Day of Atonement nor the public confession of sin implies that the sins confessed individually were not previously forgiven and removed from God's record.

[14] *Questions on Doctrine*, p. 361.

on the individual himself, and the trespass-offerings which concerned sins whose effects terminated primarily on others. Since the basic idea behind both of these sacrifices was that of expiation and propitiation, these offerings certainly symbolized atonement *provided* much more vividly than atonement *appropriated*. So we see that the distinction Adventists make between these two types of offerings — a distinction which is basic to their doctrine of the investigative judgment — is also not in harmony with the facts.

(3) A third reason why the doctrine of the investigative judgment is to be rejected is that this doctrine *is based on a mistaken application of the Old Testament sacrificial system to Christ.* This, of course, naturally follows from the previous point. If Seventh-day Adventists misunderstand the Old Testament sacrificial system, it follows that they will also misapply that sacrificial system to the work of Christ. Let us now look at this matter in detail.

First, the Adventists mistakenly apply the Old Testament sacrificial system to Christ by insisting that Christ only forgave sins previous to 1844 but did not blot them out. It will be recalled that Crosier taught this in his *Day-Star* article (see above, p. 94), and that Seventh-day Adventists today still teach this (above, p. 117). This view ties in with their understanding of the meaning of the Old Testament sacrifices, as the following quotation will show:

> In the sanctuary in heaven, the record of sins is the only counterpart of the defilement of the earthly sanctuary. That the sins of men are recorded in heaven, we shall show in the next section. It is the expunging, or blotting out, of these sins from the heavenly records that fulfills the type set forth in the services on the Day of Atonement. In that way the sanctuary in heaven can be cleansed from all defilement.[15]

The thrust of these words is that, previous to 1844, the sins of penitent believers, though forgiven, were recorded in the heavenly sanctuary; it was not until after 1844 that the process of blotting out these sins was begun.

In refutation, we reply that the conception of sins being recorded in the sanctuary is one which has been shown to rest on a misunderstanding of the Old Testament sacrificial system. Further, the thought that Christ did not blot out sins previous to 1844 is without one shred of Scriptural support. On the contrary, David exclaims in Psalm 103:12, "As far as the east is from the west, so far hath he removed (*hirchiq*, Hiphil perfect of *rachaq*,

---

[15] *Questions on Doctrine*, p. 435.

indicating completed action) our transgressions from us."[16]   In Isaiah 44:22 we read, "I have blotted out (*machithi,* perfect tense, indicating complete action), as a thick cloud, thy transgressions, and, as a cloud, thy sins. . . ." If in the Old Testament we are already told that God has blotted out the sins of His people, how can one say that Christ, the second Person of the Trinity, could not blot out sins in the New Testament era previous to 1844?

In fact, the entire distinction between the forgiveness of sins and the blotting out of sins — which is basic to Seventh-day Adventist theology — is foreign to the Scriptures.   Does David suggest that there is any such distinction when he prays, in Psalm 51:1, "Have mercy upon me, O God, according to thy lovingkindness;   According to the multitude of thy tender mercies blot out my transgressions"?   In the New Testament the word commonly used for *forgive* is *aphieemi.*   The root meaning of this word is to *let go* or to *send away*; hence it has acquired the additional meaning: to *cancel, remit,* or *pardon* sins.[17]   Is there, now, any justification for the view that one's sin can be canceled without being blotted out?   When Jesus, for example, said to the paralytic, "Son, be of good cheer; thy sins are forgiven" (Mt. 9:2), did He mean: your sins are now forgiven, but not yet blotted out; if you do not continue to live up to all my commandments, these sins may still be held against you?   Why should the paralytic have been of good cheer, if this was the meaning of these words?

Seventh-day Adventists try to justify this distinction by appealing to the Parable of the Unmerciful Servant in Matthew 18:23-35. They contend that, since the king in the parable revoked his cancellation of the unmerciful servant's debt, God may also withdraw forgiveness once granted — hence the forgiveness of sins does not necessarily mean the blotting out of sins.[18]   The flaw in this reasoning is that an earthly king cannot read hearts, whereas God can.   The point of the parable is not that God may revoke forgiveness once bestowed, but that we must be ready to forgive others if we expect to be forgiven by God.   Christ Himself expresses this point very clearly when He says, "For if ye forgive men their trespasses, your heavenly Father will also forgive you.   But if ye forgive not men their trespasses, neither will your Father forgive your trespasses" (Mt. 6:14, 15).   In other words, a man who does not forgive those who have sinned

---

16 On p. 443 of *Questions on Doctrine* the authors admit that this figure is one used in Scripture to express the complete obliteration of sin.
17 Arndt and Gingrich, *Greek-English Lexicon of the New Testament* (Chicago: University of Chicago Press, 1957), p. 125.
18 *Questions on Doctrine,* pp. 439-40.

against him has *never really had his sins forgiven* by God, though he may think so.

We conclude that the Seventh-day Adventist distinction between the forgiveness of sin and the blotting out of sin is completely foreign to Scripture and robs the believer of all assurance of salvation.

Secondly, the idea that Christ has been engaged since 1844 in a work of investigative judgment in the heavenly sanctuary is completely without Biblical support. For, according to the Scriptures, the present work of Christ in heaven is a work of intercession, not a work of judging. Note, for example, how clearly this is taught in Hebrews 7:25, "Wherefore also he is able to save to the uttermost them that draw near unto God through him, seeing he ever liveth to make intercession for them." The basic meaning of the verb *entugchanoo,* which is here used, is to *plead for someone* or to *intercede for someone.*[19] The thought of judging, of examining records, of determining whether individuals are worthy of salvation or not, is completely foreign to this word. The same verb is used in Romans 8:34, "Who is he that condemneth? It is Christ Jesus that died, yea rather, that was raised from the dead, who is at the right hand of God, who also maketh intercession for us." In both passages, the verb *entugchanoo* is in the present tense, indicating that this intercession is a continuing activity. In Hebrews 7:25, in fact, the infinitive phrase *eis to entugchanein* shows that this intercession constitutes the very purpose for which Christ now lives! On what Scriptural ground, therefore, can Adventists say that Christ is now engaged in a work of judgment?[20]

It is, of course, true that there shall be a judgment of all men. But this judgment will occur after Christ has returned, not before. Note what our Lord Himself tells us, in Matthew 25:31-32, "But when the Son of man shall come in his glory, and all the angels with him, then shall he sit on the throne of his glory; and before him shall be gathered all the nations. . . ." Christ then goes on to describe the nature of this judgment and the standard whereby men shall be judged, ending his description with the familiar words, "And these shall go away into eternal punishment; but the righteous into eternal life" (v. 46). Here,

---

[19] Arndt and Gingrich, *op. cit.,* p. 269.

[20] Adventists grant that Christ is our Advocate and that He pleads the cases of His own people in the investigative judgment (*Questions on Doctrine,* pp. 441-42). Since, however, by their own definition, the work Christ is doing since 1844 is a work of *judgment,* we can only conclude that their theology evinces a serious confusion between Christ's work as Priest and Christ's work as Judge. How can He both plead the cases of His people and judge them at the same time?

indeed, we read about an "investigative judgment" — a judgment
based on an investigation of the lives of those arraigned before the
throne; but this judgment takes place after Christ has returned in
glory. In II Thessalonians 1:7-9 we read: "And to you that are
afflicted rest with us, at the revelation of the Lord Jesus from
heaven with the angels of his power in flaming fire, rendering vengeance to them that know not God, and to them that obey not the
gospel of our Lord Jesus: who shall suffer punishment, even eternal
destruction from the face of the Lord. . . ." The work of Christ as
judge is here pictured as occurring after His return from heaven.
In Revelation 20:11-15 we also read about the judgment. It is
described as being before the great white throne (v. 11), as
involving all the dead (vv. 12 and 13) — this implies that the
resurrection must have occurred before this time — and as
being based on works (v. 12). At the end of this judgment,
we are told, death and Hades are cast into the lake of fire (v. 14);
from 21:4 we learn that the cessation of death shall be a mark of
the final state. We also learn that those who are not found written
in the book of life are cast into the lake of fire — this, too, is
an event which points to the end of time. From every indication, therefore, we observe that the judgment here pictured is
not one which is going on now, but one which will take place
just before the final state is ushered in. From the other passages cited we conclude that this must be after Christ's return
to earth.

What Scriptural warrant do Seventh-day Adventists have for
teaching that there will be a judgment according to works before
the return of Christ? The Scripture passages alluded to in
parentheses at the end of Article 16 of the *Fundamental Beliefs*
(an article dealing with the investigative judgment) do not
give the slightest support for this doctrine. The first one,
I Peter 4:17-18, "For the time is come for judgment to begin at
the house of God," simply states, in harmony with the context, that
Christians may often have to be chastised by God in this world
in order that they may become more holy; it says nothing about
any judgment in the heavenly sanctuary. The second passage,
Daniel 7:9 and 10, pictures the Ancient of Days seated on a
throne, and a judgment which involves the opening of books.
This vision, however, which is to be understood in the light of
the rest of the chapter, and particularly in the light of verses 13
and 14 (the giving of dominion and glory to the Son of Man),
does not depict any investigative judgment in the heavenly sanctuary, but vividly symbolizes the overthrow of earthly empires and
powers that are opposed to God and the establishment of Christ's

everlasting reign. The third passage, Revelation 14:6-7, describes the message of the first angel: "Fear God, and give him glory; for the hour of his judgment is come." One needs a great deal of imagination to see in this verse a reference to an investigative judgment by Christ in the heavenly sanctuary! The last text mentioned is Luke 20:35, where Jesus is reported as saying, "But they that are accounted worthy to attain to that world, and the resurrection from the dead, neither marry, nor are given in marriage." Jesus is simply saying that those who will be privileged to enjoy the resurrection of believers will not marry; He gives not the slightest suggestion that their worthiness to attain this state will be determined by an investigative judgment in the heavenly sanctuary. Anyone who sees an investigative judgment taught in the verses just examined is seeing something in these passages which simply is not there!

(4) A fourth reason why the doctrine of the investigative judgment is to be rejected is *that it violates Scriptural teaching about the sovereignty of God.* It is clearly stated, in Article 16 of the *Fundamental Beliefs,* that "this investigative judgment determines who of the myriads sleeping in the dust of the earth are worthy of a part in the first resurrection, and who of its living multitudes are worthy of translation." This statement, however, stands in violent contradiction to what is said on page 420 of *Questions on Doctrine*: ". . . As Sovereign God, He . . . knows just who will accept and who will reject His 'great salvation.'" If this is so, why should God or Christ have to examine books of record to *determine* who may be raised in glory or translated into glory? Seventh-day Adventists cannot have their cake and eat it: either God does know who will accept His great salvation, and in that case the investigative judgment is unnecessary — or He must conduct an investigation to find out who is saved, and then He cannot be said to foreknow this!

Let us see what Mrs. White, the prophetess of Seventh-day Adventism, has to say about this matter:

> . . . There must be an examination of the books of record to determine who, through repentance of sin and faith in Christ, are entitled to the benefits of His atonement. The cleansing of the sanctuary therefore involves a work of investigation, — a work of judgment. This work must be performed prior to the coming of Christ to redeem His people; for when He comes, His reward is with Him to give to every man according to his works.[21]

[21] *The Great Controversy,* p. 422.

This statement leaves us with a God who has to do homework
before He can know who are entitled to the benefits of the
atonement, and with a Christ who, like an earthly professor, must
mark his examination papers before He knows what grade to
give to each student!   What resemblance is there between this
God and this Christ on the one hand, and the God and Christ of
the Scriptures on the other?   We learn from Ephesians 1:4 that
the destinies of the saved are not only foreknown by God but
have been predetermined from eternity: "Even as he chose
us in him [in Christ] before the foundation of the world."
Crystal clear on this point is Romans 8:29-30: "For whom he
foreknew, he also foreordained to be conformed to the image
of his Son, that he might be the firstborn among many brethren;
and whom he foreordained, them he also called; and whom he
called, them he also justified; and whom he justified, them he
also glorified."   Why should God have to conduct an investigative
judgment about those whom He has foreordained from eternity
to be justified and glorified?

What about Christ?   The Bible tells us that Christ knows His
sheep, and has given them eternal life, so that no one can snatch
them out of His hand (Jn. 10:27-28); that He prayed not for
the world but for those whom the Father had given Him (John
17:9); that it is the will of Him that sent Christ that of all that
which the Father had given Him He should lose nothing, but
should raise it up at the last day (Jn. 6:39).   Does this Christ,
now, have to conduct an investigation to determine which of the
inhabitants of the earth shall be raised in glory?

Adventists try to get around this difficulty by saying:

> Were God alone concerned, there would be no need of an
> investigation of the life records of men in this judgment [the
> investigative judgment], for as our eternal Sovereign God, He is
> omniscient. . . .   But that the inhabitants of the whole universe,
> the good and evil angels, and all who have ever lived on this
> earth might understand His love and His justice, the life history
> of every individual who has ever lived on the earth has been
> recorded, and in the judgment [the investigative judgment] these
> records will be disclosed.[22]

But here is confusion worse confounded!   In the first place, the
above statement is not consistent with the assertion previously
quoted, that the purpose of the investigative judgment is to *determine* who are worthy of resurrection to glory and translation.
Further, what is said above makes sense if we think of the final
judgment, which is public, in which the reasons for the final

---

[22] *Questions on Doctrine,* pp. 420-21.

destinies of men will be made known to all.   But it makes no
sense when applied to the investigative judgment, which is not
public, and which is therefore not witnessed by men!

(5) A fifth reason why the doctrine of the investigative judgment is to be rejected is that *it jeopardizes the Biblical teaching
that we are saved by grace alone*.   We have already touched upon
this point (see above, pp. 125-28).   Let us look at this matter a bit
more closely.   Mrs. White describes those who "pass" in the investigative judgment as follows:

> All who have truly repented of sin, and by faith claimed
> the blood of Christ as their atoning sacrifice, have had pardon
> entered against their names in the books of heaven; as they
> have become partakers of the righteousness of Christ, and their
> characters are found to be in harmony with the law of God, their
> sins will be blotted out, and they themselves will be accounted
> worthy of eternal life.[23]

The stipulation that the characters of these individuals must be
found to be in harmony with the law of God before their sins can
be blotted out suggests that they must have attained a certain
legal righteousness of their own before they will receive full salvation.

In a chapter in which he discusses the investigative judgment,
William Henry Branson says:

> A Christian who through faith in Jesus Christ has faithfully kept
> the law's requirements will be acquitted [in the investigative judg-
> ment]; there is no condemnation, for the law finds no fault in
> him. If, on the other hand, it is found that one has broken
> even a single precept, and this transgression is unconfessed, he
> will be dealt with just as if he had broken all ten.[24]

In this astounding statement a prominent Seventh-day Adventist
writer tells us that the basis for acquittal in the investigative
judgment is the perfect keeping of the law's requirements!   This
is surely a far cry from the Apostle Paul's assertion, "We reckon
therefore that a man is justified by faith apart from the works of
the law" (Rom. 3:28).   To the Galatians, who were being
tempted to base their hope for salvation in part on works which
they did themselves, came Paul's stern warning: "Ye are severed
from Christ, ye who would be justified by the law; ye are fallen
away from grace" (Gal. 5:4).   If the determining factor in being
accepted in the investigative judgment is the faithfulness with
which one has kept the law's requirements, then certainly salvation is no longer by grace alone.   And if the failure to confess

[23] *The Great Controversy*, p. 483, quoted in *Questions on Doctrine*,
p. 443.
[24] *Drama of the Ages*, p. 351.

even a single transgression of the law will result in damnation, one wonders what will happen to the Psalmist who exclaimed, "Who can discern his errors?" (Ps. 19:12). We conclude that the Seventh-day Adventist doctrine of the investigative judgment does not permit Adventists to continue to claim that they teach salvation by grace alone.

THE SCAPEGOAT DOCTRINE

The other aspect of Seventh-day Adventist teaching in relation to the investigative judgment that remains to be evaluated is the view that the sins of mankind will be laid on Satan just before Christ's return to earth. It is my conviction that this doctrine, too, is completely without Scriptural support. For this judgment I advance the following four reasons:

(1) It is not at all certain that the word *Azazel* in Leviticus 16:8, and following verses, means Satan. Seventh-day Adventists insist that this is what the word means, citing a number of authorities to support their claim.[25] The plain fact of the matter, however, is that no one knows exactly what this strange word means. The early tradition rendered the word *la'aza'zeel* as follows: "for removal." The Septuagint translation of this expression was *too apopompaioo*: for the one to be sent away. From this was derived the Vulgate translation, *capro emissario*: for the goat to be sent forth. It is from this tradition that the King James rendering originated: "scapegoat" (literally, "escape-goat"). This ancient tradition still has many supporters. The Brown-Driver-Briggs Hebrew lexicon suggests that the word Azazel means "entire removal." The article on Azazel found in the *International Standard Bible Encyclopedia* suggests the same interpretation.[26] Others, however, argue from the juxtaposition of Azazel with Jahwe that the former must be a proper name. Following this interpretation, some hold that it must refer to Satan, and others suggest that it designates a wilderness demon. One must simply confess that, until further light is given, no one can be dogmatic as to the meaning of this word. It may mean Satan, but it may also mean something else.

(2) Even if it be granted, for the sake of argument, that Azazel does mean Satan, it does not at all follow that the second goat in the ceremonies of the Day of Atonement stood for Satan. For it is specifically stated in Leviticus 16:10 that the second goat was to be sent into the wilderness *la'aza'zeel: to* or *for* Azazel. If

---

[25] *Questions on Doctrine,* pp. 391-95.
[26] Ed. James Orr (rev. ed., Grand Rapids: Eerdmans, 1939), I, 342-44.

Azazel means Satan, the second goat was sent *to* or *for* Satan; to
say that the second goat *stood for Satan* is to make an unwarranted leap from the entity to whom or for whom the goat was
sent to the goat himself.

(3) It is, further, impossible to regard the second goat as
standing for Satan since, according to Leviticus 16:5, the two
goats represented one sin-offering. In the last-named verse we
read, "And he [the high priest] shall take of the congregation of
the children of Israel two he-goats for a sin-offering (*lechatta'th*)."
It is not just the slain goat, in other words, that constitutes the
sin-offering; it is the two goats together. This means that both
goats pictured the propitiation that was to be offered by Christ.
The slain goat pictured the fact that Christ was to shed His blood
to redeem us from sin, whereas the goat sent into the wilderness
pictured the fact that by His atoning work Christ was to remove
our sins from us. To suggest, as Seventh-day Adventists do, that
the second goat stood for Satan is to transfer a work of Christ
to the Prince of Darkness!

Note what Fairbairn has to say about this second goat:

> What took place with the live goat was merely intended to unfold,
> and render palpably evident to the bodily eye, the effect of the
> great work of atonement. The atonement itself was made in
> secret, while the high priest alone was in the sanctuary; and
> yet . . . it was of the utmost importance that there should be
> a visible transaction, like that of the dismissal of the scape-
> goat, embodying in a sensible form the results of the service.
> Nor is it of any moment what became of the goat after being
> conducted into the wilderness. It was enough that he was led
> into the region of drought and desolation, where . . . he should
> never more be seen or heard of. With such a destination, he
> was obviously as much a doomed victim as the one whose
> life-blood had already been shed and brought within the veil;
> he . . . exhibited a most striking image of the everlasting oblivion
> into which the sins of God's people are thrown, when once they
> are covered with the blood of an acceptable atonement.[27]

(4) That Satan will be punished for his sins is certainly taught
in Scripture, but that our sins or the sins of all men will be placed
on Satan is nowhere taught in Scripture. This idea rests, as we
have just seen, on a misunderstanding of the role of the second
goat in the ceremonies of the Day of Atonement. Further, this
conception is in direct conflict with I Peter 2:24, where we read

---

[27] *Typology of Scripture,* II, 340-41. Cf. also W. Moeller in the *I. S. B. E.*
article referred to above: "Both goats . . . represent two sides of the same
thing. The second is necessary to make clear what the first one, which
has been slain, can no longer represent, namely, the removal of the
sin. . ." (I, 343).

the following concerning Christ: "Who his own self bare our sins
in his body upon the tree. . . ." It was therefore Christ who bore
our sins and thus removed them; not Satan. To suggest that
Christ still has to take our sins from the heavenly sanctuary at the
end of time in order to lay them on Satan implies that He has
not previously borne them away, and that His atoning work was
therefore inadequate for the complete removal of sin. Moreover, if Christ lays the sins of unbelievers on Satan as well, why
must they still suffer for them? If, on the other hand, they do
suffer for them, why must *their sins* still be laid on Satan? Finally,
if it is necessary for these sins to be laid on Satan before they can
be obliterated from the universe, Satan plays an indispensable
part in the blotting out of sin. Though Seventh-day Adventists
deny that Satan makes atonement for our sins in any way, they
are nevertheless guilty of ascribing something to Satan which
should only be ascribed to Christ: the obliteration of our sins.

We conclude that the doctrines of the investigative judgment
and of the laying of sins on Satan are false teachings. Not only
do they lack all Scriptural support; they actually go contrary to
Scripture at various points, as has been shown. If Seventh-day
Adventists honestly wish to be true to Scripture alone in their
teachings, they should repudiate both of these doctrines.[28]

---

[28] The reader is further referred to Herbert Bird's *Theology of Seventh-
day Adventism,* pp. 72-92, and to Norman F. Douty's *Another Look at
Seventh-day Adventism,* pp. 118-29, for competent evaluations of both
the investigative judgment doctrine and the scapegoat teaching.

APPENDIX C

SEVENTH-DAY ADVENTIST TEACHING
ON THE SABBATH

In Chapter 3 we discussed the teaching of Seventh-day Adventists on the Sabbath insofar as it is inconsistent with their claim that they believe in salvation by grace alone (above, pp. 127-128). In this appendix we shall examine and evaluate their teaching on the question of the proper day to be observed by Christians. Are Seventh-day Adventists right in insisting that the seventh day of the week is the only proper Lord's day for us to observe, in obedience to the Fourth Commandment?

Here again we must first of all recall how their doctrine of the Sabbath originated. A retired sea captain (Joseph Bates) became convinced through reading an article in a periodical that the seventh day was the proper Sabbath to be kept. After having arrived at this conclusion, he came into contact with a group of Adventists in New Hampshire who had been influenced by a lay woman (Mrs. Rachel Oakes) to keep the seventh-day Sabbath. Having thus been confirmed in his convictions, Bates wrote two tracts about the Sabbath, in which the position still held by Seventh-day Adventists today was set forth (see above, pp. 95-96). In 1847, between the publication of Bates's first and second tracts, Mrs. White had a vision in which she was taken into the holy of holies of the heavenly sanctuary, and saw the Ten Commandments with a halo of glory around the Sabbath Commandment (above, pp. 97-98). We see, therefore, that the denomination arrived at its view about the Sabbath not through thorough, basic Bible study on the part of well-trained Biblical scholars, but through the influence of non-theologically trained lay members and through a confirmatory vision from Mrs. White. It is on the basis of this type of "guidance" that Seventh-day Adventists overthrow the first-day Sunday, which has been observed by all the churches of Christendom since the beginning of the Christian era.

Let us look at some of the arguments Adventists advance for their position.

(1) *They maintain that the Sabbath is a memorial of creation,* that it had no ceremonial significance by foreshadowing something

161

yet to come, but that it had only commemorative significance, pointing back to the creation of the world.[1] Since God created the world in six days and rested on the seventh day, the seventh-day-ness of the Sabbath was not a temporary feature of the day which was later to be changed, but always remained part of the Sabbath commandment.[2]

In answer to this argument, it should be observed that the Bible itself indicates that the Sabbath points forward as well as backward. In the fourth chapter of Hebrews a comparison is made between the rest of the Sabbath Day and the rest of heavenly glory. The inspired author is referring to future heavenly blessedness when he says, in verse 9, "There remaineth therefore a sabbath rest (*sabbatismos*) for the people of God." Obviously, therefore, the Sabbath is a type of heavenly rest, and does not have *merely* commemorative significance.

As far as the seventh-day-ness of the Sabbath is concerned, the very fact that the day was changed in New Testament times to the first day indicates that the seventh-day-ness was not an irrevocable aspect of the Sabbath commandment.[3] Geerhardus Vos, while agreeing with the Adventists that the Sabbath has its roots in creation rather than in the Mosaic ordinance, and is therefore binding upon all mankind,[4] adds that the coming of Christ has brought about a change in the order in which the day of rest is observed:

> The universal Sabbath law received a modified significance under the Covenant of Grace. The work which issues into the rest can no longer be man's own work. It becomes the work of Christ. This the Old Testament and the New Testament have in common. But they differ as to the perspective in which they each see the emergence of work and rest. Inasmuch as the Old Covenant was still looking forward to the performance of the Messianic work, naturally the days of labor to it come first, the day of rest falls at the end of the week. We, under the New Covenant, look back upon the accomplished work of Christ. We, therefore, first celebrate the rest in principle procured by Christ, although the Sabbath also still remains a sign looking forward to the final eschatological rest.[5]

The position of the historic Christian church on this matter is well set forth in the Westminster Confession of Faith:

> As it is of the law of nature, that, in general, a due proportion of time be set apart for the worship of God; so, in his Word,

---

[1] *Questions on Doctrine,* p. 158.
[2] *Ibid.,* pp. 161-65.
[3] The evidence supporting this statement will be given later in this appendix.
[4] *Biblical Theology* (Grand Rapids, Eerdmans, 1954), p. 155.
[5] *Ibid.,* pp. 157-158.

by a positive, moral, and perpetual commandment, binding all men in all ages, he hath particularly appointed one day in seven for a Sabbath, to be kept holy unto him (Ex. 20:8, 10, 11; Isa. 56:2, 4, 6, 7): which, from the beginning of the world to the resurrection of Christ, was the last day of the week; and, from the resurrection of Christ, was changed into the first day of the week (Gen. 2:2, 3; I Cor. 16:1, 2; Acts 20:7), which in Scripture is called the Lord's day (Rev. 1:10), and is to be continued to the end of the world, as the Christian Sabbath (Ex. 20:8, 10, with Mt. 5:17, 18).[6]

(2) Seventh-day Adventists *cite Revelation 14 to buttress their position on the Sabbath*: "We believe that the restoration of the Sabbath is indicated in the Bible prophecy of Revelation 14:9-12."[7] On another page the authors of *Questions on Doctrine* affirm that they understand the prophecies of Daniel 7 and Revelation 13 relating to the beast to have reference particularly to the Papacy, adding,

Thus it was that the Adventist heralds of Sabbath reform came to make a further logical application of the mark of the beast — holding it to be, in essence, the attempted change of the Sabbath of the fourth commandment of the Decalogue by the Papacy, its endeavor to impose this change on Christendom, and the acceptance of the Papacy's substitute by individuals.[8]

The reader's attention is now called to the text of Revelation 14:9-12:

And another angel, a third, followed them, saying with a great voice, If any man worshippeth the beast and his image, and receiveth a mark on his forehead, or upon his hand, he also shall drink of the wine of the wrath of God, which is prepared unmixed in the cup of his anger; and he shall be tormented with fire and brimstone in the presence of the holy angels, and in the presence of the Lamb: and the smoke of their torment goeth up for ever and ever; and they have no rest day and night, they that worship the beast and his image, and whoso receiveth the mark of his name. Here is the patience

---

[6] Chap. 21, Section 7, as found in Schaff's *Creeds of Christendom*, 4th ed. (New York: Harper, 1919), III, 648-49. The *Post Acta* of the Synod of Dort of 1618-19 contain a statement about Sabbath observance which distinguishes between a ceremonial element and a moral element in the Fourth Commandment. The ceremonial element, which has been abolished for New Testament Christians, is the observance of the seventh day. The moral element, which is still binding, is the observance of a definite day for rest and worship. This statement, which has been adopted by the Christian Reformed Church, may be found in J. L. Schaver's *Polity of the Churches* (Chicago: Church Polity Press, 1947), II, 33.

[7] *Questions on Doctrine,* p. 153.

[8] *Ibid.,* p. 181.

of the saints, they that keep the commandments of God, and the faith of Jesus.

Where, now, does one see any reference to the Sabbath in this entire passage? One can perhaps excuse a retired sea captain for imagining that he could see a denunciation of the first-day Sabbath in this passage, but for an entire denomination to adopt this interpretation is a far more serious matter. By this type of irresponsible exegesis one can prove anything from the Bible which he wishes to.

(3) Seventh-day Adventists assert that *the New Testament emphasizes the observance of the seventh day as the Sabbath.* For proof they point to the fact that both Jesus[9] and Paul[10] observed the seventh day rather than the first. This argument, however, is not difficult to meet. Our Lord observed the seventh day before His resurrection because He was at that time bound to the Old Testament regulation. It is significant to note, however, that *after* His resurrection He appeared to the apostles on two successive first days of the week. As far as the Apostle Paul is concerned, he went to Jewish synagogues on the seventh-day Sabbath because he wished to witness to Jews, whom he could find there on that day. Does the fact that Seventh-day Adventists sometimes attend Sunday church services in order to win converts to their faith imply that they believe the first day of the week to be the Sabbath? Further, it is to be remembered that Paul did address a gathering of Christians at Troas on the first day of the week — to this point we shall come back in a moment.

What proof is there now from the New Testament itself that the observance of the Sabbath was changed from the seventh to the first day of the week? Let us note the following Biblical facts:

(i) Jesus arose from the dead on the first day of the week (John 20:1), thus designating the first day as the one now to be observed.[11]

(ii) Jesus appeared to ten of His disciples on the evening of that first day of the week (John 20:19ff.).

(iii) On the following first day of the week, Jesus appeared to the eleven disciples (John 20:26ff.).

(iv) The promised coming of the Holy Spirit was fulfilled on

---

[9] *Ibid.,* p. 151, 161.

[10] Arthur E. Lickey, *God Speaks to Modern Man* (Review and Herald, 1952), pp. 424, 430. On the latter page Lickey makes the point that Luke, in the book of Acts, recorded eighty-four Sabbath services and only one first-day meeting for worship.

[11] Even Seventh-day Adventists admit that Christ arose on the first day (*Questions on Doctrine,* p. 151). Vos, quoting Delitzsch, makes the comment that, since Christ lay in the grave on the seventh day, the Jewish Sabbath was, as it were, buried in His grave (*op. cit.,* p. 158)

the first day of the week (Acts 2:1ff.). Since this was an event of as great importance as the incarnation of Christ, it is highly significant that this outpouring occurred on a Sunday.[12]

(v) On that same first day of the week the first gospel sermon was preached by Peter (Acts 2:14ff.), and 3,000 converts were received into the church (Acts 2:41).

(vi) At Troas the Christians of that city assembled for worship on the first day of the week and Paul preached to them (Acts 20: 6-7). With respect to this passage a leading Seventh-day Adventist writer says,

> The first day of the week (Bible time) begins Saturday night at sundown and ends Sunday night at sundown. Inasmuch as this meeting was held on the first day of the week and at night, it must therefore have been on what we call Saturday night, the first day having begun at sundown.[13]

Lickey's reasoning assumes that Luke was following the Jewish system of reckoning, which began a day at sundown. F. F. Bruce, however, contends that Luke was not using the Jewish mode of reckoning, but the Roman reckoning from midnight to midnight;[14] on this basis Luke was designating, not Saturday evening, but Sunday evening. Lickey further contends that this meeting was not a regular service but simply a farewell meeting for Paul, and that it therefore tells us nothing about the day on which Christians ordinarily met for worship.[15] To this it may be replied that Luke's statement, "we being gathered together to break bread" strongly suggests (though it does not finally prove) the thought that this

---

[12] The question might be asked, How do we know that the day of Pentecost mentioned in Acts 2 fell on a Sunday? The word *Penteekostee* which is here used means "fiftieth." It designated the Jewish Feast of Weeks, at which two wave-loaves of leavened bread were offered to the Lord. Lev. 23:15-16 specified that this feast was to be observed on the morrow after the seventh Sabbath after the Feast of the Passover. The Sadducean party in the first century A.D. interpreted "the morrow after the Sabbath" as being a first day of the week; on this interpretation Pentecost would always fall on a Sunday. The Pharisees of that day, however, interpreted the Leviticus passage in such a way that Pentecost fell on various days of the week. F. F. Bruce points out that, though the Pharisaic interpretation became normative for Judaism after A.D. 70, "While the temple stood, their [the Sadducees'] interpretation would be normative for the public celebration of the festival [Pentecost]; Christian tradition is therefore right in fixing the anniversary of the descent of the Spirit on a Sunday" (*Commentary on the Book of the Acts* [Grand Rapids: Eerdmans, 1955], p. 53, n. 3).

[13] Lickey, *op. cit.,* p. 430.

[14] *Op. cit.,* p. 408, n. 25. Cf. O. Cullmann, *Early Christian Worship* (London, 1953), pp. 10ff., 88ff. In either case, however, the meeting was held on the first day of the week.

[15] *Op. cit.,* p. 431. Cf. M. L. Andreasen, *The Sabbath, Which Day and Why?* (Washington: Review and Herald, 1942), pp. 167-70.

was a regular meeting at which they ate together and celebrated the Lord's Supper.[16]   If there was no special significance in the day on which the Christians met, why should Luke take the trouble to say, as he does, "on the first day of the week"?   This item of information could well have been omitted if it conveyed a fact of no importance.   That Luke mentions it shows that already at this time Christians were gathering for worship on the first day of the week.

(vii) Paul instructed the Christians at Corinth to make contributions for the poor in Jerusalem on the first day of the week: "Upon the first day of the week let each one of you lay by him in store, as he may prosper, that no collections be made when I come" (I Cor. 16:2).   As can be imagined, Adventists find in this passage no proof for the observance of the first day as a day of worship.   M. L. Andreasen, for example, contends that this passage does not refer to a collection taken in church, but that it instructs the Corinthian Christians to lay aside money at home, as they had been prospered; this would involve some bookkeeping, which would be inappropriate on the Sabbath — hence Paul instructs them to do this on Sunday.[17]   Lickey advances a similar interpretation, saying, among other things,

> A church member runs a small shop all week, let us say. Friday afternoon he closes early enough to prepare for the Sabbath.   There is no time to figure accounts.   But when the Sabbath is past, and the first day of the week comes, he is to check his net earnings and lay aside a proper sum, not at church, but at home.[18]

We shall have to agree that Paul is here probably not speaking of an offering which is to be taken at a church service.   The expression *par' heautoo tithetoo* is in all likelihood to be understood as meaning: let him lay aside by himself — that is, at home.[19]   Again, however, it is important to note that the first day of the week is specifically designated for this laying aside.   Why should Paul say this if the Corinthians regularly gathered for worship on

[16] Bruce, *op. cit.,* p. 408.   Cf. R. C. H. Lenski, *Acts of the Apostles* (Columbus: Wartburg Press, 1944), p. 826; also F. W. Grosheide, *Handelingen,* in *Korte Verklaring* (Kampen: Kok, 1950), p. 107.
[17] *The Sabbath,* pp. 172-74.
[18] *Op. cit.,* pp. 433-34.
[19] It is so understood by Grosheide, in his *Commentary on First Corinthians* (Eerdmans, 1955), p. 398; by Lenski in his *First Corinthians* (Columbus: Wartburg Press, 1946), p. 759; and by Arndt and Gingrich in their *Greek-English Lexicon,* p. 615 (though qualified by a *probably*). Charles Hodge, however, is of the opinion that Paul is referring to an offering brought to church and collected there (*First Corinthians* [Eerdmans. reprinted 1956], pp. 363-64).

Saturday? Christian giving is part of our worship; it is to be expected that we engage in this form of worship on the day on which we gather for public prayers. Surely not every member of the Corinthian church was a shopkeeper who needed to do some figuring before he could determine how much he should give; surely, also, even the shopkeepers could do their figuring on the evening before the day of worship as well as on the day after. The only plausible reason for mentioning the first day in this passage is that this was the customary day on which Christians were meeting for worship.[20]

(viii) The Apostle John wrote, in Revelation 1:10, "I was in the Spirit on the Lord's day (*en tee kuriakee heemera*). The Greek word *kuriakee* is an adjective meaning "belonging to the Lord"; literally, therefore, the expression means: *on the day belonging to the Lord.* Seventh-day Adventists contend that the expression *the Lord's day,* as here used, refers to Saturday.[21] In taking this position, however, they stand completely alone. These words have been understood universally as referring to Sunday, the first day of the week. They are so understood by the standard commentators, and by the standard lexicons.[22] If we add to this the fact that the expression is used to stand for Sunday in such early Christian writings as the *Didachee* and Ignatius's *Letter to the Magnesians,* we see on what flimsy grounds Adventists stand when they try to interpret these words as meaning Saturday. John's statement that he was in the Spirit on the Lord's Day further confirms the fact that the first day of the week was now the one commonly used for worship.[23]

(4) Seventh-day Adventists contend that "*the earliest authentic instance, in early church writings, of the first day of the week being called 'Lord's Day' was by Clement of Alexandria, near the*

---

[20] So also Grosheide, Lenski, and Hodge, in the works mentioned above.

[21] Lickey, *op. cit.,* p. 415; and Andreasen, *The Sabbath,* p. 186.

[22] Under the latter the following may be mentioned: Moulton and Milligan, *Vocabulary of the Greek Testament* (Eerdmans, 1957), p. 364; Werner Foerster, in Kittel's *Theologisches Woerterbuch zum Neuen Testament* (Stuttgart: Kohlhammer, 1938), III, 1096; and Arndt and Gingrich's *Greek-English Lexicon,* p. 459. The last-named authors say, under Lord's day: "Certainly Sunday (so in Modern Greek)."

[23] The book of Revelation was probably written during the last decade of the first century. Thus we have seen evidence that the first day of the week was being used as the day of worship by Christians as early as the first century. If, now, this was contrary to the will of God, the Apostles should have opposed its use and warned Christians against it. We find no such opposition, however; on the contrary, we find Paul supporting the first day by urging Christians to lay aside their gifts on that day.

close of the second century."[24]   That this statement is quite contrary to fact will be evident from the following quotations:

(i) Revelation 1:10, "I was in the Spirit on the Lord's Day."[25]

(ii) From the Epistle of Ignatius *To the Magnesians,* Section 9: "If then those who had walked in ancient practices attained unto newness of hope, no longer observing sabbaths, but fashioning their lives after the Lord's day, on which our life also arose through him. . . ."[26]

(iii) From the *Didachee,* or *Teaching of the Twelve Apostles,* Section 14: "And on the Lord's Day gather yourselves together and break bread and give thanks. . . ."[27]

(Though the following two quotations do not use the expression, "the Lord's Day," they do give further evidence for the early observance of the first day of the week as the day of worship.)

(iv) From the *Epistle of Barnabas,* Section 15: "Wherefore also we keep the eighth day for rejoicing, in the which also Jesus rose from the dead, and having been manifested ascended into the heavens."[28]

(v) From Justin Martyr's *First Apology,* Chapter 67: "But Sunday is the day on which we all hold our common assembly, because it is the first day on which God, having wrought a change in the darkness and matter, made the world; and Jesus Christ our Saviour on the same day rose from the dead."[29]

---

[24] *Questions on Doctrine,* p. 166.   The reference given in Clement is *Miscellanies,* V, 14.

[25] Written about A.D. 95.   See above discussion.

[26] Written about A.D. 107.   Text from J. B. Lightfoot's *The Apostolic Fathers* (Grand Rapids: Baker, 1956), p. 71.

[27] Written during the last part of the first century or the beginning of the second.   Text from Lightfoot, *op. cit.,* p. 128.

[28] Written some time between 70 and 130 A.D.   Text from Lightfoot, *op. cit.,* p. 152.

[29] Written about 155 A.D.   Text from *The Ante-Nicene Fathers* (Eerdmans, reprinted 1956), I, 186.   Seventh-day Adventists contend that what Justin speaks of here was a "festival of the resurrection" which began to be observed alongside of the seventh-day Sabbath from the middle of the second century (*Questions on Doctrine,* p. 152).   This, however, seems very unlikely.   The service held on this day, as described in the earlier part of the chapter, includes Scripture reading, a brief homily, prayer, thanksgiving, the celebration of the Lord's Supper, and an offering for the needy.   This certainly appears to be a description of a regular Sunday worship service.   If this were a festival service held alongside of Sabbath worship, one would expect some reference to this fact in the chapter.   No such reference is found, however; instead, Justin says: "Sunday is the day on which we all hold *our common assembly.* . . ." Further, in the *Dialogue with Trypho,* written some time after the *First Apology,* Justin clearly affirms that the Gentile Christians of his day did not observe the Sabbath: "But the Gentiles, who have believed on Him [Christ] . . . they shall receive the inheritance . . . even although they neither keep the Sabbath, nor are circumcised, nor observe the feasts" (Chap. 26; text from *The Ante-Nicene Fathers,* I, 207).

The statements quoted above, plus the New Testament evidence previously given, make it quite evident that the change from the seventh day to the first day was not brought about by "the Papacy," as Seventh-day Adventism contends,[30] but came about long before the Papacy arose as a strong ecclesiastical institution. We conclude that the Adventist position on the Sabbath is not only historically unwarranted, but is also without Scriptural support.[31]

[30] *Questions on Doctrine*, p. 181. We are never told, however, exactly which Pope it was who changed the day.

[31] For further treatment and elaboration of the subject discussed in this appendix, the reader is referred to Bird's *Theology of Seventh-Day Adventism*, pp. 93-118; Douty's *Another Look at Seventh-day Adventism*, pp. 80-91; and Martin's *The Truth About Seventh-day Adventism*, pp. 140-73. Older but very thorough is D. M. Canright's *The Lord's Day from Neither Catholics Nor Pagans*, subtitled "An Answer to Seventh-day Adventists on this Subject" (New York: Revell, 1915). Valuable material may also be found in J. K. Van Baalen's *Chaos of Cults*, 4th ed. (Eerdmans, 1962), pp. 240-47, 249-53.

CHAPTER FOUR

Christian Science

HISTORY

LIFE OF MARY BAKER EDDY

MARY BAKER EDDY WAS BORN AT BOW, NEW HAMPSHIRE, ON JULY 16, 1821, as the youngest of six children.[1] Her parents were devoutly religious. Her father, Mark Baker, was a stern Calvinist. Mary often disagreed with her father, particularly on such points as the final judgment day, the peril of endless punishment, and the view that God has no mercy toward unbelievers. Mary was a nervous child and missed much schooling as a result. She got her education mostly through her own efforts and through the help of her brothers and sisters, particularly her brother Albert who taught her advanced subjects during summer vacations.

For years Mary was a semi-invalid. One author states that she was afflicted with a spinal weakness which caused spasmodic seizures, followed by prostration which amounted to a complete nervous collapse.[2]

---

[1] For this brief biographical sketch I am particularly indebted to Charles S. Braden, *Christian Science Today* (Dallas: Southern Methodist University Press, 1958), pp. 11-41.

[2] Harry S. Goodykoontz, "The Healing Sects," in *The Church Faces the isms,* ed. A. B. Rhodes (New York: Abingdon, 1958), p. 197.

At the age of 17 Mary joined the Congregational Church at Tilton, New Hampshire.   In her autobiography, written when she was seventy, she asserts that she refused to accept the somewhat morbid theology of this church.   Despite this refusal, however, so she claims, she was accepted into membership.

In 1843 she was married to George Glover.   This was a happy marriage but a short-lived one, lasting only a little longer than half a year.   Glover died, leaving her with an unborn child in Charleston, South Carolina, where they were living at the time. Mary went back north and, in September of 1844, gave birth to a son whom she named George.   The trip from the South was very hard on her; it appears that from this time on she was never entirely free from pain.   It is therefore not surprising that she became preoccupied with the question of health.

In 1853 Mary married dentist Daniel Patterson.   This marriage was a very unhappy one.   Patterson was not a good provider; he often spent much time practicing in other towns, and was reputed to have become interested in other women.   This marriage lasted until 1866, when he and Mary were permanently separated. Seven years later Mary obtained a divorce on the grounds of desertion, though her own later references to this divorce make it appear that Patterson had been guilty of adultery.

During this time her health was still poor.   When reports spread through the country that in Portland, Maine, a man named Phineas P. Quimby was effecting remarkable cures without medicine, Mary decided to go to him.   She first saw Quimby in 1862; she believed herself to have been healed by him.   For a considerable time she was an enthusiastic follower of Quimby, accepting his conviction that he had rediscovered Jesus' own healing methods. Mary tried to follow Quimby's methods, not only with regard to her own health, but also in the treatment of others.   She even delivered a public lecture on Quimby's "Spiritual Science Healing Disease."

One of the most heated controversies regarding Mrs. Eddy concerns the relation between her teachings and those of Phineas P. Quimby.   Mrs. Eddy herself (who at this time, it will be recalled, was Mrs. Patterson) at first praised Quimby to the skies.   Later on, however, she repudiated any indebtedness to him, affirming that he had really borrowed most of his ideas from her, and that actually he had had an impeding effect upon her own teachings. Most non-Christian-Scientists, however, believe that she was greatly indebted to Quimby for her ideas, many writers asserting that she even copied large sections from Quimby's manuscripts, later incorporating this material into *Science and Health*.   The "official" Christian Science view is that Quimby was a "mesmerist" healer,

and that Mrs. Patterson gave him some of his best ideas. Sibyl
Wilbur, the "official" biographer of Mary Baker Eddy, questions
the existence of any original Quimby manuscripts.[3] On the other
hand, opponents of Christian Science, including George A. Quimby, Phineas's son, maintain that there were manuscripts written
by Phineas Quimby, and that Mrs. Patterson made liberal use of
them. In fact, in 1921 Horatio W. Dresser published a book ed-
ited by him, entitled *The Quimby Manuscripts*, which contained
correspondence between Mr. Phineas Quimby and his patients,
and also the Quimby manuscripts whose existence had been
questioned.[4] People have found a great many parallels between
Quimby's writings and Mrs. Eddy's *Science and Health*. Note, for
example, the following statement: "We may say at once that, as
far as the thought is concerned, *Science and Health* is practically
all Quimby."[5]

It will be rather obvious to any unbiased observer that Mrs.
Eddy owed many of her ideas to Phineas Quimby. Quimby spoke
of his system as "the Science of the Christ"; Mrs. Eddy called
her system *Christian Science*.[6] Mrs. Eddy certainly got from
Quimby her emphasis on healing by opposing "truth to error."
It must also be admitted, of course, that Mrs. Eddy went considerably beyond Quimby. The latter had no intention of founding
a separate religious movement.[7]

Phineas Quimby died in January of 1866. On February 1 of

---

[3] *The Life of Mary Baker Eddy* (New York: Concord, 1908), p. 104, 105.

[4] A copy of this rare volume, published in New York by T. Y. Crowell, and comprising 440 pages, can be found in the library of Union Theological Seminary in New York City.

[5] Ernest Sutherland Bates and John V. Dittemore, *Mary Baker Eddy: The Truth and the Tradition* (New York: Knopf, 1932), p. 156.

[6] Walter R. Martin and Norman H. Klann, *The Christian Science Myth* (Grand Rapids: Zondervan, 1955), p. 14. The authors add in a footnote that Quimby even called his system *Christian Science* some years before Mrs. Eddy adopted the name, referring to p. 388 of the *Quimby Manuscripts*. Bates and Dittemore give the exact quotation from Quimby containing the words "Christian Science," and the date when these words were written: Feb., 1863 (*op. cit.*, p. 157, n. 6).

[7] It should be added here that, according to Christian Scientists, what Mrs. Eddy may have borrowed from Quimby was of superficial value, since her system of religious thought is, in their judgment, basically different from his. See Clifford P. Smith, *Historical Sketches* (Boston: Christian Science Publishing Society, 1941), pp. 45-53. Note also the following statement, from DeWitt John's *Christian Science Way of Life* (Englewood Cliffs: Prentice-Hall, 1962): "To be sure, there are certain superficial resemblances between Christian Science and Quimbyism in certain limited directions (e.g., that there is no intelligence in matter) and also an occasional similarity of terminology (e.g., that sickness is 'error' or 'belief'). But the meaning of the terms is radically different in Christian Science" (p. 152).

that year Mrs. Patterson fell on an icy pavement and was pain-fully injured. Many years later she told the following version of this fall: this injury, she said, had been pronounced fatal by the physicians. On the third day after her fall, however, she opened her Bible to Matthew 9:2-8 (the story of the healing of the para-lytic, including Jesus' words: "Arise, take up thy bed, and go to thy house"). As she read, the healing truth dawned upon her senses; hence she now arose, dressed herself, and was ever afterward in better health than she had enjoyed before.[8] At another time she described Christian Science as a discovery made in February of 1866.[9]

There is some question, however, as to the accuracy of Mrs. Eddy's recollections about this incident. The doctor who attended her at the time, Dr. Alvin M. Cushing of Springfield, Massachu-setts, made an affidavit on August 13, 1904, in which he made the following statement:

> I did not at any time declare, or believe, that there was no hope of Mrs. Patterson's recovery, or that she was in a critical con-dition, and did not at any time say, or believe that she had but three or any other limited number of days to live; and Mrs. Patterson did not suggest, or say, or pretend, or in any way whatever intimate, that on the third day or any other day, of her said illness, she had miraculously recovered or been healed, or that discovering or perceiving the truth or the power employed by Christ to heal the sick, she had, by it, been restored to health.[10]

Further, on February 14, 1866 (hence 13 days after the fall and 10 days after the alleged cure), Mrs. Patterson sent a letter to Julius Dresser, a former pupil of Phineas Quimby, asking him to come and help her since, so she said, "I am slowly failing."[11] It seems quite evident that Mrs. Eddy's memory regarding this incident did not serve her very well.

This event was, however, a turning-point in her life. She now determined to devote her life to emphasizing the healing element of religion. During the next few years Mrs. Patterson (who after

---

[8] Mary Baker Eddy, *Miscellaneous Writings* (Boston, 1896), p. 24. See also *Retrospection and Introspection,* p. 24.

[9] Mary Baker Eddy, *Science and Health with Key to the Scriptures* (Boston, 1934), p. 107.

[10] Bates and Dittemore, *op. cit.,* p. 112. This volume contains the entire text of the affidavit. Dr. Cushing explained that these statements were based upon his own detailed medical records.

[11] The text of the letter is found on p. 109 of Bates and Dittemore's biography. Interestingly enough, though Mrs. Patterson had told Dresser that she was not placing her intelligence in matter, the latter countered, in his reply to her, "If you believe you are failing, then your intelligence is placed in matter" (*ibid.,* p. 110).

her separation from Patterson in 1866 resumed the name of Glover) carried on a growing healing practice, taught others her ideas, and even began to set them down in writing. In 1870, in Lynn, Massachusetts, Mrs. Glover was teaching pupils her system of healing, charging a fee of $300 for a dozen lessons. Though this fee seems high, it must be remembered that, after taking these lessons, one could set himself up as a doctor and charge fees comparable to those of the regular medical practitioners of the day.

In 1875 Mrs. Glover bought a house of her own in Lynn. Also during this year she finished the writing of *Science and Health,* the textbook of Christian Science. Three of her associates helped her get the manuscript into print, since no commercial firm was willing to undertake its publication. Copies of this rare first edition of 1875 are now almost priceless. Also in 1875 the first organization of a society was effected. A small group agreed to contribute regularly in order to rent a public hall; they also employed Mrs. Glover to preach for them on Sundays.

Two years later, in 1877, Mrs. Glover married Asa Gilbert Eddy, a sewing machine agent. Eddy had been the first student of Mrs. Glover to assume the title of "Christian Science Practitioner."

On August 23, 1879, *The Church of Christ* (*Scientist*) was incorporated and was given a charter; hence we may recognize this date as the official beginning of the Christian Science Church. The headquarters of this church were to be in Boston; the purpose of the incorporation was "to transact the business necessary to the worship of God."[12] The Christian Science *Church Manual* states, however, that the purpose of the church was to be: "to commemorate the word and works of our Master, which should reinstate primitive Christianity and its lost element of healing."[13] Mrs. Eddy was appointed on the committee which was to draft the tenets of the Mother Church; after the charter had been obtained, Mrs. Eddy was extended a call to become the pastor of the church.[14]

In 1881 Mrs. Eddy founded the "Massachusetts Metaphysical College" in her home at Lynn. Later she moved this institution to Boston and continued to instruct students there. During these years Mrs. Eddy continued to revise her book and to write other books and magazine articles.

It should be noted here that a retired Unitarian minister by the name of James Henry Wiggin was "literary adviser" to Mrs. Eddy

---

[12] Edwin F. Dakin, *Mrs. Eddy* (New York: Scribner, 1930), p. 151.
[13] P. 17. The edition used is the 89th, copyrighted in 1936.
[14] Note how completely Mrs. Eddy dominated this church from the very beginning.

from 1885 to 1891. Bates and Dittemore quote from an article
in the *New York World* of November 6, 1906, written six years
after Wiggin's death, by Livingston Wright, the former's literary
executor, which contains an account of what Wiggin had told
Wright about his relationship to Mrs. Eddy. Dakin also quotes
from this article, much of which was written in the first person.
Wiggin is here quoted as describing how Mrs. Eddy came to him
with a manuscript of *Science and Health,* asking him to put it into
better literary shape. She did not give him the impression that any
major revision was necessary, but that there were "doubtless a few
things here and there, that would require the assistance of a fresh
mind."[15] Wiggin's reaction to the manuscript, as reported in the
article, was as follows:

> Of all the dissertations a literary helper ever inspected, I do
> not believe one ever saw a treatise to surpass this. The misspell-
> ing, capitalization and punctuation were dreadful, but these
> were not the things that feazed me. It was the thought and the
> general elemental arrangement of the work. There were pas-
> sages that flatly and absolutely contradicted things that had pre-
> ceded, and scattered all through were incorrect references to
> historical and philosophical matters.
> . . . I was convinced that the only way in which I could under-
> take the requested revision would be to begin absolutely at the
> first page and rewrite the whole thing![16]

Wiggin further indicated, according to the *New York World* article,
that he had to rewrite practically every sentence. He found that
Mrs. Eddy knew absolutely nothing of the ancient languages, and
that her English was so poor that he virtually had to revise the
work *in toto.*[17] It would seem, therefore, that Mrs. Eddy was not
only indebted to Quimby for many of her ideas, but that she likewise owed a considerable debt to Wiggin for having put her
thoughts into readable English, and for having corrected many of
her references.

During these years Mrs. Eddy was also engrossed in problems
of organization and administration; she had to make occasional

---

[15] Dakin, *op. cit.,* p. 225.

[16] *Ibid.* Cf. Bates and Dittemore, *op. cit.,* p. 267.

[17] In reply, however, Christian Scientists state that the *New York World*
article is not reliable, since the words attributed by it to Wiggin were
actually Wright's own reconstructions of what Wiggin was reputed to
have said to him some seven years earlier (Robert Peel, *Christian Science:
Its Encounter with American Culture* [New York: Henry Holt, 1958], p.
118, n. 24). They also cite Mrs. Eddy's own statement about her
indebtedness to Wiggin in *Miscellany,* pp. 317-18, where she claims that
she only employed him to improve her grammar and to remove ambiguities
from her writing. It seems difficult to determine exactly how much
Mrs. Eddy owed to Wiggin.

trips to court to defend her interests. Under the stress of these responsibilities, ill health once more overtook her. She now began to attribute her illnesses to the evil influences of her enemies, describing these influences as forms of "malicious animal magnetism."[18] Because her teeth had to be extracted, she resorted to artificial dentures; she also began to wear glasses;[19] and, when her pain would not yield to purely metaphysical healing methods, she used to call in a doctor to administer morphine.[20] She justified her usage of these non-mental measures by various types of arguments. As an example, note the following from *Science and Health*:

> If from an injury or from any cause, a Christian Scientist were seized with pain so violent that he could not treat himself mentally — and the Scientists had failed to relieve him, — the sufferer could call a surgeon who would give him a hypodermic injection, then, when the belief of pain was lulled, he could handle his own case mentally.[21]

In 1882 Mrs. Eddy's third husband, Asa Gilbert Eddy, died from organic heart disease. Mrs. Eddy, however, announced to the newspapers that he had been murdered with arsenic mentally administered by "certain parties here in Boston who had sworn to injure" the Eddys.[22]

In 1886 the National Christian Scientists' Association was organized, indicating that the movement was becoming national in scope. In 1889 Mrs. Eddy retired from the local leadership in Boston and moved to Concord, New Hampshire. In 1892 she organized the Mother Church in Boston, calling it *The First Church of Christ, Scientist.* In her retirement at Concord she continued to revise *Science and Health* and to write extensively. In 1908 she founded the *Christian Science Monitor,* a daily which is still being published, stressing the edifying instead of the seamy

---

18 Or M. A. M. for short. The expression "animal magnetism" was coined by Friedrich Anton Mesmer (1733-1815), an Austrian physician, to describe the hypnotic influence he had on his patients. Mrs. Eddy added the adjective "malicious." It may be noted that the ascription of personal afflictions to the influence of enemies is a trait typical of paranoid personalities, and has affinities with the delusions of persecution which are so common in these personalities.

19 Peel, however (*op. cit.,* p. 95), asserts that she was healed of this eye affliction in later years.

20 Bates and Dittemore give evidence for the fact that Mrs. Eddy was addicted to morphine during part of her life, and that during most of her life she had to battle against "the morphine habit" (*op. cit.,* pp. 41-42, 151, 445).

21 P. 464. Note the interesting suggestion that a hypodermic injection can lull "the belief of pain."

22 From an article in the Boston *Daily Globe* of June 4, 1882, quoted by Bates and Dittemore, *op. cit.,* p. 219.

side of the news. The *Monitor* is, in fact, one of the outstanding
newspapers in the world, noted for the excellence of its reporting
and the wide range of its coverage.

There were troubles toward the end of her life. Augusta Stetson, head of the New York church, was banished from the church
she had built because her growing popularity began to threaten
Mrs. Eddy's supremacy. After some of Mrs. Eddy's pupils had
begun to believe that, if one became sufficiently spiritual, it would
be possible to conceive a child without the help of a man, one
of these disciples, Mrs. Josephine Woodbury, claimed that a child
born to her in 1890 had been virginally conceived. This claim —
which, needless to say, was played up by the newspapers — so em-
barrassed Mrs. Eddy that she eventually had Mrs. Woodbury ex-
communicated. When, after this excommunication, the child in
question, who had been named "the Prince of Peace," tried to
attend the Christian Science Sunday school, he was "lifted up by
his coat-collar and bodily thrown out"![23]

On December 3, 1910, Mrs. Eddy, who had taught that there
is no death, quietly "passed on." Dakin relates the following
conversation which took place shortly before her death between
Mrs. Eddy and one of her closest associates, Adam Dickey: "If
I should ever leave here, will you promise me that you will say
that I was mentally murdered?" "Yes, Mother."[24]

THE CHRISTIAN SCIENCE CHURCH

Since Mrs. Eddy's death, control of the Christian Science denomination has been vested in a self-perpetuating Board of Directors, the first members of which had been appointed by Mrs.
Eddy herself. The rules whereby the church is governed, plus
a number of by-laws, are found in the *Church Manual,* written by
Mrs. Eddy. Mrs. Eddy had incorporated into the *Church Manual* the stipulation that with respect to these rules nothing could
be adopted, amended, or annulled without the written consent of
the Leader.[25] Thus her control as long as she lived was complete,
and, since she cannot now give written consent to any change, it
is impossible to alter the rules of the church in any way today.
The Christian Science Church is therefore a highly authoritarian
organization. There have been a number of individuals within
the denomination who have resented this authoritarian control
and have pleaded for greater liberty, both in the areas of church

[23] Bates and Dittemore, *op. cit.,* p. 364-67.
[24] *Op. cit.,* pp. 504-505. Dakin is quoting from Dickey's *Memoirs of
Mary Baker Eddy.*
[25] Article 35, Sec. 3, of the 89th edition (p. 105).

government and teaching; they, however, have either stepped out of the church voluntarily or have been forced out.

Though at first Mrs. Eddy used to preach at the services, in 1895 she promulgated a by-law which "ordained the Bible and *Science and Health* as pastor on this planet of all the churches of the Christian Science denomination."[26] This means that at the present time no sermon is preached in Christian Science services. Prescribed portions of Scripture are read by the Second Reader; these are followed by the reading of correlative passages from *Science and Health* by the First Reader. The same lesson is read on a particular Sunday in every Christian Science Church the world around. Some Christian Science hymns are sung, and there is usually a selection by a soloist. There is also a period of silent prayer and the audible repetition of the Lord's Prayer — the latter, however, is followed by a quotation from *Science and Health* (pp. 16 and 17), giving Mrs. Eddy's interpretation of the "spiritual sense" of this prayer.

A Board of Lectureship has been set up; each church is expected to call for a lecturer at least once a year. Lecturers must send copies of their lectures to the clerk of the Mother Church before delivery. A Committee on Publication functions for the Mother Church in each state and in Canada for the purpose of correcting false or misleading statements in the public press concerning Christian Science or its founder. Christian Scientists are not permitted to buy from publishers or bookstores who have on sale "obnoxious books" — meaning books which are unfavorable to Christian Science. At times the church has attempted to suppress the sale of books which are unfavorable to it or to its founder. Every branch church is expected to maintain a reading room where one may read, buy, or borrow authorized Christian Science literature. The closest equivalents to the ordained pastors of Protestantism in the Christian Science Church are the practitioners: people who have received instruction in Christian Science and who devote their full time to the practice of its healing methods. Wednesday evening meetings at Christian Science churches are "testimony meetings," at which people testify about their healings.

The Christian Science Church has not experienced as rapid a growth as have the Mormons, the Seventh-day Adventists, or the Jehovah's Witnesses. One of the difficulties we encounter in attempting to assess the size of the Christian Science Church is that

---

[26] Charles S. Braden, *These Also Believe* (New York: Macmillan, 1960), p. 196. This rule, in modified form, is found in Article 14, Sec. 1, of the *Church Manual* (p. 58).

a provision of the Church Manual prohibits the numbering of members for publication. Christian Scientists are not averse, however, to publishing statistics about the number of their churches. In a letter to the author from the manager of Committees on Publication of the Mother Church in Boston, dated September 6, 1962, the total number of Christian Science churches and societies is given as 3,284. Societies are groups of Christian Scientists not large enough or strong enough to be organized as churches. From Mr. Frank A. Salisbury, local Christian Science practitioner and assistant Committee on Publication in Grand Rapids, Michigan, through whose kindness the above-mentioned letter was obtained, it was learned that Christian Science churches vary in size all the way from perhaps 1500 members in the larger cities to 50 or less in the smaller towns. It will be noted that this number of churches is considerably less than the 13,369 churches listed in the 1962 Seventh-day Adventist *Yearbook,* or the 21,557 congregations listed by Jehovah's Witnesses in the January 1, 1962, issue of the *Watchtower.* Though it is difficult to know exactly what these figures mean in terms of total membership, it seems quite obvious that Christian Science has not grown as rapidly as have the Seventh-day Adventists or the Jehovah's Witnesses. In this connection it may be recalled that the Seventh-day Adventist denomination began just sixteen years before the Christian Science Church was first incorporated, and that the Jehovah's Witnesses were first incorporated a few years after the latter date.

The total number of Christian Science practitioners at the present time, according to the above-mentioned letter, is approximately 8,000, of whom about 1,300 are outside the United States. The *Christian Science Journal* of 1958 listed 9,567 practitioners, whereas the 1931 *Journal* had listed 10,177.[27] It is clear, therefore, that the number of practitioners has been steadily declining since 1931. During this same period, however, the number of churches increased from 2,466 in 1931[28] to 3,284 in 1962.

The geographical distribution of Christian Scientists resembles that of the Mormons in at least one respect: most of the members of both groups are found in the United States. According to the Committee on Publication, about one-third of the Christian Science churches are outside the United States. If we assume that foreign and United States Christian Science Churches do not vary in size, we may conclude that out of every three Christian Scien-

[27] Braden, *Christian Science Today,* p. 271.
[28] *Ibid.,* the figure having been obtained from the 1931 *Christian Science Journal.*

tists in the world, only one would be found outside the United States. If, however, foreign Christian Science Churches are smaller in size, on the average, than United States Churches, the proportion might be three to one or even four to one. In any event, the foreign-United States ratio in the Christian Science denomination is quite the reverse of that which obtains among Seventh-day Adventists and Jehovah's Witnesses (see above, p. 16).

The various churches and societies are listed according to geographical distribution on the pages of the *Christian Science Journal.* From the September, 1962, issue we learn that the foreign country which has the largest number of Christian Science Churches is England. Next come West Germany, Canada, and the combined countries of Australia and New Zealand — each of these, however, has only about one-fourth as many churches as England has. Smaller numbers of Christian Science churches and societies are found in Africa, Asia, South America, and in such European countries as Switzerland, the Netherlands, and France. It appears quite evident that most Christian Scientists are found in English-speaking countries. It is also interesting to note that in the United States the largest number of Christian Science churches and societies in any state is found in California, Los Angeles alone having 45 churches.

From the letter sent by the Publication Committee the following information was also gleaned: Christian Scientists have one central publishing house, the Christian Science Publishing Society in Boston. Besides their daily newspaper, the *Christian Science Monitor,* Christian Scientists publish the following major periodicals: *The Christian Science Journal,* official organ of the Mother Church, published monthly; the *Christian Science Sentinel,* published weekly; *The Herald of Christian Science,* published monthly and quarterly in 11 languages; and the *Christian Science Quarterly,* containing the Bible Lessons. Religious publications include the *Christian Science Hymnal,* as well as other books and pamphlets. Mrs. Eddy's *Science and Health* is now being published in eight languages other than English, the latest translation being into Russian. Various other materials appear in 17 languages other than English.

Christian Scientists maintain a radio program, *The Bible Speaks to You,* which is broadcast regularly over approximately 700 stations in the United States and some 100 outside of the United States. The television series, *How Christian Science Heals,* has been concluded, and a new TV series is in the planning stage.

Two sanatoriums, one on the East Coast and one on the West Coast, are maintained by the Mother Church for those relying solely on Christian Science treatment. The church also maintains a home for elderly Christian Scientists who have faithfully served the denomination over a period of years. In addition, there is an independently owned and operated sanatorium for those with mental difficulties who are relying on Christian Science for healing. Institutional work in prisons, reformatories, and mental hospitals is carried on by the Mother Church locally, and by the branch churches throughout the country.

SOURCE OF AUTHORITY

Again, we begin our discussion of the doctrinal tenets of a cult with the question which is of basic importance: What is the source of authority? Christian Science ostensibly claims to accept the Bible as its final source of authority. On page 497 of *Science and Health* a brief statement of the "important points, or religious tenets" of Christian Science is given. The first of these reads as follows: "As adherents of Truth, we take the inspired Word of the Bible as our sufficient guide to eternal Life." To the same effect are the following affirmations of Mrs. Eddy:

> The Bible has been my only authority. I have had no other guide in "the straight and narrow way" of Truth.[29]
> In following these leadings of scientific revelation, the Bible was my only textbook.[30]

At first hearing, these statements make it appear as if Christian Scientists do not differ from Protestant Christians in acknowledging the Scriptures as their final authority in matters of faith and life. In actual practice, however, Christian Scientists accept the Bible only as interpreted by Mrs. Eddy, whose book, *Science and Health, with Key to the Scriptures,* is really their ultimate source of authority, and is thus placed above the Bible. In proof of this assertion, I advance the following considerations:

(1) *Mrs. Eddy is believed by Christian Scientists to have received her insights through divine revelation.* Christian Scientists accept as gospel truth the following assertion by Mrs. Eddy: "No human pen nor tongue taught me the Science contained in this book, *Science and Health.* . . ."[31] The obvious implication is that she was taught her views by a superhuman source: namely, by God Himself. This conclusion is confirmed by the following statement:

> In the year 1866, I discovered the Christ Science or divine laws of Life, Truth, and Love, and named my discovery Christian Science. God had been graciously preparing me during

[29] *Science and Health,* p. 126.
[30] *Ibid.,* p. 110.
[31] *Ibid.*

many years for the reception of this final revelation of the absolute divine Principle of scientific mental healing.[32]

Above this paragraph Mrs. Eddy placed the following Scriptural
quotation: "But I certify you, brethren, that the gospel which
was preached of me is not after man. For I neither received it
of man, neither was I taught it, but by the revelation of Jesus
Christ." At another place Mrs. Eddy maintained that, in writing
Science and Health, she was only "echoing the harmonies of
heaven":

> I should blush to write of "Science and Health with Key to
> the Scriptures" as I have, were it of human origin, and were I,
> apart from God, its author. But, as I was only a scribe echo-
> ing the harmonies of heaven in divine metaphysics, I cannot
> be super-modest in my estimate of the Christian Science text-
> book.[33]

We note thus at the outset the claim, common to all cults, that the
group in question has access to a source of direct divine revelation.

(2) *Mrs. Eddy's book,* Science and Health, *is recognized by
Christian Scientists as their final authority.* For proof I quote
from *Science and Health*:

> A Christian Scientist requires my work *Science and Health*
> for his textbook, and so do all his students and patients. Why?
> *First*: Because it is the voice of Truth to this age, and contains
> the full statement of Christian Science, or the Science of heal-
> ing through Mind. *Second*: Because it was the first book known,
> containing a thorough statement of Christian Science. Hence
> it gave the first rules for demonstrating this Science, and reg-
> istered the revealed Truth uncontaminated by human hypoth-
> eses.[34]

Note that *Science and Health* is here said to be the *voice of Truth*
and to be *uncontaminated by human hypotheses.* Since Christian
Scientists accept *Science and Health* as true, they must also accept
as true this estimate of the book — an estimate which raises it
far above every other book, including the Bible.

Small wonder, therefore, that Charles S. Braden asserts:

> *Science and Health with Key to the Scriptures* is a second
> scripture to the Christian Scientists. This is seen in the constant
> use made of it, and the authority that is accorded it, equal to or
> greater than the Bible itself, since the true meaning of the latter
> is known only through the interpretation given it in *Science and
> Health.*[35]

---

[32] *Ibid.,* p. 107. Note particularly the expression, *this final revelation.*
[33] *The First Church of Christ, Scientist, and Miscellany* (Boston, 1941),
p. 115.
[34] *Ibid.,* pp. 456-57.
[35] *These Also Believe,* p. 209.

The very fact that Christian Scientists have this book read publicly alongside of the Bible in their Sunday services substantiates Dr. Braden's affirmation.

(3) *The Bible is often said to be in error.* Note first the following significant statement:

> The decisions by vote of Church Councils as to what should and should not be considered Holy Writ; the manifest mistakes in the ancient versions; the thirty thousand different readings in the Old Testament, and the three hundred thousand in the New, — these facts show how a mortal and material sense stole into the divine record, with its own hue darkening to some extent the inspired pages.[36]

Contrast with this the assertion on page 99 of *Science and Health*: "Christian Science is unerring and divine. . . ," and the previously quoted claim that *Science and Health* is uncontaminated by human hypotheses. As Mormons contend that the Bible is full or errors whereas the *Book of Mormon* is errorless (see above, pp. 18-19), so Christian Scientists allege that the Bible has many errors, but that they have a source of authority which is not subject to these human frailties. It is becoming increasingly clear that there is much which various cults have in common!

Let us look at some examples of these supposed errors in Scripture. Christian Scientists believe that the second chapter of Genesis is grossly in error. Taking a leaf from higher criticism, Mrs. Eddy contended that two distinct documents had been used in the writing of the early part of the Book of Genesis: the Elohistic and the Jehovistic.[37] Genesis 1, representing the Elohistic document, describes man as having been created in the image of God; this account of creation is "spiritual" and true. Genesis 2, however, derived from the inferior Jehovistic document, represents man as formed of the dust of the ground; this account of creation is false and in error:

> The Science and truth of the divine creation have been presented in the verses already considered [those of Genesis 1], and now the opposite error, a material view of creation, is to be set forth. The second chapter of Genesis contains a statement of this material view of God and the universe, a statement which is the exact opposite of scientific truth as before recorded.[38]

---

[36] *Science and Health*, p. 139. Note the vagueness of this assertion. We are not told which of the ancient versions had "manifest mistakes," nor of what sort they were. Neither are we given any samples of these variant readings, most of which, as anyone conversant with the facts knows, do not affect the meaning of the passage in question to the slightest degree.

[37] *Ibid.*, p. 523.

[38] *Ibid.*, p. 521.

The Science of the first record proves the falsity of the second. If one is true, the other is false, for they are antagonistic.[39]

Is this addition to His creation [Gen. 2:7] real or unreal? Is it the truth, or is it a lie concerning man and God?

It must be a lie, for God presently curses the ground.[40]

Error, furthermore, is not limited to the Old Testament. In another book Mrs. Eddy says:

To suppose that Jesus did actually anoint the blind man's eyes with his spittle, is as absurd as to think, according to the report of some, that Christian Scientists sit in back-to-back seances with their patients, for the divine power to filter from vertebrae to vertebrae.[41]

(4) *The historical contents of the Bible are said to be unimportant.* Listen to this astounding statement, taken from a report made of one of Mrs. Eddy's sermons: "The material record of the Bible, she said, is no more important to our well-being than the history of Europe and America; but the spiritual application bears upon our eternal life."[42] What is being said here is that the life, death, and resurrection of Jesus Christ, as historical events, are no more important for our spiritual well-being than, say, the defeat of Napoleon by Wellington or the discovery of America by Columbus! Yet no less an authority than the Apostle Paul exclaims: "If Christ hath not been raised, your faith is vain; ye are yet in your sins" (I Cor. 15:17).

(5) *Christian Scientists so completely reinterpret the Bible as to read into it any meaning they wish.* The key to their method of Bible interpretation is found in the following statement of Mrs. Eddy: "The literal rendering of the Scriptures makes them nothing valuable, but often is the foundation of unbelief and hopelessness. The metaphysical rendering is health and peace and hope for all."[43]

Let us note a few examples of these "metaphysical renderings." After citing Genesis 1:1, Mrs. Eddy explains: "This creation consists of the unfolding of spiritual ideas and their identities, which are embraced in the infinite Mind and forever reflected."[44] On Genesis 1:6 ("And God said, Let there be a firmament. . ."), Mrs. Eddy comments as follows: "Spiritual understanding, by which human conception, material sense, is separated from Truth,

---

[39] *Ibid.*, p. 522.

[40] *Ibid.*, p. 524. One wonders, however, where this "lie" came from, and how it came to appear in a book which is supposed to be the "sufficient guide to eternal life," and the "only authority"!

[41] *Miscellaneous Writings* (Boston, 1896), p. 171.

[42] *Ibid.*, p. 170.

[43] *Ibid.*, p. 169.

[44] *Science and Health*, pp. 502-503.

is the firmament."[45]   Genesis 1:9, which reads, "And God said,
Let the waters under the heavens be gathered together unto one
place. . . ," is "officially" interpreted as follows: "Spirit, God,
gathers unformed thoughts into their proper channels, and un-
folds these thoughts, even as he opens the petals of a holy purpose in order that the purpose may appear."[46]   When one pages
through the Glossary found on pages 579-599 of *Science and
Health,* he is regaled by twenty pages of comparable feats of exegetical acrobatics.   It need hardly be added that by means of this
method one can read into Scripture the most fantastic ideas the
human mind can concoct.   One may admire the ingenuity with
which these interpretations are fabricated, but can one call this
listening to Scripture?

We conclude that the Bible is decidedly not Christian Science's
"only authority," but that the writings of Mrs. Eddy, particularly
Science and Health, are for Christian Science what the writings of
Joseph Smith are for Mormonism and the works of Ellen G.
White are for Seventh-day Adventism.   In other words, in Christian Science as well as in these other cults, the opinions of the
cult leader are elevated above the Bible and are recognized as the
supreme source of authority.

DOCTRINES

BASIC DENIALS

On page 27 of *Miscellaneous Writings,* Mrs. Eddy makes the
following statement: "Here also is found the pith of the basal
statement, the cardinal point in Christian Science, that matter and
evil (including all inharmony, sin, disease, death) are *unreal."*
Let us look at these "unrealities" briefly, and see what Christian
Science teaches about them.   There are four of them: matter,
evil, disease, and death.

MATTER

Mrs. Eddy says:
> My first plank in the platform of Christian Science is as fol-
> lows: "There is no life, truth, intelligence, nor substance in mat-
> ter.   All is infinite Mind and its infinite manifestation, for God
> is All-in-all.   Spirit is immortal Truth; matter is mortal error.
> Spirit is the real and eternal; matter is the unreal and temporal."[47]

Christian Science therefore contends that matter does not really
exist.   Matter is defined in the Glossary of *Science and Health*

[45] *Ibid.,* p. 505.
[46] *Ibid.,* p. 506.
[47] *Miscellaneous Writings,* p. 21.

as an illusion, as "the opposite of Truth; the opposite of Spirit; the opposite of God; that of which immortal Mind takes no cognizance; that which mortal mind sees, feels, hears, tastes, and smells only in belief" (p. 591). Mortal mind is defined on the same page as "nothing claiming to be something . . . error creating other errors; a suppositional material sense. . . ." Matter, therefore, has no real existence even in the mind; it is an illusion held by an illusion.

Why is the reality of matter denied? Because matter is the opposite of God, and God is the only real substance (p. 468).[48] When one observes that we learn to know the existence of matter through our senses, Christian Science replies by saying that our senses are deceitful (p. 395), and false; that, in fact, they defraud and lie (p. 489). The corporeal senses, therefore, are "the only source of evil and error" (p. 489).

It apparently never occurred to Mrs. Eddy that by undermining the reliability of the senses she was taking away the foundation for all knowledge, including that taught by Christian Science. If my senses only defraud and lie, the sense of sight with the help of which I read *Science and Health* also defrauds me, and thus I can learn nothing whatever about the truth. Triumphantly Mrs. Eddy explains that astronomical science contradicted the testimony of corporeal sense to the effect that the sun rises and sets while the earth stands still (p. 493); it apparently never occurred to her that Galileo arrived at his new understanding of the workings of the solar system by looking through a telescope with the aid of his corporeal senses!

EVIL AND SIN

For Christian Science evil is nothing (p. 287), unreal (p. 71), an illusion and a false belief (p. 480). Sin, which may in most cases be equated with evil, is a delusion (p. 204), an illusion (p. 494). Note the following statement:

> All reality is in God and His creation. . . . That which He creates is good, and He makes all that is made. Therefore the only reality of sin, sickness, or death is the awful fact that unrealities seem real to human, erring belief, until God strips off their disguise (p. 472).

So there is no such thing as evil or sin.

In answer to the question, "If God made all that was made, and

---

[48] Because most of the quotations and references in the remainder of this chapter will be to *Science and Health,* undesignated page references occurring in this chapter from now on are to this book. Thus (p. 468) following a statement means page 468 in the 1934 ed. of *Science and Health.*

it was good, where did evil originate?" Mrs. Eddy replies: "It never originated or existed as an entity. It is but a false belief."[49]

DISEASE

On this question Mrs. Eddy says: "The cause of all so-called disease is mental, a mortal fear, a mistaken belief or conviction of the necessity and power of ill-health. . ." (p. 377). Disease is an illusion and a delusion (p 348). ". . . The evidence of the senses is not to be accepted in the case of sickness, any more than it is in the case of sin" (p. 386). "Man is never sick, for Mind is not sick and matter cannot be" (p. 393).

Consequently, the cure of sickness for Christian Science is to help a person understand that he is not really sick, that his pain is imaginary, and that his imagined disease is only the result of a false belief.

DEATH

Death is defined in the Glossary of *Science and Health* as follows: "An illusion, the lie of life in matter; the unreal and untrue. . ." (p. 584). The definition continues: "Any material evidence of death is false, for it contradicts the spiritual facts of being." Death is only a "belief" which must finally be conquered by eternal Life (p. 380). Note the following sentences:

> If it is true that man lives, this fact can never change in Science to the opposite belief that man dies. . . . Death is but another phase of the dream that existence can be material. . . . The dream of death must be mastered by Mind here or hereafter. . . . Life is real, and death is the illusion (pp. 427-28).

It is rather embarrassing to Christian Scientists to have it pointed out to them that death still does occur in their ranks. Their position would seem to be that, though man has not yet attained to the state in which he can overcome death, such a state may finally be attained.[50] Mrs. Eddy never provided an official ritual for funerals, though she did provide orders of service for other occasions.

It seems quite surprising, too, that Mrs. Eddy herself apparently did not have enough faith to avoid death. Some of her followers did not think that she had died; Mrs. Augusta Stetson, in fact, wrote a letter in which she indignantly rejected newspaper accounts

---

[49] *Miscellaneous Writings,* p. 45. The questioner is bound to ask at this point, But where did the false belief come from? This point is, needless to say, the Achilles' heel of Christian Science. There simply is no explanation in this system for the universal "false belief" that matter exists.

[50] Bates and Dittemore, *op. cit.,* p. 451.

of her death, declaring in italics, "Mary Baker Eddy never died."[51]
Others looked hopefully for her resurrection.[52] The officers of the
church, however, issued an official statement to the effect that
they did not look for Mrs. Eddy's return to this world.[53]

DOCTRINE OF GOD

THE BEING OF GOD

It is very difficult to form a clear idea of God as He is conceived
of by Mrs. Eddy. In attempting to define God, she often simply
piles up a series of words, without defining any one of them. In
brief we may say that, for Mrs. Eddy and Christian Science,
whatever is good is God, and whatever is not God does not really
exist, though it may seem to exist to erring, mortal mind. God,
to the Christian Scientist, is divine Mind, and Mind is all that truly
exists.[54]

Mrs. Eddy summarizes her views about God in the following
four statements:

1. God is All-in-all.
2. God is good. Good is Mind.
3. God, Spirit, being all, nothing is matter.
4. Life, God, omnipotent good, deny death, evil, sin, disease.

Disease, sin, death, deny good, omnipotent God, Life (p. 113).

God is described on another page as follows: "Divine Principle,
Life, Truth, Love, Soul, Spirit, Mind" (p. 115). God is further
said to be substance, and the only intelligence of the universe, including man (p. 330). On page 331 we are told that, since God
is All-in-all, "nothing possesses reality nor existence except the
divine Mind and His ideas."

All this adds up to a pantheism which is thoroughgoing and all-
embracing: all is God and God is all. All that truly exists is God
and God is Spirit; hence everything that is not spirit does not
exist. When the question is asked whether Mrs. Eddy's God is
personal, it is difficult to give a clear and unambiguous answer.
On the one hand, the descriptions of God so far noted seem to
point to an impersonal principle rather than to a personal being.
In fact, in one place Mrs. Eddy says, "We must learn that God
is infinitely more than a person, or finite form, can contain; that

[51] James Snowden, *The Truth About Christian Science* (Philadelphia:
Westminster, 1920), p. 154, n. 1.
[52] Dakin, *op. cit.*, p. 520.
[53] Bates and Dittemore, *op. cit.*, p. 451.
[54] It is to be observed that whenever words like mind, truth, love, soul,
and the like, are capitalized in *Science and Health,* they refer to the
deity; whereas when such words are uncapitalized, they do not.

God is a divine *Whole,* and *All,* an all-pervading intelligence and Love, a divine, infinite Principle. . . ."[55] In *Science and Health,* however, she affirms, "God is individual and personal in a scientific sense, but not in any anthropomorphic sense" (pp. 336-37). Again, on another page, she says, "If the term personality, as applied to God, means infinite personality, then God *is* infinite *Person,* — in the sense of infinite personality, but not in the lower sense" (p. 116).   Braden concludes that Mrs. Eddy "oscillates continually between the personal and impersonal thought of God."[56] Though this may appear so when one compares various of her statements about God, the basic thrust of her God-concept is, however, definitely impersonal. For a God who is not above His universe but is identified with it as the All cannot be a truly personal God. This point will become more evident as we shall discuss, later in this chapter, the works of God.

Christian Science repudiates the orthodox Trinity. We read in *Science and Health:* "The theory of three persons in one God (that is, a personal Trinity or Tri-unity) suggests polytheism, rather than the one ever-present I AM" (p. 256). Though Mrs. Eddy thus denied the tri-personality of God, she apparently felt compelled to make certain concessions to the Trinitarian conception:

> Life, Truth, and Love constitute the triune Person called God, — that is, the triply divine Principle, Love. They represent a trinity in unity, three in one, — the same in essence, though multiform in office: God the Father-Mother; Christ the spiritual idea of sonship; divine Science or the Holy Comforter.[57] These three express in divine Science the threefold, essential nature of the infinite (pp. 331-32).

It should be quite evident that Mrs. Eddy's Trinity bears no more resemblance to the Trinity of the Scriptures than does that of Georg Wilhelm Hegel, for whom the Trinity was but a pictorial way of representing the impersonal Absolute, and the movement of the Absolute from thesis through antithesis to synthesis.

Reference has previously been made to the distinction Mrs. Eddy makes between the so-called Elohistic and Jehovistic documents presumed to underlie the Book of Genesis (above, p. 184). It is significant to note that this distinction between the names of

---

[55] *Miscellaneous Writings,* p. 16. Cf. the following statement from *Science and Health:* ". . . To reach his [Jesus'] example and to test its unerring Science . . . a better understanding of God as divine Principle, Love, rather than personality or the man Jesus, is required" (p. 473).

[56] *These Also Believe,* p. 202.

[57] Note that here Mrs. Eddy equates Christian Science with the third "person" of the Trinity!

God is applied by her to two distinct God-concepts. Elohim, so she asserts, is the name of the one Spirit or intelligence who is the true God (p. 591). Jehovah, however, is the name of the God "of limited Hebrew faith";[58] in *Science and Health* she says, "The Jewish tribal Jehovah was a man-projected God, liable to wrath, repentance, and human changeableness" (p. 140). In Chapter 2 it was shown that this distinction is completely untenable, since in many passages in the Hebrew Bible the two names, Jehovah and Elohim, occur side by side (see above, p. 44, n. 85). In blissful ignorance of the fact that the Hebrew of Psalm 23:1 reads, "Jehovah [*Yahweh*] is my shepherd," Mrs. Eddy renders the verse: "Divine love is my shepherd," thus equating the Jewish tribal Jehovah of limited Hebrew faith with Divine love! (p. 578).

THE WORKS OF GOD

Decrees. It is quite obvious that a God who is identified with all that exists cannot be said to foreordain what comes to pass, since he has no existence apart from the universe. Accordingly, we find that Christian Science totally repudiates the Biblical teaching that God has foreordained all that happens, including the faith of His people. In her autobiographical volume, *Retrospection and Introspection,* Mrs. Eddy tells how, while she was in her teens, the doctrine of unconditional election or predestination greatly troubled her. She further relates that her worries about this doctrine made her ill, that her father kept stressing this doctrine and others which she disliked, but that her mother bade her lean on God's love. Soon her fever was gone and, so she continues, "the 'horrible decree' of predestination — as John Calvin rightly called his own tenet — forever lost its power over me."[59]

We are therefore not surprised to find her referring, in *Science and Health,* to "the practically rejected doctrine of the predestination of souls to damnation or salvation" (p. 150). Elsewhere, referring to another teaching which she rejects, she says, "This teaching is even more pernicious than the old doctrine of foreordination, — the election of a few to be saved, while the rest are damned. . ."

---

[58] *Unity of Good* (Boston, 1936), p. 14.
[59] Pp. 13-14 (Boston, 1920). It should be noted at this point that what Calvin called a "horrible decree" (*decretum horribile*) in *Inst.* III, 23, 7 is not the decree of predestination (which he elsewhere calls a most useful doctrine and one with very sweet fruit, III, 21, 1), but the decree that Adam's fall involved his descendants in eternal death. Calvin insists that this latter decree is by no means the only decree God made.

(p. 38). In another book Mrs. Eddy denies that God either foreknew or foreordained evil, since evil does not exist.[60]

There is, then, no foreordination or predestination in Christian Science. The following statement, in fact, has universalistic overtones:

> "Which were born, not of blood, nor of the will of the flesh."
> This passage refers to man's primal, spiritual existence, created
> neither from dust nor carnal desire. . . . The apostle indicates no
> personal plan of a personal Jehovah, partial and finite; but the
> possibility of all finding their place in God's great love, the
> eternal heritage of the Elohim, His sons and daughters.[61]

Creation. Granted the Christian Science view of God, it is not possible to arrive at a real doctrine of creation. For if there is no such thing as matter, God cannot have called a material universe into being. If time is considered equivalent to matter and error (p. 595), there can be no such thing as a creation in time. And if all is God, this *all* cannot have been created by God, since God has no existence apart from the all.

This is precisely what we find as we peruse Christian Science writings. Matter, as has been seen, does not exist. The existence of a realm of spiritual beings, ordinarily called angels and demons, is also denied. Angels, it is said, are simply "God's thoughts passing to man" (p. 581). The devil, it is said, is "evil; a lie; error" (p. 584); thus his existence as a personal being is rejected. Similarly, the existence of demons is denied; Mrs. Eddy speaks of "the wicked endeavors of suppositional demons,"[62] and in *Pulpit and Press* she quotes, apparently with approval, a passage from a Christian Science sermon which speaks of "the demons of evil thought."[63]

If there is no material universe, and if there are no angels or demons, what is left to form a possible object for creation? One might reply, man. But man, it will be recalled, has no body — since the body is material and matter does not exist. How about the souls of men? The word *souls*, we are told, must never be used in the plural:

> The term *souls* or *spirits* is as improper as the term *gods*. Soul
> or Spirit signifies Deity and nothing else. There is no finite soul
> nor spirit. Soul or Spirit means only one Mind, and cannot be
> rendered in the plural (p. 466).

---

[60] *Unity of Good*, p. 19.
[61] *Miscellaneous Writings*, p. 182.
[62] *Ibid.*, p. 19.
[63] P. 29 (Boston, 1923). The minister was Judge Hanna, then pastor of the Boston Church. Cf. *Science and Health*, p. 79: "Jesus cast out evil spirits, or false beliefs."

If, however, there is no finite soul, and if Soul simply signifies Deity, it follows that man's soul was never created, but always existed. For God always existed, and man's Soul is equivalent to Deity. This point is, in fact, specifically stated: ". . . The universe, inclusive of man, is as eternal as God, who is its divine immortal Principle" (p. 554).

What, then, is creation for Christian Science? A perusal of Mrs. Eddy's commentary on Genesis (*Science and Health,* pp. 501-557) will reveal that she understands the creation narrative found in the first chapter of Genesis as referring simply to the unfolding of thoughts in the mind of God. Her comment on Genesis 1:1 has already been referred to: "This creation consists of the unfolding of spiritual ideas and their identities, which are embraced in the infinite Mind and forever reflected" (p. 503). We have also noted previously that the firmament of verse 6 is interpreted by her as meaning "spiritual understanding," and that the gathering together of the waters in verse 9 designates, for her, the gathering of unformed thoughts.[64] The dry land mentioned in verse 10 "illustrates the absolute formations instituted by Mind," whereas the water mentioned in this same verse "symbolizes the elements of Mind" (p. 507). When the 14th verse reports, "And God said, Let there be lights in the firmament of the heaven," Mrs. Eddy interprets as follows: "This text gives the idea of the rarefaction of thought as it ascends higher" (p. 509). When the creation of the two great lights is narrated in verse 16, however, the interpretation undergoes a slight shift: "The sun is a metaphorical representation of Soul outside the body, giving existence and intelligence to the universe" (p. 510).[65] On p. 511 we are told that rocks and mountains stand for solid and grand ideas, that animals and mortals represent the gradation of mortal thought,[66] and that fowls that fly above the earth correspond to aspirations soaring beyond and above corporeality (pp. 511-12). In connection with verse 26, where the creation of man in God's image is recorded, Mrs. Eddy writes: "Man is the family name for all ideas, — the sons and daughters of God" (p. 515). And with respect to the command to be fruitful and

---

[64] Pp. 505 and 506. See above, pp. 185-86.

[65] Here Mrs. Eddy has slipped into a "mortal mind" way of thinking. If there is no such thing as body, as she contends, how can Soul be "outside the body"?

[66] But "mortal mind" is defined on p. 571 as "nothing claiming to be something." Are animals and mortals, then, gradations of nothing? Besides, Gen. 1 is supposed to be a "brief, glorious history of spiritual creation," whereas the account which begins with 2:6 is said to be "mortal and material" (p. 521). Why, then, this reference to *mortal thought* in Genesis 1?

multiply (v. 28), the "scientific" interpretation is: "Divine Love blesses its own ideas, and causes them to multiply. . ." (p. 517).

We conclude, therefore, that there is in Christian Science teaching nothing even remotely resembling the Christian doctrine of creation. For Christian Scientists all that truly exists is God. What we ordinarily think of as the material universe is simply the thoughts of God. These thoughts, however, always existed. Thus, for Christian Science, the narrative of creation in Genesis 1 is not a record of God's calling a universe into existence at a certain point of time, but simply an allegorical description of something which had no beginning (see p. 502) and will have no end (see p. 503): the unfolding of the thoughts of God.

Providence. If we go by the sound of the words, it certainly seems as if Christian Scientists believe in the providence of God — that is, in God's continual preservation and government of the universe. "God creates and governs the universe, including man," we read on page 295 of *Science and Health.* When we look up the word *providence* in the concordances to Mrs. Eddy's writings,[67] we find a number of places where the word is used. So, for example, in her autobiography, called *Retrospection and Introspection,* we hear her saying, "Even so was I led into the mazes of divine metaphysics through the gospel of suffering, the providence of God, and the cross of Christ."[68] In her Message to the Mother Church at Boston for 1902, she began by saying, "Beloved brethren, another year of God's loving providence for His people in times of persecution has marked the history of Christian Science."[69] In another of her messages she urged her people to "trust the divine Providence."[70] In *Science and Health,* in fact, she insists that "under divine Providence there can be no accidents" (p. 424).

One of the aspects of divine providence is government. We note in Mrs. Eddy's writings many references to God's government. It is said, for instance, that "to fear sin is to misunderstand the power of Love . . . to doubt His government and distrust His omnipotent care" (p. 231). On another page the following advice is given: "Be firm in your understanding that the divine Mind governs, and that in Science man reflects God's government" (p. 393). We find also frequent reference to God's government of the universe. "The term Science," we are told, "properly under-

---

[67] Two of these concordances have been issued by the Christian Science Church, one to *Science and Health,* and one to works other than *Science and Health.* See bibliography.
[68] P. 30.
[69] *Message for 1902* (Boston, 1930), p. 1.
[70] *Miscellaneous Writings,* p. 320.

stood, refers only to the laws of God and to His government of the universe, inclusive of man" (p. 128). "The universe," it is said, . . . is allied to divine Science as displayed in the everlasting government of the universe" (p. 121). On page 539 the question is indignantly asked, "Has Spirit resigned to matter the government of the universe?"

The other aspect of divine providence usually distinguished is preservation. We find occasional instances in which Mrs. Eddy expresses belief in divine preservation. For example, in *Christian Science versus Pantheism* she says, "God, Spirit, is indeed the preserver of man."[71]

When read at face value, these statements certainly give one the impression that Christian Scientists accept the doctrine of providence as taught by the historic Christian church. However, whenever we see the word God used in Christian Science literature, we must remember the definition of God cited earlier: "God is All-in-all," and the implication of this definition: "nothing possesses reality nor existence except the divine Mind and His ideas" (above, p. 189). If this is so, it is impossible for God to govern or to preserve all, for God Himself is the all that is to be governed or preserved. If, now, we take another look at the statement quoted from page 295 of *Science and Health*, "God creates and governs the universe, including man," we recall that there is, strictly speaking, no doctrine of creation in Christian Science. So the first word used to describe God's activity here, *creates,* does not mean *creates* in the sense that Christians ordinarily understand creation, but means something completely different. The second word used to describe God's action here, however, the word *governs,* also does not at all mean what historic Christianity has always understood by that word. There can be no divine government in Christian Science (in the sense in which this word has usually been understood) since government implies that that which is governed is distinct from that which governs it. But this is precisely what is not the case in Christian Science. If God is all, how can he govern or preserve that which is identical with himself? If God is not a person but a principle, how can he (or it) be said to possess the kind of personal will necessary in one who governs or preserves? We conclude that there is, strictly speaking, no doctrine of divine providence in Christian Science, just as there is no doctrine of creation.

The above discussion illustrates and confirms a point made

[71] P. 4 (Boston, 1926).

by Walter R. Martin in one of his books:[72] one of the most important keys for the understanding of cultism is to keep in mind the fact that cultists use the terminology of orthodox Christianity but pour into it a completely different meaning. We have noted how Christian Scientists do this in their usage of such terms as God, the Trinity, creation, and providence. We shall see more examples of this deceptive technique as we go along. The important lesson to be learned from this is that we may never assume, when a cultist uses a theological expression which sounds familiar, that he means by it what historic Christianity has always meant by it. One must always go beneath the word used to the concept for which it stands, if one would understand what the cultist is saying.

DOCTRINE OF MAN

According to Christian Science teaching, man has not fallen into sin; hence we cannot employ the customary distinction between man in his original state, and man in the state of sin. Accordingly, our subdivisions here will differ from those previously used.

THE CONSTITUTIONAL NATURE OF MAN

Man Has No Body. As we have seen, for Christian Scientists matter does not exist. This means that man has no body; the common belief that we have bodies is simply an error of mortal mind. "Spirit is God, and man is His image and likeness. Therefore man is not material; he is spiritual."[73] A more complete statement of this point is found in *Science and Health*:

> Man is not matter; he is not made up of brain, blood, bones, and other material elements. The Scriptures inform us that man is made in the image and likeness of God. Matter is not that likeness. . . . Man is spiritual and perfect. . . . He is . . . the reflection of God, or Mind, and therefore is eternal; that which has no separate mind from God; that which has not a single quality underived from Deity; that which possesses no life, intelligence, nor creative power of his own, but reflects spiritually all that belongs to his Maker (p. 475).

According to the above, man is not material in any sense; he has no bones, no blood, no material elements whatsoever. One may counter at this point: But does not the Bible say that man was formed from the dust of the ground? Christian Scientists reply that the verse which so describes man's formation (Gen. 2:7)

---

[72] *The Christian and the Cults* (Grand Rapids: Zondervan, 1956), pp. 44-54.
[73] *Miscellaneous Writings,* p. 21.

is taken from the inferior Jehovistic document, so that this account of creation is therefore false and in error (see above, p. 184). No Christian Scientist, therefore, believes that man was made from the dust: "The belief that life can be in matter or soul in body, and that man springs from dust or from an egg, is the result of the mortal error which Christ, or Truth, destroys . . ." (p. 485).

The Image of God. Genesis 1, however, which according to Mrs. Eddy is the true, spiritual account of creation, pictures man as having been made in the image of God. What, now, do Christian Scientists understand by the image of God? That man is the image and reflection of God, particularly in the fact that he is spirit, not matter.

> Jesus taught but one God, one Spirit, who makes man in the image and likeness of Himself, — of Spirit, not of matter. Man reflects infinite Truth, Life, and Love. The nature of man, thus understood, includes all that is implied by the terms "image" and "likeness" as used in Scripture (p. 94).

> If the material body is man, he is a portion of matter, or dust. On the contrary, man is the image and likeness of Spirit; and the belief that there is Soul in sense or Life in matter obtains in mortals, *alias* mortal mind, to which the apostle refers when he says that we must "put off the old man" (p. 172).

> The Scriptures inform us that man is made in the image and likeness of God. Matter is not that likeness. The likeness of Spirit cannot be so unlike Spirit (p. 475).

Summarizing, the constitutional nature of man, according to Christian Science, is that man is only spirit or soul, and that he has no material body. "The great mistake of mortals," says Mrs. Eddy, "is to suppose that man, God's image and likeness, is both matter and spirit, both good and evil" (p. 216). On another page, after affirming that Christian Science brings to light the only true God, and man as made in His likeness, she adds, "the opposite belief — that man originates in matter and has beginning and end, that he is both soul and body, both good and evil, both spiritual and material — terminates in discord and mortality, in the error which must be destroyed by Truth" (p. 338).[74]

---

[74] It is interesting to note that Mormons and Christian Scientists arrive at opposite conclusions about the meaning of the image of God. Mormons contend that the term "image of God" applies primarily to man's physical nature, taking issue with those who see in it a reference to man's spiritual nature (see above, pp. 48-49). Christian Scientists, on the other hand, see in the expression a repudiation of man's physical, bodily existence. Both interpretations are erroneous. For a thorough and competent recent study of the concept, the reader is referred to G. C. Berkouwer's *Man, the Image of God* (Eerdmans, 1962).

THE SINLESSNESS OF MAN

The Fall of Man Denied. Christian Scientists deny that man has ever fallen into sin. "If man was once perfect but has now lost his perfection, then mortals have never beheld in man the reflex image of God" (p. 259). "In Science there is no fallen state of being; for therein is no inverted image of God. . . ."[75] What, then, do Christian Scientists do with the Biblical story of the fall recorded in Genesis 3? To begin with, they ascribe the fall narrative to a portion of Genesis which is said to be a myth (p. 530), and a history of error (p. 530). Further, they completely allegorize the account of the fall. Adam, for them, does not designate a historical person, but is a synonym for error, and stands for a belief of material mind (p. 529). Eve stands for "a finite belief concerning life, substance, and intelligence in matter" (p. 585). The serpent is at one time identified with corporeal sense (p. 533), and at another time interpreted as standing for "a lie . . . the first claim that sin, sickness, and death are the realities of life" (p. 594). The tree of life is explained as being "significant of eternal reality or being" (p. 538); whereas the tree of knowledge is said to typify unreality (p. 538). The fall, therefore, for Christian Science, was not a historical event; the Biblical narrative of it is simply an allegory picturing what is unreal and untrue in contrast to what is real and true — namely, the sinlessness of man. Their position is well summarized in the following words: "Whatever indicates the fall of man . . . is the Adam-dream, which is neither Mind nor man, for it is not begotten of the Father" (p. 282).

Man's Sinfulness Denied. Not only do Christian Scientists deny what theologians call original sin, however; they deny the existence of all sin, actual as well as original. For them there is no such thing as sin or evil. "Here also is found . . . the cardinal point in Christian Science, that matter and evil (including all inharmony, sin, disease, death) are *unreal.*"[76] ". . . Evil is naught, and good only is reality."[77] "Man is incapable of sin, sickness, and death. The real man cannot depart from holiness. . ." (p. 475).

When, therefore, we think we sin, or see someone else sin, we are simply the victims of an illusion: the illusion of mortal mind. Where mortal mind, which reveals its presence universally, comes from, however, Christian Scientists do not tell us. It cannot come from the fall of man, for there never was a fall. The persistence of mortal mind and of mortal thinking is one

---

[75] *No and Yes* (Boston, 1936), p. 17.
[76] *Miscellaneous Writings*, p. 27.
[77] *Unity of Good*, p. 21.

of the greatest mysteries in Christian Science. If all is God and God is all, mortal mind simply should not be — and yet it is!

Man Identified with God. We have already noted that, according to Mrs. Eddy, man "has no separate mind from God" (p. 475). This means that man is actually a part of God — which is already implied in their basic premise, "Whatever is, is God." We may say that, insofar as man is real, he is God; insofar as he is not God, he does not really exist. "The Science of being reveals man as perfect, even as the Father is perfect, because the Soul, or Mind, of the spiritual man is God, the divine Principle of all being. . ." (p. 302). "According to divine Science, man is in a degree as perfect as the Mind that forms him" (p. 337). So far is this identity carried that it is even said that whatever God can do, man can do: "Man is God's image and likeness; whatever is possible to God, is possible to man *as God's reflection.*"[78]

One wonders on what legitimate basis a Christian Scientist could distinguish between man as he understands him and God. Since God and man are equal, why should God be exalted above man? Christian Science, by equating man and God, completely wipes away the distinction between the creature and the Creator.

THE TIMELESSNESS OF MAN

It has become customary in Christian theology to distinguish between God as the timeless one and man as a creature subject to the limitations of time. This distinction, however, does not hold in Christian Science. Man himself is a timeless being. In connection with the doctrine of creation we noted that man had no beginning in time; his soul is identical with Soul with a capital letter, which signifies deity — hence man is as eternal as God. This point is specifically stated on page 79 of *Miscellaneous Writings*: "The spiritual man is that perfect and unfallen likeness, coexistent and coeternal with God." Note also these words from *Science and Health*: ". . . Let us remember that harmonious and immortal man has existed forever, and is always beyond and above the mortal illusion of any life, substance, and intelligence as existent in matter" (p. 302).

This means that man's birth was not a real occurrence, but only an illusion. "The belief that life can be in matter or soul in body, and that man springs from . . . an egg, is the result of . . . mortal error" (p. 485). "Can there be any birth or death for

[78] *Miscellaneous Writings*, p. 183.

man, the spiritual image and likeness of God?" (p. 206). "It [Christian Science] brings to light the only living and true God and man as made in His likeness; whereas the opposite belief — that man originates in matter and has beginning and end . . . — terminates in discord and mortality, in the error which must be destroyed by Truth" (p. 338).[79]

So, for Christian Science, the real man is not the person who was born at such and such a time and who dies on such and such a day, but someone who is utterly timeless: who has always existed and will always exist. Since death is not real, as we have seen, there is no point at which man ceases to exist. Man had no beginning and will have no end. This man is not a being who can be perceived by ordinary eyes; his existence can only be discerned by faith: Christian Science faith, that is. We conclude that Christian Science, in its anthropology, denies the reality of the body, of sin and the fall, and repudiates man's temporality and finiteness.

DOCTRINE OF CHRIST

THE PERSON OF CHRIST

The Distinction between Jesus and Christ. As is well known, Jesus is the personal name of Christ (Mt. 1:21), whereas Christ is his official name, the name which designates His office (Mt. 16:16). The name Christ is the Greek equivalent of the Hebrew word *mashiach,* meaning *the Anointed One.* These two names frequently occur together in the New Testament, sometimes as Jesus Christ, sometimes as Christ Jesus.

In the first two centuries of the Christian era there were individuals and groups who distinguished sharply between Jesus, thought of as a mere man, and Christ, thought of as a divine spirit who descended upon Jesus at the time of his baptism and then left him again before He died.[80] Christian Scientists, though not at all agreeing with these groups in the way the distinction is made, nevertheless do share with them a sharp distinction between what they call Jesus and what they call Christ. Jesus, for them, was a certain man who lived in Palestine about 1900 years ago, whereas Christ is the name for a certain divine idea.[81]

---

[79] In view of the illusory nature of man's birth, it seems strange that Mrs. Eddy found it necessary to give her students instructions as to the proper way to attend the birth of a new child (p. 463).

[80] For example, the Ebionites, Cerinthus, and certain of the Gnostics. See Reinhold Seeberg, *Textbook of the History of Doctrines,* trans. Chas. Hay (Grand Rapids: Baker, 1954), I, 88, 92, 96-97.

[81] Already at this point we have our problems with this distinction. For, as we have just learned, the real man has no beginning and no end;

Let us look at some of the evidence for this distinction. "The spiritual Christ was infallible; Jesus, as material manhood, was not Christ."[82] "In healing the sick and sinning, Jesus elaborated the fact that the healing effect followed the understanding of the divine Principle and of the Christ-spirit which governed the corporeal Jesus" (p. 141). A more elaborate statement of the distinction is found on p. 473:

> Christ is the ideal Truth, that comes to heal sickness and sin through Christian Science, and attributes all power to God. Jesus is the name of the man who, more than all other men, has presented Christ, the true idea of God. . . . Jesus is the human man, and Christ is the divine idea; hence the duality of Jesus the Christ.

Looking at this distinction a bit more closely, we go on to ask ourselves, Who, then, is Christ — or, more accurately, what, then, is Christ — for Christian Science? He is "the spiritual or true idea of God" (p. 347); "Christ, as the true spiritual idea, is the ideal of God now and forever. . ." (p. 361). So — and this is very important for the understanding of Christian Science Christology — Christ is not a person, but merely an idea.

Who, then, is Jesus? A "human man," as we saw above. Jesus was a man who lived at a certain time. "Remember Jesus, who nearly nineteen centuries ago demonstrated the power of Spirit. . ." (p. 93). "This healing power of Truth must have been far anterior to the period in which Jesus lived" (p. 146). "The corporeal man Jesus was human" (p. 332).[83]

What, now, is the relation between these two: Jesus and Christ? One way of putting this would be to say that the invisible Christ became perceptible in the visible Jesus:

---

neither birth nor death are real. How, then, can Christian Scientists speak of a certain man who lived in Palestine many years ago? Such a statement implies that, in the case of Christ at least, birth and death were real. Further, we have also learned that nothing really exists except the divine Mind and His ideas (above, p. 189). If this is so, the man Jesus could only truly exist as either part of the Divine Mind or as one of God's ideas. But if this is so, what is the difference between the real Jesus and Christ (who is supposed to be a divine idea)? If Christian Scientists were consistent, they should repudiate the very distinction just alluded to. We shall find them maintaining this distinction with great difficulty.

[82] *Miscellaneous Writings,* p. 84.

[83] So far the distinction seems to be somewhat clear: Jesus was a man whereas Christ was an idea or concept. In the Glossary of *Science and Health,* however, we find Mrs. Eddy wreaking havoc with her own distinction, when she tells us that Jesus means "the highest human corporeal concept of the divine idea. . ." (p. 589). Previously Jesus had been defined as a man; now he is only a concept! We see, thus, that the distinction between Jesus and Christ is already breaking down.

The invisible Christ was imperceptible to the so-called personal senses, whereas Jesus appeared as a bodily existence. This dual personality of the unseen and the seen, the spiritual and material, the eternal Christ and the corporeal Jesus manifest in the flesh, continued until the Master's ascension. . . (p. 334).[84]

This does not mean, however, that the invisible Christ was not in the world previous to Jesus' appearance "as a bodily existence." "Throughout all generations both before and after the Christian era, the Christ, as the spiritual idea . . . has come with some measure of power and grace to all prepared to receive Christ, Truth" (p. 333). If Christ was in the world before the Christian era, what, then, did the man Jesus do? "Jesus demonstrated Christ; he proved that Christ is the divine idea of God — the Holy Ghost, or Comforter, revealing the divine Principle, Love, and leading into all truth" (p. 332).[85] At the time of the ascension, we are told, "the human, material concept, or Jesus, disappeared, while the spiritual self, or Christ,[86] continues to exist in the eternal order of divine Science, taking away the sins of the world, as the Christ has always done, even before the human Jesus was incarnate to mortal eyes" (p. 334).

Summing up the relation between Jesus and Christ, Jesus was a man (or a concept) who presented and demonstrated Christ, a divine idea (or a spiritual self). Sometimes it is Jesus who is the person and Christ which is the impersonal idea, and then again it is Jesus which is the impersonal concept and Christ who is the spiritual self. If the going seems a bit rough here, the reader is reminded that this is but a small sample of the difficulty one encounters when he tries to determine exactly what Christian Scientists teach.

Is Jesus still alive? He should be, since, according to Christian Science teaching, there is no death and man has no beginning or end. Yet, in the passage just cited from page 334, Mrs. Eddy says that, at the time of the ascension, "the human, material concept, or Jesus, disappeared." In the light of this statement we must assume that Jesus has simply been annihilated. Mrs. Eddy also denies that the human Jesus was or is eternal (p. 333-34). The only conclusion we can arrive at is that the human Jesus no longer exists. As a matter of fact, we may as well say that, for Christian Science, there never was a Jesus. For Jesus was

---

[84] How could the corporeal Jesus be manifest in the flesh if, as Mrs. Eddy teaches, nothing corporeal really exists?

[85] Here we are told that Christ is the Holy Ghost. Thus further confusion is introduced into Christian Science teaching about the Trinity.

[86] Note that, according to this quotation, Jesus is a concept and Christ is a self, thus completely reversing the definitions previously given!

supposed to have been "a corporeal man"; for Christian science, however, corporeality does not really exist.

A Jesus who has been reduced to such small dimensions could not have been a very important person. That this was so for Mrs. Eddy is conclusively proved by the following statement which she once made in one of her classes:

> If there had never existed such a person as the Galilean Prophet, it would make no difference to me. I should still know that God's spiritual ideal is the only real man in His image and likeness.[87]

The Jesus of Christian Science, therefore, was so insignificant that if he had not lived, it would have made no essential difference! What was important about Jesus was the idea he had. Though Jesus is no more, the idea he presented and demonstrated is still in the world, in the teachings of Christian Science. Christian Science is therefore actually more important than the man Jesus!

The Incarnation and the Virgin Birth. Was there a real incarnation? Did the Word truly become flesh? Since, according to Christian Scientists, there is no such thing as matter, how can they conceive of God's having entered into a material body? We are not surprised to find them flatly denying the possibility of the incarnation: "A portion of God could not enter man; neither could God's fulness be reflected by a single man, else God would be manifestly finite, lose the deific character, and become less than God" (p. 336).

Was Jesus born of a virgin? Yes, says Christian Science, but not in a crassly material way:

> Those instructed in Christian Science have reached the glorious perception that God is the only author of man. The Virgin-mother conceived this idea of God, and gave to her ideal the name of Jesus. . . .
>
> The illumination of Mary's spiritual sense put to silence material law and its order of generation, and brought forth her child by the revelation of Truth, demonstrating God as the Father of man (p. 29).
>
> Jesus was the offspring of Mary's self-conscious communion with God (pp. 29-30).
>
> Mary's conception of him [Jesus] was spiritual . . . (p. 332).

It is admittedly difficult to follow Mrs. Eddy's reasoning here. If we read the first two sentences carefully, we get the impression that what Mary conceived was an idea, rather than a flesh-and-blood son. This position is, however, not consistent with expressions which speak of Jesus as a human man (p. 473) and

---

[87] *The First Church of Christ, Scientist, and Miscellany*, pp. 318-19.

as manifest in the flesh (p. 334). Neither is this position consistent with the distinction between Jesus and Christ. For Christ was supposed to be the divine idea, and Jesus a corporeal man, whereas it now turns out that Jesus was just an idea after all.

The Fallibility of Jesus. Although the Bible teaches the complete sinlessness of our Lord Jesus Christ, Mrs. Eddy contends that Jesus was fallible, deceptive, and in error on certain points. It will be recalled that, according to her, it was only the spiritual Christ who was infallible, since Jesus, as material manhood, was not Christ.[88] Note further the following statements:

> He [Jesus] knew the mortal errors which constitute the material body, and could destroy those errors; but at the time when Jesus felt our infirmities, he had not conquered all the beliefs of the flesh or his sense of material life, nor had he risen to his final demonstration of spiritual power (p. 53).
>
> Sometimes Jesus called a disease by name. . . . These instances show the concessions which Jesus was willing to make to the popular ignorance of spiritual Life-laws (p. 398).
>
> To accommodate himself to immature ideas of spiritual power, — for spirituality was possessed only in a limited degree even by his disciples, — Jesus called the body, which by spiritual power he raised from the grave, "flesh and bones" (p. 313).

Summing up, according to the quotation from page 53, Jesus, while on earth, entertained some "beliefs of the flesh" — which, so Christian Science teaches, are erroneous beliefs; according to the statement from page 398, Jesus deepened "the popular ignorance" instead of removing it; and, according to the assertion found on page 313, Jesus actually told an untruth in order to accommodate himself to his disciples' immature ideas. The Jesus of Christian Science, therefore, was either not sufficiently mature to have overcome erroneous beliefs, or not sufficiently frank to acknowledge his rejection of such beliefs. In other words, he was either the victim of error, or deliberately dishonest and deceptive. Is this the Christ of the Scriptures?

It is highly significant that whenever Jesus and Mrs. Eddy disagree (as, for example, on the matter of the reality of disease), it is Jesus who is wrong and Mrs. Eddy who is right.

The Deity of Jesus. After what has been said, it need hardly be added that Christian Science denies the full deity of Jesus. It will be recalled that he is called a human man, a corporeal man, and so on. The admission of the fallibility of Jesus certainly denies his equality with God. Mrs. Eddy particularly

---

[88] *Miscellaneous Writings*, p. 84.

takes up the question of Jesus' deity on page 361 of *Science and Health*:

> The Christian who believes in the First Commandment is a monotheist. Thus he virtually unites with the Jew's belief in one God, and recognizes that Jesus Christ is not God, as Jesus himself declared, but is the Son of God. This declaration of Jesus, understood, conflicts not at all with another of his sayings: "I and my Father are one," — that is, one in quality, not in quantity. As a drop of water is one with the ocean, a ray of light one with the sun, even so God and man, Father and son, are one in being.

Two things are evident from this quotation. First, Jesus is not considered fully equal to God; the term *Son of God* here is intended to mean something less than full equality with God. Second, insofar as Jesus is here said to be "one in being" with God the Father, he is so in no different way than any one of us is, since, as we have seen, what gives all of us reality is the fact that we are part of God (as the water is part of the ocean). We conclude, therefore, that Christian Science denies the unique deity of Jesus Christ.

Other Doctrines Denied. Nowhere do we see the completely anti-Christian character of Christian Science teaching as clearly as in its doctrine of Christ. Not just *some* but *all* the major elements of the Christology of historic Christianity are repudiated by this group. We have already noted a number of these; let us look at a few more examples.

According to Christian Science, *Jesus did not have a genuine human nature.* Though Mrs. Eddy says that the corporeal man Jesus was human (p. 332), and that Jesus appeared as a bodily existence (p. 334), on another page she explains what this "bodily existence" amounted to: "Wearing in part a human form (that is, as it seemed to mortal view), being conceived by a human mother, Jesus was the mediator between Spirit and the flesh, between Truth and error" (p. 315). Here the humanity of Jesus is first said to have been only partial, and later asserted to have been only a seeming one: "as it seemed to mortal view." Since *mortal mind,* according to the Glossary, is "error creating other errors" (p. 591), we may conclude that *mortal view* is an erroneous view. The thought that Jesus had a human form is, therefore, one of the errors of mortal mind which must be laid aside if we desire to understand the truth.

Further, *Jesus did not really suffer.* Though we are told on page 11 that "Jesus suffered for our sins," we are informed on page 23 that "suffering is an error of sinful sense."

Again, *Jesus did not really die.* "Jesus' students," Mrs.

Eddy tells us, ". . . did not perform many wonderful works, until
they saw him after his crucifixion and learned that he had not
died" (pp. 45-46). Farther down on the same page she speaks
of "Jesus' unchanged physical condition after what seemed to
be death" (p. 46). Jesus' death, therefore, was not real but
only apparent. He was alive all the time he was in the tomb,
doing a very important three days' work, namely, solving the
great problem of being (p. 44). Nevertheless, with a sublime disregard for all the laws of logic, Mrs. Eddy informs us, on page
45, that "our Master fully and finally demonstrated divine Science
in his victory over death and the grave." A stupendous victory
this was: over a death which had never occurred, and over a
grave which never held a dead body!

Jesus did not really arise from the dead. "Our Master," we
read on page 509, "reappeared to his students, — to their apprehension he arose from the grave, — on the third day of his
ascending thought. . . ." Note that he reappeared only to the
apprehension of his students, and that he did so, not on the
third day of his sojourn in the tomb, but on the third day of
his *ascending thought.* If his thought had been ascending for
three days, he was not really dead, and hence this was not really
a resurrection. On page 201 of *Miscellaneous Writings* we find
Mrs. Eddy saying, "When Jesus reproduced his body after its
burial, he revealed the myth or material falsity of evil. . . ."
Whereas the Bible teaches the physical resurrection of Jesus
Christ from the dead, Mrs. Eddy contends that Jesus merely
reproduced his body. Since Jesus' human form, or partial human
form, was only one that seemed to be such to erring, mortal view,
we may conclude that he had no real bodily existence before his
death. The "reproduction" after his burial, therefore, can only
mean that Jesus reproduced for his disciples the appearance of
a body.[89] When we turn to the definition of *resurrection* found
in the Glossary, we read, "Spiritualization of thought; a new and
higher idea of immortality, or spiritual existence; material belief
yielding to spiritual understanding" (p. 593). Spiritualization of
thought, however, is not the resurrection of a dead body; thus this
pivotal doctrine of Biblical Christianity is also flatly denied.

Jesus did not really ascend into heaven. "This dual personality
of . . . the eternal Christ and the corporeal Jesus manifest in
flesh, continued until the Master's ascension, when the human,
material concept, or Jesus, disappeared. . ." (p. 334). According
to this statement, what ascended was not a person but merely

---

[89] But why should he have done this, if one purpose of his ministry, as
Mrs. Eddy maintains, was to reveal the unreality of matter?

an idea: the human concept disappeared. Another explanation
of the ascension tells us: "In his final demonstration, called the
ascension, which closed the earthly record of Jesus, he arose above
the physical knowledge of his disciples, and the material senses
saw him no more" (p. 46). So here the ascension is interpreted
as meaning that the material senses of his disciples no longer
saw him;[90] this was not an ascension into heaven, therefore, but
simply a rising above his disciples' physical knowledge. Still
another interpretation of the ascension is found on the same page:
". . . After his resurrection he [Jesus] proved to the physical
senses that his body was not changed until he himself ascended,
— or, in other words, rose even higher in the understanding of
Spirit, God." The expression, *in other words,* tells us that what
follows is an explanation of what the ascension meant: Christ's
rising higher in the understanding of Spirit. In none of these three
conflicting interpretations of the ascension, however, do we find the
faintest resemblance to the Biblical teaching that Christ actually
went up to heaven in His glorified body; thus this doctrine, too,
is discarded by Christian Scientists.[91]

In summary, Christian Science denies the unity of the Person
of Jesus Christ, Jesus' present existence, the absolute necessity for
Jesus' earthly mission, the incarnation of Christ, the Virgin
birth of Jesus, the sinlessness of Jesus, the full deity of Jesus,
and Jesus' genuine humanity. In addition, they reject Jesus'
suffering, death, physical resurrection, and ascension into heaven.
By what conceivable right, therefore, do the members of this
group still dare to call themselves a church of *Christ?*

THE WORK OF CHRIST

*Jesus did not atone for our sin by shedding his blood on the
cross.* As we have seen, Christian Scientists reject Jesus' genuine
humanity, his suffering, death, and resurrection. One cannot,
therefore, expect to find them teaching that Jesus atoned for our
sin, particularly not since they deny the reality of sin. The
thought that Jesus Christ shed his blood on the cross in order
to pay the debt incurred by our sin must have been particularly

---

[90] This is also a perplexing statement. According to p. 313 Jesus called
the body he had raised from the grave "flesh and bones" only to accommodate himself to the immaturity of his disciples. In other words,
this was not a material body. But now his ascension is said to mean
that the material senses of his disciples no longer saw him whose body
was not really material in the first place!
[91] For Christian Science teaching on the Second Coming of Christ, see the
section dealing with their doctrine of the last things.

abhorrent to Mrs. Eddy, for we find her specifically disavowing
it several times:

> The real atonement — so infinitely beyond the heathen con-
> ception that God requires human blood to propitiate His justice
> and bring His mercy — needs to be understood.[92]
> That God's wrath should be vented upon His beloved Son, is
> divinely unnatural (p. 23).
> One sacrifice, however great, is insufficient to pay the debt of
> sin (p. 23).
> The material blood of Jesus[93] was no more efficacious to cleanse
> from sin when it was shed upon "the accursed tree," than when
> it was flowing in his veins as he went daily about his Father's
> business (p. 25).

The work of Jesus was rather to demonstrate the truth. We
have previously noted that, according to Christian Science teaching, Jesus came to present or to demonstrate a divine idea (*Science
and Health,* pp. 473 and 332). In harmony with this, the
significance of the crucifixion of Jesus is said to be that it
demonstrated affection and goodness: "The efficacy of the crucifixion lay in the practical affection and goodness it demonstrated
for mankind" (p. 24).[94]

Similar statements are made about the sufferings of Jesus:
"It was not to appease the wrath of God, but to show the allness
of Love and the nothingness of hate, sin, and death, that Jesus
suffered."[95] "Was it just for Jesus to suffer? No; but it was
inevitable, for not otherwise could he show us the way and the
power of Truth" (p. 40).

More specifically, *the work of Jesus was to set us an example
of the kind of life we must live.* "Jesus aided in reconciling man
to God by giving man a truer sense of Love . . . and this truer sense
of Love redeems man from the law of matter, sin, and death by
the law of Spirit. . ." (p. 19). "His consummate example was
for the salvation of us all, but only through doing the works which
he did and taught others to do" (p. 51). "Jesus did his work,
and left his glorious career for our example."[96] "Jesus taught

---

[92] *No and Yes,* p. 34.

[93] A peculiar statement, to say the least, by a person who denies that anything material can exist.

[94] We see here the attempt to treat the crucifixion as if it were something
very real when actually, according to Christian Science teaching, it cannot have been real. For if suffering and death are not real, how could
there have been a real crucifixion? The only consistent interpretation
of the above statement, on Christian Science premises, would be to say
that affection and goodness were demonstrated by an illusion.

[95] *No and Yes,* p. 35. It will be recalled, however, that Mrs. Eddy said,
on p. 23 of *Science and Health,* that suffering is "an error of sinful sense."

[96] *Miscellaneous Writings,* p. 212.

the way of Life by demonstration . . ." (p. 25). "He did life's work aright not only in justice to himself, but in mercy to mortals, — to show them how to do theirs, but not to do it for them nor to relieve them of a single responsibility" (p. 18).

Typical of the Christian Science view of Jesus is the description of him as a "Way-shower": "This [his advent in the flesh] accounts for his [Jesus'] struggles in Gethsemane and on Calvary, and this enabled him to be the mediator, or *way-shower,* between God and men" (p. 30). "The Christ-element in the Messiah made him the Way-shower, Truth and Life" (p. 228).

What Christian Scientists therefore stress about Jesus is not his Person, but the impersonal example he set before us and the impersonal truth he represented: "Our heavenly Father, divine Love, demands that all men should follow the example of our Master and his apostles and not merely worship his personality" (p. 40).[97] "Christ is Truth, and Truth is always here, — the impersonal Saviour."[98] It is not the Person of Jesus who saves, but the principle for which he stands. Mrs. Eddy relegates those who still cling to the Person of Jesus to the category of scholasticism: "Scholasticism clings for salvation to the person, instead of to the divine Principle, of the man Jesus. . ." (p. 146).

One could call the Christian Science view of the work of Jesus the *Example* or *Moral Influence* theory of the atonement. Because of the pecularities of Christian Science theology, however, their view of the atonement does not really fit into any previous category. The great difficulty in speaking of the Christian Science view of the atonement is that, for them, sin has no real existence. If this is so, how can one speak of an *atonement* in Christian Science? How can one atone for something which does not exist?

It is clear that Christian Scientists repudiate the teaching which is at the heart of the gospel: that Jesus Christ suffered and died on the cross in order to bear the burden of God's wrath against sin, so that we might be saved through His blood. We are left with a Jesus who was merely an example — an example so impersonal, in fact, that it is the principle for which He stands that saves rather than He Himself. In Christian Science one can get along very well without the Person of Jesus Christ!

DOCTRINE OF SALVATION

Here again we face a real difficulty. How can you speak of a doctrine of salvation in a system which denies that man is in

---

97 Note that here the example of Jesus is not particularly distinguished from that of his apostles. In other words, there appears to be nothing unique about it.

98 *Miscellaneous Writings,* p. 180.

need of salvation? According to Christian Science, man is not a sinner. If sin is not real, and if man has never fallen, what does man need to be saved from? The most common answer Christian Scientists give to this question is: from false beliefs. Yet this is not the whole story, as we shall see. In their teachings on the doctrine of salvation, as in so many other areas, we shall find Christian Scientists hopelessly inconsistent.

We have previously noted that, according to Christian Science, sin and evil have no real existence, but are only illusions (see above, pp. 187-88). In agreement with this view of sin, we read on page 473 of *Science and Health* that Christ "came to destroy the belief of sin." On another page Mrs. Eddy explains how we are to rid ourselves of sin:

> To get rid of sin through Science, is to divest sin of any supposed mind or reality, and never to admit that sin can have intelligence or power, pain or pleasure. You conquer error by denying its verity (p. 339).

On the basis of statements of this sort, sin is just a bad dream, and we must all learn not to believe in bad dreams. Being "saved from sin," therefore, on these terms is simply ceasing to believe that sin has any reality.[99]

Here, too, however, we find Christian Scientists guilty of the grossest inconsistencies and contradictions. We have learned that sin, sickness, and death have no real existence but are illusions, and that man is incapable of sin, sickness, and death. Yet we are also told that the Master "wrought a full salvation from sin, sickness, and death" (p. 39), and that salvation means "sin, sickness, and death destroyed" (p. 593). If we take the last statement seriously, and understand *destroyed* to mean "have no real existence," we are shut up to two possibilities: either everyone possesses salvation (since, according to Christian Science, these three things have no real existence for anybody), or sin, sickness, and death are real after all and are destroyed only for certain people. If the first of these two alternatives is true, the word *salvation* has lost all meaning, being equivalent to mere existence. If the second is true, these three evils do exist in some sense, and Christian Science has lost its main plank.

It is extremely difficult to know exactly what Mrs. Eddy means; she keeps shifting from one position to another, until the reader

---

[99] The implications of this view of sin, when carried to their logical extreme, are appalling. On this basis, one could arise from the most wicked debauchery of which man's heart is capable, and simply brush off his guilt by saying, "There is no such thing as sin!" A more dangerous weapon than this teaching was never handed to depraved mankind!

begins to suffer from intellectual vertigo. If we, however, assume that the latter alternative is true — that sin, sickness, and death do have some kind of relative existence, and that salvation means to be delivered from them — how, then, is one saved from sin in Christian Science? The answer is very simple: one just quits sinning. "The way to escape the misery of sin is to cease sinning. There is no other way" (p. 327).[100] ". . . If the sinner continues to pray and repent, sin[101] and be sorry, he has little part in the atonement, — in the *at-one-ment* with God, — for he lacks the practical repentance, which reforms the heart and enables man to do the will of wisdom" (p. 19).

When one further inquires, however, whether it is not possible in Christian Science to obtain forgiveness for sin, one receives the following answers:

> To remit the penalty due for sin, would be for Truth to pardon error. Escape from punishment is not in accordance with God's government, since justice is the handmaid of mercy (p. 36).

> Does not Science show that sin brings suffering as much today as yesterday? They who sin must suffer.[102] "With what measure ye mete, it shall be measured to you again" (p. 37).

> Justice requires reformation of the sinner. Mercy cancels the debt only when justice approves (p. 22).[103]

We are now so hopelessly trapped in the maze of Christian Science doubletalk that it does not seem as though we shall ever escape. Sin is supposed to be an illusion and a delusion; yet the

---

[100] "To cease sinning" — what can this possibly mean? In view of previous statements about the unreality of sin, does this mean merely: stop thinking you are sinning? If so, one could blithely persist in theft and murder, or whatever else his depraved heart desired. If, however, at this point Mrs. Eddy means: stop doing wrong things, then sin has some reality after all, and the entire structure of Christian Science theology topples to the ground.

[101] "If the sinner continues to sin. . . ." Meaning? How can he continue to do something of which he is incapable? Suppose I have just proved that man, not having wings like a bird, cannot fly. But now, after having proved this, I say, "If man, however, keeps on flying like a bird, he reveals his lack of true spirituality." Such a statement would make as much sense as Mrs. Eddy's affirmation about continuing in sin.

[102] Note how completely nonsensical this statement is, in the light of previous Christian Science teaching that both sin and suffering are unreal: "If one sins" (and to think that you can sin is an error of mortal sense), "one must suffer" (and to think that one can suffer is an error of sinful sense).

[103] It will be recalled that "sinner" is for Christian Scientists an impossible term to apply to man. How can one, now, *reform* a person who is incapable of sin? The term *debt*, in the latter part of the quotation, implies that some real sins have been committed. But there are no real sins, according to Christian Science teaching. How, then, can there be a debt which needs to be canceled?

only way one can avoid suffering and escape the penalty due to sin is to quit sinning! If one takes the last-quoted statements seriously, Christian Science appears to be unspeakably cruel and heartless. It seems to say: Quit your sinning completely, or else suffer the terrible penalties which your sin incurs.

No one need be very perturbed, however, by threatenings of this sort, because he can immediately turn to other pages in *Science and Health* to find statements which sound like this: "All that we term sin, sickness, and death is a mortal belief" (p. 278); "man is incapable of sin, sickness, and death" (p. 475); "sin, sickness, and death must be deemed as devoid of reality as they are of good . . ." (p. 525). So the sin which is said to bring suffering, to involve debt, and to make one liable to punishment, is just a false belief after all, and does not really exist.

We conclude, then, that for Christian Science salvation from sin is accomplished when one ceases to sin, or when one stops believing that there is such a thing as sin. In either event, the death of Christ has nothing to do with salvation; if Christ had never existed, it would have made no real difference. It is thus clear that Christian Science teaching on salvation bears not the slightest resemblance to the soteriology of historic Christianity, and has no right to call itself Christian.

DOCTRINE OF THE CHURCH AND SACRAMENTS

DOCTRINE OF THE CHURCH

In the Glossary of *Science and Health* the church is defined as follows:

> The structure of Truth and Love; whatever rests upon and proceeds from divine Principle.
>
> The Church is that institution, which affords proof of its utility and is found elevating the race, rousing the dormant understanding from material beliefs to the apprehension of spiritual ideas and the demonstration of divine Science, thereby casting out devils, or error, and healing the sick (p. 583).

From this definition it is obvious that, in common with all cults, Christian Science claims to be the only true church, thus implying that all other groups which call themselves churches are false. The position Christian Scientists take on Mrs. Eddy and her textbook already implicitly involves this claim. For, as we saw previously, they contend that Mrs. Eddy received the final revelation of the divine Principle of scientific mental healing (p. 107), and that *Science and Health* is the voice of truth, uncontaminated by human hypotheses (pp. 456-57). If this is so, it must follow that no group outside of Christian Science has or knows the truth.

This point is specifically stated by Mrs. Eddy: "Outside of Christian Science all is vague and hypothetical, the opposite of Truth. . ." (p. 545). Doctrines of churches other than the Christian Science Church are called man-made: Mrs. Eddy speaks of a time to come "when the lethargy of mortals, produced by man-made doctrines, is broken by the demands of divine Science" (p. 38). Note also these words:

> The notion of a material universe is utterly opposed to the theory of man as evolved from Mind. Such fundamental errors send falsity into all human doctrines and conclusions. . . (p. 545).

On the other hand, we are told, it is Christian Science which has brought truth to light: "Christian Science brings to light Truth and its supremacy, universal harmony, the entireness of God, good, and the nothingness of evil" (p. 293). The contrast between Christian Science and all mere "human beliefs" is highlighted in the following quotation:

> Beyond the frail premises of human beliefs, above the loosening grasp of creeds, the demonstration of Christian Mind-healing stands a revealed and practical Science. It is imperious throughout all ages as Christ's revelation of Truth, of Life, and of Love, which remains inviolate for every man to understand and to practice (p. 98).

We are further told that "Christian Science teaches only that which is spiritual and divine, and not human. Christian Science is unerring and Divine; the human sense of things errs because it is human" (p. 99). When Christian Science is, moreover, completely identified with Christianity (p. 372),[104] we are left with no alternative but that of concluding that any group which does not agree with Christian Science is, in its judgment, not genuinely Christian.

It is quite clear that there is in Christian Science, as in Mormonism, no appreciation for the doctrine of the universal church. The only true church, according to them, is the Christian Science Church, all others flounder about in error and in darkness.

DOCTRINE OF THE SACRAMENTS

It could be expected that Christian Scientists would find the sacraments, in which spiritual truths are expressed through material means, rather embarrassing. As a matter of fact, Christian Scientists have simply eliminated the sacraments from their services.

---

[104] "Christian Science and Christianity are one."

Baptism. There is no rite of baptism in Christian Science Churches, either for infants or for adults:

> Christian Science has one faith, one Lord, one baptism; and this faith builds on Spirit, not matter; and this baptism is the purification of mind, — not an ablution of the body, but tears of repentance, an overflowing love, washing away the motives for sin; yea, it is love leaving self for God.[105]

Baptism is therefore defined in the Glossary of *Science and Health* as follows: "Purification by Spirit; submergence in Spirit" (p. 581). Repeating this thought in slightly different words, Mrs. Eddy says elsewhere: "Our baptism is a purification from all error" (p. 35). In Chapter VII of *Miscellaneous Writings* Mrs. Eddy speaks of three senses in which Christian Scientists may be said to receive baptism: the baptism of repentance, the baptism of the Holy Ghost, and the baptism of Spirit;[106] nowhere, however, does she mention water-baptism.

The Lord's Supper. Christian Scientists do not administer the Lord's Supper at their services. They do hold so-called communion services in the branch churches twice a year,[107] but on these occasions neither bread nor wine is served.

Thomas L. Leishman explains the Christian Science position on this point as follows:

> To all Christian Scientists, *Communion* — in thought and in practice — possesses a deep and abiding significance, but, as in the case of baptism, we seek to attain to the *spiritual* meaning of the Eucharist, dispensing with the literal use of sacramental bread and wine, as we dispense with the use of actual baptismal water.[108]

The use of bread and wine, Mrs. Eddy teaches, hinders one from understanding the spiritual sense of the sacrament: "The true sense is spiritually lost, if the sacrament is confined to the use of bread and wine" (p. 32).[109]

Typical of Mrs. Eddy's spiritualizing exegesis is her reinterpretation of the Biblical record of Christ's last supper:

> His followers, sorrowful and silent, anticipating the hour of their Master's betrayal, partook of the heavenly manna, which

---

[105] Mary Baker Eddy, *The People's Idea of God* (Boston, 1936), p. 9.

[106] Pp. 203-205. One wonders why the baptism of Spirit is different from that of the Holy Ghost.

[107] At first, communion services were also held in the Mother Church, but Mrs. Eddy abolished these services in 1908. The reason she gave was: the number of communicants had grown so great that the church could no longer seat them (Dakin, *op. cit.,* p. 505).

[108] *Why I Am a Christian Scientist* (New York: Nelson, 1958), p. 87.

[109] Note that Mrs. Eddy thus arbitrarily removes from the Lord's Supper the very element which makes it a sacrament: the outward and visible material sign.

of old had fed in the wilderness the persecuted followers of Truth. Their bread indeed came down from heaven. It was the great truth of spiritual being, healing the sick and casting out error. Their Master had explained it all before, and now this bread was feeding and sustaining them. They had borne this bread from house to house, *breaking* (explaining) it to others, and now it comforted themselves (p. 33).

For Mrs. Eddy, therefore, the bread of the last supper was the truth of spiritual being, and Jesus' breaking of the bread simply meant that he was explaining his truth to his disciples. The entire Lord's Supper, therefore, is to be understood not in a material but in a spiritual manner:

> Our Eucharist is spiritual communion with the one God. Our bread, "which cometh down from heaven," is Truth. Our cup is the cross. Our wine the inspiration of Love, the draught our Master drank and commended to his followers (p. 35).

What kind of "communion service" do Christian Scientists hold in their branch churches? As was said, no bread or wine is served. At a certain point in the service, however, the congregation is invited to kneel in silent communion.[110] Leishman explains that this period of silent communion is one "during which we seek to realize more fully our union and spiritual relationship with Him, with a view to becoming better Christians — and Christian Scientists."[111]

When this service of silent communion is held, however, Christian Scientists do not commemorate the Last Supper of our Lord, but rather the "morning meal" which Jesus shared with His disciples after His resurrection, on the shore of the Sea of Tiberias.

> What a contrast between our Lord's last supper and his last spiritual breakfast with his disciples in the bright morning hours at the joyful meeting on the shore of the Galilean Sea! . . . This spiritual meeting with our Lord in the dawn of a new light is the morning meal which Christian Scientists commemorate. . . . They celebrate their Lord's victory over death, his probation in the flesh after death, its exemplification of human probation, and his spiritual and final ascension above matter, or the flesh, when he rose out of material sight (p. 35).

We learn from Leishman that it is at the communion service that this "morning meal" is commemorated.[112]

It need hardly be added that a period of silent meditation such as described above, though it may be spiritually helpful, is no

[110] *Church Manual*, p. 126.
[111] *Op. cit.*, p. 91.
[112] *Ibid.*, p. 92.

sacrament. Christ Himself instituted the sacraments for the strengthening of our faith; Christian Scientists, however, do not find them necessary. Once again we have found Mrs. Eddy claiming to be wiser than Jesus Christ Himself.

DOCTRINE OF THE LAST THINGS

In expounding Christian Science teachings about the last things, it is impossible to make the customary distinction between individual eschatology (the soul after death) and general eschatology (events associated with the Second Coming of Christ). For, as we shall see, there is no such thing as general eschatology in Christian Science. It will be recalled that, according to Mrs. Eddy, "nothing possesses reality nor existence except the divine Mind and His ideas" (p. 331). If the universe is thus nothing other than the divine Mind and His ideas, it follows that the universe can have no cataclysmic end or transformation, that history can have no climax, and that things must simply go on and on as they do now (or, rather, appear to go on and on, for in a pantheistic system like Christian Science there can be no real history). Since Jesus, as we have seen, neither really arose from the dead nor really ascended into heaven, he cannot return to earth in a Second Coming. It is obvious, therefore, that there can be no general eschatology in Christian Science teaching.

Christian Scientists do teach a kind of individual eschatology, though in this area, as in all others, their views are radically different from the teachings of historic Christianity.[113] Actually, their chief emphasis is on salvation as a present experience rather than as a future possession:

> "*Now,*" cried the apostle, "is the accepted time; behold, *now* is the day of salvation," — meaning, not that now men must prepare for a future-world salvation, or safety, but that now is the time in which to experience that salvation in spirit and in life (p. 39).

Though this is so, Christian Scientists will grant that salvation cannot be limited to this present life, since there is an existence after this life:

> Man is not annihilated, nor does he lose his identity, by passing through the belief called death. After the momentary belief

---

[113] Customarily, individual eschatology deals with the state of the soul between death and the resurrection. Christian Scientists, however, deny the reality of both death and the resurrection. It is therefore to be expected that their views on man's state after "the change called death" will be in a class by themselves.

of dying passes from mortal mind, this mind is still in a conscious state of existence. . . .[114]

A Time of Probation. Mrs. Eddy teaches that after "the change
called death" there will be a time of probation for everyone. "As
death findeth mortal man, so shall he be after death, until probation and growth shall effect the needed change" (p. 291). We
may not assume, therefore, that death automatically destroys the
illusion that matter, sickness, and sin exist.

> If the change called *death* destroyed the belief in sin, sickness,
> and death, happiness would be won at the moment of dissolu-
> tion, and be forever permanent; but this is not so. Perfection
> is gained only by perfection. . . .
>
> The sin and error which possess us at the instant of death do
> not cease at that moment, but endure until the death of these
> errors (p. 290).[115]

This means, then, that some kind of spiritual progress is
necessary for every man after "the change called death." This
progress is called "growth."

> The period required for this dream of material life, embracing
> its so-called pleasures and pains, to vanish from consciousness,
> "knoweth no man . . . neither the Son, but the Father." This
> period will be of longer or shorter duration according to the
> tenacity of error (p. 77).

We approach death, in other words, with certain errors and sins
which have persisted in our lives, despite our best efforts to root
them out. After we have "died," these errors and sins are still
in our consciousness, so that we must continue to fight against
them. The more tenaciously we have held to these errors and
sins in life, moreover, the longer will be the duration of this battle.
Though on the one hand, therefore, Christian Science minimizes
sin by denying its reality, on the other hand sin is, in its teachings,
so strong, and the salvation from sin which it offers man is so
weak, that man must still fight against sin and error after he
has died! This conception of "salvation" is, however, the in-

---

[114] *Miscellaneous Writings,* p. 42. Note that death is described as a mere
belief, and that "mortal mind" does not die but continues to persist after
the "change called death." Mortal mind is thus possessed of some kind of
immortality.

[115] This quotation well illustrates the "Alice-in-Wonderland" quality of
Christian Science double talk. One of the basic tenets of Christian Science
is that neither death nor matter have any real existence; yet here Mrs. Eddy
speaks of "the moment of dissolution." The bewildered reader is bound to
ask, "Dissolution of what?" It cannot be the body, for there is no body.
Neither can it be the soul, for the soul is part of God. Christian Science
also teaches that sin is an illusion and a false belief. Yet here sin is presented as an illusion so powerful and persistent that it is not banished even
by the "change called death"!

evitable consequence of Christian Science's repudiation of the atoning work of Christ. Both here and hereafter such salvation as they teach is wholly by works and not at all by grace!

A "time of probation" after death is therefore absolutely necessary:

> Man's probation after death is the necessity of his immortality; for good dies not and evil is self-destructive, therefore evil must be mortal and self-destroyed. If man should not progress after death, but should remain in error, he would be inevitably self-annihilated.[116]

If man, then, is not successful in this post-mortem warfare against sin and error, he will be self-annihilated. The only conclusion we can draw from the above statement is that this type of individual will eventually cease to exist. Christian Scientists, therefore, in agreement with Seventh-day Adventists and Jehovah's Witnesses, affirm that those in whom error and sin persists shall not be eternally tormented, but shall be annihilated. The teaching that certain people will be annihilated is, however, in flat contradiction to what Mrs. Eddy said about man's having no end, as he had no beginning (p. 338; see above, pp. 199-200).

What happens if man does continue to progress after "the change called death"? "Those upon whom 'the second death hath no power' are those who progress here and hereafter out of evil, their mortal element, and into good that is immortal; thus laying off the material beliefs that war against Spirit. . . ."[117] People who attain this goal arrive at perfection:

> The sin and error which possess us at the instant of death do not cease at that moment, but endure until the death of these errors. To be wholly spiritual, man must be sinless, and he becomes thus only when he reaches perfection (p. 290).

If a person, then, continues to progress after death, continues to grow out of evil and into good, continues to lay aside material beliefs and renounce mortal errors, he will finally reach perfection. Though elsewhere Mrs. Eddy has told us that man is incapable of sin (p. 475), here she proclaims that man has to *become* sinless, and that he can only reach this state of perfection after death, at the end of a long struggle with sin in the hereafter![118]

There is no Hell. As is evident from their teaching on annihilation, Christian Scientists deny that there is a place called hell.

[116] *Miscellaneous Writings,* p. 2.
[117] *Ibid.*
[118] Note, too, that in all of this discussion about probation after death not a word is said about the saving work of Christ or the help of the Holy Spirit or the grace of God. Surely here is a system of "salvation" from which the last vestige of the gospel of Jesus Christ has been removed!

Hell, in fact, is defined in the Glossary of *Science and Health* as follows: "Mortal belief; error; lust; remorse; hatred; revenge . . . self-imposed agony; effects of sin; that which 'worketh abomination or maketh a lie' " (p. 588).

> I am asked, "Is there a hell?" Yes, there is a hell for all who persist in breaking the Golden Rule or in disobeying the commandments of God. Physical science has sometimes argued that the internal fires of our earth will eventually consume this planet. Christian Science shows that hidden unpunished sin is this internal fire, — even the fire of a guilty conscience. . . . The advanced psychist knows that this hell is mental, not material, and that the Christian has no part in it.[119]

Hell is here identified with the fire of a guilty conscience, and is said to be mental, not material; thus its distinct existence as a place of punishment is denied. Mrs. Eddy sums up her teaching about hell in a single pithy sentence: "Sin makes its own hell, and goodness its own heaven" (p. 196).

There is no Heaven. If hell as a distinct locality is denied, we would expect that heaven would be repudiated as well. And so it is. Heaven is defined in the Glossary as follows: "Harmony, the reign of Spirit; government by divine Principle; spirituality; bliss; the atmosphere of Soul" (p. 587). Harmony or spirituality, needless to say, do not designate a place; if there is a heaven which a Christian Scientist may enjoy, it must be one which he carries along with him. Clear and unambiguous is the following statement: "Heaven is not a locality, but a divine state of Mind in which all the manifestations of Mind are harmonious and immortal, because sin is not there. . ." (p. 291). For Christian Scientists, therefore, both heaven and hell are portable.

There is no Second Coming. At times Mrs. Eddy interprets Biblical references to the Second Coming of Jesus Christ as pointing to the rise of Christian Science: "The second appearing of Jesus is, unquestionably, the spiritual advent of the advancing idea of God, as in Christian Science."[120] In the following quotation this interpretation is made even more explicit:

> It is authentically said that one expositor of Daniel's dates fixed the year 1866 or 1867 for the return of Christ — the return of the spiritual idea to the material earth or antipode of heaven. It is a marked coincidence that those dates were the first two years of my discovery of Christian Science.[121]

---

[119] *The First Church of Christ, Scientist, and Miscellany,* p. 160.
[120] *Retrospection and Introspection,* p. 70.
[121] *The First Church of Christ, Scientist, and Miscellany,* p. 181. Note that the return of Christ is explained as "the return of the spiritual idea to the material earth." Elsewhere, however, she teaches that there is no material earth.

This conception of the Second Coming is consistent with Mrs. Eddy's understanding of Jesus as a man who no longer exists, and of Christ as the divine idea which Jesus most fully represented and demonstrated. To affirm, however, that the second appearance of Jesus coincided with the rise of Christian Science is to make Mrs. Eddy equivalent in importance to Jesus Himself. Again we observe a trait typical of the cult: exalting the human leader to equality with, if not superiority to, Jesus Christ.

At another place, however, a Scripture passage referring to the Second Coming of Christ is construed as pointing to a time apparently still future:

> In Colossians (3:4) Paul writes: 'When Christ, who is our life, shall appear [be manifested], then shall ye also appear [be manifested] with him in glory.' When spiritual being is understood in all its perfection, continuity, and might, then shall man be found in God's image (p. 325).

The future tense of the verb "shall be found" in the above quotation indicates that, in this instance, the second appearance of Christ is understood as having not yet occurred. Whichever of the two above-mentioned interpretations of the Second Coming we accept as being the more typical of Christian Science teaching, however, it is quite clear that Christian Scientists categorically deny the literal return to earth of our glorified Saviour at the end of this age.

There will be no Resurrection of the Body. It will be recalled that Christian Scientists deny Christ's resurrection from the dead (above, p. 206). It will also be recalled that the word *resurrection* is defined in the Glossary of *Science and Health* as meaning "spiritualization of thought . . . material belief yielding to spiritual understanding." We are not surprised, therefore, to read on page 291 of *Science and Health*: "No resurrection from the grave awaits Mind or Life, for the grave has no power over either." Nothing is said in the above quotation about a resurrection which might await the body. But since for Christian Science the body does not really exist, it is obvious that there is no room whatever in Christian Science thinking for the doctrine of the resurrection of the body — a doctrine which has been from the very beginning one of the distinctive marks of Christianity.

There will be no Final Judgment. This cardinal teaching of historic Christian eschatology is also repudiated by Christian Science: "No final judgment awaits mortals, for the judgment-day of wisdom comes hourly and continually, even the judgment by which mortal man is divested of all material error" (p. 291).

There will be no New Heaven and New Earth. On pages 572-

574 of *Science and Health* Mrs. Eddy gives her interpretation of the passage from Revelation 21 which speaks of the new heaven and the new earth. She affirms that this new heaven and new earth cannot be terrestrial or material, but must be spiritual — at least to the illumined, "scientific" consciousness. This point is made unmistakably clear elsewhere:

> In the Apocalypse it is written: 'And I saw a new heaven and a new earth; for the first heaven and the first earth were passed away; and there was no more sea.' In St. John's vision, heaven and earth stand for spiritual ideas. . . (p. 536).

We have thus seen that Christian Science repudiates every major tenet of Christian eschatology: the teaching that at death one's eternal destiny is irrevocably determined, the existence of hell, the existence of heaven, the Second Coming of Christ, the resurrection of the body, the final judgment, and the new heaven and new earth which will usher in the age to come. As was the case in the other areas of doctrine we have considered, so it is in the area of eschatology: Christian Scientists flatly reject every major doctrine of historic Christianity. Christian Scientists, therefore, have no more right to apply to themselves the title *Christian* than have Buddhists or Hindus — with whose teachings, indeed, Christian Science has greater affinity than with those of Christianity. We conclude that, strictly speaking, Christian Science is neither Christian nor a science.

CHAPTER FIVE

Jehovah's Witnesses

HISTORY

CHARLES TAZE RUSSELL

THE HISTORY OF JEHOVAH'S WITNESSES IS VERY CLOSELY TIED IN with the history of the three presidents of the organization who have so far held office. The first of these was Charles Taze Russell (1852-1916).[1] He was born in the town of Allegheny, now part of Pittsburgh, Pennsylvania, on February 16, 1852. His parents were Presbyterians of Scotch-Irish descent. At the age of fifteen Russell was already in partnership with his father, operating a chain of men's clothing stores. By this time he had joined the Congregational Church, finding it more to his liking than the Presbyterian.

Russell was soon troubled, however, by some of the doctrines taught in this church, the doctrines of predestination and eternal punishment giving him particular difficulty. By the time he was seventeen, in fact, he had become an avowed skeptic, discarding

[1] This biographical sketch is based chiefly on material found in two Watchtower publications: *Qualified to be Ministers* (Brooklyn, 1955), pp. 297-312; and *Jehovah's Witnesses in the Divine Purpose* (Brooklyn, 1959), pp. 14-63. Except where otherwise indicated, the information which follows has been gathered from the above-mentioned volumes.

the Bible altogether. He explains how this happened in these
words:

> Brought up a Presbyterian, indoctrinated from the Catechism,
> and being naturally of an inquiring mind, I fell a ready prey
> to the logic of infidelity, as soon as I began to think for myself.
> But that which at first threatened to be the utter shipwreck of
> faith in God and the Bible was, under God's providence, over-
> ruled for good, and merely wrecked my confidence in human
> creeds and systems of Bible misinterpretations.[2]

One day in 1870 he dropped into a dusty, dingy basement hall
near his Allegheny store

> to see if the handful who met there had anything more sensible
> to offer than the creeds of the great churches. There, for the
> first time, I heard something of the views of Second Adventism,
> by Jonas Wendell. . . .
>
> Though his Scripture exposition was not entirely clear, and
> though it was very far from what we now rejoice in, it was
> sufficient, under God, to re-establish my wavering faith in the
> Divine inspiration of the Bible. . . .[3]

His interest in Bible study aroused to fever pitch, Russell now
organized a Bible class of six members who agreed to meet regularly. This group met in Pittsburgh from 1870-1875. Russell and
his associates were disappointed by the Adventist view that
Christ was coming again in the flesh, being convinced that His
Second Coming would be a spiritual or invisible one. Russell
therefore issued a pamphlet entitled *The Object and Manner of
the Lord's Return,* of which some 50,000 copies were published.

In 1876 Russell came into contact with N. H. Barbour of Rochester, New York. Barbour was the leader of a group of disaffected
Adventists who had left that movement because they, like Russell,
believed that the Second Coming of Christ was to be a spiritual,
non-visible one. The Pittsburgh group and the Rochester group
now joined, with the result that the magazine *The Herald of the
Morning,* formerly published by Barbour, became a joint venture.

---

[2] *Watchtower* magazine, 1916, pp. 170-71; quoted in *Jehovah's Witnesses in the Divine Purpose,* p. 14. Note here a typical cult phenomenon:
the rejection of all "human creeds."

[3] *Jehovah's Witnesses in the Divine Purpose,* p. 14. It is important to
note that, by his own admission, it was the Adventists who delivered Russell
from his early skepticism. Though the term "Second Adventism" which is
used in the quotation does not represent any known Adventist denomination,
I conclude, from the similarities which exist between Seventh-day Adventist
doctrines and Jehovah-Witness teachings, that this group was either a Seventh-day Adventist congregation, or a group of Adventists who held doctrines similar to those of Seventh-day Adventism. From the Adventists Russell obviously borrowed such doctrines as the extinction of the soul at
death, the annihilation of the wicked, the denial of hell, and a modified
form of the investigative judgment.

In 1877 Barbour and Russell jointly published a 194-page book entitled *Three Worlds or Plan of Redemption.*

This book set forth their belief that Christ's second presence began invisibly in the fall of 1874 and thereby commenced a forty-year harvest period. Then, remarkably accurately, they set forth the year 1914 as the end of the Gentile times. . . .[4]

In a few years, however, Russell broke with Barbour because the latter began to deny that the death of Christ was the ransom price for Adam and his race. Russell now started a new periodical called *Zion's Watch Tower and Herald of Christ's Presence,* the first issue coming off the press on July 1, 1879.[5]

The new magazine proved to be an important factor in the expansion of the movement. By 1880, for example, some thirty congregations had come into existence in seven states. Zion's Watch Tower Tract Society was established as an unincorporated body in 1881, with Russell as its manager. On December 13, 1884, this Society was granted a legal charter and was organized as a corporation; we may therefore recognize this date as the official beginning of the Jehovah's Witness movement.[6] The purpose of the society, as stated in Article II of the charter, was "the dissemination of Bible truths in various languages by means of the publication of tracts, pamphlets, papers and other religious documents, and by the use of all other lawful means. . . ."[7]

In accordance with this purpose Russell now issued the first of what was eventually to become a 7-volume series of doctrinal books. This first volume, appearing in 1886, was called *The Divine Plan of the Ages.* The entire series, first called *Millennial Dawn,* later came to be called *Studies in the Scriptures.* These books had a wide circulation; over six million copies of the first volume were distributed.

In 1889 the society acquired a building in Allegheny, Pennsylvania, which served as its headquarters for the next twenty years. Russell made his first trip abroad in 1891, and in 1900 the society's

---

[4] *Qualified to be Ministers,* p. 300. It will be noted, therefore, that as early as 1877 Russell specified that Christ had invisibly returned in 1874.

[5] Though at first this magazine was published monthly, in 1892 it began to appear semi-monthly. In 1909 its name was changed to *The Watch Tower and Herald of Christ's Presence;* in 1939 the name became *The Watchtower and Herald of Christ's Kingdom;* later in that same year the title by which it still appears was assumed: *The Watchtower Announcing Jehovah's Kingdom (Jehovah's Witnesses in the Divine Purpose,* p. 21, note m).

[6] Though at first the society went by the above-mentioned name, in 1896 the name was changed to Watch Tower Bible and Tract Society of Pennsylvania (*Qualified to be Ministers,* p. 303).

[7] *Ibid.,* p. 304.

first branch office was established in London.   Soon books and
pamphlets began to be published in languages other than English.
In 1903, while Russell was on a second European tour, a branch
of the society was set up in Germany; in 1904 one was opened in
Australia.

A new avenue of expansion opened up when, in 1908, Joseph
Franklin Rutherford, the society's legal counselor, obtained property for the society in Brooklyn, New York.   In order to hold this
property, the society had to form another corporation; hence in
1909 the People's Pulpit Association of New York was incorporated.[8]

In *Jehovah's Witnesses in the Divine Purpose* it is said that
during the years 1909-1914 Russell's sermons were sent out weekly
to about 3,000 newspapers in the United States, Canada, and
Europe (p. 50).   Martin and Klann, however, in their *Jehovah
of the Watchtower,* give documentary evidence to prove that in
many cases these sermons were never delivered, as reported, in
the places claimed.   From the *Brooklyn Daily Eagle* of February
19, 1912, the authors quote a news story affirming that a sermon
allegedly delivered by Russell in Honolulu on a certain date was
never preached.[9]   On a later page the authors reproduce a photostatic copy of a letter sent to the *Brooklyn Daily Eagle* by a Honolulu editor stating that on the designated day Russell had stopped
in Honolulu for a few hours, but had made no public address.[10]

Martin and Klann also tell how Russell's periodical once adver-
tised so-called "Miracle Wheat" for one dollar a pound, claiming
that it would grow five times as fast as any other brand.   After
the *Brooklyn Daily Eagle* had published a cartoon ridiculing the
"Pastor" and his "miracle wheat," Russell sued the newspaper for
libel.   When this wheat was investigated by government depart-
ments, however, it was found to be, not five times as good as, but
slightly inferior to, ordinary wheat.   Needless to say, the *Eagle*
won the suit.[11]

---

[8] In 1956 the name of this corporation was changed to the one it now
bears: Watchtower Bible and Tract Society of New York, Inc.   There
is also a British corporation, which was formed in 1914, under the name
International Bible Students Association; it has a Brooklyn address as
well as a London address.   The work of the organization is done by
all three of these corporations; it is the Pennsylvania corporation, however, which is the controlling body and which provides the other corporations with financial support (*Jehovah's Witnesses in the Divine Purpose,* pp. 48-49).

[9] Walter R. Martin and Norman H. Klann, *Jehovah of the Watchtower,*
rev. ed. (Grand Rapids: Zondervan, 1959), pp. 15-17.

[10] *Ibid.,* opposite p. 30.

[11] *Ibid.,* p. 14.   The authors quote from the Nov. 1, 1916, issue of the
Daily Eagle, which contained an obituary article about Russell.

It should be mentioned at this point that Russell was married in 1879 to Maria Frances Ackley. No children were born of this union. For many years Mrs. Russell was active in the Watchtower Society, serving as the first secretary-treasurer of the society and for many years as associate editor of the *Watch Tower*. In 1897, however, she and Russell separated. In 1913 Mrs. Russell sued her husband for divorce on the grounds of "his conceit, egotism, domination, and improper conduct in relation to other women."[12]

Russell's appalling egotism is evident from a comment made by him about his *Scripture Studies* series:

> . . . Not only do we find that people cannot see the divine plan in studying the Bible by itself, but we see, also, that if anyone lays the "Scripture Studies" aside, even after he has used them, after he has become familiar with them, after he has read them for ten years — if he then lays them aside and ignores them and goes to the Bible alone, though he has understood his Bible for ten years, our experience shows that within two years he goes into darkness. On the other hand, if he had merely read the "Scripture Studies" with their references and had not read a page of the Bible as such, he would be in the light at the end of two years, because he would have the light of the Scriptures.[13]

Russell, in other words, considered his books so indispensable for the proper understanding of Scripture that without them one would simply remain in spiritual darkness.

In June, 1912, the Rev. Mr. J. J. Ross, pastor of the James Street Baptist Church of Hamilton, Ontario, published a denunciatory pamphlet about Russell entitled *Some Facts about the Self-styled "Pastor," Charles T. Russell*.[14] Russell sued Ross for libel. In the trial, which took place the following year, Russell was proved to be a perjurer. When asked by Attorney Staunton, Ross's lawyer, whether he knew the Greek alphabet, Russell replied, "Oh, yes." When he was further asked to identify the Greek letters on top of a page of the Greek Testament which was handed him, he was unable to do so, finally admitting that he was not familiar

---

[12] Bruce M. Metzger, "The Jehovah's Witnesses and Jesus Christ," *Theology Today*, April, 1953, pp. 65-66. Dr. Metzger refers his readers to Herbert H. Stroup's *The Jehovah's Witnesses* (New York: Columbia University Press, 1945), pp. 9-11, for a more detailed account of the divorce proceedings.

[13] *Watch Tower*, Sept. 15, 1910, p. 298; quoted in Martin and Klann, *op. cit.*, p. 24. See also J. K. Van Baalen's *Chaos of Cults*, 3rd ed.. p. 269, n. 2, where this same passage is quoted from the July, 1957, *Watchtower*.

[14] Martin and Klann, *op. cit.*, p. 18.

with the Greek language.[15]   Russell, furthermore, had previously claimed to have been ordained by a recognized religious body. Staunton also pressed him on this point, finally asking him point-blank, "Now, you never were ordained by a bishop, clergyman, presbytery, council, or any body of men living?"   Russell answered, after a long pause, "I never was."[16]   In this trial, therefore, Russell's deliberate perjury was established beyond doubt, and the real character of the man looked up to by his followers as an inspired religious teacher was clearly revealed.

Russell died on October 31, 1916, while aboard a train near Pampa, Texas, on his way home from a California speaking trip. It is claimed by Jehovah's Witnesses that during his lifetime he traveled more than a million miles, gave more than 30,000 sermons, and wrote books totalling over 50,000 pages.[17]

JOSEPH FRANKLIN RUTHERFORD

On January 6, 1917, Joseph Franklin Rutherford, who had been serving as the society's legal counselor, became the second president of the Watchtower Society.[18]   Rutherford was born on November 8, 1869, in Booneville, Missouri, of Baptist parents. When he was sixteen years old, he entered college for the purpose of studying law.   At the age of twenty-two he was admitted to the bar and began to practice law, later serving four years as public prosecutor for Booneville.   Still later he was appointed special judge for the Fourteenth Judicial District of Missouri.   During this time he occasionally served as substitute judge when the regular judge was ill.   Hence he came to be called "Judge" Rutherford.   In 1894 Rutherford came into contact with representatives of the Watchtower Society; in 1906 he joined the movement; and in 1907 he became the society's legal counselor.

When he became president, Rutherford proceeded at once to reorganize the Brooklyn office and to encourage the members of the society to engage in a more active program of witnessing. Shortly after Rutherford's accession to the presidency, dissatisfaction arose within the ranks of the society.   This dissatisfaction culminated in open rebellion, after which the leaders of the dis-

---

[15] *Ibid.*, p. 20.   The authors quote from a copy of the Russell-vs.-Ross transcript on file in the Brooklyn headquarters of the Watchtower Society.

[16] *Ibid.*, p. 22.   For the entire story of this trial, which includes other examples of Russell's deliberate lying under oath, the reader is referred to pp. 18-22 of Martin and Klann.

[17] *Qualified to be Ministers*, p. 310.

[18] This sketch of the history of the Jehovah's Witnesses during Rutherford's presidency is based chiefly on pp. 312-32 of *Qualified to be Ministers*, and on pp. 64-195 of *Jehovah's Witnesses in the Divine Purpose*.

affected group were dismissed from their official positions. This dismissal led to the formation of certain schismatic groups.

In July of 1917 the seventh volume of the *Studies in the Scriptures* series, *The Finished Mystery,* was published. This book, which was compiled by Watchtower editors from the writings of Charles T. Russell, was chiefly a commentary on Revelation and Ezekiel. A 4-page extract from this book entitled "The Fall of Babylon" was distributed in great quantities to church members, beginning on December 30, 1917. According to this tract, Catholic and Protestant religious organizations together form present-day Babylon which, it was predicted, would soon pass into oblivion. The furor which the tract aroused soon led to governmental action. In February of 1918 the Canadian government forbade anyone to possess copies of Watchtower publications; it was alleged that they contained seditious and anti-war statements.[19] William J. Schnell, a former Jehovah's Witness who left the movement, asserts that during this time Rutherford was pursuing "a seemingly anti-war editorial policy" in the *Watchtower* magazine.[20] In May of 1918 warrants were issued by the United States District Court of Eastern New York for the arrest of eight of the society's leaders, including Rutherford, charging them with conspiring to cause insubordination and refusal of duty in United States military and naval forces.[21] On June 20 the eight were found guilty of these charges, and the next day they were sentenced to twenty years imprisonment in the federal penitentiary at Atlanta, Georgia.[22]

The Brooklyn headquarters were now closed, operations of the society being conducted, for the time being, from Pittsburgh. After the war ended in November of 1918, society members began to petition their congressmen and governors for the release of the Watchtower leaders. On May 14, 1919, the convictions of the eight leaders were reversed, and soon thereafter they were set free.[23]

The Brooklyn office was now reopened, and the society received a new lease on life. During the course of this year a second magazine, *The Golden Age,* was launched, the first issue appearing on October 1, 1919.[24]

---

[19] *Jehovah's Witnesses in the Divine Purpose,* pp. 75-76.

[20] *Thirty Years a Watch Tower Slave* (Grand Rapids: Baker, 1956), p. 37.

[21] *Qualified to be Ministers,* p. 315.

[22] *Ibid.* Actually, to eighty years, since they were sentenced to twenty years each on four different counts (*Jehovah's Witnesses in the Divine Purpose,* p. 80).

[23] *Qualified to be Ministers,* p. 316.

[24] The name of this semi-monthly was changed in 1937 to *Consolation;* in 1946 the name was changed to *Awake,* under which title it is still published (*Jehovah's Witnesses in the Divine Purpose,* p. 89, note v).

Printing activities were now expanded, the society deciding to do all its own printing. In 1921 the society published *The Harp of God,* the first of a series of books by Rutherford, who proved to be an even more prolific writer than Russell had been.[25]   Soon the Rutherford books were replacing Russell's volumes as standard expositions of Watchtower doctrine.

In 1920 all the members of the congregations who participated in the witnessing work of the society were required to turn in weekly reports. William J. Schnell, whose *Thirty Years a Watch Tower Slave* is a revealing account of the inner workings of the movement, contends that during Rutherford's presidency there emerged a basic change in Watchtower policies. Whereas emphasis had previously been laid on Bible study, character development, and the cultivation of the fruits of the Spirit, all the stress came to be laid on the placing of literature, the making of calls, and the reporting of these calls to Watchtower Headquarters. Schnell claims that as a result of this change of purpose, more than three-fourths of the Bible Students originally associated with the movement left the group.[26]

In connection with the increased emphasis on witnessing, there began to appear, in October of 1922, a monthly service sheet of instructions called *The Bulletin.* Though these instructions had been issued since 1917 to "pioneers," who devoted full time to witnessing, they were now made available to all members of the society to help them in their propagandizing activities.[27]

In 1931, at a convention held at Columbus, Ohio, the members of the society adopted a resolution affirming that, from then on, they were to be known as *Jehovah's Witnesses,* basing this new name particularly on the words of Isaiah 43:10, "Ye are my witnesses, saith Jehovah, and my servant whom I have chosen. . . ."[28]

In 1940 the society began its street distribution of the *Watchtower* and *Consolation* magazines, offering them to people on street corners. This policy is still followed. Another witnessing method which had been in vogue from 1934 — the playing of phonograph records at the doors of homes — was abandoned in 1944, however, in favor of personal presentations by the members.[29]

During World War II the policy of neutrality which the society

[25] See the bibliography for Rutherford's other publications.
[26] *Op. cit.,* pp. 29, 41, 42.
[27] In 1935 the name of this monthly was changed to *Director;* in 1936, to *Informant;* and in 1956, to *Kingdom Ministry (Jehovah's Witnesses in the Divine Purpose,* p. 104 and p. 148, n. u).
[28] *Jehovah's Witnesses in the Divine Purpose,* pp. 125-126. The entire text of the resolution is there reproduced.
[29] *Qualified to be Ministers,* p. 334.

had adopted in 1917 was reaffirmed, with the result that many Jehovah's Witnesses were convicted and imprisoned for refusing to serve in the armed forces. After 1940 most male witnesses were able to establish their ministerial status before their local draft boards so as to obtain 4-D exemptions from military service. Not all were successful in obtaining such exemptions, however; hence some 3,500 Witnesses were imprisoned during the war years.[30] It is significant to note that the number of Jehovah-Witness "ministers" doubled between the years 1939 and 1945, the number given for the latter year being 141,606.[31]

On January 8, 1942, Rutherford died. He had been president of the society for twenty-five years. During his presidency the society moved from a more or less democratic organization to a "theocratic" one,[32] in which the directors of the various local congregations were no longer elected by local assemblies, but were appointed by the governing body in Brooklyn.[33]

NATHAN HOMER KNORR

On January 13, 1942, Nathan H. Knorr was elected to be the society's third president.[34] He was born in 1905 in Bethlehem, Pennsylvania. At the age of sixteen he had already resigned his membership in the Reformed Church and had associated himself with the Allentown, Pennsylvania, congregation of Jehovah's Witnesses. At the age of eighteen he became a full-time preacher, and joined the headquarters staff in Brooklyn. Soon he was made co-ordinator of all printing activities in the society plant, becoming general manager of the publishing office and plant in 1932. In 1934 he became one of the directors of the New York corporation,

---

[30] *Ibid.,* pp. 327-31. The statement about "most male witnesses" is found on p. 331. On pp. 223-24 of *Jehovah's Witnesses in the Divine Purpose,* however, we are told that, during these war years, only a few Jehovah's Witnesses were given ministerial exemption. One wonders how these two apparently contradictory statements can be reconciled.

[31] *Qualified to be Ministers,* p. 332. "Ministers" are Jehovah's Witnesses who are actively engaged in witnessing. Even those who do not devote their full time to these religious activities are considered by the group to be "ministers."

[32] "Theocratic" means *God-ruled.* Since Jehovah's Witnesses believe that they are directly ruled by God, the adjective "theocratic" is applied by them not only to their type of organization, but also to all their activities: they speak of "theocratic ministry," "theocratic warfare," and so on.

[33] *Qualified to be Ministers,* p. 320.

[34] The following information about the history of the Jehovah's Witnesses since 1942 is based chiefly on pp. 332-45 of *Qualified to be Ministers,* and on pp. 196-295 of *Jehovah's Witnesses in the Divine Purpose.*

and in 1940 he became vice-president of the Pennsylvania corporation.[35]

Knorr is not as well known as the previous two society presidents were; few outsiders even know his name. One of his major concerns while in office has been the improvement of the society's training program. A major step in this new educational program was the establishment, in 1943, of the Gilead Watchtower Bible School in South Lansing, New York (near Ithaca). An important next step was the organization of "theocratic ministry schools" in every Jehovah's Witness congregation. In order to aid the congregations in their local training programs, three textbooks, containing information about Bible contents, witnessing methods, and history, were published over a ten-year period: *Theocratic Aid to Kingdom Publishers* (1945), *Equipped for Every Good Work* (1946), and *Qualified to be Ministers* (1955).

In addition to the above titles, a new series of doctrinal books is being published during Knorr's presidency. Unlike previous Watchtower publications, however, these books are not the work of a single author. Although it is surmised that Mr. Knorr is their primary author, the books pass through several hands before publication,[36] and are issued anonymously. One of the first of these books, which are now considered authoritative doctrinal guides by the Witnesses, taking the place of previous publications by Russell and Rutherford, was *The Truth Shall Make You Free,* published in 1943. In 1946 came *Let God Be True,* a Jehovah-Witness doctrinal summary, which was revised in 1952, and of which, so it is claimed, more than 17,000,000 copies have been printed, in 50 languages. *Make Sure of All Things,* which first appeared in 1953 and was revised in 1957, is a compilation of Scripture passages on seventy topics; Jehovah's Witnesses use this volume as a handy Scripture reference book when making calls. *From Paradise Lost to Paradise Regained,* published in 1958, represents a new format: the type is larger and easier to read than that used in the other books, and there are many illustrations. By means of these publications, which have been sold by the millions, the society now spreads its teachings far and wide.[37]

Another important project carried out during Knorr's presidency has been the translation of the Bible into modern English. In

---

[35] *Jehovah's Witnesses in the Divine Purpose,* p. 196.

[36] This information was obtained from Mr. Ulysses V. Glass, Press Secretary to Mr. Knorr, in an interview at Brooklyn Headquarters on June 6, 1962.

[37] For other titles published since Knorr assumed the presidency, see the bibliography.

1950 the first of these translations appeared: *The New World Translation of the Christian Greek Scriptures.* The translation of the Old Testament has been released in portions: Volume I was published in 1953, Volume II in 1955, Volume III in 1957, Volume IV in 1958, and Volume V in 1960. In 1961 the entire Bible in the *New World Translation* was published in one volume. The translators make clear that this one-volume edition may be considered a revised edition of the *New World Translation,* since certain changes from previous editions have been made in it.[38] The names of the members of the New World Bible Translation Committee which did the translating are not divulged; the members of this committee have requested that they remain anonymous even after their death.[39] This translation is by no means an objective rendering of the Bible into English; it incorporates many features which support Jehovah-Witness doctrines.[40]

During Knorr's regime as president, there has been a tremendous expansion of the work into foreign countries. Whereas in 1942 witnessing was carried on in only 54 countries, in 1961 work was done in 185 countries.[41]

One of the most publicized aspects of Jehovah-Witness activity during the past ten years has been the Yankee Stadium conventions in New York City, which were attended by Witnesses from all over the world. The Yankee Stadium Assembly held in 1950 attracted a peak attendance of 123,707;[42] the 1953 assembly reported a top attendance of 165,829;[43] and the 1958 assembly, held simultaneously in Yankee Stadium and the Polo Grounds, drew a record attendance on Sunday, August 3, of 253,922 persons.[44]

STATISTICS AND ACTIVITIES

Though the Watchtower Society keeps no membership roll, it does keep a record of the preaching activities of all Jehovah's Witnesses. Since 1948, the January 1 issue of the *Watchtower* magazine has contained the so-called "Service Year Report" for the preceding year. From the January 1, 1962, issue we report

[38] *New World Translation of the Holy Scriptures,* revised A D 1961 (Watchtower Society, 1961), p. 6.
[39] *Jehovah's Witnesses in the Divine Purpose,* p. 258.
[40] For scholarly and competent analyses of these translations, the reader is referred to Bruce M. Metzger, *op. cit.,* pp. 67, 74-80; and to Walter E. Stuermann, "Jehovah's Witnesses," *Interpretation,* Vol. V, No. 3 (July, 1956), pp. 323-45. See below, pp. 238-42.
[41] *Qualified to be Ministers,* p. 340; *Watchtower,* Jan. 1, 1962, p. 25.
[42] *Qualified to be Ministers,* p. 342.
[43] *Ibid.,* p. 344.
[44] *Jehovah's Witnesses in the Divine Purpose,* p. 291.

the following: in 1961 the average number of active Jehovah's Witnesses throughout the world was 884,587.[45]

Jehovah's Witnesses do not recognize ordination in the sense in which Christian churches do; every active Witness is called a "minister." The closest analogy to an ordained minister among the Jehovah's Witnesses is a "pioneer publisher" — person who devotes his full time to witnessing and distributing literature. In 1961 the average number of pioneer publishers throughout the world was 29,844.[46] The total number of congregations listed for the year 1961 was 21,557.[47]

What is the geographical distribution of Jehovah's Witnesses? The average number of publishers in the United States for 1961 was 248,681.[48] This figure represents twenty-eight percent of the average number of publishers, or active witnesses, in the world during that year. Thus, approximately thirty percent of the members of this group are to be found in the United States, whereas approximately seventy percent are in foreign countries. In other words, approximately two out of every three Jehovah's Witnesses are to be found outside the United States.

From the above-mentioned issue of the *Watchtower* we learn, further, that the foreign country in which the most Jehovah's Witnesses are found is West Germany (67,814 active Witnesses listed for 1961). Next is Great Britain, with 44,974; then Canada, with 36,459. The number of publishers said to be active in Africa is quite astounding: 31,195 in Nigeria and South Cameroun, and 27,988 in Northern Rhodesia. 29,190 active Jehovah's Witnesses are listed for the Philippines, 22,235 for Mexico, and 21,806 for

[45] *Watchtower*, Jan. 1, 1962, p. 25. This is the figure given for "1961 Av. Pubs." *Pubs.* stands for *publishers*, a common designation for active Witnesses. Since it is said on p. 20 of this issue that these individuals devoted some time every month to "declaring the good news of God's kingdom," we may assume that this figure represents the total number of regularly active Witnesses for the year. This figure is larger by 33,209 than the corresponding figure given for 1960. It should be observed, however, that when those who attended the observance of the Memorial, or Lord's Supper, in 1961 are listed, the number is much larger: 1,553,909. (Note: the Jan. 1, 1963, *Watchtower*, giving figures for the year 1962, lists 920,920 average publishers, an increase of 36,333 over the preceding year. The same issue, on p. 29, indicates that 69,649 individuals were baptized in 1962. The world-wide Memorial attendance in 1962 is given as 1,639,681 — an increase of 85,772 over 1961.)

[46] *Ibid.*, p. 25. It is significant to note that this represents a reduction of 740 from the average total for 1960 (*1961 Yearbook of Jehovah's Witnesses*, p. 42).

[47] *Watchtower*, Jan. 1, 1962, p. 25. This figure represents an increase of 549 congregations over the previous year (cf. *1961 Yearbook*, p. 43).

[48] *Ibid.*, p. 22.

Brazil. Other countries in which the Witnesses are active include Argentina, Australia, Belgium, Cuba, Denmark, Finland, France, Ghana, Italy, the Netherlands, Nyasaland, South Africa, Southern Rhodesia, and Sweden.[49]

During the year 1961 Jehovah's Witnesses claim to have put in 132,695,540 hours of witnessing and to have distributed 14,650,615 pieces of literature and 105,281,876 individual magazines! They further state that they made 45,004,266 back calls and conducted 622,665 Bible studies in 1961.[50]

As we previously noted, the two chief Jehovah-Witness magazines are *Watchtower* and *Awake,* each of which appears biweekly, one alternating with the other. In the January 1, 1962, issue of the *Watchtower* it is claimed that 3,850,000 copies of this issue were printed, in 62 languages. The June 22, 1962, issue of *Awake* reports that 3,600,000 copies of that issue were printed, in 25 languages.

Most of the literature of the society is printed and bound at their own printing plant in Brooklyn, New York. In 1961, 5,851,105 Bibles and other bound books and 13,084,075 booklets were produced there.[51] All those working at the printing plant receive room and board, a small clothing allowance, and fourteen dollars a month.[52] This extremely low salary is undoubtedly one of the biggest reasons why Jehovah's Witnesses can sell most of their bound books for as little as fifty cents a copy.

Office workers at Bethel Headquarters (as the Brooklyn apartment and office building is called) work for the same "salary" as the employees of the printing plant. In addition, there are two "Kingdom farms" — one near Ithaca, New York, and one about fifty miles from New York City — which provide vegetables, fruit, and dairy products for the "Bethel family."

For approximately thirty years the Watchtower Society owned and operated Radio Station WBBR on Staten Island, New York.

---

[49] This list includes all countries where the Witnesses claim to have had at least 5,000 active workers in 1961. In addition, they list a great many more countries where a smaller number of publishers are found. It must be remembered, of course, that I am simply reproducing Jehovah-Witness figures here. We are not told how these figures have been arrived at, nor what criterion is used to determine whether a person is a publisher.

[50] *Watchtower,* Jan. 1, 1962, p. 25.

[51] *Ibid.,* p. 26.

[52] It should be remembered, however, that the people thus housed are either single individuals or married couples without children. There are no facilities at Bethel Headquarters in Brooklyn for married couples with children.

In 1937, however, the society withdrew from the commercial use of radio, and in 1957 Radio Station WBBR was sold.[53]

As far as is known, the society operates no hospitals, sanatoriums, clinics, or dispensaries. There are no Jehovah-Witness elementary schools, high schools, or colleges. It has been noted, however, that in 1943 the Gilead Watchtower Bible School was opened. In 1960 this school was moved from its former location in upper New York State to 107 Columbia Heights in Brooklyn — across the street from Bethel Headquarters.[54] The facilities formerly used by this school in South Lansing, New York, are now being used for a "Kingdom Ministry School,"[55] which will provide short training periods for workers who cannot attend the regular ten-month course at the Gilead School.[56] There are also plans to open more training schools in foreign countries such as England, Germany, and France.[57] These schools give training on the Bible-school level for various types of Jehovah-Witness ministries.

As far as the organization of the Watchtower Society is concerned, mention has already been made of the three corporations under which the society operates, and of its "theocratic" method of appointing people to positions of leadership. Below the central controlling powers are the so-called "regional servants," of which there are six in the United States. These supervise the work done in their areas, and report to the Board of Directors. Under these are the "zone servants," which number 153 in the United States. These must work with the congregations in their zones and must conduct occasional "zone assemblies" at which the constituent groups meet together.[58] The local groups, which are never larger than two hundred, are called "companies" or "congregations," and the person in charge of each congregation is called a "company servant."[59] The congregations meet in unpretentious buildings called "Kingdom Halls."[60]

Though Jehovah's Witnesses do not actually prohibit smoking, the practice is frowned upon. It is said that smoking pollutes the body and should therefore be avoided. There is no specific ban

---

[53] *Jehovah's Witnesses in the Divine Purpose,* pp. 120, 138, 283.
[54] *1961 Yearbook,* p. 59.
[55] *Ibid.,* p. 61.
[56] *Jehovah's Witnesses in the Divine Purpose,* pp. 292-93. The regular training period at the South Lansing Gilead school was six months; after the school was moved to Brooklyn, the training period was lengthened to ten months.
[57] *Ibid.,* p. 293.
[58] *Ibid.,* pp. 189-90.
[59] *Ibid.,* p. 189.
[60] For most of the above information I am indebted to Charles S. Braden, *These Also Believe,* pp. 365-66.

on drinking alcoholic beverages, but anyone drinking to excess will be disfellowshiped.[61]

Jehovah's Witnesses consider Christmas to be "a celebration that is neither commanded nor mentioned in Scripture, but that was borrowed from . . . pagan celebrations"[62]; they oppose the use of Christmas trees.[63] They are unalterably opposed to blood transfusions,[64] and they refuse to salute the flag of any nation.[65] Though they do pay taxes and make social security payments, they do not vote or hold political office.[66] In times of war Jehovah's Witnesses take a position of strict neutrality. They claim that "the preaching activity of Jehovah's ministers entitles them to claim exemption from performing military training and service in the armed forces," adding that they have conscientious objections to noncombatant as well as to combatant military service.[67]

There have been a number of defections from the Jehovah-Witness movement. One of the best known is the so-called *Dawn Bible Students' Association,* which broke away from the parent group after Russell's death; its headquarters are in East Rutherford, New Jersey. Another prominent splinter group is the so-called *Laymen's Home Missionary Movement,* which originated in 1917. The first leader of this group was Paul S. L. Johnson; its headquarters are in Philadelphia. Kurt Hutten is of the opinion that approximately twenty groups have left the Jehovah's Witnesses.[68]

SOURCE OF AUTHORITY

BASIS FOR INTERPRETING SCRIPTURE

As we begin our examination of the doctrinal teachings of Jehovah's Witnesses, we shall first of all take up the question of their source of authority. The Watchtower Society has not issued a set of statements of belief comparable to the "Fundamental Beliefs of Seventh-day Adventists," or the "Articles of Faith" of the Mormons. To find the teachings of Jehovah's Witnesses on various doctrinal points we must consult their publications. It will be recalled that the anonymous books and booklets published since 1942 are now considered their authoritative doctrinal guides, re-

[61] Letter to the author from Watchtower Headquarters dated Jan. 21, 1963.
[62] *Awake,* Dec. 8, 1961, p. 8.
[63] Braden, *These Also Believe,* p. 379.
[64] *Make Sure of All Things,* p. 47.
[65] *Let God Be True,* 2nd ed. (1952), pp. 242-43.
[66] Personal interview with Ulysses V. Glass, June 6, 1962.
[67] Letter from Watchtower Headquarters, Jan. 21, 1963.
[68] *Die Glaubenswelt des Sektierers* (Hamburg: Furche-Verlag, 1957) p. 96.

placing earlier publications authored by Russell and Rutherford.

When we approach these publications with the question, What do Jehovah's Witnesses consider to be their ultimate source of authority? the answer seems to be the same as that given by the Protestant churches: namely, the Bible. "The Holy Scriptures of the Bible are the standard by which to judge all religions."[69] Scripture, it is said, is the written revelation of the true God[70]; the Bible is therefore not a human product, but a book of which God is the primary author and inspirer.[71]

In *Let God Be True,* the most widely circulated and perhaps best known Jehovah-Witness doctrinal book, it is unequivocally stated: "We shall let God be found true by turning our readers to his imperishable written Word."[72]   On another page it is said,

> To let God be found true means to let God have the say as to what is the truth that sets men free. It means to accept his Word, the Bible, as the truth. Hence, in this book, our appeal is to the Bible for truth. Our obligation is to back up what is said herein by quotations from the Bible for proof of truthfulness and reliability.[73]

And another statement appears later in the volume: "The Word of the Most High God is the dependable basis for faith."[74] From both Old Testament and New Testament it is shown that the oral traditions of men were not considered authoritative either by the Bible writers or by Jesus Christ; hence the authors of *Let God Be True* decisively reject such a second source of authority next to the Bible.[75]

We gratefully recognize that Jehovah's Witnesses thus clearly state their dependence on Scripture as their final source of authority.   As we examine their theology, however, it will become quite evident that this is by no means a fair and honest statement of the case.   Instead of listening to Scripture and subjecting themselves wholly to its teachings, as they claim to do, they actually impose their own theological system upon Scripture and force it to comply with their beliefs.

As evidence for this I advance, first, the fact that their *New World Translation* of the Bible is by no means an objective rendering of the sacred text into modern English, but is *a biased translation in which many of the peculiar teachings of the Watchtower*

[69] *What Has Religion Done for Mankind?*   (Brooklyn: Watchtower Bible and Tract Society, 1951), p. 32.
[70] *Ibid.,* p. 26.
[71] *Ibid.,* pp. 29-31.
[72] Rev. ed. (Brooklyn, 1952), p. 18.
[73] *Ibid.,* p. 9.
[74] *Ibid.,* p. 121.
[75] *Ibid.,* pp. 11-18.

Society are smuggled into the text of the Bible itself. The Watchtower Society, for example, has intruded into the *New World Translation* its own peculiar teaching about the Holy Spirit. Jehovah's Witnesses deny both the personality and the deity of the Holy Spirit, defining the Holy Spirit as "the invisible active force of Almighty God which moves his servants to do his will."[76] So pervasively has this teaching been incorporated into the *New World Translation* that no person reading this Bible without previous theological training would ever get the impression that the Holy Spirit is a divine Person.

Let us observe how this is done. Though we are not told why the *New World Translation* capitalizes words which have to do with God, we may assume that they do so as a means of designating deity (for example, God, Lord Jehovah, Rock, King, Shepherd, and so on). As is well known, Jehovah's Witnesses deny the full deity of Jesus Christ, maintaining that Christ is "a god" but not "Jehovah God," that He is not equal to the Father, and that He is not the Second Person of the Holy Trinity. It is, however, quite striking that the *New World Translation* capitalizes various titles which designate Jesus Christ: for example, Word (Jn. 1:1, 14), Son (Mt. 11:27), Saviour (Lk. 2:11), and Lord (Jn. 20:28). The capitalization of these titles presumably indicates that, though Christ is not recognized as equal to the Father, He is nevertheless honored as the highest of all God's creatures.

Against this background it is highly significant that the word *spirit,* when used to designate the Holy Spirit, is never capitalized in the *New World Translation.* In Matthew 28:19, for example, we read, "Go therefore and make disciples of people of all the nations, baptizing them in the name of the Father and of the Son and of the holy spirit." By this type of translation Jehovah's Witnesses are affirming that they refuse to ascribe to the Holy Spirit even the honor paid to Christ as the highest of all God's creatures. This rendering thus not only denies the deity of the Holy Spirit, but even denies His equality with Jesus Christ, who is considered inferior to the Father. A comparable passage is II Corinthians 13:14, "The undeserved kindness of the Lord Jesus Christ and the love of God and the sharing in the holy spirit be with all of YOU."[77] To cite a few more examples, the words *spirit* or *holy spirit* also occur in uncapitalized form in the following passages: Isaiah 63:10 ("But they themselves rebelled and made his holy

---

[76] *Ibid.,* p. 108.
[77] *You* is printed in capitals in the *New World Translation* to indicate that the pronoun is in the plural number.

spirit feel hurt"); John 14:26 ("But the helper, the holy spirit, which the Father will send in my name, that one will teach YOU all things and bring back to YOUR minds all the things I told YOU"); Acts 8:29 ("So the spirit said to Philip: 'Approach and join yourself to this chariot' "); and I Corinthians 12:3 (". . . nobody can say: 'Jesus is Lord!' except by holy spirit").[78]

Despite their claim to be only listening to Scripture, Jehovah's Witnesses are here reinterpreting the Bible in line with their Unitarian ideas about God. Most emphatically does the Bible teach the deity of the Holy Spirit. This is evident even from the *New World Translation* of Acts 5:3-4. In this passage, after Luke has recorded Ananias' sin, he reports Peter's words to him: "Ananias, why has Satan emboldened you to play false to the holy spirit. . . . You have played false, not to men, but to God."[79] The Holy Spirit, to whom Ananias has "played false," is here unmistakably designated as being God. What clearer proof could be asked for the fact that Jehovah's Witnesses pervert the Scriptures to suit their purpose?

There is, however, another way in which Jehovah's Witnesses pervert Biblical teaching about the Holy Spirit by means of their translation of the Bible. As was noted, they also deny the personality of the Holy Spirit. This denial, too, they obtrude into their supposedly objective rendering of God's Holy Word. Let us note a few examples of this. John 14:26, in the *New World Translation,* reads as follows: "But the helper, the holy spirit which the Father will send in my name, that one will teach YOU all things and bring back to YOUR minds all the things I told YOU." The relative pronoun *which* conveys to the unsuspecting reader the thought that the "holy spirit" here spoken of is not a person but an impersonal power (since, in modern English, *whom* is used to designate a person and *which* to designate a thing).[80]

---

[78] One cannot appeal to the Greek text to settle the question of whether Holy Spirit ought to begin with capital letters, since in the oldest manuscripts of the New Testament all the letters of every word were capitals. The capitalization of words in a translation, therefore, reflects the judgment of the translator or editor.

[79] Since there are some variations between the text of the *New World Translation of the Christian Greek Scriptures* which was published in 1950 and revised in 1951 and the later edition of the entire Bible, it should be noted that all quotations from the *New World Translation* appearing in this book, unless otherwise designated, are from the 1961 edition of the *New World Translation of the Holy Scriptures.*

[80] Because *which* as a relative pronoun could be used to designate persons in 17th-century English, the King James Version of 1611 could properly render the opening words of the Lord's Prayer, "Our Father which art in heaven" (Mt. 6:9, Lk. 11:2). In modern English, however, *which* may not be used to refer to persons; hence recent versions have substituted *who* for *which* in Mt. 6:9.

The Greek, to be sure, has *ho,* which is the neuter singular form of the relative pronoun. The reason for this, however, is that the antecedent of the relative is *pneuma* (spirit), which is a neuter noun in Greek. That the Evangelist did not intend to say that the helper whom the Father would send was a thing or an impersonal force is evident from the form of the demonstrative pronoun, *ekeinos* (translated *that one* in the *New World Translation*). Though there is a neuter singular form of this pronoun, *ekeino,* it is not the neuter form which is here used but the masculine singular form, *ekeinos.* The meaning is clear: *that one, that person,* will teach you all things. The *New World* rendering, *"which* the Father will send," is therefore a biased rendering which denies the personality of the Holy Spirit.[81]

Another example of this type of mistranslation is Romans 8:16, "The spirit itself bears witness with our spirit that we are God's children." Still another example is found in Ephesians 4:30, "Also, do not be grieving God's holy spirit, with which YOU have been sealed for a day of releasing by ransom." If any Scripture passage teaches the personality of the Holy Spirit, surely it is this one; for how can one grieve an impersonal force — say, an electrical current? Yet the New World Translation again uses *which* instead of *whom.* It should be clear by now that these impersonal renderings of pronouns referring to the Holy Spirit are not objective translations but perversions of the Bible.[82]

There are other ways in which the *New World Translation* dis-

---

[81] How would Jehovah's Witnesses explain the latter half of the verse, "that one will teach you all things," in the light of their insistence that the Holy Spirit is "the invisible active force of Almighty God"? Can an impersonal force "teach all things"?

[82] If Jehovah's Witnesses wish to justify their use of the pronoun *which* with reference to the Holy Spirit on the ground of the fact that *pneuma* is a neuter noun in Greek, we would remind them that the *New World Translation* at other times uses a masculine or feminine pronoun to refer to a neuter noun. For example, in Mt. 14:11 we read, "And his head was brought on a platter and given to the maiden (*korasion*), and she brought it to her mother." The Greek verb translated "she brought" is *eenegken,* a third person singular form. This form may be translated either as "he brought," "she brought," or "it brought." The implied subject of the verb is *korasion,* a neuter noun, meaning *little girl* or *maiden.* If a neuter noun always called for a neuter pronoun, the translation should have read, "*it* brought it to her mother." Here, however, the translators correctly interpreted the neuter noun as standing for a person, and hence rendered the clause, "and *she* brought it to her mother." We can only conclude, therefore, that when the New World translators refer to the Holy Spirit as *it* or *which,* their choice of pronouns is not based upon grammatical grounds but upon their own preconceived conception of the impersonality of the Holy Spirit.

torts the text of Scripture. More passages of this type will be examined in detail in Appendices D and E. Enough evidence has been given on the preceding pages, however, to establish the point that Jehovah's Witnesses are not simply going back "to the Bible alone" when they use their *New World Translation,* but are putting into people's hands a biased rendering of the sacred text, by means of which their heretical doctrines are subtly insinuated into the minds of unsuspecting readers.

A second ground for the assertion made above (namely, that Jehovah's Witnesses do not subject themselves to the claims of Scripture but impose their own beliefs upon Scripture, thereby forcing it to comply with their teachings) is that *their method of using Scripture is to find passages which seem to support their views, and to ignore passages which fail to provide such support.* As an example of this technique, I present their attempt to disprove the doctrine of the Trinity in *Let God Be True.*

After asserting that the doctrine of the Trinity originated not with God but with Satan, the authors of this volume adduce four Scripture passages which, so they say, are "the main scriptures used to support the trinity doctrine"[83]: I John 5:7, John 10:30, I Timothy 3:16, and John 1:1. They then proceed to show that I John 5:7 is probably spurious.[84] On this point they are correct — this verse is not found in the oldest manuscripts of the Greek New Testament and hence, though found in the King James Version, it is omitted in all the modern versions, including both the ASV and the RSV.[85] It should be added at once, however, that no reputable theologian from any evangelical denomination would use this passage today as a proof-text for the Trinity!

The authors next proceed to interpret John 10:30 ("I and the Father are one") as teaching merely that Jehovah and Christ are regarded as "one in agreement, purpose and organization."[86] What the authors fail to mention, however, is that, according to verse 31, the Jews took up stones to stone Jesus, giving as their reason for this action, "For a good work we stone thee not, but for blasphemy; and because that thou, being a man, makest thyself God" (verse 33, ASV). A mere claim of agreement in purpose with God would never have made the Jews cry "blasphemy!" The clear implication of this word, understood against

---

[83] *Let God Be True,* p. 102.

[84] *Ibid.,* p. 103.

[85] In the King James Version I John 5:7 reads, "For there are three that bear record in heaven, the Father, the Word, and the Holy Ghost: and these three are one." Though these later versions do have a verse which is called verse 7, the words which comprise this verse were part of verse 6 in the King James Version.

[86] *Ibid.,* p. 104.

the background of Jewish monotheism, is that the Jews understood Jesus to be claiming full equality with God the Father.

The authors of *Let God Be True* next cite I Timothy 3:16.
Here the King James Version reads, "And without controversy
great is the mystery of godliness: God was manifest in the flesh
. . . ." The authors reject this reading in favor of the rendering
found in the American Standard Version: "He who was manifested in the flesh," adding that Moffatt has also adopted this
reading.[87]   They might have added that all the modern translations (including the RSV, the New English, the Berkeley Version,
and Phillips) have "he who" instead of "God," because the
manuscript evidence for the former reading is much stronger than
that for the latter.   The above facts should make it clear that the
churches which confess the doctrine of the Trinity do not base
this tenet upon the older rendering of I Timothy 3:16, as Jehovah's Witnesses claim.

The last passage adduced as supporting the Trinity doctrine is
John 1:1.   In agreement with the *Emphatic Diaglott*[88] and the
New World Translation, the authors render the last part of this
verse, "and the Word was a god."   In Appendix D it will be
demonstrated that this rendering of the Greek text is a mistranslation.   Suffice it to say here that the entire argumentation of this
paragraph is based on this mistranslation.[89]

After discussing these four passages, the authors of *Let God be
True* go on: "In the four scriptures which the clergy erroneously
quote as supporting the trinity. . . ."[90]   This assertion, however,
is quite misleading, since no reputable "clergyman" or theologian
today who accepts the Trinity would use I John 5:7 in the King
James Version as a proof for that doctrine, and since no modern
version of the New Testament contains the reading of I Timothy
3:16 to which Jehovah's Witnesses object.

Confusion is worse confounded when the authors say, "Therefore, if, as claimed, it [the doctrine of the Trinity] is the 'central
doctrine of the Christian religion,' it is passing strange that this
complicated, confusing doctrine received no attention by Christ
Jesus, by way of explanation or teaching."[91]   The authors are
here guilty of deliberate misrepresentation, for they have failed

---

[87] *Ibid.,* pp. 104-105.
[88] An interlinear Greek Testament, originally published in 1864 by
Benjamin Wilson, a self-educated newspaper editor of Geneva, Illinois.
Because many of Mr. Wilson's theological conceptions were similar to
Watchtower teachings, the Watchtower Society now publishes the *Emphatic Diaglott.*
[89] *Let God Be True,* p. 106.
[90] *Ibid.,* p. 107.
[91] *Ibid.,* p. 111.

even so much as to mention the Great Commission of Matthew
28:19, where Jesus clearly teaches the Trinity: "Go ye therefore,
and make disciples of all the nations, baptizing them into the
name of the Father and of the Son and of the Holy Spirit"
(ASV). Nor has any mention been made by them in this
chapter of the Apostolic Benediction of II Corinthians 13:14,
the Trinitarian implications of which are quite obvious: "The
grace of the Lord Jesus Christ, and the love of God, and the
communion of the Holy Spirit, be with you all" (ASV). Neither
has there been the slightest reference to I Peter 1:1 and 2, a passage
which gives equal honor to all three Persons of the Trinity:
"Peter, an apostle of Jesus Christ, to the elect who are so-
journers of the Dispersion . . . according to the foreknowledge of
God the Father, in sanctification of the Spirit, unto obedience
and sprinkling of the blood of Jesus Christ. . ." (ASV).

Many more passages could be quoted to show that the Bible
definitely does teach the doctrine of the Trinity; passages of this
sort can easily be found in any standard evangelical textbook
of Christian doctrine. Enough of these passages have been cited
above, however, to demonstrate that, in "proving" their doctrines
from Scripture, the Witnesses deliberately select passages which
can be twisted so that they seem to favor their views, while dis-
regarding other texts which fail to support their views. Again we
see that, instead of listening to Scripture, Jehovah's Witnesses
impose their own ideas upon Scripture.

A third ground for the above-mentioned charge is *the organization's insistence that their adherents may only understand the
Scriptures as these are interpreted by the leaders of the Watchtower
Society*. Though ostensibly Watchtower leaders claim the Bible
alone as their sole source of authority, actually they say to their
adherents: You must understand the Bible as we tell you to, or
else leave the movement and thus run the risk of everlasting
destruction! For proof of this accusation I advance the following
evidence:

(1) Charles Taze Russell affirmed that anyone who studied only
the Bible, without the aid of his *Studies in the Scriptures*, would
soon be in spiritual darkness.[92]

(2) During the 1890's, while Mrs. C. T. Russell was an associate editor of the *Watch Tower* magazine, she tried to

> secure a stronger voice in directing what should appear in the
> *Watch Tower*. . . . When Mrs. Russell realized that no article
> of hers would be acceptable for publication unless it was con-
> sistent with the Scriptural views expressed in the *Watch Tower*,

[92] See above, p. 227.

she became greatly disturbed and her growing resentment led her eventually to sever her relationship with the society and also with her husband.[93]

Well might she be disturbed and resentful! For the editorial policy of the magazine was obviously this: Whatever you write must agree wholly with the interpretation of Scripture taught by the group in control; if it does not, your contribution will not be accepted.

(3) In 1909 certain leaders of study classes were asking that *Watch Tower* publications should no longer be referred to in their meetings, but only the Bible. Russell himself replied to this suggestion in a *Watch Tower* article:

> This [the suggestion just made] sounded loyal to God's Word; but it was not so. It was merely the effort of those teachers to come between the people of God and the *Divinely provided light upon God's Word.*[94]

A moment's reflection on the implications of these words will reveal that, according to Russell himself, the interpretations of the Bible furnished by *Watch Tower* writers are not at all in the category of helpful but fallible guides for the understanding of Scripture. On the contrary, these interpretations are alleged to be "the Divinely provided light upon God's Word." Surely at this point we are not far removed from the position of the Mormons, who affirm that God gave His people additional revelations through Joseph Smith which are determinative for the proper understanding of the Bible.

(4) To meet the possible objection that what has been described above may have been true in Russell's day but is no longer true today, let us see what *Let God Be True,* the Witnesses' best-known and most widely distributed doctrinal book, has to say about this question. After quoting Luke 12:37, the authors of this book go on to say that Jesus Christ is today the provider of spiritual food for his people and that he does so "through a visible instrument or agency on earth used to publish it [this spiritual food] to his slaves."[95] Matthew 24:45-47 is then quoted in the *New World Translation*: "Who really is the faithful and discreet slave whom his master appointed over his domestics to give them their food at the proper time? Happy is that slave if his master on arriving finds him doing so. Truly I say to you, He will appoint him over all his belongings." Now follows this statement:

---

[93] *Jehovah's Witnesses in the Divine Purpose,* p. 45.
[94] *Watch Tower,* 1909, p. 371; quoted in *Jehovah's Witnesses in the Divine Purpose,* p. 46 (the italics are Russell's).
[95] *Let God Be True,* rev. ed. of 1952, p. 199.

This clearly shows that the Master would use *one* organization, and not a multitude of diverse and conflicting sects, to distribute his message. The "faithful and discreet slave" is a company following the example of their Leader. That "slave" is the remnant of Christ's spiritual brothers. God's prophet identifies these spiritual Israelites, saying: "Ye are my witnesses, saith Jehovah, and my *servant* whom I have chosen" (Isa. 43: 10).

From and after A.D. 1918 this "slave" class has proclaimed God's message to Christendom which still feeds on the religious traditions of men. The truth so proclaimed does a dividing work, as foretold, the ones accepting the truth being taken to the place of security, and the others abandoned. Those who have been favored to comprehend what is taking place, and who have taken their stand for Jehovah's Theocracy, have unspeakable joy now. The light of his truth is not confined to a small place, or one corner of the globe. Its proclamation is world-wide. In the thirty-three years from 1919 to 1952 inclusive Jehovah's Witnesses distributed more than half a billion bound books and booklets, hundreds of millions of magazines, tracts and leaflets, and delivered hundreds of millions of oral testimonies, in over 90 languages.[96]

As we study this quotation, several points become clear:

(1) The "faithful and discreet slave" in Jesus' parable is understood as designating an organization, namely, the "remnant of Christ's spiritual brothers." This means, in Jehovah-Witness terminology, the "anointed class," or 144,000, who play a leading role in directing the Watchtower Society and who hold all the more important offices.[97]

(2) The "domestics" over whom the "faithful and discreet slave" is placed are, apparently, the "other sheep," or "great crowd" — Jehovah's Witnesses who do not belong to the "anointed class," but who take an active part in the work.[98]

(3) The great task of the "anointed class" is that of providing

---

[96] *Ibid.*, p. 200.

[97] *Ibid.*, p. 303. How these authors have come to apply the term "faithful and discreet slave" to an organization is one of the mysteries of Jehovah-Witness exegesis. In earlier days the expression was applied by this group to C. T. Russell. It was during Rutherford's time that the term came to be applied to the anointed class, this shift being, in fact, the occasion for a rather serious split within the movement (*Jehovah's Witness in the Divine Purpose,* pp. 69ff.). Actually, it will be apparent to any careful reader that Jesus in this parable is not referring to any earthly organization at all, but to spiritual overseers over God's people (like pastors or teachers), considered as individuals, who are either faithful or unfaithful to their task.

[98] This point is made clear in a discussion of this passage found in another Watchtower publication: *Qualified to be Ministers,* p. 353. See also *New Heavens and a New Earth,* 1953, p. 260.

spiritual food for the "other sheep." This implies that the "other sheep" must constantly look to the "anointed class" for the proper interpretation of the Bible and that they are not allowed to engage in any independent investigation of the Scriptures.

(4) The "spiritual food" which the "anointed class" provides is "his [Christ's] message," "God's message" [in distinction from "the religious traditions of men"], "his [God's] truth." This truth is of decisive importance since all those who accept it will find spiritual security, whereas those who do not accept it will be abandoned by God.

(5) It is this truth which is being disseminated throughout the world by means of the various publications of the Watchtower Society and by means of the oral testimonies of its members.

It is now quite evident that, despite the claim of this movement to depend on the Bible alone, the real source of authority for Jehovah's Witnesses is the interpretation of the Bible handed down by the "anointed class" at Watchtower headquarters. To use their own language, the Witnesses insist that the Watchtower Society is "the instrument or channel being used by Jehovah to teach his people on earth."[99] All Christian groups outside their fold are thus alleged to be walking in darkness, no matter how diligently they may study the Scriptures; only the Jehovah's Witnesses are said to be walking in the light, since their "anointed class" is God's channel of enlightenment for all people on earth.[100]

Instead of really listening to Scripture, therefore, Jehovah's Witnesses superimpose their own system of interpretation on the Bible, allowing it to say only what they want it to say. As an example of this type of treatment of Scripture, I present their interpretation of Romans 13:1-7. From the earliest years of the Christian era this passage has been understood as applying to earthly governments and as teaching that lawfully appointed civil magistrates have been ordained by God. The reference to the sword in the ruler's hand (v. 4) and to the payment of tribute (v. 6) make it quite clear that the Apostle Paul was here discussing the believer's attitude toward governmental authorities. One wonders how, in the light of this passage, Jehovah's Witnesses can justify their insistence that all governmental authorities are part of the devil's organization.

Their reply is really quite simple: the church has never properly understood Romans 13!

> In 1929 the clear light broke forth. That year *The Watchtower* published the Scriptural exposition of Romans chapter 13.

[99] *Qualified to be Ministers*, p. 318.
[100] Yet, in *Let God Be True*, pp. 11-18, the authors solemnly claim to recognize no second source of authority next to the Bible!

It showed that Jehovah God and Christ Jesus, rather than worldly rulers and governors, are "The Higher Powers". . . .[101]

In another volume we are told that the submission which Romans
13 tells us to render to Jehovah God and Jesus Christ, as our
"Superior Authorities," includes "Theocratic submission" to those
who have divine authority in the Theocratic organization — in
other words, to the "anointed class."[102] The authors of *This
Means Everlasting Life* further inform us that the *sword* of verse
4 is to be understood in a symbolic sense, as standing for God's
power of executing judgment.[103] Most inconsistently, however,
the *tribute* of verse 6 is interpreted quite literally, as referring
to the payment of taxes to the government![104] Why the sword is
to be understood symbolically and the tribute must be interpreted
literally, we are not told. Is further proof required to show that
Jehovah's Witnesses do not arrive at their interpretations of
Scripture by thorough, diligent, contextual study of the Word,
but by imposing their preconceived ideas upon the Word?

Kurt Hutten, one of the ablest students of the cults in our time,
has aptly summed up the Witnesses' claim to be Jehovah's sole
channel of truth in the following words:

> The members of the [Jehovah-Witness] organization are obli-
> gated to unconditional obedience. This obligation includes
> the duty of accepting the word of God only in the interpreta-
> tion offered them by the Brooklyn publications. The Watch-
> tower Society has divine authority and hence also possesses
> a monopoly on the truth and on the proper proclamation of the
> Gospel. It is forbidden to nourish oneself from other sources
> or to think one's own thoughts. Those who do this disregard
> "the light which comes to them through God's channel with
> reference to His Word," and imply that *"The Watchtower* is not
> sufficient for our time." They thereby commit an offense
> which entails disastrous consequences, and are by Jehovah not
> reckoned as belonging to the "sheep" but to the "goats." For
> to despise the Theocratic organization is to despise Jesus
> Christ.[105]

---

[101] *The Truth Shall Make You Free,* 1943, p. 312. See also *Let God
Be True,* p. 248, and *What Has Religion Done for Mankind?,* 1951, p.
292. Note the implication of the statement quoted above: previous
to 1929 no one properly understood this passage!
[102] *This Means Everlasting Life,* 1950, p. 203.
[103] *Ibid.,* p. 199.
[104] *Ibid.,* p. 200.
[105] *Seher, Gruebler, Enthusiasten,* 6th ed. (Stuttgart: Quell-Verlag, 1960),
p. 105 [translation mine]. It is significant that this complete domination
of Scripture interpretation by Watchtower leaders is precisely what
William J. Schnell experienced during his thirty years with the movement.
See, e.g., p. 43 of his *Thirty Years a Watchtower Slave,* where he ex-

METHOD OF INTERPRETING SCRIPTURE

It is, of course, conceivable that someone might say, Granted that the Jehovah's Witnesses recognize a superior source of authority in their own Watchtower publications, might it not be possible that the Watchtower publication staff does a fairly competent job of interpreting Scripture? By way of anticipating this type of question, I should like to describe briefly the methods of Scriptural interpretation used by this group. As we examine these methods, it will again become quite clear that Jehovah's Witnesses do not really subject themselves to the authority of God's Word, but simply manipulate the Scriptures so as to force them to agree with Watchtower teachings.

The interpretation of Scripture found in Jehovah-Witness publications is often characterized by *absurd literalism*. For example, Jehovah's Witnesses prohibit their members from receiving blood transfusions, justifying this prohibition by an appeal to Scripture passages which forbid the eating of blood. A sample of the type of passage involved is Leviticus 17:14, ". . . I said unto the children of Israel, Ye shall eat the blood of no manner of flesh. . . ."[106] On the basis of Biblical passages of this sort they assert that blood transfusion is a "feeding upon blood," and is therefore "an unscriptural practice."[107] Certain that they have thus discerned Jehovah's will in this matter, Jehovah's Witnesses will deliberately let a loved one die rather than to permit a blood transfusion.[108]

---

plains how the leaders of the society put themselves "into the sole position of giving the Organization's instructions on how to worship, what to worship with, and what to believe." Note also what is said by him on p. 107 about the indoctrination methods of the society whereby "their brain [that of the Jonadabs or 'other sheep'] became totally washed of any other ideas they might ever have loosely held about the Bible, themselves, or other people. Their own thoughts were thus replaced by a narrow sphere or circumscribed area of thought, or as the Watch Tower put it, a 'channel.' "

[106] Other Old Testament passages adduced by them in this connection include Gen. 9:3-5; Lev. 7:26, 27; Lev. 17:10-12; Deut. 12:16. It is added that the prohibition of blood was also enjoined upon Christians in New Testament times, according to Acts 15.28, 29 (*Make Sure of All Things,* rev. ed., 1957, p. 47).

[107] *Ibid.*

[108] It should be observed, however, that (1) the blood which was prohibited in the Levitical laws was not human blood but animal blood; (2) what was forbidden was the eating of this blood with the mouth — which is something quite different from receiving blood into one's veins as a medicinal measure; (3) the reason for this Old Testament prohibition is stated in Lev. 17:11, namely, that God had appointed the blood of animals as a means of making atonement, and that therefore such blood was not to be used as food (cf. C. F. Keil and F. Delitzsch, *Commentary on the Pentateuch* [Edinburgh: Clark,

Another example of absurd literalism is mentioned by Charles S. Braden: Jehovah's Witnesses forbid the use of Christmas trees on the basis of Jeremiah 10:3 and 4, ". . . The customs of the peoples are vanity; for one cutteth a tree out of the forest, the work of the hands of the workman with the axe. They deck it with silver and with gold. . . ." This must be, so they say, a Biblical reference to the Christmas tree; since verse 2 of this chapter says, "Learn not the way of the nations," it is obvious that the Christmas tree stands condemned![109]

These are but two examples of Jehovah-Witness literalism; many more could be given. It must not be inferred, however, that Jehovah's Witnesses always interpret the Bible literally. On the contrary, they are quite ready to spiritualize Scripture passages when such spiritualization fits into their preconceived ideas. For example, they spiritualize the sword in Romans 13:4,[110] and the twelve tribes in Revelation 7:4-8.[111] They are opposed to the literal interpretation of Christ's physical resurrection,[112] of prophecies concerning the return of the Jews to their land,[113] and of prophecies regarding Christ's physical and visible return to earth.[114]

At other times the interpretation of Scripture found in Jehovah-Witness publications is characterized by *absurd typology*. So, for example, it is said that Noah in the Old Testament typified Jesus Christ; that Noah's wife pictured the "bride of Christ," that is, the "Christian congregation of 144,000 anointed members"; that Noah's three sons and three daughters-in-law pictured the "great crowd" (namely, the "other sheep," or larger class of Jehovah-Witness adherents). The ark pictured the "new system

---

1891], II, 410); and (4) the reason why Gentile Christians were asked to abstain from blood, according to Acts 15:20 and 29, was that they might not give offense to Jewish Christians, who at this time still shrank with horror from the eating of blood (cf. F. F. Bruce, *Commentary on Acts* [Grand Rapids: Eerdmans, 1955], and Lenski, *ad loc.*). It is quite clear, therefore, that neither the Old Testament nor the New Testament passages adduced by Jehovah's Witnesses on this matter have anything to do with the current medical practice of blood transfusion. (For fuller treatment of this question, see Martin and Klann, *op. cit.*, pp. 115-26).

[109] *These Also Believe,* p. 379 (unfortunately, Dr. Braden does not mention the source of his information). It will be quite clear to even a casual reader of Jeremiah 10, however, that what is forbidden and ridiculed in vv. 3-5 is the making of wooden idols.

[110] See above, p. 248.

[111] *Let God Be True,* p. 130. Jehovah's Witnesses take literally the number 144,000 mentioned in these verses, but symbolically the distribution of these 144,000 into the twelve tribes of Israel.

[112] *Ibid.,* p. 40.

[113] *Ibid.,* p. 217.

[114] *Ibid.,* pp. 197ff.

of things according to the new covenant mediated by Jesus Christ."
The flood symbolized the coming Battle of Armageddon.[115]

Another example of absurd typology is the Jehovah-Witness
interpretation of the Parable of the Rich Man and Lazarus,
found in Luke 16:19-31. This parable, we are told, tells us
nothing about the state or condition of people after death, but
simply pictures two classes existing on earth today:

> The rich man represents the ultraselfish class of the clergy of
> Christendom, who are now afar off from God and dead to his
> favor and service and tormented by the Kingdom truth pro-
> claimed. Lazarus depicts the faithful remnant of the "body
> of Christ." These, on being delivered from modern Babylon
> since 1919, receive God's favor, pictured by the "bosom posi-
> tion of Abraham," and are comforted through his Word.[116]

William G. Schnell gives a further example of this kind of
typology. In 1931, he claims, the Watchtower Society interpreted the Parable of the Laborers in the Vineyard, found in
Matthew 20:1-16, as follows: the twelve hours of the parable
stood for the twelve years which had elapsed since 1919 (when
the society had received a new lease on life after the discharge
of its leaders from prison). The shilling which every laborer received, regardless of the length of time he had served, stood for
the new name which each member of the organization received
that year, whether he had been with the movement from the beginning or had just joined: the name *Jehovah's Witness!*[117]

A third common characteristic of Jehovah-Witness Scripture
study is what might be called *"knight-jump exegesis."* Kurt
Hutten, who devotes several pages to an analysis of Watchtower
exegetical methods,[118] has coined this expression to describe the
way Witnesses jump from one part of the Bible to another, with
utter disregard of context, to "prove" their points.[119] He goes on
to affirm that the Bible should be interpreted in an organic fashion,

---

[115] *New Heavens and a New Earth*, pp. 310-11; cf. *You May Survive
Armageddon into God's New World*, 1955, p. 292; and *The Truth Shall
Make You Free*, 1943, pp. 323-27. To see Noah as a type of Christ,
and Noah's family as a type of the church is, of course, quite in
harmony with Biblical typology. But by what stretch of the imagination
are we justified in separating Noah's wife from Noah's children, as
standing for two different groups within the church?

[116] *Let God Be True*, p. 98. The reader is also referred to *What
Has Religion Done for Mankind?*, 1951, pp. 246-56 and 302-12, for
a fuller discussion of this parable.

[117] *Thirty Years a Watchtower Slave*, p. 97.

[118] *Seher, Gruebler, Enthusiasten*, pp. 119-25.

[119] *"Der Roesselsprung," ibid.*, p. 120. A knight-jump in chess is a move
of three squares over the chessboard so that the piece passes over any
adjacent square whether occupied or not, and alights on a square of
different color from that which it started.

in a manner which does full justice to the differences between Old
and New Testament, between poetic books and prophetic books,
between histories and epistles, and which takes into account
the fact that revelation is progressive — that it advances from
lesser to greater clarity. Since Jehovah's Witnesses cannot draw
their teachings from the Bible when so interpreted, however, they
must, Hutten continues, resort to "knight-jump" methods to arrive
at their conclusions.[120] The Bible, for them, is like a flat surface
in which every text has equal value.

> They [Jehovah's Witnesses] . . . can jump blithely from a
> passage in the Pentateuch to a passage in the prophets or in the
> book of Revelation. They can thus draw their lines in all di-
> rections [*kreuz und quer*] through the Bible, gleefully combine
> them in zigzag fashion, and put them together again in the
> most fantastic way.[121]

Hutten also compares their method of using Scripture to that of
children building various structures with building blocks, the
Bible being, for the Witnesses, the box which contains the blocks.
The only difference, so the author continues, is that, whereas
children do this type of thing in a playful spirit, being perfectly
ready to knock down their houses as soon as (or very soon after)
they have built them, Jehovah's Witnesses use this method in dead
earnest, believing that they are thus honoring the revelation of
God![122]

An outstanding example of this method of Bible interpretation
is their manner of arriving at the date 1914 as the year when
Christ's Kingdom was established. Jehovah's Witnesses claim
that "Christ the Messiah did not set up God's kingdom at his
first advent or at once after ascending to heaven."[123] How, then,
can we determine the time when the kingdom was established?
From Luke 21:24 it is learned that "Jerusalem will be trampled
on by the nations, until the appointed times of the nations are
fulfilled" (NWT).[124] The "appointed times of the nations,"
it is said, "indicated a period in which there would be no representative government of Jehovah on earth, such as the kingdom
of Israel was; but the Gentile nations would dominate the earth."[125]
These times were running already in Jesus' day, since Jerusalem
was then in bondage to Rome. When, then, had these "times of

---

[120] *Ibid.,* pp. 121-22.
[121] *Ibid.,* p. 121 [translation mine].
[122] *Ibid.,* pp. 121-22.
[123] *The Truth Shall Make You Free,* p. 241.
[124] The abbreviation NWT will be used from now on for the 1961
edition of the *New World Translation.*
[125] *Let God Be True,* p. 250.

the nations" begun? In 607 B.C., when Israel, which was a theocracy, lost her sovereignty and was carried away to Babylon.[126]

From Daniel 7:14, it is said, we learn that Christ was to receive a kingdom which will never be destroyed. It is then naively added, "When would Christ receive this never-to-be-destroyed kingdom? At the end of the 'appointed times of the nations.' "[127]

When, then, will these "appointed times of the nations" end? For the answer we switch to Daniel 4, which contains the account of Nebuchadnezzar's dream of the tree and his subsequent period of living like a beast of the field. This vision, we are told, was a "prophetic vision . . . concerning the times of the nations and the restoration of Jehovah's Theocracy."[128] Nebuchadnezzar is told that after he shall have been reduced to the status of a beast, "seven times" shall pass over him; following this his kingdom shall be restored to him (Dan. 4:25-26). These "seven times," it is said, depict symbolically the length of the "times of the nations."[129]

How, then, do we determine the length of these "seven times"? In the case of Nebuchadnezzar they meant seven literal years. Obviously this cannot be the prophetic meaning of the "seven times," for then Christ would have ascended his throne already in the Old Testament era. When we compare Revelation 12:6 with Revelation 12:14, however, we learn that "a time, and times, and half a time" is equivalent to 1260 days. Obviously, a time, and times, and half a time" are three and a half times. But three and a half times constitute half of seven times; hence seven times must equal twice 1260 days, or 2,520 days.[130]

We are still not through with our calculation, however, since 2,520 literal days would only bring us seven years beyond the

---

[126] *Ibid.*, pp. 250-51. In *Paradise Lost* (this abbreviation will be used from now on for *From Paradise Lost to Paradise Regained*), 1958, p. 172, it is specifically stated: "The king of Babylon took Zedekiah off 'Jehovah's throne' in the year 607 B.C. and laid his city and territory desolate. So that year God's earthly kingdom ended. And that year, 607 B.C., the 'appointed times of the nations' began." Unfortunately, however, the facts do not bear out this assertion, which is pivotal for Jehovah-Witness chronology. Old Testament scholars are virtually unanimous in dating the capture of Zedekiah and the fall of Jerusalem, not in 607 B.C., but in 587 or 586 B.C. (cf. J. D. Douglas, ed., *The New Bible Dictionary*, p. 1357; *The Westminster Dictionary of the Bible*, p. 108; *The Westminster Historical Atlas to the Bible*, p. 15; and Merrill F. Unger, *Archaeology of the Old Testament*, p. 284).

[127] *Paradise Lost*, p. 173.

[128] *Let God Be True*, p. 251. How the Watchtower editorial staff can be so sure that this vision, which was given to Nebuchadnezzar to reveal what God was about to do to him and to his kingdom, pertains to the "times of the nations," we are not told.

[129] *Ibid.*, p. 251; cf. pp. 251-54.

[130] *Ibid.*, p. 252.

beginning of the "appointed times of the nations." There must be some deeper meaning hidden in this figure of 2,520 days. We find this deeper meaning when we turn to Ezekiel 4:6. There we read, in the King James Version, "I have appointed thee every day for a year."[131] Thus we have our clue:

> By applying this divine rule the 2,520 days means 2,520 years. Therefore, since God's typical kingdom with its capital at Jerusalem ceased to exist in the autumn of 607 B.C., then, by counting the appointed times from that date, the 2,520 years extend to the autumn of A.D. 1914.[132]

Thus, by a calculation which involves a conglomeration of figures derived with great ingenuity from assorted passages taken from Luke, Daniel, Revelation, and Ezekiel, we have arrived at the year 1914. Here is "knight-jump exegesis" with a vengeance! Yet Jehovah's Witnesses assure us that by this type of procedure they are listening to the Word of God instead of to the traditions of men!

A fourth characteristic of Jehovah-Witness exegesis is what we might call the *"rear-view method" of interpreting prophecy.* Hutten indicates that much of their prophetic interpretation rests upon a rather primitive kind of trick: they first pounce on certain happenings in the recent past, then find some Biblical texts which can somehow be made to fit these events, after which they triumphantly point to the events in question as "fulfilled prophecies."[133]

As an example of this technique, I suggest the Jehovah-Witness interpretation of Revelation 11:11-13. This passage describes the two witnesses who, after having been killed, were revived again. The Witnesses say this prophecy was fulfilled in 1919, when Judge Rutherford and other leaders of the movement were released from prison and thus enabled to resume their witnessing activities![134]

Another example of this type of "rear-view" exegesis is the Jehovah-Witness explanation of Revelation 17:3-6. This passage depicts a woman sitting on a scarlet-colored beast, on whose forehead has been written the name, "Babylon the Great, the mother of the harlots and of the disgusting things of the earth"

---

[131] Even the casual reader of this chapter will note that the expression quoted above designates the meaning of the symbolic action the prophet is commanded to engage in: each day the prophet lies on his side stands for a year in the history of the house of Israel or the house of Judah. To draw from this passage a rule applicable to a figure derived from the book of Revelation is, to say the least, dubious exegesis!

[132] *Let God Be True,* p. 252.

[133] *Seher, Gruebler, Enthusiasten,* p. 123.

[134] *You May Survive Armageddon* [this abbreviation will be used from now on for *You May Survive Armageddon into God's New World*], pp. 116-120. See also *New Heavens and a New Earth,* pp. 255-56.

(NWT). Jehovah's Witnesses interpret this woman as standing for "the visible organization of the religious heads of heathendom and Christendom."[135] The beast the woman rides, it is further said, is

> this peace beast, formerly known as the League of Nations but now since its reappearance in 1945 the United Nations. Its having sixty member nations in 1951 was well symbolized in the peace beast's having seven heads and ten horns.[136]

In *Let God Be True* we are given a further reason why this identification of the beast with the present-day United Nations organization must be true: "As for that many-membered beastly association of nations, the 'wild beast that you saw was, but is not [during World War II], and yet is destined to ascend out of the abyss [as the United Nations]'."[137]

Having briefly examined some typical methods of Scripture interpretation used by Jehovah's Witnesses, we conclude that they do not really subject themselves to the authority of the Bible alone, apart from human traditions, as they claim to do. Rather, as we now see more clearly, their very method of interpreting the Scriptures makes it impossible for them really to listen to God's Word. Given the methods described above, one can draw from the Bible virtually any doctrine his imagination can concoct. These doctrines may be interesting, novel, and appealing — but they suffer from one fatal defect: they do not rest upon the authority of God's Word, but upon the fabrications of man's mind!

DOCTRINES

DOCTRINE OF GOD

THE BEING OF GOD

The Trinity. As is well known, Jehovah's Witnesses reject the doctrine of the Trinity. They claim, in fact, that this doctrine

---

[135] *What Has Religion Done for Mankind?*, 1951, p. 328. Note the utterly arbitrary way in which all heathen religions and all forms of Christianity are lumped together as constituting "the great whore" of Rev. 17. For Jehovah's Witnesses, therefore, there is no religiously significant difference between, say, a Nigerian animist and a devout Lutheran Christian.

[136] *Ibid.*, pp. 328-29. How 60 member nations are pictured by 7 heads and 10 horns we are not told.

[137] P. 258. The words between single quotation marks have been quoted from Revelation 17:8 in the 1951 ed. of the NWT, comments between brackets having been inserted by the authors of *Let God Be True*. For Jehovah's Witnesses, therefore, the fact that the beast is described as one that "was, is not, and is destined to ascend out of the abyss" proves conclusively that this Scripture passage predicted the rise of the League of Nations, its disappearance, and the subsequent rise of the United Nations!

originated with the ancient Babylonians at about 2200 B.C.[138]
It is said that the Babylonians had a kind of divine triad: Cush,
the father; Semiramis, the mother (Cush's wife); and Nimrod, the
first ruler of Babylon, who was the son of Semiramis but later
became her husband. Since all three of these individuals were
deified by the Babylonians, this is where the idea of the trinity
originated.[139] Later the Hindus, it is claimed, borrowed this idea
of a divine triad from the Babylonians. In the Hindu religion this
trinity assumed the following form: Brahma the Creator, Vishnu
the Preserver, and Siva the Destroyer. These three together composed the one god Brahm.[140] There was even a kind of trinity in
Egypt: the goddess Isis, her sister Nephthys, and Osiris, the son of
Nephthys, who was adopted by Isis as her son, but who also became Isis's husband.[141] We conclude, it is said, that the doctrine
of the trinity had its origin in the demon-religions of ancient Babylon, India, and Egypt. "The obvious conclusion is, therefore, that
Satan is the originator of the Trinity doctrine."[142]

According to Jehovah's Witnesses, the only true God, in one
person, is Jehovah. Before He began to create, Jehovah was all
alone in universal space.[143] It is recognized that the name *Elohim*
is also applied to God in the Old Testament; it is, in fact, specifically affirmed that the plural form of *Elohim* does not denote
the persons of the Trinity but is a plural of majesty, which describes
a single person.[144] The Witnesses claim, however, that Jehovah,
which they prefer to use, is God's true and exclusive name. While
granting that perhaps this name should be pronounced *Yahweh,*
they favor the form *Jehovah* because this is the most familiar and
popular way of rendering the divine name.[145]

This divine name is therefore consistently rendered *Jehovah* in
the Old Testament section of the *New World Translation* — a
practice to which no exception can be taken, particularly since
this was also done by the translators of the American Standard

---

[138] *Make Sure of All Things,* p. 386.
[139] *Religion for Mankind* [this abbreviation will be used from now
on for *What Has Religion Done for Mankind?*], pp. 92-95. On p. 95
it is added that, since Nimrod had married his mother, one could say
that he was his own father and his own son. Thus, it is said, the way
was prepared for the doctrine of the trinity.
[140] *Ibid.,* p. 193.
[141] *Ibid.,* p. 109.
[142] *Let God Be True,* p. 101.
[143] *Ibid.,* p. 25.
[144] *New Heavens and a New Earth,* pp. 35-36.
[145] *Let God Be True,* p. 23; *New World Translation of the Christian
Greek Scriptures,* 1951 ed., pp. 10, 25.

Version. Without any Scriptural warrant whatsoever, however, Jehovah's Witnesses have also introduced the name Jehovah 237 times into the text of the *New World Translation* of the New Testament.[146]

Jehovah's Witnesses deny the full deity of Jesus Christ, and his complete equality with Jehovah. He may be called *a god,* but not *Jehovah God;* he is *a mighty one* but not *almighty* as Jehovah God is.[147] He was created by Jehovah as the first son brought forth by Him; "hence he is called 'the only begotten Son' of God, for God had no partner in bringing forth his first-begotten

---

[146] *New World Translation of the Christian Greek Scriptures,* p. 24. On what basis do they justify this practice? Their argument runs as follows: A papyrus manuscript of the second half of Deuteronomy in the LXX translation has recently been found, which has been dated from the second or first century B.C. This manuscript, called Papyrus Fouad 266, consistently has the tetragrammaton (JHVH, the Hebrew form rendered Jehovah in the ASV) in Aramaic characters for the divine name instead of the common renderings of the name: *Kurios* (Lord) or *Theos* (God). From this fact it is concluded that the original manuscripts of the LXX, which were written in the 3rd and 2nd centuries B.C., also must have had the divine name in its tetragrammaton form instead of in the forms *Kurios* or *Theos,* and it is implied that later copyists of the LXX deliberately substituted *Kurios* or *Theos* for the tetragrammaton (pp. 11-12). This being so, Christ and his disciples must have had copies of the LXX which had the divine name in its tetragrammaton form (p. 12). The writers of the New Testament, therefore, must have used the tetragrammaton for the divine name in their Greek writings, which would include the books of the New Testament (p. 18). Hence it is obvious that the text of the New Testament has been tampered with and that copyists have eliminated the tetragrammaton from these manuscripts, substituting for it either *Kurios* or *Theos* (p. 18). Therefore, Jehovah's Witnesses say, we are justified in replacing *Kurios* or *Theos* with the tetragrammaton (in the form *Jehovah*) in 237 instances (p. 19).

In reply, the following may be said: (1) The fact that an early fragment of the LXX used the tetragrammaton exclusively does not prove that the entire LXX text originally followed this practice. This fragment may simply have represented one type of LXX text. If the tetragrammaton were used exclusively in the original manuscripts, how do we account for its complete disappearance from the 4th and 5th century uncials of the LXX? (2) Even if the LXX did originally use the tetragrammaton, this fact would give us no warrant for tampering with the text of the New Testament which has *Kurios* or *Theos* for God but never JHVH, not even where JHVH did occur in Old Testament passages quoted (see Moulton and Geden's *Concordance to the Greek Testament* under *Kurios*). To assume that the text of the New Testament has been corrupted in 237 places *without one shred of textual evidence* is to engage in a most dangerous kind of speculation! (3) The fact, alluded to by them, that some translations of the New Testament into Hebrew use the tetragrammaton to designate God proves precisely nothing! For how otherwise would Hebrew translators render a Greek word which was originally JHVH?

[147] *Let God Be True,* pp. 32, 33.

Son."[148] Since Christ was the first creature of Jehovah, he had a beginning.[149] It is obvious therefore, that Christ is not the second person of the Trinity.[150]

As has already been stated, the Holy Spirit is, for Jehovah's Witnesses, "the invisible active force of Almighty God which moves his servants to do his will."[151] At another place it is added: "It [the Holy Spirit] is the impersonal, invisible active force that finds its source and reservoir in Jehovah God and that he uses to accomplish his will even at great distances, over light years of space."[152] The Holy Spirit is therefore neither God nor a person; he is merely an impersonal force — we have previously noted how Jehovah's Witnesses have insinuated this conception of the Holy Spirit into their *New World Translation*.[153]

Strictly speaking, therefore, Jehovah's Witnesses are Unitarians. For them, God exists only in one Person — the Person of Jehovah. Jesus Christ, though a person, is not a divine Person; the Holy Spirit is neither a person nor a divine Person.

The Attributes of God. The Witnesses usually speak of four attributes of Jehovah: justice, power, love, and wisdom. No attempt is made by them to distinguish between incommunicable and communicable attributes, it being specifically said that the same four attributes or qualities which are found in God are also found in man.[154]

Are any of these attributes given prominence above others? It has frequently been said that Jehovah's Witnesses minimize the love of God, and tend to exalt the power of God as His outstanding attribute. Charles Braden, for example, makes this assertion[155]; John H. Gerstner implies the same.[156] Kurt Hutten is of the opinion that the vindication of Jehovah is, for Jehovah's Witnesses, the theme of world history — a vindication which will finally reveal itself in a spectacular kind of public triumph over Satan and his hosts. What the Witnesses fail to see, he continues, is that according to Scripture God glorifies Himself

---

148 *Ibid.,* p. 32.
149 *Ibid.,* p. 33.
150 Further details about their view of Christ will be given under the Doctrine of Christ.
151 *Let God Be True,* p. 108.
152 *Let Your Name Be Sanctified,* 1961, p. 269. Note the word *reservoir,* which suggests that the Holy Spirit is a kind of substance which is stored in God.
153 See above, pp. 239-41.
154 *Your Will Be Done* [this abbreviation will be used from now on for *Your Will Be Done on Earth,* 1958], p. 21. On p. 191 of *Make Sure of All Things,* however, the omnipresence of Jehovah is denied.
155 *These Also Believe,* p. 371.
156 *Theology of the Major Sects* (Grand Rapids: Baker, 1960), p. 36.

especially through His love, revealed in the sending of His Son into the world to seek and to save that which was lost.[157]

What shall we say about this? To be fair to the Witnesses at this point, we must grant that they do stress the importance of the love of God. They make love, as we have seen, one of the main attributes of God. Further, in the booklet entitled *God's Way is Love,* published in 1952, great emphasis is laid on this attribute of God. We are here told, for example, that God's love is opposed to both purgatorial torment after death and eternal torment in hell (p. 12), that God showed his love in creating the universe (pp. 14-17), and in putting man into an earthly paradise of pleasure (p. 18). After Adam and Eve had sinned, God showed his love for mankind by giving man the promise of Genesis 3:15 (p. 20). The Bible, we are told, is a gift of God's love (p. 22). The reign of Christ, which began in 1914, is an expression of God's love for mankind (p. 27). Even the Battle of Armageddon is an expression of God's love for man since it will be a blessing for man to have the wicked destroyed (p. 28). God's provision of redemption for mankind is said to be a manifestation of his love (p. 31). In fact, "everything God has done and will do in the future is prompted by love" (p. 13).

It is therefore not correct to say that Jehovah's Witnesses lay no stress on the love of God. It is true, however, that for them the vindication of Jehovah or of Jehovah's name is the primary purpose of world history:

> . . . Today the great issue before all heaven and earth is, Who is supreme? Who in fact and in right exercises the sovereignty over all the universe? Jehovah's primary purpose is to settle this issue. To do so means the vindication of his universal sovereignty or domination.[158]

It is further said that the great means whereby Jehovah will vindicate Himself will be the war of Armageddon and that the vindication of His reproached name is more important than the salvation of men.[159]

It should further be observed that the vindication of Jehovah is also the primary purpose for which Jesus came to earth: "After this announcement of the Kingdom Jesus went to John, showing

---

[157] *Seher, Gruebler, Enthusiasten,* pp. 129-30.

[158] *Let God Be True,* pp. 27-28. See also p. 163: ". . . Vindication of Jehovah's name and sovereignty is the foremost doctrine of the Bible. . . ."

[159] *Ibid.,* p. 29. Note that, in the light of this statement, the primary purpose of Armageddon is not to reveal God's love to man but to vindicate Jehovah over against his enemies. Cf. on this point also *You May Survive Armageddon,* pp. 25-26, where it is specifically said that Armageddon will be a manifestation of God's justice rather than of His love.

the primary purpose for which he came to earth, namely, to bear witness to God's kingdom which will vindicate the sovereignty and holy name of Jehovah God."[160] It is granted that Jesus also came to earth to redeem man, but this is said to have been a secondary purpose:

> Thus John showed the secondary purpose for which the Son of God came to earth, namely, to die as a holy sacrifice to Jehovah God in order to cancel the sins of believing men and to free them from death's condemnation, that they might gain eternal life in the righteous new world which God has promised to create.[161]

I conclude, therefore, that, though Jehovah's Witnesses do stress the love of God in various ways, in the totality of their theology Jehovah's love is subordinated to His power and His justice. For this judgment I advance the following reasons: (1) It is clearly stated by them that the vindication of Jehovah is the primary purpose of world history and of the coming of Christ. This vindication of Jehovah means that He will prove Himself superior to His enemies, both in regard to the rightness of His cause and the greatness of His power. This vindication will be dramatized especially by the great climax of world history, the Battle of Armageddon, at which He will overwhelmingly demolish His foes. (2) Even in God's plan of redemption, which is secondary to His main purpose, it is not so much the love of God for unworthy sinners which is magnified as His just recognition of the worthiness of His true followers. As will become evident when we discuss Jehovah-Witness soteriology, Jehovah's true people, whether belonging to the anointed class or to the other sheep, are chosen by Him because of their worthiness in believing on Him and in dedicating their lives to Him. During the millennium the millions who will be raised from the dead will be given a new opportunity to show their faithfulness and obedience to Jehovah, on the basis of which their final destiny will be determined. Even the way of salvation, therefore, in Jehovah-Witness theology, serves primarily to vindicate Jehovah's justice rather than to reveal His love.

THE WORKS OF GOD

Decrees. One of the first doctrines Russell doubted was predestination. It will be of interest, therefore, to see what present-day Witnesses teach about this doctrine.

---

[160] *Let God Be True*, p. 37.
[161] *Ibid.*, p. 38. In the light of these quotations it would seem that God's provision of redemption for mankind as a manifestation of his love is only a secondary purpose for Christ's coming to earth.

Only with respect to Jesus Christ do Jehovah's Witnesses teach the predestination of an individual: "Only in the case of the chief member of the new creation did God foreordain and foreknow the individual, his only-begotten Son."[162]   Having used Christ in forming the heavens and the earth, Jehovah then used him also in forming His new creation: namely, the people that were to constitute His new nation.   Of this people Jesus Christ was chosen to be the head.[163]

What about the members of this new nation?

> In the case of the others [those other than Christ] he [Jehovah] did not choose to predestinate the individuals, although he did foreordain the number of them and their nationality.   But he left it open to those favored with the opportunity in his foreordained time to prove themselves worthy of being incorporated finally into the new creation.[164]

God foreordained the exact number of this new nation: 144,000. This number has been derived from Revelation 7:4-8, and 14:1 and 3; Jehovah's Witnesses take this number literally, but they take the fact that these 144,000, according to Revelation 7:5-8, were selected out of the twelve tribes of Israel, figuratively![165] It was therefore foreordained by Jehovah that this group would be no larger than 144,000 and that its members would be drawn from various nations.[166]

It is clear that this is not predestination in the Reformed sense or even in the Arminian sense.   God has simply determined the number of people that will belong to this class, but He has not chosen them as individuals.   The following passage adds the thought that God has simply determined beforehand what should be the requirements for belonging to this class:

> God has foreknowledge of the elect [another name for the 144,000]; not meaning that he chose to foreknow the individuals, but that he purposed or predestinated that there should be such an elect company. . . . He did not have to concern himself with the individuals and their names and personal identities.   He simply determined beforehand or predestinated what should be the requirements for membership in this class and

---

162 *New Heavens and a New Earth*, p. 159.
163 *Ibid.*, p. 160.   The "new nation" means the anointed class or 144,000.   From time to time in this exposition, the distinction between "anointed class" and "other sheep" will be referred to, since one cannot understand any phase of Jehovah-Witness theology apart from this distinction.   A more complete description of these two groups will be given under the Doctrine of the Church.
164 *Ibid.*, p. 159.
165 *Let God Be True*, p. 130.
166 *New Heavens and a New Earth*, pp. 168-69.

what standards they had to meet and what qualities they had to display.[167]

How about the "other sheep"? Has their number also been determined beforehand by God? No. Since Revelation 7:9 and 10 tells us about a "great crowd which no man was able to number," distinct from the 144,000 mentioned in the earlier verses of the chapter, Jehovah's Witnesses conclude that the other sheep are not limited in number. "Anyone may become one of this great crowd of sheeplike people who will gain everlasting life on a paradise earth."[168] How? By hearing the voice of the Right Shepherd and coming into the New World Society.[169] This means, of course, subjecting themselves to the Society's requirements for other sheep.

Jehovah's Witnesses thus deny that God has chosen from eternity those who are to be saved, whether they be members of the anointed class or of the other sheep. By thus rejecting divine pre-destination they impugn the sovereignty of God. At this point it would seem that the "vindication of Jehovah's sovereignty" is not coming off very well.

Creation. Jehovah's Witnesses affirm that God created all that exists and therefore vigorously oppose all evolutionary theories.[170] God's various creations, however, took place at various points in time.

The first creature Jehovah made was Jesus Christ. Previous to this time Jehovah had been sonless; now He for the first time became a father. Jehovah did not form Christ out of pre-existent matter or with the help of a "female principle"; He formed Christ out of nothing. Christ was therefore the only direct Son of God; hence he may be called the only-begotten Son.[171]

With the co-operation of this Son, Jehovah afterwards brought forth all His other sons.[172] In other words, Jehovah used His Son as a working partner or co-worker through whom all other things, including angels and men, were brought into existence.[173]

Next God created a realm of spirits. "The creating of the spirit realm was long before the creating of the material universe with its billions of independent galaxies like our own Milky

---

[167] *The Kingdom Is at Hand*, 1944, pp. 291-92.
[168] *Paradise Lost*, p. 195.
[169] *Ibid.*, p. 196.
[170] *Let God Be True*, Chap. 7.
[171] *New Heavens and a New Earth*, pp. 24-25. Note that the Witnesses do not recognize the kind of distinction suggested in the Nicene Creed: "begotten, not made"; for they maintain that Christ was both created by the Father and begotten by the Father.
[172] *Ibid.*, p. 25.
[173] *Ibid.*, pp. 62-63; *Let God Be True*, p. 33. Cf. *The Truth Shall Make You Free*, p. 48.

Way."[174] This spirit realm consisted of myriads of angels, sometimes called "sons of God" in the Bible. Thus, in a sense, the angels are brothers of Jesus Christ, the first-created Son (who in his pre-human state was the archangel Michael).[175] Since Satan was originally one of the spirit-sons of Jehovah, we may say that Satan, too, was originally a brother of Jesus Christ.[176] The prophet Daniel was given a vision of hundreds of millions of angels before God's throne (Daniel 7:9, 10). All these angels are organized and placed in various positions of service.[177]

> All together, they [the angels] form the invisible heavenly organization of Jehovah God, in complete subjection to him and lovingly obedient to him as their theocratic Head and Lifegiver. From the time of Jehovah's prophetic utterance at Genesis 3:15 concerning the seed of the woman, this heavenly universal organization has been compared to a faithful wife of a husband and has been spoken of as Jehovah's woman or wife. He, the Creator of this heavenly organization, is its husband, who fathers the seed or offspring it brings forth.[178]

At another place, after Genesis 3:15 has been quoted, it is said,

> By saying that the serpent would be bruised in the head God meant that Satan would be destroyed. And it would be done by the one whom God would choose. That one was the Seed of the woman. The woman was not disobedient Eve, but rather God's heavenly organization of faithful spirit creatures.[179]

The realm of angels, therefore, constitutes Jehovah's woman or the heavenly mother. The chief Son of this heavenly mother is Jesus Christ, who is the seed of the woman alluded to in Genesis 3:15.[180]

[174] *New Heavens and a New Earth*, p. 20.
[175] *Ibid.*, pp. 26-28.
[176] *Let God Be True*, p. 57.
[177] *New Heavens and a New Earth*, p. 32.
[178] *Ibid.*
[179] *Paradise Lost*, p. 34. The Hebrew word used for woman in Gen. 3:15 is *'ishshah*. This word is used throughout the chapter to designate Eve. By what exegetical legerdemain do Jehovah's Witnesses arrive at the astounding conclusion that *'ishshah* in the 15th verse means myriads of angels?
[180] *Ibid.* It is not easy to determine when, according to the Witnesses, the heavenly woman brought forth Jesus. It is said at one place that God's woman was childless until A.D. 29, when Jesus was baptized and the Father said, "This is my Son, the beloved" (NWT). These words, it is stated, mean that the Father now begot Jesus as His spiritual son, and that the Father's woman, the heavenly organization [also called "the Jerusalem above"], had now brought forth the first of her seed (*New Heavens and a New Earth*, p. 153). On p. 201 of this same volume, however, we are told that it was not until Christ's resurrection that the heavenly woman became mother to her first divine, immortal, royal Son. And on pp. 220-21 we are told that God did not open the womb of His woman for the birth of her royal First-born until 1914.

"Just ten days after Jesus' ascension to heaven, God used his heavenly Zion to bring forth other spiritual children." This happened on the Day of Pentecost, when the holy spirit was poured out, and when many faithful Israelite followers were begotten as spiritual sons.[181] It is further said that the heavenly organization produces all the other members of the anointed class[182]; thus this heavenly organization, and not the earthly church, is the mother of the 144,000. The earthly congregation of anointed ones is, in fact, the visible representation of God's woman on earth.[183]

Next God called into being all the tremendous masses of matter that comprise the material universe; it is this divine act of creation which is referred to in Genesis 1:1.[184] On pages 34 and 35 of *New Heavens and a New Earth* (published in 1953) a guarded and qualified admission is made that the universe may be billions of years old; on page 43 of *Your Will Be Done On Earth* (published in 1958), however, it is stated without qualification that the inanimate material universe is billions of years old. A long period of time is therefore said to have elapsed between this original creation and the beginning of the actual week of creation.[185]

At length, however, the creative week began:

> The time had now come to start getting the earth ready for the animals and humans that would later live on it. So a period began that the Bible calls the "first day." This was not a day of twenty-four hours, but was instead 7,000 years long.[186]

Man was created towards the end of the sixth day, after almost 42,000 years of the creation week had gone by.[187] The seventh

---

[181] *New Heavens and a New Earth,* p. 203.

[182] *Make Sure of All Things,* p. 75.

[183] *New Heavens and a New Earth,* p. 185. As we shall see when we discuss the fall, some of these angels, under Satan's leadership, rebelled against God and thus became part of the devil's organization.

[184] *Ibid.,* p. 34.

[185] *Paradise Lost,* p. 10. In *What Do the Scriptures Say About "Survival After Death"?* (a booklet published in 1955), p. 58, it is specifically stated that the visible universe is 4½ billion years old. Cf. *You May Survive Armageddon* (1955), p. 21.

[186] *Ibid.* How have the Witnesses arrived at this figure? Since the 7th day, on which God rested from His creative work, is said to be still in progress, and since it is assumed that 6,000 years have elapsed from the time of man's creation to the present, with another 1,000 years to be added to this Sabbath during the coming millennium, it is inferred that the 7th day is to be 7,000 years long. From this it is concluded that each of the creation days was of this length (*Let God Be True,* pp. 168, 178).

[187] *Paradise Lost,* p. 18. It is interesting to note that, though the Witnesses are willing to accept in one area the results of scientific discoveries which have led many in our day to conclude that the universe is very old, they refuse to accept such scientific evidence in another area: namely, as it concerns the age of man.

day, on which God rests from creating, is also a 7,000-year day, and is now in progress.

Providence. Since Jehovah is recognized as Creator and as sovereign, and since all of history is said to be firmly under His control, it may be safely assumed that Jehovah's Witnesses accept the doctrine of divine providence, though the term is not listed in their indexes. It is said in *Let God Be True* (p. 169) that God has ordained the Sabbath of creation as a means of vindicating Him "as the Creator of what is good and . . . as the Maintainer and Preserver of such good." This statement implies that God does uphold and preserve His universe.

DOCTRINE OF MAN

THE ORIGINAL STATE OF MAN

The Constitutional Nature of Man. According to Genesis 2:7 man is a combination of two things: the "dust of the ground" and the "breath of life." "The combining of these two things (or factors) produced a living soul or creature called *man*."[188] A study of the way in which the Hebrew word *nephesh* and the Greek word *psuchee* (the Biblical words usually translated *soul*) are used in the Scriptures reveals that these terms are nowhere associated with such words as "immortal, everlasting, eternal, or deathless"; it is concluded, therefore, that the Bible nowhere teaches that the human soul is immortal.[189] On the contrary, the Bible teaches that the human soul is mortal: witness such passages as Ezekiel 18:4, "the soul that sinneth, it shall die," and Isaiah 53:12, where Christ, who is there predicted, is said to have "poured out his soul unto death."[190]

At another place *soul* is defined as follows:

> A soul, heavenly or earthly, is a living, sentient (or sense-possessing, conscious, intelligent) creature or person. A soul, heavenly or earthly, consists of a body together with the life principle or life force actuating it.[191]

---

[188] *Let God Be True*, p. 68.
[189] *Ibid.*, p. 69.
[190] *Ibid.*, pp. 70-71. On Mt. 10:28, however, which reads: "Do not become fearful of those who kill the body but cannot kill the soul; but rather be in fear of him that can destroy both soul and body in Gehenna" (NWT), their comment is: "the word 'soul' is used [here] as meaning future life as a soul" (*ibid.*, p. 71). This interpretation, however, is not at all consistent with the view advanced on earlier pages that the soul is mortal and may die. The fact is that in Mt. 10:28 we are plainly told that it is possible to kill the body (*sooma*) without killing the soul (*psuchee*); this passage therefore militates against the Jehovah-Witness contention that the soul in Scripture is always mortal.
[191] *Make Sure of All Things*, p. 349.

These statements declare that there can be no soul that exists apart from the body. A man, it is said, *is* a soul; he does not *possess* a soul.[192] Nothing in Scripture, we are told, indicates that Adam after his fall into sin would only *appear to die,* but that his soul would live on forever.[193]

Jehovah's Witnesses therefore oppose the view that man consists of body and soul; they teach that man is a soul which consists of a body together with a life principle which actuates it. They therefore vigorously repudiate the doctrine of the inherent immortality of human souls as the foundation of false religion. It was the devil, in fact, who originated this doctrine, when he said to the woman, "Ye shall not surely die" (Gen. 3:4).[194] On the basis of Ecclesiastes 3:19 and 20 it is further affirmed that men and beasts die alike.[195]

The Image of God. Jehovah's Witnesses declare that man was created in the image of God. This means that man was endowed with God's attributes.

> To man as a creature with God's attributes was granted the privilege of holding dominion over the earth and its forms of life: the birds, fish and animals. Toward these he had the responsibility of exercising the same attributes as his Creator: wisdom in directing the affairs charged to him, justice in dealing with other creatures of his God, love in unselfishly caring for the earth and its creatures, and power in properly discharging his authority to carry on the right worship of the Universal Sovereign in whose image he was created. — Genesis 1:26-28.[196]

On the basis of Psalm 8:4-8 in the King James version it is implied that man was made a little lower than the angels.[197] Man is, however, superior to the animals, not because he has an immortal soul, but because (1) he is a higher form of creature, and (2) he was originally given dominion over the lower forms of animal life.[198]

---

[192] *Ibid.*
[193] *Let God Be True,* p. 74.
[194] *Ibid.,* pp. 74-75.
[195] *Ibid.,* p. 75. Note that Jehovah-Witness teaching on the constitutional nature of man is virtually identical with that of Seventh-day Adventism (see above, pp. 110-11). It will be recalled that Russell was delivered from his early skepticism by the teachings of an Adventist minister; it would appear, therefore, that he borrowed his view of the soul, which was basically the same as that of present-day Witnesses, from the Adventists (see above, pp. 223-24).
[196] *Let God Be True,* p. 145. No attempt is here made to indicate any distinction between these attributes as they occur in God and in man.
[197] *Ibid.,* p. 67; cf. p. 41.
[198] *Ibid.,* p. 68.

MAN IN THE STATE OF SIN

The Fall of Man. God created Adam perfect. In support of this assertion Deuteronomy 32:4 is quoted: "his [God's] work is perfect."[199] This perfect man did not have to die:

> God did not appoint the perfect man to die, but God opened to him the opportunity of everlasting life in human perfection in the Edenic paradise. Only if the perfect man disobeyed would God sentence him to death, and he would cease to exist as a soul.[200]

So then, if man had not sinned, he would not have died. "Had perfect Adam not sinned, it would have been possible for him, though mortal, to live on earth forever and to bequeath life to his children."[201] The words, "though mortal," imply that Adam, even if he had remained sinless, would never have obtained immortality. Yet he would have continued to live on earth forever. How would this have been possible? We get the answer from *Make Sure of All Things*:

> Everlasting life: Life in a perfect organism, fleshly for humans who gain life on earth, spiritual for faithful angels who continue to live in heaven. . . . God through his organization protects the life of such individuals for all eternity. Such a person, by his very creation, is dependent upon food, subject to God's laws governing created things.[202]

Adam and Eve, however, did not remain obedient to God; they fell into sin. The Witnesses accept as literal history the story of the fall found in Genesis 3. One of God's good angels, who had been placed in Eden as the overseer of humankind, rebelled against God.[203] Filled with pride, he desired to be equal to God; hence he planned to cause disobedience among God's sons and thus to gather a group of persons who would serve him instead of God.[204] He it was, therefore, who spoke to Eve through the serpent. Be-

---

[199] *Ibid.,* p. 117. The application of this passage to the creation of man is, however, of doubtful warrant. A careful reading of the passage, which occurs in the Song of Moses, will reveal that the point of the Hebrew word *tamim* which is here used is that God is beyond reproach in His providential dealings with man.

[200] *This Means Everlasting Life,* p. 32.

[201] *Let God Be True,* p. 74.

[202] P. 243. Thus Adam would have been sustained everlastingly by the food of his earthly paradise home, and his body would never have become old (*Paradise Lost,* p. 26). Incidentally, we note that the angels, too, would have to be sustained by food (!), since their immortality is denied (*Make Sure of All Things,* p. 247).

[203] *Let God Be True,* pp. 57-58.

[204] *Paradise Lost,* p. 30.

guiled by this rebellious spirit, called the Devil or Satan, Eve first
and then Adam ate the fruit of the forbidden tree and thus disobeyed God.[205]

The penalty for this first sin was death — not eternal torment
in hell but physical death.[206] Such physical death meant annihilation for man:[207]

> Death did not mean that a soul taken from heaven and en-
> cased in Adam's earthly body would escape and return to heaven
> and live there immortally. No! At death Adam would return
> to the dust.[208]

God did not, however, immediately execute this death penalty,
since Satan had now raised an issue which affected the whole universe, namely, that of the sovereignty of Jehovah.[209] Because
Jehovah's sovereignty had to be vindicated, Satan was not destroyed at once; he was given time to bring forth seed, against
whom Jehovah would wage war.[210] Adam and Eve were also not
put to death at once since they had to be permitted to bring children into the world — so that men might learn about God and so
that Jehovah might be vindicated.[211] When Adam was 930 years
old he died. He did not live out a full thousand-year period, but,
since with God one day is as a thousand years, we may say that
Adam did die in the same day that he ate of the forbidden fruit.
Thus God's word was vindicated: "In the day that thou eatest
thereof thou shalt surely die."[212]

> There is not a scrap of evidence that Adam repented. He
> was a willful rebel and was beyond repentance, and his sentence
> is beyond recall. . . . Adam died and went nowhere but to
> the dust from which he had been taken.[213]

[205] *Ibid.*, pp. 30-32.
[206] *This Means Everlasting Life*, p. 44.
[207] *New Heavens and a New Earth*, p. 84; *Paradise Lost*, p. 28.
[208] *New Heavens and a New Earth*, p. 88.
[209] *This Means Everlasting Life*, p. 42.
[210] *Let God Be True*, pp. 58-59. By the seed of Satan is meant people
and spirits who are in league with him and form part of his organization.
Cain was the first of Satan's seed (*New Heavens and a New Earth*, p. 91).
A large group of angels joined Satan in his rebellion and became demons.
It is contended that the fall of the angels is depicted in Genesis 6:1-4, the
"sons of God" in this passage being interpreted as angels who "materialized
in flesh," and the "daughters of men" being understood to have been human
women (*ibid.*, pp. 91-94).
[211] *This Means Everlasting Life*, p. 42.
[212] *The Truth Shall Make You Free*, pp. 111-113. Though the days
of creation are thus said to have been 7,000 years long, and though in
prophetic sections of the Bible a day is said to equal a year, the day in
which Adam lived is alleged to have been 1,000 years long!
[213] *Ibid.*, p. 113.

Original Sin. What were the results of Adam's sin for his descendants? Adam brought death not only on himself but on all the race descended from him.[214] Other results of Adam's fall included inborn sin, imperfection, and disease.[215] Though we do not have anywhere a clear exposition of what this inborn sin involves, *Let God Be True* speaks of both condemnation and disability. On page 119 we read about the "inherited condemnation of Adam's descendants," and also of the "inherited disability under which all are born." On page 117 the results of Adam's sin are expressed as follows: "All his [Adam's] children, we and our ancestors, were born following his sin."

It should be added, however, that Jehovah's Witnesses do not at all have the same understanding of "inborn sin" that is found, say, in the Westminster Confession, the Heidelberg Catechism, or the Augsburg Confession. According to Romans 8:7 no one who still has the "mind of the flesh" can be subject to the law of God, and according to I John 5:1 no one who is not born again or begotten of God can believe that Jesus is the Christ. The Witnesses, however, do not agree with this clear teaching of Scripture. They declare that only the 144,000 have been and will be born again or begotten of God. Since this congregation of 144,000 began to be gathered after Pentecost,[216] no one could have been regenerated before Pentecost. Yet many served God faithfully in Old Testament times, according to them, and will therefore be raised as other sheep during the millennium. Furthermore, since Pentecost, and particularly since 1931 (they are rather vague on the period between Pentecost and 1931), the vast majority of Jehovah's Witnesses have been, and are still, other sheep. These other sheep however, *cannot be born again.* Yet they are said to be able to exercise true faith,[217] to be faithful to Jehovah,[218] to belong to "obedient mankind,"[219] and to dedicate themselves to do God's will.[220] The Witnesses, therefore, teach that a person can believe and be faithful to Jehovah without having been born again!

I conclude that, though Jehovah's Witnesses appear to teach an inherited disability on account of Adam's sin, their theology belies this assertion. For a "disability" which enables unregenerate man to have true faith, to dedicate his life to God, and to remain faithful to Jehovah is no disability at all!

214 *New Heavens and a New Earth,* p. 89.
215 *Religion for Mankind,* p. 63.
216 *New Heavens and a New Earth,* p. 203.
217 *This Means Everlasting Life,* p. 295.
218 *Let God Be True,* p. 231.
219 *New Heavens and a New Earth,* p. 336.
220 *Let God Be True,* p. 298.

DOCTRINE OF CHRIST

THE PERSON OF CHRIST

The Prehuman State. In order to understand Jehovah-Witness teaching on the person of Christ, we shall have to distinguish between a prehuman, a human, and a posthuman state. To begin with the prehuman state, Christ, it is said, was the first creature of Jehovah.[221] During this prehuman state, which lasted from the time of the Son's creation to the time when he was born of Mary, Christ was the Logos or Word of the Father. This does not mean, however, that he was equal to the Father; the title Logos only implies that the Son was the spokesman for God the Father to other creatures that were called into being after him.[222] Thus the Son was the Chief Executive Officer of Jehovah and, as such, superior to all other creatures.[223]

Jehovah's Witnesses insist, however, that neither in this state nor in any subsequent state is the Son equal to Jehovah. As a matter of fact, during his prehuman state the Son was really an angel. Previous to the Son's coming to earth as a man he was not known in heaven as Jesus Christ, but as Michael; when we read in Jude 9 about Michael the archangel, we are to understand this expression as a designation of Jesus Christ in his prehuman state.[224] Between Christ in his prehuman state and the angels, therefore, there is a difference only of degree but not of kind; it will be recalled that, according to the Witnesses, the angels are higher than man, but only creatures.

Yet, though the Son was only a creature during his pre-human state, Jehovah's Witnesses insist that he was at that time some kind of god. On the basis of their translation of John 1:1 ("In [the] beginning the Word was, and the Word was with God, and the Word was a god," NWT), they call the Word "a god,"[225] or say that he had "a godly quality."[226] The Witnesses interpret the so-called *kenosis* passage of Philippians 2:5-8 as meaning that the Son "did not follow the course of the Devil and plot and scheme to make himself like or equal to the Most High God and to rob God or usurp God's place."[227] To support this interpretation they ap-

---

[221] See above, p. 257.
[222] *Let God Be True,* p. 33; *The Truth Shall Make You Free,* p. 44.
[223] *The Truth Shall Make You Free,* p. 44.
[224] *New Heavens and a New Earth,* pp. 28-30. These pages also contain the Scriptural evidence adduced to prove this point.
[225] *Let God Be True,* p. 34.
[226] *The Word — Who Is He?* (booklet pub. in 1962), p. 56.
[227] *Let God Be True,* pp. 34-35.

peal to their own renderings of the passage in the *New World Translation* and in the *Emphatic Diaglott*.[228]

While he was in this prehuman state, the Son, in common with the other angels, did not possess immortality. Later, however, Jehovah "opened up to his Son the opportunity to gain immortality."[229]

The Human State. The following quotation from a recent book sets forth in some detail the Jehovah-Witness view of the conception, birth, and nature of Jesus Christ while he was on earth:

> To become born of Mary the heavenly Son had to lay aside all his heavenly glory and position. At God's due time for his only-begotten Son to become a man, Jehovah took the perfect life of his only-begotten Son and transferred it from heaven to the egg cell in the womb of the unmarried girl Mary. God, by his almighty power, was able to take the personality of his only-begotten Son, his life pattern, and put this personality within the powers of the tiny bundle of live energy that he placed into the womb of Mary. Thus God's Son was conceived or given a start as a human creature. It was a miracle. Under Jehovah's holy power the child Jesus, conceived in this way, grew in Mary's womb to the point of birth.
>
> Thus the child Jesus was born with all the marvelous qualities of righteousness in him just as a child inherits qualities from his father. Having a perfect Father as his life source, Jesus did not inherit imperfection from his imperfect mother Mary.[230]

From these paragraphs it is clear that the Witnesses do not deny the virgin birth of Christ, as has recently been alleged.[231] Note that what is said to have been transferred from heaven to Mary's womb was the "life," the "personality," or the "life pattern" of the Son of God, who, it will be recalled, was never equal to Jehovah but was only a created angel. What happened when Jesus was born, therefore, was not the incarnation of God. ". . . Jesus' birth on earth was not an incarnation."[232] Christ was therefore not God in the flesh.

---

[228] *Ibid.*, pp. 32, 35. These passages, and others adduced by Jehovah's Witnesses to substantiate their view of the person of Christ, will be dealt with more fully in Appendix D.

[229] *The Truth Shall Make You Free*, p. 44. Cf. above, n. 202, and see discussion of Christ's posthuman state.

[230] *Paradise Lost*, p. 127. Cf. *Let God Be True*, p. 36; *The Kingdom is at Hand*, p. 49; *New Heavens and a New Earth*, pp. 150, 153. On the last-named page the work of the spirit in overshadowing Mary is also mentioned.

[231] John H. Gerstner, *The Theology of the Major Sects*, p. 36.

[232] *Religion for Mankind*, p. 231. It is quite revealing to note what the Jehovah-Witness conception of incarnation is: "Moreover, if a mere incarnation of the Son of God had been intended, then it would not have been necessary for him to have his life transferred to an embryo in the virgin's womb and to be developed there and finally born as a helpless infant."

But now the question arises: Is there real continuity between the Son of God in his prehuman and his human state? Was the child born of Mary really the same individual who existed previously in heaven as the Archangel Michael? To this question it is difficult to give an unambiguous answer. On the one hand, Jehovah's Witnesses frequently speak of "Christ's prehuman existence,"[233] say that the angel Michael was actually Jesus Christ in his prehuman spirit form,[234] and assert that it was God's only-begotten Son who became a man.[235] Other passages from their writings, however, imply that there was no real continuity between Michael and the man Jesus Christ:

> That the Son of God born on earth was no mighty spirit person clothing himself with a baby's fleshly form and pretending to be absolutely ignorant like a newborn infant is proved by the scripture (Philippians 2:5-8), which shows he laid aside completely his spirit existence. . . .[236]
> By this miracle [the virgin birth] he was born a man (Philippians 2:7 . . .). He was not a spirit-human hybrid, a man and at the same time a spirit person. He was not clothed upon with flesh over an invisible spirit person, but he WAS flesh.[237]

If Christ, however, was not a spirit person during his human state, but only a man, was not his birth the birth of a new individual, rather than a transfer of a heavenly life to the womb of Mary? If Christ completely laid aside his previous spirit existence, how could he still be the individual who had lived in that spirit existence? The thrust of the above two quotations is clearly this: when Christ was born of Mary, he stopped being a spirit person and became a man — nothing more than a man.

One point has become very clear: Jehovah's Witnesses do not believe that Christ had (or has) two natures. While on earth Christ had only one nature: the nature of a man. Since previous to his birth from Mary, the Son of God is said to have had a spirit nature, of which he divested himself at the time he came to earth, we must conclude, according to Watchtower teaching, that the

---

He could still have remained a spirit person and materialized a fully developed fleshly body and clothed himself with it, just as . . . the angel Gabriel did when appearing visibly to Mary" (*The Truth Shall Make You Free*, p. 245). Actually, however, what is here described is not an incarnation but a temporary assumption of a body for the purpose of bringing a message.
[233] *Let God Be True*, p. 34; *New Heavens and a New Earth*, p. 28; *The Word — Who Is He*, p. 38.
[234] *New Heavens and a New Earth*, p. 27; cf. p. 30.
[235] *Paradise Lost*, p. 127.
[236] *The Truth Shall Make You Free*, p. 246.
[237] *Religion for Mankind*, p. 231.

Christ who was born in Bethlehem is not the same individual who existed previously as the Archangel Michael.[238]

It should further be added that Christ was born as "a perfect human creature."[239] The reason for this is that Christ had to be the absolute equivalent of the perfect man Adam in Eden. Since, according to Deuteronomy 19:21, God had said "Soul (*nephesh*) will be for soul, eye for eye, tooth for tooth . . ." (NWT), it is obvious that another perfect man must be sacrificed to undo the harm wrought by Adam's fall.[240] "Hence as the human life privileges had been forfeited for the human race by its perfect father Adam, through sin, those life privileges had to be repurchased by the sacrifice of a perfect human life like Jesus'."[241]

Before we go on to consider Christ's posthuman state, something should be said about the significance of Christ's baptism since this will shed light on the Witnesses' view of his person. When Jesus was baptized, there came a voice from heaven saying, "This is my son, the beloved, whom I have approved" (Mt. 3:17, NWT). This meant that "as God by his spirit overshadowing Mary transferred his Son's life from heaven to her womb, now God by that same spirit begot Jesus to become his spiritual son."[242] The coming down of the spirit upon Christ in the form of a dove represented the fact that Christ was now anointed with God's spirit, thus becoming Jehovah's High Priest.[243] By this act Christ became " 'a new creation' with spirit life in the invisible heavens in view."[244] By this act Christ also became God's Anointed One or Christ — the Heir of the heavenly Kingdom.[245]

---

[238] It is thus evident that Jehovah's Witnesses reject Chalcedon as well as Nicaea. The Witnesses might counter the above argumentation by saying that since the *life* of the heavenly being was transferred to Mary's womb there is some continuity after all. In reply I would say: But the life which was transferred was not the life of a spirit person. Where, then, is the continuity? Since Jehovah's Witnesses do not teach the pre-existence of man, we must conclude that the life of Jesus as a man began with his miraculous conception. But this was a human life, not an angelic life.

[239] *New Heavens and a New Earth*, p. 151.

[240] *Ibid.*, pp. 151-52.

[241] *Ibid.*, p. 152.

[242] *Ibid.*, p. 153. At another place it is said that at this time God "begot Jesus to be his spiritual Son once more instead of a human Son" (*Let God Be True*, p. 38). The words "once more" imply that the Son was a spiritual Son during his prehuman state, but that he ceased being a spiritual Son when he was conceived and born of Mary. This statement thus underscores the discontinuity that exists between the first and second states of Christ's existence.

[243] *New Heavens and a New Earth*, p. 153.

[244] *Your Will Be Done*, p. 138. It is implied that if Christ had not been thus spirit-begotten, he would not have been entitled to enjoy spirit life in heaven when his earthly life was over.

[245] *Ibid.*

According to the above statements Christ was not Jehovah's
High Priest, nor the Messiah, nor the Heir of the heavenly Kingdom until he had been baptized!   More serious still, these statements clearly avow that Christ was not a spiritual or spirit-begotten
Son of God until his baptism.   Since the members of the anointed
class must also become spiritual sons,[246] and be begotten by God's
spirit,[247] it is obvious that there is a very close analogy between
Christ and the members of the anointed class.   Since Christ while
on earth was not God, and not a spirit person, but only a man
(though a sinless man), we may say that the difference between
Christ and the 144,000 is not one of kind but only one of degree.

The Posthuman State. Jehovah God raised Christ from the
dead, "not as a human Son, but as a mighty immortal spirit
Son. . . ."[248]   The physical resurrection of Jesus Christ is therefore denied; Christ was raised not with the same body which he
had before, but as a "spirit Son, no longer flesh.[249]   The reasoning
behind this teaching is as follows: In order to atone for the sin
of Adam, Christ had to sacrifice his human body.   This means
that he had to renounce it permanently and could not get it
back again.   Therefore God raised him as a spirit Son.[250]   The
Scripture passage usually cited to substantiate this view is I Peter
3:18, "Being put to death in the flesh, but being made alive in the
spirit" (NWT).

What happened to the body of Christ?   ". . . Jehovah God disposed of that body in his own way, just as he disposed of the body
of Moses, who was a type of Christ Jesus; but no one knows
how."[251]   Rutherford had surmised that the Lord may have preserved it somewhere to exhibit to the people in the millennial
age.[252]

At another place it is stated that Christ was raised not with a
body of flesh, but "in a spirit body."[253]   This "spirit body," however, which Christ had after his resurrection, was not a visible
body.   How, then, did Christ reveal himself to his disciples after
his resurrection?   "By materializing fleshly bodies on the occasions

---

[246] *Let God Be True,* p. 300.
[247] *This Means Everlasting Life,* p. 121.
[248] *Let God Be True,* p. 40.
[249] *Religion for Mankind,* p. 259; cf. *Make Sure of All Things,* p. 314.
[250] *Religion for Mankind,* p. 259.
[251] *The Truth Shall Make You Free,* p. 264.
[252] *The Harp of God,* 1928, p. 173.   If, however, it had to be demonstrated that Christ had permanently renounced his body, why was his body not
left in the tomb?
[253] *The Truth Shall Make You Free,* p. 264.   Cf. *Make Sure of All
Things,* p. 349, where we read that a heavenly soul, as well as an earthly
soul, consists of "a body together with the life principle or life force actuating it."

of his appearances," each such body being different from the others.[254] These were temporary materializations, comparable to those in which angels had occasionally appeared to men.[255]

At the time of his resurrection Christ was given immortality as a reward for his faithful course on earth; he was, in fact, the first creature to receive this gift.[256] God now exalted his Son to be higher than he was before he lived and died as a man, and made him to be Head under Jehovah of God's capital organization over the universe.[257] The Son now resumed the name Michael, "to tie him with his prehuman existence."[258]

Since, according to Watchtower teaching, there is no such thing as an immaterial soul which persists after death, and since Christ's material body was not raised, we are forced to conclude that Christ was actually annihilated when he died. While on earth Christ was only a man, with a nature which was only human; this human nature, however, was sacrificed on the cross[259] so completely that he could not get it back again. It will not do to say that Christ sacrificed only his human body and not his human soul, since the Witnesses recognize no human soul which survives the body. The life which Christ now enjoys is not human life, nor the life of a divine Person with a human nature, but angelic life — life as a spirit-creature called Michael. It is obvious, therefore, that Christ after his resurrection is for the Witnesses not in any sense human, or a being with a human nature. Thus there is no real continuity, either, between the second and the third state of Christ's existence. For this reason Jehovah's Witnesses cannot really speak of the exaltation of Christ, since the individual who is exalted is not the same being as the individual who was humiliated.

I conclude that what the three states of Christ's existence in Watchtower theology really amount to is this: angel — man — angel, with no real continuity between the three. A little reflection will reveal how devastating this view is of the Christology of the

---

[254] *The Truth Shall Make You Free*, pp. 265-67.
[255] *Let God Be True*, p. 40.
[256] *Ibid.*, p. 74.
[257] *Ibid.*, p. 40.
[258] *Your Will Be Done*, p. 316.
[259] Jehovah's Witnesses prefer to speak of "torture stake" instead of "cross," since they believe that Jesus was put to death on a simple upright stake, without a crossbar; their NWT, therefore, also renders the Greek verb *stauro-oo* (crucify) as "impale." H. J. Spier, in his *De Jehovah's Getuigen en de Bijbel* (Kampen: Kok, 1961), pp. 132-33, has shown the untenability of this interpretation. See also Alfred Edersheim, *Life and Times of Jesus the Messiah* (New York: Longmans, Green, & Co., 1901), II, 584-85; and J. D. Douglas, ed., *The New Bible Dictionary* (Eerdmans, 1962), p. 279.

Scriptures. The individual who laid down his life at Calvary was not the individual who existed previously in heaven and was God's agent in creation; the individual who is now ruling over his heavenly Kingdom is not the individual who died on the cross for us. Really, Jehovah's Witnesses have three Christs, none of whom is equal to Jehovah and none of whom is the Christ of the Scriptures.

THE WORK OF CHRIST

The Atonement. As we have seen, because of Adam's sin all men have inherited physical death and inborn sin. Jesus Christ, the Witnesses teach, made atonement for us and thus removed for believers the results of Adam's sin. The word *atonement,* it is said, is drawn from the expression *at one,* and means that what makes satisfaction for another thing which has been forfeited must be "at one" with that other thing, that is, must be exactly equivalent to it.[260] When applied to the work of Christ, atonement means that "the human life that Jesus Christ laid down in sacrifice must be exactly equal to that life which Adam forfeited for all his offspring; it must be a perfect human life, no more, no less."[261]

This human life which Jesus sacrificed for his people is called a *ransom.* A ransom is defined as "that which buys back, loosens or releases . . . more especially, releasing from inherited sin and from prospects of eternal death as a result of sin."[262] God provided through Christ a redemptive price whereby "those of men who have faith in God's provision may come into harmony with him and, serving him faithfully, they may receive the gift of life, being freed from inherited sin and from eternal death as a result of sin."[263]

Since what was lost in Adam was perfect human life with its rights and earthly prospects, what is redeemed or bought back is also perfect human life with its rights and earthly prospects.[264] This is exactly what Jesus laid down in death: a perfect human life, with all its rights and earthly prospects. Since this human life was not given back to Jesus, this sacrificed human life remained effective,

> a thing of value with purchasing power, hence with ransoming or redemptive power. The value of the perfect human life was

---

[260] *You May Survive Armageddon,* pp. 38-39. Webster's *New Collegiate Dictionary,* 1956 ed., agrees that *atone* comes from *at one,* but defines *at one* in this sense as meaning "in concord or friendship" (p. 55). It would appear that the Jehovah-Witness derivation of this word is not accurate.
[261] *You May Survive Armageddon,* p. 39.
[262] *Make Sure of All Things,* pp. 293-94.
[263] *Let God Be True,* p. 113. By "eternal death" in this quotation is meant annihilation.
[264] *Ibid.,* p. 114.

now available for use on behalf of faithful men needing to be ransomed thereby.[265]

It is expressly denied that the atonement of Christ was a satisfaction of divine justice:

> Justice was satisfied in mankind's suffering death, the just penalty of sin. So the ransom is an expression of God's mercy, his undeserved kindness toward mankind.[266]

This statement must be understood against the background of Jehovah-Witness teaching that the penalty for Adam's sin was not eternal torment in hell but physical death which was to be followed by annihilation. The purpose of Christ's death, then, was to rescue men from the annihilation in which they would otherwise have remained after death. The question, however, must now be raised: what happens to the justice of God when people are raised from the dead? Since God's justice required man's death *and annihilation,* how can it be said that the justice of God is satisfied by the death of people who are later raised again? If Christ did not in any sense satisfy God's justice by his atoning work, we shall have to conclude that, for Jehovah's Witnesses, the justice of God is so weak that He simply relaxes its demands in the case of those who come to believe in Christ.

What is said about Christ's removal of the curse, however, is not consistent with the above. It is taught that Christ had to hang on the "stake" as an accursed one in order to deliver the Jews from the curse of the law which rested upon them for their transgressions, particularly for their rejection of God's Messiah.[267] At another place we are told that Christ died not just for the curse on the Jews, but for the "condemnation of sin on all mankind."[268] If this is so, there must be a sense in which Christ's death did satisfy God's justice or appease God's wrath. For how otherwise could God remove the curse of the law or the condemnation of sin?

The Extent of the Atonement. For whom did Christ make this atonement? Not for everyone. It is specifically stated that Adam is not included among those ransomed.[269] Those who remain eternally dead and are thus permanently annihilated are also said

---

[265] *Ibid.,* p. 116.
[266] *Ibid.,* p. 115. The implication is that the ransom was an expression of God's mercy but not in any sense an expression of God's justice.
[267] *This Means Everlasting Life,* pp. 109-10; *Paradise Lost,* p. 144.
[268] *Religion for Mankind,* p. 148.
[269] *Let God Be True,* p. 119. The reason here given is: "Because he was a willful sinner, was justly sentenced to death, and died deservedly, and God would not reverse his just judgment and give Adam life." Apparently the Witnesses exclude the possibility that Adam may have repented of his sin, and may have exercised faith in the promise of salvation recorded in Gen. 3:15 (see above, n. 213).

not to have been ransomed.[270]   It is further stated that Christ laid down his life for the other sheep as well as for the bride class,[271] for non-Jews as well as for Jews,[272] for all the "worthy ones of Adam's children,"[273] and for all the believers of Adam's family.[274] This ransom provides the basis for the "resurrection of the dead who are in God's memory and their eventual gaining of life."[275] The ransom, in fact, extends its benefits even to those who "practiced vile things" on earth, but who will be raised during the millennium and will then be given the opportunity of responding to the gospel.[276]

As we reflect upon this view of the atonement, we note how far it falls short of Biblical doctrine. First, the sacrifice brought by Christ, for the Witnesses, was not of infinite value since it was the sacrifice of a mere human life. There is no hint in their teachings of the thought expressed in Anselm's *Cur Deus Homo* that the "price paid to God for the sin of man [must] be something greater than all the universe besides God,"[277] and that therefore the one who pays this price must in his own person be God.

It should further be pointed out that, though Jehovah's Witnesses repeatedly say that God sent His Son Christ Jesus to earth to provide this ransom,[278] and that the one who did the ransoming work was therefore the same individual who was previously with God in heaven,[279] their teachings about the person of Christ do not warrant this conclusion. For, as has been pointed out, there is no real continuity between Christ as he appeared in the flesh and the previously existing Archangel Michael.[280] For the Witnesses, therefore, God did not really send his only-begotten Son (even if one understands this term as designating the created Logos) into the world to ransom man from his sins. Rather, He caused a sin-

---

[270] *Make Sure of All Things,* p. 296.
[271] *You May Survive Armageddon,* p. 230.
[272] *Let God Be True,* p. 119.
[273] *Paradise Lost,* p. 143.
[274] *Let God Be True,* p. 119.
[275] *Ibid.,* p. 120.
[276] *Ibid.,* p. 280. As will be seen when we discuss the doctrine of salvation and the doctrine of the last things, however, what really determines the salvation of those to whom Christ's ransom is to be applied is not the merits of Christ but the works of men. Note, e.g., the following statement: ". . . the course of an individual determines whether he will ultimately receive benefit from the ransom sacrifice of Christ or not" (*ibid.,* p. 120).
[277] Translated by Sidney Deane (La Salle: Open Court, 1959), p. 244 (Book II, Chap. 6). Scripture proof for the full deity of the Saviour will be given in Appendix D. Suffice it here to say that Phil. 2:5-8, when properly interpreted, teaches that the one who died on the cross was fully God.
[278] *Let God Be True,* p. 113.
[279] *Ibid.,* p. 115.
[280] See above, pp. 272-73.

less man to be miraculously conceived by Mary; this man was not even a "spirit-begotten son of God" at birth, but only a human son. He was different from other men only in two respects: (1) he had been born of a virgin, and (2) he lived a perfect life. But Jehovah's Witnesses cannot consistently maintain that the individual whom they call Jesus Christ was the same individual who had existed previously with God as His only-begotten Son and who had been God's agent in creation.

At this point the question cannot be suppressed: Why should the sacrificed life of Jesus Christ have so much value that it can serve to ransom millions of people from annihilation? It was a perfect human life which was sacrificed, to be sure; we must not minimize this point. But it was the perfect human life of someone who was *only a man.* Could the life of a mere man, offered in sacrifice, serve to purchase a multitude which no man can number?[281]

DOCTRINE OF SALVATION

Who will benefit from the ransom of Christ? At this point the anti-Reformation character of Watchtower teachings becomes very clear: "By willingly laying down his human life he [Christ] could use its right to buy back the worthy ones of Adam's children."[282] It is, however, impossible to discuss Jehovah-Witness soteriology without distinguishing between the "anointed class" and the "other sheep," since the way of salvation is not the same for both:

> All who by reason of faith in Jehovah God and in Christ Jesus dedicate themselves to do God's will and then faithfully carry out their dedication will be rewarded with everlasting life (Romans 6:23). However, that life will not be the same for all. The Bible plainly shows that some of these, that is, 144,000, will share in heavenly glory with Christ Jesus, while the others will enjoy the blessings of life down here on earth (Revelation 14:1, 3; Micah 4:1-5).[283]

The Anointed Class. Since the way of salvation is more elaborate and complex for the anointed class than it is for the other sheep, we shall first look at the doctrine of salvation as it applies to the anointed class or 144,000. How do they obtain salvation? They must first believe and repent. Faith is defined as follows:

> Faith means that by reason of Bible knowledge one has a firm assurance that God exists and that he will reward those who earnestly seek him, and that the Bible is his truth and

---

[281] What the Witnesses teach about the work of Christ (that is, the spirit creature who "arose" from Jesus' grave) since his "resurrection" will be treated under the Doctrine of the Last Things.
[282] *Paradise Lost,* p. 143. Cf. n. 276 above.
[283] *Let God Be True,* p. 298.

man's sure guide. It further means to accept Jesus not only as
a Teacher and Example but also as one's Savior and Ransomer.
Such faith causes one to be converted or turned, to change his
course of action.[284]

This faith includes not only knowledge of the message of the Bible
but also acceptance of Christ, followed by a change of life.[285]

Repentance is also required. In *Make Sure of All Things* repentance is thus defined: "Recognition and admission of a wrong
condition or course of action, and a sincere sorrow with determination, motivated by a wholehearted desire to conform to right
principles, to turn forever from such wrong course and take a
course in harmony with God's will" (p. 307). In the light of what
was said about faith, it is evident that repentance is a fruit of true
faith.

True faith and true repentance thus require that one should
"give up one's selfish course and dedicate oneself to do God's will,
just as Jesus did."[286] Dedication, which is required of all who
want to serve God, is defined as follows:

> Christian dedication is the act of a person in setting himself
> apart by solemn agreement, unreservedly and unconditionally,
> to do the will of Jehovah God through Christ Jesus, as that will
> is set forth in the Bible, being made plain by God's holy spirit.
> It means one must live a holy life, separate from this world,
> and serve God henceforth to eternity.[287]

Since Jesus publicly confessed his dedication to do his Father's
will by being baptized, everyone who has similarly agreed to do
God's will should be baptized, as a symbol of his dedication. This
baptism, however, must be by immersion.[288]

In order to enter into the heavenly glory for which they are
destined, the members of the anointed class "must undergo the
sacrifice of all human life right and hopes, even as Jesus did."[289]
Since, however, these people are sinners, they do not have either
the right to life or an acceptable body to offer as a sacrifice. Hence
they must first be justified or declared righteous before they can
undergo the sacrifice of human life-right and hopes.[290]

[284] *Ibid.*, pp. 295-96.
[285] It is said in *Make Sure of All Things*, p. 120, that faith is a gift from
God. On the other hand, however, after the authors of *Paradise Lost*
have described faith, repentance, and dedication, they go on to say, "This
much the individual can do. The rest [meaning the other steps necessary
for becoming a member of the anointed class, here called "the spiritual
nation"] depends upon God" (p. 152).
[286] *Let God Be True*, p. 296.
[287] *Make Sure of All Things*, p. 91.
[288] *Let God Be True*, pp. 296-98.
[289] *Ibid.*, p. 299.
[290] *Ibid.*

When and how does this justification occur? It is not easy to answer the first of these two questions since it is said that God declares such a person righteous "because of his faith in Christ's blood."[291] Actually, these individuals already exercised faith in Christ's blood before their baptism since faith is a prerequisite for baptism.[292] It appears, however, that this justification does not take place until after one has been baptized.[293] As far as the "how" of this justification is concerned, we read in *Let God Be True*:

> Christ Jesus then [after one has exercised faith and has dedicated himself to God] acts as an advocate, covering the sins of such a dedicated one by the merit of his sacrifice. The dedicated one is now in position to be justified or declared righteous by God, and thus he has access to God through Christ Jesus. He has an acceptable body and the right to perfect life on earth, and all this can be presented for sacrifice with Christ Jesus.[294]

It is to be noted that the justification of the 144,000 is solely for the purpose of enabling them to sacrifice their right to life on earth so that they can share the life of Christ in heaven.[295]

What is the next step? "God now choosing them [the 144,000], he accepts the High Priest's sacrifice of the dedicated ones and causes his active force or holy spirit to act upon them so as to bring them forth as spiritual sons with the hope of life in the heavens and he [God] acknowledges them as his sons."[296] So the members of the anointed class are now brought forth as spiritual sons of God. At this time God gives to such persons his holy spirit;[297] they now also have "prospects and hopes for spirit life by resurrection to heaven."[298]

---

[291] *Paradise Lost*, p. 152.
[292] *Ibid.*
[293] *Ibid.* Cf. *Let God Be True*, p. 299.
[294] P. 299. See also *Paradise Lost*, p. 152. What is puzzling, however, is that, though this justification is described in these two places as an act in which God declares these people righteous, in *New Heavens and a New Earth*, p. 167, we read, "For their [the members of the anointed class] proving faithful imitators of his Son to the close of their earthly life, making their calling and their being chosen certain, Jehovah God will pronounce them righteous. . . ." Is there a difference between "declaring righteous" and "pronouncing righteous"? If so, the latter occurs at the close of the earthly life of the 144,000, and is based not on faith, but on works. If not, Jehovah's Witnesses are not consistent on this point.
[295] Cf. *This Means Everlasting Life*, pp. 120-21.
[296] *Let God Be True*, pp. 299-300. It will be remembered that Christ was also begotten or brought forth as a spiritual son of God at the time of his baptism.
[297] *Paradise Lost*, p. 152.
[298] *Make Sure of All Things*, p. 48. This is the reason, I presume, why the other sheep do not need to be born again — they have no prospects of spirit life in heaven.

These persons now become members of Christ's body, and thus receive of his anointing.[299] God now consecrates them or sets them apart for a holy work;[300] this anointing or consecration means that they are made kings and priests of God, in which double capacity they will rule, together with Christ, over the rest of mankind.[301] The holy spirit is for the anointed ones a pledge guaranteeing their heavenly inheritance.[302]

These anointed ones do not yet have immortality at this time, but have a hope of it set before them and therefore seek it as a prize. "To gain that incorruptible prize they must be loyal to God even at the cost of their human lives."[303]

> Before such members of Christ's body can receive their heavenly inheritance they must be set apart more and more from this world and to the holy service of Jehovah God. demonstrating their dependability by carrying out their dedication faithfully until death. This work of setting them apart the Scriptures speak of as "sanctification". . . .[304]

The anointed ones, therefore, are also sanctified; in this process both the Creator and the dedicated ones have a part.[305]

The anointed ones must preach the good news of Christ's Kingdom. If they maintain their integrity until death, they will receive immortality. God is now using these consecrated members of Christ's body to direct the work of proclaiming his Name and Kingdom. The earthly remnant of his body is known as the "faithful and discreet slave";[306] it is the task of this remnant to provide spiritual food for those who hunger and thirst after truth.[307]

As we reflect on the way of salvation for the 144,000, we remember what was said in *Paradise Lost,* p. 152, about the earlier stages of this process: "This much the individual can do. The rest depends upon God." Jehovah's Witnesses teach that the selection of the 144,000 is a sovereign act on God's part. This selection, however, is made on the basis of their having met the requirements for membership in this class.[308] One is chosen to

---

[299] *Let God Be True,* p. 300.
[300] *Paradise Lost,* p. 152.
[301] *New Heavens and a New Earth,* p. 307; *Paradise Lost,* p. 153.
[302] *Let God Be True,* p. 300.
[303] *This Means Everlasting Life,* p. 121.
[304] *Let God Be True,* p. 301.
[305] *Ibid.* Strange to say, however, the passage quoted to support this point is Lev. 20:7, 8. But the anointed class (who are the only ones that will be sanctified in this sense) did not begin to be gathered until Pentecost! (See above, p. 264).
[306] *Let God Be True,* pp. 302-303. By earthly remnant is meant the members of the anointed class who are still left on earth at any one time.
[307] *Ibid.,* p. 132.
[308] See above, p. 261.

belong to this group, therefore, on the basis of his worthiness. We must remember, too, that the first steps in the process which leads to salvation for this class are faith, repentance, and dedication to Christ — steps which these individuals themselves must take. It is only after they have taken these steps that God justifies, regenerates, and sanctifies them. It should further be noted that much emphasis is laid on continued faithfulness to God. These people must "demonstrate their dependability by carrying out their dedication faithfully until death."[309] If they turn back from this dedication, such turning back "would mark them as agreement-breakers, worthy of death, annihilation."[310] As a matter of fact, salvation for the Witnesses is not something which one receives when he becomes a Christian, but something which is not fully attained until one's earthly course is finished.[311]

Hence, though Jehovah's Witnesses claim that salvation is of grace, and that all credit for salvation belongs to Jehovah,[312] we conclude that in Watchtower theology it is not really God's sovereign grace that saves even the 144,000, but rather man who saves himself by grasping the ransom, by showing himself worthy of being selected as a member of the anointed class, and by carrying out his dedication to Jehovah faithfully until death. Another point should here be noted. What Christ earned by his ransom, as we have seen, was a perfect human life with its rights and earthly prospects. When the anointed ones are justified, they receive this right to perfect life on earth. This right, however, they now proceed to sacrifice, as Jesus had done before them; by so doing they obtain the right to share heavenly life with Christ after death.[313] Thus they obtain the right to heavenly life, not through Christ's sacrifice (since he earned only the right to perfect life on earth), but through their own sacrifice of their earthly prospects in the Paradise of the New World. It is therefore literally true that these 144,000 earn their own way to heaven!

The Other Sheep. How do the other sheep obtain salvation? They, too, need to have faith in Jehovah and in Jesus Christ; they, too, must dedicate themselves to do God's will and must faithfully carry out their dedication[314]; they, too, must be baptized by immersion as a symbol of their dedication.[315]

Note, however, the following differences between the way of

---

[309] *Let God Be true*, p. 301.
[310] *Ibid.*, pp. 302-3.
[311] *Make Sure of All Things*, p. 332.
[312] *Ibid.*, p. 336.
[313] *Let God Be True*, pp. 299-300. Cf. *This Means Everlasting Life*, p. 120; *New Heavens and a New Earth*, p. 309.
[314] *Let God Be True*, p. 298.
[315] *Make Sure of All Things*, p. 30.

salvation for the other sheep and for the anointed class:

(1) The other sheep do not need to sacrifice the prospect of perfect human life in the coming earthly Paradise.[316]

(2) Hence God does not need to justify them — at least not during their present existence.[317]

(3) God therefore does not need to regenerate the other sheep; in fact, they cannot be born again.[318]

(4) Neither does God need to consecrate or anoint them to be kings and priests.[319]

(5) Neither does God need to sanctify them.[320]

Since the vast majority of Jehovah's Witnesses today belong to the other sheep, and since the vast majority of those who will be resurrected and saved during the millennium will belong to the other sheep as well, I conclude that, according to Watchtower teaching, most of those who are to be saved will attain this salvation without being regenerated, justified (in the Christian sense), anointed to office, and sanctified (in the Christian sense). This means that, without having their sinful natures renewed, this "great crowd" will be able to have faith in Christ, to dedicate their lives wholly to him, and to remain faithful to the end! This means that the vast majority of believers are not priests or kings — Jehovah's Witnesses thus deny the universal priesthood of believers, one of the basic truths of the Protestant Reformation.

---

[316] *New Heavens and a New Earth,* p. 309.

[317] The reason for the qualification is this: the Witnesses teach that there will be a justification of the other sheep at the end of the millennium. After describing how the other sheep who have been given new bodies during the millennium resist Satan's final attempt to draw them away from God, the authors of *You May Survive Armageddon* say: "God will be vindicated as true by their unbreakable steadfastness and he will judge them worthy of the right to everlasting life in the earthly paradise. He will accordingly justify them [the other sheep], and the names of these unchangeably righteous ones will be 'written in the book of life'" (p. 360; cf. *New Heavens and a New Earth,* pp. 355-56; *This Means Everlasting Life,* p. 304). This type of "justification," however, is something quite different from that which the 144,000 are said to receive when they believe. For the justification of the 144,000 is said to be by faith, whereas that of the other sheep is a justification earned by their works.

[318] *Make Sure of All Things,* pp. 48-49. See, e.g., the discussion in *This Means Everlasting Life,* pp. 120-21, which makes it quite clear that only those destined for heavenly life will be begotten by God's spirit.

[319] *Make Sure of All Things,* p. 91: "Consecration . . . . applies only to Christ and the anointed, spirit-begotten members of his body."

[320] *You May Survive Armageddon,* p. 252. Again we note the tendency to use theological terms in a variety of ways: "They [the other sheep] are not 'saints' or sanctified ones. . . . However, . . . they are sanctified for the warfare and must aid in keeping the camp of the theocratic warriors clean, unworldly, pleasing to God." It is clear, however, that this latter kind of sanctification is not the sanctification of which the Bible speaks.

This means, too, that the vast majority of believers are not justified by faith but must earn their justification by their "unbreakable steadfastness" during the millennium — thus the Witnesses repudiate the so-called material principle of the Reformation: justification by faith. Looking at all this, one is forced to the conclusion that, in this theological system, man is saved not primarily by the grace of God shown to unworthy sinners, but rather by his own demonstration of his worthiness to be saved.

William J. Schnell points out that during his years with the movement the other sheep were told that if they stayed close to the Watchtower organization, listened attentively to its indoctrination, went out regularly to distribute literature, and rigidly reported the time spent in doing so, they *might* be saved at Armageddon! All the emphasis, he insists, was on works, particularly on witnessing, as the way to arrive at a reasonable certainty of future salvation, rather than on faith in Jesus Christ as Saviour.[321] Kurt Hutten similarly suggests that the real core of the way of salvation for Jehovah's Witnesses is witnessing; the harder one works at his witnessing, the more prominent the role he will play in the earthly paradise to come![322]

One more observation should be made. By their sharp division of believers into two classes, the Watchtower Society actually makes a large part of the Bible, particularly of the New Testament, meaningless for the majority of its adherents. For all Scriptural passages dealing with regeneration, sanctification, anointing, and consecration; all passages which speak of being sealed by the Spirit, filled with the Spirit, or testified to by the Spirit; all passages which describe the body of Christ, the bride of Christ, the new creation, the holy nation, and the elect (the list is far from exhaustive) are intended, so the Witnesses say, only for the anointed class and mean nothing for the other sheep. Surely this is a kind of divisive criticism of the Bible that is just as damaging to its authority and comfort as are the irreverent scissors of the higher critic!

DOCTRINE OF THE CHURCH AND SACRAMENTS

DOCTRINE OF THE CHURCH

The attitude of Jehovah's Witnesses toward the Christian church in general is so utterly bigoted as to be almost unbelievable. They — the Witnesses — alone are God's true people; all others are followers of the devil. The "great whore" of Revelation 17,

---

[321] *Op. cit.*, p. 104.
[322] *Seher, Gruebler, Enthusiasten*, p. 108.

as we saw, is organized religion, Christian as well as heathen.[323]
The devil's organization, constantly at war against Jehovah's theocratic organization, has two parts: an invisible section, consisting
of the demons, and a visible section. The latter section includes
all the political organizations of this world and all its religious systems, including apostate Christendom — that is, all of Christendom except for the Watchtower Society and its members.[324]
Though the Roman Catholic Church is singled out as the false
church in its worst form,[325] all denominations of Christendom
are included in the devil's organization.[326]   Organized Christianity, especially from the fourth century onward, was the beginning of the "man of lawlessness"; the various Protestant denominations have now joined with the Roman Catholic Church in
"making up that great combine, the organized clergy of Christendom, the 'man of lawlessness.' "[327]   The religious clergy, in fact,
are the direct visible link between mankind and the invisible
demons![328]

True religion, according to *Religion for Mankind,* was established in the Garden of Eden before man fell (pp. 44-47); false
religion, however, was introduced by Satan when he tempted Eve
(pp. 49-53). In various ways false religion and apostasy revealed
itself before the flood (pp. 58-74), after the flood (pp. 74-91),
and during the later history of Israel (pp. 177-190). The Babylon
from which the Jewish remnant was delivered in 537 B.C. fore-
shadowed the deliverance of the present-day true church, that is,
the Jehovah-Witness organization, from modern Babylon, that is,
the false religions of the present world, including particularly organized Christendom (p. 190; cf. p. 328). Jesus Christ again
introduced true religion, but very soon apostasy began once
more.[329]   The Council of Nicaea in A.D. 325, which defined the
doctrine of the Trinity, was a great victory for apostate Christianity.[330]   Virtually the entire history of the Christian church through
the ancient and medieval periods was a history of apostasy.[331]
Though the Reformation brought some reforms, various gross errors, such as the Trinity, the immortality of the soul, and hell-fire,

[323] *Religion for Mankind,* p. 328.
[324] *Ibid.,* p. 307.
[325] *Ibid.,* pp. 272-77.
[326] *Jehovah's Witnesses in the Divine Purpose,* pp. 107-9.
[327] *Qualified to be Ministers,* pp. 288, 291.
[328] *The Kingdom is at Hand,* p. 186.
[329] *Qualified to be Ministers,* pp. 283-84.
[330] *The Truth Shall Make You Free,* p. 281; cf. *Religion for Mankind,*
pp. 271-72.
[331] *Qualified to be Ministers,* pp. 283-291.

continued to be perpetuated.[332] The real restoration of the church to true religion did not take place until the 1870's when Russell began his Bible class;[333] the complete release of God's true people from "Babylonish captivity," however, did not occur until 1919.[334]

Basic to Jehovah-Witness ecclesiology is, once again, the distinction between the anointed class and the other sheep. We shall therefore look at each of these classes in turn.

The Anointed Class. This designates the "congregation of faithful Christians who [will] win the heavenly reward."[335] The number of this group, when completed, will be 144,000.[336] Since only the 144,000 properly belong to the church, or "congregation," as it is usually called,[337] it is clear that the true church of Jehovah will have only 144,000 members. Whenever the expression "congregation of God" occurs in Jehovah-Witness literature, therefore, it must be understood as referring only to the 144,000.

A rather bewildering variety of names are, however, applied to this group. Among these are the following: Anointed, Body of Christ, Bride of Christ, Chosen Ones, Elect, Holy Nation, Israel of God, Kingdom Class, Little Flock, New Creation, New Nation, Royal House, Royal Priesthood, Sanctuary Class, Sons of Levi, Spirit-Begotten, Spiritual Israel, Spiritual Sons.[338]

The relationship of this group to the heavenly theocratic organization has been previously described.[339] Because the heavenly theocratic organization is "God's woman" or "wife," and because the members of the anointed class are children of this woman, they can properly be said to be children of God. The anointed class is the earthly counterpart of Jehovah's heavenly theocratic organization, and hence plays a leading role in directing the activities of the Watchtower Society.

---

[332] *Ibid.,* p. 292.

[333] *Ibid.,* p. 296.

[334] *Ibid.,* p. 297. See references to this date in various Watchtower publications. The implication of all this is obvious: anyone who does not join the Jehovah-Witness organization today but remains in a Christian church is a devotee of false religion.

[335] *Your Will Be Done,* p. 15.

[336] See above, p. 261.

[337] "Scripturally 'church' means a congregation called out from the world for God's purpose; and so the *New World Translation* renders the Greek Word *ekklesia* by the English word 'congregation' " (*Let God Be True,* p. 125).

[338] *Watch Tower Publications Index of Subjects Discussed and Scriptures Explained, 1930-1960* (Pub. in 1961), p. 64. Note that the term "elect" is applied only to the 144,000. It will be remembered that the living members of this group existing on earth at any time are called the "remnant."

[339] See above, p. 264. It will be remembered that the anointed class began to be gathered at Pentecost.

As will be described more fully under the DOCTRINE OF THE
LAST THINGS, the anointed class is destined to spend eternity in
heaven with Christ; they will not live in the Paradise of the new
earth.

The Other Sheep. Charles T. Russell had already distinguished
between two classes of spirit-begotten people: A higher class,
which he called class *n,* the members of which will be the Bride
of Christ, the "little flock," and will sit with the Lord in his throne
in glory; and a lower class, which he called class *m,* who shrink
from the death of the human will and therefore will not sit with
the Lord in his throne of glory, but will finally reach birth as spirit
beings of an order lower than the divine nature. This latter group
Russell called, in fact, the "Great Company," a name very similar
to one of the names given the "other sheep" class today: "the
great crowd."[340]   There are important differences, however, between these two classes as described by Russell and the two classes
distinguished by Jehovah's Witnesses today.   For Russell both of
these classes were spirit-begotten; for Jehovah's Witnesses, however, the other sheep, or lower class, cannot be spirit-begotten.
Russell taught that the members of the *m* class would eventually
become spirit beings, whereas the Witnesses say that the other
sheep will never become spirit beings.   If Russell was once considered the mouthpiece of God, he is obviously no longer considered such by present-day Jehovah's Witnesses.[341]

Russell had also taught that at the end of the "time of harvest"
in 1918 the door to immortality would be closed since every place
in the bride class would be taken.[342]   Because large numbers came
into the movement after that date, however, Jehovah's Witnesses
began to gather in addition to the anointed class another group,
called "other sheep," in 1931.[343]   In 1936, it is said, the Watchtower Society received clear Scriptural evidence that this "other
sheep" class was destined to live on earth after Armageddon.[344]

As was the case with the anointed class, various names have
been given to this second class of believers.   The name "great

---

[340] *Studies in the Scripture,* Series I, *The Plan of the Ages* (orig.
pub. 1886; this ed. pub. in Allegheny, Pa., in 1907), pp. 235-36, 240.

[341] At this point a significant question arises: If Russell's teachings on a
matter like the above can be so changed, what right do Jehovah's Witnesses
have to follow him as slavishly as they do on other points? (see Martin
and Klann, *op. cit.,* pp. 37-41). Suppose he were wrong on other matters
as well!

[342] *Op cit.,* Series III, *Thy Kingdom Come* (orig. pub. 1891; this ed.
pub. in Allegheny, Pa., in 1907), pp. 205-23; cf. Kurt Hutten, *Seher,
Gruebler, Enthusiasten,* p. 104.

[343] *Jehovah's Witnesses in the Divine Purpose,* p. 139; *New Heavens and
a New Earth,* p. 308; *Paradise Lost,* p. 195.

[344] *Jehovah's Witnesses in the Divine Purpose,* p. 140.

multitude" or "great crowd" is derived from Revelation 7:9, where, so it is alleged, this group is distinguished from the 144,000 mentioned in the fourth verse of the chapter.[345] The name "other sheep" is derived from John 10:16, where Jesus is recorded as saying, "other sheep I have, which are not of this fold."[346] Another common name for this group is "Jonadabs," a name derived from II Kings 10:15-28, and Jeremiah 35. Jonadab (or Jehonadab), a son of Rechab, was the head of a Kenite tribe which dwelt among the Israelites. Jehu took Jonadab along with him and used his help in suppressing Baal worship in Samaria. Jonadab was thus a person who was not an Israelite, but who assisted in the work of an Israelite king.[347] Comparably, Jonadabs today are not regarded as brethren in Christ, but nevertheless may be spared from the destruction of Armageddon if they work along with the anointed class.

Jehovah's Witnesses display a fantastic kind of exegetical ingenuity in finding Biblical symbols or types for the "other sheep" class. In *You May Survive Armageddon,* for example, the other sheep are said to be pictured by the famine-stricken Egyptians (pp. 328-29), the foreigners of David's army (pp. 251-52), the Gibeonites (pp. 241-44), Jephthah's daughter (pp. 323-25), Joseph's ten half-brothers (pp. 327-28), the mariners with Jonah (pp. 149-150), the mixed company that left Egypt (pp. 122-25), the Nethinim, non-Israelites who became temple slaves (pp. 142-48), Noah's sons and daughters-in-law (pp. 290-93), the prodigal son (p. 363), and Rebekah's nurse (pp. 224, 226, 229. Pp. 367-68 of this volume, in fact, list 42 Biblical types of the other sheep!).

The other sheep whom Christ is gathering now are, however, just the beginning of this group. The vast majority of these other sheep will be gathered during the millennium, when most of those in the grave will be raised.[348] During Christ's thousand-year reign the other sheep become "the earthly children of the Lifegiver Jesus Christ and hence are technically in the position of being 'grandchildren' of God."[349]

As will be set forth more fully under the DOCTRINE OF THE LAST THINGS, the other sheep will not get to heaven after death,

---

[345] *You May Survive Armageddon,* p. 180.
[346] *Ibid.,* p. 68; *Let God Be True,* p. 231.
[347] *You May Survive Armageddon,* pp. 276-81; *Let God Be True,* p. 231.
[348] *You May Survive Armageddon,* p. 168.
[349] *Let God Be True,* p. 163. This would imply that the other sheep are not children of God, but only grandchildren. Inconsistently, however, Watchtower authors say elsewhere that the other sheep will remain forever on the new earth as "the justified human sons of Jehovah God" (*New Heaven and a New Earth,* p. 356).

but will be raised with physical bodies and will, if they pass the necessary tests, spend eternity in the Paradise of the new earth.

Reflecting upon Jehovah-Witness ecclesiology, we observe that, whereas the Scriptures say that there is one body and that we have been called to one hope of our calling (Ephesians 4:4), Jehovah's Witnesses have split the church[350] into two bodies, with two separate and distinct hopes for the future. Whereas the Scriptures say, "You are all, in fact, sons of God through your faith in Christ Jesus" (Gal. 3:26, NWT), the Witnesses say, Among those who believe, some are sons of God, but others are grandsons of God. Whereas the Scriptures say, of those who are in Christ, "There is neither Jew nor Greek, there is neither slave nor freeman, there is neither male nor female; for you are all one [person] in union with Christ Jesus (Galatians 3:28, NWT), the Watchtower says, There is, however, a most important distinction among the people of God which Paul here has forgotten to mention: that between the anointed class and the other sheep. Whereas the Scriptures say, in Revelation 21:2, that the holy city comes down out of heaven from God, prepared as a bride adorned for her husband (implying that this bride will be on the new earth thereafter, so that heaven and earth now become one), Jehovah's Witnesses, in defiance of Scripture, wish to keep the bride of Christ in heaven throughout eternity, and to leave the lower class of adherents on earth. Whereas the Scriptures say that Jesus Christ gave himself for us that he might "cleanse for himself a people peculiarly his own, zealous for fine works" (Titus 2:14, NWT), Watchtower teachers say that Christ really came to cleanse for himself not one people, but two peoples, and that these two peoples shall remain forever separate. I conclude that the ecclesiology of the Jehovah's Witnesses is a perversion of Scriptural teaching about the church.

DOCTRINE OF THE SACRAMENTS

Baptism. Baptism by immersion is required of all converts.[351] Any male Jehovah's Witness may perform this rite.[352] Conventions and assemblies of the Witnesses are usually occasions for mass baptisms. Candidates must be baptized "in the name of the Father and of the Son and of the holy spirit." This means that the person to be baptized must recognize Jehovah as Supreme, must recognize the part the Son performs in Jehovah's purpose,

---

[350] It is granted that, according to Watchtower teaching, only the 144,000 constitute the church. But surely this kind of terminological jugglery does not justify their chopping the people of God into two severed fragments!
[351] *Let God Be True,* p. 297; cf. *New Heavens and a New Earth,* p. 301; *Make Sure of All Things,* p. 30.
[352] *The Kingdom is At Hand,* p. 296.

and must recognize the holy spirit as God's active force which will help him carry out his dedication.[353]

What is the significance of baptism? Baptism is defined in *Make Sure of All Things* as "an outward symbol, as a testimony before witnesses, of the baptized one's complete, unreserved and unconditional dedication and agreement to do the will of Jehovah God. . ." (p. 27). Immersion is essential to the symbolism: "The being dipped under water pictures the death of one's past course. The being lifted out of it pictures being raised and made alive to the doing of God's will."[354] Infant baptism is said to be unscriptural since repentance and faith must precede baptism.[355] Though the children of Jehovah's Witnesses are therefore not to be baptized in infancy, they must yet be treated by their parents as "something 'holy' to God."[356]

For all those who submit to this rite, baptism is a symbol of one's dedication to be God's minister.[357] This would therefore be true for both the anointed class and the other sheep. The other sheep, however, enjoy, in addition to their water baptism, a baptism into the Greater Noah.[358] This baptism means that they will be enabled to survive Armageddon, provided they remain loyal to God.[359]

For the anointed class, moreover, there is also a baptism additional to their water baptism. This is "another baptism which no human being on earth can administer. This is the baptism of the holy spirit, which Christ Jesus administers as Jehovah's Servant."[360] This baptism of the holy spirit (sometimes called a baptism with the holy spirit) indicates that the person has been baptized into the body of Christ, and that he has been baptized into Christ's death.[361] This baptism into Christ's death means baptism into a kind of death that parts with all prospect of perfect human life in the new world.[362]

The other sheep, however, do not receive this baptism *of* or *with*

---

[353] *Let God Be True*, pp. 297-98.
[354] *Ibid.*, p. 297.
[355] *Make Sure of All Things*, pp. 32, 30.
[356] *This Means Everlasting Life*, p. 256. The Scripture reference given here is I Cor. 7:14.
[357] *Make Sure of All Things*, p. 265. It will be remembered that every active Witness is called a minister, even though he does not devote full time to his witnessing.
[358] *New Heavens and a New Earth*, p. 309. Baptism into the Greater Noah is described on p. 293 of *You May Survive Armageddon* as baptism into Jesus Christ.
[359] *New Heavens and a New Earth*, p. 311.
[360] *The Kingdom is at Hand*, p. 296.
[361] *Ibid.*, pp. 296-98.
[362] *New Heavens and a New Earth*, p. 309.

the holy spirit, though "they do enjoy a measure of God's spirit."[363]
They are not members of Christ's body, and are not baptized into
Christ's death. They do not inherit God's kingdom,[364] or become
part of it,[365] and they can only be the *subjects* of the kingdom of
God,[366] over whom Christ and the 144,000 will rule eternally.

The Lord's Supper. Jehovah's Witnesses celebrate the Lord's
Supper once a year, after sundown on the "exact day of the year
that he [Christ] died, the true Passover date of the Jews. This
would be Abib or Nisan 14."[367] This date usually occurs within
what we call passion week; yet it may fall on any day of the
week.[368]

Though at first the Bible Students called this meal the "Anniversary Supper," today Witnesses call it the "Memorial."[369] At this
Memorial unleavened bread and fermented wine are served.[370]
Jehovah's Witnesses reject transubstantiation (the view that the
bread and wine change into the actual body and blood of Christ),
maintaining that the loaf of bread merely symbolizes Jesus' fleshly
body and that the cup of wine symbolizes Jesus' blood.[371]

When we look at the purpose of the Memorial, it becomes quite
clear that it is intended for the 144,000 only. Its purpose, according to *Make Sure of All Things,* is to help the communicant remember Jesus' sacrifice (p. 260), whereby the forgiveness of sins
has been obtained (pp. 261-62), and whereby a way has been
opened for him and for his fellow anointed ones to go to heaven
(p. 261). The communicant remembers that Jesus' blood put
into force a new covenant between Jehovah and the 144,000
(p. 261), and thus exercises partnership with his fellow communicants and with Jehovah and Christ Jesus (p. 262).

It is specifically taught that Jesus "set up this evening meal
with those who were to be taken into the covenant for the
Kingdom."[372] A few lines farther along we read that the " 'other
sheep' have personal Scriptural evidence that they are not in that
Kingdom covenant."[373] In other words, the Memorial was intended by Christ to be celebrated by the 144,000 only! The only
semblance of Scripture proof given for this limitation of the

---

[363] *Ibid.*
[364] *Let God Be True,* p. 138.
[365] *Ibid.,* p. 136.
[366] *Ibid.,* pp. 138-39; *This Means Everlasting Life,* p. 275.
[367] *Jehovah's Witnesses in the Divine Purpose,* p. 24.
[368] *Make Sure of All Things,* p. 169.
[369] *Jehovah's Witnesses in the Divine Purpose,* p. 24.
[370] *Your Will Be Done,* p. 155; *Make Sure of All Things,* p. 260.
[371] *Make Sure of All Things,* p. 257.
[372] *Your Will Be Done,* p. 156.
[373] *Ibid.* We are not told what this "personal Scriptural evidence"
is.

Memorial to the anointed class is the quotation of Luke 22:28-30 in the *New World Translation,* according to which Jesus makes a covenant with his disciples for a Kingdom. In utterly arbitrary fashion, the authors proceed to assert dogmatically that the other sheep have no part in this "Kingdom covenant." Thus Jehovah's Witnesses prohibit the vast majority of their adherents from partaking of a sacrament which Christ appointed for all His people.

Though the other sheep may not partake of the elements, they are instructed to attend the Memorial annually and to observe its celebration.[374] Thus the number of partakers of the Memorial is always a very small portion of those who attend. In 1961, for example, though there was a world-wide Memorial attendance of 1,553,909, only 13,284 partook of the meal.[375]

DOCTRINE OF THE LAST THINGS

INDIVIDUAL ESCHATOLOGY

The State of Man After Death. It has been shown above that Jehovah's Witnesses deny the immortality of the soul, define soul as a living person, and say that man does not possess a soul but is a soul.[376] It will be obvious, therefore, that they disavow any conscious existence of the soul after death. Let us look into this matter a bit more in detail.

This disavowal is explicitly stated in a booklet published in 1955 entitled *What Do the Scriptures Say about "Survival After Death"?* On page 26 of this booklet they affirm that the human soul cannot exist apart from the human body. The human soul, therefore, is not immortal but mortal; a number of Scripture passages are cited in proof of this point (pp. 35-43). It is further contended that, since there is no sense in which any aspect of man continues to exist consciously after death, "in this respect mankind, because of the condemnation to death that they inherited from Adam, are like the lower animals that die. . ." (p. 31).[377]

The Meaning of Sheol and Hades. In this connection we should note what Jehovah's Witnesses teach about such Biblical words as Sheol and Hades. The Hebrew word Sheol, rendered *hell, grave,*

---

374 *Make Sure of All Things,* p. 263.

375 *Watchtower,* Jan. 1, 1962, p. 25.

376 See above, pp. 265-66.

377 The similarity between this view of the state after death and that of the Seventh-day Adventists is quite apparent. Note that, as in the case of Seventh-day Adventist teaching, the Jehovah-Witness position on the state after death cannot properly be described as *soul-sleep,* since, according to them, there is no soul that sleeps after death. The soul simply ceases to exist after death; hence their view, like that of the Adventists, can more accurately be described as *soul-extinction.*

or *pit* in the King James Version, means "mankind's common grave or the pit of burial"; it is emphatically denied that the word Sheol can ever mean "a fiery place of torture or a place of two compartments, one of bliss and one of fiery torment."[378] A number of Scripture passages are adduced to support this contention.[379] It is further asserted that Hades, the Greek equivalent of Sheol, also means "mankind's common grave."[380] Since the Bible teaches that after death man goes to either Sheol or Hades, and since both of these words simply mean grave, the Scriptures, so it is claimed, do not teach that there is any immaterial aspect of man which survives after death. When man dies, he totally ceases to exist.

Conditional Immortality. It must not be inferred from the above description of the state of man after death, however, that, according to Watchtower teaching, death is the final end for every human being. The Witnesses do indeed maintain that this is so for certain men, as will be shown later. But they also affirm that for most members of the human race some type of existence after death is to be expected. This type of existence, however, is not a continued subsistence, either in conscious or unconscious fashion, of the soul, but will take the form of some kind of resurrection. This resurrection may occur in either a physical or a non-physical way. The members of the anointed class have been or will be "resurrected" as spirits with "bodies" that are spiritual but not in any sense physical. The members of the other sheep, however, as well as the vast majority of the rest of mankind, will be raised with physical bodies during the millennium.[381]

We thus observe that Jehovah's Witnesses, while denying the inherent immortality of the human soul, do teach a kind of conditional immortality. *Conditional immortality* may be defined as the view that holds that, though man is inherently mortal, immortality is conferred on certain members of the human race as a divine gift. The Witnesses teach that immortality belongs primarily and originally to Jehovah.[382] Immortality in a secondary sense (not *inherent* but *bestowed* immortality), however, is given only to Christ and to the members of the anointed class:

[378] *Let God Be True,* pp. 89-90.

[379] *Ibid.,* pp. 90-92. The Witnesses are not wholly consistent on this point, however. For on pp. 93-94 we are told that the hell pictured in Isa. 14:9, into which the king of Babylon — who stands for Satan — is said to descend, is the abyss into which Satan is cast at the beginning of the millennium (Rev. 20:1-3). The word here translated hell is, however, Sheol. In this instance Sheol obviously does not mean grave, since the devil has no body which can be cast into a grave.

[380] *Ibid.,* p. 93.

[381] These teachings will be examined in greater detail and carefully documented later in this chapter.

[382] *Make Sure of All Things,* p. 349.

> Christ Jesus was first to receive immortality as a reward for his
> faithful course on earth, and it [immortality] is now also given in
> reward to those who are of the true congregation or "body of
> Christ." Immortality is a reward for faithfulness.[383]

This does not mean, however, that all other human beings besides the anointed class will finally be annihilated. The other
sheep and the majority of the rest of mankind will be raised with
physical bodies; after they shall have passed the tests to which
they must submit during the millennium, they will be granted everlasting life. But this everlasting life should be distinguished from
immortality, which is bestowed only on the anointed class.[384] For
Jehovah's Witnesses, to receive immortality, therefore, means to
be "raised" without a physical body; everlasting life in a physical
body is not considered equivalent to immortality.[385]

In summary, we may say that, according to Watchtower teaching, one of four possible destinies awaits a person when he dies:
(1) he may remain in the condition of nonexistence into which
death has plunged him; (2) he may be "raised" with a "spirit
body," thus receiving immortality, after which he will go directly
to heaven to reign there with Christ; (3) he may be raised with a
physical body and then, after having passed the millennial tests,
receive everlasting life on the renewed earth; or (4) he may, after
having been raised with a physical body, still fail to pass the millennial tests, and thus eventually be annihilated.[386]

GENERAL ESCHATOLOGY

The Kingdom of God. In order to understand Jehovah-Witness
teaching about the so-called "second presence" of Christ, we must
first examine their doctrine of the kingdom of God. Here, too, we
shall find the Witnesses differing sharply from evangelical Christians. Let us look first at a rather comprehensive definition of the
kingdom of God:

> The Kingdom of God is a Sovereign-empowered theocratic
> government under an administration of divinely appointed Kings.
> Jehovah himself is the great Everlasting King. . . . He has taken

---

[383] *Let God Be True,* p. 74. Cf. *Make Sure of All Things,* pp. 136,
350, 246, 247.
[384] *Make Sure of All Things,* pp. 248, 243. Cf. *Let God Be True,* p. 75.
[385] Cf. what was said on p. 267 above about the everlasting life Adam
would have attained if he had not sinned. Quite inconsistent with
this position, however, is the denial of the immortality of the angels, who,
like the glorified members of the anointed class, do not have physical
bodies (see above, p. 267).
[386] See Appendix E for a critical evaluation of Jehovah-Witness teaching
on soul-extinction, conditional immortality, and the annihilation of the
wicked.

into association as co-regent his Son Christ Jesus. God has pur-
posed the Kingdom as the capital or ruling part of his universal
organization. It is comprised of the King Christ Jesus and
144,000 associate kings taken from among men. It is entirely
heavenly, having no earthly part. All becoming members must
be resurrected and given spirit bodies.[387]

From this definition we learn that, though Jehovah is the King
of this kingdom, Jesus Christ is His co-regent and that this kingdom is the "ruling part" of Jehovah's organization. It is also quite
clear from this statement that only the 144,000 belong to this
kingdom. Even the 144,000, however, do not belong to the kingdom until after their "resurrection" with spirit bodies. The kingdom of God, therefore, is in no sense earthly; it is exclusively a
heavenly kingdom.[388]

When we now ask Jehovah's Witnesses when this heavenly kingdom was established, we get the following kind of answer: God
foretold the coming of this kingdom in Old Testament times, the
first of these prophecies being Genesis 3:15.[389] During the history
of Israel, God set up a theocracy, in which He Himself was the
ruler of His people; this, however, was not the kingdom promised
in Eden, but only a picture or type of the greater kingdom that
was to come.[390] When Christ came he proclaimed that the kingdom of God had drawn near; this, however, did not mean that the
kingdom had actually been established, but only that the anointed
king was now personally in the midst of the people of Israel.[391]
Though the disciples also proclaimed the presence of the kingdom
in this sense at the time when Christ was upon earth, "there is no
record that they continued to do so after his [Jesus'] ascension
on high," since "such an announcement would not be appropriate

[387] *Make Sure of All Things,* p. 226.
[388] The kingdom of God, therefore, for the Witnesses, does not designate a
group of people on earth — this despite the fact that they name their
places of worship "Kingdom Halls." It is specifically stated that "all
selected for the kingdom must die in order to enter it" (*ibid.*, p. 235).
Though the kingdom of God is a heavenly organization, this kingdom
does have earthly subjects: the other sheep (*Let God Be True,* p. 139;
This Means Everlasting Life, p. 275). Since only the 144,000 are members of the kingdom, the other sheep are subjects but not members. Even
the angelic hosts who serve as faithful messengers of the king are not
members of this kingdom but only subjects (*Let God Be True,* p. 138).
[389] *Let God Be True,* p. 134.
[390] *Ibid.,* p. 135.
[391] *Ibid.,* p. 140. In this connection Lk. 17:21 is quoted: "Look, the
kingdom of God is in your midst" (NWT). The Witnesses evade the
clear teaching of this passage — that the kingdom of God had then
already been established — by contending that these words only mean
that the King of the kingdom was then in the midst of the Pharisees (cf.
also *The Truth Shall Make You Free,* p. 299).

until his return and second presence."[392]   Christ, therefore, did not establish the kingdom of God at the time of his first advent. Neither did he establish this kingdom at once after he had ascended into heaven; his ascension was only the beginning of a long period of waiting for the establishment of the kingdom of God.[393]

When, then, was the kingdom of God actually established? In the year A.D. 1914. We have previously noted the fantastic calculations whereby the Witnesses have arrived at this date.[394] On October 1 of the year 1914, it is contended, the "appointed times of the nations" ended, and God's heavenly kingdom, with Christ enthroned as king, began.[395]   It can therefore now properly be said that the kingdom of God is here.[396]   Since the kingdom of God is here, we are now living in the "time of the end" — a period which began in 1914 and will end when the devil's world is destroyed in the Battle of Armageddon.[397]

The "Return" of Jesus Christ. Since Jehovah's Witnesses identify the establishment of the kingdom of God with the "return" of Jesus Christ, we next turn our attention to this "return." I have put quotation marks around the word *return* for two reasons: (1) This so-called "return" of Christ was neither a physical nor a visible one, since Christ after his resurrection has no physical body[398]; and (2) this was not really a "return" at all, since Christ did not go back to earth but simply began to rule over his kingdom from heaven.[399]   Thus there is actually no resemblance whatever between Jehovah-Witness teaching on the "return" of Christ and evangelical Protestant teaching about Christ's Second Coming.[400]

---

[392] *Let God Be True,* p. 140. But how would Jehovah's Witnesses interpret Acts 8:12, where Philip's preaching to the Samaritans is described as "preaching good tidings concerning the kingdom of God"; or Acts 19:8, where Paul is said to have taught in the synagogue at Ephesus for three months, "reasoning and persuading as to the things concerning the kingdom of God"?

[393] *The Truth Shall make you Free,* p. 241; *Let God Be True,* p. 140; *Make Sure of All Things,* p. 234. See also *New Heavens and a New Earth,* pp. 315, 317; and *This Means Everlasting Life,* p. 220.

[394] See above, pp. 252-54.

[395] *Paradise Lost,* pp. 173-74. Cf. *You May Survive Armageddon,* p. 100; *Let God Be True,* p. 141.

[396] *Let God Be True,* p. 141.

[397] *Paradise Lost,* pp. 178, 203. Further details about the nature and functioning of this kingdom will be given as we go along.

[398] *Let God Be True,* pp. 198-99; *Make Sure of All Things,* p. 321.

[399] *Paradise Lost,* pp. 173-74; *New Heavens and a New Earth,* p. 317.

[400] Watchtower publications usually prefer the designation "second presence" (using the word *presence* as a translation of the Greek word *parousia*), but they occasionally speak of Christ's *return* (*Let God Be True,* p. 198; *Make Sure of All Things,* p. 319). If, however, Christ was already in heaven prior to 1914, and if in 1914 he simply assumed a throne in heaven, how can this action possibly be called a *return?* The

To understand better what the Witnesses mean by Christ's "return," let us compare two statements from their writings. The first, from *This Means Everlasting Life,* p. 220, reads: "When he [Christ] ascended to heaven he sat down at God's right hand to wait for that time of entering into his authority and ruling like Melchizedek over his enemies as his footstool." The second is from *You May Survive Armageddon,* p. 100: ". . . Jehovah the heavenly Father brought forth his kingdom by bringing forth his anointed King-Priest Jesus Christ and elevating him to the active kingship in the throne at God's right hand." Putting these two statements together, we learn that from the time of his ascension to October 1, 1914 (when the kingdom was brought forth), Christ was sitting at the right hand of God the Father, and that on October 1, 1914, the Father placed the Son on the throne at His right hand. Thus the "return" or "second presence" of Christ simply means that Christ, who had been sitting at the Father's right hand in heaven since his ascension, now ascends the throne of his kingdom at the Father's right hand in heaven. The "return" of Christ is, for Jehovah's Witnesses, an exclusively heavenly transaction, consisting merely in Christ's exchanging an "ordinary" [401] seat at the Father's right hand for a throne. Watchtower teachings on this point, therefore, not only deny Christ's physical and visible return to earth, but also imply that Christ did not exercise His kingly office prior to 1914.

According to Jehovah-Witness teaching, therefore, we need no longer look for Christ's "return" or "second presence," because this "return" has already taken place. Christ "became King of the earth at the time of his second presence, A.D. 1914."[402]

This "second presence" of Christ, however, was also the occasion for an upheaval in the demonic world. Jehovah's Witnesses see in Revelation 12:1-9 a description of events which occurred at the time of this "second presence." The birth of the man-child depicted in verse 5 symbolically pictures the birth of the heavenly

---

word *return* is used meaningfully when a return to earth is thought of, but it has no intelligible meaning when it is used to describe the Jehovah-Witness conception of the "second presence" of Christ.

[401] By what stretch of the imagination, however, can Jehovah's Witnesses interpret the Biblical phrase "sitting at the right hand of God" as designating anything less than Christ's kingly reign from heaven? See I Pet. 3:22 and Eph. 1:20-23.

[402] *Make Sure of All Things,* p. 234. It should be noted that on this point present-day Jehovah's Witnesses are not true to the teachings of Russell who, as we have seen, taught that Christ's second presence began in the fall of 1874 (see above, p. 225). If Russell could be wrong about this crucial matter, how can the Witnesses be so sure that their present leaders are right about the new date?

kingdom and the placing of Christ on the throne of this kingdom.[403] The dragon's attempt to devour the man-child pictures the devil's unsuccessful endeavor to destroy the newborn government.[404] Since, for the Witnesses, Michael is another name for Christ in his glorified state, the war which is next described, between Michael and his angels on the one hand and the dragon and his angels on the other, is simply a dramatic picture of a great battle between Christ and the devil.[405] As a result of this great battle, the devil was hurled out of heaven and was cast down to the earth (v. 9).[406]

After Satan had been hurled out of heaven, however, he proceeded to vent his rage upon the peoples of the earth.

> Furious at the successful birth of the theocratic government, Satan determined to destroy all people ere they learned of the newly established kingdom. This was why he plunged the nations into the war of 1914-1918. It was the first time in history that so great a conflict had taken place.[407]

Driving home their point, the authors of *Let God Be True* go on to say: "It [the beginning of World War I] is conclusive proof that the 'appointed times' have ended, Satan's rule is interfered with, and the enthronement of Christ Jesus has taken place."[408]

Christ's Coming to His Temple. Though at the time when Christ became king of the heavenly kingdom of God in 1914 he ruled alone, it was not his intention to continue ruling as a solitary monarch. ". . . Men and women from upon the earth have been raised out of death to heavenly life to rule with him."[409] The number of the members of this group, we are further told, is to be 144,000; thus we know that those who either have or will have the privilege of ruling with Christ in this sense are the members of the anointed class. This group, however, did not begin to reign with Christ in heaven at the moment when the kingship was bestowed upon him, but a few years later.[410]

In explaining when the members of the anointed class did begin to reign with Christ, the authors of *Paradise Lost* point to a

---

[403] *New Heavens and a New Earth,* pp. 209-10.
[404] *Let God Be True,* p. 202.
[405] *Paradise Lost,* p. 176.
[406] *Ibid.*
[407] *Let God Be True,* p. 254.
[408] *Ibid.* It takes a bit of imagination to understand how the beginning of the worst war in history, fought largely by non-Jews, can be construed as proof that the "appointed times of the nations" — times during which Gentile nations would dominate the earth (see above, p. 252) — have ended, that Satan's rule has been interfered with, and that Christ's enthronement has now taken place!
[409] *Paradise Lost,* p. 213.
[410] *Ibid.*

parallel between Christ's first presence on earth and his "second presence." Christ was anointed with God's spirit — it is said — during his first presence in A.D. 29; three and a half years after this he cleansed the temple at Jerusalem; six days after this he arose from the dead. A similar time period, we are further told, is found during Jesus' "second presence." In the fall of 1914 he was crowned as king; three and a half years after that he cleansed Jehovah's spiritual temple; a very short time after the temple's cleansing, still in the year 1918, the heavenly resurrection of certain Christians occurred, and these then began to live and reign with Christ in heaven.[411]

Examining this matter in somewhat greater detail, we ask what Jehovah's Witnesses mean by the spiritual temple which Christ is supposed to have cleansed in 1918. This spiritual temple is understood to have been the Jehovah-Witness earthly organization, for we are told that during this year "Christians who had selfish hearts and wrong ideas toward his [Christ's] service dropped out of his organization."[412]

A short time after this cleansing of the spiritual temple, the members of the anointed class who had died by that time were "raised" with spiritual (that is, non-physical) bodies, and were placed on the throne with Jesus Christ.[413] At another place it is said that these risen ones were now "put in their places in the heavenly temple"[414]; from these words it appears that there is a temple in heaven corresponding to the earthly spiritual temple which Christ had just cleansed, and that the "raised" members of the anointed class are now in this heavenly temple — or, perhaps, constitute this temple.[415]

---

[411] *Ibid.*

[412] *Ibid.* See *Qualified to be Ministers*, pp. 313-14, where it is made clear that Jesus' coming to his temple for judgment in the spring of 1918 resulted in the separation of the "faithful and discreet slave" class from the "evil slave" group. The latter group, it is added, then subdivided and left the movement (see also *Jehovah's Witnesses in the Divine Purpose*, pp. 70-73). The above, in other words, is the official Jehovah-Witness explanation for the formation of certain schismatic groups in the year 1918 (see above, pp. 228-29).

[413] *Paradist Lost*, p. 213; *New Heavens and a New Earth*, p. 319.

[414] *You May Survive Armageddon*, p. 117.

[415] There is a great deal of ambiguity in Jehovah-Witness writing about this heavenly temple. Often one gets the impression that this heavenly temple is simply another name for the 144,000 after they have been translated to heaven, and that this temple will only be completed after the last of the 144,000 have been "raised" from the dead: "Jehovah's temple . . . consists of more than Jesus alone. It includes his congregation of 144,000 spiritual members, the spiritual body of which Jesus Christ is Head" (*You May Survive Armageddon*, p. 81). Members of the anointed class are often described as "living stones" of that temple (*ibid.*, pp. 96, 108; *Let Your Name Be Sanctified*, p. 274). At other

The Witnesses thus try to show that prophecy was fulfilled in 1918 as well as in 1914. Which prophecy? The prophecy of Malachi 3:1, "And suddenly there will come to his temple the [true] Lord, whom you people are seeking, and the messenger of the covenant in whom you are delighting" (NWT). There was, so they say, an "initial" or "miniature" fulfillment of this prophecy, and a final fulfillment. The initial fulfillment occurred when Christ cleansed the temple during his earthly ministry, and when certain subsequent events occurred.[416] The final fulfillment came in 1918, when Christ again came to his temple.[417]

In trying to show how this final fulfillment occurred, however, the Watchtower authors become quite badly confused. According to *Paradise Lost,* Christ's coming to the temple in 1918 was his coming to the earthly Jehovah-Witness organization to cleanse it of rebellious members.[418] According to the authors of *The Truth Shall Make You Free* and *You May Survive Armageddon,* however, the temple Christ came to in 1918 was not the earthly organization but the heavenly temple.[419] So there is ambiguity as to which temple he came to. Even if one understands Jehovah's Witnesses to mean by the temple to which Christ came in 1918 the heavenly one rather than the earthly organization, one is still at a loss to know exactly what they are trying to say. For, (1) if the heavenly temple is just another name for the 144,000, it is not correct to say that Christ came to them in 1918, for they were then "raised" to be with him in heaven; it would be more correct to say that, in 1918, the temple came to Christ. If, however, (2) the heavenly temple is the name of a certain place in heaven, we wonder where this place is. From *New Heavens and a New Earth,* p. 319, we learn that the 144,000 who are "raised" "are by such a spiritual, heavenly resurrection granted to sit with Jesus Christ in his throne, even as he conquered this old world and sat down with

---

times, however, one receives the impression that this heavenly temple is a place in heaven to which the members of the anointed class go after they die: "They [the deceased anointed ones] are now with him [Christ] at the temple, that is, in the condition of unity with him in the place invisible to human eyes, which place is symbolized by the 'air'" (*The Truth Shall Make You Free,* p. 304).

[416] *You May Survive Armageddon,* pp. 91-97.

[417] *Ibid.,* pp. 98ff.; *The Truth Shall Make You Free,* pp. 303, 324.

[418] *Paradise Lost,* p. 213.

[419] *The Truth Shall Make You Free,* pp. 303-4; on p. 324 this coming to the heavenly temple is called Christ's *epiphaneia* or "appearing" in distinction from his *parousia,* which occurred in 1914. Cf. *You May Survive Armageddon,* pp. 103-4; on the latter page it is said that the resurrection of the sleeping temple stones took place shortly after the arrival of Adonai [the Lord] and His messenger at the spiritual temple on the heavenly Mount Zion.

his Father in His throne." These words imply that the place to which the "raised" 144,000 go is the place where Christ is (for Christ has been seated on the throne since 1914). If this is so, how can Christ be said to "come to his temple" in 1918? How can one "come to" a place where he already is?[420]

The "first resurrection." We should now examine in greater detail what Jehovah's Witnesses mean by the "resurrection" of the deceased members of the anointed class which occurred in 1918. The Witnesses distinguish between a *first* or *earlier* resurrection and later resurrections.[421] These resurrections, however, are distinguished not just in time but also in manner; the "first" or "earlier" resurrection is said to be a nonphysical one, whereas the later resurrections are said to be physical.

What is the nature of this "first resurrection"? The following rather lengthy quotation describes both types of resurrection:

> Resurrection is a restoration to life of the nonexistent dead. . . . It is an act of God dependent entirely upon God's marvelous power through Christ and upon His memory of the dead. It is the reactivating of the life pattern of the creature, a transcription of which is on record with God, and is referred to as being in His memory. Resurrection does not involve the restoring of the original identical body of the creature. The life pattern is the personal life-long record of the creature built up by his thoughts and by the experiences in the life he has lived resulting from certain habits, leanings, mental abilities, memories and history. It is also a register of the individual's intellectual growth and his characteristics, all of which make up one's personality. Hence, according to God's will for the creature, in a resurrection one is restored or re-created in either a human or a spirit body and yet retains his personal identity by the setting in motion again of the distinctive life pattern of that individual.[422]

Note that resurrection is here defined as a restoration to life of the nonexistent dead, that it is dependent upon God's memory of the dead, that it is a reactivation of the life pattern of the creature

---

[420] On p. 275 of *This Means Everlasting Life* it is unequivocally asserted that the throne from which Christ rules in heaven is at the same time the place where he ministers in the heavenly temple: "It is from heaven that Christ and his 144,000 associate kings rule, for Christ Jesus sits at God's right hand. . . . The throne, heaven, is the place for kings to rule from, and not the footstool, the earth. Moreover, it is the Most Holy of all, the heaven itself of God's presence, where the High Priest of God applies the merit of his sacrifice for the sake of humankind."

[421] They call the "resurrection" of the 144,000 the "first resurrection," basing this on Rev. 20:6 (*Let God Be True*, p. 277); at times, however, they also refer to this as the "earlier resurrection," basing this designation on the NWT of Phil. 3:11, where the Greek word *exanastasis* is rendered, wholly without lexical warrant, *earlier resurrection* (*ibid.*, p. 282).

[422] *Make Sure of All Things*, p. 311.

rather than a restoring of the creature's original body, and that it is by this reactivation of the life pattern that the personal identity of the individual is to be retained. Note, too, that one may be restored in "either a human or a spirit body." In the "first resurrection" individuals are restored in *spirit bodies*.[423]

This "first resurrection" follows the pattern of Christ's resurrection. As he was "raised" without a physical body in order to partake of heavenly life, so also are the members of the anointed class. Only Christ and the 144,000, therefore, participate in this "first resurrection." When the Bible says that Christ is the "firstfruits of them which are asleep" (I Cor. 15:20), this does not mean that he was the firstfruits of all believers who have died, but only of the 144,000.[424]

This "first resurrection" was therefore not a bodily resurrection in the sense that these individuals were raised with physical bodies. It is called, as a matter of fact, a "spiritual, heavenly resurrection."[425] The members of the anointed class "raised" in 1918 are said to have been raised with "spirit bodies" to join Christ at the spiritual temple,[426] to have become "invisible spirit creatures,"[427] and to have entered upon "spirit life in the heavens."[428] We are, in fact, given the distinct impression that this "spirit life" is a more perfect form of life than one which would involve a physical resurrection: "The 'resurrection of life' includes the 'first resurrection,' which is the resurrection to instantaneous perfection of life, spirit life, in which Jesus himself participated and in which only the 144,000 joint heirs participate with him."[429]

Since this was a "resurrection" to a heavenly, spirit existence, it was invisible to human eyes.[430] In the case of those "raised" in 1918, this event was a transition from nonexistence to spirit-existence, possible only because God had on record a trans-

---

[423] The expression "spirit body" will be puzzling to most readers. It will be recalled that, according to Watchtower teaching, a heavenly soul "consists of a body together with the life principle or life force actuating it" (above, p. 265). So there are "heavenly" bodies as well as earthly, physical bodies. The author was told by Mr. Ulysses Glass, a member of the Watchtower staff, that these "heavenly bodies" will be vastly superior to the bodies of those on earth (personal interview, June 6, 1962).

[424] *Let God Be True*, pp. 276-77.

[425] *New Heavens and a New Earth*, p. 319.

[426] *Let God Be True*, p. 203.

[427] *Ibid.*, p. 138.

[428] *Paradise Lost*, p. 231.

[429] *You May Survive Armageddon*, pp. 354-55. One is tempted to ask: if perfection of life is spirit life, how could Jesus have lived a perfect life on earth in a body? One senses at this point a kind of Gnostic devaluation of the body.

[430] *Let God Be True*, p. 278; *The Kingdom is at Hand*, p. 304.

scription of the life patterns of these individuals.[431]   Actually,
therefore, God re-created them on the basis of His memory of
what they were like before they died.

Jehovah's Witnesses do not teach, however, that in 1918 the
total number of the anointed class was "raised" with a spiritual
resurrection.   A "remnant" of the 144,000 was still alive in
1918; a "remnant" is still alive today; and there will be a "remnant"
of this group left on earth during the coming millennium.[432]   So
the question arises: What happens to the members of this remnant
when they die?   The answer is: they undergo the "first resurrection" at the moment of their death.   Immediately at death
they enter into an "eternal spirit existence,"[433] are "resurrected
in the spirit,"[434] are "changed instantaneously to spirits immortal,
incorruptible,"[435] and "receive an immediate change to spirit
life."[436]   They are changed from being human creatures to being
spirit creatures in heaven with Christ.[437]   At another place we
are told: ". . . At death they are changed from human to divine,
incorruptible, immortal, spiritual, in but a moment or twinkling
of an eye. . . ."[438]

As this last quotation indicates ("changed from human to
divine"), this "first resurrection" is a kind of deification of the
members of the anointed class.   This does not mean, of course,
that the "little flock" now become equal to Jehovah God, but
they do become virtually equal to Christ — who is also "divine,"
though not equal to Jehovah.   Note the following parallels between what happens to the members of the anointed class and
what happened to Christ: (1) Like Christ, they are "raised"
with spirit bodies for life in heaven; (2) like Christ, they have
sacrificed their rights to life on earth in order to earn the right

[431] Make Sure of All Things, pp. 311, 313.
[432] *Let God Be True*, p. 278; *Paradise Lost*, p. 231; *New Heavens and
a New Earth*, p. 321.   In the last-named reference it is specifically stated
that "the thousand-year reign does not have to wait until they [the last
of the remnant] are glorified in the heavens. . . ."
[433] *Let God Be True*, p. 129.   In this connection the authors quote I
Cor. 15:51-52, "We all shall not sleep but we shall all be changed, in a
moment, in the twinkling of an eye, at the last trump. . ." (cf. *Paradise
Lost*, p. 232).   Apparently the "last trump" is thought to sound every
time a member of the remnant dies!
[434] *Let God Be True*, p. 279.
[435] *This Means Everlasting Life*, p. 235.
[436] *Let God Be True*, p. 203.   Cf. *This Means Everlasting Life*, p. 231;
Paradise Lost, p. 231.
[437] *Paradise Lost*, p. 232.
[438] *New Heavens and a New Earth*, p. 320.   Cf. *Make Sure of All
Things*, p. 247, where we are told that Christ and the 144,000 in heaven
share a "divine nature."

to life in heaven;[439] (3) like Christ, they attain immortality — an immortality which is shared by no other creatures, not even the angels; (4) like Christ, they have been begotten by God's spirit to become spiritual sons of God; (5) like Christ, they reign after death from a heavenly throne. Thus, as has been previously observed,[440] the difference between Christ and the 144,000, for the Witnesses, is not one of kind but only one of degree. And at this point we may well wonder whether one is justified in affirming even a difference of degree![441]

In referring to this "first resurrection" I have been putting the word *resurrection* between quotation marks since I do not believe that this can properly be called a resurrection. I make this judgment for two reasons:

(1) As was noted previously in the case of the Seventh-day Adventists,[442] this is not really a resurrection because, at least in the case of those "raised" in 1918, these individuals had been completely annihilated when they died; hence it would be more accurate to call their "restoration" to life in 1918 a new creation.

(2) The word *resurrection* has always been understood by the Christian church to mean resurrection with a physical body. Giving to people who had previously been annihilated a new existence as "spirit creatures" (or transforming people instantaneously from physical beings to "spirit creatures," in the case of those "raised" after 1918) is not a resurrection but rather a change into a different kind of existence.

In the history of the Christian church, people who taught that the "resurrection" was a nonphysical one were branded as heretics. The early fathers vigorously defended the resurrection of the body (in a physical sense) as a distinctively Christian doctrine over against those who, under the influence of Greek philosophy or Gnostic speculation, denied this teaching.[443] Yet today Jehovah's Witnesses, claiming to be listening to Scripture alone, are again reviving this ancient heresy!

It should now be added, by way of evaluation, that, as was observed in the case of the "resurrection" of Jesus Christ,[444] so

[439] See above, pp. 280, 283.
[440] See above, p. 274.
[441] On p. 275 of *This Means Everlasting Life* the astounding suggestion is made that the 144,000 must help to bring back the dead who are in the graves!
[442] See above, p. 140.
[443] See, e.g., Polycarp, *To The Philippians,* 7; *The Epistle of Barnabas,* 5 and 21; *II Clement,* 9; Justin Martyr, *First Apology,* 18-19; Tatian, *To the Greeks,* 6; Theophilus, *To Autolycus,* I, 7; Athenagoras, *The Resurrection of the Dead,* 18-25; Irenaeus, *Against Heresies:* II, 29, 2; IV, 5, 2.
[444] See above, p. 275.

here also there is no real continuity between the state of being in the flesh and the "resurrection" state. Christ by his "resurrection" was changed from a human being to a spirit creature. So it is with the 144,000: by their "resurrection" they are changed from being human creatures to being spirit creatures.[445] From their own description of this change, therefore, we learn that, for the Witnesses, the 144,000 cease to be human beings after their "resurrection." They enter into an entirely different kind of existence: a spirit existence. It would not be inaccurate to say that the 144,000 are, at death, changed into angels (angels, that is, who are now immortal, in distinction from ordinary angels, who remain mortal). The "resurrection" of the 144,000 is, therefore, really the creation of a new type of being — not a resurrection of human beings.

The Judgment of the Nations. Jehovah's Witnesses distinguish various *judgment days*.[446] One of these days of judgment began when Christ came to the temple in 1918.[447] "In the spring of 1918," it is said, "he [Christ] came as Jehovah's Messenger to the temple and began judgment first of the 'house of God' and then of the nations of this world."[448]

This judgment which began at the house of God is, however, variously interpreted. In one place we are told that this judgment was accomplished by the "resurrection" of the anointed class, by which a favorable judgment was rendered to the house of God.[449] At another place in the same book, however, we are informed that this judgment consisted in the following: The faithful ones who took up the witnessing work in 1918 and 1919, and who began to serve spiritual food to the spiritually hungry at this time, were judged by Jehovah to be the "faithful and discreet slave class." Thus, it is alleged, Jehovah indicated who were His true people, distinguishing them from those who falsely claimed to be the "house of God," namely, the churches of Christendom.[450] One may apparently adopt either interpretation, or both.

---

[445] *Paradise Lost*, p. 232.

[446] *Make Sure of All Things*, pp. 219-25.

[447] *Let God Be True*, p. 277. We note here some similarity to the "investigative judgment" of the Seventh-day Adventists. It will be recalled that Russell had some early associations with the Adventists. As the Watchtower understanding of this judgment at the temple is unfolded, however, it will become evident that the teaching of the Witnesses here is quite different from that of Seventh-day Adventism.

[448] *Ibid.*, p. 287. In connection with the judgment which began at the "house of God," I Peter 4:17 is quoted.

[449] *You May Survive Armageddon*, p. 117.

[450] *Ibid.*, pp. 207-208. To understand what Jehovah's Witnesses mean by the "faithful and discreet slave class," see above, pp. 245-46.

In the spring of 1918 Christ also began his judgment of the nations. This teaching is derived from Matthew 25:31-46, the passage which speaks of the judgment of the sheep and the goats.[451] This judgment, it is said, takes place during the "time of the end," that is, from the spring of 1918 to the Battle of Armageddon.[452] Christ, now seated on the throne of his glory, is busy separating the people of the nations into two classes, called sheep and goats.[453] The basis for this judgment is the attitude people take toward the kingdom message and its bearers, the remnant.[454] The goats are those who have no appreciation for the kingdom message and who show no help or kindness to the bearers of this message;[455] this group will include Christendom because it has had no charity for the remnant of Christ's brothers.[456] The sheep, however, are those who rejoice at the coming of the kingdom and do good to the remnant who bear the message.[457] By the time of the Battle of Armageddon this judging of the nations will have been completed; the sheep will have been gathered at the king's right side, into company with the remnant, whereas the goats will have been gathered at his left side.[458] At the Battle of Armageddon the judgment against the nations will be executed.[459] Then the goats will be destroyed and annihilated, whereas the sheep will live through the battle and "enter upon the opportunities for everlasting life in the new world."[460]

The Battle of Armageddon. Before the glorious new world can be ushered in, however, there will occur a battle more terrible than anything the world has ever seen. "Armageddon will be the worst thing ever to hit the earth within the history of man."[461] What kind of battle will this be?

We find a brief definition of it on page 24 of *Make Sure of All Things*:

> The battle of Jehovah God Almighty in which his executive officer Christ Jesus leads invisible forces of righteousness to de-

---

[451] *Let God Be True*, p. 290.
[452] *You May Survive Armageddon*, p. 160.
[453] *Let God Be True*, p. 204.
[454] *Ibid.*, p. 290; *You May Survive Armageddon*, p. 163.
[455] *Let God Be True*, p. 290.
[456] *You May Survive Armageddon*, pp. 165-66.
[457] *Let God Be True*, p. 290; *You May Survive Armageddon*, pp. 164-65.
[458] *You May Survive Armageddon*, pp. 164-68.
[459] *Let God Be True*, p. 287.
[460] *You May Survive Armageddon*, pp. 165-67. The moral is obvious: if you want to survive Armageddon and enter the paradise of the new world, you must leave Christendom and join the Jehovah-Witness movement!
[461] Statement made by Nathan Knorr at the 1953 Yankee-Stadium Assembly, quoted in *You May Survive Armageddon*, p. 11.

stroy Satan and his demonic and human organization, eliminating wickedness from the universe and vindicating Jehovah's universal sovereignty.

From this definition we learn that Armageddon will be Jehovah's decisive (though not final) battle against His enemies, both demonic and human; that Christ will be Jehovah's executive officer, leading invisible forces to victory; and that this battle will result in the elimination of wickedness and the vindication of Jehovah's sovereignty.[462]

The background for the Battle of Armageddon is the tribulation brought upon Satan's world by Christ, who has taken action to unseat Satan from his position as ruler of the earth. Actual combat against Satan and his demon horde began with Christ's enthronement in A.D. 1914. This combat was cut short in A.D. 1918, to be resumed at Armageddon.[463] "In between, while this tribulation is cut short, there is a work of proclaiming the Kingdom and its day of vengeance, and of exposing Satan's filthy organization. . . ."[464] Because it is believed that only those who are members of the Watchtower organization, whether as anointed ones or other sheep, will survive Armageddon,[465] and because it is further believed that no one who dies at Armageddon will be raised from the dead during the millennium,[466] Jehovah's Witnesses preach with great urgency: Come into Jehovah's theocratic organization now, or be forever annihilated in the Battle of Armageddon![467]

This great battle will not be a conflict between capitalism and communism, nor will it be a destruction of the nations through atomic energy, but it will be Jehovah's fight in which both the invisible and visible parts of Satan's world will be completely destroyed.[468] Armageddon, the "war of the great day of God

---

[462] It will be recalled that the vindication of Jehovah's sovereignty is, for the Witnesses, the primary purpose of world history (see above, pp. 259-60).

[463] *Make Sure of All Things,* p. 390. The astounding implication of these words is that Christ did not engage in actual combat with Satan previous to 1914, and that he does not do so between 1918 and Armageddon!

[464] *Ibid.*

[465] *Paradise Lost,* p. 210; *You May Survive Armageddon,* pp. 217, 347.

[466] "The unrighteous 'goats' will be everlastingly cut off from all life in the battle of Armageddon with which this old world will end" (*Paradise Lost,* p. 202).

[467] *Let God Be True,* pp. 260, 201. In the latter passage the role of Jehovah's Witnesses is compared to that of Noah before the flood.

[468] *Ibid.,* p. 259. This statement must not be taken entirely at face value, however, since Satan is only "abyssed" at Armageddon, to be loosed again at the end of the millennium.

the Almighty" (Rev. 16:14),[469] will be a war in which the nations of the world will fight against God's kingdom headed by His Anointed One, Jesus[470]; it will be a battle between those who are for and those who are against Jehovah's universal sovereignty.[471] Jehovah will actually welcome this fight, for it will give Him the opportunity of vindicating His universal sovereignty over the earth.[472]

Satan is now grouping his forces in preparation for the war of Armageddon.[473] His demons are leading the nations to prepare to do battle against those who visibly represent the kingdom of God, the remnant and their companions in the New World Society.[474]

Where will this battle be fought? Though the word *Armageddon,* or *Har-Magedon,* derived from Rev. 16:16, means "mountain of Megiddo," this battle will not be fought just at the field of Megiddo in Palestine since this battlefield would be too small to hold all the kings of the earth and their armies.[475] The battle will be fought in all quarters of the globe.[476] The reason why this battle is called that of Armageddon is that the battles fought in ancient times at Megiddo in Palestine were decisive: the armies that won there won complete victories, whereas those that lost suffered total defeat.[477]

When will this battle be fought? At the close of the "time of the end," which will be very soon.[478] It was affirmed in 1952 that this war would begin inside our generation.[479] In a volume published in 1958 we are told that many people alive since 1914 will still be living when Armageddon begins.[480]

Just before Armageddon begins, the devil will attack the New World Society.[481] This attack will provoke Jehovah to anger; He will then unleash the Battle of Armageddon by giving Christ

[469] *Paradise Lost,* p. 203.
[470] *You May Survive Armageddon,* p. 333.
[471] *Ibid.,* p. 338.
[472] *Ibid.,* p. 334. Note the conception of the nature of Jehovah which underlies this statement!
[473] *Let God Be True,* p. 259.
[474] *You May Survive Armageddon,* pp. 333-34. At this point Rev. 12:17 is quoted, the same passage to which Seventh-day Adventists appeal to support their conception of the "remnant church." Cf. *Paradise Lost,* p. 203, where a similar statement is made, buttressed by a reference to Rev. 16:14, 16.
[475] *Paradise Lost,* pp. 203-4.
[476] *You May Survive Armageddon,* p. 337.
[477] *Paradise Lost,* p. 203.
[478] *Ibid.,* p. 205.
[479] *Let God Be True,* p. 179.
[480] *Paradise Lost,* p. 205.
[481] *Ibid.,* p. 206.

the command to destroy the devil's wicked world.[482] The invisible "appearance" of Christ at this time is called "the revelation of the Lord Jesus from heaven" depicted in II Thessalonians 1:7-10[483]; this revelation (*apokalupsis*) is distinguished from the second presence of Christ (*parousia*) which occurred in 1914.[484] This "appearance" of Christ on earth is called "the final revelation of the King"[485] and is even referred to as his "return."[486]

Who will be drawn up in battle array at the War of Armageddon? On the one side will be all the nations of the world, the members of the United Nations (the beast of Rev. 17), the religious heads of heathendom and Christendom (the woman who rides the beast), and all the goats that have been separated from the sheep by the judgment of the nations just concluded (this last group will include most of Christendom).[487] On the other side will be the remnant of spiritual Israel (that is, the members of the 144,000 left on earth at that time) and the "great crowd" of other sheep[488] — a crowd, however, which will look very small compared to the vast hordes which oppose them. In addition to these visible forces there will be invisible combatants as well. Fighting against God will be the devil and all the demons.[489] Fighting on the side of the remnant and the other sheep, however, will be Jesus Christ and, following his leadership, the unseen hosts of heaven (that is, the angels) together with those of his anointed followers who have been "resurrected."[490]

The remnant and the other sheep do not need to fight at Armageddon; Christ and his heavenly armies will do all the fighting for them.[491] When we ask what weapons will be used by the

[482] *Ibid.,* p. 207.
[483] *You May Survive Armageddon,* p. 27.
[484] *This Means Everlasting Life,* p. 222.
[485] *Let God Be True,* p. 205.
[486] *Ibid.,* p. 206. So there are two "returns" of Christ: the first one, which occurred in 1914, when he ascended the throne of his kingdom; and a second one, which will occur when he comes to earth to conduct the Battle of Armageddon! It is therefore not quite correct to say that Jehovah's Witnesses do not look for *any* future "return" of Christ. Even this future return, however, will be an invisible one (*ibid.,* p. 205).
[487] *You May Survive Armageddon,* p. 338; see above, pp. 254-55. It is evident from this description why Jehovah's Witnesses attack not only all churches but also all political organizations and governments. All governments and all churches are part of the devil's visible organization. The Witnesses therefore refuse to salute the flag of any nation since, so they say, such an act ascribes salvation to the nation for which the flag stands, and is an act of idolatry (*Let God Be True,* pp. 242-43).
[488] *You May Survive Armageddon,* pp. 338-39.
[489] *Paradise Lost,* p. 203.
[490] *You May Survive Armageddon,* pp. 338-39. The revelation of Christ at Armageddon will, however, be an invisible one. Thus neither Christ nor his heavenly armies will be seen by men.
[491] *Paradise Lost,* p. 204.

rebellious nations, we get an ambiguous answer. On the one hand we are told that the nations will use their military, naval, and air equipment,[492] and that they will release atomic bombs, hydrogen bombs, disease-germ bombs, and chemical gas bombs.[493] Yet on the other hand we are informed that the wood of the weapons of Gog's hordes (that is, those of the devil) will make so large a pile that it will take seven years to use it up as fuel. These weapons are then designated as follows: shields, bows and arrows, handstaves, and spears.[494] Jehovah, however, will completely exterminate His enemies by unleashing such terrors as cloudbursts, floods, earthquakes, hailstones, fires, and flesh-eating plagues.[495] The fire of Armageddon will, in fact, be far more destructive than literal fire; it will completely envelop the devil's visible and invisible organizations.[496]

The results of this terrible battle will be worse than those of any previous war in history. Over two billion people will die.[497] All of Christendom will be wiped out,[498] and all the nations will be destroyed.[499] "Satan's entire world or system of things, its invisible demonic heavens and its visible wicked human earth, will be destroyed. . . ."[500] Dead bodies will be everywhere, from one end of the earth to the other; these shall neither be wept over nor buried.[501] Not a single human being who was against Jehovah's organization will survive.[502]

Only faithful Jehovah's Witnesses — members of the remnant or of the other sheep — will survive Armageddon; these "will stand and see the salvation of Jehovah for them."[503] Jehovah will not allow His executioners to touch them.[504] These Armageddon survivors will be assigned the duty of gathering up the bones that

---

[492] *You May Survive Armageddon,* p. 337.
[493] *Ibid.,* p. 340.
[494] *Ibid.,* p. 343.
[495] *Paradise Lost,* pp. 207-208.
[496] *New Heavens and a New Earth,* p. 294.
[497] *You May Survive Armageddon,* p. 341.
[498] *Ibid.,* p. 217.
[499] *Ibid.,* p. 57.
[500] *Ibid.,* p. 346.
[501] *Paradise Lost,* p. 210.
[502] *You May Survive Armageddon,* p. 342.
[503] *Ibid.,* p. 347. Note that what determines survival at Armageddon is not first of all faith in Jesus Christ as Saviour, but membership in the New World Society. Faith in the all-sufficient atonement of Christ will not save from total annihilation any member of "Christendom" unaffiliated with the Watchtower organization.
[504] *Ibid.,* p. 217. When we ask how anyone can be expected to live through this devastating holocaust, or how Jehovah's Witnesses will be kept safe from enemy bullets and bombs, we are told that "Jehovah will perform a stupendous miracle in preserving them [His people] through the terrifying destruction" (*This Means Everlasting Life,* p. 266).

are left of the slain, and of burying them (not the bodies; just the bleached bones).[505]   The survivors are also given the task of converting whatever instruments of combat are left on the earth into implements of peace.[506]

To complete the story of the Battle of Armageddon, it should be mentioned that, at the end of the battle, Satan and his demons are cast into the "abyss" by Christ, who is said to be the angel referred to in Revelation 20:1.[507] The abyss is not a symbol for the condition of nonexistence; it stands for a deathlike state of inactivity.[508]   Thus, both the devil and his demons having been rendered inactive, the world is ready for the millennium which now begins.

The Millennium. Jehovah's Witnesses understand the thousand years of Revelation 20 as pointing to a literal thousand-year period, beginning immediately after Armageddon, during which God's new world is to be established on earth.   This period is referred to in their literature as that of Christ's millennial reign,[509] or of his thousand-year reign.[510]   God's new world is said to consist of "new heavens and a new earth." By the new heavens the Witnesses understand "the righteous new heavenly ruling powers, Christ Jesus with his 'bride' of 144,000 members."[511] By the new earth they mean "not a new earthly globe, but the righteous earthly subjects of the King living under a new social arrangement."[512]

This leads us to consider the role of the 144,000 during the millennium.   They are, of course, not on earth but in heaven (except for those few still living on earth after Armageddon, who will join the heavenly assembly as soon as they die).[513]   The

[505] *Paradise Lost,* p. 211.
[506] *The Truth Shall Make You Free,* p. 360.
[507] *Paradise Lost,* p. 211.
[508] *Ibid.*
[509] *New Heavens and a New Earth,* p. 321.
[510] *Paradise Lost,* p. 226.   At this point a question arises: Since Christ began ruling from his heavenly throne in 1914, why is this period referred to as "the thousand years of Christ's reign" (*Let God Be True,* p. 270)? And how can the 144,000 be said to reign a thousand years with Christ during the millennium (*ibid.,* p. 137), when they actually began to reign with him in 1918?
[511] *Religion for Mankind,* p. 377.   Actually, the new heavens in this sense began to come into existence in 1918, when the first group of anointed ones began to be "raised"; these new heavens, further, are not complete until some time after the millennium has begun since there will still be members of the remnant living on earth after Armageddon.
[512] *Ibid.*   It will be recalled that in the Battle of Armageddon Satan's demonic heavens and wicked human earth were destroyed (see above, p. 311).
[513] *New Heavens and a New Earth,* p. 321; *You May Survive Armageddon,* p. 352.

144,000 in heaven are, during the millennium, the invisible part of the new world,[514] the ruling body of Jehovah's universal organization.[515] In the capacity of priests and kings they reign with Christ during the millennium.[516] They may therefore be called "associate kings" and "royal priests"[517]; since the power of judging has also been bestowed upon them,[518] they may in addition be called "associate judges."[519] It may be gathered from the above that the 144,000 will therefore help Christ in carrying out his kingly, priestly, and judicial activities. We are told, in fact, that they "join him [Christ] in dispensing the benefits of Christ's ransom sacrifice to the believers of mankind during the thousand years of the Kingdom rule."[520] We are further informed that they must officiate as priests "for the everlasting good of mankind, even to bringing back all the dead who are in the graves."[521] Christ, in fact, will not even be able to bring the inhabitants of God's new world to perfection without the help of his heavenly bride:

> The ministry of the heavenly High Priest together with the 144,000 who will be his underpriests and "priests of God" will lift up the antitypical twelve tribes of Israel to human perfection by the end of the thousand years of Christ's reign.[522]

What will the earth be like during the millennium? The earth, it is said, will be cleansed after Armageddon.[523] Soon after the devastation of Armageddon has been removed, the earth will become a new paradise, replacing the paradise lost at the dawn of history.[524] The whole earth will be made into a garden; under Jehovah's direction, aided by an ideal climate and the absence of destructive pests, the survivors of Armageddon will replant the earthly paradise.[525] Man will again subdue the earth and have dominion over the lower creation; all the beasts will now be at

---

[514] *Let God Be True*, p. 138.

[515] *Ibid.*, p. 130.

[516] *Ibid.*, p. 137.

[517] *This Means Everlasting Life*, p. 275.

[518] *You May Survive Armageddon*, p. 276.

[519] *Make Sure of All Things*, p. 221.

[520] *This Means Everlasting Life*, pp. 274-75. Christ therefore needs the services of the 144,000 in applying the fruits of his atonement to his people.

[521] *Ibid.*, p. 275. Apparently Christ cannot raise the dead without the help of the 144,000.

[522] *You May Survive Armageddon*, p. 353.

[523] *Paradise Lost*, p. 216. Yet this cleansing is not final. For, on p. 239 of the same volume, we are told that it is not until the execution of judgment over Satan and his followers at the end of the millennium that the perfect earth will be cleansed.

[524] *Ibid.*, pp. 220ff.

[525] *Ibid.*, p. 221.

peace with each other and with man.[526]   On this new earth there
will be neither thorns nor thistles.[527]   There will be no more
famine or drought; no diseases, aches, or pains; and no more old
age, since perpetual youth will be the lot of all the faithful.[528]
Death will also be largely eliminated[529] — the only ones who will
die during the millennium will be those members of the remnant
that survived Armageddon and those inhabitants of the new earth
who refuse to obey Jehovah (these as we shall see, will be
annihilated). All results of sin in human social life will also have
been removed.   There will be no more war, no crime, no lawlessness or vice — since all people who want to do bad things
have been killed at Armageddon.[530]   Hence there will be no need
for armed troops or for police forces.[531]   All will be at peace with
each other since all will be united in the worship of the one true
God.[532]

During the millennium the earth, which was denuded of all
human inhabitants except Jehovah's Witnesses by the Battle of
Armageddon, will be repopulated.   How will this repopulation
take place?   First, by the birth of children to the Armageddon
survivors, and, second, by a series of resurrections.   Let us look
at each of these methods in detail.

Children Born During the Millennium.   Children will be
born to the survivors of Armageddon.[533] These Armageddon survivors may expect to receive a mandate from God through Christ
enjoining them to reproduce their kind.[534] Since not all of these survivors were married when Armageddon came, there will be marriages during the millennium.[535] Because children so born will not
die — unless they prove rebellious — and because room must be
left on the earth for those who will be raised from the dead, God
will see to it that, at a certain point of time, childbearing will
cease.[536]

[526] *Let God Be True*, p. 267.
[527] *New Heavens and a New Earth*, p. 344.
[528] *Let God Be True*, pp. 267-68.
[529] *Ibid.*, p. 268.
[530] *Ibid.*, p. 267; *Paradise Lost*, pp. 221-22.
[531] *Let God Be True*, p. 267.
[532] *Ibid.*, p. 266.
[533] *You May Survive Armageddon*, p. 351.
[534] *New Heavens and a New Earth*, pp. 331-32.
[535] *Let God Be True*, p. 269.
[536] *Paradise Lost*, p. 225.   There appears to be some ambiguity in
Jehovah-Witness teaching on the question of whether only Armageddon
survivors will be able to bring forth children during the millennium,
or whether this privilege will be extended also to the other sheep raised
from the dead after Armageddon.   On pp. 362-64 of *The Truth Shall
Make You Free* (published in 1943) we are told that the other sheep
raised after Armageddon will have a part in fulfilling the divine mandate

A word should be said about the nature of these children. Infant death, needless to say, will no longer occur during the millennium; neither will any of these children be cripples.[537] Yet they will not be perfect; "being born of not yet perfect although righteous parents,[538] these children will not be born any more perfect than their parents then."[539] Though imperfect, the children born to Armageddon survivors will not grow older, however, nor weaker and impaired with age, but will grow "young, strong, and gradually freed from all blemishes and marks of imperfection."[540] Their parents will teach them to do right, transmitting to them God's instructions. Though Godfearing parents before the millennium train their children in an imperfect way, during the millennium parents will be able to perform this task "in a perfect and complete way under God's direction."[541]

Resurrections During the Millennium. Before discussing the various groups that will be raised during the millennium, we should examine the nature of these resurrections. According to Jehovah-Witness teaching, there is no soul which survives after death. When a man dies he totally ceases to exist.[542] Yet the Witnesses do teach that people will be "raised" from the dead. We have already looked at their teaching on the so-called first or nonphysical "resurrection" which the members of the anointed class experience. There are others, however — their number will far exceed that of 144,000 — who will be raised with physical bodies. Yet even these resurrections with physical bodies are not, strictly speaking, resurrections. Since these individuals were totally annihilated when they died, it would be more accurate to call the "resurrections" which are now said to occur *new creations.*[543] Interestingly enough, Watchtower authors even use the word *create* to describe this type of resurrection: "through Jesus Christ who died for them [people to be raised during the millennium], God will create new bodies for them."[544]

---

to bring forth children. In later publications, however, it is said that only Armageddon survivors will have this privilege (*Let God Be True,* pp. 268-69; *Paradise Lost,* pp. 224, 226). Perhaps there has been a shift in Watchtower thinking on this point.

[537] *Paradise Lost,* p. 225.

[538] A strange combination, to say the least!

[539] *New Heavens and a New Earth,* p. 346.

[540] *You May Survive Armageddon,* p. 353.

[541] *Paradise Lost,* pp. 224-25. Another strange combination: parents who are still imperfect will be able, during the millennium, to do a perfect job of training their children!

[542] See above, pp. 293-94.

[543] See the comment made about the Seventh-day Adventist conception of the resurrection on p. 140 above.

[544] *Paradise Lost,* p. 234.

This type of resurrection is described as a "reactivating of the life pattern of the creature."[545] This is possible only because the life pattern of every creature to be so raised is on record with God. God therefore re-creates these individuals on the basis of His memory of what they were like before they died.[546] "People who have been kept in God's memory will be brought back to life from their death state to enjoy the benefits of God's righteous new world."[547] A human being so raised will retain his personal identity "by the setting in motion again of the distinctive life pattern of that individual."[548] Such a person will have the same personality that he had when he died; he will therefore be recognizable by acquaintances.[549]

It should be noted that those who are physically raised during the millennium are not raised with perfect human bodies. Their new bodies, it is said, will match the personalities of the individuals who are raised — personalities which were neither sinless nor perfect at the moment of death.[550] These individuals, therefore, are raised in a fallen condition; only by the end of the millennium will they have been lifted out of their fallen condition and brought to a condition of human perfection.[551]

A great number of people will be raised with physical bodies

---

[545] *Make Sure of All Things,* p. 311 (see above, p. 302, where this rather detailed description is quoted in full).

[546] *Ibid.*

[547] *Paradise Lost,* p. 227. The implication is that some have not been kept in God's memory and will therefore not be brought back to life. This point is made explicit on p. 364 of *The Truth Shall Make You Free.* Here, speaking of people who are cast into Gehenna, the place of final destruction, the authors say, ". . . They are not spoken of as 'in the tombs' or 'in the graves,' which is to say, in the memory of God as having an opportunity for redemption by Christ's blood. . . . God will not remember them in the time of 'resurrection of the dead, both of the just and unjust.' "

[548] *Make Sure of All Things,* p. 311.

[549] *Survival After Death,* p. 38. It is significant that, for the Witnesses, a resurrection with a physical body is of lower value than one with a nonphysical body, since the latter is experienced only by Christ and the 144,000, whereas the former is experienced by the more numerous other sheep. Again we see in Watchtower teaching a kind of Gnostic disparagement of the physical body.

[550] *Paradise Lost,* p. 234.

[551] *Ibid.,* p. 238; *Let God Be True,* p. 293. At the beginning of the millennium, therefore, all three groups that make up the population of the new earth are still imperfect: the Armageddon survivors, the children born to them, and those raised from the dead. Gradually, however, as the millennium progresses, they advance toward perfection, through the ministry of the heavenly High Priest and the 144,000 (*You May Survive Armageddon,* p. 353). This perfecting does not take place without the obedient cooperation of millennial mankind with Christ during the thousand years (*This Means Everlasting Life,* p. 304).

during the millennium. One statement, in fact, gives the impression that most people who have ever lived will be so raised: "The greater mass of humankind will find life here on earth amid paradise conditions."[552] There will be some, however, who will not be brought back from death. Christ himself will judge who deserve to be raised or who could profit from being raised.[553]

Those Not Raised During the Millennium. Let us now note which individuals will not be raised from the dead. As we have previously observed, none of those killed at Armageddon will be raised. All those who knowingly and deliberately did wrong will not be raised.[554] Those who died wicked beyond reform or correction and beyond redemption by Christ's blood will not be raised.[555] This group includes all who have sinned against the holy spirit.[556] Among those included in the number of people who will not be raised are Adam and Eve[557]; it is said that, since Adam had his final judgment in the garden of Eden, and was sentenced there, he will not be raised for any further judgment during the millennium.[558] Others who will not be raised include Cain,[559] those who died in the flood, the people of Sodom,[560] Judas Iscariot, and the religious hypocrites of Jesus' day.[561] All these will simply be left in the nonexistence into which death has plunged them.

The "Resurrection of Life." Jehovah's Witnesses distinguish between two kinds of resurrection during the millennium: a "resurrection of life" and a "resurrection of judgment." They base this distinction on the words of Jesus recorded in John 5:28-29:

---

[552] *Let God Be True*, p. 279. Jehovah's Witnesses are not universalists, since they teach that some will be annihilated. Yet the above statement suggests that, in their judgment, the number of those annihilated will be small in comparison with the number of the saved.

[553] *You May Survive Armageddon*, p. 354. The statement "who could profit from being raised" is puzzling, in view of the fact that some who are raised during the millennium will disobey God and consequently be annihilated. Did these individuals really "profit" from their resurrection? Could not Christ have foreseen their disobedience and simply have left them in the condition of nonexistence in which they were before their resurrection?

[554] *Paradise Lost*, p. 229.

[555] *Let God Be True*, p. 289.

[556] *Ibid.* How can one, however, sin against an impersonal force?

[557] *Paradise Lost*, p. 236.

[558] *Let God Be True*, p. 289. It is striking to note the difference between the view of Adam held by Mormons and Jehovah's Witnesses. By the latter, he is not even considered worthy of being raised from the dead; by the former, however, he is hailed as one of the noblest characters that ever lived and is even looked upon as a god! (above, pp. 51, 41).

[559] *You May Survive Armageddon*, p. 354.

[560] *Paradise Lost*, p. 236.

[561] *You May Survive Armageddon*, p. 354.

". . . the hour is coming in which all those in the memorial tombs
will hear his voice and come out, those who did good things to a
resurrection of life, those who practiced vile things to a resurrection
of judgment" (NWT). The "resurrection of life" includes the
resurrection of faithful men of God who lived before Pentecost,
and of other sheep who died before Armageddon.[562] The "resurrection of judgment" is that of the rest of mankind who have not
been judged worthy of being destroyed.[563]

The "resurrection of life" includes, first, that of Old Testament
people who were faithful to God and that of others who lived
at the time of Christ but died before Pentecost.[564] "These men
knew that their hope was in a resurrection to life right here on
earth. And they really had strong faith in the fact that they would
be resurrected."[565] When these ancient worthies are raised, they
will become "other sheep" of the Right Shepherd.[566]

Many of these Old Testament saints will be made theocratic
princes — that is, will be given princely or leading positions in the
new earth, as the visible representatives of Christ.[567] Among
these will be Enoch, Noah, Abraham, Isaac, Jacob, David,[568]
Moses, and Daniel.[569] However, some of the other sheep who
have survived Armageddon will also be made princes[570]; since
many of them occupy positions as theocratic princes in the New
World Society today, before Armageddon, they will carry these
princely responsibilities with them through Armageddon.[571] Thus
the inhabitants of the new earth will be given good rulers, chosen
for this purpose by Jesus Christ himself.[572]

Since those who are to be made princes must serve as rulers
of the new earth, they will be raised first.[573] The next group to
be raised, also as part of the "resurrection of life," will be the
other sheep who died before Armageddon.[574] These, though
unable to share the heavenly blessedness of the 144,000, will be
able to enjoy everlasting life on the paradise earth if they remain

---

[562] *Paradise Lost*, p. 228. On p. 231 it is said that the resurrection of
the 144,000 was also part of the "resurrection of life."
[563] *Ibid.*, p. 229.
[564] *You May Survive Armageddon*, p. 355.
[565] *Paradise Lost*, p. 228.
[566] *You May Survive Armageddon*, p. 355. They cannot become members of the 144,000 because they died before Pentecost, when the anointed
class began to be gathered.
[567] *Ibid.*, p. 355.
[568] *Ibid.*
[569] *Religion for Mankind*, p. 339.
[570] *Let God Be True*, pp. 139, 263.
[571] *You May Survive Armageddon*, pp. 355-56.
[572] *Paradise Lost*, p. 218.
[573] *Ibid.*, p. 232.
[574] *Ibid.*

faithful to God.[575] Though Jesus expressly said that they would inherit the kingdom prepared for them (Mt. 25:34), we are given to understand that this is not the kingdom of heaven but the earthly realm of the kingdom of heaven.[576]

The "Resurrection of Judgment." After the princes and the other sheep have been raised, there follows the "resurrection of judgment."[577] This is the resurrection of people "whose hearts may have been wanting to do right, but who died without ever having had an opportunity to hear of God's purposes or to learn what He expects of men."[578] These individuals are further described as having been sincere in their belief, but having lacked an opportunity to learn of righteousness from God. This opportunity they will now receive.[579] This group will include the penitent thief.[580] Along with him, billions of others will be brought back for this "resurrection of judgment."[581] These resurrections will be spread out over a long period so that people who have been raised earlier can help to get things ready for those who are yet to return.[582]

After this "resurrection of judgment" has begun, an ambitious educational program will be inaugurated. Those now raised from the dead must be taught the truth and shown what is right.[583] An extensive educational work will therefore be necessary to give instruction in God's law to these unrighteous dead as they arise from their tombs.[584] During the millennium they will be learning righteousness from the Judge and through his earthly princes.[585]

The Day of Judgment. Jehovah's Witnesses speak of a "Judgment Day" for mankind; this day, however, is not to be a twenty-four-hour day but is to extend through the first thousand years of the new world.[586] The inhabited earth which, according to Paul's

---

[575] *Let God Be True*, p. 282.
[576] *Paradise Lost*, p. 202.
[577] *Ibid.*, p. 233.
[578] *Ibid.*, p. 229.
[579] *Ibid.*
[580] *Ibid.* To justify their position, the authors punctuate Lk. 23:43 as follows: "Verily I say unto thee this day, With me shalt thou be in Paradise."
[581] *Ibid.*, p. 232.
[582] *Ibid.*
[583] *Ibid.*, p. 229.
[584] *Let God Be True*, p. 270.
[585] *Ibid.*, p. 293. Note that nothing is said in this connection about the atoning work of Jesus Christ. The emphasis is all on doing right and learning God's laws! Christ's ransom has provided the basis for their resurrection from the dead, but their acquisition of everlasting life is dependent solely on their obedience to God's laws.
[586] *Ibid.*, p. 286. For proof the authors quote II Peter 3:8, "one day is with the Lord as a thousand years, and a thousand years as one day."

words in Acts 17:31, is to be judged by Christ is not the present
world (which has been judged and condemned at Armageddon),
but the world to come, that is, the inhabited earth as it exists
during the millennium.[587]   Anyone not inhabiting the earth in the
new world will therefore not be involved in this judgment.[588]
All those who will be on earth during the millennium, however,
will be involved in this judgment,[589] which is also called a thousand-
year day of test.[590]

The basis for this judgment will not be the lives people have
lived before they died, but the works they perform during the millennium.[591]   Armageddon survivors will be judged according to
their faithfulness to God and Christ throughout the thousand-year
judgment day; if they are approved, they will receive the right to
eternal life.[592]   Children born of Armageddon survivors will have
full opportunity for life through Christ the King; they will also be
judged on the basis of their works — any of them not desiring
to serve Jehovah will be executed.[593]   All those raised from the
dead during the millennium will likewise be judged. Those raised
in the "resurrection of judgment" will be judged according to what
they do with the training they now receive; if they obey God's
commands, they will get everlasting life; but if they do not obey,
they will go into everlasting death.[594]

> Jesus Christ the Right Shepherd died for them [those raised
> in the "resurrection of judgment"] not to put them on judgment
> for their past vile lives, but to provide for them a period of
> judgment in the new world in hope of their reforming and prac-
> ticing good things and deserving to be lifted up to human per-
> fection, thus to be judged according to their future works under
> the Kingdom. They will have the opportunity to become "other
> sheep" by listening to the voice of the Shepherd King and
> obediently following him, that he may gather them into the "one
> flock."[595]

In the case of some this judgment will result in annihilation.
Those who refuse to obey God's kingdom, after a long enough
trial, will be sentenced to everlasting destruction [annihilation] be-

[587] *Ibid.,* pp. 285-86.
[588] *Ibid.,* p. 286.
[589] *Ibid.,* p. 288.
[590] *Make Sure of All Things,* p. 224.
[591] *Ibid.,* p. 225; *Let God Be True,* p. 293.
[592] *Let God Be True,* p. 290.
[593] *Ibid.,* p. 269.
[594] *Paradise Lost,* p. 229.
[595] *You May Survive Armageddon,* p. 356. Note once again that the
ultimate basis for the salvation of these individuals is not the work of
Christ for them but their "reforming and practicing good things." This is
not salvation by grace but salvation by works!

fore the end of the millennium.[596] Risen ones who prove unreformable or turn rebellious will be executed.[597] The vast majority, however, will pass the judgment-test and receive everlasting life on the new earth.[598]

We see therefore that, according to Jehovah-Witness teaching, most of the inhabitants of the earth will have a second opportunity to make life's most momentous decision after they have died. The Watchtower conception of the judgment day is radically different from that of historic Christianity since, as we have seen, the judgment is based, for them, not on deeds done in this life but on what is done during the millennium.[599]

Satan's Final Battle. Though the "Day of Judgment" extends throughout the millennium, this is still not the last judgment; "the final judgment will not come until the end of Christ's thousand-year reign."[600] At this point the King, Jesus Christ, steps aside to allow the Supreme Judge, Jehovah, to make the final test.[601] This last test or judgment will occur by means of Satan's final battle. At the end of the millennium Satan and his demons will be loosed or released from the abyss in which they have been confined for a thousand years.[602] Satan, his mental attitude unchanged, will once again seek to usurp Jehovah's position of sovereignty over the universe, and will once again try to turn mankind against God.[603] He will use some sly appeal to selfishness, making people think they will be better off if they follow him.[604] This attempt of Satan will be a final test of obedience which everyone on earth will have to face — even the princes and the Armageddon survivors.[605] The human race which thus faces its final trial is, it must be remembered, a perfected one.[606]

Sad to say, however, some of earth's perfected inhabitants will

---

[596] *Paradise Lost,* p. 237.
[597] *You May Survive Armageddon,* pp. 356-57.
[598] *Let God Be True,* p. 279.
[599] At this point we may well ask whether the Battle of Armageddon is really a revelation of God's justice, as the Witnesses claim. For is it not true that many of those killed in this battle have not had an opportunity to hear God's purposes or to learn what He expects of men? In the case of millions of these Armageddon victims, if they had happened to die one week — or, for that matter, one day — before Armageddon, they would have been among those raised in the "resurrection of judgment," and given a new opportunity to learn about God's kingdom. But, because they happened to have the misfortune of living at the time of Armageddon, they were put to death without any hope of resurrection. Is this divine "justice"?
[600] *Paradise Lost,* pp. 237-38.
[601] *New Heavens and a New Earth,* p. 353.
[602] *Let God Be True,* pp. 270, 293.
[603] *Ibid.,* p. 270.
[604] *Paradise Lost,* p. 239.
[605] *Ibid.,* p. 238.
[606] *You May Survive Armageddon,* p. 357.

be led astray by Satan and will join him.[607]   Satan, his demons, and his followers now assault the "camp of the holy ones," made up of perfect humanity, and the "beloved city," challenging Jehovah's sovereignty for the last time.[608]   Fire comes down out of heaven, however, and devours all those who follow Satan.[609]   All human rebels, all the demons, and Satan himself will now be cast into the lake of fire and sulphur, which stands for everlasting destruction.[610] All these will be consigned to the "second death," which means annihilation.[611]   They will be as if they had never existed; "their cursed name will rot."[612]

Those who do not yield to Satan's temptation, however, and who thus pass this final test, will be declared righteous by Jehovah,[613] and will be given the right to perfect life on the paradise earth forever.[614]   Thus the inhabitants of the new world will receive what Adam lost long ago: everlasting life on a paradise earth.[615]   The earth has now been finally cleansed, since everyone who would disobey Jehovah has been annihilated, and everyone who remains will have proved that he intends to obey God forever.[616]   The great controversy that has raged throughout the universe is now settled[617]; Jehovah's sovereignty has now been ultimately vindicated!

The Final State.   As has already been implied, Jehovah's Witnesses repudiate the doctrine of eternal torment for the finally impenitent, claiming that this doctrine is based on Satan's original lie in Eden.[618]   They advance four reasons why this doctrine is to be rejected: (1) it is wholly unscriptural; (2) it is unreasonable; (3) it is contrary to God's love; and (4) it is repugnant to justice.[619]

In this connection we should briefly examine Watchtower

---

[607] *Let God Be True,* p. 270; *New Heavens and a New Earth,* p. 354. Another strange phenomenon! Earlier we saw that imperfect parents will be able during the millennium to do a perfect job of training their children (above, p. 315). Now we observe that perfect people can still be led astray by Satan and can still rebel against God!

[608] *New Heavens and a New Earth,* p. 354.

[609] *Paradise Lost,* p. 239.

[610] *Let God Be True,* p. 270.

[611] *Ibid.,* p. 293.

[612] *New Heavens and a New Earth,* p. 355.

[613] This is the final justification of the other sheep alluded to in n. 317, above.   Remember that this is a justification based on works rather than on faith.

[614] *Paradise Lost,* p. 240; *Let God Be True,* pp. 280, 293.

[615] *Paradise Lost,* p. 234.

[616] *Ibid.,* p. 239.

[617] *New Heavens and a New Earth,* p. 351.

[618] *Make Sure of All Things,* p. 155.

[619] *Let God Be True,* p. 99.

teachings about Gehenna, the New Testament word usually rendered *hell* in our English translations. In a note found on pages 766-67 of their *New World Translation of the Christian Greek Scriptures,* the authors explain that the word Gehenna is the Greek form of the Hebrew *Gei-Hinnom,* which means "valley of Hinnom." This valley, which lay west and south of ancient Jerusalem, came to be the dumping place and incinerator for the filth of the city. Fires were kept burning there continually. The bodies of dead animals or of executed criminals were sometimes thrown into this valley; occasionally these bodies landed on a ledge, in which case they were devoured by worms which did not die until they had consumed the fleshy parts. No living animals were ever thrown into Gehenna. Hence, it is said, this place could never symbolize a region where human souls are "tormented in literal fire and attacked by undying immortal worms for ever and ever."

> Because the dead criminals cast here were denied a decent burial in a memorial tomb, which symbolizes the hope of a resurrection, Gehenna was used by Jesus and his disciples to symbolize everlasting destruction, annihilation from God's universe, or "second death," an eternal punishment.[620]

The word Hades, as we have seen,[621] is interpreted to mean simply the grave. A further refinement is added to the definition of Hades, however, on page 155 of *Make Sure of All Things:*

> After Jesus introduced the truth about life and immortality, only the willfully wicked were spoken of as being in Gehenna, the expression *Hades* [translated "hell" in English] being applied to the dead in God's memory, those with opportunity or hope of a resurrection.

Gehenna, therefore, is for Jehovah's Witnesses a symbol of annihilation — an annihilation from which there is no awakening,[622] and no resurrection.[623] People who are cast into Gehenna do not remain in the memory of God.[624] Gehenna, "the second death," and "the lake that burneth with fire and brimstone" all stand for the same thing: total annihilation.[625] Such total annihilation is therefore the doom of the "goats" at the Battle of Armageddon[626]; of all those who will not be raised during the millennium; of all those who, though living on the new earth during the millennium,

[620] P. 767. Cf. *Let God Be True,* pp. 95-96; *Make Sure of All Things,* p. 155.

[621] Above, pp. 293-94.

[622] *Make Sure of All Things,* p. 155.

[623] *Let God Be True,* p. 96.

[624] *The Truth Shall Make You Free,* p. 364.

[625] *Ibid.*

[626] *Let God Be True,* p. 97.

refuse to obey God's kingdom[627]; and of all who follow Satan in his final battle.[628]

Jehovah's Witnesses, however, do not claim to be denying the doctrine of eternal punishment; they insist that total annihilation *is* eternal punishment since it is total, final, and therefore eternal destruction. The authors of *Let God Be True* render the first part of Matthew 25:46 as follows: "These [the 'goats'] will depart into everlasting cutting-off [Greek, *kolasis*]. . . ,'' adding the comment, "So the everlasting punishment of the 'goats' is their everlastingly being cut off from all life."[629]

We see, therefore, that in the final state all who have rebelled against Jehovah and have refused to obey the laws of His kingdom will have been annihilated, and that only those members of the human race and of the angelic hosts who have proved loyal to Jehovah are still in existence. Let us now note what Jehovah's Witnesses teach about each of these remaining groups.

The other sheep, including all who were raised during the millennium and have passed the millennial tests, will remain forever on the renewed earth.[630] These other sheep are not given immortality, but will continue to exist everlastingly, though still dependent on food.[631] No other creature in the universe can now cause their death. "It is in this sense that these loyal ones gain the endless world to come and can never die any more."[632] It must be remembered, however, that the "second death" is always within God's power to administer to possible rebels.[633] God does

---

[627] *Paradise Lost*, p. 237; *You May Survive Armageddon*, p. 356.

[628] *Let God Be True*, p. 270.

[629] P. 97. This passage, as well as the entire question of the denial of eternal torment, will be further discussed in Appendix E. Note that, in this interpretation, no room is left for any gradation in the punishment of the finally impenitent — a gradation which is clearly called for by Lk. 12:47-48. Cf. the position of Seventh-day Adventists on this matter (above, p. 142).

[630] This is taught despite the fact that in Rev. 7:9 the "great crowd" is pictured as standing "before the throne and before the Lamb," and that in verse 15 we are told that the members of the great crowd "are rendering him [God] sacred service day and night in his temple" (NWT). The Witnesses also teach, however, that the throne of God is in heaven rather than on earth (*New Heavens and a New Earth*, p. 16), and that the Lamb is now in heaven (above, p. 298). They further teach that the temple at which the 144,000 have been united with Christ is in heaven (*Let God Be True*, p. 132). What Biblical basis, then, do Jehovah's Witnesses have for insisting that the "great crowd" of other sheep never gets to heaven but remains eternally upon the earth?

[631] *Make Sure of All Things*, p. 243.

[632] *This Means Everlasting Life*, p. 305.

[633] *New Heavens and a New Earth*, p. 356; cf. *This Means Everlasting Life*, p. 303. So there exists the possibility that even these finally perfected inhabitants of the earth may still rebel against God! The above statement, however, does not seem to agree with what we find on pp. 239-40 of

not intend to transport these other sheep to different planets or to heaven; He will keep them on the earth as expert gardeners to maintain it as a glorious paradise.[634] This earth will never come to a flaming end, as some scientists predict, but will endure forever.[635]

From this new earth all illness, sorrow, tears, and religious confusion will have been abolished.[636] All men will obey God's commands.[637] The purpose of life on this new earth will be the worship and praise of God and the unselfish service of man.[638] Love will therefore prevail: "love first to God with all one's heart, mind, soul, and strength, and love for one's perfect, godly neighbor as for oneself."[639] Everyone will be eternally happy in the paradise of the new earth.[640]

What about the 144,000? The "resurrection" of the last of the 144,000, which has occurred during the millennium, will have completed the marriage of Christ, the Lamb of God, to his bride.[641] It will be recalled that only the 144,000 and Christ are given immortality, which is defined as follows: "Deathlessness, that is, the life principle of the person possessing it cannot be taken away."[642] The 144,000 remain in heaven throughout eternity; they never come down again to inhabit the earth.[643] They continue to reign with Christ as his joint-heirs and co-rulers in Jehovah's glorious theocracy.[644] The heavenly kingdom, consisting of Christ and the "resurrected" 144,000, remains forever as the invisible or heavenly part of the new world.[645] This kingdom will bring unheard-of increase of blessings throughout eternity.[646]

A word should be said about the continued existence of the angels. The sentence of death pronounced upon the devil in paradise proves that "holy angels, such as Satan had been up till

---

Paradise Lost: ". . . We can be sure that, when he [Jehovah] says that everyone who is living on earth is worthy of life [after the final test], never again will there be even a single case of rebellion or disobedience against him anywhere on earth!"

[634] *New Heavens and a New Earth*, p. 360.
[635] *Ibid.*, pp. 356-67.
[636] *Let God Be True*, p. 271.
[637] *Paradise Lost*, p. 240.
[638] *New Heavens and a New Earth*, p. 361.
[639] *You May Survive Armageddon*, p. 361.
[640] *New Heavens and a New Earth*, p. 360.
[641] *Ibid.*, p. 322.
[642] *Make Sure of All Things*, p. 243.
[643] *Let God Be True*, p. 132. On the legitimacy of the view that the anointed class remains eternally in heaven while the other sheep are on the earth, see above, p. 290.
[644] *Let God Be True*, p. 132.
[645] *Ibid.*, p. 138.
[646] *Make Sure of All Things*, p. 233.

his rebellion, are not immortal, indestructible, but their living forever is hinged upon their perfect obedience to God."[647]   Theoretically, therefore, the holy angels can still be annihilated by God, since it is possible that they may become disobedient.   Since angels are not immortal, they must be sustained by food.[648]

We may summarize the Jehovah-Witness conception of the final state in their own words:

> Forever the new earth and the new heavens will remain in tune in the unifying worship of the only true God and in the unswerving love of righteousness.   Perfect mankind's home and its radiant sun and silvery moon will endure as long as God's kingdom by Christ Jesus, the great Son and Seed of David, and that is forever.[649]

[647] *Survival After Death,* p. 62.
[648] *Make Sure of All Things,* pp. 247 and 243.   See above, p. 267.   We are not told what this food is.
[649] *New Heavens and a New Earth,* p. 356.

APPENDIX D

JEHOVAH-WITNESS TEACHING ON THE
PERSON OF CHRIST

In the preceding chapter the teachings of Jehovah's Witnesses about the person of Christ have been set forth. In this appendix these teachings will be critically evaluated. It is important that we do this, since the confession of the full deity of Jesus Christ and of His equality with God the Father has always been one of the distinguishing marks of Christianity.

A REVIVAL OF ARIANISM

A bit of historical orientation will first be in order. Essentially, the Jehovah-Witness view of the person of Christ is a revival of the Arian heresy of the fourth century A.D. Arius (who lived from approximately A.D. 280 to 336) and his followers (called Arians) taught that the Son, whom they also called the Logos or Word, had a beginning, that the term *beget* when applied to the generation of the Son meant to *make,* and that therefore the Son was not of the same substance as the Father but was a creature who had been called into existence by the Father.[1] The Arians taught that there was a time when God was alone and was not yet a Father.[2] Arius went on to ascribe to Christ only a subordinate, secondary, created divinity.[3] He asserted that such titles as *God* or *Son of God* when applied to Christ were mere courtesy titles: " 'Even if He is called God,' wrote Arius, 'He is not God truly, but by participation in grace. . . . He too is called God in name only.' "[4] Up to this point, there is virtual identity between the teachings of Arius and those of present-day Jehovah's Witnesses on the person of Christ.

It should be borne in mind, however, that there are also differences between Arian teachings and those of the Watchtower.

[1] J. N. D. Kelly, *Early Christian Doctrines* (London: Adam & Chas. Black, 1958), pp. 227-28.
[2] Reinhold Seeberg, *Textbook of the History of Doctrines,* trans. Chas. Hay (Grand Rapids: Baker, 1954), I, 203.
[3] D. S. Schaff, "Arianism," in *The New Schaff-Herzog Encyclopedia of Religious Knowledge* (Grand Rapids: Baker, reprinted 1960), I, 281.
[4] Kelly, *op. cit.,* p. 229. The quotation is from Athanasius' *Contra Arianos,* I, 6.

Among these differences the following may be mentioned: Arius
and the Arians taught that Christ, the created being through whom
God made the world, did in the course of time assume a human
body, though this was a human body without a rational soul.[5]
Thus Arius would not agree with Jehovah's Witnesses that Christ,
who was a created angel, became a mere man and ceased to be an
angel while he was on earth.   Arius held that Christ continued to
be the Logos during his stay on earth but assumed a human body
and directed its activities; the Logos thus took the place of the
human soul in the being which resulted from this union.   Arius
would therefore repudiate the discontinuity between Christ's prehuman and human stages which is implicit in Jehovah-Witness
Christology.   Further, Arius did not deny the personality of the
Holy Spirit.   He taught that the Holy Spirit was an "hypostasis" or
person, but that his essence was utterly unlike that of the Son.
The later Arians amplified this thought so as to teach that the
Holy Spirit was the noblest of the creatures produced by the
Son at the Father's bidding.[6]   While denying the deity of the Holy
Spirit, therefore, the Arians did not deny His personality, as
Jehovah's Witnesses do.[7]

On the basic question, however, of the equality of the Son to
the Father, the Witnesses take the Arian position: the Son is not
equal to the Father but was created by the Father at a point in
time.   As is well known, the church rejected the Arian position
at the Council of Nicaea in A.D. 325. The Nicene Creed, drafted by
this council and accepted universally by Christians today, made
the following affirmation about the deity of Christ:

> We believe . . . in one Lord Jesus Christ, the Son of God, be-
> gotten from the Father, only-begotten, that is, from the substance
> of the Father . . . begotten not made, of one substance with the
> Father. . . .[8]

Specifically directed against the Arians was the closing statement:

> But as for those who say, There was when He was not, and,
> Before being born He was not, and that He came into existence
> out of nothing, or who assert that the Son of God is from a dif-
> ferent . . . substance, or is created, or is subject to alteration or
> change — these the Catholic [that is, universal] Church anathe-
> matizes.[9]

---

[5] Kelly, *op. cit.,* pp. 281, 283.
[6] *Ibid.,* pp. 255-56.
[7] It could therefore be observed that, though Jehovah's Witnesses are
basically Arian in their view of Christ and the Trinity, they are actually
more heretical than the Arians were.
[8] Kelly, *op. cit.,* p. 232.
[9] *Ibid.*

By assuming once again the Arian position on the person of Christ, Jehovah's Witnesses have separated themselves from historic Christianity. Since the Watchtower Christology is essentially Arian, it may be noted that one finds in the writings of Athanasius (295-373 A.D.), the arch-enemy of Arianism, an effective refutation of the teachings of the Witnesses about the person of Christ.[10] Note, for example, the following statement: "Those who call these men [the Arians] Christians are in great and grievous error, as neither having studied Scripture, nor understanding Christianity at all, and the faith which it contains."[11] He adds that to call the Arians Christians is equivalent to calling Caiaphas a Christian and to reckon Judas as still among the apostles.[12] Athanasius further comments that, though the Arians use Scriptural language, and frequently quote Scripture, their doctrine is thoroughly unscriptural[13] — a statement which could with equal propriety be made about Jehovah's Witnesses today. At another place he accuses the Arians of harboring the same error as that of the Jews who crucified Jesus since the latter also refused to believe that Jesus was truly God, charging Him with blasphemy because He claimed to be equal with God.[14] Arians, Athanasius alleges, are cloaking Judaism with the name of Christianity.[15]

As can be expected, many of the Scripture passages to which the ancient Arians appealed are also adduced by Jehovah's Witnesses today: passages such as Proverbs 8:22, Colossians 1:15, John 14:28, Mark 13:32, and so on. A large part of Discourse I, all of II, and most of III are occupied with the task of refuting the Arian interpretation of these passages. Though present-day Biblical scholars would not agree with all of Athanasius's exegeses, much of what he says in these Discourses is still valuable for us as we encounter Watchtower misinterpretations of these and kindred passages.

Appealing to John 1:3, which tells us that without the Word nothing was made, Athanasius asks, How then did the Word Himself come into being, if He was one of the "things that were

---

[10] A number of these works are to be found in Vol. IV of the *Nicene and Post-Nicene Fathers,* Second Series. Among the more important of these are *On the Incarnation of the Word,* and the *Four Discourses Against the Arians,* both of which are contained in Vol. IV. As one reads the latter work, one is struck again and again by the similarities between Arianism and Watchtower teachings.

[11] *Four Discourses Against the Arians* (trans. by Cardinal Newman), Discourse I, Section 1, in *Nicene and Post-Nicene Fathers* (Grand Rapids: Eerdmans, 1953), Second Series, IV, 306.

[12] *Ibid.,* I, 2 (i.e., Discourse I, Section 2).

[13] *Ibid.,* I, 8.

[14] *Ibid.,* III, 27.

[15] *Ibid.,* III, 28.

made"? If, on the contrary, all things were made through the Word, the Son Himself cannot have been made, cannot be a mere created work.[16] Athanasius reveals the soteriological motive for his opposition to Arius when he says, "For if, being a creature, He [Christ] had become man, man had remained just what he was, not joined to God; for how had a work been joined to the Creator by a work?"[17] To the same effect is the following:

> But this would not have come to pass [the blessings of our fu-
> ture life in glory], had the Word been a creature; for with a crea-
> ture the devil, himself a creature, would have ever continued the
> battle, and man, being between the two, had been ever in peril
> of death, having none in whom and through whom he might be
> joined to God and delivered from all fear.[18]

Athanasius's point here is well taken: If Christ was only a creature, as the Arians asserted, what guarantee have we that He really conquered the devil, who is also a creature, and that He truly united us to God? How can a mere creature deliver us from the power of another creature? The same devastating criticism can be leveled against the Christology of the Watchtower.

CRITIQUE OF WATCHTOWER EXEGESIS

We proceed next to examine some of the more important Watchtower interpretations of Scripture passages bearing on the person of Christ. It will be remembered that the Witnesses claim to be guided only by the Word of God and not at all by the opinions of men. Let us see whether their use of Scripture in connection with the alleged creatureliness of Christ supports their claim.[19]

Old Testament Passages. Beginning with Old Testament passages, let us look first at a text to which Jehovah's Witnesses appeal as teaching that Christ was a created being, Proverbs 8:22. In *What Has Religion Done for Mankind?* this passage is quoted in Moffatt's translation, "The Eternal formed me first of his creation, first of all his works in days of old"; previous to this quotation the comment is made: "In the proverbs of wisdom he [Jehovah's only-begotten son] speaks of himself as wisdom and calls attention to his being a creation of the eternal heavenly Father."[20]

---

[16] *Ibid.,* II, 71.
[17] *Ibid.,* II, 67.
[18] *Ibid.,* II, 70.
[19] Needless to say, no attempt will here be made to give an exhaustive survey of the Biblical evidence for the deity of Christ. The material which follows is an endeavor to refute the type of Biblical interpretation the Witnesses adduce to support their view of Christ.
[20] P. 37. Cf. *The Truth Shall Make You Free,* p. 43, where a similar use is made of the passage.

It is interesting to observe that the ancient Arians also used this passage to support their views of the person of Christ, utilizing the Septuagint translation of the verse, "The Lord created me *(ektise)* . . . ."[21] So much did the Arians make of this text, in fact, that Athanasius felt it necessary to devote the major part of his second Discourse against the Arians to an exposition of this passage.[22]

Though Proverbs 8:22 figured largely in the Christological controversies of the early centuries, most modern interpreters agree that the purpose of the author of Proverbs here was not to give a dogmatic description of the "origin" of the Second Person of the Trinity, but rather to set forth the value of wisdom as a guide to be followed by believers. In pursuit of this purpose, the author presents a poetic personification of wisdom. By this personified wisdom the statement is made, "Jehovah possessed me in the beginning of his way, before his works of old."[23] The point of the passage is that wisdom is older than creation and therefore deserves to be followed by all. To use Proverbs 8:22 as ground for a denial of the eternity of the Son — a doctrine clearly taught in the rest of Scripture — is to use the passage in an unwarranted manner.[24]

Isaiah 9:6 is commonly understood by Christians to be one of the clearest Old Testament attestations to the deity of Jesus Christ found anywhere. In the *New World Translation* it reads as follows: "For there has been a child born to us, there has been a son given to us; and the princely rule will come to be upon his shoulder. And his name will be called Wonderful Counselor, Mighty God, Eternal Father, Prince of Peace." It is acknowledged even by Jehovah's Witnesses that this passage predicts the coming Messiah. Yet the Witnesses evade the clear teaching of the passage when they say, "He [Jesus Christ] is a 'mighty God,' but not the Almighty God who is Jehovah (Isa. 9:6)."[25] The fact of the matter is, however, that the Hebrew expression here translated *Mighty God* (*'eel gibboor*) is also used in Isaiah 10:21, where the *New World Translation* has: "A mere remnant will

---

[21] Kelly, *op. cit.,* p. 230.
[22] Discourse II, Sections 18-82.
[23] ASV. A marginal note appended to the word *possessed* reads: "or formed." The Hebrew verb here used, *qanah,* may also be rendered *begat* (see C. F. Burney, "Christ as the ARCHEE of Creation," *Journal of Theological Studies,* XXVII [1926], 160-77).
[24] Cf. Franz Delitzsch, *Commentary on Proverbs, ad loc.;* W. H. Gispen, *De Spreuken Van Salomo* (Kampen: Kok, 1952), pp. 133-34; and Kenneth S. Kantzer, "Wisdom," in Baker's *Dictionary of Theology* (Grand Rapids: Baker, 1960), p. 554.
[25] *The Truth Shall Make You Free,* p. 47.

return, the remnant of Jacob, to the Mighty God." It becomes clear from verse 20 of this chapter that the "Mighty God" to whom the remnant of Jacob is said to be about to return is none other than Jehovah, the Holy One of Israel. Yet precisely the same Hebrew expression, *'eel gibboor,* is used in Isaiah 10:21 and in Isaiah 9:6. If *'eel gibboor* in 10:21 means Jehovah, by what stretch of the imagination may the same phrase in 9:6 be interpreted to mean someone less than Jehovah?

In this connection it ought also to be observed that the Hebrew word *'eel* in Isaiah usually denotes Jehovah, the only true God; when it does not do so (in 44:10, 15, 17; 45:20; 46:6), it is used to describe an idol made by men's hands. Surely Isaiah did not intend to say that the coming Messiah would be an idol god! It ought also to be noted that the expression *'eel gibboor* is, in Old Testament literature, a traditional designation of Jehovah — see Deuteronomy 10:17, Jeremiah 32:18, and Nehemiah 9:32.[26] We are forced to conclude that Jehovah's Witnesses have not listened to Scripture here, but have simply imposed their preconceived view of Christ upon the Bible.

New Testament Passages. Probably the best-known New Testament passage to which the Witnesses appeal is John 1:1, which is translated in the 1961 edition of the *New World Translation* as follows: "In [the] beginning the Word was, and the Word was with God, and the Word was a god." Note that the word *God* is capitalized the first time it occurs in the text but not the second time, and that in the second instance it is preceded by the indefinite article. The impression this translation intends to convey is that the Word (Jesus Christ) is not God but *a god* — not equal to Jehovah God but a subordinate deity.

By way of refutation, it should be observed, first, that Jehovah's Witnesses thus take a polytheistic position, affirming that there exists, besides Jehovah God, someone who is a lesser god. This position is, however, in direct conflict with Scripture, which affirms in Deuteronomy 4:35, "You have been shown, so as to know that Jehovah is the [true] God; there is no other besides him" (NWT); and in I Corinthians 8:4, "We know that an idol is nothing in the world, and that there is no God but one" (NWT). How, then, can the Witnesses affirm that Jesus Christ is *a god?* To be sure, the New Testament does occasionally speak of gods other than Jehovah, but then only in the sense of false gods. So, for

---

[26] The only difference between these expressions and the one in Isa. 9:6 is the addition of the word *gadool* (meaning great), and of the definite article. In Isa. 10:21, however, the definite article is also missing; yet the reference is unmistakably to Jehovah. Cf. Delitzsch's *Commentary on the Prophecies of Isaiah* on Isa. 9:6.

example, in Acts 28:6 the term *a god* (*theon*) describes what the superstitious inhabitants of Malta thought Paul was after they had observed that the viper did not harm him.[27]   And in Galatians 4:8 Paul observes, "Nevertheless, when you did not know God, then it was that you slaved for those who by nature are not gods (*theois*)" (NWT).   Do the Watchtower theologians intend to teach that Jesus Christ is a god in one of the two senses just described?   Yet the only times the New Testament speaks of gods (*theoi*) other than Jehovah is when it is describing false gods or idols.[28]   By calling Jesus Christ *a god,* therefore, Jehovah's Witnesses are actually making themselves guilty of idolatry and polytheism.

In an appendix found on pages 773-77 of their *New World Translation of the Christian Greek Scriptures* (published in 1951), the Watchtower editors explain why they have rendered John 1:1 as they did.   They make clear that when the word *theos* (the Greek word for God) first appears in this verse, it occurs with a definite article (*pros ton theon*), whereas when it appears the second time, it does not have the definite article (*kai theos een ho logos*).   The editors go on to justify their translation, "and the Word was a god," by saying,

> Careful translators recognize that the articular construction of the noun [that is, the construction in which a noun appears with the definite article] points to an identity, a personality, whereas an anarthrous construction [a construction in which a noun appears without a definite article] points to a quality about someone (p. 774).

In refutation, let it be emphatically stated that this observation is simply not true to fact.   In the article on *theos* in the most recent Greek-English Lexicon of the New Testament, it is said that *theos* is used in the New Testament "quite predominantly of the true God, sometimes with, sometimes without the article."[29]   As a matter of fact, Jehovah's Witnesses do not follow the above-mentioned rule themselves in their *New World Translation.*   In the very chapter in which John 1:1 is found, for example, the word *theos* occurs at least four other times without the definite

[27] Cf. also Acts 14:11, where the multitude at Lystra is reported as saying about Paul and Barnabas, "The gods [*hoi theoi*] have . . . come down to us" (NWT).

[28] It might be objected that in Jn. 10:34 and 35 the term gods (*theoi*) is applied to Old Testament judges.   Yet surely the Witnesses do not intend to say that Christ is a god only in the sense in which these judges could be called gods since they affirm that Christ is superior to all other creatures.

[29] Wm. F. Arndt and F. Wilbur Gingrich, *Greek-English Lexicon of the New Testament* (Chicago: University of Chicago Press, 1957), p. 357.

article, and yet in each instance it is rendered *God,* not *a god.* In John 1:6 we read, in the *New World Translation,* "There arose a man that was sent forth as a representative of God; his name was John." Since the Greek has *para theou* (no definite article), the Witnesses, to be consistent with their observation about the function of the definite article, ought to translate: "sent from *a god.*" Yet here they render the anarthrous *theos* by *God.* In verse 12 the expression *tekna theou* (again the anarthrous *theos*) is rendered "God's children," and in verse 13 the words *ek theou egenneetheesan* are translated "born . . . from God." Why not "children of *a god,*" and "born from *a god*"? In the 18th verse we read: "No man has seen God at any time." But the Greek again has the anarthrous *theos: Theon oudeis heooraken.* Why do the Witnesses not translate, "No man hath seen *a god* at any time"? The above makes clear that Jehovah's Witnesses do not really believe their own statement about the articular and anarthrous construction of the noun since they do not follow this rule in their own translation. We are compelled to conclude that they translate John 1:1 as they do, not on the basis of careful grammatical study of the Bible, but on the basis of their own doctrinal presuppositions.

In the particular construction in which *theos* occurs in the last part of John 1:1, it functions as a predicate noun preceding the copulative verb *een,* meaning *was.* The authors of the appendix alluded to above contend that the absence of the article before the predicate noun in John 1:1 indicates that the predicate noun designates merely the class to which the subject is referred and excludes the idea that the Word is the same God as the God with whom he is said to be (pp. 774-75).

In reply, however, it should be observed that, according to a recognized Greek scholar,

> A definite predicate nominative has the article when it follows the verb; it does not have the article when it precedes the verb. . . . The opening verse of John's Gospel contains one of the many passages where this rule suggests the translation of a predicate as a definite noun. . . . The absence of the article [before *theos*] does *not* make the predicate indefinite or qualitative when it precedes the verb; it is indefinite in this position only when the context demands it. The context makes no such demand in the Gospel of John, for this statement cannot be regarded as strange in the prologue of the gospel which reaches its climax in the confession of Thomas [John 20:28, "My Lord and my God"].[30]

---

[30] Ernest C. Colwell, "A Definite Rule for the Use of the Article in the Greek New Testament," *Journal of Biblical Literature,* LII (1933), 13, 21.

In the light of Colwell's rule, a definite article is not needed before the second *theos* in John 1:1 in order to make it definite. As a matter of fact, the Witnesses themselves testify to the validity of Colwell's rule in their translation of John 19:21, which in the *New World Translation* reads as follows: "However, the chief priests of the Jews began to say to Pilate: 'Do not write, "The King of the Jews," but that he said, "I am King of the Jews" '." Though in the earlier part of the verse the word for king has the definite article (*ho basileus*), in the latter part the word occurs without the definite article (*basileus eimi toon Ioudaioon*). The construction here is quite parallel to that in John 1:1, since *basileus* is a predicate noun, preceding the copulative verb *eimi* (I am). In accordance with previous policy, therefore, the Watchtower translators should have rendered these words: "I am *a king* of the Jews." Quite inconsistently, however, they here consider the predicate noun definite, though it lacks the definite article: "I am King of the Jews." Why, then, did they not consider the predicate noun definite in John 1:1?

The answer is not difficult to find. Jehovah's Witnesses themselves tell us why they have adopted their rendering of John 1:1 on page 774 of the afore-mentioned appendix:

> . . . It is presumptuous to say . . . that the sentence should therefore be translated "and the Word was God." That would mean that the Word was the God with whom the Word was said to be. This is unreasonable; for how can the Word be with the God and at the same time be that same God?[31]

It has thus become clear that the ultimate ground for the Witnesses' translation of this important passage is not the authority of Scripture, but their own rationalistic, anti-Trinitarian theology. What they are saying, in effect, is this: we refuse to accept as Scriptural what our minds cannot grasp!

At this time the reader's attention is called to what is perhaps the most scholarly refutation of Watchtower teachings on the person of Christ ever penned: *The Jehovah's Witnesses and Jesus Christ,* by Bruce M. Metzger, Professor of New Testament Language and Literature at Princeton Theological Seminary.[32] In this twenty-page article Professor Metzger adduces several Scrip-

---

[31] Trinitarians would reply that, though the relationship between the Father and the Son is not rationally explicable, it is nevertheless not contrary to reason. If the Triune God consists of three Persons in one Being, the Son can be both with God and God.

[32] Originally published in the April, 1953, issue of *Theology Today,* this article has been reprinted in pamphlet form and may be obtained from the Theological Book Agency, Princeton, N. J., at 15 cents per copy, or eight copies for one dollar.

ture passages which prove the full deity of Jesus Christ and then proceeds to attack the Jehovah-Witness translations and exegeses of a number of New Testament passages dealing with the person of Christ. Anyone desiring a competent evaluation of Watch-tower exegetical methods should obtain a copy of Metzger's article.

Professor Metzger shows, for example, on pages 76-77 of this article that the Witnesses have without any warrant whatever in-serted the word *other* four times into their translation of Colossians 1:15-17. The latter part of the 16th verse, for example, which in the American Standard Version reads as follows, "all things have been created through him, and unto him," has been trans-lated by Jehovah's Witnesses as follows: "All other things have been created through him and for him." Since the word *other* is not found in the Greek text in any one of these places, Metzger concludes that the word has simply been inserted by the translators "in order to make the passage refer to Jesus as being on a par with other created things." We see again that the Witnesses have smuggled their own theology into their translations.[33]

On page 78 one will find a discussion of the Watchtower trans-lation of Philippians 2:6, "Who [Christ], although he was existing in God's form, gave no consideration to a seizure, namely, that he should be equal to God." The impression given by this trans-lation is that Christ was not equal to God and even scorned such an equality. Metzger proceeds to show that this translation rests upon a misunderstanding of the Greek.

Next Dr. Metzger indicates that the *New World Translation* obscures the clear attestation of two New Testament passages to the deity of Christ: Titus 2:13 and II Peter 1:1 (p. 79). He cites Granville Sharp's rule, that when a Greek *kai* (and) "connects two nouns of the same case, if the article precedes the first noun and is not repeated before the second noun, the latter always refers to the same person that is expressed or described by the first noun." On the basis of this principle of Greek grammar, Metzger contends that Titus 2:13 should be translated, "the appearing of the glory of our great God and Saviour Jesus Christ";

---

[33] Whereas in the 1951 ed. of the *New World Translation of the Christian Greek Scriptures* the word *other* was simply inserted into the text without any punctuation marks, in the revised ed. of 1961 brackets have been placed around the word *other* in these four instances. On p. 6 of the latter ed. we read, "Brackets enclose words inserted to complete or clarify the sense in the English text." Though the addition of brackets makes it clear that the word *other* is not found in the original, the retention of the word in the revised edition indicates that the interpretation underlying this mis-translation has not been repudiated.

and that II Peter 1:1 should be rendered, "the righteousness of our God and Saviour Jesus Christ."[34]

On pages 79-80 Metzger criticizes the *New World* rendering of Revelation 3:14, which makes the exalted Christ refer to himself as "the beginning of the creation by God." He points out that "by God" would have required the preposition *hupo,* whereas the Greek has the genitive case, *tou Theou,* which means *of God* and not *by God.* The passage, Metzger concludes, does not teach that Christ was created by God but rather that He is the origin or primary source of God's creation.

On pages 81-82 Metzger takes up passages which seem to teach a subordination of the person of the Son to the Father. He makes clear, for example, that John 14:28, "My Father is greater than I," does not intend to picture a permanent subordination of the Son to the Father, but rather describes Christ's condition while in the state of humiliation in contrast to the celestial glory which He was about to receive.

Christ as the Son of God. The most recent Jehovah-Witness publication in which their view of the person of Christ is set forth and defended is a 64-page booklet published in 1962, entitled *"The Word" — Who Is He? According to John.* Though much that is found in this booklet simply repeats what had been taught in earlier publications, one or two points made here will require some attention. The authors claim that the title *Son of God,* ascribed to Christ by John the Baptist, Nathanael, John the apostle, Martha, and the Jews, implied that Christ was not the Second Person of the Trinity but a person inferior to God the Father (pp. 19-20; 24ff.). In proof of this contention the authors adduce Christ's discussion with the Jews who had taken up stones to stone him, recorded in John 10. Though Jesus here said, "I and the Father are one," the authors contend, he did not claim to be equal to the Father, but rather claimed to be less than God (pp. 25-26). Though the Old Testament spoke of certain judges as "gods" (verse 35 of John 10, referring to Ps. 82:6), Jesus, it is said, here only claimed to be the *Son* of God; hence the Jews were quite in error when they thought Christ was uttering blasphemy (pp. 27-28).

By way of refutation, it should first be pointed out that, according to John 5:18, the Jews sought to kill Jesus "because not only was he breaking the Sabbath but he was also calling God his own Father, making himself equal to God" (NWT). The

---

[34] It is significant to note that at both of these places the RSV, which some years ago was accused by certain conservative theologians of having liberal leanings, gives a clearer testimony to the deity of Christ than either the KJ or the ASV!

Jews, therefore, did not understand the expression *Son of God* as Jehovah's Witnesses apparently do. For the latter, the term means someone inferior to the Father. By the Jews of Jesus' day, however, the term was interpreted as meaning full equality with the Father, and it was on account of this claim that they sought to kill him.[35]

This point becomes quite clear when we compare John 10:33 with 10:36. The former verse reads, "We [the Jews] are stoning you [Jesus], not for a fine work, but for blasphemy, even because you, although being a man, make yourself a god" (NWT).[36] The latter passage reads, "Do you say to me whom the Father sanctified and dispatched into the world, 'You blaspheme,' because I said, I am God's Son?" (NWT). Putting together these two verses (if we translate verse 33 as in the standard versions), we see that Christ's calling himself the Son of God was interpreted by the Jews as a claim to equality with the Father.

When Jesus was tried by Caiaphas, furthermore, He was asked, "By the living God I put you under oath to tell us whether you are the Christ the Son of God!" (Mt. 26:63, NWT). After Jesus had answered this question in the affirmative, the high priest is reported to have said, "He has blasphemed! What further need do we have of witnesses?" (v. 65, NWT). Obviously, the high priest understood the expression *Son of God* as meaning full equality with the Father since he called Jesus' assumption of this title blasphemy. If Jesus meant by the term *Son of God* something less than equality with the Father, He would by His affirmative answer be guilty of uttering an untruth, since for the Sanhedrin this title meant such equality. Surely if Jesus did not intend His words to be understood as meaning what the high priest and the rest of the Sanhedrin thought they meant, He could have and should have corrected their understanding of these words.

When, after the trial before Caiaphas, Jesus appeared before Pilate, the Jews said to the governor, "We have a law, and according to the law he [Jesus] ought to die, because he made himself

---

[35] According to Lev. 24:16 one who blasphemed the name of Jehovah was to be put to death by stoning. Since, in the eyes of these Jews, Jesus was a mere man, his claim to equality with the Father was considered blasphemy by them — a sin worthy of the death penalty.

[36] Here the NWT is quite misleading. In the light of John 5:18, quoted above, what the Jews accused Jesus of was the claim of being equal to Jehovah God. Though the definite article is missing before *theon* in 10:33 (it occurs only in p[66], *prima manus*), it is found in 5:18, where the reason why the Jews sought to kill Jesus is also stated: he made himself equal to God (*too theoo*). 10:33 should therefore be rendered as in the KJ, ASV, and RSV: "make yourself God."

God's son" (Jn. 19:7, NWT).[37]   Again it is crystal-clear that
the Jews understood the expression *Son of God,* which Jesus
acknowledged as descriptive of himself, as meaning nothing less
than full equality with the Father.   Is it likely, now, that present-
day Jehovah's Witnesses know better what Jesus claimed to be,
when He called Himself the Son of God, than the Jews who were
His contemporaries?

Christ as the Proper Object of Worship.   What do Jehovah's
Witnesses do with what is perhaps the clearest direct affirmation
of the deity of Christ in the New Testament, the words of Thomas
to the risen Jesus, "My Lord and my God"?   Four pages of
"The Word" — Who is He? According to John are devoted to an
exposition of this passage (pp. 48-51).   Before evaluating the
interpretation of this text found in this booklet, however, we must
first observe what the rest of the New Testament teaches about
Christ as a proper object of worship.

The Greek word *proskuneoo,* usually translated worship, is
used some sixty times in the New Testament.   It may occasionally
designate the deference given by one man to another who is his
superior, as in Matthew 18:26, where the RSV translates "im-
ploring him."   The word is used in Revelation 3:9 to describe
the honor which will be rendered to the church at Philadelphia
by those who were of the synagogue of Satan.[38]

The word *proskuneoo* is, however, much more frequently used
to describe the worship of God.   It is so used in the following
passages: Matthew 4:10, Luke 4:8, John 4:21-24, I Corinthians
14:25, Revelation 4:10, 7:11, 14:7, 19:4, 10, 22:9.   Christ
Himself, in fact, affirms with unmistakable clarity that worship
in the sense of religious veneration may be offered to God alone.
For when the devil asks Jesus to fall down and worship him
(*proskuneoo*), Jesus replies, "It is Jehovah your God you must
worship (*proskuneoo*), and it is to him alone you must render
sacred service" (Mt. 4:10, NWT).[39]   On the basis of these
words of Jesus, therefore, it should be clear that, if Jesus Christ
is not the same being as Jehovah, he may not be worshiped by

---

[37] Why in this instance the NWT does not capitalize the word *son,* whereas in Mt. 26:63, giving the high priest's question to Jesus, the word *son*
is capitalized, we are not told.

[38] Lenski, however, is of the opinion that *proskuneoo* here designates
the worship of the exalted Christ in the presence of the Philadelphian church
(*The Interpretation of St. John's Revelation,* p. 143).

[39] Jesus is here quoting Deut. 6:13, where the Hebrew has *Yahweh Eloo-
heykha,* Jehovah your God. In both the Matthew passage and the parallel
passage in Luke (4:8), in fact, Christ is reported as having added a word
which does not occur in the Hebrew: the word *alone* (NWT) or *only*
(KJ, ASV, & RSV).   Christ thus makes the command even more explicitly
exclusive than it is in Deuteronomy.

men. Jehovah's Witnesses teach that Jesus Christ is not the same being as Jehovah. We should therefore expect to find the New Testament forbidding the worship of Christ. On the contrary, however, we find that in the New Testament the worship of Christ is not only permitted but praised.

By way of negation, we should observe that the worship of certain individuals other than Jehovah or Christ is specifically forbidden. As we just saw, Jesus refused to worship the devil. In the book of Revelation the worship of the beast — an apocalyptic symbol of anti-Christian worldly power — is considered the epitome of rebellion against God, punishable by everlasting torment (Rev. 14:9-11). In three specific instances in the New Testament, worship is offered to individuals only to be rejected by them. When Cornelius falls down to worship Peter, the latter declines to be so honored, saying, "I myself am also a man" (Acts 10:25-26, NWT). When John the Apostle falls down to worship the one who has been speaking to him, the latter says, "Be careful! Do not do that! All I am is a fellow slave of you and of your brothers who have the work of witnessing to Jesus. Worship God" (Rev. 19:10, NWT).[40] And when John again falls down in worship, this time before the feet of the angel that had been showing him the things he had seen, the angel says, "Be careful! Do not do that! All I am is a fellow slave of you and of your brothers who are prophets and of those who are observing the words of this scroll. Worship God" (Rev. 22:9, NWT). Note that in the last two passages it is explicitly asserted that John may not worship creatures but may worship only God![41]

What, now, about Jesus Christ? Is there any indication in the New Testament that Christ prohibited people from worshiping him, as Peter did and as the angel did? Did Christ ever say to anyone: "Do not worship me, for I am only a creature. Worship God but do not worship me"? There is no such indication. On the contrary, we find numerous instances where people do worship Christ; in some of these the worship is commended or recognized as evidence of true faith, and in none of these is this worship forbidden.

Let us look at some of these instances. The leper described in Matthew 8:2 worshiped Jesus (ASV).[42] A ruler, identified by the

---

[40] Some commentators hold that the individual here spoken of is an angel, whereas others suggest that he was a fellow man. In either interpretation, he was only a creature; hence John was not permitted to worship him.

[41] In each passage alluded to in the above paragraph, the Greek word for worship is *proskuneoo*.

[42] The NWT here renders the verb *proskuneoo* as *doing obeisance*, though in many of the passages previously discussed it rendered this verb with the

other Synoptists as Jairus, is reported as worshiping Jesus (Matt. 9:18, ASV). After Jesus had walked on the water and had quieted the wind, the disciples are said to have worshiped him, saying, "Of a truth thou art the Son of God" (Mt. 14:33, ASV).[43] The Canaanitish woman worshiped Jesus, saying, "Lord, help me" (Mt. 15:25, ASV). The man born blind, having been informed by Jesus that He was the Son of man, said, "Lord, I believe. And he worshiped him" (Jn. 9:35, 38, ASV).[44] After Jesus' resurrection, the women who ran from the empty tomb and the disciples on the mountain in Galilee are said to have worshiped Him (Mt. 28:9 and 17, ASV). In each of the above instances the same word is used which is used of the worship of God: *proskuneoo*. In each of the above instances Jesus willingly receives the worship rendered to Him, and in no case does He tell anyone not to worship Him. And yet this is the same Jesus who had said to Satan, "Thou shalt worship (*proskuneoo*) the Lord thy God, and him only shalt thou serve" (Mt. 4:10, ASV). And the same New Testament which clearly forbids the worship of a creature — even of an angelic creature — both permits and approves the worship of Jesus Christ. Surely here is clear proof of Christ's deity!

To all of this Jehovah's Witnesses might reply: the obeisance

---

word *worship*. On p. 9 of the 1951 ed. of the *New World Translation of the Christian Greek Scriptures*, it is said, "To each major word [of the New Testament] we have assigned one meaning and have held to that meaning as far as the context permitted." In the case of the word *proskuneoo*, however, the translators of the NWT have not assigned the same meaning throughout; sometimes they render this word *worship*, and sometimes *do obeisance*. It will be granted, of course, that there are instances in the New Testament where *proskuneoo* does not mean worship in the full sense of the word (e.g., in Mt. 18:26, in Mk. 15:19, and probably in Rev. 3:9). But the question is whether Jehovah's Witnesses are warranted in using the weaker expression, *do obeisance*, in every instance where *proskuneoo* is used in connection with Jesus (except in Heb. 1:6 where even the NWT has *worship*). One suspects that it is not grammatical but theological considerations which have led them to translate the verb in this way.

[43] Though the NWT again has *did obeisance* rather than *worship*, it is quite clear that the honor shown to Christ by the disciples at this time was not mere deference to a superior creature, but the worship of one recognized as equal to God. Earlier Matthew had recorded the words of the Father at Jesus' baptism: "This is my beloved Son, in whom I am well pleased" (3:17). In the light of these earlier words, in the light of Jewish monotheism, and in the light of what was said about the Jewish understanding of the expression *Son of God*, surely nothing less could have been meant here than the worship of Christ as one who was God!

[44] Though the ASV text here has *Son of God, Son of man* is found in the older mss., and is therefore the better reading. It is quite evident from the context, however, that what is denoted here by *proskuneoo* is not mere respect for a person in authority, but religious worship — worship which is, in fact, an act of faith.

which was shown to Jesus by these various individuals was only a kind of respect shown to a superior creature, and does not imply that Jesus was God. How shall we answer this objection?

It will be granted that the word *proskuneoo* when used by New Testament writers does not always designate the adoration of God. As we have seen, it may occasionally be used of an act of respect paid to a creature. But it is clear from Jesus' own words, as recorded in Matthew 4:10, that when *proskuneoo* designates an act of religious veneration, it means *worship,* and that such worship as is described by this word may be offered *only to God.* And it will also be clear to anyone who takes the trouble to study the instances just enumerated that the act described in these passages by *proskuneoo* was nothing less than religious veneration.[45]

It should further be noted that, according to Watchtower teaching, Jesus Christ while on earth was only a man, the exact equivalent of Adam before the fall.[46] When Peter told Cornelius not to worship him (Acts 10:25-26), the former gave as his reason for refusing this worship: "I myself am also a man" (NWT). Here the *New World Translation* renders *proskuneoo* with *did obeisance.* If, now, Peter had to tell someone not to do obeisance to him because he was only a man, by what right could Jesus Christ, who according to Watchtower teachings was only a man, receive obeisance from people without rebuking them?

After Jesus' resurrection, so the Witnesses teach, he became a spirit-creature, higher in status than he had been when he lived on earth as a man, but still only a creature. The life he now enjoys is not the life of a divine Person with a human nature but the life of an exalted angel called Michael.[47] In Revelation 22:9, however, the angel who had been speaking to John told the latter not to fall down and worship him (*proskuneoo*), but to worship (*proskuneoo*) only God. If Christ after his resurrection was only an angel — higher, to be sure, than the other angels, but less than God — how could he accept the worship (*proskuneoo*) of the women and the disciples without rebuking them?

All these instances in which Jesus was worshiped come to a

---

[45] Though this is not specifically stated in the instances of the leper and of Jairus, it will be remembered that both of these men prostrated themselves before Jesus because they believed that He could perform a miracle for them. Though this act may not yet have been an expression of true, saving faith at that moment, it was certainly an act of religious veneration in each case. One might counter by saying that the apostles, who were only human, also performed miracles. True, but people did not prostrate themselves before the apostles in worship. When one person began to do so, he was rebuked (Acts 10:25-26).

[46] See above, pp. 272-73, 275.

[47] See above, pp. 274-76.

climax in the adoration of Thomas recorded in John 20:28. When Thomas saw Jesus the week after he had expressed disbelief in Jesus' resurrection, he said to Him, "My Lord and my God!" (NWT). If Jesus were not God, he should have rebuked Thomas at this point. Instead of rebuking him, however, Jesus praised Thomas, saying, "Because you have seen me have you believed? Happy are those who do not see and yet believe" (v. 29, NWT). Surely here is indisputable proof that Jesus recognized Himself to be God and not only permitted but encouraged believers to worship Him as such!

What, now, do Jehovah's Witnesses do with this verse? On one occasion a Witness who came to the author's door affirmed that when Thomas said, "My Lord," he was looking at Jesus, but that when he said, "My God," he was looking up to heaven and addressing the Father. As Professor Metzger has pointed out, however, the introductory words make this interpretation impossible: "Thomas said to him [that is, to Jesus]: 'My Lord and my God!' " (NWT).[48]

In *"The Word" — Who is He? According to John* the Witnesses now grant that Thomas did say all of these words to Jesus. They go on to assert, however, that if Thomas had meant that Jesus was the only true God, Jesus would certainly have reproved him. Since Jesus did not reprove him, so they argue, Thomas could not have meant this (p. 50). What, then, did Thomas mean when he said to Jesus, "My God"? He meant what the Apostle John meant: that Jesus was the Son of God (20:31). John did not say that Jesus was *God the Son;* he only said that Jesus was the *Son of God.* By *Son of God* John meant a being who was not the Second Person of the Trinity but a created being inferior to the Father (pp. 50-51).[49]

This interpretation, however, is a bold attempt to evade the clear teaching of the passage. In refutation of the Jehovah-Witness exegesis of John 20:28, I offer the following considerations:

(1) What can the expression "my God" possibly mean other than "my true God"? As we saw above, the New Testament recognizes no true God beside Jehovah God; any god other than Jehovah is for New Testament writers a false god or an idol. Thomas, being a Jew, was a strict monotheist; for him there was no God beside Jehovah. When he said, "my God," he could have meant nothing other than "my one and only true God."[50]

---

[48] *Op. cit.,* p. 71, n. 13.
[49] The same general interpretation of this passage, though in greatly condensed form, is found in *The Truth Shall Make You Free,* p. 266.
[50] Though it is true that the definite article is found with *theos* in the Greek of this passage (*ho theos mou,* the god of me), we cannot attach

(2) The argument the Witnesses use to bolster their interpretation boomerangs against them. Here was a monotheistic Jew saying to Jesus: "My God!" The fact that Jesus did not rebuke Thomas but commended him for his faith proves decisively that Jesus was equal to the Father, that He was Himself very God! When thus understood, Jesus' willingness to be called God by Thomas is quite in harmony with the testimony of the rest of the Bible about Him, and with His willingness to permit men to worship Him.

(3) That the Jehovah-Witness understanding of the expression *Son of God* is erroneous, and that *Son of God* in John's Gospel can mean nothing less than full equality with the Father, has already been shown. There is therefore no contradiction whatever between Thomas' ascription of full deity to Jesus and John's statement, "These [things] have been written down that you may believe that Jesus is the Christ the Son of God. . ." (20:31, NWT).

The Jehovah-Witness denial of the deity of Christ must therefore be rejected by all true believers as a heresy which cuts the very heart out of the Bible. Athanasius put it well: "Jesus whom I know as my Redeemer cannot be less than God!"

---

decisive significance to its occurrence here, since the nominative used as a vocative very often takes the definite article as a Semitic idiom (C. F. D. Moule, *An Idiom-Book of New Testament Greek,* pp. 116-117; cf. F. Blass and A. Debrunner, *A Greek Grammar of the New Testament,* trans. R. W. Funk, Sec. 147, (3)). A. T. Robertson (*A Grammar of the Greek New Testament in the Light of Historical Research,* p. 465) makes the same admission. Yet the latter also says, on p. 462, "When Thomas said, '*Ho kurios mou kai ho theos mou*' (Jn. 20:28), he gave Christ full acceptance of his deity and of the fact of his resurrection."

APPENDIX E

THE TEACHINGS OF SEVENTH-DAY ADVENTISTS AND JEHOVAH'S WITNESSES ON THE LIFE AFTER DEATH

In this appendix attention will be given to two aspects of the eschatological teaching of both Seventh-day Adventists and Jehovah's Witnesses: the question of soul-extinction and the question of the annihilation of the wicked.

SOUL-EXTINCTION

It was pointed out in Chapter 3 that, according to Seventh-day Adventists, there is no soul which survives after the body dies, that after death nothing of man survives, and that therefore at death man becomes completely nonexistent. Though they do teach that all men will be raised from the dead, the condition of man between death and the resurrection is, for them, not one of consciousness but of non-existence; hence their view, in distinction from the view usually called *soul-sleep,* can better be characterized as that of *soul-extinction.*[1]

In Chapter 5 it was found that Jehovah's Witnesses have basically the same view of what happens after death. For them, too, there is no soul which survives when the body dies, since the soul cannot exist apart from the body. No aspect of man continues to exist consciously after death; hence when man dies he totally ceases to exist.[2] Thus their view, too, can be called that of *soul-extinction.* Though the Witnesses claim that not all people will be raised from the dead, but that some will remain in the condition of nonexistence into which death has plunged them, and though the Witnesses also teach that members of the 144,000 who die now do not sink into nonexistence, but are immediately changed into immortal spirits, it remains true, for them, that all who do not fall into the latter category will experience *soul-extinction* when they die.

What shall we say about this view? It should first be observed

[1] See above, pp. 110-11, 135-36.
[2] See above, pp. 265-66, 293-94.

345

that this view of the future of man between death and the resurrection has never been held by any recognized branch of the
Christian Church. Though there have been groups which have
embraced similar views,[3] and though there have been and are
occasional theologians who are so inclined,[4] the position sketched
above has never been incorporated into any of the historic Christian creeds.

It must be admitted, of course, that the Scriptures do not say
a great deal about the so-called *intermediate state,*[5] and that what
is central in the Biblical message about the future life is the
doctrine of the resurrection of the body. It must also be granted
that the Bible does not give us a theoretical exposition of the
nature of the intermediate state. G. C. Berkouwer, for example,
in a recent book on eschatology, concedes that the New Testament
nowhere gives us an anthropological description of man in the
intermediate state, nowhere explains how man can still be
conscious when separated from his body.[6] The New Testament,
he continues, does not satisfy our curiosity about the "how" of
this intermediate state; it only tells us that we shall be *with Christ*
— and this ought to be sufficient.[7] Berkouwer does, however,
make clear, in Chapter Two of this volume, that he believes
in a conscious existence of man in the intermediate state, even
though he finds it impossible to describe the nature of this
existence.

The word "psuchee." Let us, then, examine the Scriptural evidence for the conscious existence of man between death and the
resurrection. As we have seen, Seventh-day Adventists contend
that there is nothing in the use of either *nephesh* or *psuchee*
(the Hebrew and Greek words for soul) which implies that there
is in man a conscious entity that can survive the body.[8] On
the basis of their own studies of these same Biblical words Jeho-

---

[3] E.g., the Anabaptists and Socinians of the 16th century, who maintained
that the souls of men, though still in existence after death, exist in a state
of complete unconsciousness (cf. H. Bavinck, *Gereformeerde Dogmatiek,*
3rd ed., IV, 672-73).

[4] G. C. Berkouwer, in his *Mens het Beeld Gods* (Kampen: Kok, 1957),
mentions such recent theologians as G. Vander Leeuw and Paul Althaus
(p. 282). A similar position has been taken by a Reformed pastor in the
Netherlands, B. Telder, in his *Sterven . . . en Dan?* (Kampen: Kok, 1960).
The last-named work, however, evoked a storm of protest both in the
Netherlands and elsewhere.

[5] The condition of man between death and the resurrection.

[6] *De Wederkomst van Christus* (Kampen: Kok, 1961), I, 62.

[7] *Ibid.,* I, 64. Cf. Oscar Cullmann, *Christ and Time,* trans. F. Filson
(Philadelphia: Westminster Press, 1950), p. 241.

[8] See above, pp. 110-11.

vah's Witnesses contend that there can be no soul that exists apart from the body.[9]

In reply, it should be pointed out first of all that the Greek word *psuchee* (to restrict ourselves to the New Testament word for soul) may have a variety of meanings. Arndt and Gingrich, in their Greek-English lexicon, suggest that *psuchee* in the New Testament may mean life, soul as the center of man's inner life, soul as the center of a life which transcends the earth, that which possesses life, a living creature, soul as that which leaves the realm of earth at death and lives on in Hades.[10]

There are at least two instances in the New Testament where the word *psuchee* is used to designate that aspect of man which continues to exist after death. The first of these is Matthew 10:28, "And be not afraid of them that kill the body, but are not able to kill the soul (*psuchee*); but rather fear him who is able to destroy both soul and body in hell." In this passage *psuchee* cannot be another name for the whole person (compare the common Seventh-day-Adventist and Jehovah-Witness assertion: man does not *have* a soul but *is* a soul); for, if so, the *psuchee* would be dead when the body is killed. What Jesus is saying here is this: There is something about you which those who kill you cannot touch! That something is that aspect of man which continues to exist after the body has been lowered into the grave.[11]

The second of these two instances is Revelation 6:9-10, "And when he [the Lamb] opened the fifth seal, I saw underneath the altar the souls (*psuchas*) of them that had been slain for the word of God, and for the testimony which they held; and they cried with a great voice, saying, How long, O Master, the holy and true, dost thou not judge and avenge our blood on them that dwell on the earth?" *Souls* here cannot simply mean living creatures or persons, for it makes no sense to say, "the people of those that had been slain," or "the living creatures of those that had been slain." If *psuchas* here was intended to stand for persons, we would expect that the case of the perfect passive participle which follows would be the same as that of the word *psuchas,* so that the passage would read, "the slain persons," or "the persons that had been slain." Instead, the participle is in the genitive case (*esphagmenoon*), so that the words must be translated, the souls *of* them that had been slain." The reference here is obviously to the *souls of people* who have been slain as martyrs for their loyalty to God — to souls, in other words, who still exist after

---

[9] See above, pp. 265-66.
[10] Wm. F. Arndt and F. Wilbur Gingrich, *Greek-English Lexicon of the New Testament* (Chicago: University of Chicago Press, 1957), pp. 901-902.
[11] See above, p. 265, n. 190.

death and who are conscious. That these souls are in a conscious
state is evident from the fact that they cry out, and that they are
spoken to (v. 11). It is clear that these souls have not yet experienced the resurrection from the dead, for (1) the end of
history has not yet come since they themselves affirm that their
blood has not yet been avenged; and (2) they are told to rest
yet for a little while, until their fellow servants should have fulfilled their course (v. 11).

So we have pictured here for us, in symbolic fashion, the souls
of people who have been slain, who have not yet taken part in the
resurrection from the dead, who are still waiting for the final
consummation of all things. Both the content of their cry and the
words addressed to them indicate that their happiness is still
incomplete, that they are waiting for and looking forward to
the final denouement, in which justice will be completely administered and God will be fully glorified.[12]

The objection might be raised that, since Revelation is a symbolic book, we have no right to draw teachings about the intermediate state from such symbols. The point is, however, that if
there is no conscious existence between death and the resurrection, the entire passage becomes meaningless. Since the text
cannot refer to people still living on earth, nor to people who
have already received their resurrection bodies, it must have
reference to individuals enjoying some kind of conscious existence
between death and the resurrection.

Though this passage is not referred to in *Questions on Doctrine,*
we do find a discussion of it in a Jehovah-Witness publication,
The Kingdom is at Hand, pages 336-37. Here the passage is
quoted in the translation of the *Emphatic Diaglott,* which renders
psuchas by *persons.* The Witnesses have corrected themselves
on this score, however, since in their *New World Translation* the
word is rendered *souls.* These *persons* or *souls* are interpreted
in the first-named volume as standing for members of the anointed
class or 144,000. The "white robe" which is said to have
been given to each of them (v. 11) is understood to mean their
"resurrection" as spirit creatures in 1918. At this point we must
remind the Witnesses that, according to their own teaching,[13] this
so-called "first resurrection" was a transition from non-existence
to spirit existence. If these *persons* or *souls* were non-existent
between their death and their spiritual resurrection, how could
they possibly be said to cry out during this period? On the basis

[12] See Berkouwer's discussion of this passage in *Wederkomst van Christus,*
I, 154-55. Cf. also Cullmann, *op. cit.,* pp. 240-41.
[13] See above, pp. 302-6.

of their own interpretation of the passage, therefore, Jehovah's Witnesses must admit that these *persons* or *souls* existed in a conscious state between their death and their resurrection.[14]

The word "pneuma." Seventh-day Adventists also contend that neither the Hebrew word *ruach* nor the Greek word *pneuma* (the two words usually translated *spirit*) ever denotes a separate entity capable of conscious existence apart from the physical body.[15] Since Jehovah's Witnesses take a similar position, it may be assumed that they would agree with the Adventists that *ruach* or *pneuma* cannot mean "an entity" capable of conscious existence apart from the body; the various meanings assigned to these two words on page 357 of *Make Sure of All Things* do not include the one just mentioned.

Restricting ourselves to the Greek word *pneuma,* let us note that in at least three New Testament instances *pneuma* must refer to that aspect of man which continues to exist after death. (1) There is, first, Luke 23:46, Jesus' seventh word from the cross, "Father, into thy hands I commend my spirit (*pneuma*)." According to Arndt and Gingrich, *pneuma* may have the following range of meanings: wind, breath, life-spirit, soul, the spirit as a part of the human personality, state of mind, a spirit as an independent being, the Spirit of God, the Spirit of Christ, the Holy Spirit.[16] To commend one's breath to the Father is meaningless. To commend one's state of mind also makes little sense. By a process of elimination we discover that the only meanings of *pneuma* that make sense here are soul, or spirit as a part of the human personality. Jesus thus commends or entrusts his human soul or spirit to the Father. Since He was not immediately raised from the dead, we conclude that His human spirit went to be with the Father in heaven during the time when His body was in the tomb.

Jehovah's Witnesses comment on this passage as follows:

> In the light of the foregoing it is clear that when Jesus, dying on the tree, said, "Father, into thy hands I commend my spirit," he was commending to his heavenly Father his power of life. He trusted that on the third day God would restore the power of life and would raise him from the dead (Lk. 23:46).[17]

As can be seen, however, from a perusal of the above range of meanings, *pneuma* never means "power of life." On the page

---

[14] The above discussion does not imply agreement with the Watchtower interpretation of this passage, but is an attempt to refute the Witnesses on their own grounds.

[15] See above, p. 111.

[16] *Op. cit.,* pp. 682-84.

[17] *The Truth Shall Make You Free,* p. 109.

preceding the one from which the above quotation is taken, it is said that "the spirit" which returns to God after death means "the life forces or the power of life which is sustained by breathing." It would appear that this power of life no longer exists after one has stopped breathing. Was it, then, this non-existent power which Christ commended into His Father's hands?

(2) Let us look next at Acts 7:59, where the dying Stephen is reported as saying, "Lord Jesus, receive my spirit (*pneuma*)." This passage is to be understood in the same way as Jesus' seventh word from the cross. Note that whereas Jesus had commended His spirit to the Father, Stephen asks Jesus to receive his spirit, thus equating Jesus with the Father and confessing Christ's full deity. What would be the point of Stephen's asking Jesus to receive his spirit if his spirit simply ceased to exist at death?

(3) Finally, let us examine Hebrews 12:22, 23: "Ye are come . . . unto the city of the living God, the heavenly Jerusalem, and to innumerable hosts of angels, to the general assembly and church of the firstborn who are enrolled in heaven, and to God the Judge of all, and to the spirits of just men made perfect . . . (*pneumasi dikaioon teteleioomenoon*)." You should appreciate your spiritual privilege as those who belong to the new covenant, the author of Hebrews is saying to his readers. As you have come into the fellowship of God's people through faith in Christ, you have not come to a mountain that burned with fire, which even beasts might not touch, but you have come to the heavenly Jerusalem, you have come into fellowship with "innumerable hosts of angels" and with "the spirits of just men made perfect."

Pneumasi, the dative plural of *pneuma,* cannot here mean angels, since angels have just been mentioned. Neither can *pneumasi* designate people still on earth, for (1) why would the author describe people on earth as spirits? If he had intended to refer to people on earth, why did he not simply write, *dikaiois teteleioomenois* ("to just men made perfect")? (2) Can we say, moreover, that people on earth have been made perfect? Paul, in fact, tells us in Philippians 3:12 that he has not yet been made perfect, using the same tense of the same verb: *teteleioomai.* The reference here is clearly to the *spirits* of just or righteous men, who are here said to have been perfected, to have been brought to their goal (*telos*). It is to the spirits of such perfected men that the readers are said to have come. This expression therefore points to the spirits of perfected saints who are now in heaven. The author does not have resurrected saints in mind, since his readers are said to have already come (*proseleeluthate*) to these spirits: that is, already to have a kind of fellowship with them, in the sense of knowing themselves to be one with them.

Though the manner of their existence is not described, this passage does reveal that the spirits of believers who have been translated to heaven do have some kind of existence between death and the resurrection. The *New World Translation* renders this passage, "and the spiritual lives of righteous ones who have been made perfect." This is, however, a mistranslation. The Greek does not say, "spiritual lives"; it says *spirits: pneumasi.*

In Christ. Approaching the question of the intermediate state from a different angle, we must next observe that the New Testament frequently speaks of the believer as being "in Christ." The expression "in Christ," or a cognate expression such as "in the Lord" or "in him," occurs 164 times in the writings of Paul alone.[18] The idea that the believer is in Christ is therefore a central concept in the New Testament. From eternity believers have been chosen in Christ (Eph. 1:4), believers are united with Christ in regeneration (Eph. 2:4, 5), and Christ continually lives in them (Gal. 2:20). Believers are said to die in Christ (Rom. 14:8), to be about to be raised with Christ (I Cor. 15:22), and to be destined for eternal glorification with Christ (I Thess. 4:17). Does it seem likely, now, that believers who were chosen in Christ from eternity and who are in Christ during this life will, at the time of their death, lapse into nonexistence, only to be recreated at the time of the final resurrection? If Christ is God and if, as our Lord Himself tells us in John 10:28 and 29, no one can ever snatch believers out of either Christ's hand or the Father's hand, does it seem likely that death can do so? One might counter that, since these believers are held in God's memory and are bound to be raised again, death does not really snatch them out of Christ's hand. But how can one be said to be still in Christ's hand if he no longer exists?

Consider also the testimony of Romans 14:8, "For whether we live, we live unto the Lord; or whether we die, we die unto the Lord; whether we live therefore, or die, we are the Lord's." According to the last part of the verse, we are the Lord's whether we live or die. In what sense, however, can we be the Lord's if we are nonexistent? If Seventh-day Adventists and Jehovah's Witnesses were right, Paul should have said, "Whether we live, therefore, or arise again, we are the Lord's"; on their basis he ought never to have said, "whether we die, we are the Lord's."

Consider further the testimony of I Thessalonians 4:16, "the dead in Christ shall rise first," and of I Corinthians 15:23,

---

[18] B M. Metzger, *The Jehovah's Witnesses and Jesus Christ*, p. 68.

"But each [shall be made alive] in his own order: Christ the firstfruits; then they that are Christ's, at his coming." How could Paul speak of the "dead in Christ" if the dead are completely nonexistent? How could he speak of "they that are Christ's," meaning those who died as believers, if the dead no longer exist in any way? The implication of the passages just quoted is clear: if we are once truly in Christ, we shall remain in Christ forever, even after we die. This fact precludes the possibility of nonexistence between death and the resurrection.

The God of the Living. In connection with what has just been said, let us look at Luke 20:27-38. The story is a familiar one: The Sadducees come to Jesus with a "parable" about the resurrection, and with a question: "Whose wife shall she be?" In reply Jesus quotes the well-known words, "I am the God of Abraham, of Isaac, and of Jacob." Jesus then adds, "Now he is not the God of the dead but of the living; for all live unto him" (v. 38). Jesus thus proves the doctrine of the resurrection of the body, which the Sadducees denied, from the Pentateuch, which they accepted as authoritative.

For our purpose, however, it is significant to note something else. Josephus tells us that the Sadducees denied the continued existence of the soul after death as well as the resurrection of the body: "But the doctrine of the Sadducees is this: that souls die with the bodies. . . ."[19] Note now that in his reply Jesus was correcting their view of the intermediate state as well as their denial of the resurrection. He was saying, in effect, "Abraham, Isaac, and Jacob, though they died many years ago, are actually living today. For God, who calls Himself the God of Abraham, Isaac, and Jacob, is not the God of the dead but of the living." To be sure, in order that these patriarchs may live in the full sense of the word, their bodies must be raised. But Jesus' words imply that the patriarchs are living even now, after their death, but before their resurrection. This point is made explicit by the words recorded only by Luke: "For all live unto him." Though the dead seem to us to be completely nonexistent, they are actually living as far as God is concerned. Note that the tense of the word for live is not future (which might suggest only that these dead will live at the time of their resurrection) but present, teaching us that they are living now. This holds true not only for the patriarchs but for all who have died. To suggest, now, that Abraham, Isaac, and Jacob are nonexistent between death and the resurrection

---

[19] *Antiquities,* XVIII, 1, 4. It would appear, therefore, that the Sadducees were the first proponents of the "soul-extinction" theory in the Christian era. Their position on this point seems to have been identical to that of present-day Seventh-day Adventists and Jehovah's Witnesses.

violates the thrust of these words, and implies that God is, with respect to these patriarchs, for a long period of time the God of the dead rather than the God of the living.[20]

The Second Word from the Cross. Let us look next at the words of Jesus to the penitent thief, recorded in Luke 23:43, "Verily I say unto thee, Today shalt thou be with me in Paradise." Both Seventh-day Adventists and Jehovah's Witnesses punctuate the words as follows, in order to evade the teaching that this man would be in Paradise that very day: "Verily I say unto thee today, Thou shalt be with me in Paradise."[21] Though it is true that the oldest manuscripts of the New Testament have no punctuation, and though the above punctuation is grammatically possible, it does not make good sense. For when else could Jesus say these words to the thief but today?

To understand why Jesus said *today,* we must note what the thief asked: "Jesus, remember me when thou comest in (or into) thy kingdom" (v. 42). This man believed that Jesus would come into His kingdom at the end of the world, and therefore asked to be remembered by Him at that time. Jesus' reply, however, promises him even more than he had asked for: "Today [not just at the end of the world] shalt thou be with me in Paradise."

The word *paradeisos* is used only here and in two other New Testament passages: II Corinthians 12:4 and Revelation 2:7. In the II Corinthians passage Paul tells us that he was caught up into Paradise in a vision; the expression *Paradise* is parallel to *third heaven* in v. 2. Here, therefore, Paradise means heaven, the realm of the blessed dead, and the special habitation of God.[22] In Revelation 2:7 we read about the tree of life which is in the Paradise of God — a passage which reminds us that *paradeisos* is the Septuagint translation of the Hebrew word *gan* in the expression, "garden of Eden." The reference to the tree of life (compare 22:2) tells us that this is a picture of "Paradise regained"; here again Paradise refers to heaven, though to the final state rather than the intermediate state. We conclude that Jesus prom-

---

[20] On this passage, see K. J. Popma, *Levensbeschouwing* (Amsterdam: Buijten en Schipperheijn, 1958), III, 196, 210.

[21] Seventh-day Adventists justify this punctuation by quoting from Mrs. White's *Desire of Ages* (*Principles of Life from the Word of God*, p. 323). Jehovah's Witnesses thus punctuate the verse in their NWT; in their other publications they interpret the verse as meaning that during the millennium the thief will be raised in the "resurrection of judgment," and given an opportunity to live in the paradise of the new earth (*This Means Everlasting Life*, pp. 281-83; *New Heavens and a New Earth*, p. 349; *Paradise Lost*, p. 229).

[22] See note on "The Third Heaven" in Philip E. Hughes, *Paul's Second Epistle to the Corinthians* (Eerdmans, 1962). pp. 432-34.

ised the penitent thief that the latter would be with Christ in heavenly bliss that very day. Surely there would have been no point to Jesus' words if the thief would, at the moment of his death, enter a state of unconsciousness or nonexistence!

To Depart and Be With Christ. We turn now to a very significant passage, Philippians 1:21-23, which in the American Standard Version reads as follows:

> For to me to live is Christ, and to die is gain. But if to live in the flesh, — if this shall bring fruit from my work, then what I shall choose I know not. But I am in a strait betwixt the two, having the desire to depart and be with Christ; for it is very far better. . . .

Note that Paul here calls death gain. How could he do this, if death meant entering a state of nonexistence? One could argue, I suppose, that Paul thinks here only of the final resurrection, which, as far as his subjective experience is concerned, will follow immediately after his death. Verse 23, however, sheds light on what Paul has in mind. Paul's desire to depart is not a morbid longing for death as such, but an eagerness to be closer to Christ than he is while still on earth — and this eventuality, he says, would be very far better.

The Greek here reads: *teen epithumian echoon eis to analusai kai sun Christoo einai. Analusai, to depart,* is an aorist infinitive, depicting the momentary act of death. Linked with *analusai* by a single article is the present infinitive, *einai, to be.* The single article ties the two infinitives together, so that the actions depicted by the two infinitives are to be considered two aspects of the same thing, or two sides of the same coin.[23] What Paul is therefore saying here is that the moment he departs or dies, that very same moment he will be with Christ. Since the verb *to be* denotes continuing existence, Paul implies that he will then not only *be* with Christ but *continue to be* with Christ.

Paul does not tell us exactly *how* he will be with Christ, but he does clearly affirm that this *being with Christ* will begin as soon as he dies. If Paul were here referring only to the resurrection of the body, he could have made this plain — see his unambiguous allusion to the resurrection which will occur at Christ's *parousia* in 3:20, 21. Here, however, he is simply thinking of the moment

---

[23] See A. T. Robertson, *Grammar of the Greek Testament in the Light of Historical Research* (Nashville: Broadman Press, 1934), p. 787: "Sometimes groups more or less distinct are treated as one for the purpose in hand, and hence use only one article." Cf. F. Blass and A. Debrunner, *A Greek Grammar of the New Testament,* trans. R. W. Funk (Chicago: University of Chicago Press, 1961), sec. 276, (3).

of his death — and he has no guarantee that the resurrection of his body will occur at that moment. At that very moment of death, he says, I will be with Christ. This condition, he adds, will be "very far better" than his present existence, clearly refuting the thought that after death one enters a state of nonexistence. How could such a state be "very far better" than Paul's state while still on earth, in which he does have conscious, though imperfect, fellowship with Christ?

Seventh-day Adventists interpret this passage as referring to Paul's being with Christ at the time of the resurrection of the body.[24] But if this were what was in Paul's mind, he would have no problem. There would be no advantage to his departing at once, since he would then not be with Christ one moment sooner than if he should remain alive. He tells us here, however, that he has a problem, for to die and be with Christ now (not, many years from now) would be very far better than remaining alive.[25]

Jehovah's Witnesses try to make this passage refer not to Paul's death, but to the time of Christ's return and Second Presence. They teach, in other words, that Paul will not be with Christ until the members of the anointed class are "raised" in 1918. They base this interpretation simply on a dogmatic assertion: "Such getting to be with Christ the Lord will first be possible at Christ's return, when the dead in Christ will rise first. . . ."[26] This view has, however, been sufficiently answered by the above discussion.

Absent from the Body, at Home with the Lord. Another very important passage in this connection is II Corinthians 5:6-8. This passage reads as follows:

> Being therefore always of good courage, and knowing that, whilst we are at home in the body, we are absent from the Lord (for we walk by faith, not by sight); we are of good courage, I say, and are willing rather to be absent from the body, and to be at home with the Lord.

Let us look carefully at the two verbs used in these verses: *endeemeoo* and *ekdeemeoo*. These verbs are compound forms derived from *deemos,* meaning *people; endeemeoo* thus means to be in among one's people or to be at home, whereas *ekdeemeoo* means to be away from one's people, or to be away from home. Moulton and Milligan cite an instance in which *ekdeemeoo* means

---

[24] *Questions on Doctrine*, pp. 527-28.
[25] See on this point Herbert S. Bird's *Theology of Seventh-Day Adventism* Eerdmans, 1961), p. 49. Cf. also Berkouwer's *Wederkomst van Christus,* I, 64-66; and Cullmann, *op. cit.,* pp. 239-40.
[26] *New World Translation of the Christian Greek Scriptures* (1951 ed.), p. 781.

to *go abroad.*[27] Note also the tenses used: present tenses in verse 6, aorists in verse 8.

"We are of good courage or good cheer," Paul says in verse 6, "knowing, as we do, that while we continue to be at home in the body (*endeemountes,* a present participle, implying continuing action), we are continually away from home as regards the Lord" (*ekdeemoumen,* a present indicative, again stressing the continuation of the action). These words sound strange. How can Paul say that he is now absent from the Lord? Does he not have fellowship with the Lord in this life? Yes, Paul replies in verse 7, but the fellowship which we have with Christ during this life is a walking by faith, not by sight. That is to say, our present fellowship with Christ, good though it be, is still incomplete, still leaves much to be desired.

In the light of this background, we approach verse 8, where the thought is continued. "We are of good courage, I say and deem it better (*eudokoumen mallon*) to be once-for-all away from home as to the body (*ekdeemeesai ek tou soomatos* — an aorist infinitive, suggesting momentary or snapshot action), and once-for-all at home with the Lord (*endeemeesai pros ton kurion* — another aorist infinitive). Whereas the present tenses in verse 6 picture a continuing at-homeness in the body and a continuing away-from-homeness as to the Lord, the aorist infinitives of verse 8 point to a once-for-all momentary happening. What can this be? There is only one answer: death, which is an immediate transition from being at home in the body to being away from home as to the body. The first aorist infinitive, *ekdeemeesai,* should probably be construed as an ingressive or inceptive aorist, indicating the momentary beginning of an action which thereafter continues.[28] Note, now, that this first aorist infinitive is followed by a second, *endeemeesai.* This second aorist is probably also to be construed as ingressive, parallel to the first. In a moment, says Paul, I shall begin to be at home with the Lord. At what moment? Obviously, at the same moment indicated by *ekdeemeesai,* the moment of death. If we look back at verse 6 again, we note that the time of *endeemountes* and *ekdeemoumen* is simultaneous: while we are at home in the body, we are away from home as to the Lord. Following this analogy, we expect that the two aorist infinitives in verse 8 also point to simultaneous time, only now to the instantaneous occurrence which ushers in a new condition: the moment we are away from home as to the body (the moment of death), that very

[27] J. H. Moulton and George Milligan, *The Vocabulary of the Greek Testament Illustrated from the Papyri* (Eerdmans, 1957; originally published in 1930), p. 192.
[28] Blass-Debrunner, *op. cit.,* sec. 331.

moment we shall be at home with the Lord. Observe, too, that the word *pros* suggests a very close fellowship, a face-to-face fellowship, implying that the fellowship with Christ which Paul expects to enjoy after death will be far closer than that which he has experienced here on earth. The passage thus teaches that at the moment of death the believer goes, not into an unconscious state or a state of nonexistence, but into a state of fellowship with Christ which is closer than that which he has enjoyed on earth.

Seventh-day Adventists contend that "there is nothing in this text to justify our coming to the conclusion that the being 'present with the Lord' will occur immediately upon being 'absent from the body.' "[29] We have seen, however, that both the tenses of the infinitives in verse 8 and the parallelism between verse 8 and verse 6 indicate that being present with the Lord does occur the moment one dies. The authors of *Questions on Doctrine* further assert, on page 530, that what the apostle has in mind when he says that he desires to be present with the Lord is the resurrection day. The difficulty with this position, however, is that he speaks here about being absent from the body and present (or at home) with the Lord. Surely receiving a resurrection body is not a being *absent* from the body! If the Adventist interpretation of this passage were correct, we would have expected Paul to say something like this: "are willing rather to be absent from *this body* and to be at home in the *new body*"![30]

The Parable of the Rich Man and Lazarus. We shall look finally at the parable of the rich man and Lazarus recorded in Luke 16:19-31. Though we may not interpret every detail of this parable literally, we may and must ask what is the main point of the story. As becomes quite clear from the context, that main point is the contrast between the lot after death of the unbelieving Pharisees (pictured by the rich man) and that of the publicans and sinners who believed on Jesus (pictured by Lazarus). Though on earth the rich man enjoyed luxury and Lazarus suffered poverty, after death the rich man is in torment, whereas Lazarus is comforted. It is quite obvious, now, that if after death people simply lapse into a state of unconsciousness or nonexistence, this parable would lose all point.

---

[29] *Questions on Doctrine*, p. 528.
[30] This is not to deny that Paul will still be "at home with the Lord" after he has received his new body. It is, however, unwarranted to make this passage refer exclusively to the resurrection body. Cf. on this passage also Cullmann, *op. cit.*, pp. 238-40; Berkouwer, *Wederkomst van Christus*, I, 68-73; and Hughes, *op. cit.*, pp. 175-85. Hughes reacts critically to the position taken on these verses by E. Earle Ellis in Chap. II of the latter's *Paul and His Recent Interpreters* (Eerdmans, 1961).

One might reply, however, that the parable pictures conditions as they will be after the resurrection of the body has occurred, since the rich man is said to have a tongue, and Lazarus is described as having fingers. Against this interpretation the following objections can be registered: (1) In verses 27 and 28 the rich man refers to his five brothers who are still living on earth and whom he wishes to warn; this situation would not be possible if the general resurrection had occurred and the final state had been ushered in. (2) Verse 31 implies that the resurrection from the dead has not yet occurred at the time pictured by the parable: "If they hear not Moses and the prophets, neither will they be persuaded, if one rise from the dead."

The diversified conscious existence of the rich man and Lazarus pictured symbolically in this parable, therefore, must be a reflection of conditions during the intermediate state. As such, the parable confirms what we have learned from other New Testament passages, namely, that believers immediately after death go to be with Christ in order to enjoy a provisional happiness in His presence (provisional because their bodies have not yet been raised), whereas unbelievers at death go at once to a place of provisional punishment.

The Watchtower interpretation of this parable, which was given previously,[31] is so palpably absurd as to require no further comment. By means of this interpretation, which flatters their own egos, the Witnesses have simply closed their ears to what Christ is saying to them here. Seventh-day Adventists, while admitting that the parable portrays allegorically conditions before the resurrection,[32] insist that "the story of the rich man and Lazarus in no way proves the consciousness of the dead. . . ."[33] They go on to assert that, though Christ knew perfectly well that there is no consciousness after death, He simply met the Pharisees on their own ground in the parable, placing His own teachings into the framework of their errors in order to reveal the unsoundness of their position.[34] This interpretation, however, implies that Jesus could use a lie to teach a truth! Though we are not permitted to draw from this parable a detailed description of conditions in the intermediate state, the story would be utterly without point if believers did not exist in conscious blessedness and if unbelievers did not

---

[31] See above, p. 251.
[32] *Questions on Doctrine*, p. 560.
[33] *Ibid.*, p. 558.
[34] *Ibid.*, p. 564. This understanding of the parable is based on a quotation from Mrs. White's book, *Christ's Object Lessons* (found on p. 263 of the latter volume).

suffer conscious torment immediately after death. How could Jesus have used this parable as a vehicle of divine revelation if the main lesson which it was intended to convey was based on a misconception about the future life?

In connection with the parable just discussed, the reader's attention is called to II Peter 2:9, which clearly teaches that the ungodly will endure conscious pain during the intermediate state: "The Lord knoweth how to deliver the godly out of temptation, and to keep the unrighteous under punishment unto the day of judgment." The last part of the text reads as follows in the Greek: *"adikous de eis heemeran kriseoos kolazomenous teerein."* Peter has been expounding the severity of divine judgments over the angels that sinned, over the ancient world, and over Sodom and Gomorrah. Verse 9 is a summary statement which serves, in turn, to introduce a further description of the terrible wickedness of the false teachers he has been writing about. The unrighteous mentioned in the text, in other words, are certainly inclusive of human beings who are unrighteous.

The same God who delivers the godly out of temptation, Peter says, knows how to keep unrighteous men (and angels) under punishment unto the day of judgment. *Kolazomenous* is a present passive (or middle) participle from *kolazoo,* to punish. God knows how to keep these unrighteous ones *kolazomenous,* says Peter; literally, keep them *being punished,* until the day of judgment. The present tense of the participle implies that this punishment is a continuing one. The words *eis heemeran kriseoos* tell us that what is here described is not the final punishment of the wicked, but a punishment which will precede the judgment day. It cannot be maintained, further, that the punishment here spoken of is one which is administered only during this life since the words "unto the day of judgment" clearly extend this punishment to that day. We learn from this passage, therefore, that the souls of the unrighteous will not be unconscious after death, but will undergo a continuing punishment even before their bodies are raised at the time of the final judgment.

We conclude that the position of Seventh-day Adventists and Jehovah's Witnesses on the condition of man between death and the resurrection is not in harmony with Scripture, and ought therefore to be abandoned by both of these groups.[35]

---

[35] On the entire question of *soul-extinction* see, in addition to the literature already noted, Chap. II of Norman F. Douty's *Another Look at Seventh-day Adventism* (Grand Rapids: Baker, 1962); and Bird, *op. cit.,* Chap. III.

THE ANNIHILATION OF THE WICKED

Both Seventh-day Adventists and Jehovah's Witnesses teach the final annihilation of the wicked and deny that there is a place of eternal torment called hell. It will be recognized that we are now no longer discussing the so-called intermediate state between death and the resurrection, but that we are now treating an aspect of the doctrine of the final state — the state into which men enter after the resurrection of the body.

Seventh-day Adventists teach that, after Satan's final assault on the "camp of the saints," fire will come down from heaven and will annihilate Satan, his evil angels, and all the wicked. Before this happens, however, those to be annihilated will be subjected to gradations of suffering, depending on the guilt of the persons or demons involved; Satan himself will suffer the longest and will therefore be the last to perish in the flames. At the end of this period of suffering, however, all those who have rebelled against God will be wiped out of existence.[36]

The teaching of Jehovah's Witnesses on this point is a bit more complicated. Whereas Seventh-day Adventists affirm that all those who have died will be raised again, no matter how wicked they may have been, the Witnesses assert that certain individuals will not be raised but will remain in the nonexistence into which they were plunged by their death: those killed at Armageddon, Adam and Eve, those who died in the flood, and so on.[37] Individuals raised from the dead during the millennium who do not obey God's kingdom will be annihilated before the end of the millennium.[38] Satan and his demons, loosed at the end of the millennium, will succeed in leading some of earth's inhabitants astray; this host he will head in a final assault on the "camp of the holy ones." Fire will come down from heaven, however, and will annihilate this entire rebellious army.[39] The possibility always remains that some who are left on the new earth after Satan's destruction may still have to be annihilated.[40] In distinction from Seventh-day Adventists, however, Jehovah's Witnesses do not teach a gradation of suffering previous to the annihilation of the wicked.

The word apollumi. The doctrine of the annihilation of the wicked is, however, not in agreement with Scripture. In order to refute this teaching, we must first of all look at some of the more

---

[36] See above, p. 142.
[37] See above, p. 317.
[38] See above, pp. 320-21.
[39] See above, pp. 321-22.
[40] See above, p. 324.

common words used in the New Testament to describe the final punishment of the wicked. The word most commonly used for this purpose is the verb *apollumi,* usually translated *destroy* or *perish* (in the middle or passive voice). Seventh-day Adventists, on pages 536 and 537 of *Questions on Doctrine,* give the impression that the word *apollumi* when used in the New Testament of the fate of the wicked means to annihilate. Jehovah's Witnesses give the same impression. On page 97 of *Let God Be True* they quote Matthew 10:28, where the word *apollumi* is used to describe what God does to both soul and body in hell (Gehenna), and conclude: "Since God destroys soul and body in Gehenna, this is conclusive proof that Gehenna, or the valley of the son of Hinnom, is a picture or symbol of complete annihilation, and not of eternal torment." The implication is clear: *apollumi* must mean annihilation.

How can it be shown that *apollumi* in the New Testament never means annihilation? We note first of all that this word never means to annihilate when it is applied to other things than man's eternal destiny. Let us observe the range of meaning of this New Testament word:

(1) Sometimes *apollumi* simply means *to be lost.* It is so used in the three "lost" parables in Luke 15, to designate the lost sheep, the lost coin, and the lost son. In the case of the son, his being lost meant that he was lost to the fellowship of his father since he went against his father's purpose.

(2) The word *apollumi* may be applied in a somewhat related way to mean *become useless.* So in Matthew 9:17 it is used to show what happens to old wineskins when you pour new wine into them: the skins "perish" or become useless. And in Matthew 26:8 a related word is used for what the disciples thought was a waste of money — the pouring of ointment on Jesus' head: "To what purpose is this waste?" (the word rendered *waste* is *apooleia,* the noun derived from *apollumi*). In neither of these instances can the word or its derivative possibly mean annihilation.

(3) Sometimes *apollumi* is used to mean *kill.* For example, note Matthew 2:13, "for Herod will seek the young child to destroy (*apolesai*) him." Even aside from the fact that Jesus is involved here, is killing annihilation? As we have learned from Matthew 10:28, one is not annihilated when he is killed. Further, strictly speaking, one does not even annihilate the body when he kills a man. The particles of a decaying body pass into other forms of matter.

(4) There is a significant type of passage in which *apollumi* cannot possibly mean annihilation: Luke 9:24, "For whosoever would save his life (*psuchee*) shall lose it; but whosoever shall lose his

life for my sake, the same shall save it." *Lose his life* in the second half of the verse is a translation of *apolesee teen psucheen*. One could render *psuchee* by soul, if he wished. In either case, annihilation is out of the question. If *apollumi* meant annihilation in the second half of this text, the person who would enter into a state of annihilation would be the saved person! To lose one's life or soul must mean something quite different from annihilation: to be willing to subordinate one's own interests to those of the Kingdom of God.

(5) We come now to those passages in which *apollumi* is used to describe the future destiny of the wicked. In the light of the usages we have noted, we certainly would not expect the word to mean annihilation in these instances. If it did have this meaning when applied to man's future state, *apollumi* would have undergone a rather abrupt change of meaning. Now in the abstract such a change of meaning would be possible. But if this were so, there would have to be a clear indication in the relevant passages that the meaning of the word had thus changed. If this were so, moreover, descriptions of the final destiny of the wicked in which the word *apollumi* is not used should unambiguously support the idea of annihilation.

The Meaning of Gehenna. Let us now examine some of these descriptions. We look, first, at a word which occurs twelve times in the New Testament and is usually translated *hell,* the Greek word *ge-enna*. Seventh-day Adventists understand this word to refer to the fires of destruction which shall finally annihilate the wicked; Jehovah's Witnesses interpret the word as a symbol of annihilation.[41] In Matthew 18:9, however, the phrase, "the Gehenna (or hell) of fire" is parallel with the expression, "the eternal fire" (*to pur to aioonion*) in verse 8. So the fire of Gehenna is not a temporary one but an eternal or endless one.[42] If the fire of Gehenna is eternal, we must conclude that the punishment of which the fire is symbolic will also be eternal. For what would be the point of keeping the fire of Gehenna burning after the last individual had been annihilated by it?

Note further that in Mark 9:43 the word *ge-enna* occurs in parallel construction with the expression, "the unquenchable fire" (*to pur to asbeston*). If the fire of Gehenna is unquenchable, will it not be an everlasting fire? Observe also that in Mark 9:48 Gehenna is described in words quoted from Isaiah 66:24, "where their worm dieth not, and the fire is not quenched." These expressions clearly

---

[41] *Questions on Doctrine,* p. 558; see above p. 323.
[42] That *aioonios* means endless when used in this sense will be shown later in this appendix.

indicate that there is no end to the punishment of Gehenna. Jehovah's Witnesses reply that what is here said not to die is the worms and not man."[43] What Jesus says here, however, is, *"their worm dieth not."* Since the worm stands for the punishment suffered by the wicked, we are compelled to conclude that the symbol of the undying worm is simply a picture of unending punishment.[44]

Much is made by both Seventh-day Adventists and Jehovah's Witnesses of the figurative nature of the descriptions of the punishment of the wicked found in the New Testament. To be sure, these descriptions are figurative and symbolic, but the figures are intended to convey meaning. Though we cannot apply every detail of these figures literally, we must accept the teaching they are intended to convey, namely, that the punishment of the wicked will be everlasting. The Biblical descriptions of Gehenna, therefore, rule out annihilationism, for creatures who have been annihilated cannot be everlastingly punished.

The Smoke of Their Torment. Let us now turn to another passage which describes the final state of the wicked: Revelation 14:11, "And the smoke of their torment goeth up for ever and ever, and they have no rest day and night, they that worship the beast and his image, and whoso receiveth the mark of his name." These words obviously refer to the punishment of the lost.[45] The smoke of the torment of these lost ones is said to go up for ever and ever. Though we must not think of literal smoke here, the expression is meaningless if it is not intended to picture, in a vivid way, punishment which will never end. The words "for ever and ever" read as follows in the Greek: *eis aioonas aioonoon* (literally, unto ages of ages). In Revelation 4:9 God is described as the one

[43] *Let God Be True*, p. 95.

[44] When Mr. Ulysses Glass of the Watchtower staff, whom the author interviewed on June 6, 1962, was asked why the Scriptures say that this fire will not be quenched, he replied, "The fire is not quenched because there will always be a place of punishment." The implication of his statement was that, after the wicked shall have been annihilated, the fire of Gehenna will be kept going in order to punish possible rebels who might still appear on the scene. Cf. *Watchtower*, Nov. 15, 1955, p. 703; and note what is said on p. 303 of *This Means Everlasting Life*: "Second death could at any time throughout eternity be inflicted upon any who might choose to sin. That always remains within God's power." That this interpretation of the "unquenchable fire" is a deliberate attempt to evade clear Scriptural teaching is evident from Jesus' words, *"Their* worm dieth not." When this clause is followed by the words, "the fire is not quenched," it is obvious that this is so because the fire continues to punish *them.*

[45] Seventh-day Adventists, as we have seen, apply this passage to those who, after having received the coming enlightenment about the obligation of the true Sabbath, still refuse to keep the seventh day (see above, pp. 127-28). Adventists would, however, agree that the punishment here described is that of the eternally lost.

that liveth for ever and ever" (*eis tous aioonas toon aioonoon*).
Except for the addition of the definite articles, this is the same
expression as that used in 14:11 of the ascending smoke of the
torment of the lost. From a comparison of these two passages,
therefore, we learn that the torment of the lost is as endless as God
Himself! Moreover, the word for torment, *basanismos,* cannot
possibly refer to an eternal state of unconsciousness or non-existence. If these lost were reduced to non-existence, how could the
smoke of their torment go up endlessly?[46]

Note further that we are told in Revelation 14:11 that the individuals here described have no rest day and night. Annihilation
cannot be pictured here, for annihilation would mean a kind of
rest. The lot of these lost ones is contrasted with the lot of the
saved in verse 13: "Blessed are the dead who die in the Lord
from henceforth; yea, saith the Spirit, that they may rest from
their labors. . . ." The saved, therefore, will have rest after they
die, whereas the lost will have no rest day or night. Can the latter
expression possibly picture a condition of unconsciousness or nonexistence?

We return now to the question of the meaning of the word *apollumi* when applied in the New Testament to the future destiny of
the wicked. In the light of the usage of this word when it does
not refer to man's final destiny, of passages like Revelation 14:11
where the future state of the wicked is described as one of endless
torment, and of Biblical descriptions of Gehenna, we are compelled to conclude that *apollumi* when used of the final lot of the
wicked cannot mean annihilation. We must therefore not be led
astray by the sound of words like *destroy* or *perish,* when these
are used in translations, as if they proved that the wicked shall be

---

[46] Seventh-day Adventists attempt to evade the thrust of this passage (and
of Rev. 19:3 and 20:10, where similar expressions are used) by pointing
to Isa. 34:10, where the expression, "the smoke thereof shall go up for
ever (*le'oolam*)" is used in a chapter depicting the judgment which shall fall
upon Edom. Since the unquenchable fire and unending smoke here pictured ended in desolation for Edom, and since obviously the fire that destroyed Edom is no longer burning, so they reason, it is clear that Rev.
14:11 and similar passages are only vivid ways of describing the complete
annihilation of the wicked (*Questions on Doctrine,* pp. 542-43).
    In reply, it may be said that Isaiah in Chap. 34 is using Edom as repre-
sentative of all powers that are hostile to the church of God, and that
therefore God's judgment on Edom is pictured in terms some of which
can only apply to His final judgment on all the wicked: "The unquenchable fire . . . and the eternally ascending smoke (cf. Rev. 19:3), prove that
the end of all things is referred to" (F. Delitzsch, *Commentary on Isaiah*
[Edinburgh: T. & T. Clark, 1881], II, 72; cf. p. 70). How would Seventh-
day Adventists explain the 4th verse of this chapter, "And all the host of
heaven shall be dissolved, and the heavens shall be rolled together as a
scroll. . ."? Were these words also fulfilled at the time of the destruction
of Edom?

annihilated.[47] *Apollumi* when used of the ultimate destiny of the wicked means everlasting perdition, a perdition consisting of endless loss of fellowship with God, which is at the same time a state of endless torment or pain.

This understanding of *apollumi,* which agrees fully with the teachings of such passages as Mark 9:48 and Revelation 14:11, does not at all go contrary to the first usages of the word discussed, but supplements them. For example, one could say that to "perish" in the sense of everlasting perdition means to become useless (meaning 2), to experience eternal death in distinction from eternal life (meaning 3; compare the expression, "the second death," in Rev. 20:6), and to remain permanently lost as the Prodigal Son was lost for a time — that is, permanently out of fellowship with God (meaning 1).

The word olethros. Another word used occasionally in the New Testament to describe the punishment of the wicked is the word *olethros.* Though Seventh-day Adventists do not quote the Greek word, they cite II Thessalonians 1:9, where *olethron aioonion* is translated "everlasting destruction," to prove the doctrine of the annihilation of the wicked.[48] Jehovah's Witnesses find in I Thessalonians 5:3, where the expression *aiphnidios olethros* is rendered "sudden destruction" in the *New World Translation,* a description of the sudden annihilation which shall overtake all non-Witnesses at the time of the Battle of Armageddon.[49]

It can readily be shown, however, that *olethros* can never mean annihilation when it is applied to the final lot of the wicked. This word is used four times in the Greek New Testament. A puzzling usage is that found in I Corinthians 5:5, where the Corinthian church is told by Paul "to deliver such a one [the fornicator in their midst] unto Satan for the destruction (*olethros*) of the flesh, that the spirit may be saved in the day of the Lord Jesus." Though

---

[47] Though the editors of the 1951 ed. of the *New World Translation of the Christian Greek Scriptures* assert that they have assigned only one meaning to each major word (p. 9), it is significant to note that the word *apollumi* is translated variously in this volume by *lose* (Lk. 15:4), *be ruined* (Mt. 9:17, *perish* (Lk. 21:18), and *be destroyed* (Jn. 3:16). The Watchtower translators would therefore have to grant, on the basis of their own New Testament, that the word *apollumi* is often used in ways in which it cannot mean *annihilate.*

[48] *Questions on Doctrine,* pp. 537 and 539. Note that in the middle paragraph on p. 537 four texts are quoted to prove that the wicked shall be "destroyed." No indication is given, however, of the fact that the word translated *destroyed* in these passages represents four different words in the original: one Hebrew word (*shamadh*) and three Greek words (*apollumi, olethros, katargeoo*). Is this responsible scholarship?

[49] *New Heavens and a New Earth,* pp. 292-93.

commentators are divided on the meaning of the word *olethros* as here used,[50] it is clear that the word does not at this place describe the final lot of the wicked, since the hope is expressed that this man may yet be saved. In I Thessalonians 5:3 the word *olethros* is used to describe what happens to the wicked on the "day of the Lord": "When they are saying, Peace and safety, then sudden destruction (*olethros*) cometh upon them, as travail upon a woman with child. . . ." If the sudden *olethros* here described meant utter annihilation, it would be impossible for these individuals to appear before the judgment-seat of Christ. But Scripture teaches plainly that all men, both good and evil, shall appear before that judgment-seat (II Cor. 5:10).[51] The word *olethros* as here used must therefore mean sudden ruin, sudden "loss of all that gives worth to existence."[52]

There are two passages where *olethros* is used to describe the final state of the wicked. One of these is I Timothy 6:9, where we read, "But they that are minded to be rich fall into a temptation and a snare and many foolish and hurtful lusts, such as drown men in destruction (*olethron*) and perdition (*apooleian,* the noun derived from *apollumi*)." Since, as we have seen above, *apooleia* and *apollumi* cannot mean annihilation, it is obvious that *olethros,* which is here used in apposition with *apooleia,* cannot mean annihilation either. Neither can *olethros* mean annihilation in II Thessalonians 1:9, "who [those that know not God and obey not the gospel of Jesus] shall suffer punishment (*dikeen*), even eternal destruction (*olethron aioonion*) from the face of the Lord and from the glory of his might." The word here translated punishment, *dikee,* cannot mean annihilation; it is used in Jude 7, in fact, to describe the eternal punishment of the inhabitants of Sodom and Gomorrah: "suffering the punishment (*dikeen*) of eternal fire." *Olethros* cannot, therefore, mean annihilation either, since it stands in apposition to *dikee.* Furthermore, how could there be an eternal annihilation? Annihilation, by definition, must take place in a moment; what sense does it make to speak of "endless

---

[50] Some hold that it refers to the visitation of bodily affliction upon this man, while others insist that it means the eventual subjugation of this man's evil nature. In neither case could the word mean annihilation.

[51] Seventh-day Adventists contend that the wicked, though annihilated at the time of Christ's coming, shall again be "raised" at the end of the millennium. It should be noted, however, that the "annihilation" thus attributed to the word *olethros* is of a temporary nature. If *olethros* means only this kind of annihilation when applied to the final state of the wicked, how do we know that God will not at some point again bring them back to life?

[52] Moulton and Milligan, *op. cit.,* p. 445, quoting Milligan on I Thessalonians. See also Leon Morris, *The First and Second Epistles to the Thessalonians* (Eerdmans, 1959), pp. 153-54.

annihilation"?[53] The doom of the wicked, as here described, means a ruin which is everlasting, a punishment which will never end.

The word kolasis. A third word used in the New Testament to describe the final state of the wicked is *kolasis.* This word is used in Matthew 25:46, "And these [those on the left hand] shall go away into eternal punishment (*kolasin aioonion*); but the righteous into eternal life (*zooeen aioonion*)." This passage occurs at the end of the section in which Jesus describes the judgment of the sheep and the goats. Jehovah's Witnesses translate the first part of this verse as follows: "And these will depart into everlasting cutting-off" (NWT). By means of this translation they give the impression that *kolasis* means annihilation. Though it is true, as their footnote on page 112 of the 1951 edition of the *New World Translation of the Christian Greek Scriptures* indicates, that the stem *kolazoo* originally meant pruning, there is no justification for the above translation. The word *kolasis* is rendered "punishment" by Thayer, Arndt-Gingrich, and Moulton-Milligan. Josephus, who lived from A.D. 37 to 100, indicates that the Pharisees of his day believed in the eternal punishment of the wicked;[54] if Jesus had felt it necessary to correct them (as He did correct the Sadducees on the matter of the resurrection of the body), he certainly should have done so.

The people of Jesus' day, however, understood the word *kolasis* as meaning not annihilation, but punishment. In the *First Epistle of Clement,* written in A.D. 96 or 97, section 11, the following expression occurs: ". . . He forsaketh not them which set their hope on Him, but appointeth unto punishment (*kolasin*) and torment (*aikismon*) them which swerve aside."[55] Had the writer understood *kolasis* as meaning annihilation, how could he have placed it first? Surely one cannot torment an annihilated person! Moulton and Milligan quote a fragment from an uncanonical gospel written during the early centuries of the Christian era in which the word *kolasis* is used in apposition with *basanos,* which means torment. The passage reads, in part, "for the evil-doers among men . . . await punishment (*kolasin*) and much torment (*polleen basanon*)." If *kolasis* was thought to mean annihilation, one would have expected the writer to use *basanos* first and *kolasis*

---

[53] "The very fact that this 'destruction' is 'everlasting' shows that it does not amount to 'annihilation' or 'going out of existence.'" Quoted from Wm. Hendriksen, *Exposition of I and II Thessalonians* (Grand Rapids: Baker, 1955), p. 160. See also Morris, *op. cit.,* pp. 205-206.
[54] *Antiquities,* XVIII, 1, 3; cf. *Jewish Wars,* II, 8, 14: "They [the Pharisees] say . . . that the souls of bad men are subject to eternal punishment."
[55] The translation is that of Lightfoot.

later, for the reason mentioned above.[56]   It is therefore clear beyond doubt that *kolasis* at the time the New Testament was written
meant punishment, not annihilation.[57]

We may further observe that in the only other New Testament
passage where *kolasis* occurs, I John 4:18, the *New World Translation* renders the word as follows: "fear exercises a restraint"
(*kolasin echei*).   To be consistent, the Witnesses should have
translated: "fear has cutting-off" (which, of course, makes no
sense).   Certainly restraint is not annihilation. We can further
check the meaning of *kolasis* by noting the two instances in which
the verb from which *kolasis* is derived, *kolazoo*, is used in the New
Testament: Acts 4:21 and II Peter 2:9. In the former passage even
the *New World Translation* has: "they did not find any ground on
which to punish (*kolasoontai*) them." The latter passage, as we
saw above, can best be rendered, "The Lord knoweth how . . . to
keep the unrighteous being punished (or under punishment, ASV;
the Greek has *kolazomenous*) unto the day of judgment." Since
the verb *kolazoo* is used in both instances in the sense of *punish,*
and since *kolasis* in I John 4:18 means restraint (NWT), punishment (ASV), or torment (KJ), it is clear that *kolasis* in Matthew
25:46 cannot by any stretch of the imagination mean annihilation,
but must mean punishment. This punishment is there described as
being everlasting or eternal.

The word aioonios. This leads us to consider the meaning of
the word *aioonios,* usually rendered *eternal* or *everlasting* in our
translations.   We have already seen that this word is applied to
God in Revelation 4:9, where God is said to live *eis tous aioonas
toon aioonoon* (literally, into the ages of the ages).   In Romans
16:26 Paul speaks about the commandment *tou aiooniou Theou,*
of the eternal God.   Surely no annihilationist would wish to deny
that God is without end!

When the word *aioonios* is used to describe future time, moreover, it denotes time without end.[58] The word is therefore frequently used in the New Testament to describe the endless future
blessedness of God's people. We find it so used in Matthew 25:

---

[56] *Op. cit.,* p. 352. The quotation is from Grenfell and Hunt's *Oxyrynchus
Papyri,* V, 840, 6. The editors of the latter volume indicate that, though
the papyrus itself was probably written in the 4th century, the original gospel of which it was a partial copy dates from the second half of the 2nd
century A.D. (pp. 1 and 4).

[57] Matthew is generally considered to have been written some time between 50 and 70 A.D. For other references to *kolasis* in writings contempo-
rary with the New Testament, see Joh. Schneider, "*Kolasis,*" in Kittel's
Theologisches Woerterbuch zum Neuen Testament, III, 817.

[58] Arndt and Gingrich, *op. cit.,* p. 28. Cf. Thayer, *op. cit.,* p. 20; and
H. Sasse, "*Aioonios,*" in Kittel, *op. cit.,* I, 209.

46, quoted above. We also find it so used in John 10:28, "And I give to them eternal life (*zooeen aioonion*), and they shall never perish, and no one shall snatch them out of my hand." Besides, we find *aioonios* used to describe the eternal glory which awaits believers in II Timothy 2:10, the eternal weight of glory in II Corinthians 4:17, an eternal inheritance in Hebrews 9:15, and an eternal heavenly building in II Corinthians 5:1. In II Corinthians 4:18, in fact, the word *aioonios* is used to modify "the things which are not seen," in contrast to "the things which are seen," called temporal (*proskaira*, lasting only for a time). No annihilationist would, one may be sure, care to deny that the future blessedness of God's people will be without end. Neither Seventh-day Adventists nor Jehovah's Witnesses do in fact deny that the future glory of the saints, described in the Scriptures as *aioonios,* is endless.

If, however, the word *aioonios* means "without end" when applied to the future blessedness of believers, it must follow, unless clear evidence is given to the contrary, that this word also means "without end" when it is used to describe the future punishment of the lost. *Aioonios* is so used in Matthew 25:46 and in II Thessalonians 1:9. Since the word *kolasis*, used in the former passage, and the word *olethros*, used in the latter, do not mean annihilation, but punishment, as has been shown, it follows that the punishment which the wicked will suffer after this life will be as endless as the future happiness of the people of God.

Seventh-day Adventists admit that the word *kolasis* in Matthew 25:46 does mean punishment. Since they also grant that *aioonios* as used in this verse means endless, it would seem to follow that they should accept the doctrine of the endless punishment of the lost. They have found a way out, however. Referring to such expressions as "eternal redemption" (Heb. 9:12) and "eternal judgment" (Heb. 6:2), they affirm, "In the expression 'eternal punishment,' just as in 'eternal redemption' and 'eternal judgment,' the Bible is referring to all eternity — not as of *process,* but as of *result.* It is not an endless process of punishment, but an effectual punishment, which will be final and forever (*aioonios*)."[59]

By way of refutation, it must be said that in the parallel expression, eternal life (*zooeen aioonion*), the word *aioonios* is used to picture a life which is not just everlasting in its result, but everlasting in its duration or continuance. Seventh-day Adventists admit that eternal life is everlasting in its duration since they hold that immortality is bestowed upon the righteous at the Second

---

[59] *Questions on Doctrine,* p. 540. Cf. p. 506, note.

Coming of Christ,[60] and that Abraham and his seed shall possess the new earth throughout the endless ages of eternity.[61] If *aioonios* in the last part of Matthew 25:46 means *endless in duration,* what right do they have to restrict the meaning of *aioonios* in the first part of this verse to *endless in result?*[62]

Degrees of Punishment. A further consideration against annihilationism is the fact that the New Testament speaks of degrees in the punishment of the wicked: Luke 12:47, 48, "And that servant, who knew his lord's will, and made not ready, nor did according to his will, shall be beaten with many stripes; but he that knew not, and did things worthy of stripes, shall be beaten with few stripes." It is here clearly taught that not all the lost will be punished in the same way. If, however, the wicked are annihilated, how can there be degrees of punishment? Can there be degrees of annihilation?

We may well challenge Jehovah's Witnesses to show how their view of the destiny of the wicked leaves any room for the variation in punishment taught by Jesus in the above passage. Seventh-day Adventists try to answer this objection by contending that there will be degrees of punishment previous to annihilation, some suffering longer than others.[63] It was taught by Mrs. White that this graded suffering is to occur after fire shall have come down from heaven to devour the devil, the evil angels, and all the wicked.[64] Satan, it is said, will suffer the longest, and will therefore be the last to perish in the flames.[65] In reply, it should be noted that it is specifically stated in the context of the passage which describes the descent of fire from heaven (Rev. 20:9) that the devil shall be tormented (*basanistheesontai*), not just for a long period of time, but "day and night for ever and ever" (*eis tous aioonas toon aioonoon*).[66]

In conclusion, we may well take note of I. M. Haldeman's comment on Christ's words about Judas, recorded in Matthew 26:24, "Woe unto that man through whom the Son of man is betrayed! good were it for that man if he had not been born." While Russell was still living, Mr. Haldeman, then pastor of the First Baptist

---

[60] *Fundamental Beliefs,* Art. 9.
[61] *Ibid.,* Art. 22.
[62] On this point, see also Bird, *op. cit.,* pp. 58-59.
[63] See above, pp. 141, 142.
[64] *Early Writings* (1882), p. 294; quoted by Douty, *op. cit.,* p. 140.
[65] See above, p. 142.
[66] Rev. 20:10. It will be recalled that precisely the same expression is used in Rev. 4:9 to describe the eternity of God. The attempt of Seventh-day Adventists on pp. 542-43 of *Questions on Doctrine* to tone down the meaning of this expression by an appeal to Isa. 34:8-10 has been answered earlier in this appendix. See on this point also Douty, *op. cit.,* pp. 157-58.

Church of New York City, wrote a brochure against the "Russell-ites" entitled *Millennial Dawnism*. The following words, taken from that brochure, are a devastating refutation not only of the teachings of present-day Jehovah's Witnesses on the future life, but of the eschatology of Seventh-day Adventism as well:

If death means the extinction of being, why should life be worse for him [Judas] than any other wicked traitor? No matter how great his guilt, death would end it all. . . .

Never to have been born means never to have come into existence.

If death means going out of existence,[67] then never to have been born and to die are equivalent conditions; they mean the same thing — non-existence.

Why, then, did the Lord say it would have been good not to come into existence? Why did he not say (seeing the man was born and there was no use in wasting regrets over his birth) — why did he not say, "It will be good for that man when he dies, for when he dies he will then be just as if he had never been born — non-existent"?

If death means non-existence, this is what he *ought* to have said.

To say anything else — if death means non-existence — was utterly meaningless.

But if death does not mean the end of existence; if death means an eternity of condition; if in this conditioned eternity of being Judas is to suffer for his deed of betrayal, then it is comprehensible why the Son of God should say it would have been good for that man if he had never been born — if he had never come into existence.

On no other basis is the "Woe to that man" of any intelligent force.[68]

We conclude that the teaching of both Seventh-day Adventists and Jehovah's Witnesses on the annihilation of the wicked is contrary to Scripture and robs the proclamation of the Christian gospel of its deepest earnestness.

---

[67] It will be recalled that according to current Jehovah-Witness teaching Judas will not be raised again (above, p. 317); hence he did go out of existence when he died. According to Seventh-day Adventists, moreover, Judas will be raised after the millennium and will have to endure a period of punishment for his sins; after that, however, he will be annihilated. Despite the differences in teaching between these two groups, therefore, Haldeman's comment is applicable to both positions.

[68] *Millennial Dawnism* (New York: Charles C. Cook, n.d.), pp. 29-30. For a similar use of this passage, see Douty, *op. cit.*, pp. 158-59.

CHAPTER SIX

The Distinctive Traits of the Cult

THE PURPOSE OF THIS CHAPTER WILL BE TO SET FORTH THE DIS-
tinctive traits or characteristics of the cult, so that we may better
understand what it is that makes a cult a cult, and what it is that
distinguishes a cult from a branch of the church of Jesus Christ.
After this has been done, a question previously referred to, namely,
whether Seventh-day Adventism should be listed among the cults
or should be classed with the historic Christian churches, will be
discussed.

In attempting to discern the traits of the cult, our aim will not
be merely to find undesirable characteristics in the cults so that
we may whitewash the churches. As was said in the opening
chapter, there is much which the churches can learn from the
cults. Besides, as we shall see, certain undesirable cultic traits
are also found, to a lesser degree, in the church. One of the
most important lessons the church may learn from a study of the
cults is that of always being on its guard against the danger of
imitating those characteristics of the cult which are definitely anti-
Scriptural.

Terminology. A word should be said about terminology. In
this chapter, as in the rest of the book, the term *cult* will be used
to designate the type of religious group being described, in preference to the term *sect*. Though in some ways these two terms are

synonymous, the word *sect* has a wider range of meaning than the word *cult*. *Sect,* derived from the Latin *sequi,* meaning to follow, may describe any dissenting or schismatic religious body, which may or may not have parted company with a longer-established communion.[1] What is called a sect depends on the point of view taken. In New Testament times, the Pharisees and Sadducees were called sects though they did not break away from Judaism (see Acts 5:17 and 15:5). In the sense of the definition given above, Christianity could be called a sect of Judaism, Protestant churches could be called sects of the Roman Catholic Church, and the Christian Reformed Church could be called a sect of the Reformed Church in America. The word *cult,* however, when applied to a religious group, has a more restricted meaning. Webster's *Third New International Dictionary* gives the following as the fourth meaning of the word *cult*: "A religion regarded as unorthodox or spurious; also a minority religious group holding beliefs regarded as unorthodox or spurious." Since the groups we are studying are minority groups which answer to this description, the term *cult* can be applied to them with greater accuracy than the term *sect*.

No attempt will be made, however, to give a precise, one-sentence definition of a cult in the above-named sense. Because of the wide variations that exist between various cults, this is not possible. Rather, the distinctive traits of the cult will be unfolded as this chapter continues.

Some General Characteristics. We may begin by observing that cults or sects have sprung up in each of the three major divisions of Christendom: Eastern Orthodoxy, Roman Catholicism, and Protestantism. We are concerned, however, with those cults which have arisen within Protestantism, and particularly with the four groups which have been discussed in this book. Restricting ourselves, then, to this latter group, what are some of the basic traits which differentiate the cult from the church?

It is extremely difficult to answer this question since there are a number of characteristics found in the cults which are also found, to a lesser degree, in the churches. We may, for example, observe that there is in all cults *an abrupt break with historic Christianity, and with its confessions.* Because the cult believes that the entire Christian church has become apostate and that God has given to the members of the cult new light on saving truth, it has severed itself from the church and has become completely independent of it. Church history for the cults is

---

[1] See Webster's *Third New International Dictionary* (Springfield: G. & C. Merriam Co., 1961), under *sect*.

therefore a very easy subject; nothing of real significance happened to the church from the time of Christ to the time when the founder of the cult began the organization of what is now hailed as the only true group of God's people. Though this trait is found in all cults, this point is not uniquely characteristic of the cults since to a lesser degree the same thing is true of many churches. A mere scanning of the table of contents of Frank Mead's *Handbook of Denominations in the United States*[2] will be sufficient to reveal the great number of splinter groups which have left the old established churches and have formed separate ecclesiastical organizations here in the United States. One could say, of course, that the various church bodies mentioned by Mead have not made as complete a break with historic Christianity as have the cults. This is true, and yet there is often much isolationism in these smaller church bodies. One could further observe that the difference between a cult and a Christian denomination which has separated from a parent body is that the denomination regrets the fragmented condition of the body of Christ, whereas the cult is happy about its separation and perfectly content to remain separated. And yet we must in all candor admit that there is often within the denominations much complacency about the fragmented nature of Protestant Christendom. The trait under discussion, therefore, can be applied to the cults, but only in a somewhat relative way.

We may further note that the cults have a *tendency to major in minors*. That is to say, cults tend to take certain peripheral truths (or teachings which are held to be truths) and to elevate them to a prominence far greater than they deserve, whereas matters of major importance are played down. The result is that the theology of the cult becomes lopsided and distorted.[3] So, for example, Mormons have assigned to celestial marriage and baptism for the dead such crucial importance that one cannot attain the highest level of salvation unless he has fulfilled these requirements (see above, pp. 62 and 65). Similarly, Jehovah's Witnesses have so exalted the duty of door-to-door witnessing that this — rather than a living faith in Jesus Christ — has become for them virtually the way to salvation. In Christian Science the healing of the body has been so emphasized that this teaching has led to the denial of the reality of sickness, matter, sin, and death. And in Seventh-day Adventism the so-called "third angel's message" — the summons to keep the seventh day as the proper

[2] New York: Abingdon Press, 1961.
[3] See on this point F. Boerwinkel, *Kerk en Secte* ('s-Gravenhage: Boekencentrum, 1956), pp. 26-27.

Sabbath — has been so blown up that it has actually become more prominent in their theological system than saving faith in the Redeemer.[4]

We should again observe, however, that though the above-mentioned trait is characteristic of the cults to an extreme degree, it is not true exclusively of them. Does not a church which has separated from a parent body always tend to lay undue emphasis on those points of doctrine or practice which occasioned the secession? Is it not true, for example, that the churches of the Reformation often reacted so strongly against Rome that certain one-sidednesses developed? Is not the doctrine of "entire sanctification" raised to undue prominence in Nazarene Churches precisely because this doctrine had been neglected by the Methodist Church previous to the origin of the later body? Is it not true that in the so-called Liberated Churches of the Nether-lands in the 1940's the doctrine of the covenant of grace was unduly emphasized because it was around this doctrine that a dispute had arisen with the parent body? It will be granted that these distortions do not go to such extremes in the churches as they do in the cults; yet must we not admit that the trait in question can be applied to cults only in a relative way?

Another trait which may be ascribed to the cults is a *tendency to perfectionism*. There is among the members of a cult a feeling of superior holiness to those in other groups, particularly to the members of the established churches.[5] The sense of sin is not prominent in the cult: the conviction that we daily fall short of doing what God requires of us. Instead, we hear Jehovah's Witnesses claim that they are more obedient to God than ordinary church members since they do far more door-to-door witnessing than the latter. We hear a prominent Mormon author say that in order to receive the highest grade of celestial exaltation one must keep the commandments of the Lord in all things — implying that this can be done, and is done by many Mormons (see above, p. 61).[6] And we note that Seventh-day Adventists apply to them-selves as a group the description of Revelation 12:17, "which keep the commandments of God," thus suggesting that they, in

---

[4] For, in the end-time, what finally determines whether one is saved is not saving faith, but obedience to the third angel's message. See above, pp. 127-28.

[5] See Boerwinkel, *op. cit.*, pp. 23-24.

[6] Note also the following statement by the same Mormon author: "We [the Mormons] are, notwithstanding our weaknesses, the best people in the world. I do not say that boastingly, for I believe that this truth is evident to all who are willing to observe for themselves. We are morally clean, in every way equal, and in many ways superior to any other people" (Joseph Fielding Smith, *Doctrines of Salvation*, I, 236).

distinction from others, are God's commandment-keeping people today (see above, pp. 124, 128). Whereas the churches are said to be filled with hypocrites and nominal Christians, the cult claims to be a group of dedicated saints who sacrificially do God's will. Again we may say, however, that though this trait is characteristic of the cults, it can only be attributed to the cult in a relative manner. For there are also denominations whose members claim that they are able to live almost without sin and who accuse other churches of far greater moral and spiritual laxity than is found within their own communion.

Up to this point, therefore, we cannot say that we have been able to put our fingers on precisely what it is that distinguishes a cult from a branch of the church of Jesus Christ. In this connection the reader's attention is called to the most penetrating study of the phenomenon of cultism which has thus far appeared. This is a work by the Lutheran theologian, Kurt Hutten, which appeared originally in German in 1957 under the title, *Die Glaubenswelt des Sektierers* (The Faith-world of the Sectarian).[7] The reason why Hutten wrote this book can be stated as follows: After having devoted a major share of his theological labors to a thoroughgoing analysis of the cults, having published an earlier descriptive work on the cults totaling over 700 pages,[8] he asked himself: "But what actually makes a cult a cult? What do the cults have in common? How can we see them, despite their great diversity, as a unified phenomenon?" Dissatisfied with the answers usually given to these questions, which all seemed superficial to him, he decided to write a book on this subject himself, and thus *Die Glaubenswelt des Sektierers* came to be written. In this volume Hutten tries to get at the root of the phenomenon of cultism, tries to put his finger on the distinctive characteristics of the cult. In what now follows, I gratefully acknowledge my indebtedness to him.

THE DISTINCTIVE TRAITS OF THE CULT

In setting forth what I believe to be the distinctive traits of the cult, I do not wish to give the impression that not the slightest trace of these characteristics is to be found in the churches. If we are honest with ourselves, we shall find vestiges of these characteristics in the churches too. I venture to affirm, however, that

[7] Hamburg: Furche-Verlag. This book has been translated into Dutch by J. J. Poort under the title *Geloof en Sekte* (Franeker: Wever, n.d.). References to this volume, which ought to be translated into English, will be in terms of both the German and the Dutch editions.

[8] *Seher, Gruebler, Enthusiasten* (Stuttgart: Quellverlag, orig. pub. in 1950, and now in its 6th ed.).

the traits which will now be described are so uniquely characteristic of the cult that any group in which they play a leading role
can no longer be recognized as belonging to the true church of
Jesus Christ.

(1) *An Extra-Scriptural Source of Authority*. As the first of
these distinctive traits of the cult, I instance the presence of an
extra-Scriptural source of authority. Hutten aptly calls this trait
"a Bible in the left hand." Recalling the ordination of a Sweden-
borgian minister, who held a Bible in his right hand and one of
Swedenborg's books in his left, Hutten observes that every cult
has such a "Bible in the left hand," which actually supersedes the
Bible in the right hand.[9] It should be added here that the cults
face a kind of dilemma with respect to the question of authority.
Since, in distinction from non-Christian religions, they claim to
be Christian groups, they must somehow appeal to the authority
of the Bible. Yet in order to justify their peculiar doctrines they
must either correct Scripture, reinterpret Scripture, or add other
sources of authority to Scripture. Their attitude toward Scripture is therefore always an ambivalent one: a mixture of apparent
subjection to its authority and of arbitrary manipulation of its
teachings.[10]

That this matter of ultimate authority is of determinative importance in evaluating the cults has already been implied by the
inclusion of a section on "Source of Authority" in the discussion
of each of the cults treated in this volume. It was found that every
cult discussed did, indeed, find its ultimate ground of authority in
some extra-Scriptural source. Mormons, it was seen, consider the
Bible to be full of errors and in dire need of supplementary material; hence their ultimate source of authority is found not in
the Bible, but in the *Book of Mormon, Doctrine and Covenants,*
and *The Pearl of Great Price*. If there should be a contradiction
between what is taught in the Bible and what is taught in these
supplementary sacred books, it is the teachings of the latter which
are determinative for Latter-day Saints (see above, pp. 18-30),
For Christian Scientists, the final source of authority is Mrs. Eddy's
Science and Health, with Key to the Scriptures; although the
Bible is read at their Sunday services, it is *Science and Health*
which determines how the Bible is to be understood (see above,
pp. 182-86). Though Jehovah's Witnesses claim that the only
basis for their teachings is the Bible, it has been seen that their
New World Translation is a biased rendering of the Scriptures

---

[9] *Glaubenswelt* (this abbreviation will be used from now on for *Die
Glaubenswelt des Sektierers*), p. 104 (Dutch translation, p. 109).
[10] *Ibid.*, pp. 104-105 (Dutch translation, p. 109).

into which they have smuggled many of their own heretical teachings, that their method of using Scripture is to find passages which seem to support their view and to ignore passages which fail to provide such support, and that they insist that the Bible may only be understood as it is interpreted by the leaders of the Watchtower Society (see above, pp. 237-48).[11]

The reader is reminded of the discussion found on pages 30-33, above, where it was pointed out that the Bible itself condemns the attempt to supplement it with any additional source of authority. These "Bibles in the left hand" are never innocent appendages to Scripture; they always overmaster and overshadow the truth of Scripture. Whenever a cult raises a book or a set of books to the level of Scripture, it does violence to the Word of God. God is no longer allowed to speak as He does in the Bible; He may now speak only as the sect deems proper. Thus the Word of God is brought under the yoke of man.[12]

The claim of the cults to have a source of revelation beyond the Scriptures — for that is what these "Bibles in the left hand" really amount to — is a claim which places them outside the pale of Christian churches. It may be added, by way of warning, that whenever a denomination of Christendom gives so much veneration to a human teacher or group of teachers that he or they are thought to be virtually infallible, it is in this respect manifesting a trait of the cult! People in the Corinthian Church who said that they belonged to Paul, Apollos, or Cephas were rebuked by Paul as being carnally minded; they were told, instead, that Paul, Apollos, and Cephas belonged to them! (I Cor. 3:21-23). Christians today who might be tempted to say that they belong to, say, Calvin or Luther, should learn from this passage that the Biblical way of expressing our relationship to human leaders is this: they (the human leaders) belong to us, but we belong to Christ. If these leaders belong to us, their writings may never be considered superior in authority to the Word of God. *Sola Scriptura* must remain the motto of every truly Protestant Church!

(2) *The Denial of Justification by Grace Alone.* A second distinctive trait of the cult is the denial of the doctrine of justification by grace alone. Grace is no longer considered the free gift of God to the unworthy sinner, but a reward which has been earned by the faithful keeping of various conditions and requirements.[13] Hutten, in fact, calls this trait the most basic character-

---

[11] The question of whether this trait of the cults, as well as the traits which follow, is also found in Seventh-day Adventism will be taken up in the second half of this chapter.

[12] Hutten, *Glaubenswelt*, pp. 110-11 (Dutch translation, p. 115).

[13] *Ibid.*, p. 34 (Dutch translation, p. 35).

istic of the cult. The Reformation, he contends, asserted the
principle of *sola gratia*: man is saved by grace alone. Salvation,
the Reformers taught, does not depend on any human or ecclesiastical co-operation with God. The concept *gratia* implies that
salvation is given freely by God apart from any conditions which
man may fulfill or which the church may make available. Even
those responses to the Gospel which take place in man through
the working of God's Spirit — his faith, his conversion, his works,
and his walk — are not meritorious, since they are all the fruits
of God's grace. Precisely because salvation is all of grace, it
can never be a ground for Pharisaic pride but must always move
us to deep humility and gratitude.[14]

This demand for humility, however, goes against the grain of
human nature. Man wants to be his own lord and master. This
is especially so in the matter of his salvation. He shrinks from
taking the leap of faith — a leap in which he must trust wholly
in God for his salvation. He prefers to take his future destiny into
his own hands; he does not wish to surrender this destiny to a
strange, unknown power. This fundamental human drive, Hutten
continues, is the real root of the cult's protest against the church.
The basic antithesis of the cult to the church is therefore the
cult's antipathy toward the central message of the Reformation:
the message of justification by grace alone and by faith alone
(*sola gratia, sola fide*). Though there are variations in the degree
to which the different cults reject this doctrine, they all do reject
it. As a matter of fact, Hutten adds, the church must always be
on its guard against slipping into this cultic manner of thinking
about the way of salvation. Only when the church has completely
conquered this cultic tendency within its own borders, will it have
the strength to oppose the cult on this point.[15]

It will not be difficult to show that the trait described above is
found in the cults we have studied. Mormons, as has been seen,
reject the doctrine of justification by faith as a pernicious doctrine
which has exercised an influence for evil in the church. They
further teach that individual salvation (entrance into one of the
three Mormon heavens) is to be merited by man through his own
acts, and that one can only become eligible for the highest degree
of salvation by keeping the commandments of the Lord in all
things (see above, pp. 59-62). Christian Scientists decisively
reject justification by grace alone; for them, salvation from sin is
accomplished when one ceases to sin, or when one stops believing
that there is such a thing as sin — on either interpretation salva-

14 *Ibid.*, p. 29 (Dutch translation, p. 29).
15 *Ibid.*, pp. 30-34 (Dutch translation, pp. 31-34).

tion is achieved by human works and not by the grace of God (see above, p. 212, and compare pp. 209-12). Though Jehovah's Witnesses claim that salvation is of grace and that all credit for salvation belongs to Jehovah (see above, p. 283), a careful study of their writings will reveal that they, too, reject justification by grace. In the case of the 144,000, man saves himself by exercising faith, repentance, and dedication to Christ (functions in which he is said not to be dependent on God), by showing himself worthy of being selected as a member of the anointed class, and by carrying out his dedication to Jehovah faithfully until death (see above, pp. 282-83; compare pp. 279-83). In the case of the other sheep, these, without having had their natures renewed, are able to exercise faith in Christ, to dedicate their lives to him, and to remain faithful to the end — this faithfulness to be revealed chiefly by diligent witnessing (see above, pp. 283-85). After the millennium has begun, these other sheep, whether as survivors of Armageddon or as resurrected beings, are to be judged on the basis of their obedience to Jehovah during the millennium. If they continue to obey God during Satan's final battle, they will be "justified," that is, given the right to perfect life on the new earth — this "justification," however, is based not on faith, but on works.[16] As far as others are concerned, billions of those who, though sincere in their belief, lacked an opportunity to learn of righteousness from God will be raised during the millennium, will be instructed in God's law, and will receive everlasting life on the new earth if they now obey God's commandments.[17]

It is clear, therefore, that these three cults definitely and deliberately reject the doctrine of justification by grace alone. Though they may speak of the grace of God, their theologies have no room for grace in the real sense of the word. For, as the Bible says, "If it [the remnant according to the election of grace] is [saved] by grace, it is no more of works; otherwise grace is no more grace" (Rom. 11:6). Note also the severe judgment leveled by Paul against this position in Galatians 5:4, "Ye are severed from Christ, ye who would be justified by the law; ye are fallen away from grace." Crystal clear is Titus 3:5: "Not by works done in righteousness which we did ourselves, but according to

[16] See above, pp. 318-19, 320, 322. Note that what is decisive in determining the salvation of these other sheep is not their faith in Christ while on earth, but their obedience to Jehovah during the millennium. Strictly speaking, therefore, the other sheep cannot claim to have any assurance of their salvation when they die; they must still earn their salvation after their resurrection.

[17] See above, pp. 319-21. Note again that the basis for the salvation of these individuals is not the work of Christ for them but their "reforming and practicing good things" (p. 320, n. 595).

his mercy he saved us. . . ." By taking the position sketched
above, therefore, the cults deny one of the cardinal teachings of
Scripture.

(3) *The Devaluation of Christ.* In the third place, all cults
are guilty of a devaluation of Christ. Hutten points out that,
since the cult has assumed a determinative role in the distribution
of salvation, the result is bound to be a minimizing of Christ as
the only Mediator. This, he adds, does not need to mean a complete denial of Christ's mission and work; it may express itself
simply in a *shifting of emphasis.*[18] We shall see this tendency
revealing itself in a twofold way: in a devaluation of the Person
of Christ and in a depreciation of His work. The latter is particularly characteristic of the cult; since salvation for the cult is
not determined by the grace of God revealed at the cross of Christ,
that cross is robbed of its unique soteriological significance.

Let us see how this trait can be found in the cults we have
studied. Mormons teach that Jesus Christ was the firstborn of
the spirit-children of Elohim; since, however, all men are spirit-
children of Elohim, it is evident that the difference between
Christ and men (even, for that matter, between Christ and Satan)
is one of degree but not one of kind (see above, pp. 53-54).
Christ is considered by Mormons not to be equal to the Father;
he shared with other pre-existent spirits like Adam and Joseph
Smith the task of "creating" this earth, and his incarnation is not
unique, for other gods before him were incarnated on other earths
(see above, p. 54). In fact, Christ's incarnation was only
illustrative of what happens to every man who perfectly fulfills
all the ordinances of the Gospel: he, too, was once a pre-existent
spirit, is now incarnate, and will some day be a god (see above,
pp. 54, 61-62, 72). As far as the work of Christ is concerned,
Mormons affirm that the atoning death of Christ was necessary to
deliver all men from death, and did provide for all the right
to be raised from the dead (see above, pp. 57-58). As was just
observed, however, Christ's atonement does not provide individual
salvation for man since this is to be merited by man's own acts;
thus the Mormon Christ does not save in the full sense of the
word but only gives man an opportunity to save himself (see above,
pp. 58-61).

According to Christian Science, Jesus was not God but only a
man, whereas Christ is the name for a certain divine idea: the
idea that sickness and sin can be healed through Christian Science
(see above, pp. 200-202). Jesus was therefore simply a man who
demonstrated a divine idea. So unimportant, in fact, is Jesus in

---

[18] *Glaubenswelt,* pp. 57-58 (Dutch translation, p. 60).

Christian Science that Mrs. Eddy could say that if such a person as Jesus had never existed, it would make no difference to her! (see above, p. 203). As far as the work of Jesus is concerned, Christian Scientists deny that he atoned for our sins by shedding his blood on the cross — after all, since sin has no real existence, why does it need to be atoned for? Jesus' work was rather that of demonstrating the truth of Christian Science and of setting us an example of the kind of life we must live. Even this example, however, is not uniquely distinguished from that of the apostles (see above, pp. 207-9).

What Jehovah's Witnesses do with the person of Christ is well known: he was, for them, not equal to Jehovah, but the first creature of Jehovah. In his prehuman state he was a created angel; during his stay on earth he was nothing more than a man; and after his stay on earth he was again nothing higher than a created angel, though now endowed with immortality. In none of these three stages, therefore, was or is Christ equal to Jehovah (see above, pp. 270-76). As regards the work of Christ, the Witnesses teach that Christ did lay down his human life for his people as a ransom. By means of this ransom Christ redeemed man from inherited sin and from the prospect of eternal death as a result of that sin (see above, pp. 276-77); his ransom provides a resurrection from the dead for all except certain classes of people (see above, p. 317). Christ did not, however, earn the right to everlasting life in heaven for the 144,000 since he earned only a perfect human life with its rights and earthly prospects; the 144,000 must themselves earn the right to heavenly life by sacrificing their earthly prospects (see above, p. 283). As for those who will spend eternity on the new earth, they, as we saw, will receive this blessing only if they have obeyed Jehovah's commandments during the millennium. Neither the 144,000 nor those who will inhabit the new earth, therefore, are really saved by the work of Christ; Christ's ransom has only served the purpose of enabling them to earn their future blessedness, either in heaven or on earth, by their own achievements.

It is quite clear, therefore, that the cults leave us with a Christ who is not the Christ. Neither in his person nor in his work is the Christ of the cult the Christ of the Bible. For the cultist, it is not really Christ who saves but man who must save himself. This position, however, cuts the very heart out of the Bible: "For God so loved the world, that he gave his only begotten Son, that whosoever *believeth on him* should not perish, but have eternal life" (Jn. 3:16). The words of Paul to the Galatians, directed against those who in that day taught that one was saved partly through faith in Christ and partly through performing certain works of the law, are equally applicable to the cults of our day: "But though we, or an angel from heaven, should preach unto you any gospel other than that which we preached unto you, let him be anathema" (Gal. 1:8).

(4) *The Group as the Exclusive Community of the Saved.* A fourth distinctive trait of the cult is that it absolutizes itself as the exclusive community of the saved. Hutten points out that the anti-ecclesiastical polemic which is so characteristic of the cult is but the converse side of its own self-justification. Since the cult is convinced that it is the only true community of God's people, it must try to show that the church is either an apostate organization or an actual instrument of the devil.[19] There is among the cults no appreciation for the Biblical doctrine of the "one holy catholic Church" — that is, of the universal church of Christ, composed of Christ's true people of all the ages and from all the nations. Every cult says, "We alone are the people of God." The cult, so to speak, takes God by the arm, insisting that His evaluation of people must agree with its own.[20]

Let us see how this trait is found in the cults we have studied. Mormons contend that the church of Jesus Christ was in a state of apostasy until God revealed Himself to Joseph Smith in 1820; when Smith and Oliver Cowdery received the Aaronic and Melchizedek priesthoods from heavenly messengers in 1829 and 1830, the Restoration of the Church took place. The Mormon Church is therefore the only true church — because it alone has the Priesthood of the Almighty, and it alone since the time of Christ has received and may still receive divine revelation. One of the early apostles of the Mormon Church claimed that non-Mormon churches have no right to call themselves Christian since Christ has nothing to do with them, and a recent Mormon writer has said that there is no salvation outside the Church of Jesus Christ of Latter-day Saints (see above, pp. 62-64). It may be noted that the possibility of salvation for those who died in ignorance of Mormon teaching only confirms the point under discussion since such people can be saved only if Mormons have been baptized for them (see above, pp. 64-66).

Christian Science also claims to be the only true church. Since Mrs. Eddy is said to have received the final revelation of the divine principle of scientific mental healing, and since *Science and Health* is said to be the voice of truth uncontaminated by

[19] *Glaubenswelt,* p. 78 (Dutch translation. p. 81).
[20] *Ibid.,* p. 52 (Dutch translation, p. 54).

human hypotheses, it follows that, according to them, no group outside of Christian Science has or knows the truth (see above, pp. 183, 212-13). Though individual Christian Scientists may express appreciation for other Christian groups, it is clear from the statements just alluded to that the views of all other churches about the Bible and the way of salvation must officially be considered basically erroneous while Christian Science is held to be unerring and divine (see above, p. 184).

In Jehovah-Witness ecclesiology we reach the ultimate in bigotry. It is said by them that Jehovah's Witnesses alone are God's true people and that all others, without exception, are followers of the devil. The Watchtower Society is now the only instrument or channel whereby Jehovah teaches His people on earth (see above, p. 247). The "great whore" of Revelation 17 is organized religion, Christian as well as heathen. The visible part of the devil's organization on earth includes all of Christendom, Protestant as well as Roman Catholic. The religious clergy are, in fact, the direct link between mankind and the demons (see above, pp. 285-86). At Armageddon all of earth's inhabitants except Jehovah's Witnesses will be wiped out of existence (see above, p. 311). Only Jehovah's Witnesses, therefore, will survive Armageddon; during the millennium non-Witnesses who are raised from the dead will be given an opportunity to save themselves in response to the preaching and teaching of the princes, prominent among whom will be those who occupied leading positions with the New World Society on earth (see above, pp. 318-21).

Whenever a group takes the position that it is the only community of the saved, however, it violates an important aspect of Scripture teaching. Christ Himself warned against this type of bigotry when his disciples said to Him, "Master, we saw one casting out demons in thy name, and we forbade him, because he followeth not with us." Jesus replied, "Forbid him not; for he that is not against you is for you" (Lk. 9:49, 50). We should therefore remember that whenever a denomination slips into a kind of thinking similar to that described above, it reveals a tendency toward cultic behavior.

(5) *The Group's Central Role in Eschatology.* The last distinctive trait of the cult I would like to mention is this: the cult plays a central role in the eschatological climax of history. The cult is convinced that it has been called into existence by God for the purpose of filling in some gap in the truth which has been neglected by the ordinary churches. The birth of the cult thus marks the final climax of sacred history, the beginning of the

latter days.[21]   Eschatology thus plays a determinative role in the theology of the cult: it becomes the arena in which the glorification of the cult will complete itself.   The cult is therefore the messenger and way-preparer for the imminent return of Christ;[22] it is God's partner in the drama of the end-time; it is the ark of safety for the coming flood; it is the instrument of divine judgment on unbelievers; it shall finally triumph in the sight of all the world as the group particularly favored by God.[23]

This type of procedure Hutten calls a cultic perversion of Biblical eschatology.   Whenever the cult has developed an eschatology, he continues, it places itself in the very center of it.   The drama of the last things thus becomes the means whereby the cult is glorified and all its enemies are overwhelmingly defeated. Though the cult may now be small and insignificant, when the final climax of history arrives, it will receive from God the place of honor it deserves as a reward for its faithfulness to His commandments.   The antithesis between God and Satan which has run through history will in the last days reach its climax as an antithesis between the cult and the rest of mankind, particularly the church.[24]

As we attempt now to see how this trait is revealed in the cults we have studied, we must first make an important exception. Because of the absence of a real historical dimension in Christian Science, the latter has no general eschatology; hence it cannot be precisely fitted into the category just described.   Christian Science denies that there will be a literal Second Coming of Christ, a general resurrection, a final judgment, and a new earth (see above, pp. 219-21).   Though there is a kind of individual eschatology in this system, there is no general eschatology in the sense of a final, dramatic climax of history.   Yet Christian Scientists do manifest a trace of the characteristic in question, since Mrs. Eddy contended more than once that what the Bible calls the Second Coming of Jesus Christ actually coincided with the rise of Christian Science (see above, p. 219).   By statements such as these Mrs. Eddy did, in a sense, place Christian Science in the center of eschatology.

---

[21] Note, for example, that the Mormons call themselves "The Church of Jesus Christ of Latter-day Saints," and that Jehovah's Witnesses designate their group as the "New World Society."

[22] Though one might object that this could not be true of Jehovah's Witnesses since they believe that Christ has already returned, it will be remembered that the Witnesses also speak of a "return" which is still future: the "revelation" of Christ at the time of the Battle of Armageddon (above, p. 310, n. 486).

[23] Hutten, *Glaubenswelt,* pp. 97-98 (Dutch translation, pp. 101-102).

[24] *Ibid.,* pp. 99-102 (Dutch translation, pp. 103-105).

It will not be difficult to show the presence of the trait under discussion in the other two cults being considered. Mormons very definitely place themselves in the center of the eschatological drama, giving themselves a position of special privilege in it. The Mormons, God's "Latter-day Saints," consider themselves the bearers of the Restored Gospel — the Gospel which must now be proclaimed by them to all the world as God's last word to mankind (see above, pp. 62-64). Before Christ returns, there will be a series of gatherings. Ephraim or the Ephraimites must be gathered first to prepare the way for the rest of the tribes of Israel when the time comes for them to be gathered to Zion. Since most Mormons today are said to be Ephraimites, it is obvious that the gathering of Ephraim is going on at the present time. Ephraim is being gathered to Zion, the gathering-place on the North American continent.[25] The "lost ten tribes" will later be gathered to Zion, where they will receive "crowning blessings" from Ephraim — that is, from the Mormons. During the millennium Christ will rule over the Mormon Zion as well as over Jerusalem in Palestine (see above, pp. 67-69). At this time Mormons on earth will be joined by a heavenly group, the City of Enoch (see above, p. 69). Also during the millennium Mormons will preach to non-Mormons who are still alive, and will be baptized for the dead who have lived from the beginning of time (see above, p. 70). In the final state Mormons who have fully kept the commandments of the Gospel will enjoy the highest grade of blessedness in the celestial kingdom; non-Mormons can enter the celestial kingdom only if Mormons have been baptized for them (see above, pp. 66, 72-73). Most non-Mormons, however, will spend eternity in one of the two lower kingdoms, the terrestrial or the telestial (see above, pp. 73-74).

Jehovah's Witnesses teach that the kingdom of God was not established until A.D. 1914, that this kingdom is now the ruling part of God's universal organization, and that this kingdom is comprised of Jesus Christ and those members of the 144,000 who are now in heaven (see above, pp. 295-97). These heavenly members of the anointed class (who were, for the most part, Jehovah's Witnesses on earth) not only rule with Christ now, but are actually changed from human beings to divine beings (see above, p. 304). Between 1918 and the Battle of Armageddon, a judgment of the nations is taking place, in which all those who do not accept the Jehovah-Witness message and who show no kindness to its bearers are doomed to destruction at Armageddon

---

[25] Though the gathering-place now appears to be Salt Lake City, it will eventually be Independence, Missouri (above, p. 68).

— a destruction from which there will be no reawakening (see above, pp. 306-7). The Battle of Armageddon will therefore be a stupendous victory for Jehovah's Witnesses, who will be the only survivors of this worldwide catastrophe (see above, p. 311). Armageddon survivors will have a favored position on the renewed earth during the millennium; many of them will be made princes (see above, pp. 311, 314, 318). Jehovah's Witnesses who have died before Armageddon will have the privilege of being raised from the dead before the rest of earth's inhabitants. Those who were active in the New World Society before the millennium will take a leading part in instructing newly-resurrected people in the laws of Jehovah (see above, pp. 318-19). For Jehovah's Witnesses, therefore, the climactic antithesis of history will be that between God's true people, the Witnesses, and all others, including the churches of Christendom.

Whenever a religious group places itself in the center of the eschatological drama, it makes itself guilty of spiritual pride. Overlooking its own shortcomings and sins, it magnifies the sins of others. It blandly assumes that because of its own superior worthiness it has become God's special favorite. When Christ came across a similar kind of pride among the Jewish leaders of His day, He rebuked it in no uncertain terms: "I say unto you, that many shall come from the east and the west, and shall sit down with Abraham and Isaac, and Jacob, in the kingdom of heaven; but the sons of the kingdom shall be cast forth into the outer darkness. . ." (Mt. 8:11, 12).[26]

IS SEVENTH-DAY ADVENTISM A CULT?

We must now turn to a question which has been considerably discussed of late: whether Seventh-day Adventism is to be considered as belonging to the cults, or as a denomination which may be classed with the evangelical churches. In a series of articles which appeared in *Eternity* magazine from September, 1956, to January, 1957, Donald G. Barnhouse and Walter R. Martin advanced the view that Seventh-day Adventism is not a cult, as had long been believed, but a branch of evangelical Christianity, though distinguished from other churches by certain peculiar ideas. In 1960 Martin published his *Truth About Seventh-day Adventism*,[27] in which he reasserted this position. In this volume he discusses and criticizes such Adventist teachings as "the

---

[26] The five distinctive traits of the cult discussed above, though of primary importance, are by no means the only ones that could be mentioned.
[27] Grand Rapids: Zondervan, 248 pp.

sleep of the soul,"[28] the annihilation of the wicked, the seventh-day Sabbath, the investigative judgment, the scapegoat doctrine, the remnant church, and the recognition of Mrs. White as the "spirit of prophecy." In spite of his strictures on the above teachings, however, he asserts, "Not one of the deviations in Seventh-day Adventism is a deviation from the cardinal doctrines of the Christian faith which are necessary to salvation" (p. 229). Martin therefore pleads with the members of the evangelical denominations to exercise spiritual fellowship with Seventh-day Adventists:

> We hope that many who have looked upon Adventists as dangerous non-Christian cultists will revise this view. In the providence of God, and in His own good time, we trust that evangelical Christianity as a whole will extend the hand of fellowship to a group of sincere, earnest fellow Christians, distinguished though they are by some peculiar views, but members of the Body of Christ and possessors of the faith that saves (pp. 236-37).

By including Seventh-day Adventism in a volume entitled *The Four Major Cults,* I have already implied that I do not share the evaluation of this movement given by Barnhouse and Martin. While not denying that the Adventists teach certain doctrines in common with evangelical Protestant churches and in distinction from most of the cults (for example, the doctrine of the full deity of Jesus Christ), I am of the conviction that Seventh-day Adventism is a cult and not an evangelical denomination. In support of this evaluation, I propose to show that the traits which we have found to be distinctive of the cults do apply to this movement.

(1) *An Extra-Scriptural Source of Authority.* Seventh-day Adventists do have an extra-Scriptural source of authority in the writings of Ellen G. White, which are accepted by them as "inspired counsels from the Lord" (see above, p. 103). That this is so has been shown on pages 100-108, above; the argumentation there given will not be repeated here. The reader is further invited to page through such Seventh-day Adventist publications as *The Seventh-day Adventist Bible Commentary, Principles of Life from the Word of God,* and *Questions on Doctrine* to note how frequently a doctrinal position or the exegesis of a Scripture passage is based on a quotation from Mrs. White. We conclude that Seventh-day Adventists interpret the Bible in the light of the

---

[28] As has been pointed out, however, this is not an accurate way of describing Seventh-day Adventist teaching, which affirms, not that the soul sleeps after death, but that after death the soul ceases to exist (see above, p. 136).

writings of Mrs. White, and that the books and testimonies of Mrs. White are for them, therefore, a source of authority superior to the Bible. This type of procedure, however, as we have seen, is a distinctive mark of the cult.

(2) *The Denial of Justification by Grace Alone.* Here we encounter one of the real problems involved in evaluating Seventh-day Adventist teachings: the baffling fact that the Adventists often theoretically take a certain position but then proceed to repudiate that position in the further elaboration of their theology. Regarding the doctrine in question, we find Seventh-day Adventists theoretically agreeing that we are justified by grace alone and not at all by obedience to law (see above, p. 123). Yet we also find them teaching that one's forgiveness can be cancelled after it has been bestowed, and that forgiven sins are not immediately blotted out because subsequent deeds and attitudes may affect the final decision (see above, p. 119). Adventists further teach that it is possible for a person through subsequent sinful deeds and attitudes to lose the justification he once received. This teaching implies that one can only be sure of retaining his justification if he continues to do the right kind of deeds and to maintain the right attitudes throughout the rest of his life (see above, p. 125).

(i) *The Investigative Judgment.* It has already been shown that the Adventists' doctrine of the investigative judgment (a doctrine which has no basis in Scripture) is not consistent with their claim that they teach justification by grace alone (see above, pp. 117-20, 126-27, 157-58). This is actually the Seventh-day Adventist position: (a) The investigative judgment *determines* who of the myriads sleeping in the dust are worthy of a part in the first resurrection.[29] (b) What is examined in the investigative judgment are the lives of the individuals in question: particularly their faith in Christ, their confession of every single sin, and their faithfulness in keeping the law's requirements.[30] (c) What therefore determines whether a person will be saved is not *primarily* what Jesus Christ has done for him on the cross, but *primarily* what the individual has done in his life. He must have kept the law's

---

[29] *Fundamental Beliefs,* Article 16.
[30] *Questions on Doctrine,* p. 443; Ellen G. White, *The Great Controversy* (Mountain View: Pacific Press, 1911), pp. 482, 490; William H. Branson, *Drama of the Ages* (Nashville: Southern Pub. Co., 1950), p. 351. Note particularly Branson's statement: "A Christian who through faith in Jesus Christ has faithfully kept the law's requirements will be acquitted; there is no condemnation, for the law finds no fault in him. If, on the other hand, it is found that one has broken even a single precept, and this transgression is unconfessed, he will be dealt with just as if he had broken all ten." It will be remembered that Mr. Branson was president of the General Conference of Seventh-day Adventists from 1950-1954.

requirements, must have continued to do the right kinds of deeds so that his forgiveness has not been cancelled, and must have confessed every single sin. It is thus clear that *what determines whether one is saved is the kind of life the investigative judgment reveals him to have lived,* particularly his blameless keeping of the law's requirements. And this position contradicts the Scriptural assertion that one is justified by grace alone.

How can anyone "faithfully keep the law's requirements"? Do we not all fall very far short of keeping these requirements? Does not the Apostle John say, "If we say that we have no sin [and to have sin means to fail in some respects to keep the law's requirements], we deceive ourselves and the truth is not in us" (I Jn. 1:8)? The Apostle Paul, in fact, makes it unmistakably clear that no one can ever "faithfully keep the law's requirements" when he says, in Romans 3:19 and 20:

> Now we know that what things soever the law saith, it speaketh to them that are under the law; that every mouth may be stopped, and all the world may be brought under the judgment of God; because by the works of the law shall no flesh be justified in his sight; for through the law cometh the knowledge of sin.

He then goes on to say, "But now apart from the law a righteousness of God hath been manifested, being witnessed by the law and the prophets; even the righteousness of God through faith in Jesus Christ unto all them that believe . . ." (vv. 21, 22). He ends this brief exposition of the way of salvation by saying, "We reckon therefore that a man is justified by faith apart from the works of the law" (v. 28). Elsewhere Paul tells us that he counted all things to be loss that he might gain Christ, "and be found in him, not having a righteousness of mine own, even that which is of the law, but that which is through faith in Christ, the righteousness which is from God by faith" (Phil. 3:9). Paul, therefore, knew that he was saved, not on the basis of a future heavenly investigation of his keeping of the law, or of his own personally achieved righteousness, but on the basis of the righteousness which he had received from God through faith! How, then, can Seventh-day Adventists teach that man is saved on the basis of his "faithful keeping of the law's requirements" as revealed by the investigative judgment?

The doctrine of justification by grace alone teaches that a person is saved because of what Christ has done for him. The doctrine of the investigative judgment, however, teaches that Christ does not know whether a given individual has been justified until his life has been investigated. If, as the Bible teaches, "the Lord knoweth them that are his" (II Tim. 2:19), and the Good Shepherd knows His own (Jn. 10:14, 27), why should Christ not know apart from this investigative judgment who are to be raised in the resurrection of the just? The only possible answer is: because he does not fully know what kind of lives these individuals have lived. But if this is so, what is decisive in determining whether one is to be saved is his faithful keeping of the law's requirements. This position, however, vitiates the doctrine of justification by grace alone!

(ii) *The Keeping of the Sabbath.* It has also been shown above that Seventh-day Adventist teaching on Sabbath-keeping is inconsistent with the doctrine of justification by grace alone (see above, pp. 125-28). The Adventist position, briefly, is as follows: In the last days, after the world shall have been enlightened concerning the obligation of the true Sabbath, anyone who shall still refuse to keep the seventh day as the Sabbath shall receive the mark of the beast and be lost. It is clear that at that time at least, salvation will not be determined only by faith in the atoning work of Christ, but by faith plus works — specifically, the work of keeping the seventh-day Sabbath.

Let us see how Mrs. White describes the crucial role of Sabbath-keeping in the drama of the latter days. Just previous to Christ's return, so she writes, there will appear in the sky a hand holding two tables of stone folded together. In this way "that holy law, God's righteousness, that . . . was proclaimed from Sinai as the guide of life, is now revealed to men as the rule of judgment."[31] The hand opens the tables, the words of which are so plain that all can read them. This public display of God's law brings consternation to the hearts of those "who have trampled upon God's holy requirements"; what is particularly called to the reader's attention, however, is the despair of those who "have endeavored to compel God's people to profane His Sabbath." "Now," it is said, "they are condemned by that law which they have despised."[32] It is therefore particularly failure to keep the seventh-day Sabbath which will be the unpardonable sin of the last days!

To the same effect are the following words:

> The enemies of God's law, from the ministers down to the least among them, have a new conception of truth and duty. Too late they see that the Sabbath of the fourth commandment is the seal of the living God. Too late they see the true nature of their spurious sabbath, and the sandy foundation upon which

[31] *The Great Controversy,* p. 639.
[32] *Ibid.,* pp. 639-40.

they have been building. They find that they have been fighting against God. Religious teachers have led souls to perdition while professing to guide them to the gates of Paradise.[33]

The point is clear: religious leaders have led souls to *perdition* by failing to teach them to observe the seventh-day Sabbath! They and their people, therefore, will be consigned to perdition, not because they failed to believe in Jesus Christ as Saviour and as the Atoner for sin, but because they failed to keep one of the ten commandments!

Next, according to Mrs. White, there comes the voice of God from heaven which declares the day and hour of Jesus' coming and delivers the everlasting covenant to His people. "And when the blessing is pronounced on those who have honored God by keeping His Sabbath holy, there is a mighty shout of victory."[34] Thus the primary reason why God's true people, here called "the Israel of God," are blessed is not that they have trusted in Christ as their Savior, but that they have properly kept the fourth commandment!

Even if we should grant (which we do not) that Seventh-day Adventists are right in observing the seventh day as the Sabbath, we would still emphatically reject their contention that a sin against one of God's commandments, committed by people who have always trusted in Christ for salvation and have always tried to serve Him sincerely, can be the basis for their everlasting perdition — since this is a sin committed in ignorance, and a sin which is repented of.[35] Conversely, neither is it in harmony with Scripture to affirm that one must keep at least the fourth commandment perfectly in order to be saved.[36] For the Scriptures teach that we

---

[33] *Ibid.,* p. 640.

[34] *Ibid.*

[35] Both of these points are implied in the quotations just given from pp. 639-40 of *The Great Controversy*. These individuals, it is there said, "have a new conception of truth and duty," implying that they did not understand the truth or know their duty before this time. If these people are true believers, they will repent of their sin as soon as it is pointed out to them. Further, since it is specified by Mrs. White that these individuals will include ministers and religious teachers, we may assume that these are people who have been faithfully worshiping God on the first day of the week all their lives. Do Seventh-day Adventists mean to say that such people will be sent to perdition solely because, though they did keep the fourth commandment, they unintentionally kept it on the wrong day?

[36] As a matter of fact, how can Seventh-day Adventists be so sure that all who do keep the seventh day as the Sabbath are properly keeping the fourth commandment? Would Jews who reject Christ as the Messiah but keep the seventh day thus be saved, while Christians who accept Christ as Savior but keep the first day are lost? Christ Himself often severely rebuked the Pharisees for their misinterpretation of the Sabbath command, even though they did observe the seventh day (Mt. 12:1-8 and parallel passages; Mt. 12:9-14 and parallel passages; Lk. 13:10-17, 14:1-6; Jn. 5:10-18, 7:22-

all continue to fall short (*husterountai,* a present indicative), of
the glory of God (Rom. 3:23), and that no one can keep God's
commandments perfectly (I Jn. 1:8). We are saved, not because of our faithfulness in keeping any of God's commandments,
but because of what our Savior has done for us, and because His
perfect righteousness has been imputed to us! We conclude that,
though Seventh-day Adventists claim to teach justification by grace
alone, their doctrine of the investigative judgment and their views
on the Sabbath command are inconsistent with that claim.

(3) *The Devaluation of Christ.* At this point we must first
acknowledge with gratitude that Seventh-day Adventists do not,
like Mormons, Jehovah's Witnesses, and Christian Scientists, deny
the full deity of Jesus Christ or the doctrine of the Trinity. Though
some earlier Adventist writers had contended that the Son was not
wholly equal to the Father, Seventh-day Adventists today affirm
Christ's complete equality with the Father, and the pre-existence
of the Son from eternity (see above, pp. 112-13). Adventists
also accept the doctrine of the Trinity, and that of the personality
and full deity of the Holy Spirit (see above, pp. 108-9).

As far as the work of Christ is concerned, Seventh-day Adventists teach the vicarious, substitutionary atonement of Christ (see
above, p. 115). Yet there remains some ambiguity in their teachings on the question of whether the atonement has been finished
on the cross, since Mrs. White says on more than one occasion
that Christ is making atonement for us today and frequently refers
to a "final atonement" after the one completed on the cross (see
above, pp. 115-17).

While appreciating the Adventists' recognition of Christ as fully
divine, however, we must reluctantly observe that there are aspects of Seventh-day Adventist teaching which detract from the
splendor of Christ's deity and do in fact constitute a devaluation
of Him:

(i) Christ is said not to have been able to blot out sins previous to 1844 but only to have been able to forgive them (see above,
p. 117). The forgiveness of sins only means, however, that these
sins remain on record in the heavenly sanctuary; this forgiveness
may be cancelled later if a person's subsequent deeds and attitudes
prove unacceptable (see above, p. 119). This view, which
was discussed and criticized in Appendix B (see above, pp. 151-
53), robs Christ of His divine prerogatives. The Pharisees accused
Jesus of speaking blasphemy when He said to the paralytic, "Thy

---

24, 9:13-16). Surely, therefore, no one may naively assume that the mere
observance of the right day (if Adventists are correct about the day) in
itself guarantees the proper keeping of the fourth commandment!

sins are forgiven thee." "For," they said, "who can forgive sins but God alone?" (Lk. 5:20, 21). In Romans 8:33 and 34, moreover, we read, "Who shall lay anything to the charge of God's elect? It is God that justifieth; who is he that condemneth?" The clear implication of the latter passage is that when God the Father has forgiven a sinner, his sins have been permanently blotted out; no one can bring charges against him any more. If the forgiveness of sins which Christ could bestow, however, only meant the placing of such transgressions on record in the heavenly sanctuary and did not mean the complete blotting out of those sins, Christ's power to forgive was considerably less than the Father's. By this teaching, therefore, Seventh-day Adventists are guilty of devaluating Christ.

(ii) Jesus Christ does not know who are His, since He must conduct an investigative judgment to determine "who . . . are worthy of a part in the first resurrection. . . ."[37] In Appendix B it was pointed out that this Seventh-day Adventist teaching leaves us with a Christ who must do homework before he can determine who are entitled to the benefits of His atonement (see above, pp. 155-57). Surely this doctrine, too, robs Christ of His sovereignty and thus devaluates Him.

(iii) The very nature of the investigative judgment implies, as we have seen, that it is not one's unbreakable connection with Christ that determines whether one is saved, but one's deeds while on earth. In Seventh-day Adventist teaching, therefore, what is ultimately determinative for salvation is not Christ's work but man's work. This teaching, too, devaluates Christ.

(iv) The crucial importance attached to the keeping of the fourth commandment after the final enlightenment likewise detracts from the saving power of Christ. To quote Mrs. White once more, "When the blessing is pronounced on those who have honored God by keeping His Sabbath holy, there is a mighty shout of victory."[38] What is here all-important and all-determinative for salvation is not the atoning work of Christ in our stead, but the keeping of the fourth command! This exaltation of Sabbath-keeping and minimizing of the work of Christ also constitutes a devaluation of Christ.[39]

(v) Seventh-day Adventists teach that the sins of all men will be laid on Satan just before Christ returns, and that only in this

---

[37] *Fundamental Beliefs,* Article 16.
[38] *The Great Controversy,* p. 640.
[39] For it is presumed that thousands of those who at this time receive the mark of the beast for failing to keep the seventh day did believe in Christ as their Savior.

way will sin finally be "eradicated" or "blotted out" of the universe. This teaching also detracts from the all-sufficiency of Christ. While we appreciate the Adventists' insistence that Satan is not a sin-bearer and that he does not make atonement for sin, it must be pointed out that they do, however, assign to Satan an indispensable role in the blotting out of sin from the universe (see above, pp. 120-22). But this, as was also pointed out in Appendix B (see above, pp. 158-60), is to ascribe to Satan what should only be ascribed to Christ: the obliteration of our sins. If Christ completely bore our sins in His body on the tree, as I Peter 2:24 tells us, why should Satan still have to help eradicate these sins from the universe?

We conclude that, in these various ways, Seventh-day Adventists are guilty of devaluating Christ, and that the full deity which they officially ascribe to Christ is overshadowed by certain teachings which detract from His majestic sovereignty.

(4) *The Group as the Exclusive Community of the Saved.* Here again, we appreciate the insistence of the authors of *Questions on Doctrine* that Seventh-day Adventists do not believe that they alone constitute the true children of God, or that they are the only true Christians in the world, or the only ones who will be saved.[40] At the same time, however, the Adventists do call themselves the *remnant church,* for two reasons: because they keep the commandments of God, particularly by observing the seventh-day Sabbath; and because they have the "spirit of prophecy" in the person of Ellen G. White (see above, p. 128).

At this point we should ask ourselves exactly what Seventh-day Adventists mean by the *remnant church.* It was pointed out above, on pages 128-29, that according to Adventist teachings the remnant church means the last segment of the true church left on earth. This judgment is confirmed by a statement found in a Seventh-day Adventist Bible-study textbook: "What, then, would be the 'remnant church'? The last church, what is left at the end of time of God's church on earth."[41] If this is so, the Seventh-day Adventist claim that they are the *remnant church* really means: we are the last true church left on earth, and all other groups which claim to be churches are not true but false churches.

Do Seventh-day Adventists actually teach that they are *the true church of God?* Yes, they do. This will become evident from the following quotations from the writings of Mrs. White, their inspired prophetess:

[40] Pp. 187, 191-92; (see above, p. 129).
[41] *Principles of Life from the Word of God* (Mountain View: Pacific Press, 1960), p. 395.

The decree that will finally go forth against the remnant people of God will be very similar to that issued by King Ahasuerus against the Jews. Today the enemies of *the true church* see in the little company keeping the Sabbath commandment, a Mordecai at the gate.[42]

I saw that the holy Sabbath is, and will be, the separating wall between *the true Israel of God* and unbelievers; and that the Sabbath is the great question to unite the hearts of *God's dear waiting saints.*[43]

When the final warning shall be given, it will arrest the attention of these leading men through whom the Lord is now working, and some of them will accept it [the message about the seventh-day Sabbath], and will stand with *the people of God* through the time of trouble.[44]

To those who reverence His holy day the Sabbath is a sign that God recognizes them as *His chosen people.* It is a pledge that He will fulfill to them His covenant.[45]

The keeping of the Sabbath is a sign of *loyalty to the true God.*[46]

As the Sabbath was the sign that distinguished Israel when they came out of Egypt to enter the earthly Canaan, so it is the sign that now distinguishes *God's people* as they come out from the world to enter the heavenly rest. The Sabbath is a sign of the relationship existing between *God and His people,* a sign that they honor His law. It distinguishes between *His loyal subjects* and transgressors.[47]

In the light of the above statements, what conclusions must we draw with respect to the other churches of Christendom? We are compelled to conclude that, according to Mrs. White, these other churches are not part of the true church, are not the true Israel of God, are not God's chosen people, are not loyal to the true God, are not God's loyal subjects, but transgressors. In fact, Christians who belong to churches which keep the first day as the Lord's Day are said to be the victims of one of Satan's most intensive campaigns against God's law: "Satan strives to turn men

[42] *Prophets and Kings* (Mountain View: Pacific Press, 1917), p. 605 [italics mine, in this and in the next five quotations].

[43] Taken from a letter to Joseph Bates written on April 7, 1847; found in *A Word to the "Little Flock"* (1847), pp. 18-19.

[44] *The Great Controversy*, p. 611.

[45] *Testimonies*, Vol. VI, p. 350; quoted in *Principles of Life from the Word of God*, p. 131.

[46] *The Great Controversy*, p. 438.

[47] *Testimonies*, Vol. VI, p. 349; quoted in *Principles of Life from the Word of God*, p. 135. It is to be noted that statements like these do not agree with what is said by the authors of *Questions on Doctrine*, "we do *not* believe that we *alone* constitute the true children of God — that we are the only true Christians — on earth today" (p. 187). Since the statements quoted above were made by Mrs. White, Seventh-day Adventists cannot in good conscience repudiate them.

from their allegiance to God, and from rendering obedience to His law; therefore he directs his efforts especially against that commandment which points to God as the Creator [the fourth]."[48]

We go on now to ask: Does Seventh-day Adventist teaching about the remnant church mean that those who are not members of this remnant group cannot be saved? In other words, do Seventh-day Adventists believe that their group is the exclusive community of the saved?

With respect to people who will be living on earth after the great enlightenment about the Sabbath day has been given (see above, p. 127), when the final test of loyalty with regard to Sabbath-keeping shall have come,[49] the Adventists do teach that all who then remain outside their group will be lost. Seventh-day Adventists contend that "before the final hour of crisis and testing all God's true children — now so widely scattered — will join with us in giving obedience to this message [the one brought by the Seventh-day Adventist movement], of which the seventh-day Sabbath is a basic part."[50] On the other hand, those who then refuse to join the remnant church in keeping the seventh-day Sabbath will receive the mark of the beast and be lost:

> . . .When Sunday observance shall be enforced by law, and the world shall be enlightened concerning the obligation of the true Sabbath, then whoever shall transgress the command of God, to obey a precept which has no higher authority than that of Rome, will thereby honor popery above God. . . . As men then reject the institution which God has declared to be the sign of His authority, and honor in its stead that which Rome has chosen as the token of her supremacy, they will thereby accept the sign of allegiance to Rome — "the mark of the beast."[51]

It is clear, therefore, that Seventh-day Adventists do consider that their group will be the exclusive community of the saved at the

---

[48] *The Great Controversy*, p. 54. We appreciate the fact that the authors of *Questions on Doctrine* seem not to wish to draw all these conclusions. Yet what is said in the above paragraph is clearly implied by the statements of Mrs. White quoted previously. The authors of *Questions on Doctrine* will therefore either have to admit that Mrs. White was mistaken when she made these statements, or that her words did not mean what she apparently intended them to mean. On the question of the attitude of Seventh-day Adventism toward other churches, see N. Douty, *Another Look at Seventh-day Adventism* (Grand Rapids: Baker, 1962), pp. 193-203.

[49] *The Great Controversy*, p. 605.

[50] *Questions on Doctrine*, pp. 195-96.

[51] *The Great Controversy*, p. 449, quoted in *Questions on Doctrine*, p. 184. See also *The Great Controversy*, p. 605. Since those who receive the mark of the beast, according to Rev. 14:9-11, will be tormented with fire and brimstone, we conclude that people who fall into this category will be eternally lost.

time of the end, since all who then remain outside their group will be lost. We conclude that at this point the Adventists do reveal one of the distinctive traits of the cult.

With respect to people who are living now, the question is more complicated. It will be remembered that, according to Adventist teaching, those who fail to keep the seventh day as the Sabbath are transgressing the most important commandment of the decalogue (see above, p. 127). The question now arises: Can Christians who repeatedly break this most important commandment still be saved?

Seventh-day Adventists answer: yes, since these Christians who are members of the other churches of Christendom are breaking this command in ignorance. For it is said by the authors of *Questions on Doctrine,* "Seventh-day Adventists firmly believe that God has a precious remnant, a multitude of earnest, sincere believers, in every church, not excepting the Roman Catholic communion, who are living up to all the light God has given them."[52] The implication is that these Christians do not have the full light on the Sabbath question which God has given to the Adventists and hence can be temporarily excused from the obligation of keeping the fourth commandment properly. Note the following statement by Mrs. White:

> But not one is made to suffer the wrath of God [visited upon those who shall refuse to keep the Creator's rest day] until the truth has been brought home to his mind and conscience, and has been rejected. There are many who have never had an opportunity to hear the special truths for this time. The obligation of the fourth commandment has never been set before him in its true light.[53]

According to this statement, one cannot be punished for failing to keep the Sabbath law until the truth about this law has been brought home to his mind and conscience and has been deliberately rejected.

This means, then, that Christians outside the Seventh-day Adventist communion today can be saved even though they continually break the fourth commandment because they are still transgressing this command in ignorance of the truth which is recognized and taught by Seventh-day Adventism. This, however, puts the so-called recognition of the universal church of Christ by Seventh-day Adventists in a rather uncomplimentary light: there is such a universal church, to be sure, but it is completely in error in its understanding of and obedience to the most important commandment of the decalogue!

[52] P. 192.
[53] *The Great Controversy,* p. 605.

If, furthermore, the salvation of those outside Seventh-day Adventism depends on their remaining in ignorance of God's real Sabbath requirement, the implication would seem unavoidable that, if these people wish to be saved, they should remain in ignorance of the Sabbath law. As we saw above, Mrs. White said that no one shall suffer the wrath of God "until the truth has been brought home to his mind and conscience, and has been rejected." Suppose, now, that a Christian had heard the Seventh-day Adventist message about the seventh day but had concluded that this teaching was erroneous — could he after this still claim to be "transgressing" the fourth commandment in ignorance? In 1847 Mrs. White wrote, "And if one believed and kept the Sabbath and received the blessing attending it and then gave it up and broke the holy commandment, they would shut the gates of the Holy City against themselves, as sure as there was a God that rules in heaven."[54] The people here described were lost, obviously, because they "sinned" against better light. But what about people who have examined the evidence Seventh-day Adventists advance and have rejected it? Would not their salvation be equally in jeopardy?

If the situation is as the Adventists picture it, would it not be far better for those in the regular churches of Christendom to come out of those churches and to join the Seventh-day Adventists? This is precisely what is held before us as the goal toward which Christ is working: "The Great Shepherd of the sheep recognizes them [God's true children now outside the Adventist fold] as His own, and He is calling them into one great fold and one great fellowship in preparation for His return."[55] If this is Christ's great purpose, it is clear that true children of God now outside Adventism who have come into contact with Seventh-day Adventism and yet remain in their churches are going contrary to Christ's purpose.

We conclude that though theoretically granting that people outside their community can be saved Seventh-day Adventists actually undermine that concession by their teaching on the remnant church. Since they claim to be *the* remnant church, in distinction from all other Christian bodies, they do manifest the cultist trait under discussion, though in a somewhat ambivalent manner.

(5) *The Group's Central Role in Eschatology.* It will not be difficult to show that this distinctive mark of the cult is prominently and clearly discernible in Seventh-day Adventism. In analogous fashion to the other cults studied, Seventh-day Adventism claims

---

[54] Letter to Joseph Bates, April 7, 1847, found in *A Word to the "Little Flock,"* pp. 18-19; quoted in Douty, *op. cit.,* p. 77.
[55] *Questions on Doctrine,* p. 192.

to have been called into existence to fill a particular gap in the truth. Adventists assert that God raised them up "for the completion of the arrested Protestant Reformation and for the full and final restoration of gospel truth."[56] God has brought the Adventist movement into being, so they allege, to bring His last great message to mankind.[57] The rise of Seventh-day Adventism therefore marks the beginning of the final climax of sacred history.[58] This movement has been called into being in order to prepare the church of the last days to meet her returning Lord.[59]

As we look more closely at the Seventh-day Adventist delineation of the events preceding the return of Christ, we note that they place their own movement in the very center of the eschatological drama. We find these events pictured in great detail in the closing chapters of Mrs. White's *The Great Controversy*. The announcement of the fall of Babylon (which designates various forms of apostate religion)[60] is followed by the call, "Come out of her, my people"; this is the final warning given to the inhabitants of the earth.[61] The various powers of the earth, including civil powers, Papists, and Protestants, now make a decree that all shall "conform to the customs of the church by the observance of the false sabbath."[62] After this decree has been promulgated, all who, in opposition to Seventh-day Adventism, continue to observe "the false sabbath" [Sunday], shall receive the mark of the beast, whereas those who keep the true Sabbath, in obedience to God's law, will receive the seal of God.[63]

Those opposing the seventh-day Sabbath will now inaugurate a terrible persecution against keepers of the true Sabbath [Seventh-day Adventists and those who have joined them].[64] Now comes the "close of probation," when Christ ceases His intercession in the sanctuary, after which there is no further opportunity for anyone to receive mercy and be saved.[65] There now follows the "time of trouble" predicted in Daniel 12:1, during which frightful

---

[56] *Ibid.*, p. 615.
[57] *Ibid.*, pp. 190, 194, 195.
[58] *Ibid.*, p. 617.
[59] *Ibid.*, pp. 615-617.
[60] *The Great Controversy*, p. 381.
[61] *Ibid.*, p. 604. In the light of the entire context (see particularly pp. 606-607), it is obvious that Babylon here stands for churches which, among other things, continue to teach that Sunday is the day of the Lord.
[62] *Ibid.*, p. 604; cf. p. 606.
[63] *Ibid.*, p. 605.
[64] *Ibid.*, pp. 608-610.
[65] *Ibid.*, pp. 613-14. This "close of probation" is supposed to be indicated by Rev. 22:11 (p. 613). Cf. pp. 428, 490-91.

plagues will be poured out on the enemies of God's people [that is, those who refuse to keep the seventh day].[66] Just when these enemies are about to wipe the Sabbath-keepers off the face of the earth, God sends deliverance, and strikes terror into the hearts of the would-be murderers.[67]

Now occurs the "special resurrection," in which two special groups are raised from the dead: those who were responsible for the trial and crucifixion of Christ, and those who died in the faith of the third angel's message — that is, faithful Seventh-day Adventists and others who have been keeping the seventh day who have died since 1846.[68] Note that at this point Seventh-day Adventists are given a special position of privilege: they shall be raised from the dead before other believers, so that they may be able to see Christ return to earth!

The doom of the wicked is now declared from heaven, producing consternation in the hearts of those who have been breaking the law of God.[69] God's commandment-keeping people, however, who have sacrificed all for Christ, and have evinced their fidelity to Him, now sing a triumphant song.[70] Opponents of the true Sabbath realize too late that they were wrong, whereas blessing is pronounced from heaven on those who have honored God by keeping His Sabbath holy.[71] Now Christ returns,[72] and calls forth the other believers from their graves.[73] The living righteous are now transformed,[74] whereas the wicked are all put to death.[75] God's people are now taken up to heaven for the millennium which follows (see above, pp. 140-41); after the annihilation of the wicked they will everlastingly inhabit the new earth (see above, p. 143).

For Seventh-day Adventists, therefore, eschatology is the arena in which the glorification of their own movement completes itself and in which they shall be completely vindicated over against their enemies. Since "the Sabbath will be the great test of loyalty" in the last days,[76] we see that the antithesis between God and Satan becomes in the end the antithesis between Seventh-day Adventism and those who refuse to follow its special teachings. We conclude

---

[66] *Ibid.*, pp. 613-34.
[67] *Ibid.*, pp. 635-36.
[68] *Ibid.*, p. 637; see above, pp. 139-40.
[69] *The Great Controversy*, p. 638.
[70] *Ibid.*, pp. 638-39.
[71] *Ibid.*, p. 640.
[72] *Ibid.*, p. 641.
[73] *Ibid.*, p. 644; see above, p. 140.
[74] *The Great Controversy*, p. 645.
[75] *Ibid.*, p. 657.
[76] *Ibid.*, p. 605.

that since Seventh-day Adventists do picture themselves as playing a central role in eschatology this distinctive trait of the cult is also clearly applicable to their movement.

An Appeal to Seventh-day Adventists. It is recognized with gratitude that there are certain soundly Scriptural emphases in the teaching of Seventh-day Adventism. We are thankful for the Adventists' affirmation of the infallibility of the Bible, of the Trinity and of the full deity of Jesus Christ. We gratefully acknowledge their teachings on creation and providence, on the incarnation and resurrection of Christ, on the absolute necessity for regeneration, on sanctification by the Holy Spirit, and on Christ's literal return. It is, however, my conviction that the Adventists have added to these Scriptural doctrines certain unscriptural teachings which are inconsistent with the former and undermine their full effectiveness. It is also my conviction that, because of the Adventists' acceptance of these additional teachings, Seventh-day Adventism must be classified, not as an evangelical church, but as a cult. The reasons for this judgment have been detailed above.

This does not mean, however, that there cannot be true children of God among the Seventh-day Adventists. This I would be the last to deny. What must be criticized, often severely, are the teachings of this group, not the individuals who hold to these teachings. Teachings we can and must evaluate in the light of God's Word; individuals we must leave to the judgment of God, who alone can read the hearts of men.

In a spirit of Christian love toward members of the Seventh-day Adventist denomination, therefore, and with grateful recognition of the soundly Scriptural elements in their teaching, I plead with my friends, the Adventists, to repudiate the cultic features and unscriptural doctrines which mar Seventh-day Adventism and to return to sound, Biblical Christianity. Whether the Scriptural emphases in Seventh-day Adventism will eventually gain the victory over these unscriptural teachings, or whether those in the group who wish to be loyal to Scripture alone should come out of it, is a question which only God can answer. But false teachings which cast a shadow over the faith once for all delivered to the saints must be repudiated by all who truly love the Lord.

CHAPTER SEVEN

Approaching the Cultist

In this chapter an attempt will be made to suggest ways and means of approaching cultists or of dealing with cultist when they contact us. The treatment of this topic must of necessity be quite broad. The approach to a cultist is bound to vary from one instance to another, depending, as it must, upon the cult involved and the individual encountered.

Difficulties

The Rev. J. K. Van Baalen has rightly said that the adherents of the cults are the most difficult people to evangelize,[1] Let us note at the outset some of the reasons why this is so. To begin with, the cultist is not a religiously indifferent person; he is "deeply religious" to the point of fanaticism. Having rejected historic Christianity, he can be counted on to be antagonistic to the testimony of a Christian believer. Second, the cultist firmly believes that he has found the truth, and hence he considers the message of historic Christianity to be inferior to the doctrines he has obtained through "special revelation," or through some inspired channel of truth. He therefore looks down upon regular church members with something of the same disdain with which a high-school senior looks

---

[1] *Chaos of Cults* (4th ed.; Eerdmans, 1962), p. 359.

down his or her nose at a mere freshman. Third, cultists are victims of a kind of mass delusion of grandeur, coupled with a great
deal of personal pride. They are God's only true people — so
they think — and all others must either join their group in some
way or be eternally lost. Fourth, cultists are acutely aware of the
shortcomings of the church, particularly of the lamentable divided-
ness of the church, and do not hesitate to remind us of these things.
"At least we are united," they will boast, "whereas you churches
can't agree on anything." Fifth, the cultist has probably — in
many cases, at least — had to endure considerable ridicule from
his kith and kin since joining the cult, and is even now sacrificing
much of his time and effort in making propaganda for the group.
Hence it is not going to be easy to induce him to leave the cult.[2]

Though the task of witnessing to cultists is not an easy one, we
do have a responsibility toward these people, who are so thoroughly
enmeshed in error while firmly convinced that they are in the
right. It will be granted, however, that one should not overlook
the difficulty of the task. In addition to the obstacles just mentioned, there is the need of being well grounded in the Scriptures
and in Christian doctrine, and of being well informed about the
teachings of the cult in question. Surely the mere reading of a
pamphlet or brochure on a particular cult does not qualify one for
conducting a thoroughgoing polemic against that cult.

Let no untrained church member, therefore, consider it an eva-
sion of duty if he does not present a systematic refutation of the
doctrines of a cultist who may happen to ring his doorbell. Let
him rather give the cultist a sincere testimony of his own personal
faith in Jesus Christ and of the joy he experiences in fellowship
with his Redeemer. This is actually one of the most effective
ways to meet a cultist; the latter may have ready answers to all
kinds of arguments, but he will find himself unable to refute a
personal testimony! A person who had formerly been a Jehovah's
Witness reported that while she was a Witness she encountered
three types of responses. Some slammed the door in her face.
These people made her feel good, since their action was construed
to be persecution for the sake of her faith. A second group of
people argued heatedly and belligerently. These only strengthened
her convictions, since she had ready answers for their arguments.
A third group gave her a personal testimony of their faith in Christ.
These, so she said, made the most lasting impression on her;
when she went to bed at night, she would think about these people

---

[2] For the thoughts expressed in the above paragraph, I am particularly
indebted to Van Baalen, *op. cit.,* pp. 359-61; and to Walter R. Martin,
The Christian and the Cults (Grand Rapids: Zondervan, 1956), pp. 84-88.

and reflect on what they had said. Surely every true believer ought to be able to give this kind of testimony.

Others, however, ought to do more than this. The pastor who comes to the realization that cultists are very active among the members of his congregation should make it his business to master the teachings of the group in question so that he is able to refute them publicly. The personal evangelist who encounters a member of a cult in his neighborhood should be prepared to work intensively with that person. The missionary who observes that cultists are trying to wean new converts away from the Christian faith and into the cult should certainly make a thorough study of the doctrines of the group involved, so that he can give the proper guidance to his people. Thorough, systematic refutation of cult teachings is properly the task of theologically-trained persons. Yet all Christians should be ready "always to give answer to every man that asketh you a reason concerning the hope that is in you" (I Peter 3:15). The answer need not always be detailed, but it ought to be forthright.

APPROACHING THE CULTIST AS A TOTAL PERSON

Our first concern in approaching the cultist must be to approach him as a total person. It is of crucial importance that we keep this in mind. Professor F. Boerwinkel is of the opinion that the approach to the cult is often too exclusively intellectual:

> People continue to act as if belonging to a cult is in the first and most important place a question of wrong intellectual concepts. When, however, one has had more intimate contact with members of the cults, it becomes quite evident that all kinds of other factors, such as those of a psychological and sociological nature, play a far greater role than intellectual considerations.[3]

For these reasons, Boerwinkel insists, an approach to the cultist merely on the intellectual level is often largely ineffectual. We have learned from recent psychological studies, he continues, that man is directed in his actions only to a small degree by purely rational considerations. This does not mean, it is added, that there should be no intellectual approach to the cultist, but only that other factors often weigh more heavily than the rational, and that therefore our approach must not be exclusively or primarily intellectual.[4]

People join cults and stay in them not primarily because their

---

[3] *Kerk en Secte* ('s-Gravenhage: Boekencentrum, 1956), p. 159 [translation mine].
[4] *Ibid.,* pp. 159-60.

doctrines are so attractive, but for other reasons. Boerwinkel suggests what some of these reasons may be: (1) People find in the cult a warm and brotherly fellowship which they have failed to find in a church.[5] (2) People find in the cult a center of integration, a place where each member plays an important role and fills a necessary function, a place where one is known and needed.[6] (3) People find in the cult a certain sense of security, since the cult provides not only what is thought to be an immediate contact with God and God's will, but also an organization which will never forsake them and will stand by them in time of trouble.[7] (4) The cult provides an outlet for the drive toward greater intensity and radicalness in one's religious life. Whereas the churches are inclined to look askance at these radical tendencies, the cult welcomes them and satisfies them. So, for example, when the cult asks of its members a greater readiness to sacrifice than does the church, or a greater willingness to endure ridicule, this request meets the need of persons with a certain type of psychological structure.[8] (5) The cult answers a need for specific instruction in the techniques of various religious practices and for specific advice on various types of moral problems. People receive from the cults definite instructions on how to conduct family worship, how to study the Bible, how to pray, how to witness, and so on — instructions which they have failed to receive from the churches. At a time when older moral patterns are being abandoned and new ones have not yet been found, many find satisfaction in turning from the less specific answers of the churches to the more specific answers of the cults, which often provide a rather detailed code of behavior for their adherents.[9]

By way of illustration of the point being made, we may observe that Mormons provide elaborate recreational facilities for their young people, open avenues of church activity for all their members (boys are ordained to the Aaronic priesthood at the age of 12), and maintain a welfare plan so comprehensive that jobs can quickly be found for unemployed Mormons and material relief is available at any time for any Mormon who needs it.[10] Surely it is obvious that many factors other than the purely intellectual are involved in one's joining and remaining in the Mormon Church! I have heard, moreover, of a young lady who joined the

[5] *Ibid.,* p. 160.
[6] *Ibid.,* pp. 124-27. It is added that this is especially significant in today's world, where the individual often seems to count for little.
[7] *Ibid.,* pp. 127-28.
[8] *Ibid.,* pp. 128-31.
[9] *Ibid.,* pp. 136-38.
[10] LeGrand Richards, *A Marvelous Work and a Wonder* (Salt Lake City: Deseret Book Co., 1950), pp. 403-5.

Jehovah's Witnesses because, so she said, "I was looked down upon in my social group and community; but when I joined the Witnesses, I was cordially welcomed, respected by all, and given work to do — so that, for the first time in my life, I really felt important!"

A further illustration of this point is the following incident, reported to me by one of my students. A Jehovah's Witness came to this student's door and was invited in. After some preliminary discussion, the student asked his caller: "Why did you join Jehovah's Witnesses? What was it that attracted you to this group?" The cultist, a bit flattered perhaps by this interest in his personal history, began to unfold a moving tale about a former church in which he had been elected treasurer and had been serving faithfully for some time. After a few years in office, however, he was falsely accused of embezzlement. The anxiety which resulted from this false accusation led him to quit his job, drove him to drink, and even brought about an attempted suicide. At this propitious moment a Jehovah's Witness appeared on the scene, agreed with the man that all churches were bad — were, in fact, part of the devil's organization — and induced him to join their group.

Experiences similar to these may often explain why individuals join cults. This would not, of course, invariably be the case; in many instances one might be in a cult because his parents were members. Yet it is probably true that a great many Jehovah's Witnesses were formerly members of Christian churches, since this group generally does its proselyting among church-members. It is probably also true that many of the people who join the other cults were church-members at one time.

In view of all this, our first aim, as we approach the cultist, must be to approach him as a total person — that is, not just as someone whose doctrines need to be refuted, but as someone whom we love, about whom we are concerned in the totality of his life. We should therefore try to find out, if we can, why he joined this cult. Did he previously belong to a church? If so, why did he leave it? What shortcomings did he find in it? In what way did the church fail to satisfy his needs? What benefits is he deriving from membership in the group to which he now belongs? What does this group do for him which the church failed to do? What activities does he now engage in, which he neglected before? What sacrifices does he now make which he did not make before? What has this group done for him?

If we can find out some of the answers to the above questions, the next step is to show this person that his individual needs

can be filled much better in and through living fellowship with the
Lord Jesus Christ. It is important that we do not at this juncture
begin to compare the cult with the church. For it may very well
be that this individual has had some disillusioning experiences with
the church or with members of the church. When the cultist
thinks of the church, he thinks of the weaknesses of the church,
and usually of those weaknesses which show up most glaringly
in comparison with the cult.

We must not, therefore, confront the cultist with the church but
with the Word and with Christ as the heart of that Word. Getting
back to basic motivations, we must try to show this man that the
needs he is trying to satisfy through membership in the cult can
only be fully and completely satisfied through living faith in Christ.
The deepest security that can be found on earth is found in the
conviction that we belong not to ourselves, but to Jesus Christ,
our Saviour, for time and for eternity,[11] and that no one can ever
pluck us out of His hand! Right at this point the cultist should be
asked, Do you have complete assurance of salvation? Jehovah's
Witnesses, for example, cannot answer this question in the affirmative, since at best they have only a conjectural assurance that they
may be spared at Armageddon,[12] and since even after Armageddon they must still pass the millennial tests of obedience in order
to inherit everlasting life on earth. For Mormons, salvation is
something which is to be achieved by man through his own works;
hence one can never be sure that he has salvation here and now.
A Seventh-day Adventist can never be certain of his salvation
since, as we have seen, whatever forgiveness of sins he has obtained may be cancelled by future deeds or attitudes, and since it
is the investigative judgment, to be conducted some time after his
death, which must determine whether he will be raised in the resurrection of the just.

Over against this uncertainty we must place the granite certainty
of the Christian faith: "I know whom I have believed, and am
persuaded that he is able to keep that which I have committed unto
him against that day" (II Tim. 1:12, KJ). This is the most basic
question of life: Am I truly saved from sin? Do I have the security of belonging to Christ for time and eternity, or do I not?
Am I building on the sand or on the rock? We must here appeal
to the very deepest springs of human behavior and squarely confront the cultist with the question: Do you or do you not have
salvation? At this point the importance of a ringing personal
testimony cannot be overemphasized. Let us dare to say to this

[11] Heidelberg Catechism, Question 1.
[12] Wm. J. Schnell, *Thirty Years a Watchtower Slave,* pp. 104-5.

man: "I know Christ as my Savior, and I know that in Him I have eternal life here and now. Do you?"

We must go on to show the cultist that the other basic needs of man are also completely satisfied only in Christ. Is he lonely? Christ, who has promised to be with us always, is a Friend whose fellowship is sweeter than that of any earthly companion. Is he afraid of being lost in the crowd? Does he feel the need of filling a place of importance in God's kingdom? In Christ we are all prophets, priests, and kings (Mt. 10:32, Acts 1:8, I Peter 2:9); whatever we do to one of the least of His brethren we do to Him (Mt. 25:40). Does he feel a lack of deep emotional satisfaction? Jesus said, "These things have I spoken unto you, that my joy may be in you, and that your joy may be made full" (Jn. 15:11).

Precisely here is the point at which our encounter with the cultist is the most difficult and at the same time the most crucial. For here it is not merely a question of doctrine versus doctrine, or Bible text versus Bible text, but of the meaning of a living experience of fellowship with Christ over against the lack of such an experience. Here the reality and vitality of our own faith and of our own Christian experience becomes most important. What we wish to offer this man is not just an organization, or a set of doctrines, but Christ in all His fulness and richness. And it is probably true that we cannot bring another closer to Christ than we stand ourselves. Or, to put it differently, "If you want others to see what Christ can do for them, let them see what Christ has done for you."[13]

Approaching the Cultist on the Intellectual Level

Although, as we have seen, we should first of all approach the cultist as a total person, an approach on the intellectual level will also be necessary in any serious encounter. If there is any desire on the part of the cultist to go more deeply into the question of whether or not his group teaches the truth, we should, if we are properly prepared, discuss with him the main doctrines taught by his cult.

In this connection a word should be said about II John 10 and 11, "If any one cometh unto you, and bringeth not this teaching, receive him not into your house, and give him no greeting; for he that giveth him greeting partaketh in his evil works." By some

---

[13] Needless to say, all this must be done with much prayer and in the confident expectation that God answers prayer. The hand of Him who changed Saul the persecutor into Paul the missionary has not been shortened!

Christians this passage is understood to mean that we may never receive a cultist into our homes, not even for the purpose of refuting his teachings. This is, however, a misinterpretation of the passage. From the preceding context it is obvious that the heresy involved is of such a serious nature that it undermines the Gospel. A person who teaches such a heresy, John says, is not to be received into your house: that is, is not to be shown the kind of hospitality that will enable him to use your house as a base of operations.[14] For such hospitality would mean cooperating with him in his nefarious work. The expression, "give him no greeting," is to be understood as follows: "do not welcome him as a brother." Obviously, therefore, this passage forbids working together with people who deny cardinal truths of the Christian faith, and thus helping them advance their cause. But this text by no means condemns the receiving of such people into our homes in order to reveal to them the errors of their way and to lead them to Christ. In fact, the passage implies that the latter course of action is our Christian duty!

GENERAL SUGGESTIONS

In connection with this approach on the intellectual level, I should like first to make a few general suggestions:

(1) We must approach the cultist with *genuine love*. Though we may never love his errors, we must love him as a person. This would seem so obvious that it does not need to be said — yet too often an encounter of this type degenerates into a mere battle of wits, in which concern for the cultist's salvation is sacrificed to a concern for the vindication of our own position. Our primary purpose, however, may never be to defeat the cultist in argument or to demolish his position, but to win him for Christ. We must remember, too, that the cultist has been taught that the members of the regular churches regard him with hostility; the most effective way to disabuse him of that notion is to reveal a loving concern quite different from what he has been led to expect. This implies, needless to say, that we must never lose our tempers during the encounter but must remain calm and self-controlled.

(2) We should approach the cultist with *humility*. We must not give him the impression that we know it all or that we have all the answers, since this would be to assume the cultic attitude we are trying to combat. Our purpose is to place the cultist under the Word of God — but this implies that we at the same time place

---

[14] This warning was particularly appropriate at a time when itinerant teachers usually looked for private homes which they could make their headquarters, since there were very few inns.

ourselves under that Word. And this means that we must be as ready to see our shortcomings as those of the cult. Further, we must also be ready to confess that we grasp only a part of the truth and not the whole of it.[15] Hutten warns us not to confuse our confession of the truth with the truth itself. Truth is always bigger than our grasp of it. Our confession of the truth as such, moreover, will not save us; it is conceivable that one who belongs to a cult might, despite the errors in which he is enmeshed, be in living fellowship with Christ, whereas someone belonging to a church with a sound, orthodox creed might stand outside of that fellowship.[16] Living communion with Christ is on a deeper level than that of mere intellectual understanding.

(3) We must be ready to recognize the *lessons we can learn from the cult*. This point need not be elaborated, since it has already been developed in Chapter 1.

(4) We must *know the teachings of the cult*. Needless to say, our success in refuting the doctrines of the cult will depend in large measure on our familiarity with its teachings, and on our understanding of its mentality. It is extremely important that we do our utmost to be fair in analyzing and reproducing cult teachings. Sometimes it happens that people who claim to set forth cult teachings distort those teachings to such an extent that the cultist can hardly recognize his position in what is attributed to him. We owe it to the cultist to make as thorough an effort as possible to understand him. Hence the importance cannot be over-stressed of using primary sources, and of making sure that these sources are not outdated or no longer recognized as authoritative.[17]

SPECIFIC SUGGESTIONS

With regard to the actual encounter with the cultist on the intellectual level, I should like to make the following specific suggestions:

(1) Let the main purpose of this encounter be to give *a positive testimony to the truth of God's Word*. The chief goal, in other words, may never be merely negative (the overthrowing of the opponent's position) but must be positive. Encountering a cultist is not a type of debate but a way of witnessing to the saving truth of the Gospel.

---

[15] "For we know in part and we prophesy in part" (I Cor. 13:9). Cf. on this point Kurt Hutten, *Glaubenswelt,* pp. 137-38 (Dutch translation, pp. 142-43).

[16] *Seher, Gruebler, Enthusiasten,* p. 726.

[17] The most important primary sources for each of the cults discussed in this book are listed in the bibliography. It should be added, however, that personal contact with cultists is necessary for those who wish to get a complete picture of the cult's way of life.

(2) *Face the question of your source of authority.* This must be done at the very beginning of the encounter. If you are talking to a Mormon, you must first show him from the Bible, which he does recognize as a sacred book, that Scripture itself teaches its own sufficiency and condemns the attempt to add other sources of revelation to it (see above, pp. 23-24, 30-33). It may be necessary at this point to go into the question of the genuineness of the *Book of Mormon* (see above, pp. 75-87). Even if this is done, however, the purpose of the discussion must not be simply to reject the *Book of Mormon,* but to defend the final authority of the Bible. Only when the Mormon is willing to listen to the Bible as authoritative can the discussion proceed with profit. If he continues to insist that his additional sacred books are just as authoritative as the Bible, there is no point in continuing the discussion.

In case you are dealing with a Jehovah's Witness, you must first ask him whether the Bible is his final source of authority. He should answer this question affirmatively, since this is what official Watchtower publications claim (see above, p. 238). If he does so, you should then proceed to show him, by careful explanation of relevant Scripture passages, that many of his teachings are wrong. He will try to answer you by quoting other texts. You must, however, constantly challenge him to show how a passage he quotes proves what he thinks it does and not simply let him rattle off texts. And you must, by going carefully into the context, by comparing Scripture with Scripture, prove that his teachings are not in harmony with the Bible.[18] If he still insists that he is right, you must then confront him with the fact that his real authority is thus not the Word of God but the teaching of a group of fallible men.[19]

Christian Scientists also theoretically claim to accept the Bible as their only authority (see above, p. 182). You must proceed to show the Christian Scientist that he cannot continue to claim to rest on the authority of the Bible alone while bowing with complete submissiveness to the interpretations of Mrs. Eddy. Is he at all willing to recognize that Mrs. Eddy might not be infallible? If so, there is point in continuing the discussion. If not, the dis-

[18] If you have enough knowledge of the original languages of the Bible to be able to appeal to them during this discussion, so much the better.

[19] A converted Jehovah's Witness has given this piece of advice to those dealing with Witnesses: Before beginning your discussion, ask the Witness whether he knew his Bible before joining the group. If he answers in the negative, as most Jehovah's Witnesses will, point out to him that he has therefore never really studied the Bible in an unbiased way (see above, p. 248, and n. 105).

cussion has reached an impasse.   The question of authority must be settled first.

Seventh-day Adventists claim that the writings of Ellen G. White are not to be placed above Scripture (see above, pp. 100-102). They should be shown that their actual use of her writings belies this claim (see above, pp. 102-8).   Since the Adventists do recognize the authority of Scripture, however, you do have a basis on which to proceed.

(3) *Present the evidence for the major doctrines of the Christian faith.*   Here again your purpose must be not just to defend the specific teachings that set your denomination apart from other Christian denominations, but to defend the Biblical teachings which are held in common by all evangelical Christians.   Your goal, it must be remembered, is not primarily to win this man for your church, but to win him for Christ!

Stick to the major doctrines; do not allow yourself to be side-tracked into discussing minor issues.   After all, the difference between you and the cult is not just a matter of this doctrine or that one; it is one which involves the interpretation of the central message of the Bible: that of salvation by grace alone.   You must, therefore, be prepared to show the cultist that the Bible clearly teaches salvation by grace alone.   You must be ready to marshall a carefully planned group of Bible passages which teach this. These passages should not be treated in isolated fashion, but in the light of the context in which they occur.

Other major doctrines of the Christian faith will also have to be defended, not on the basis of creeds or confessions, but by direct appeal to Scripture.   The best way to be prepared to meet the cultist, therefore, is to know your Bible well, and to know how to show the Biblical basis for the cardinal doctrines of Christianity. In Appendices C, D, and E an attempt has been made to set forth the Scriptural basis for such doctrines as the first-day Sabbath, the deity of Christ, man's conscious existence between death and the resurrection, and the eternal punishment of the wicked.   One may find suggestions for giving a Scriptural defense of other Christian teachings which cultists deny by consulting the doctrinal books listed on pp. 33-34 above, or by using the anti-cult literature mentioned in the bibliography.   In many cases, however, the pastor or missionary who is working with a cultist may have to do his own personal research on specific doctrinal points.[20]

---

[20] In connection with this doctrinal discussion the reader is reminded of a point made earlier, namely, that you must make sure that you and the cultist agree on your use of terms.   Christian Scientists, for instance, use such terms as *God, Trinity, creation,* and *providence* in a sense quite different from that which historic Christianity ascribes to them (see above,

(4) *Follow up the contact made.* This may be done by making further calls at the cultist's home. If the cultist reveals some interest in learning more about the teachings of the Bible, offer to conduct a Bible-study class for him (and for any others who may be interested). In a letter I received from a former student it was reported that a certain Jehovah's Witness was converted to Christianity through the patient witnessing of one Christian family, who sat down with him once a week for six months and explained the Scriptures to him. If more of this kind of witnessing were done by Christians, probably many more slaves of the cults would become liberated!

(5) *Keep on praying.* Promise the individual with whom you are working that you will pray for him, and then keep on doing so. The Jehovah's Witness mentioned in the above paragraph was not converted until three years after the six-month Bible class; but the Christian family had been praying for him all that time. "Ask, and it shall be given you; seek, and ye shall find; knock, and it shall be opened unto you" (Luke 11:9).

---

pp. 195-96). We have noted, too, that Jehovah's Witnesses use the terms *justification* (see above, pp. 280-81, 284) and *sanctification* (see above, pp. 282, 284) in various ways. Unless there is precise agreement on the meaning of theological terms, you and the cultist may find yourselves continually talking past each other.

Bibliography

An attempt has been made to list the most important publications on each of the cults treated.

GENERAL WORKS

BOOKS:

Atkins, G. C. *Modern Religious Cults and Movements.* New York: Revell, 1923.

Bach, Marcus. *They Have Found a Faith.* New York: Bobbs-Merrill, 1946.

————. *Faith and My Friends.* New York: Bobbs-Merrill, 1951.

Blanke, Fritz. *Kirchen und Sekten.* 2nd enlarged ed. Zurich: Zwingli Verlag, 1955.

Boerwinkel, F. *Kerk en Secte.* 's Gravenhage: Boekencentrum, 1956. Analyzes the differences between the cult and the church.

Braden, Charles S. *These Also Believe.* New York: Macmillan, 1951.

Chery, H. Ch. *L'offensive des Sectes.* Paris: Editions du Cerf, 1954.

Clark, Elmer T. *The Small Sects in America.* Rev. ed. Nashville: Abingdon, 1949.

Davies, Horton. *The Challenge of the Sects.* A rev. and enlarged ed. of his *Christian Deviations.* Philadelphia: Westminster, 1961.

Delleman, Th. *Tussen Kerk en Tegenkerk.* Aalten: Graafschap, 1957. Attempts to answer the question: What makes a cult a cult?

Ferguson, Charles W. *The Confusion of Tongues.* New York: Doubleday-Doran, 1928.

Ferm, Vergilius (ed.). *Religion in the Twentieth Century.* New York: Philosophical Library, 1948.

Gerstner, John H. *The Theology of the Major Sects.* Grand Rapids: Baker, 1960.

Hutten, Kurt. *Seher, Gruebler, Enthusiasten.* 6th ed. Stuttgart: Quellverlag, 1960 (first pub. in 1950). Describes the various cults active in Europe. An extensive work.

————. *Die Glaubenswelt des Sektierers.* Hamburg: Furche, 1957. A penetrating analysis of the distinguishing characteristics of the cults.

————. *Geloof en Sekte.* A Dutch translation of the above work by J. J. Poort. Franeker: Wever, n.d.

Kok, A. B. W. M. *Verleidende Geesten.* Kampen: Kok, 1953.

Lindeboom, J. *Stiefkinderen van het Christendom.* Groningen: M. Nijhoff, 1929.

Martin, Walter R. *The Rise of the Cults.* Grand Rapids: Zondervan, 1955.

————. *The Christian and the Cults.* Grand Rapids: Zondervan, 1956. Discusses methods of approaching the various cults.

417

Mathison, Richard R. *Faiths, Cults, and Sects of America.* Indian-
apolis: Bobbs-Merrill, 1960.

Mayer, F. E. *Religious Bodies of America.* St. Louis: Concordia,
1954.

Mead, Frank S. *Handbook of Denominations in the United States.*
2nd rev. ed. Nashville: Abingdon, 1956.

Neve, J. L. *Churches and Sects of Christendom.* Rev. ed. Blair, Neb.:
Lutheran Pub. House, 1952.

Rhodes, A. B. (ed.). *The Church Faces the Isms.* New York: Abingdon, 1958.

Rosten, Leo (ed.). *A Guide to the Religions of America.* New York:
Simon and Shuster, 1955.

Sanders, J. O., and Wright, J. Stafford. *Some Modern Religions.* London: Tyndale Press, 1956.

Van Baalen, J. K. *The Chaos of Cults.* 4th rev. and enlarged ed.
Grand Rapids: Eerdmans, 1962.

PERIODICALS:

Braden, Charles S. "Why are the Cults Growing?" *Christian Century,*
Vol. LXI, Nos. 1-4 (Jan.-Feb., 1944), pp. 45-47, 78-80, 108-110,
137-40.

————. "What Can We Learn From the Cults?" *Religion in Life,*
Vol. XIV, No. 1 (Winter, 1944-45), pp. 52-64.

Kuizenga, John E. "The Cults: Phenomenon and Challenge," *Theology Today,* Vol. I, No. 1 (April, 1944), pp. 34-46.

MORMONISM

PRIMARY SOURCES:

The Book of Mormon, Doctrine and Covenants, and *The Pearl of
Great Price.* All three are published by the Church of Jesus Christ
of Latter-day Saints at Salt Lake City, Utah.

(Note: Versions of *The Book of Mormon* and of *Doctrine and
Covenants* published at Independence, Missouri, by the Reorganized
Church of Jesus Christ of Latter-day Saints differ in some im-
portant respects from those published at Salt Lake City.)

Inspired Version of the Holy Scriptures. An Inspired Revision of the
Authorized Version, by Joseph Smith, Jr. A New Corrected Edition. Independence: Herald Pub. House, 1955 (copyrighted in
1944).

(Note: This is the Bible version used by the Reorganized Mormon
Church. Though Utah Mormons use the King James Version,
they do accept all the changes made in the King James by Joseph
Smith which have been incorporated into the "Inspired Version.")

Smith, Joseph Fielding, compiler. *Teachings of the Prophet Joseph
Smith.* Salt Lake City: Deseret News Press, 1958. Excerpts from
doctrinal sermons and writings of Joseph Smith.

Widtsoe, John A., compiler. *Discourses of Brigham Young.* Salt Lake
City: Deseret Book Co., 1954. Selections gathered from the *Journal of Discourses,* arranged under 42 topics. 11-p. index.

BIOGRAPHICAL WORKS:

Biographies of Joseph Smith:

Brodie, Fawn M. *No Man Knows my History.* New York: Knopf,
1957.

Vander Valk, M. H. A. *De Profeet der Mormonen, Joseph Smith,
Junior.* Kampen: Kok, 1921. Contains a 31-p. bibliography, with
1395 entries.

Biographies of Brigham Young:

Cannon, Frank J. and Knapp, George L. *Brigham Young and his
Mormon Empire.* New York, 1913.

Gates, Susa Young. *The Life Story of Brigham Young.* London, 1930.
Written by one of Young's daughters.

Werner, M. R. *Brigham Young.* New York: Harcourt, Brace, and
Co., 1925.

WORKS DEALING PARTICULARLY WITH THE BOOK OF MORMON:

Budvarson, Arthur. *The Book of Mormon Examined.* La Mesa,
Calif.: Utah Christian Tract Society, 1959. Now published by
Zondervan under the title, *The Book of Mormon: True or False?* A
critical examination of the Book of Mormon by a former Mormon.

Hunter, Milton R. *Archaeology and the Book of Mormon.* Vol. I.
Salt Lake City: Deseret Book Co., 1956. An attempt to verify the
truth of the Book of Mormon by means of archaeological evidence,
chiefly from Central America.

Jonas, Larry W. *Mormon Claims Examined.* Grand Rapids: Baker,
1961. Contains correspondence from the Smithsonian Institution
denying Mormon claims about the use of the Book of Mormon as
a guide for archaeologists.

Kirkham, Francis W. *A New Witness for Christ in America.* 2 vols.
Independence: Zion's Press, 1951. Pro-Mormon. Discusses the
"divine origin of the Book of Mormon" and analyzes "the many
attempts to prove the book man-made."

Reynolds, George. *A Complete Concordance to the Book of Mormon.* Salt Lake City: Deseret Book Co., 1957.

———. *The Story of the Book of Mormon.* Salt Lake City: Deseret
Book Co., 1957. A "sacred" history, describing the events recorded in the Book of Mormon.

Roberts, Brigham H. *New Witnesses for God.* 3 vols. Salt Lake City:
Deseret News Press, 1927. Cites many "external and internal
evidences of the truth of the Book of Mormon."

Shook, Charles A. *The True Origin of the Book of Mormon.* Cincinnati: Standard Pub. Co., 1914. Anti-Mormon, by one who left the
Mormon Church.

Sjodahl, J. M. *An Introduction to the Study of the Book of Mormon.*
Salt Lake City: Deseret News Press, 1927.

Webb, R. C. *Joseph Smith as a Translator.* Salt Lake City: Deseret
News Press, 1936. An attempt to show that Smith really did
translate from Egyptian.

Wood, Wilford C. *Joseph Smith Begins his Work.* Salt Lake City:
Deseret News Press, 1958. A photostatic copy of the first (1830)
edition of the Book of Mormon. A comparison of this edition
with the current one will reveal the many changes which have
been made in the Book of Mormon.

WORKS DEALING PARTICULARLY WITH POLYGAMY:

Young, Ann Eliza. *Wife Number 19.* · Hartford: Dustin, Gilman,
1879. An autobiography of Brigham Young's apostate wife.

Young, Kimball. *Isn't One Wife Enough?* New York: Holt, 1954.
An exposition of plural marriage "in all its success and in all its
sadness," by a grandson of Brigham Young.

WORKS DEALING PARTICULARLY WITH THE HISTORY OF MORMONISM:

Bancroft, Hubert H. *History of Utah.* San Francisco, 1890. Largely
a history of the Mormons in Utah.

Beadle, John H. *Life in Utah;* or, The Mysteries and Crimes of
Mormonism. Philadelphia, 1870.

Birney, Hoffman. *Zealots of Zion.* Philadelphia, 1931. A history
of the early years of Mormonism.

Cannon, Frank J., and O'Higgins, Harvey J. *Under the Prophet in
Utah*: The National Menace of a Political Priestcraft. Boston,
1911. A history of Mormonism in Utah from 1888 to 1911.

Hafen, Leroy R. *Handcarts to Zion.* Glendale: A. H. Clark, 1960.
The story of a unique western migration (1856-1860).

————. *Journals of Forty-Niners.* Glendale: A. H. Clark, 1954.
Salt Lake City to Los Angeles, with diaries.

Hinckley, Gordon B. *What of the Mormons?* Salt Lake City: Church
of Jesus Christ of Latter-day Saints, 1954. Mostly historical;
well illustrated.

Howe, Eber D. *Mormonism Unveiled.* Painesville, Ohio, 1834.

Howells, Rulon S. *The Mormon Story*: A Pictorial Account of
Mormonism. Salt Lake City: Bookcraft, 1957 (10th ed., 1962).
History, organization, practices, doctrines. Profusely illustrated.

Kelly, C., and Birney, H. *Holy Murder*: The Story of Porter Rockwell.
New York, 1934. The biography of the executioner of early
Mormonism.

Linn, W. A. *The Story of the Mormons* (from the date of their origin
to the year 1901). New York: Macmillan, 1923 (copyrighted in
1902). Though old, one of the best historical studies.

Roberts, Brigham H. *A Comprehensive History of the Church of
Jesus Christ of Latter-day Saints.* 6 vols. Salt Lake City: Deseret
News Press, 1930.

Smith, Joseph, Jr. *The History of the Church of Jesus Christ of Latter-day Saints* (often referred to as the *Documentary History of the Church*). 6 vols. Salt Lake City: Deseret News, 1902-12.

Smith, Joseph Fielding. *Essentials in Church History.* 13th ed. Salt Lake City: Deseret News Press, 1953. An official history of the Mormon Church by the church historian.

West, Ray B., Jr. *Kingdom of the Saints.* The Story of Brigham Young and the Mormons. New York: Viking Press, 1957. A well-researched, appreciative history of Mormonism by a former Mormon.

(Note: the following is a history of Mormonism from the standpoint of the Reorganized Church:

Davis, Inez Smith. *The Story of the Church.* 6th ed.; 2nd revision. Independence: Herald Pub. House, 1959. Includes both the early history and that of the Reorganization.)

REFERENCE WORKS ON MORMONISM:

Brooks, Melvin R. *L. D. S. Reference Encyclopedia.* Salt Lake City: Bookcraft, 1960.

Jenson, Andrew. *Encyclopedic History of the Church of Jesus Christ of Latter-day Saints.* Salt Lake City: Deseret News Press, 1941. Gives historical details about various Mormon settlements and stakes.

DOCTRINAL STUDIES BY MORMON AUTHORS:

Bennion, Lowell L. *An Introduction to the Gospel.* Salt Lake City: Deseret Sunday School Union Board, 1955. A course of study for Sunday Schools.

————. *The Religion of the Latter-day Saints.* Salt Lake City: Latter-day Saints' Department of Education, 1940. A guide to Mormon doctrines for college students.

Berrett, Wm. E. *Teachings of the Doctrine and Covenants.* Salt Lake City, 1954. A Sunday School Manual.

Hunter, Milton R. *The Gospel Through the Ages.* Salt Lake City: Deseret Book Co., 1958 (copyrighted in 1945). A doctrinal study intended especially for Mormon missionaries.

McConkie, Bruce R. *Mormon Doctrine.* Salt Lake City: Bookcraft, 1958. A detailed exposition of Mormon doctrine in encyclopedic form.

Richards, LeGrand. *A Marvelous Work and a Wonder.* Salt Lake City: Deseret Book Co., 1950. An exposition of Mormon doctrines particularly intended for missionaries.

Smith, Hyrum M., and Sjodahl, Janne M. *Doctrine and Covenants Commentary.* Rev. ed. Salt Lake City: Deseret, 1960 (copyrighted in 1951). Historical and explanatory notes.

Smith, Joseph F. *Gospel Doctrine.* 12th ed. Salt Lake City: Deseret News Press, 1961 (copyrighted 1939). Selections from the sermons and writings of Joseph F. Smith (1838-1918), the 6th

president of the Mormon Church and the father of Joseph Fielding Smith.

Smith, Joseph Fielding. *Answers to Gospel Questions.* 3 vols.
Salt Lake City: Deseret Book Co., 1958. A series of answers to
questions pertaining to Scripture, doctrine, and history, submitted
over a period of years, and answered in the Mormon periodical,
The Improvement Era.

————. *Doctrines of Salvation.* 3 vols. Salt Lake City: Bookcraft,
1960 (copyrighted 1954-56). Compiled from the sermons and
writings of Joseph Fielding Smith, current president of the Council
of Twelve Apostles, by Bruce R. McConkie. The most complete
and most recent discussion of Mormon doctrine presently available.

Talmage, James E. *A Study of the Articles of Faith. 36th ed.*
Salt Lake City: Church of Jesus Christ of Latter-day Saints,
1957 (first published in 1899). An exposition of the Mormon
Articles of Faith. A standard source-book for Mormon doctrines.

————. *The Vitality of Mormonism.* Boston: R. G. Badger, 1919.
Brief essays on distinctive Mormon doctrines.

Widtsoe, John A. *Evidences and Reconciliations.* Arranged by G. H.
Durham. 3 vols. in 1. Salt Lake City: Bookcraft, 1960. A
series of answers to questions, involving doctrine, science, history,
ethics, and church rules, submitted to the author over a period of
years.

————. *A Rational Theology.* 6th ed. Salt Lake City: Deseret
Book Co., 1952 (copyrighted in 1915). An exposition of Mormon
theology, somewhat philosophically oriented.

(Note: The following volume is a study of the differences in doctrine and practice between the Reorganized Church and the Utah
Church:

Ralston, Russell F. *Fundamental Differences Between the Reorganized
Church and the Church in Utah.* Independence: Herald Pub.
House, 1960. 244 pp.)

GENERAL WORKS:

BOOKS:

Arbaugh, George B. *Gods, Sex, and Saints*: The Mormon Story.
Rock Island: Augustana Press, 1957. Deals with polytheism, other
Mormon doctrines, and the approach to Mormons.

————. *Revelation in Mormonism.* Chicago: University of Chicago
Press, 1932. A doctoral dissertation dealing with the Mormon
conception of divine revelation.

Bennett, Wallace F. *Why I am a Mormon.* New York: T. Nelson,
1958.

Ericksen, Ephraim E. *The Psychological and Ethical Aspects of
Mormon Group Life.* Chicago: University of Chicago Press, 1922.

Kinney, Bruce. *Mormonism: The Islam of America.* Rev. and enlarged ed. New York: Revell, 1912. The author was formerly
superintendent of Baptist missions in Utah.

La Rue, Wm. E. *The Foundations of Mormonism.* New York: Revell, 1919.

Martin, Walter R. *The Maze of Mormonism.* Grand Rapids: Zondervan, 1962. History, doctrines, public relations. Has chapter on how to meet Mormon missionaries.

McNiff, W. J. *Heaven on Earth*: A Planned Mormon Society. Oxford, Ohio: Mississippi Valley Press, 1940. A study of Mormon culture.

O'Dea, Thomas F. *The Mormons.* Chicago: University of Chicago Press, 1957. Based partly on a Harvard dissertation. Includes historical, psychological, and sociological insights.

Sheldon, Henry C. *A Fourfold Test of Mormonism.* New York: Abingdon Press, 1914.

Snowden, James H. *The Truth about Mormonism.* New York: George H. Doran, 1926. A study of the history, doctrines, and practices of Mormonism.

Tanner, Jerald. *Mormonism*: A study of Mormon History and Doctrine. Obtainable from the Utah Evangel Press, P. O. Box 108, Clearfield, Utah. In this mimeographed book, published in 1962, the author, a former Mormon, exposes the unwillingness of the Mormon Church to permit early Mormon documents to be examined or microfilmed by non-Mormons, and reveals the many changes that have been made in the Mormon sacred books and in Mormon doctrines. He also gives much well-documented evidence about embarrassing historical episodes like the Mountain Meadows Massacre and the work of the Danites. Reflects a great deal of research in Mormon writings.

Van Dellen, I. *Het Mormonisme.* Kampen: Kok, 1911. A study of Mormonism by a Christian Reformed minister.

Vander Valk, M. H. A. *De Mormonen*: Hun Profeet, Leer, en Leven. Kampen: Kok, 1924. A popular study by the author of *De Profeet der Mormonen* (see above).

PAMPHLETS:

(Note: Pastors and missionaries desiring inexpensive booklets for distribution to parishioners and inquirers are referred to the following list.)

Anderson, Einar. *Mormonism* (A Personal Testimony). Chicago: Moody Press, 1956. 32 pp.

Biederwolf, Wm. E. *Mormonism under the Searchlight.* Grand Rapids: Eerdmans, 1945. 68 pp.

Fraser, Gordon H. *Is Mormonism Christian?* An Examination of Mormon Doctrine as Compared with Orthodox Christianity. Chicago: Moody Press, 1957. 122 pp. An excellent brief survey.

Martin, Walter R. *Mormonism.* Grand Rapids: Zondervan, 1957. 32 pp.

Nutting, John D. *Mormonism Today and its Remedy.* Cleveland: Utah Gospel Mission, 1927. 20 pp. Brief account of doctrines, practices, and history.

Smith, John L. *Has Mormonism Changed?* Clearfield, Utah: Utah
Evangel Press, 1959. 59 pp. Discusses missionary work among
Mormons, history, and doctrines.

———. *Hope or Despair.* Clearfield, Utah: Utah Evangel Press,
1959. 35 pp. Brief criticism of Mormon doctrines, including
10 photostatic reprints, some from the *Journal of Discourses.*

Talbot, Louis T. *What's Wrong with Mormonism?* Findlay, Ohio:
Dunham Pub. Co., 1957. 48 pp.

Triezenberg, Henry J. *The Bible and Mormonism.* Faith, Prayer,
and Tract League; 1016 11th St., Grand Rapids, Mich. 20 pp.

(Note: Some of the above pamphlets can be obtained from Religion Analysis Service, 902 Hennepin Ave., Minneapolis 3, Minn.)

PERODICALS:

Boyd, Robert F. "Mormonism," *Interpretation,* Vol. X, No. 4 (Oct.,
1956), pp. 430-46.

Spence, Hartzell. "The Mormon Church: A Complete Way of
Life," *Reader's Digest,* April, 1958.

Walters, Wesley P. "Mormonism," *Christianity Today,* Vol. V, No.
6 (Dec. 19, 1960), pp. 8-10.

SEVENTH-DAY ADVENTISM

PRIMARY SOURCES:

White, Ellen Gould. *Patriarchs and Prophets.* Mountain View, Calif.:
Pacific Press Pub. Association, 1913 (first pub. in 1890). (Vol.
I of the Conflict of the Ages Series).

———. *Prophets and Kings.* Mountain View: Pacific Press, 1917.
(Vol. II of the Conflict of the Ages Series).

———. *The Desire of Ages.* Mountain View: Pacific Press, 1940
(first pub. in 1898). (Vol. III of the Conflict of the Ages Series).

———. *The Acts of the Apostles in the Proclamation of the Gospel
of Jesus Christ.* Mountain View: Pacific Press, 1947 (first pub.
in 1911). (Vol. IV of the Conflict of the Ages Series).

———. *The Great Controversy Between Christ and Satan.* Mountain
View: Pacific Press, 1911 (first pub. in 1888). (Vol. V of the
Conflict of the Ages Series).

———. *Christ's Object Lessons.* Washington, D.C.: Review and
Herald Pub. Association, 1941. A discussion of the parables of
Jesus.

———. *Counsels on Stewardship.* Washington, D.C.: Review and
Herald, 1940.

———. *Education.* Mountain View: Pacific Press, 1942 (first
pub. in 1903).

———. *Gospel Workers.* Washington, D.C.: Review and Herald,
1915.

———. *The Ministry of Healing.* Mountain View: Pacific Press,
1942 (first pub. in 1905).

————. *The Sanctified Life.* Washington, D.C.: Review and Herald, 1937.

————. *Steps to Christ.* Washington, D.C.: Review and Herald, 1921 (first pub. in 1892).

————. *Testimonies for the Church.* Vols. I-IX (1855-1909).

————. *Thoughts from the Mount of Blessing.* Mountain View: Pacific Press, 1928 (first pub. in 1896).

HISTORIES OF SEVENTH-DAY ADVENTISM:

Department of Education, General Conference of Seventh-day Adventists. *The Story of Our Church.* Mountain View: Pacific Press, 1960 (copyrighted in 1956). An official, though popularized, history.

Froom, Leroy Edwin. *The Prophetic Faith of Our Fathers.* The Historical Development of Prophetic Interpretation. 4 vols. Washington, D.C.: Review and Herald, 1946-54. A voluminous study of the history of the interpretation of prophecy. Vol. IV contains the history of the beginnings of the Seventh-day Adventist denomination.

Loughborough, John N. *The Great Second Advent Movement.* Washington, D.C.: Review and Herald, 1909.

Nichol, Francis D. *The Midnight Cry.* Washington, D. C.: Review and Herald, 1945. A defense of the character and conduct of Wm. Miller and the Millerites.

Olsen, Mahlon E. *A History of the Origin and Progress of Seventh-day Adventists.* 2nd ed. Washington, D. C.: Review and Herald, 1926.

Spalding, Arthur W. *Captains of the Host.* Washington, D.C.: Review and Herald, 1949. A history of Seventh-day Adventism up to 1900.

————. *Christ's Last Legion.* Washington, D.C.: Review and Herald, 1949. The history of Seventh-day Adventism since 1900.

SEVENTH-DAY ADVENTIST PUBLICATIONS:

Andreasen, M. L. *God's Holy Day.* Washington, D. C.: Review and Herald, 1949.

————. *The Sabbath, Which Day and Why?* Washington, D. C.: Review and Herald, 1942.

————. *The Sanctuary Service.* 2nd ed., rev. Washington, D. C.: Review and Herald, 1947.

Bible Readings for the Home. Rev. ed. Washington, D. C.: Review and Herald, 1949.

Branson, Wm. H. *In Defense of the Faith.* Washington, D. C.: Review and Herald, 1933. A reply to Canright's book, *Seventh-day Adventism Renounced.*

————. *The Drama of the Ages.* Nashville: Southern Pub. Association, 1950. God's plan for saving man from sin.

Department of Education, General Conference of Seventh-day Adventists. *Principles of Life from the Word of God.* A Systematic

Study of the Major Doctrines of the Bible. Mountain View: Pacific Press, 1952 (4th printing, 1960). Intended for classroom use.

Haynes, Carlyle B. *The Christian Sabbath.* Nashville: Southern Pub. Assn., 1949.

————. *Life, Death, and Immortality.* Nashville: Southern Pub. Assn., 1952.

————. *Our Lord's Return.* Nashville: Southern Pub. Assn., 1948.

————. *Seventh-day Adventists, their Work and Teachings.* Washington, D. C.: Review and Herald, 1940. Discusses major doctrines, activities, finances, institutions, leadership, customs.

Lickey, Arthur E. *Fundamentals of the Everlasting Gospel.* Washington, D. C.: Review and Herald, 1947. Brief statement of fundamental beliefs, suitable for the instruction of converts.

————. *God Speaks to Modern Man.* Washington, D. C.: Review and Herald, 1952. A rather thorough discussion of Adventist teachings.

Nichol, Francis D. *Answers to Objections.* Washington, D. C.: Review and Herald, 1952. Contains some of the material found in *Reasons for our Faith,* but has much additional material. An extensive work.

————. *Ellen G. White and her Critics.* Washington, D. C.: Review and Herald, 1951. An attempt to answer various criticisms of Mrs. White.

————. *Questions People Have Asked Me.* Washington, D. C.: Review and Herald, 1959. The questions concern ethical, practical, and doctrinal problems.

————. *Reasons for our Faith.* Washington, D. C.: Review and Herald, 1947. Discusses questions vital to the proper understanding and effective presentation of certain Adventist teachings.

Seventh-day Adventist Bible Dictionary. Don F. Neufeld, ed. Authors: Siegfried H. Horn, et. al. Washington, D. C.: Review and Herald, 1960.

Seventh-day Adventist Bible Commentary. Francis D. Nichol, ed. 7 vols. Washington, D. C.: Review and Herald, 1953-57. Contains general articles on doctrinal and Biblical topics, as well as a verse-by-verse commentary.

Seventh-day Adventist Church Manual. General Conference of Seventh-day Adventists, 1959. Beliefs, church government, membership, duties of officers, services and meetings, auxiliary organizations, finances, standards of Christian living, church discipline.

Seventh-day Adventists Answer Questions on Doctrine. An Explanation of Certain Major Aspects of Seventh-day Adventist Belief. Prepared by a Representative Group of Seventh-day Adventist Leaders, Bible Teachers, and Editors. Washington, D. C.: Review and Herald, 1957. Contains answers to questions submitted to the denomination by Walter R. Martin. It may be considered the most recent official statement of Seventh-day Adventist doctrine.

Smith, Uriah. *The Prophecies of Daniel and the Revelation.* Rev. ed. Nashville: Southern Pub. Assn., 1946 (first pub. in 1874).

Spicer, Wm. Ambrose. *Our Day in the Light of Prophecy.* Washington, D. C.: Review and Herald, 1918.

Walker, Allan. *The Law and the Sabbath.* Nashville: Southern Pub. Assn., 1953.

Yearbook of the Seventh-day Adventist Denomination. Published annually by the Review and Herald Pub. Co., Washington, D. C. Gives information about world statistics, mission work, educational institutions, hospitals and sanitariums, publishing houses and denominational workers.

GENERAL WORKS:

BOOKS:

Bird, Herbert S. *Theology of Seventh-day Adventism.* Grand Rapids: Eerdmans, 1961. A competent analysis, based on recent sources.

Canright, D. M. *The Lord's Day from Neither Catholics nor Pagans.* New York: Revell, 1915.

————. *Seventh-day Adventism Renounced.* Grand Rapids: Baker, 1961. Originally published in 1889. A former Seventh-day Adventist gives the reasons why he left the denomination, and offers a searching critique of Adventist doctrines.

Douty, Norman F. *Another Look at Seventh-day Adventism.* Grand Rapids: Baker, 1962. A careful, detailed analysis, based on *Questions on Doctrine,* and on a great number of other Seventh-day Adventist publications.

Herndon, Booton. *The Seventh Day.* New York: McGraw-Hill, 1960. A very sympathetic treatment. Deals mostly with mission work, but includes brief statements on history, beliefs, and practices.

Martin, Walter R. *The Truth about Seventh-day Adventism.* Grand Rapids: Zondervan, 1960. Defends the view that Seventh-day Adventism is not a cult but a branch of evangelical Christianity. The author is, however, very critical of many Adventist doctrines.

Mitchell, David. *Seventh-day Adventists: Faith in Action.* New York: Vantage Press, 1958. Very sympathetic, though written by a non-Adventist.

Sheldon, Henry C. *Studies in Recent Adventism.* New York: Abingdon, 1915.

Smay, L. J. U. *The Sanctuary and the Sabbath.* Cleveland: Evangelical Association, 1915.

PAMPHLETS:

(Note: These are inexpensive, and may be ordered in quantities for distribution.)

Biederwolf, Wm. E. *Seventh-day Adventism: The Result of a Predicament.* Eerdmans, n. d. 48 pp.

De Korne, J. C. *The Bible and Seventh-day Adventism.* Faith,

Prayer, and Tract League; 1016 11th St., Grand Rapids, Mich. 15 pp.

Rowell, J. B. *Seventh-day Adventism Examined.* Susanville, Calif.: Challenge Pub. Co., 1952. 52 pp.

Talbot, Louis T. *What's Wrong with Seventh-day Adventism?* Findlay, Ohio: Dunham Pub. Co., 1956. 55 pp.

Tanis, Edward J. *What the Sects Teach.* Grand Rapids: Baker, 1958. 89 pp. A brief critical treatment of Seventh-day Adventism (and of Jehovah's Witnesses, Christian Science, and Spiritism).

(Note: Some of the above pamphlets can be obtained from Religion Analysis Service, 902 Hennepin Ave., Minneapolis 3, Minn.)

PERIODICALS:

Barnhouse, Donald G., and Martin, Walter R. A series of articles on Seventh-day Adventism, which appeared in *Eternity* magazine, Vol. VII, No. 9 — Vol. VIII, No. 1 (Sept., 1956 to Jan., 1957). In these articles the authors first advanced the view that Seventh-day Adventism is not a cult but a branch of evangelical Christianity.

Bear, James E. "The Seventh-day Adventists," *Interpretation,* Vol. X, No. 1 (Jan., 1956), pp. 45-71.

Bird, Herbert S. "Another Look at Adventism," *Christianity Today,* Vol. II, No. 15 (April 28, 1958), pp. 14-17.

Lindsell, Harold. "What of Seventh-day Adventism?" *Christianity Today,* Vol. II. Nos. 13 & 14 (March 31 & April 14, 1958), pp. 6-8, 13-15.

Martin, Walter R. "Seventh-day Adventism," *Christianity Today,* Vol. V, No. 6 (Dec. 19, 1960), pp. 13-15.

Yost, Frank H. "A Seventh-day Adventist Speaks Back," *Christianity Today,* Vol. II, No. 21 (July 21, 1958), pp. 15-18. A reply to Lindsell and Bird.

CHRISTIAN SCIENCE

PRIMARY SOURCES:

Eddy, Mary Baker. *Science and Health with Key to the Scriptures.* Boston: Trustees under the Will of Mary Baker Eddy,[1] 1934 (first pub. in 1875).

―――. *Christian Healing.* Boston: Trustees, 1936 (first pub. in 1886).

―――. *Christian Science Versus Pantheism.* Boston: Trustees, 1926 (first pub. in 1898).

―――. *The First Church of Christ, Scientist, and Miscellany.* Boston: Trustees, 1941 (first pub. in 1913).

―――. *Messages to the Mother Church.* Boston: Trustees, 1900, 1901, 1902.

―――. *Miscellaneous Writings.* Boston: Trustees, 1924 (first pub. in 1896).

―――――――――――

[1] Cited hereafter as Trustees.

————. *No and Yes.* Boston: Trustees, 1936 (first pub. in 1891).

————. *The People's Idea of God.* Boston: Trustees, 1936 (first pub. in 1886).

————. *Pulpit and Press.* Boston: Trustees, 1923 (first pub. in 1895).

————. *Retrospection and Introspection.* Boston: Trustees, 1920 (first pub. in 1891).

————. *Rudimental Divine Science.* Boston: Trustees, 1936 (first pub. in 1891).

————. *Unity of Good.* Boston: Trustees, 1936 (first pub. in 1887).

————. *Prose Works Other Than Science and Health.* Boston: Trustees, 1925. Contains all of Mrs. Eddy's prose works other than *Science and Health* in one volume.

————. *Manual of the Mother Church.* 89th ed. Boston: Trustees, 1936 (first pub. in 1895).

CONCORDANCES:

A Complete Concordance to Science and Health. Compiled by Albert F. Conant. Boston: Christian Science Pub. Soc., 1916.

A Complete Concordance to the Writings of Mary Baker Eddy Other Than Science and Health. Compiled by Albert F. Conant. Boston: Trustees, 1934 (first pub. in 1915).

BIOGRAPHIES OF MRS. EDDY:

"OFFICIAL":

Orcutt, Wm. D. *Mary Baker Eddy and her Books.* Boston: Christian Science Pub. Soc., 1950.

Powell, Lyman P. *Mary Baker Eddy, A Life-size Portrait.* Boston: Christian Science Pub. Soc., 1950 (first pub. in 1930).

Smith, Clifford P. *Historical Sketches from the Life of Mary Baker Eddy and the History of Christian Science.* Boston: Christian Science Pub. Soc., 1941.

Tomlinson, Irving C. *Twelve Years with Mary Baker Eddy.* Recollections and Experiences. Boston: Christian Science Pub. Soc., 1945.

Wilbur, Sibyl. *Life of Mary Baker Eddy.* New York: Concord Pub. Co., 1908. This is *the* approved official Biography.

"NON-OFFICIAL":

Bates, Ernest S., and Dittemore, John W. *Mary Baker Eddy, the Truth and the Tradition.* New York: Knopf, 1932.

Dakin, E. F. *Mrs. Eddy, the Biography of a Virginal Mind.* New York: Scribner, 1930.

Milmine, Georgine. *The Life of Mary Baker Eddy and the History of Christian Science.* New York: Doubleday, Page, and Co., 1909.

Springer, Fleta Campbell. *According to the Flesh.* New York: Coward-McCann, 1930.

(Note: Important for the light it sheds on Mrs. Eddy's relationship to Phineas Quimby is Horatio Dresser's *The Quimby Manuscripts*. New York: T. Y. Crowell, 1921; reprinted in 1961 by the Julian Press, N. Y.)

HISTORIES OF CHRISTIAN SCIENCE:

Beasley, Norman. *The Cross and the Crown*, The History of Christian Science. New York: Duell, Sloan, and Pierce, 1952.
————. *The Continuing Spirit*. New York: Duell, Sloan, and Pierce, 1956. History of Christian Science since 1910.
Braden, Charles S. *Christian Science Today*: Power, Policy, Practice. Dallas: Southern Methodist Univ. Press, 1958. History of Christian Science since 1910.
Swihart, Altman K. *Since Mrs. Eddy*. New York: Holt, 1931. Dissident movements which have arisen out of Christian Science.

GENERAL WORKS:

BOOKS:

Bellwald, A. M. *Christian Science and the Catholic Faith*. New York: Macmillan, 1922.
Clemens, C. *Awake to a Perfect Day*. New York: Citadel, 1956.
Clemens, Samuel L. (Mark Twain). *Christian Science, with Notes Containing Corrections to Date*. New York: Harper, 1907.
Fisher, Herbert A. L. *Our New Religion*: An Examination of Christian Science. New York: Cape and Smith, 1930.
Gillespie, John. *Scriptural References Sustaining the Doctrines of Christian Science*. Boston: Christian Science Pub. Soc., 1901.
Gray, James M. *The Antidote to Christian Science; or, How to Deal With it from the Bible and Christian Point of View*. New York: Revell, 1907.
Haitjema, Th. L. *Christusprediking Tegenover Moderne Gnostiek*. Wageningen: Veenman, 1929.
Haldeman, Isaac M. *Christian Science in the Light of Holy Scripture*. New York: Revell, 1909.
John, DeWitt. *The Christian Science Way of Life*. With Canham, Erwin D., *A Christian Scientist's Life*. Englewood Cliffs, N. J.: Prentice-Hall, 1962. Written by Christian Scientists. The first book contains some account of Christian Science beliefs.
Johnston, Allen W. *The Bible and Christian Science*: A Review of *Science and Health* in Relation to Holy Scripture. New York: Revell, 1924.
Leishman, Thomas L. *Why I am a Christian Scientist*. New York: Nelson, 1958.
Martin, Walter R., and Klann, Norman H. *The Christian Science Myth*. Rev. ed. Grand Rapids: Zondervan, 1955. History, doctrine, public relations, Christian Science cures.
Moehlmann, Conrad H. *Ordeal by Concordance*. New York: Longmans, Green, 1955. An answer to W. M. Haushalter's *Mrs. Eddy Purloins from Hegel*.

Peabody, F. W. *The Religio-Medical Masquerade*: A Complete Exposure of Christian Science. New York: Revell, 1915.

Peel, Robert. *Christian Science: Its Encounter with American Culture*. New York: Holt, 1958. Written by a Christian Scientist. A study of the relationship between Christian Science and transcendentalism.

Sheldon, Henry C. *Christian Science So-Called*: An Exposition and an Estimate. Cincinnati: Jennings and Graham, 1913.

Snowden, James Henry. *The Truth About Christian Science*: The Founder and the Faith. Philadelphia: Westminster Press, 1920.

Steiger, H. W. *Christian Science and Philosophy*. New York: Philosophical Library, 1948.

Whitney, Adeline D. *The Integrity of Christian Science*. Boston: Houghton-Mifflin, 1900.

Wolcott, P. *What is Christian Science?* New York: Revell, 1896.

PAMPHLETS:

(Note: These are inexpensive, and may be ordered in quantities for distribution.)

Biederwolf, Wm. E. *The Unvarnished Facts About Christian Science*. Grand Rapids: Eerdmans, n. d. 41 pp.

Martin, Walter R. *Christian Science*. Grand Rapids: Zondervan, 1957. 32 pp.

Parks, H. J. *Christian Science*. London: Church Book Room Press, 1961. 20 pp.

Talbot, Louis T. *What's Wrong with Christian Science?* Findlay, Ohio: Dunham Pub. Co. 48 pp.

Tanis, Edward J. *What the Sects Teach*. Grand Rapids: Baker, 1958. 89 pp. A brief critical treatment of Christian Science (and of Jehovah's Witnesses, Seventh-day Adventism, and Spiritism).

Wassink, A. *The Bible and Christian Science*. Faith, Prayer, and Tract League; 1016 11th St., Grand Rapids, Mich. 19 pp.

Wertheimer, Max. *Why I Left Christian Science*. Findlay, Ohio: Dunham Pub. Co., 1934. 60 pp.

(Note: Some of the above pamphlets can be obtained from Religion Analysis Service, 902 Hennepin Ave., Minneapolis 3, Minn.)

PERIODICALS:

Gerstner, John H. "Christian Science," *Christianity Today*, Vol. V, No. 6 (Dec. 19, 1960), pp. 5-7.

Wyckoff, Albert Clark. "Christian Science," *Interpretation*, Vol. XII, No. 4 (Oct., 1958), pp. 424-440.

JEHOVAH'S WITNESSES

PRIMARY SOURCES:

Russell, Charles T. *Studies in the Scriptures.* 7 Vols. Brooklyn:
  Watchtower Bible and Tract Soc., 1886-1917.
Rutherford, Joseph F. The following are his major books:
  Children (1941).
  Creation (1927).
  Deliverance (1926).
  Enemies (1937)
  Government (1928)
  The Harp of God (1921). A doctrinal summary.
  Jehovah (1934).
  Life (1929).
  Light (2 vols.; 1930).
  Preparation (1933).
  Preservation (1932).
  Prophecy (1929).
  Reconciliation (1928).
  Religion (1940).
  Riches (1936).
  Salvation (1939).
  Vindication (3 vols.; 1931 and 1932).

Note: Though Russell's and Rutherford's publications are referred to in *Jehovah's Witnesses in the Divine Purpose,* the authoritative doctrinal guides for the movement today are the volumes
  which follow. These books, published by the Watchtower Bible
  and Tract Society since Rutherford's death, have no indication of
  authorship. They are listed in chronological order.
The New World (1942).
The Truth Shall Make You Free (1943).
The Kingdom is at Hand (1944).
Theocratic Aid to Kingdom Publishers (1945).
Let God Be True (1946; revised in 1952). A summary of the
  main doctrines taught by Jehovah's Witnesses.
Equipped for Every Good Work (1946). A survey of the contents
  of the Bible books.
This Means Everlasting Life (1950).
What has Religion Done for Mankind? (1951).
New Heavens and a New Earth (1953).
Make Sure of All Things (1953; revised in 1957). A compilation
  of Scripture passages on 70 topics.
Qualified to Be Ministers (1955). How to study the Bible, how to
  conduct meetings, and how to witness.
You May Survive Armageddon into God's New World (1955).
From Paradise Lost to Paradise Regained (1958).
Your Will be Done on Earth (1958).
Let Your Name Be Sanctified (1961).

The Watchtower Society has published a great number of booklets. Four of the more important titles are listed below:

Defending and Legally Establishing the Good News (1950). This 96-p. booklet, written by Hayden C. Covington, general counsel for Jehovah's Witnesses, gives advice to the Witnesses on legal procedures and lists court decisions upholding their legal rights.

What Do the Scriptures Say about "Survival After Death"? (1955). 96 pp. Discusses the immortality of the soul, and related questions.

Blood, Medicine, and the Law of God (1961). 64 pp. Deals with the question of blood transfusion.

"The Word" — Who Is He? According to John (1962). 64 pp. John's teachings about the Logos.

OFFICIAL GREEK TESTAMENT AND BIBLE TRANSLATIONS:

Wilson, Benjamin. *The Emphatic Diaglott.* Brooklyn: Watchtower Society, 1942 (first pub. in 1864). An interlinear Greek Testament, based on the recension of J. J. Griesbach (1806).

The New World Translation of the Hebrew Scriptures. Pub. in 5 vols.: Vol. I, Genesis through Ruth (1953); Vol. II, I Samuel through Esther (1955); Vol. III, Job through Song of Solomon (1957); Vol. IV, Isaiah through Lamentations (1958); Vol. V, Ezekiel through Malachi (1960).

The New World Translation of the Christian Greek Scriptures. First pub. in 1950, rev. in 1951.

The New World Translation of the Holy Scriptures. A rev. ed. of the entire translation in one volume, without footnotes. Pub. in 1961. The latest official edition of the *New World Translation.*

HISTORIES OF JEHOVAH'S WITNESSES:

Jehovah's Witnesses in the Divine Purpose. Brooklyn: Watchtower Bible and Tract Society, 1959. This is the official history of the movement.

Qualified to Be Ministers (1955), pp. 297-360, contains a brief history.

Macmillan, A. H. *Faith on the March.* Englewood Cliffs: Prentice-Hall, 1957. A history of the movement told in autobiographical fashion by one of its leaders.

REFERENCE WORKS:

Watchtower Publications Index of Subjects Discussed and Scriptures Explained, 1930-1960. Brooklyn, 1961. Indexes subjects treated and Scripture passages commented on in all Watchtower publications for these years, including periodicals.

Yearbook of Jehovah's Witnesses. Published annually. Contains statistics and service reports for the preceding year.

GENERAL WORKS:

BOOKS:

Axup, Edward J. *The Jehovah's Witnesses Unmasked.* New York: Greenwich, 1959.

Cole, Marley. *Jehovah's Witnesses: The New World Society.* New York: Vantage Press, 1955. A highly sympathetic treatment, acclaimed by Jehovah's Witnesses, but criticized by Martin and Klann, in an appendix to *Jehovah of the Watch Tower,* as not true to fact.

————. *Triumphant Kingdom.* New York: Criterion Books, 1957.

Czatt, Milton. *The International Bible Students: Jehovah's Witnesses.* New Haven: Yale University Press, 1933. Essay based on a doctoral dissertation.

Dencher, Ted. *The Watchtower Heresy Versus the Bible.* Chicago: Moody Press, 1961. A defense of Christian doctrines against Jehovah-Witness perversions, by a former Witness. Makes much use of Scripture. Includes chapter on methods of approach.

Haldeman, I. M. *Millennial Dawnism:* The Blasphemous Religion which teaches the Annihilation of Jesus Christ. New York: Chas. Cook, n.d. (before 1914). A refutation of Millennial Dawnism — an early name for Russellism.

Hebert, Gerard, S. J. *Les Temoins de Jehovah.* Montreal: Les Editions Bellarmin, 1960. A critical study by a Jesuit father, treating history and doctrine. Lists every Watchtower publication from Russell's time to the present.

Martin, Walter R., and Klann, Norman H. *Jehovah of the Watch Tower.* Rev. ed. Grand Rapids: Zondervan, 1959. History, methods, and teachings; refutation of major doctrines. One of the more important secondary sources.

McKinney, George D., Jr. *The Theology of the Jehovah's Witnesses.* Grand Rapids: Zondervan, 1962. A systematic exposition of doctrinal teachings. A competent work, though occasionally outdated quotations are used.

Pike, Royston. *Jehovah's Witnesses: Who They Are, What They Teach, What They Do.* New York: Philosophical Library, 1954. An objective treatment, more complete than most accounts on their eschatology.

Schnell, Wm. J. *Thirty Years a Watchtower Slave.* Grand Rapids: Baker, 1956. A revealing account of the inner workings of the movement by one who was a Jehovah's Witness for thirty years. Makes a contribution no other book has made.

————. *Into the Light of Christianity.* Grand Rapids: Baker, 1959. Discusses and refutes the main doctrines of Jehovah's Witnesses.

————. *Christians: Awake!* Grand Rapids: Baker, 1962. Deals chiefly with methods of witnessing to Jehovah's Witnesses.

Spier, H. J. *De Jehovah's Getuigen en de Bijbel.* Kampen: Kok, 1961. Paperback. A competent analysis and refutation of the main doctrines. Includes a 19-p. glossary of Watchtower terms.

Stroup, Herbert H. *The Jehovah's Witnesses.* New York: Columbia

Univ. Press, 1945. An objective, scholarly study, based on a doctoral dissertation.

Whalen, Wm. J. *Armageddon Around the Corner.* New York: John Day Co., 1962. A Roman Catholic layman writes about the movement, touching on its history, theology, organization, court activities, and schisms.

PAMPHLETS:

(Note: These are inexpensive, and may be ordered in quantities for distribution.)

Biederwolf, Wm. E. *Russellism Unveiled.* Grand Rapids: Eerdmans, 1949. 35 pp.

Burrell, M. C. *Jehovah's Witnesses.* London: Church Book Room Press, 1960. 20 pp. History, methods, and doctrines.

Kneedler, Wm. Harding. *Christian Answers to Jehovah's Witnesses.* Chicago: Moody Press, 1953. 64 pp. A brief exposition and refutation of the main doctrines.

Martin, Walter R. *Jehovah's Witnesses.* Grand Rapids: Zondervan, 1957. 64 pp. History, doctrines, and practices.

Mayer, F. E. *Jehovah's Witnesses.* St. Louis: Concordia, 1957. Rev. ed. (first pub. in 1942). 61 pp. Mayer was professor of systematic theology at Concordia Seminary. Leans chiefly on Rutherford; no reference to later publications.

Metzger, Bruce M. *The Jehovah's Witnesses and Jesus Christ.* A reprint from *Theology Today*, Vol. X, No. 1 (April, 1953), pp. 65-85; obtainable from the Theological Book Agency, Princeton, N. J. Metzger is professor of New Testament at Princeton Seminary. A scholarly refutation of the Jehovah-Witness view of Jesus Christ.

Strauss, Lehmann. *An Examination of the Doctrine of Jehovah's Witnesses.* New York: Loizeaux Bros., 1955 (first pub. 1942). 47 pp.

Talbot, Louis T. *What's Wrong with Jehovah's Witnesses?* Findlay, Ohio: Dunham Pub. Co. 50 pp.

Tanis, Edward J. *What the Sects Teach.* Grand Rapids: Baker, 1958. 89 pp. A brief critical treatment of Jehovah's Witnesses (and of Christian Science, Seventh-day Adventism, and Spiritism).

Wassink, A. *The Bible and Jehovah's Witnesses.* Faith, Prayer, and Tract League; 1016 11th St., Grand Rapids, Mich. 18 pp. Outdated in some respects, but still useful.

(Note: Some of the above pamphlets can be obtained from Religion Analysis Service, 902 Hennepin Ave., Minneapolis 3, Minn.)

PERIODICALS:

Schnell, Wm. J., ed. *The Converted Jehovah's Witness Expositor.* Published every 3 months at 2889 Guss Ave., Youngstown, Ohio. Contains material for use in witnessing to Jehovah's Witnesses.

Stuermann, Walter E. "Jehovah's Witnesses," in *Interpretation*, Vol. V, No. 3 (July, 1956), pp. 323-45. History, organization, and the New World Translations.

Index

The following abbreviations will be used in the index:

> **M** Mormonism
> **SDA** Seventh-day Adventism
> **CS** Christian Science
> **JW** Jehovah's Witnesses

Adam — M: Michael before he came to earth, 45; helped Elohim create the earth, 45; Eve only one of his wives, 40-41; baptized by immersion, 20; a god, 41; holds the keys of salvation, 51; JW: died on the same day that he ate the fruit, 268; beyond repentance, 268; not to be raised from the dead, 317; difference between Mormon and Jehovah-Witness views of, 317

Adam-God theory, 40-41

Age of the universe: SDA, 109-10; JW, 264

Angels—CS: existence of denied, 192; JW: created before the material universe, 263; brothers of Jesus Christ, 263; higher than men, 270; not immortal, 267, 325-26; can still be annihilated, 326; must be sustained by food, 326

Annihilation of Christ, 275 (*see also* Jesus)

Annihilation of Satan and the demons: SDA, 142; JW, 322

Annihilation of the wicked: SDA, 142, 360-71; JW, 308, 320-21, 322, 323-24, 360-71; Scriptural teachings on, 360-71

Anointed class, 246, 247; the exact number of foreordained, 261; children of God's woman, 264; began to be gathered after Pentecost, 269; difference between them and Christ only one of degree, 274; way of salvation for, 279-83; earn their way to heaven by sacrificing earthly prospects, 281, 283; described, 287-88; names applied to, 287; children of God, 287; heavenly destiny, 288; baptism of or with the holy spirit, 291; raised with "spirit bodies" in 1918, 300, 302-303; parallels between Christ and, 304-305; role of during the millennium, 312-13; last ones "raised" during the millennium, 325; reign eternally with Christ in heaven, 325 (*see also* remnant; 144,000)

Anointing, of Christ, 273; of the anointed class to be kings and priests of God, 282; not necessary for the other sheep, 284

Anthon, Prof. Chas. S., 12, 85-86

Approaching the cultist, 405-16; difficulties, 405-407; importance of personal testimony, 406-407, 410-11; approaching the cultist as a total person, 407-11; reasons why people are attracted to cults, 408; assurance of salvation, 410; approaching the cultist on the intellectual level, 411-16; II John 10-11, 411-12; general suggestions, 412-13; specific suggestions, 413-16

Challenge of the cults, the, 1-8; having convictions, 2; knowing the Scriptures, 2-3; zeal for witnessing, 3-4; use of the printed page, 4-5; sense of urgency, 5; role of laymen, 5-6; sense of dedication, 6; techniques for witnessing, 7; enduring ridicule, 7-8; contribution to good health, 8

Christ—M: Pre-existence of, 53-54; incarnation not unique, 54; brother to the devil and the demons, 54; polygamous marriage of, 56; SDA: pre-existence of, 113; human nature of, 113-15; CS: a divine idea, 200-202; JW: foreordained, 261; created in time, 262; God's co-worker in creation, 262; a brother of Satan, 263; prehuman state, 270-71; human state, 271-74; a perfect human creature, 273; significance of his baptism, 273-74; posthuman state, 274-76; lack of continuity between these three states, 275-76 (*see also* Christ, deity of; Jesus; virgin birth of Christ)

Christ, coming to his temple, 299-302; parallel between Christ's first and second presence, 300; occurred in 1918, 300; involved the "resurrection" of the 144,000, 299-300; involved the cleansing of the spiritual temple, 300-302; the temple cleansed was the earthly organization, 300; involved a heavenly temple, 300-302

Christ, deity of: M, 54; SDA, 109, 112-13, 130, 394-96; JW: Christ not equal to Jehovah, 270; an archangel, 270; a god, 270; Scriptural teachings on, 327-44 (*see also* Christ, person of; Jesus; only-begotten Son; Son of God)

Christ, devaluation of, found in all the cults, 382-84; 394-96

Christ, distinction between Jesus and, 200-202, 204

Christ, person of: appendix on Jehovah-Witness view of, 327-44; Watchtower view of, a revival of Arianism, 327-30; *critique of Watchtower exegesis*, 330-44; OT passages: Prov. 8:22, 330-31; Is. 9:6, 331-32; NT passages: John 1:1, 332-35; Col. 1:15-17, 336; Phil. 2:6, 336; Tit. 2:13, 336-37; Rev. 3:14, 337; John 14:28, 337; Christ as the Son of God, 337-39; Christ as the proper object of worship, 339-44; John 20:28, 343-44

Christ, priestly ministry of, two phases in, 94, 151-53

Christ, return of: M, 67, 68, 69; SDA, 137, 138; CS, 219-20; JW, 224, 297-99; not a visible return, 297; not a return to earth, 297; occurred in 1914, 298; made Christ King of the earth, 298; caused upheaval in the demonic world, 298-99; a second "return" at the Battle of Armageddon, 310

Christian Science, said to be unerring and divine, 213; identified with Christianity, 213; its rise coincided with the second appearance of Jesus, 219-20

Christian Science, basic denials of: matter, 186-87; evil and sin, 187-88; disease, 188; death, 188-89

Christian Science Church: history, 171-82; given a charter and incorporated, 175; government, 178; services described, 179; Committee on Publication, 179; reading rooms, 179; practitioners, 179-80; statistics, 179-80; geographical distribution, 180-81; periodicals, 181; institutions, 181-82

Christmas, Jehovah's Witnesses do not celebrate, 237; Christmas trees opposed, 237, 250

Church: M, 62-64; SDA, 128-32; CS, 212-13; JW, 285-90; includes only the anointed class, 287; evaluation of Watchtower ecclesiology, 290

Church, invisible or universal: M, 64; SDA, 129-32, 396-400; CS, 213; JW, 285-86; doctrine of, denied by all cults, 384-85, 396-400

Church of Jesus Christ of Latter-day Saints; *see* Mormon Church

Coffee and tea: M, 18; SDA, 133

Conditional immortality: SDA, 136; JW, 294-95

Continuity, lack of, between Christ's prehuman and human state, 272-73; between Christ's human and posthuman state, 275; between all three states of Christ's existence, 275-76

statistics and activities, 233-37; numbers, 233-34; geographical distribution, 235-36; hours of witnessing, 235; distribution of literature, 235; salaries of workers, 235; government, 236; attitude toward politics and war, 237; schisms, 237; Watchtower explanation of 1918 schisms, 300

Jesus (Christian Science): annihilation of, 202; existence of unimportant, 203; fallibility of, 204; deity of denied, 204-205; human nature of denied, 205; suffering of, 205-206; death of denied, 205-206; resurrection denied, 206; ascension of denied, 206-207

Judgment day, the millennial, 319-21; concerns only those living on the earth during the millennium, 320; basis for judgment, 320; results, 320-21; involves a "second chance" to be saved, 321

Judgment, final: SDA, 142-43; CS, 171, 220-21; JW, 321-22

Judgment of the nations, 306-307; time of, 307; basis for, 307; completed by the time of Armageddon, 307; executed at the Battle of Armageddon, 307

Judgments, various, distinguished by Jehovah's Witnesses: Adam's judgment in the Garden of Eden, 317; the judgment which began at the house of God in 1918, 306; the judgment of the nations from 1918 to the Battle of Armageddon, 306-307; the millennial thousand-year day of judgment, 319-21; the final judgment at the end of the millennium, 321-22

Justification: M, 59-60; SDA, 123, 124-25; JW: of the anointed class, 281; purpose of, 281; not necessary in the usual sense for the other sheep, 284; another type of, necessary for the other sheep, 284, 322; justification by grace alone denied by all the cults, 379-82, 390-94

Kingdom of God, 295-97; other sheep subjects but not members, 292, 296; defined, 295-96; only Christ and the 144,000 belong to, 296; angels subjects but not members, 296; established in 1914, 296-97

Knorr, Nathan H., 231-33; joins Jehovah's Witnesses, 231; becomes third president, 231; improves training program, 232; new series of doctrinal books, 232; Bible translation, 232-33; foreign expansion, 233

Laborers in the Vineyard, parable of, Jehovah-Witness interpretation of, 251

Lamanites, received a "skin of blackness," 26; ancestors of the American Indians, 26; dark skin to be removed, 26; killed the Nephites, 27

Legalism, 125-28

Life after death: appendix on the teachings of Adventists and Jehovah's Witnesses on, 345-71; *soul-extinction,* 345-59; not held by any recognized branch of the Christian church, 345-46; the word *psuchee,* 346-49; the word *pneuma,* 349-51; in Christ, 351-52; the God of the living, 352-53; the second word from the cross, 353-54; to depart and be with Christ, 354-55; absent from the body and at home with the Lord, 355-57; parable of the rich man and Lazarus, 357-59; II Pet. 2:9, 359; *the annihilation of the wicked,* 360-71; the word *apollumi,* 360-62, 364-65; the meaning of Gehenna, 362-63; the smoke of their torment, 363-64; the word *olethros,* 365-67; the word *kolasis,* 367-68; the word *aioonios,* 368-70; degrees of punishment, 370

Liquor: M, 18; SDA, 133; JW, 236-37

Logos, Christ the, 270, 327, 328

Lord's Supper: M, 66-67; administered weekly, 66; bread and water used, 66; SDA, 134-35; administered quarterly, 134; preceded by footwashing, 134; significance, 135; unleavened bread and unfermented wine used, 135; CS, 214-16; communion services, 214-15; neither bread nor wine used, 214; JW, 292-93; administered once a year, 292; unleavened bread and fermented wine used, 292; intended for the 144,000 only, 292; significance, 292; the other sheep must attend, 293

various names given to, 288-89; Biblical types of, 289; grandchildren of God, 289; earthly destiny, 289-90; baptism into the Greater Noah, 291; resurrection of, 318-19; OT saints will become, 318; some will become princes, 318; final destiny, 324

Pantheism, 189

Pearl of Great Price described, 29

Perfection, reached only after death, 218

Perfectionism, 124, 376-77

Polygamy, 28, 29, 56

Predestination: M, 41-42; SDA, 109; CS, 191-92; JW, 223, 260-62

Princes: many OT saints will become, 318; some other sheep who survive Armageddon will become, 318; will give instruction in God's law to those raised from the dead, 319

Probation, a time of, after death, 217-18

Probation, the close of, 138, 401

Providence: M, 45-46; SDA, 110; CS, 194-96; JW, 265

Races, reason for discrimination between, 48

Ransom, the, 276-77; bought back a perfect human life with earthly prospects, 276, 283; benefits of, 278; who brought, 278-79; value of, 279; who will benefit from, 279 (*see also* atonement)

Rapture: M, 69-70; SDA, 137, 140-41, 402

Reformation, the, incomplete: M, 62; SDA, 129, 401; JW, 286-87

"Reformed Egyptian," 11, 76, 77-80, 81, 83

Regeneration: the anointed ones undergo, 269, 281, 284; the other sheep do not need, 269, 284

Remnant, the, 282, 287, 304, 307, 309, 310, 314 (*see also* anointed class)

Remnant church, 98, 102, 104, 128-32, 133, 396, 398, 400; not exegetically defensible, 131-32; not doctrinally defensible, 132

Reorganized Church of Jesus Christ of Latter-day Saints, 18, 19, 21, 66

Repentance: necessary for the anointed class, 280; must precede baptism, 291

Resurrection appearances of Christ: M, 10, 27; CS, 206; JW, 274-75

Resurrection of believers: M, 69; SDA, 140, 402 (*see also* resurrections; resurrection, the first; resurrection, the special)

Resurrection of Christ: SDA, 113; CS, 206; JW, 274-75

Resurrection of the body, denied by Christian Science, 220

Resurrection of the wicked: M, 70-71, 74; SDA, 141 (*see also* resurrections; resurrection, the special)

Resurrection, the first (Jehovah's Witnesses), 302-306; only Christ and the 144,000 participate in, 303; not a bodily resurrection, 303; took place in 1918, 302-303; a transition from nonexistence to spirit-existence, 303-304; experienced by the remnant at death, 304; a kind of deification, 304; parallels between Christ and the anointed class, 304-305; properly a new creation, 305; an ancient heresy, 305; no continuity between being in the flesh and this "resurrection" state, 306

Resurrection, the special (Seventh-day Adventists), 139-40, 402

Resurrections: M, 69-71, 74; SDA, 136, 139-40, 141, 402; JW: definition of two types of, 302; the first resurrection, 302-306; resurrections during the millennium, 315-19; nature of these resurrections, 315-16; the number of those raised, 316-17; those not raised, 317; the "resurrection of life," 317-19; the "resurrection of judgment," 319

Revelations, received by presidents of the Mormon Church, 29-30